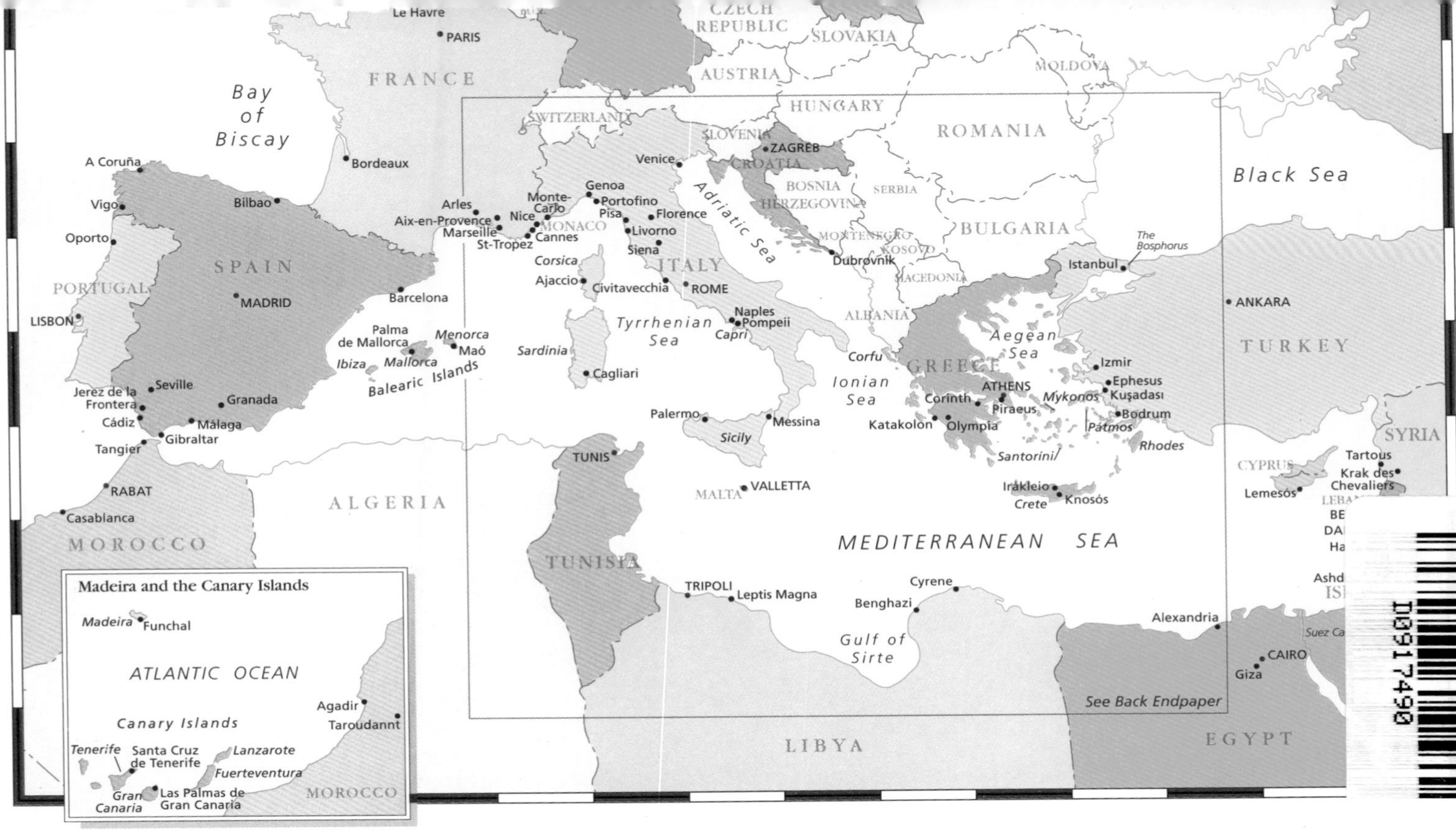

Le Havre
PARIS
FRANCE
Bay of Biscay
CZECH REPUBLIC
SLOVAKIA
AUSTRIA
MOLDOVA
HUNGARY
ROMANIA
SWITZERLAND
SLOVENIA
ZAGREB
CROATIA
BOSNIA HERZEGOVINA
SERBIA
MONTENEGRO
KOSOVO
MACEDONIA
ALBANIA
BULGARIA
Black Sea
The Bosphorus
Istanbul
ANKARA
TURKEY
A Coruña
Bordeaux
Vigo
Bilbao
Oporto
PORTUGAL
SPAIN
MADRID
LISBON
Barcelona
Arles
Aix-en-Provence
Marseille
St-Tropez
Nice
Monte-Carlo
MONACO
Cannes
Genoa
Portofino
Pisa
Livorno
Florence
Siena
Venice
Adriatic Sea
Dubrovnik
Corsica
Ajaccio
Civitavecchia
ITALY
ROME
Naples
Pompeii
Capri
Tyrrhenian Sea
Sardinia
Cagliari
Palma de Mallorca
Menorca
Maó
Ibiza
Mallorca
Balearic Islands
Seville
Jerez de la Frontera
Cádiz
Granada
Málaga
Gibraltar
Tangier
RABAT
Casablanca
MOROCCO
ALGERIA
TUNIS
TUNISIA
Palermo
Sicily
Messina
MALTA
VALLETTA
Corfu
Ionian Sea
GREECE
Aegean Sea
ATHENS
Corinth
Piraeus
Katakolon
Olympia
Mykonos
Izmir
Ephesus
Kuşadası
Bodrum
Patmos
Rhodes
Santorini
Irákleio
Crete
Knosós
MEDITERRANEAN SEA
SYRIA
Tartous
Krak des Chevaliers
CYPRUS
Lemesós
TRIPOLI
Leptis Magna
Cyrene
Benghazi
Gulf of Sirte
LIBYA
Alexandria
CAIRO
Giza
EGYPT
See Back Endpaper
Madeira and the Canary Islands
Madeira
Funchal
ATLANTIC OCEAN
Agadir
Taroudannt
Canary Islands
Tenerife
Santa Cruz de Tenerife
Lanzarote
Fuerteventura
Gran Canaria
Las Palmas de Gran Canaria
MOROCCO

EYEWITNESS TRAVEL

CRUISE GUIDE TO

EUROPE

& THE MEDITERRANEAN

EYEWITNESS TRAVEL

CRUISE GUIDE TO EUROPE & THE MEDITERRANEAN

DK

LONDON, NEW YORK,
MELBOURNE, MUNICH AND DELHI
www.dk.com

PROJECT EDITOR Felicity Crow
PROJECT ART EDITOR Gillian Andrews
ART EDITORS Tessa Bindloss, Simon J M Oon
EDITORS Catherine Day, Kevin McRae
DESIGNER Elly King
PICTURE RESEARCHERS Brigitte Arora, Katherine Mesquita
MAP CO-ORDINATOR Casper Morris
DTP DESIGNERS Jason Little, Conrad van Dyk

MAPS
ERA-Maptec Ltd

PHOTOGRAPHERS, ILLUSTRATORS & CONTRIBUTORS
(See Acknowledgments *pp380–83)*

Reproduced by Colourscan, Singapore
Printed and bound by South China Printing Co. Ltd., China

First published in Great Britain in 2001
by Dorling Kindersley Limited
80 Strand, London WC2R 0RL
11 12 13 14 10 9 8 7 6 5 4 3 2 1

Reprinted with revisions 2004, 2007, 2011

A CIP CATALOGUE RECORD IS AVAILABLE FROM THE BRITISH LIBRARY.

ISBN: 978-1-40535-889-7

FLOORS ARE REFERRED TO THROUGHOUT IN ACCORDANCE WITH EUROPEAN USAGE, IE THE "FIRST FLOOR" IS THE FLOOR ABOVE GROUND LEVEL.

Front cover main image: Cruise ship Asuka II, passing Venice.

MIX
Paper from responsible sources
FSC www.fsc.org FSC™ C018179

The information in this DK Eyewitness Travel Guide is checked regularly.

Every effort has been made to ensure that this book is as up-to-date as possible at the time of going to press. Some details, however, such as telephone numbers, opening hours, prices, gallery hanging arrangements and travel information are liable to change. The publishers cannot accept responsibility for any consequences arising from the use of this book, nor for any material on third party websites, and cannot guarantee that any website address in this book will be a suitable source of travel information. We value the views and suggestions of our readers very highly. Please write to: Publisher, DK Eyewitness Travel Guides, Dorling Kindersley, 80 Strand, London WC2R 0RL, Great Britain, or email: travelguides@dk.com.

◁ **Cruise ship moored at the quayside in Nice on the French Riviera**

CONTENTS

Lavishly costumed entertainment, a feature on many cruise ships

Evocative advertising poster from the Golden Age of cruising

PORTS OF CALL

Panoramic views from Firá on the Greek island of Santorini

Swimming and sunbathing on board ship in the Mediterranean

SURVIVAL GUIDE

DIRECTORY OF CRUISE LINES

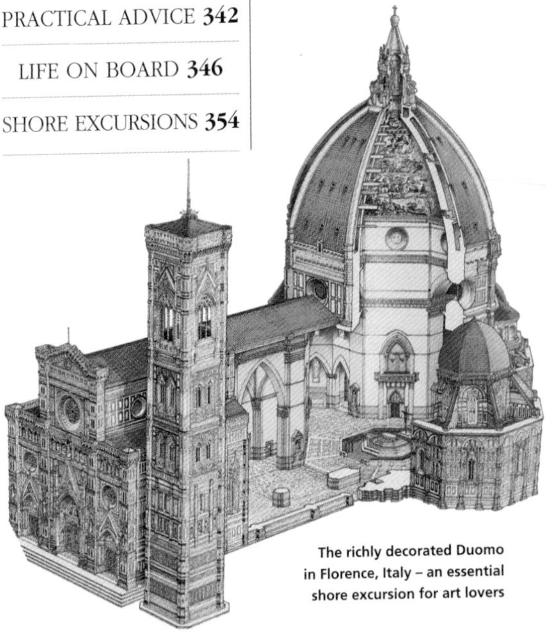

The richly decorated Duomo in Florence, Italy – an essential shore excursion for art lovers

HOW TO USE THIS GUIDE

This guide will help you get the most from your cruise holiday, providing expert recommendations and concise practical information. *Introducing Cruise Travel* gives useful background information, providing a brief history of cruising and covering the options open to anyone planning a cruise. The *Ports of Call* section of the guide is arranged by country and gives descriptions of the most popular stopping places for cruise ships. It covers all the important sights in or near each port. The *Survival Guide* covers all you need to know about the practicalities of cruising, from planning and booking your cruise to on-board facilities and shore excursions.

PORTS OF CALL

The guide follows an itinerary around Europe and the Mediterranean from north to south, starting at the North Cape of Norway and travelling south through the coastal countries of nothern Europe, then around to Spain and Italy. The southern Mediterranean coast is followed from west to east, then onwards to Turkey and Greece.

ITALY
SARDINIA 210–211 • GENOA 212
PORTOFINO 213 • VENICE 214–219
PISA 220–221 • FLORENCE 222–227
SIENA 228–229 • ROME 230–239
NAPLES 240–241 • POMPEII 242–243
CAPRI 244–245 • PALERMO 246 • MESSINA 247

1 Country Chapters

Each chapter begins with an introductory page featuring a map of the area. Ports of call and major excursion destinations are marked with black spots and listed below the map with page numbers. Capital cities are marked in red for reference, though not necessarily featured in the text.

A country map shows the location of all the ports of call featured in that chapter.

A concise map shows the centre of the city, the main streets and the key sights.

2 City Feature

These two pages highlight the most famous sights, allowing visitors with a tight schedule to set their priorities at a glance.

A Fact File provides concise, practical details, pointing out the best local characteristics of the city.

3 Exploring the Key Sights

For cities with a wealth of historical and artistic heritage, these pages give more detailed descriptions of all the entries in the Key Sights list. The *Exploring* paragraphs will guide visitors towards shopping or other specific areas. Feature boxes provide extra background information.

4 Ports and Towns in Brief
These distill the essence of smaller ports of call or excursion sites in a single page – ideal for visitors who may have only a few hours to spend ashore.

A name in brackets tells you which is the nearest port to the destination described.

The Locator Map shows the destination in relation to the nearest port of call.

The Key Sights list provides an at-a-glance summary of the most interesting places to visit while ashore. Those marked with a star are especially rewarding.

The Locator Map situates the illustrated 3-D street-by-street map within the greater area of the city.

5 Street-by-Street Map
The most important sightseeing areas of selected cities are illustrated in 3-D with accurate drawings of buildings and monuments.

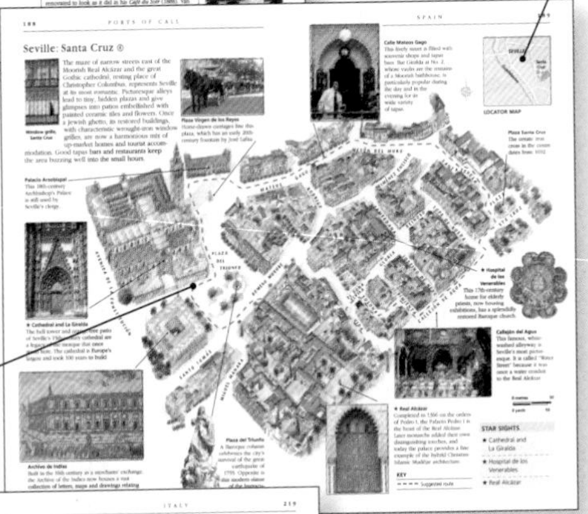

A suggested walking route covers the most interesting streets in the area.

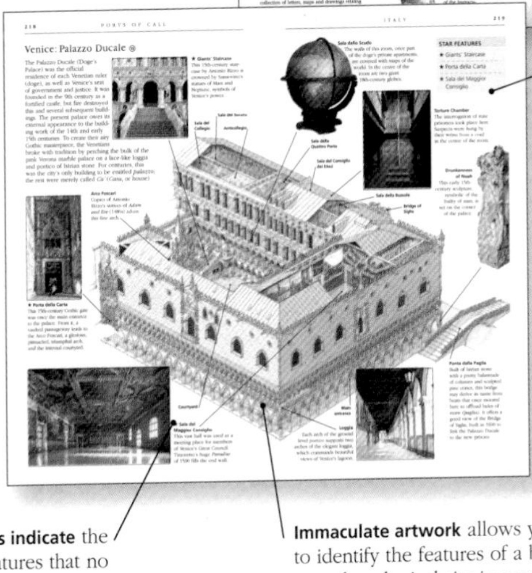

The Star Features box highlights the most spectacular rooms, areas or features at a glance.

6 The Top Sights
Historic buildings are dissected to reveal their interiors and Classical ruins are reconstructed to help you visualize them in their former glory.

Stars indicate the features that no visitor should miss.

Immaculate artwork allows you to identify the features of a building or archeaological site in great detail.

STRATHAIRD
P&

INTRODUCING

CRUISE TRAVEL

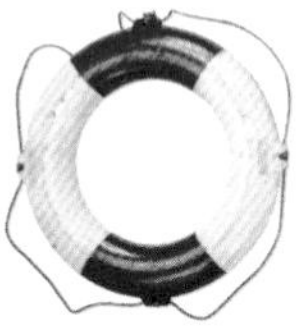

THE HISTORY OF CRUISE TRAVEL

Humankind has always had a close relationship with the sea. From earliest times, people have built ships for trade, defence or exploration, and cities such as London, Barcelona and New York have grown wealthy on the back of maritime commerce. More recently, the sea has become increasingly synonymous with leisure.

THE VICTORIAN ERA

It was not until the middle of the 19th century that anyone took to the seas purely for pleasure. The very beginnings of cruise travel can be traced back to 1837 – the year Queen Victoria came to the throne in England – when the Peninsular Steam Navigation Company (later renamed P&O) was founded. In 1839 Samuel Cunard, born in Canada, came to Britain and with the paddle-steamer *Britannia* founded the British and North American Royal Mail Steam Packet Company (later renamed the Cunard Line). Two of the world's most well-known cruise lines had been born. Voyaging for pleasure received a boost in the 1840s when William Makepeace Thackeray and Charles Dickens wrote of their maritime adventures, while a P&O voyage from London to the Black Sea in 1843 was featured in Mark Twain's popular novel *The Innocents Abroad*. The first real "cruise" is said to have been offered in 1858 aboard the P&O steamship *Ceylon*, with the wealthy passengers paying to act out their dreams of maritime adventure; the ship was not fitted for passengers and so facilities were very basic. Refitted in 1881, the *Ceylon* became the first purpose-built passenger ship. Such ships began to offer trips to the Canary Islands, the Norwegian fjords and the Mediterranean, and by the late 19th century, wealthy travellers could sail from Europe as far as the West Indies.

1920s poster advertising the White Star Line

Crew and officers of the *Benares*, part of P&O's 19th-century fleet

THE ROARING TWENTIES

Among the best-known ships of the 1920s were Cunard Line's *Mauretania, Aquitania and Berengaria*, White Star Line's *Majestic*, French Line's *Ile de France*, Germany's *Bremen* and Sweden's *Gripsholm*. In the USA, during the Prohibition era (1920–33)

short "booze cruises" from US ports allowed passengers to indulge in drinking and gambling and the pleasures of destinations such as Cuba, Bermuda and the Bahamas.

In 1922 Cunard Line's *Laconia* sailed on a world cruise, starting and finishing in New York. Although a relatively small ship (20,000 grt), she had a three-class capacity of over 2,000 berths, more than many of the much larger ships in service today.

On the North Atlantic, Europe's shipping lines excelled themselves, introducing ever more opulence. Ships had palatial dining rooms adorned with marble, sumptuous salons hung with works of art and fitted with windows 4.5 m (15 ft) high, and hot and cold running water supplied to every cabin. The most impressive ship of the times was P&O's *Viceroy of India*, introduced in 1929. She played a dual role as a liner to India and as a luxury cruiser, was P&O's first turbo-electric-powered ship and boasted the company's first indoor ship's swimming pool.

Indoor swimming pool of P&O's 1929 *Viceroy of India*, one of the first on a cruise liner

A NEW ERA

The Thirties ushered in an era of much larger, faster ships. Union-Castle Line with its "weekly Royal Mail Service" began to offer "Holiday Tours to South Africa", departing from the English port of Southampton, with highly competitive return fares to Cape Town of £90 for first class, £60 for second class and £30 for third class.

By 1930 Cunard Line was working on a grand plan for a new generation of ships to replace their existing liners. This would lead to the introduction of the two most illustrious liners of the day: *RMS Queen Mary* and *RMS Queen Elizabeth*. Each around 80,000 grt, with speeds in excess of 30 knots, their weekly service between Southampton and New York became famous for its unrivalled levels of luxury and attentive service, and became a potent symbol of cruise travel at its most opulent.

THE BLUE RIBAND

At the beginning of the 20th century, competition between the shipping lines was becoming intense, with speed, as always, a major selling point. The Blue Riband award was introduced for the fastest transatlantic crossing, and was monitored by an international committee. Cunard Line's *Mauretania* managed the superb feat of holding the Blue Riband from 1907 until 1929, improving its record-breaking average speed over 20 years from 22.21 to an incredible 27.22 knots.

Cunard Line's *SS Mauretania* being towed into dock in 1922

The Golden Age of Cruising

In the period between the two world wars, cruising became a fashionable activity for the wealthy. Ships became larger and grander as British, French, German and American companies competed to produce the biggest and fastest liners the world had ever seen. Famous ships such as the *Mauretania, Normandie, Franconia*, and *Queen Mary* plied the oceans, offering unprecedented standards of luxury. The *Franconia* boasted a two-deck-high smoking room built in the style of El Greco's 15th-century home, while the *Normandie* featured a winter garden with live caged birds. Passengers, who often took their servants with them, were pampered in style, with fine food and wine and staff to attend to their every need as they were transported between exotic ports of call.

Advertisement for Cunard Line, illustrating a liner's interior

Bright Young Things
Cruise travel in the 1920s and 1930s became extremely popular with the fashionable set around the world – so much so that sea travel became synonymous with glamour.

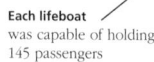

Cunard's red and black funnels
Each lifeboat was capable of holding 145 passengers

THE *QUEEN MARY*

With accommodation for up to 2,000 passengers, this ship, built for the Cunard Line, captured the hearts of a generation. One of the most opulent ships of her day, she was launched at Clydebank in 1934. With 1,174 officers and crew, the ship's passenger to crew ratio was less than two to one, giving unmatched service. Royalty, heads of state, film stars and captains of industry fell in love with this elegant liner, and clamoured to be seen aboard her.

Art Deco Interior
The dominant interior furnishing style of this period, Art Deco, was employed to great effect on luxury cruise liners. The bar of the *Queen Mary* was one of the most opulent examples.

THE ORIGINS OF "POSH"

In the days before air-conditioning, the voyage through the Suez Canal and Red Sea was feared due to the intense heat. On the outward voyage the cabins on the port side got the early morning sun, but had the whole day to cool off. On the return journey the reverse was true. P&O were in the habit of allocating the cooler cabins to government officials and dignitaries, whose papers were marked "Port Outward – Starboard Homeward". This became shortened to POSH and a new word entered the English language.

A 1920s cruise liner in the Suez Canal

QUEEN MARY
Bridge
Over 2,000 portholes cover the sides of the ship's hull.
The two bow anchors of this gigantic ship weighed 16 tonnes each.
The bow-wave at full speed was more than 3 m (10 ft) high.

MENU
P&O

1930s Menu
Cuisine on ships of this period reflected the style of the luxurious surroundings in which it was served. Caviar and champagne were, of course, staples, and many other lavish, beautifully prepared meals would have been served. The menus themselves often featured exquisitely-drawn Art Deco designs.

P&O
TOURIST CLASS
CRUISES
1933

P&O Poster
Advertisements from this period emphasize grace, style and luxury. This P&O poster, featuring an officer in his immaculate white uniform, also conveys a strong sense of calm and discipline – key qualities in the days when cruise liners and merchant ships served the four corners of the world.

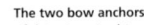

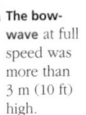

Cunard Line's *Queen Mary* entering New York harbour in 1936

THE OPULENT THIRTIES

In 1931 the Canadian Pacific company introduced its luxury liner *Empress of Britain*, which dominated the sealanes between Britain and Montreal for much of the decade.

Meanwhile the French had entered the race by introducing their own super-luxury liner, the *Normandie*, in May 1935. Conceived on a grand scale, she had 14 deluxe suites, as well as private dining rooms and sitting rooms. Her public rooms and stairways were designed to remind passengers of the Palace of Versailles near Paris *(see p149)*.

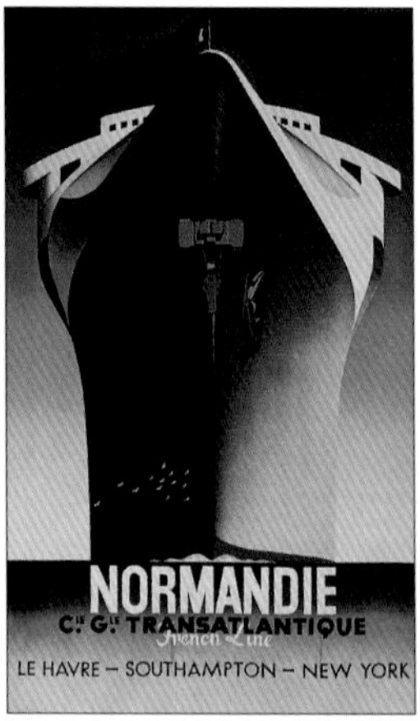

1935 poster for the French cruise liner *Normandie*

At the beginning of the 1930s the USA had two ships, *Manhattan* and *Washington*, which operated weekly services between New York and Britain, France and Germany. In 1934 the United States Line began construction of a new oil-fired liner, designed to be capable of an average speed of 25 knots. Named *SS America*, she was, at the time, the largest cruise liner ever built.

THE END OF AN ERA

The *Queen Mary* was in the mid-Atlantic when World War II was declared in September 1939. Loaded with passengers, she ran a zig-zag course using blackout at night to avoid detection, and arrived safely in New York on 4 September. By the time *SS America* entered service in July 1940, Europe was at war, and the USA's entry into the war was not far off. In June 1941 *SS America* was, like the two giant "Cunard Queens" and many other liners, commissioned to help the war effort as a troop carrier; she was repainted and refitted, and renamed *USS West Point*.

In 1946, *SS America*, like the *Queen Mary* and the *Queen Elizabeth*, resumed passenger service between New York and Europe.

In the post-World War II years, despite the fact that Britain's Empire had begun to shrink, British shipping lines were able to resume the dominant position on the world's sealanes that they had established 20 years earlier. The main difference now was that most passengers were businessmen, servicemen or government employees; few people were travelling for pleasure.

AIR TRAVEL BRINGS RAPID CHANGE

By the time the first commercial jet crossed the Atlantic in 1958 there were over 100 passenger shipping lines. Before long, however, it became cheaper, and faster, to travel by air than by sea, and passenger liners were forced to seek new markets. The first ship designed primarily for modern cruising was the Furness Withy company's *Ocean Monarch*, which entered service in May 1951 on a round-trip from New York to Bermuda. Older ships in use at this time were forced into retirement, and several shipping companies simply went out of

Queen Mary used as World War II troop carrier

business. Those with vision and suitable ships relocated to ports in Florida, offering cruises to the Bahamas and the Caribbean, and to the US west coast where cruises were operated to Alaska in summer and Mexico in winter. By 1960 companies were offering to fly passengers to join their ships at faraway ports – the era of fly-cruises had begun.

In the 1960s older transatlantic liners found themselves unable to compete with jumbo jets, and vast numbers went to the scrapyard. Cunard Line's *Queen Mary* went out of service in 1967, and has ended her days as a hotel and museum ship berthed in Long Beach, California. The following year the *Queen Elizabeth* was withdrawn; and after a disastrous fire while out of service, she was scrapped altogether. One note of optimism was the launch in 1969 of the *Queen Elizabeth II*, still today, after extensive refurbishment and new engines, the only passenger liner in regular service between Europe and New York.

MASS CRUISING

Since the early 1970s, tour operators and cruise lines in Europe and the USA have offered cruises as a holiday experience. Carnival Cruise Lines, now part of the world's largest cruising corporation, started in 1971 when the former transatlantic liner *Empress of Canada* was renamed *Mardi Gras* and began Caribbean cruising from Miami. Leisure cruising in the USA received a boost when the popular TV series *The Love Boat* aired for nine years from 1977. With cruises now operating in six continents and new, larger ships entering service all the time, passengers are spoilt for choice. In fact the industry has never been so buoyant; more than 40 new cruise ships, worth US$10 billion, entered service at the beginning of the 21st century. Among them were two super cruisers, Royal Caribbean International's *Voyager of the Seas* *(see pp12–13)* and Cunard Line's *Queen Mary II*. These huge ships are surely the shape of things to come.

Royal Caribbean International's *Voyager of the Seas*, one of a new generation of "superliners"

STYLES OF CRUISING

Cruises come in a wide variety of styles and can be taken on vessels of many kinds, including luxury sailing yachts, small ships with themed itineraries, working ships and giant "superliners", some of which carry over 3,000 passengers. On many cruises shipboard life is the focus of the trip, leaving little desire to disembark, while on others, onshore destinations are the key.

Large, well-appointed luxury suite, available on many ships

Apart from obvious material factors affecting people's choice of cruise, such as the cabin and the amenities available, there is also the question of atmosphere. Cruising may claim to have shed its "stuffy" image, but inevitably some degree of formality on board ship survives. Large US ships, working ships and cruises that welcome children are among the least formal, but smaller luxury ships still encourage old-style maritime formality. As a rule of thumb, the higher the price, the more attention passengers need to pay to etiquette.

TYPES OF CRUISES

Competition has made cruising more affordable, and trips are available in a range of grades, generally defined by the style of ship and grade of cabin on offer (for example, economy, stateroom, suite – *see p340)*. Budget travelling is also possible, for there are cruises to suit most pockets, and it is worth noting that a higher-grade cabin on a middle-of-the-range ship has a similar price to a lower-grade cabin on a ship with more facilities.

For those not on a tight budget, there is a vast array of cruise options. The cruise industry is doing well at present and many people are paying large sums of money for top-class cruises, due entirely to the increase in quality and choice. Companies such as Crystal Cruises, Cunard Line, Radisson Seven Seas Cruise Lines, Seabourn Cruise Line and Silversea Cruises are the leaders in this field, but if a very large ship with a broad range of facilities is preferred, it is worth looking at ruises offered by Celebrity Cruises and Royal Caribbean International, among others.

THEMED CRUISES

On most cruises the Cruise Director holds informal meetings to introduce the next port of call, shore excursions,

Star Clippers' four-masted barquentine *Star Flyer*

Hurtigruten ferry, off the coast of Norway

shopping opportunities, currency and so on, but on some voyages, such as P&O Theme Cruises, sports personalities, musicians, cookery experts and celebrities give demonstrations and talks. Themes vary enormously, from chamber music and jazz to bridge, cookery or golf. The leader in this area is Swan Hellenic, whose 5-star ship *Minerva* carries a maximum of 474 guests on Discovery Cruises all over Europe and the Mediterranean. Accompanied by a number of guest speakers, who talk on a wide range of destination-related subjects, travellers follow an itinerary adhering to a cultural, geographical or historical theme.

A very different style of cruise can be had with Star Clippers, who offer Mediterranean sailing cruises aboard the 110-m (360-ft) *Star Flyer* (2,556 grt), a four-masted barquentine of the kind that battled round Cape Horn a century ago, and the *Royal Clipper*, a beautiful 134-m (440-ft) five-masted sailing ship (5,000 grt) that entered service in May 2000. Windstar Cruises offer informal cruising on ships that are a cross between 19th-century sailing ships and an Americas Cup yacht. The daily programme varies according to the number of passengers, but activities include scuba-diving, kayaking and wind surfing.

WORKING CRUISES

One of the best options for budget travellers is to sign up on a working cargo ship, many of which cater for ten or twenty passengers. Lodgings and food are always excellent, and peace and quiet are guaranteed. No entertainment is provided, and the crew may not speak English, but a freighter has a workaday authenticity that glitzier liners lack. To reach some truly remote and otherwise inaccessible destinations, smaller merchant vessels are well worth looking into. Hurtigruten, for example, are express coastal steamers that offer a year-round service between Bergen and Kirkenes in the far north of Norway. Their routes are claimed to provide "The World's Most Beautiful Voyage" and are served by a fleet of 11 working ships, linking 35 ports over a distance of 4,200 km (2,500 miles). Operated by Norwegian Coastal Voyages, these unique cruises take 11 days, although passengers can join them at any port of call.

CRUISES FOR CHILDREN

Children love cruising and it can be an exciting, educational experience for them. It is best to choose a ship that particularly welcomes children; there are free children's "clubs", entertainment and amenities on some ships, as well as special menus, cots and high chairs. For very young children, babysitting services may be available, but at extra cost. If the cruise is carefully chosen, adults can also have plenty of time to themselves.

Ship's pool, always popular with children

A romantic honeymoon aboard ship

HONEYMOON CRUISES

Cruises are ideal for honeymoons and second honeymoons. Most companies will make special arrangements for honeymooners or those celebrating a major anniversary, often with gifts, photographs, flowers and champagne. More and more couples are choosing to marry, or at least renew their vows, aboard ship. Princess Cruises' *Grand Princess* even has a wedding chapel in which, following maritime tradition, the Captain performs the ceremony.

TYPES OF CRUISE SHIP

There is a wide range of cruise ships in service, from small ships such as Silversea Cruises' *Silver Wind* (16,927 grt) to P&O's superliner *Aurora* (76,000 grt) and Royal Caribbean International's *Voyager of the Seas* (138,000 grt), so far the largest cruise ship ever built.

Large ships are generally reckoned to be those that cruise with more than 1,500 passengers. The larger the ship, the newer she is likely to be. Some of the latest cruise ships, those with a capacity for over 2,500 passengers, are dubbed "mega-ships" or "superliners", and have a vast range of cabins and an equally astonishing range of on-board facilities.

Very large ships, though, can have disadvantages. In an atmosphere like that of a floating town, passengers may find themselves having to queue for embarkation, disembarkation, in the Purser's office, at the bar and even for informal buffet meals. Service on ships of this size can be rather impersonal and it may be difficult to learn the layout of the ship – new friends made in the bar or restaurant may never be seen again. Some ports are unable to accept large ships, so the itinerary may be restricted for those wishing to make shore excursions. On the other hand, large ships have so many on-board facilities that you may never get round to trying them all: not just a choice of bars and restaurants, but an extraordinary range of activities and entertainment, almost all at no extra cost. Also, on a very large ship, there is almost no sense of movement, even in rough weather so passengers are unlikely to suffer from motion sickness.

Medium-sized cruise ships generally carry between 500 and 1,500 passengers. Some of these ships may be over 30 years old and are likely to have undergone refurbishment and modernization, possibly more than once. Older ships tend to be used at the slightly cheaper end of the cruise

Jogging on the sports deck aboard the *Grand Princess*

Luxury mall on a Royal Caribbean cruise ship

market, and can be quite crowded. However, they offer excellent value for money and tend not to be as formal as more upmarket ships. Many luxury ships fall into the "medium-sized" category. Typically, they offer more space, beautiful cabins, highly trained staff and a variety of dining options. Such benefits, of course, mean higher prices for passengers. For those who like such things, the atmosphere of these ships will also be considerably more formal and ship's etiquette more rigidly adhered to.

Smaller ships, with under 500 passengers, offer far fewer activities and less on-board entertainment, and are more susceptible to pitching or rolling in heavy weather. Yet many people prefer the more intimate atmosphere, the sense of really being at sea, the feeling of camaraderie when making new friends and sharing experiences and the opportunity to chat with the Captain and the ship's crew. Smaller ships also tend to visit more ports. In addition, there is a good chance of passengers being allowed to visit the bridge, a huge bonus for anyone interested in charts, satellite navigation, engine power and the running of the ship.

SHIPS' TONNAGE

The figures given for a passenger ship's tonnage have nothing to do with the vessel's weight, nor how much water it displaces. They relate to available volume capacity and are expressed in gross register tonnes (grt). One gross tonne equals 2.83 cubic metres (100 cubic feet), *tonne* being an Old French word meaning a "large barrel". Centuries ago, wine was shipped from France to England in casks of a standard size, so a ship carrying ten casks was said to measure ten tonnes.

Silver Wind
(Silversea Cruises)
Length: 156 m (514 ft)
Speed: 20.5 knots
Passengers: 298
Weight: 16,927 grt

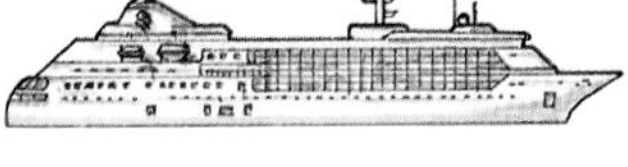

Emerald
(Louis Cruise Lines)
Length: 183 m (599 ft)
Speed: 20 knots
Passengers: 1,172
Weight: 26,431 grt

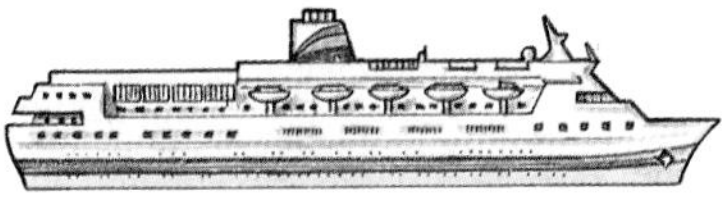

Voyager of the Seas
(Royal Caribbean International)
Length: 311 m (1,020 ft)
Speed: 24 knots
Passengers: 3,114
Weight: 138,000 grt

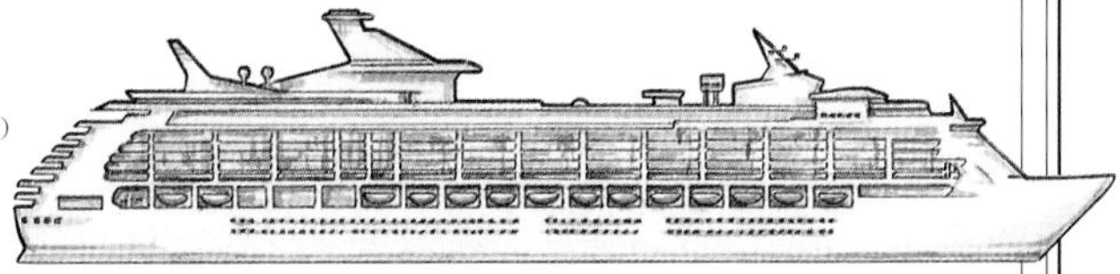

Comparative ships' sizes
The differences in size between ships can be quite staggering. Even the smallest ships are large by most comparisons, while the largest can seem almost like floating cities, with a wide range of facilities to match.

WHERE TO CRUISE

There is hardly any part of coastal Europe that is not accessible by cruise ship. In the Mediterranean alone, probably the most popular cruise destination, more than 50 companies offer cruises ranging in duration from one night to three weeks. Other popular cruise routes include voyages to the beautiful Scandinavian fjords, around the scenic coast of Great Britain and to North Africa.

Cruising around the majestic Norwegian fjords

SCANDINAVIA AND THE BALTIC

A wide range of itineraries to Scandinavia and the Baltic ports is available, in summer only, which means passengers cruising in the Arctic Circle can enjoy the phenomenon of 24-hour daylight. Typical destinations on a Norwegian cruise include Norway's beautiful fjords, found along the west coast and the North Cape. The Scandinavian capitals of Stockholm (Sweden), Oslo (Norway), Helsinki (Finland) and Copenhagen (Denmark) are all popular destinations and offer a mixture of traditional culture and modern European city life.

Further east, the old Russian capital of St Petersburg has many sights of architectural and historical importance and remnants of pre-Revolution Imperial Russia. Most notably, the Hermitage *(see pp64–7)* is home to one of the largest collections of paintings and sculptures in the world. Tallinn (Estonia), Riga (Latvia) and Gdansk (Poland), previously satellites of the Soviet Union, reveal a world that was hidden from Western scrutiny for most of the 20th century. By contrast, Hamburg is the major port of Europe's strongest economy, Germany.

NORTHWESTERN EUROPE

Cruises to northwestern Europe generally run in summer only. Ports of call include cities such as Amsterdam (the Netherlands), a city whose connection to the sea is emphasized by its pattern of canals, and its opulent townhouses, the product of maritime trade that once encompassed much of the world.

Round-Britain cruises include stop-offs at Dover for the English capital, London. Arguably the most exciting and cosmopolitan city in Europe, London boasts modern architecture,

Crowds watching the military tattoo at Edinburgh Castle, Scotland

Monte-Carlo in the south of France

fine bars and restaurants and a myriad of museums. Further north, Leith is the main port for the Scottish capital, Edinburgh, a city rich in pomp and tradition. Other routes include Dublin (Ireland), while others concentrate on the wilderness of the Hebrides and other Scottish islands.

Le Havre (northern France) offers direct access to the beautiful French capital, Paris, while Bordeaux, further south, is a must for wine lovers, as this port is in one of the world's most renowned wine-producing regions.

SOUTHERN EUROPE

Over 50 companies operate cruises in the Mediterranean, offering a wide range of durations and ports of call. The season for Mediterranean cruises generally runs from April to October. Ports of call include cities such as Nice and Monte-Carlo (southern France), which are located on the beautiful Côte d'Azur, while Cádiz, Seville and Barcelona are a fantastic introduction to the Iberian Peninsula. Barcelona, in particular, has long been a cultural and economic powerhouse and retains a vibrancy found in few other cities.

Destinations in Italy include Civitavecchia for Rome, Naples for Pompeii, Livorno for Florence, Siena and Pisa, and Venice. All offer the visitor an unrivalled chance to explore the finest art and architecture that civilization offers: from ancient Roman cities to Byzantine cathedrals and Renaissance palaces. Modern Italy, too, boasts high culture, high fashion and some of the world's finest food.

Further east, Piraeus, for Athens, offers a glimpse of "the cradle of civilization", as well as being a springboard for Crete, Mýkonos, Santoríni and many of the other Greek islands.

NORTH AFRICA AND THE MIDDLE EAST

Because of the hotter temperatures, cruises to North Africa and the Middle East have a longer season, running earlier and later in the year than other Mediterranean cruises.

Ports of call in North Africa include destinations such as Agadir, Casablanca, Tangier and Tunis, whose names alone evoke images of exotic markets and exquisitely-designed mosques. Tripoli is the gateway to the magnificent Roman ruins of Leptis Magna *(see pp264–5)*, while Alexandria, further east, gives access to Cairo and the ancient pyramids at Giza *(see pp268–9)*.

In the Middle East, Jerusalem, from Ashdod, is a key destination for those fascinated by Christianity, Judaism and Islam. Syria's Crusader fort of Krak des Chevaliers *(see pp290–91)* and the Roman city of Ephesus in Turkey *(see pp296–7)* offer still more history. Last, but not least, Istanbul, a city over 2,500 years old and where East meets West, has an abundance of ancient mosques and churches.

Market in the North African port of Tunis

Cruise ship moored in Venice ▷

PORTS OF CALL

NORWAY

North Cape
Honningsvåg
Tromsø
Arctic Circle
Trondheim
Bergen
OSLO
Stavanger

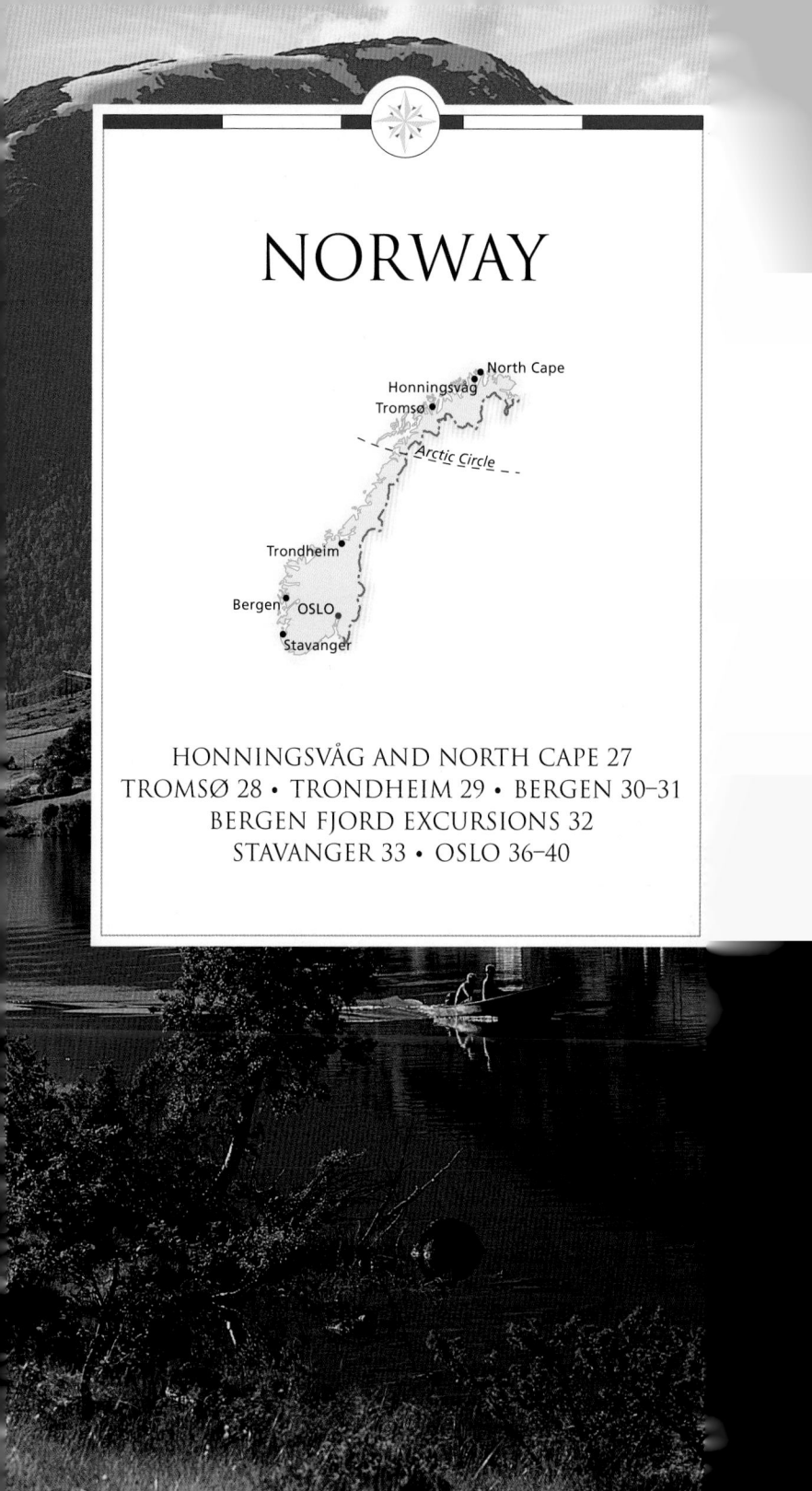

Honningsvåg and North Cape

Mountainous arctic scenery dominates the northern tip of Norway, stretching 250 km (155 miles) east to the Russian border, and 300 km (186 miles) south to Finland. Most travellers to the north of Norway head for the North Cape (Nordkapp) of Magerøya, a treeless island renowned as Europe's most northerly point. The cliff here drops 307 m (1,007 ft) into the sea and a tunnel leads through the rock to the cavernous North Cape Hall (Nordkaphallen), a popular centre for watching the midnight sun (from June to August) and the wintertime Northern Lights. Although the adjacent Knivskjellodden peninsula lies at a slightly higher latitude, the preference for the Cape dates to prehistoric times when local *Sami* (or Lapp) people saw the site as a source of earthly power. *Sami* families still lead a largely nomadic life in the region, herding and exporting reindeer; they are one of Europe's oldest peoples.

Honningsvåg, Magerøya's largest settlement, lies 34 km (21 miles) south of the Cape. The village contains a museum of local history and a small wooden church that alone survived the fires of World War II.

Honningsvåg
The port and fishing village of Honningsvåg stands on a southern tip of Magerøya, sheltered by the hills overlooking the Porsangerfjord. A ramshackle assortment of modern buildings, it lies 160 km (99 miles) northeast of Hammerfest, the world's most northerly town.

Children of the Earth Monument
A modern monument celebrates the North Cape's heritage as a place of earthly power. In prehistoric times local Sami people performed ritual sacrifices nearby.

KEY SIGHTS

Earth Monument
Honningsvåg
North Cape ★
North Cape Hall

FACT FILE

TOURIST INFORMATION

Nordkapphuset, Honningsvåg. ***Tel*** *(78) 47 25 99.* ◯ *summer: daily to 8pm; winter: Mon–Fri to 4pm.*

LOCAL SPECIALITIES

Crafts
Carpentry (wooden trolls, furniture), jewellery, knitwear, silverware, fur.

Dishes
Reinsdyrsuppe (reindeer soup).
Meldalsodd (meatball soup).
Gammeldags sursild (marinated herring).
Tilslorte bondepiker (apple and biscuit dessert).

EXCURSIONS

Tana Bru 129 km (80 miles) SE of Honningsvag. A ***Sami*** settlement by the River Tana. Offers excellent salmon fishing.

Hammerfest 160 km (99 miles) SW of Honningsvag. One of the most northerly towns. Visit the local museum.

Vardø 220 km (132 miles) E of Honningsvåg. Norway's most easterly town. 18th-century fort.

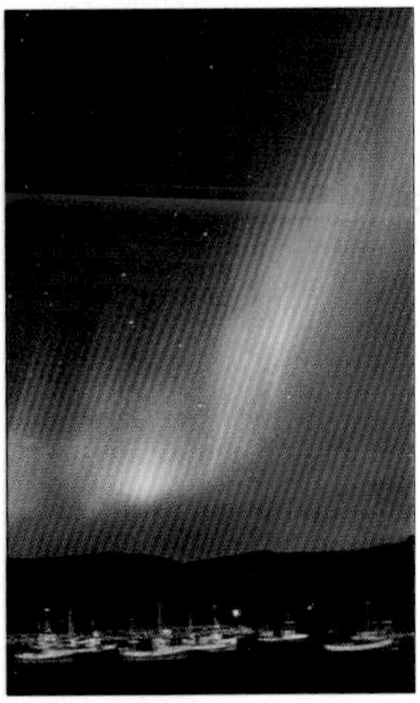

Northern Lights
Although rare, the Northern Lights can be seen all over Norway. They are caused by charged particles entering the earth's magnetic field at the poles.

◁ **The midnight sun, seen from the vantage point of North Cape Hall**

Tromsø

Roald Amundsen, Norway's most famous explorer

Tromsø is a lively university town with a mountainous, fjord-side location. Known as the capital of northern Norway, it lies well inside the Arctic Circle and is best seen in summer, when the midnight sun shines from mid-May to mid-July. It is a famous starting point for polar expeditions, and the history of these (including Roald Amundsen's pioneering trip to the South Pole in 1912) and the town's fishing and hunting industries is recounted in the Polaria and the Polar Museum. Home to some 64,000 people, Tromsø is remarkably compact and stands on an island connected to the mainland by a bridge. A cable car (Fjellheisen) provides access to Mount Storsteinen, a peak that affords stunning views of the town and the surrounding landscape.

KEY SIGHTS

Arctic Cathedral ★

Art Museum of Northern Norway

Mount Storsteinen

Polaria

Polar Museum

FACT FILE

TOURIST INFORMATION

Kirkegata 2. ***Tel*** *(77) 61 00 00.*
summer: Mon–Fri to 7pm; Sat & Sun to 5pm; winter: Mon–Sat to 4pm.

LOCAL SPECIALITIES

Dishes

Reinsdyrstek (reindeer steak).
Pinnekjøtt (salted lamb ribs).
Rakfisk (fermented fish).
Koldtbord (midday buffet).

EXCURSIONS

Tromsø Museum 1.5 km (1 mile) S of Tromsø. Regional history. Exhibits on Sami indigenous culture.

Botanical Gardens 3 km (2 miles) N of Tromsø. Arctic flora.

Lofoten Islands 200 km (124 miles) SW of Tromsø. Remote and mountainous archipelago, popular for winter fishing.

Arctic Cathedral

Tromsø's best-known sight is the Arctic Cathedral. Completed in 1965, it is intended to resemble a *Sami* (Lapp) tent. Its eastern wall has the tallest stained-glass window in Europe.

Lofoten Islands

At the end of the year cod migrate from the Barents Sea to spawn in the waters off Norway, making outposts like the Lofoten Islands vital for winter fishing. The Lofoten Wall (Lofotenveggen) is a range of mountains stretching 160 km (100 miles) across the archipelago.

Art Museum of Northern Norway

This museum displays a broad range of work by several Norwegian artists. Edvard Munch *(see p36)* and Odd Nerdrum are both featured, as are works by the lesser-known Adolph Tidemand, Johan Dahl and Axel Revold. Temporary exhibitions often feature major foreign works.

Trondheim

Detail from a gate at Stiftsgården

Trondheim has benefited from having a good harbour as well as being situated at the head of what is, by Norwegian standards, a wide and fertile valley – the Trøndelag region. Known as Nidaros ("mouth of the River Nid") until the 16th century, it was founded in AD 997 and was the religious and political capital of Norway for many centuries. The earliest Norse Parliament (or *Ting*) was held here, and the construction of Nidaros Cathedral, which survived an otherwise devastating fire in 1682, began in 1077. The much-restored Archbishop's Palace and several wharves are also medieval, but most of the buildings date from the 18th century, a time when the fishing and timber industries were prominent. The wooden Stiftsgården, for example, was built as a private home in the 1770s; it is now the king's official residence in Trondheim and remains the largest timber building in northern Europe. Trondheim also has a number of excellent museums, among the best of which is the Museum of Decorative Arts, whose collection features furniture, ceramics, silver and glassware dating from the 16th century, plus a particularly fine collection of Art Nouveau artifacts.

KEY SIGHTS

Archbishop's Palace
Bakklandet ★
Museum of Decorative Arts
Nidaros Cathedral ★
Stiftsgården

FACT FILE

TOURIST INFORMATION

Munkegaten 19. ***Tel*** *(73) 80 76 60.* *May–Aug: daily to 6pm (May & Jun: Sat & Sun to 4pm); Sep–Apr: Mon–Fri to 4pm.*

MARKETS

Seafood Ravnkloa fish market, Fjordgata; Mon–Fri.

LOCAL SPECIALITIES

Dishes

Geitost (brown goats' milk cheese).
Fårikål (mutton and cabbage stew).
Gammelost (sour milk cheese).

Drinks

Mjød (fermented honey and water).

EXCURSIONS

Stiklestad 59 km (35 miles) NE of Trondheim. Site where Olav Haraldsson (St Olav) was slain. A museum chronicles his life.

Bakklandet
Dominated by brightly painted 18th-century warehouses, Bakklandet is the most scenic part of Trondheim. It boasts many of the city's most popular bars and restaurants.

Stiftsgården
Originally the provincial governor's home, the timber Stiftsgården is a handsome example of how the town looked in the 18th century. It is now a royal residence and the interior can be viewed by guided tour.

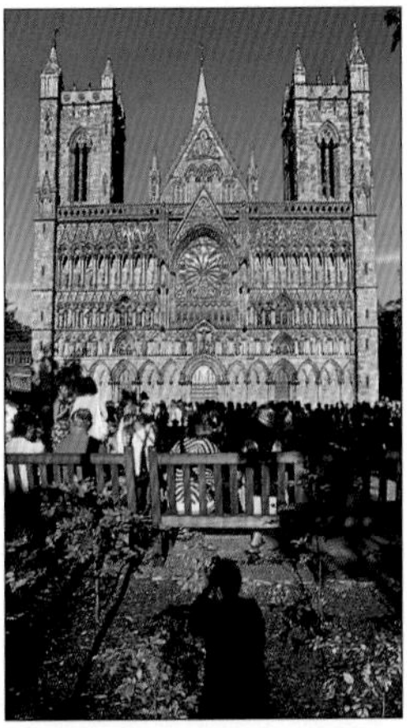

Nidaros Cathedral
One of Norway's architectural highlights, the medieval cathedral has a Gothic arched nave and a magnificent stained-glass rose window. Since 1988 the Norwegian Crown Jewels have been kept here; the regalia of the king, queen and crown prince are on display in a side chapel.

Bergen

Founded in 1070, Bergen was the largest city in medieval Norway and remained the country's busiest port until well into the 19th century. A divisive era dawned in the 14th century when Hanseatic merchants from northern Germany *(see p88)* established a trading station here; a rich class of traders flourished at the expense of local fishermen, a system that continued even after the Norwegians regained control in the 1550s. Nevertheless, the Bryggen (the old waterfront trading centre) has since become the city's architectural treasure, and is now one of UNESCO's World Heritage Sites. The Leprosy Museum and the Bergen Art Museum are other local highlights, while the port is the main gateway to the dramatic and untamed west coast *(see p32)*.

Mariakirken ③
Dating from the 12th century, this twin-towered church is the oldest building in Bergen. Its Baroque pulpit is a 17th-century addition.

Rosenkrantz Tower ②
This reconstructed tower was first built in 1565 by Erik Rosenkrantz, a governor of the city. Standing opposite the harbour, it was intended as a residence and a defence point. Today it is possible to climb to the top for views over the city.

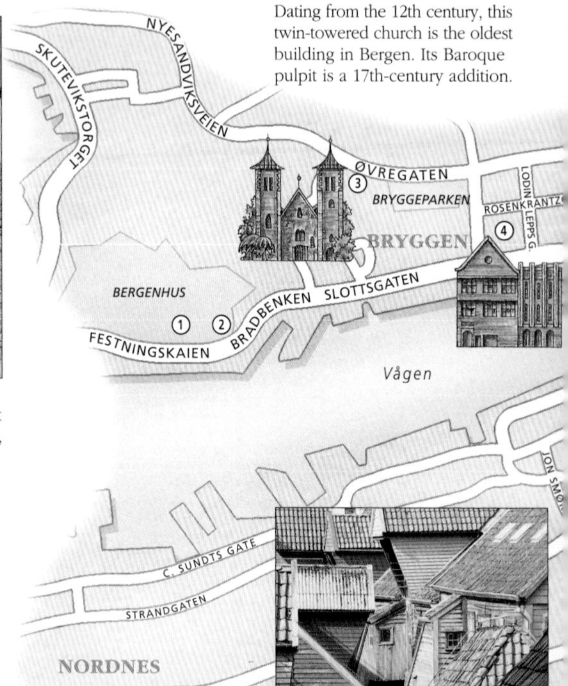

Håkon's Hall ①
Originally built for King Håkon in 1260, Håkon's Hall was reconstructed after World War II. Both the hall and the Rosenkrantz Tower were badly damaged when a German ammunition ship exploded in 1944.

Bryggen ④
Bergen's main wharf was once called "German Quay", after the Hansa merchants who formerly controlled it. Most of the beautifully preserved buildings date from the 18th and 19th centuries.

EDVARD GRIEG (1843–1907)

Born in Bergen, the son of a fish merchant, Edvard Grieg was one of Norway's greatest composers. Along with Henrik Ibsen *(see p39)* he was a prominent figure in the Norwegian nationalist movement, which led to the dissolution of the union with Sweden in 1905. Much of his music, which he once said even tasted of cod, celebrates the Norwegian sea and countryside. For many years he lived in Troldhaugen, just south of Bergen.

Statue of Edvard Grieg at Troldhaugen

Torget Fish Market (5)
All kinds of marine life can be bought at this popular open-air market, as well as fruit, vegetables and flowers.

Leprosy Museum (6)
Housed in St Jørgen's Hospital, this museum tells the story of Norway's struggle with leprosy. The leprosy bacillus was discovered at the hospital by Armauer Hansen in 1873.

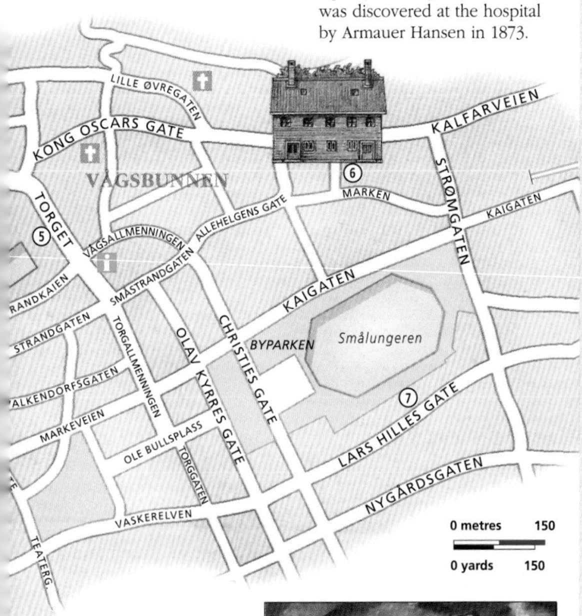

Bergen Art Museum (7)
Divided between three buildings, the Bergen Art Museum contains numerous works by local Norwegian artists, including paintings of the town itself, such as this evocative painting of the old harbour by Nils Krantz dating from 1924.

KEY SIGHTS

(1) Håkon's Hall
(2) Rosenkrantz Tower
(3) Mariakirken
(4) Bryggen ★
(5) Torget Fish Market
(6) Leprosy Museum ★
(7) Bergen Art Museum

FACT FILE

TOURIST INFORMATION

Vagsallmenningen 1. ***Tel** (55) 55 20 00.* ◻ *Jun–Aug: daily to 10pm; May & Sep: daily to 8pm; Oct–Apr: Mon–Sat to 4pm.*

MARKETS

Seafood Torget; daily.

LOCAL SPECIALITIES

Crafts
Traditional woodwork, ironwork, furniture, enamelware, fur, woodcarving (including wooden trolls), silverware, knitwear.
Dishes
Fiskekabaret (seafood and vegetables in aspic).
Shillingsboller (sugar-coated spiral bun).
Skolebrød (custard roll with coconut icing).
Drinks
Hansa (beer).

EXCURSIONS

Gamle Bergen Museum 3 km (2 miles) N of Bergen. An open-air architectural museum, with buildings dating from the 18th and 19th centuries. The interiors have been refurbished in keeping with the age of the buildings.
Fantoft Stave Church 5 km (3 miles) S of Bergen. A painstakingly restored 12th-century building, originally modelled on the stave church in Borgund *(see p32)*. The Borgund church is the best of its kind in Norway.
Troldhaugen 8 km (5 miles) S of Bergen. This is the former lakeside home of the composer Edvard Grieg, who spent the last 22 years of his life here. The building is now a museum dedicated to his life and works, with guided tours available. Grieg and his wife are buried just a few minutes' walk from the house.

Around Bergen's Fjords

Bergen is the perfect base for exploring the western fjords. Hurtigruten (or "rapid route") ferries ply northwards from Bergen to Kirkenes, connecting with routes leading into Sognefjord, Nordfjord, Aurlandsfjord and even more remote places; the further north one travels the bleaker and more forbidding the scenery becomes. Hardangerfjord, to the south, is also accessible from Bergen. Less dramatic than Sognefjord and its tributaries, it leads to the pretty town of Ulvik, which is famous for its orchards, and Eidfjord to the northeast – a lonely fjord deep enough for cruise ships to enter. From Eidfjord it is a short distance to the Hardangervidda National Park, a high-lying area of lake-dotted moorland dominated by a 1862-m (6109-ft) high peak. The Hardangerjøkulen glacier can be also reached from Eidfjord, but accompanied walking is advised.

Sognefjord
At 200 km (120 miles) long and 1,300 m (4,260 ft) deep, Sognefjord is the largest fjord in the world. It passes through some of Norway's lushest territory and is best seen in May when the trees are in bloom. Its banks are scattered with villages, and Balestrand and Fjaerland are popular places to visit. Neroyfjord and Fjaerlandsfjord are two spectacular tributaries.

Aurlandsfjord
Ferry services operate daily between Bergen and the remote town of Flåm. This tiny resort stands at the end of Aurlandsfjord, a narrow inlet overlooked by sheer cliffs and cascading waterfalls.

Borgund Stave Church
The road between Oslo and Bergen passes one of the finest medieval churches in Norway. Located at Borgund, near the head of Sognefjord, the building is made of vertical timbers slotted into wooden frames, or "staves".

KEY SIGHTS

Aurlandsfjord
Borgund Stave Church ★
Hardangerfjord ★
Sognefjord ★

FACT FILE

TOURIST INFORMATION

The town centre, Aurland. **Tel** *(57) 63 33 13.* ☐ *daily to 3:30pm (Jun–Aug: Sat to 5pm).*

The harbour, Balestrand. **Tel** *(57) 69 12 55.* ☐ *mid-May–mid-Sep: Mon–Fri to 6pm, Sat & Sun to 2pm.*

The passenger ferry, Fjaerland. **Tel** *(57) 69 32 33.* ☐ *mid-May–mid-Sep: daily to 5:30pm.*

The train station, Flam. **Tel** *(57) 63 21 06.* ☐ *May & Sep: daily to 4pm; Jun–Aug: daily to 7:30pm.*

The waterfront, Ulvik. **Tel** *(56) 52 63 60.* ☐ *mid-May–mid-Sep: daily to 5pm; mid-Sep–mid-May: Mon–Fri to 2pm.*

LOCAL SPECIALITIES

Crafts Knitwear, fur.

EXCURSION

Norwegian Glacier Museum
Fjaerland, 150 km (93 miles) NE of Bergen. Glaciers explained.

Stavanger

A tin of Stavanger fish

Stavanger is one of Norway's great success stories. After flourishing in the 19th century, the city survived the collapse of the local herring industry and blossomed again with the discovery of North Sea oil in the 1960s. The Norwegian Petroleum Museum tells the story of this venture, while various buildings around town, including Ledaal Manor (a royal residence), Breidablikk (a restored villa), and the entire old quarter, recall the days of 19th-century prosperity. Other highlights include a 12th-century cathedral, a picturesque marina and the Canning Museum, which highlights another of the city's major industries. The best view over Stavanger can be seen from the Valberg Tower, a 19th-century fire look-out.

Gamle Stavanger

In contrast to the modern town centre, Old Stavanger is characterized by 19th-century wooden houses. Built by merchants during the herring boom, they are in perfect condition today, with gas lamps and tiny terraced gardens. A former sardine-canning factory in the old quarter houses the Canning Museum; packaging imported fish became an important industry when herring became scarce in the 1870s.

KEY SIGHTS

Breidablikk
Canning Museum
Cathedral
Gamle Stavanger ★
Ledaal Manor
Marina
Norwegian Petroleum Museum
Valberg Tower

FACT FILE

TOURIST INFORMATION

Domkirkeplassen 3.
Tel *(51) 85 92 00.* ◯ *summer: daily to 6pm; winter: Mon–Fri to 4pm, Sat to 2pm.*

MARKETS

Flowers & fruit Torget; daily.
Seafood Along the quayside; daily.

LOCAL SPECIALITIES

Crafts
Traditional woodwork, ironwork.
Dishes
Laks (salmon).
Fenalår (cured leg of mutton).
Ferske reker (fresh prawns).
Gomme (sweet milk dessert).
Drinks
Akevitt (Norwegian aquavit).

EXCURSIONS

Haugesund 52 km (31 miles) N of Stavanger. The grave of Harald Hårfager, who united Norway in AD 872. An obelisk marks the spot.
Preikestolen (Pulpit Rock) 25 km (15 miles) NE of Stavanger. A sheer 600-m (1,967-ft) drop into the Lysefjord. Often crowded, but offering breathtaking views.

Marina

Once crowded with fishermen, coopers and net-makers, the marina at Stavanger is relatively tranquil today and makes an ideal place to spend a few quiet hours. The area becomes quite lively at night, however, particularly along Skagenkaien, which has a number of night-clubs and bars. The clientele is an interesting mixture of travellers, office workers, fishermen and, at weekends, workers from the oil rigs.

The Fjords

Among the world's most spectacular geological formations, the Norwegian fjords are long, narrow inlets stretching deep into the surrounding mountains. At their innermost reaches, their depth often matches the height of the cliffs above, while shallower waters connect them to the sea. They were created by a gradual process of glacier erosion during the last Ice Age (around 110,000 to 13,000 BC) when enormous glaciers crept through the valleys, gouging steep-sided crevices into the landscape, often far below the surface of the sea. When the glaciers finally melted, sea water burst in and filled the hollows left by the ice.

Waterfalls can be seen where glaciers and torrents of water once cut vertical precipices into the mountain sides.

At the fjords' mouths on the Atlantic coast the tree-covered mountains rise steeply. Fir and birch are the most common species. In the north, however, the cliff faces are usually bare all the way down to the shore.

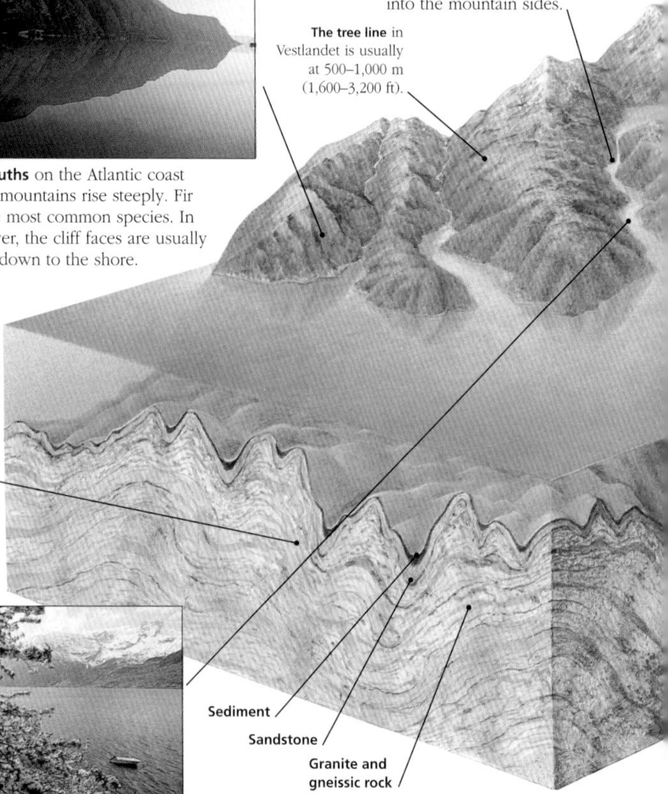
The tree line in Vestlandet is usually at 500–1,000 m (1,600–3,200 ft).
The threshold between fjord and sea often has a depth of just one tenth of the fjord at its deepest point.
Sediment
Sandstone
Granite and gneissic rock

Fruit and vegetable cultivation is a thriving industry at the inner reaches of the more southern fjords. Here the climate is more favourable than by the coast.

THE STRUCTURE OF A FJORD

This cut-away artwork shows a typical fjord, with a threshold of shallow water at the mouth falling steeply down to great depths further inland, and inlets radiating from the main fjord. The sea bed, like the surrounding mountains, consists of granite and gneiss with a layer of sediment on top.

Glaciers covered coastal areas during the last Ice Age, creating fjords as they melted. A reminder of these powerful formations can still be seen in clefts higher up in the mountains.

The high, snow-covered peaks can reach heights of 1,500 m (4,900 ft) just a short distance from the shore.

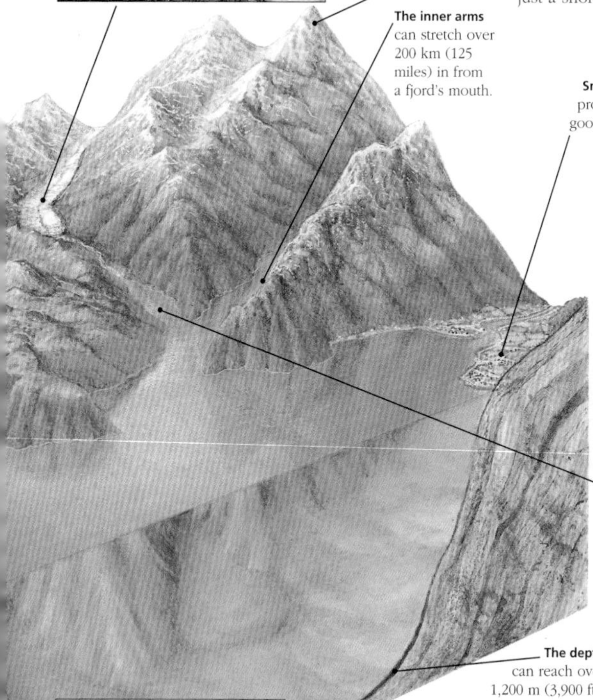

The inner arms can stretch over 200 km (125 miles) in from a fjord's mouth.

Small towns have developed in protected bays where the soil is good for cultivation and farming.

The inlets can be very long and often branch into several tributaries. The glaciers carved through the rock wherever the surface was weak.

The depth can reach over 1,200 m (3,900 ft).

Car ferries criss-cross the fjords at many points. Although not as quick an alternative as road tunnels and bridges, they remain a popular choice for the scenic views they offer.

TUNNELS UNDER THE FJORDS

Communications along the Atlantic coast of Norway have always been a challenge, with fjords cutting long clefts into the land and the risk of avalanches and the mountains themselves creating other obstacles. However, great improvements to the infrastructure have been made possible thanks to the riches from the North Sea oil fields. Using modern engineering and drilling techniques, huge tunnels have been driven through mountain ranges and under fjords, making transport easier between the small communities.

The Lærdal Tunnel, an impressive 24.5 km (15 miles) long

Oslo

Founded around 1050 by King Harald Hårdråde, Oslo came into prominence in the 14th century when Håkon V moved from Bergen *(see pp30–31)* to Oslo's fortress of Akershus. Under Danish rule (1397–1814) its fortunes initially waned, only to flourish again after Christian IV rebuilt the town in 1624. "Christiania" prospered in the 19th century and became the capital of an independent Norway in 1905, after 90 years of union with Sweden. Reverting to its original name in 1925, Oslo consolidated its role as a university town throughout the 20th century. Now a wealthy modern city, Oslo has two cultural centres, one focused on Karl Johans Gate, the main thoroughfare, the other on the Bygdøy Peninsula.

Royal Palace ⑥
This 19th-century palace has gardens open to the public. A statue of its builder, King Karl Johan (1818–44), stands by the gate.

Vigeland Sculpture Park and Museum ⑤
Located in the Frognerparken, the Vigeland Sculpture Park is a showcase of the art of Gustav Vigeland. The fantastic bronze figures were still in the making when Vigeland died in 1943, nearly twenty years into the project.

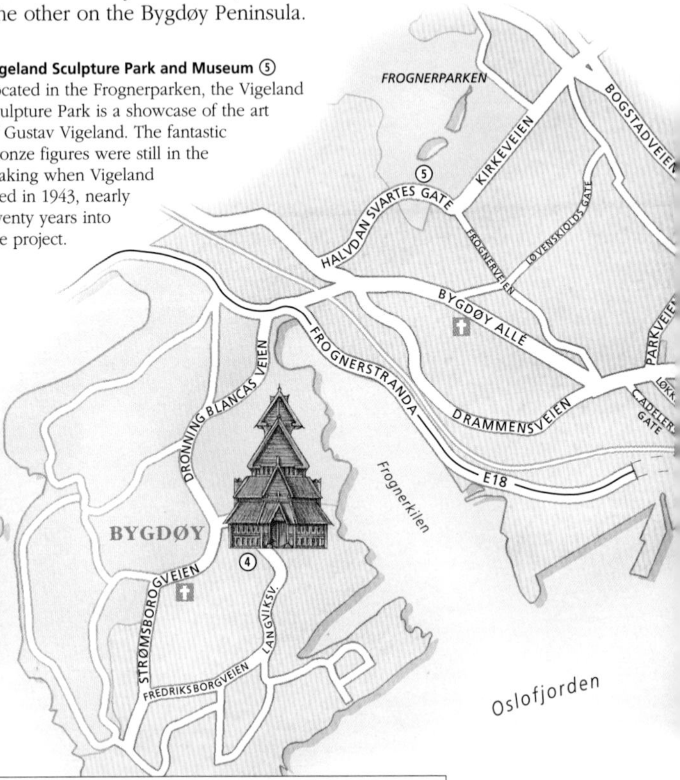

0 metres 500

0 yards 500

EDVARD MUNCH

One of Scandinavia's leading artists, Edvard Munch (1863–1944) left an incredible 1,100 paintings, 4,500 drawings and 18,000 graphic works to the city of Oslo when he died. Despite a life plagued by depression, he was a highly prolific artist whose intensely psychological work remains one of the great cornerstones of early modern art. Munch is widely considered to be the father of the Expressionist movement.

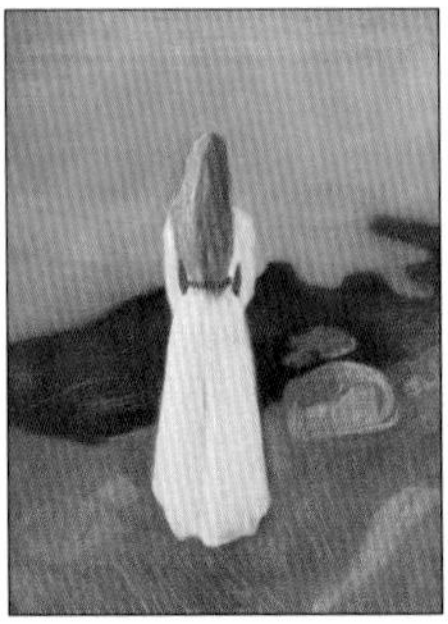

***Young Girl on a Jetty* (1896) by Edvard Munch**

Bygdøy Peninsula ④
As important as the city centre itself, the Bygdøy Peninsula boasts some of Norway's finest museums. The Viking Ships Museum alone justifies a visit, with its trio of 9th-century longboats discovered on the shores of Oslofjorden.

Rådhuset ②
Oslo's Modernist City Hall opened in 1950 to mark the city's 900th anniversary. The interior design celebrates all things Norwegian, including this Viking warrior carved into one of the doors.

Domkirke ⑩
Standing in what was once the city's main square, the Domkirke (Cathedral) has a combination of Baroque and contemporary decoration. The tower was rebuilt in 1850.

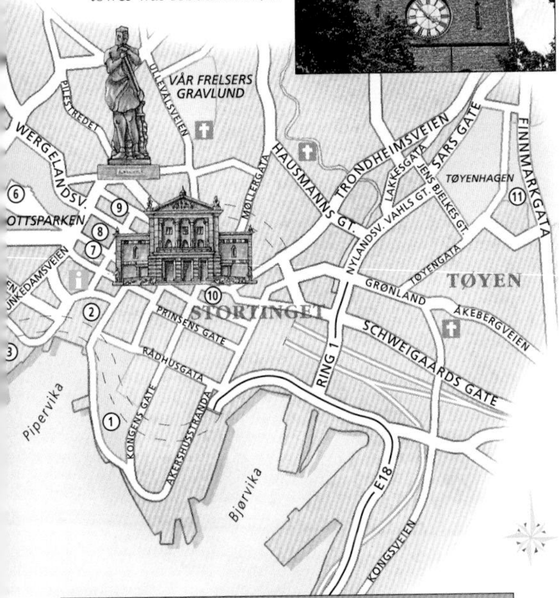

Aker Brygge ③
Formerly a shipyard, Aker Brygge is a commercial area built around a modern sculpture court. It contains some of Oslo's most popular bars, many of which have views of Akershus Castle and the fishing boats on the opposite quay.

KEY SIGHTS

① Akershus Castle ★
② Rådhuset
③ Aker Brygge
④ Bygdøy Peninsula ★ *(see p40)*
⑤ Vigeland Sculpture Park and Museum ★
⑥ Royal Palace
⑦ National Theatre
⑧ Oslo University
⑨ National Gallery ★
⑩ Domkirke
⑪ Munch Museum ★

FACT FILE

TOURIST INFORMATION

Jernbanetorget 1. ***Tel*** *(81) 53 05 55.* ◻ *May–Sep: to 8pm; Oct–Apr: to 6pm, public hols to 4pm.*

MARKETS

Fruit and flowers Stortorvet; Mon–Sat.

LOCAL SPECIALITIES

Crafts
Traditional woodwork, ironwork, furniture, enamelware, fur, woodcarving (including wooden trolls), silverware, knitwear.

Dishes
Ferske reker (freshly boiled shrimps).
Lutefisk (air-dried white fish, soaked and then poached).
Rømmegrøt (sour cream porridge).
Multer med krem (cloudberries and cream).

Drinks
Ringnes (beer).

EXCURSIONS

Nordmarka 3 km (2 miles) N of central Oslo. A wilderness area popular with hikers and skiers, offering hills, lakes and forests.

Henie-Onstad Art Centre 6 km (4 miles) W of central Oslo. Prestigious modern art centre including work by Matisse, Picasso and various Expressionist artists.

Fredrikstad 88 km (54 miles) S of Oslo. Old fortress town with moats, gates and a drawbridge. Originally constructed by Frederick II in 1567, it was rebuilt in the 17th century to become Norway's strongest fortress.

Akershus Castle, Oslo's monument to medieval times

Exploring Oslo

All the main sights in central Oslo lie within walking distance of each other, as do those of the neighbouring Bygdøy Peninsula *(see p40)*. The main street, Karl Johans Gate, cuts through the Neo-Classical heart of town, stretching westwards from Oslo Central Station past Oslo University and the Parliament building to the Royal Palace in the Slottsparken. The city has undergone a cultural and social rebirth in recent years and now has a good restaurant scene and nightlife.

Akershus Castle ①

Overlooking Oslofjorden, Akershus Castle is the city's finest memorial to medieval times. Built around 1300, it was transformed in the 1620s by King Christian IV who turned it into a Renaissance residence. He surrounded the structure with a fortress (the Akershus Festning), complete with bastions to protect against artillery bombardments. During World War II, the Nazis occupied the castle and killed many of the Norwegian Resistance movement in its grounds. Today, a Resistance Museum stands by the castle gates, its largely pictorial displays detailing the history of Norway's war, from occupation to resistance and liberation. Parts of the fortress are still in military use.

Rådhuset ②

The Rådhuset is by far Oslo's most noticeable building when viewed from the fjord. Many considered it an un-Norwegian addition to the city when it opened in 1950 to commemorate Oslo's 900th anniversary, but the Rådhuset has since become a popular symbol of civic pride. Contrasting with the austere exterior, all manner of colourful murals, sculptures and frescoes celebrate Norwegian achievements inside. Since 1990, the main hall has hosted the presentation of the Nobel Peace Prize, an award established by Swedish chemist Alfred Nobel (1833–1910). The four other Nobel Prizes (for physics, chemistry, medicine and literature) are presented in Stockholm *(see pp44–9)*.

Aker Brygge ③

The old Aker shipyard is now a glass-and-chrome shopping and restaurant complex built around an open sculpture court. The area is particularly popular on long, summer evenings, when people gather at waterfront bars and watch the central harbour. The waterways are always busy with ferries shuttling between the many delightful islands of Oslofjord.

Bygdøy Peninsula ④

See p40.

Vigeland Sculpture Park and Museum ⑤

Clustered in Frogner Park, the weird and wonderful sculptures of Gustav Vigeland (1869–1943) depict a strange world of fighting and playing figures. Fifty-eight bronzes of men, women and infants flank the footbridge over the river, and his most famous creation, a 17-m (56-ft) high granite obelisk adorned with 121 intertwined figures, stands in the centre of the park. Only a short walk from the obelisk is a museum devoted to Vigeland himself, who lived and worked in the building for nine years. Numerous items relating to his life and

The Vigeland Sculpture Park, viewed from the central obelisk

work are on display, including plastercasts and drawings, plus photographs of the park while it was being built.

Royal Palace ⑥

Completed in 1848, a year when monarchies throughout Europe were being overthrown, the Royal Palace, with its lack of walls or railings, is a symbol of Norwegian openness. Though the interior is out of bounds to the public, the gardens are open to all and make a popular meeting spot in summer. An equestrian statue of the builder of the palace, King Karl Johan (reigned 1818–44), stands in the square in front of the building. A one-time general in Napoleon's army, he abandoned the French revolutionary cause and was elected king of Sweden – and therefore king of Norway, as the country had passed into Swedish control in 1814.

Statue of King Karl Johan, outside the Royal Palace

National Theatre ⑦

Built in 1899, this Neo-Classical theatre is flanked by statues of the great 19th-century Norwegian playwrights Bjørnsterne Bjørnson (1832–1910), who won the Nobel Prize for Literature in 1903, and Henrik Ibsen (1828–1906), one of the founders of modern drama.

The auditorium has been restored to its original design and can be seen by guided tour. All performances are given in Norwegian.

Oslo University ⑧

The 19th-century university stands at the western end of Karl Johans Gate. One of the great attractions inside is the main hall, or Aula, with its huge murals by Edvard Munch *(see p36)*. Although completed in 1909, the murals were unveiled only in 1916, following a typically controversial reception. The images, including *Sun, Alma Mater* and *The History* have an optimism that is not usually associated with his work.

Also within the university grounds is the History Museum, which has an excellent Viking and early medieval section. An ethnographic display features numerous *Sami* (Lapp) artifacts.

National Gallery ⑨

Norway's largest and most comprehensive collection of fine art is housed in a grand 19th-century building situated close to the university.

French Impressionist paintings by Manet, Monet and Degas hang alongside Post-Impressionist works by Cézanne and Gauguin and early 20th-century Modernists Picasso and Braque.

The Munch room contains a number of important works by Edvard Munch, including *The Sick Child* (1885), which portrays a young person's farewell to an unlived life, and one of many versions of his world-famous expression of existential angst *The Scream* (1893). A room of Norwegian paintings includes 19th-century landscapes by Johan Christian Dahl and Thomas Fearnley, both of whom depicted local scenery. All works by artists born after 1920 are now on display in the National Museum of Contemporary Art.

Exterior of the National Gallery

Domkirke ⑩

Standing next to the Basarhallene (the 19th-century home of the city's food market), the Domkirke is a late-17th-century cathedral with a remodelled tower dating from 1850. The interior has been restored to its original, dazzling colour scheme, and the imposing royal box remains directly in front of the lavish Baroque pulpit. The stained-glass windows were created in 1910 by Emanuel Vigeland, the younger brother of Gustav Vigeland, the creator of Oslo's Sculpture Park.

Munch Museum ⑪

No trip to Oslo is complete without a visit to the Munch Museum. It contains a huge collection of the artist's work, only a fraction of which can be shown at any one time. The paintings span the whole of Munch's career and feature all of his most famous images (including the popular version of *Red Virginia Creeper* and *The Scream*), plus numerous self-portraits that reveal much of the mind of their creator.

Munch's pioneering woodcuts and lithographs are also on display, alongside many of his earlier works. A separate exhibition highlights the life and times of one of Norway's most troubled artists.

The National Theatre, with statues of playwrights Ibsen and Bjørnson

Oslo: Bygdøy Peninsula ④

No trip to Oslo is complete without a visit to the Bygdøy Peninsula, an area of natural beauty lying southwest of the city centre, offering beaches, walking paths, the royal family's summer residence and numerous historic sites. Several halls, including the Viking Ships Museum, are devoted to Norway's maritime past, while a Folk Museum celebrates traditional ways of life. The schooner that took explorer Roald Amundsen to the Antarctic now has its own museum, as do the remarkable vessels built by Thor Heyerdahl for his pioneering expeditions to Polynesia and the Caribbean.

The balsawood Kon-Tiki raft used by Thor Heyerdahl in 1947

Kon-Tiki Museum
The Kon-Tiki Museum houses the incredibly fragile-looking vessels used by Norwegian explorer Thor Heyerdahl on his legendary journeys across the Pacific and Atlantic oceans. The balsawood *Kon-Tiki* raft carried him and his crew all the way from Peru to Polynesia in 1947, confirming his theory that the first Polynesian settlers may have come from pre-Inca South America. In 1970 he also sailed a tiny papyrus boat, called *Ra II*, from Morocco to the Caribbean, proving that the ancient Egyptians may have had contact with the Americas. Next to the boats themselves, the eventful sagas of these expeditions are described in the exhibition.

Norwegian Folk Museum
Established in 1894, this excellent semi-outdoor museum is largely devoted to Norwegian rural life. The buildings include reconstructed dwellings, barns, storehouses and a magnificent original stave church, complete with shingle-covered roofs, dating from the 13th century.

Inside, displays include examples of folk art, dolls and dollhouses, *Sami* (Lapp) handicrafts, regional folk dresses, the playwright Henrik Ibsen's study and a reassembled Norwegian Parliament chamber. There are also regular shows of traditional local culture, including folk dancing, flatbread baking and weaving.

A restored grass-roofed house at the Norwegian Folk Museum

Detail of the Oseberg ship in the Viking Ships Museum

Viking Ships Museum
No museum pays homage to the Viking explorers better than this specially built hall containing three beautifully preserved 9th-century vessels. All three were unearthed from burial mounds in Norway, and funerary goods from each are on display, including ceremonial sleighs, chests and tapestries. Viewing platforms allow visitors to study the magnificent 22 m by 5 m (72 ft by 16 ft) Oseberg ship and the slightly larger Gokstad ship, both of which were discovered on the western side of Oslofjorden. Fragmented sections of the smaller Tune ship remain much as they were when they were found on the eastern side of the fjord in 1867.

Fram Museum
Built in 1892 by Scottish-Norwegian shipbuilder Colin Archer, the tiny schooner *Fram* is a unique smooth-sided vessel that was ideal for polar voyages. It is best known as the ship that carried Roald Amundsen on his pioneering journey to the South Pole in 1912 (ahead of Britain's Captain Scott). The ship's living quarters are incredibly cramped, but visitors can ease themselves between the beams and braces that hold the vessel together. Much of Amundsen's equipment is on display, ranging from delicate surgical instruments to an unlikely form of seafaring entertainment: a piano.

The Vikings

From the 8th to the 11th century the Vikings, or Northmen, sailed from their overpopulated fjords in Scandinavia and made their way across Europe, plundering, looking for trade and offering mercenary service. The Swedes established themselves throughout the Baltic and controlled the overland route to the Black Sea, while the Danes invaded England, Portugal and France. The adventures of the Norwegians, however, were unparalleled in their success and became the stuff of Viking legend.

Gold and silver box brooch

After overrunning the Orkneys, Hebrides, Shetlands, Faroes, eastern Ireland and Iceland, the Norwegian Vikings discovered Greenland and quite possibly sailed to North America (Vinland) under Eric the Red in around AD 1000.

The Vikings were undoubtedly the most feared Europeans of their day, and their impact on history was immense. Fear of the Viking raid unified many otherwise disparate tribes and kingdoms, and many new political states were created by the Vikings themselves.

Burial "ships" made of stone were provided for warriors from poorer families

VIKING RELIGION

The Vikings' supreme gods were Odin (god of war), Thor (thunder) and Frey (fertility), and Valhalla was their equivalent of heaven. Warriors were buried with whatever the afterlife required, and the rich were entombed in ships, often with their servants. Most had converted to Christianity by the late 10th century, but Sweden remained pagan well into the 11th century.

Frey, god of fertility

THE LONGBOAT

The longboat was the main vessel of the Viking raid. Longer, slimmer and faster than the usual Viking ship, it had a large rectangular sail and between 24 and 50 oars. The sail was used in open sea and navigation was achieved by taking bearings from the stars.

The prow, curled into a "shepherd's crook", formed a high defensive barrier.

The keel was characteristically shallow to allow for flat beach landings.

The beautifully restored Oseberg ship, unearthed in 1904, on display at the Viking Ships Museum in Oslo

Weapons and armour were the very backbone of Viking culture, so the blacksmith's art was always in demand. Bronze and iron swords were endlessly produced, many of which followed their bearers to the grave. Arrows, axes, shields, helmets and coats of mail were standard military gear, many examples of which survive in pristine condition today. Most existing items were found in graves throughout Scandinavia.

Viking helmet with noseguard

Gold arm ring from Denmark

Jewellery design often showed Arab and eastern European influence, which illustrates the extent of Viking domination. Gold and silver were a sign of great wealth and prestige, and many such pieces were buried in Viking tombs. Equally beautiful ornaments were made of bronze, pewter, coloured glass, jet and amber.

Picture stones were memorial blocks that celebrated bravery in battle and the glory of dead relatives. Set in public places, they were carved with stories told in pictures and runic writing.

Picture stone from Sweden

Stockholm archipelago, Sweden ▷

SWEDEN

Stockholm

An unbelievably beautiful city, Stockholm is surrounded by clear water and unspoilt countryside that stretches right into the heart of the urban area. The city's 750-year history has produced many attractive buildings and plenty of cultural treasures – now on display in its many fine museums. The generally accepted founder of Stockholm is the 13th-century regent, Birger Jarl, who built a fort to protect Lake Mälaren from pirates. Initially important as a trading centre, the city did not become the capital of Sweden until the 16th century. Over the centuries, Stockholm's reputation as a rustic capital has been superseded by its current distinction as a dynamic centre of information technology.

The National Historical Museum ⑤
This well-preserved Madonna figure, Maria from Viklau, is part of the medieval collection.

City Hall ③
The Stadshuset was probably Sweden's biggest architectural project of the 20th century. Completed in 1923, it has become a symbol of the city and serves as a backdrop for the annual regatta on the Riddarfjärden. The Nobel Prize festivities are also held here.

Royal Palace ①
Erik XIV's crown, made by Cornelius ver Weiden in 1561, is kept in the treasury of the Royal Palace. Built in the 18th century, the palace is no longer a royal residence, though the King and Queen have offices here.

Mariaberget ⑩
Mariaberget's stone buildings on the steep slopes down towards Riddarfjärden are among Stockholm's most distinctive. After a fire destroyed the old buildings in 1759, the area was rebuilt according to a law forbidding the construction of wooden houses in this part of the city.

Skansen Open Air Museum ⑦
The world's first open-air museum, founded in 1891, shows the Sweden of bygone days. Farms, urban scenes, craft working and traditional festivals can be experienced in a setting of Nordic flora and fauna.

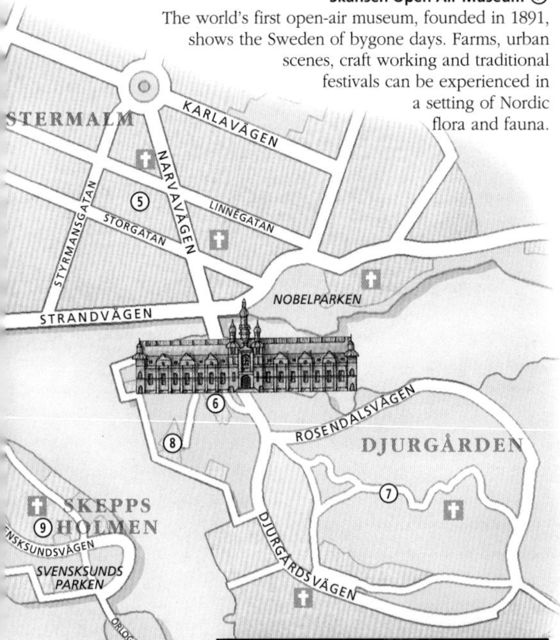

★ **Vasa Museum ⑧**
A fatal capsizal in 1628, and a successful salvage operation 333 years afterwards, gave Stockholm its most popular museum, the Vasamuseet. The eponymous warship *Vasa* is now 95 per cent intact after painstaking renovation.

KEY SIGHTS

① Royal Palace ★
② Storkyrkan
③ City Hall ★
④ Kungsträdgården
⑤ The National Historical Museum
⑥ Nordic Museum
⑦ Skansen Open Air Museum ★
⑧ Vasa Museum ★
⑨ Skeppsholmen and Modern Museum
⑩ Mariaberget

FACT FILE

TOURIST INFORMATION

Vasagatan 14.
Tel *468 508 285 08.* ☐ *Mon–Fri to 7pm, Sat to 5pm, Sun to 4pm.*

MARKETS

Traditional Christmas market Skansen; Sundays in December.
Fruit & vegetables Hötorget; Mon–Sat. Östermalmshallen, Humlegårdsgatan 1–3; Mon–Sat. Söderhallarna Medborgarplatsen 3; Mon–Sat.

LOCAL SPECIALITIES

Crafts
Dalahäst wooden horses, hand-painted clogs, hand-knitted garments, glass and crystal.
Dishes
Böckling (smoked herring). *Gubbröra* (anchovy, beetroot, onion and capers). *Gravad Lax* (marinated salmon). *Köttbullar med lingon* (meatballs with lingonberries).
Drinks
Brännvin (flavoured schnapps).

EXCURSIONS

Drottningholm Lovön island, 10 km (6 miles) W of Stockholm. This 17th-century palace is a UNESCO World Heritage site, and home of the Swedish royal family.
Birka Björkö island, 30 km (19 miles) W of Stockholm. The museum and archaeological digs show the history of Scandinavia's first town, founded in the 8th century by the king of Svea.

Stockholm: Gamla Stan

The city's Gamla Stan (Old Town) grew up on three islands linked by bridges. Relics of its earliest history *(see p44)* can be found on the largest island, Stadsholmen, the whole of which is an area of historical heritage. The greatest sights are the Royal Palace and monuments in the surrounding streets, shown here. The steep hill of Slottsbacken runs past the palace's most attractive façade, providing the route for ceremonial processions and the daily Changing of the Guard at midday. At the top end is the Storkyrkan, the city's cathedral, finished in the area's characteristic warm ochre plaster. The narrow streets brim with bookstores and antiques and souvenir shops, and many medieval cellars are now restaurants and cafés.

Statue of Olaus Petri
Sweden's greatest Lutheran reformer *(see p48)* is buried in the Storkyrkan.

Palace of Axel Oxenstierna
Built in 1653 this is, for Stockholm, an unusual example of Roman Mannerism. Axel Oxenstierna (1583–1654) was chancellor to King Gustav II Adolf, and an influential figure in Swedish politics.

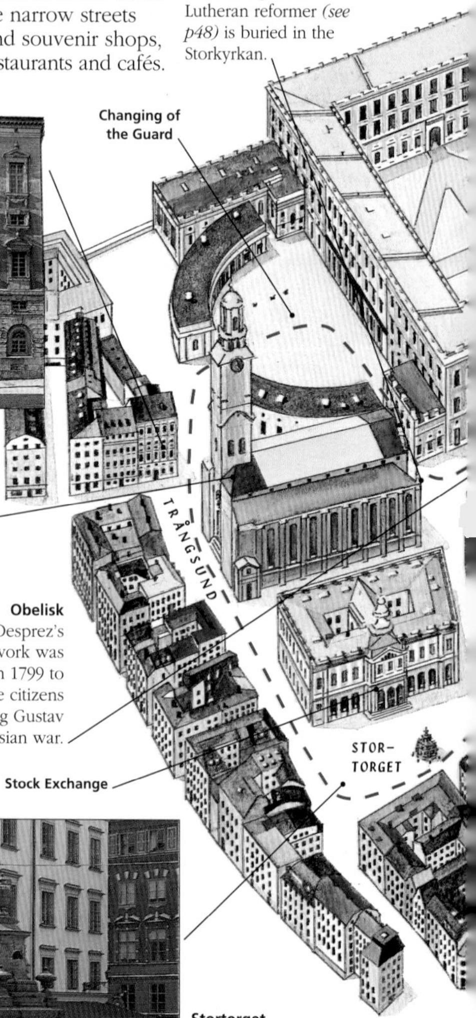

Changing of the Guard

Obelisk
Louis Jean Desprez's striking work was erected in 1799 to thank the citizens for backing Gustav III's Russian war.

Stock Exchange

★ Storkyrkan
The late-Gothic interior of this cathedral is filled with treasures from different eras, including this Baroque pulpit (see p48) above Olaus Petri's grave.

Stortorget
This square, with a well dating from 1778, is at the heart of Stockholm's Old Town. Eighty Swedish noblemen were beheaded here during the Stockholm Bloodbath of 1520.

STAR SIGHTS

- ★ Storkyrkan
- ★ Livrustkammaren
- ★ Royal Palace

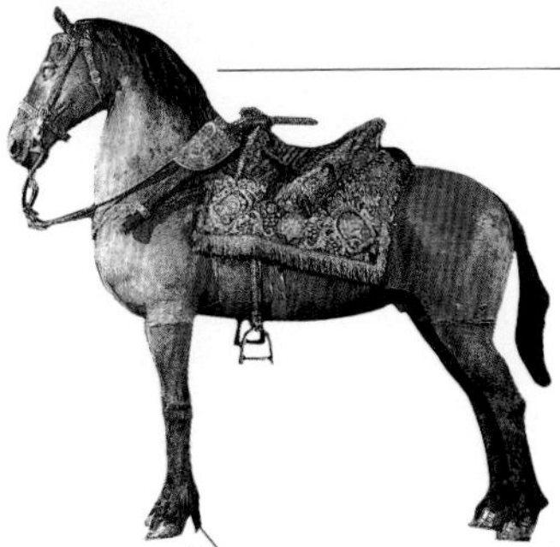

★ Livrustkammaren
Sweden's oldest museum, founded in 1633, displays royal weaponry, clothing and carriages from over five centuries. Among the exhibits is Gustav II Adolf's stuffed stallion, Streiff, which the king rode at the battle of Lützen in 1632.

LOCATOR MAP

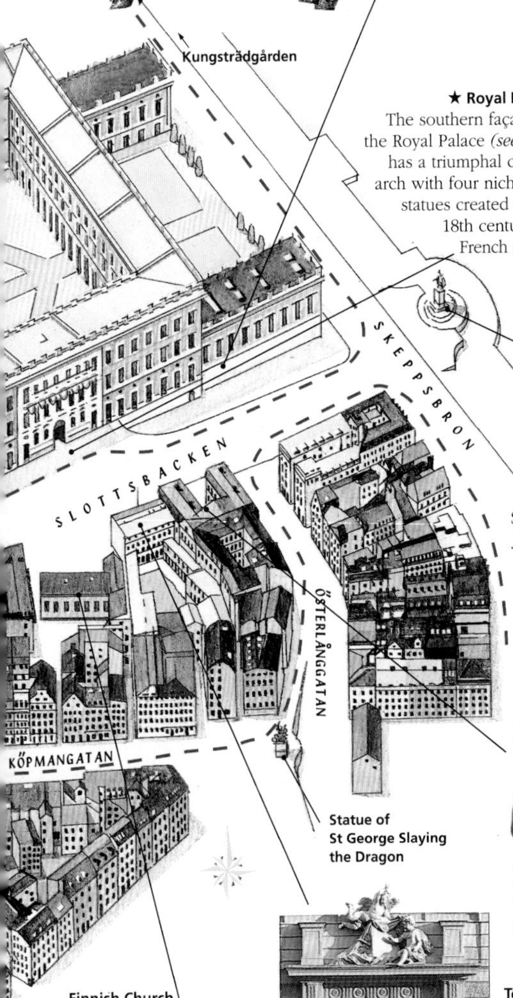

★ Royal Palace
The southern façade of the Royal Palace *(see p48)* has a triumphal central arch with four niches for statues created in the 18th century by French artists.

Gustav III's statue
Sculpted in 1799, J T Sergel's work honours the "charming king" who was murdered in 1792.

Kungliga Myntkabinettet
The Royal Coin Cabinet has the world's largest stamped coin, weighing almost 20 kg (44 lb) and dating from 1644.

Statue of St George Slaying the Dragon

Tessin Palace
Built between 1694 and 1697, by and for Nicodemus Tessin the Younger, architect of the Royal Palace, this palace has been the residence of the Governor of Stockholm County since 1968.

Finnish Church
Slottsbacken's oldest building dates from the 1640s. It was originally a royal ball-games court, but since 1725 it has been the religious centre for the city's Finnish community.

0 metres 100
0 yards 100

KEY

– – – Suggested route

Storkyrkan's Italian Baroque façade, seen from Slottsbacken

Exploring Stockholm

Stockholm is a perfect city for pedestrians. Distances between sights are usually short, and around every corner there is something interesting to discover. The capital extends across a large number of islands, affording eye-catching vistas and pleasant waterfront scenes.

Royal Palace ①

Defensive installations have stood on the island of Stadsholmen since the 10th century. The Tre Kronor (three crowns) fortress was completed in the mid-13th century and became a royal residence during the next century. In the 16th century, the fortress was turned into a Renaissance palace, which burned to the ground in 1697. In its place, Stockholm's city architect, Nicodemus Tessin the Younger, created a simple yet beautiful palace with an Italianate exterior and French interior tempered by Swedish influences. The palace's 608 rooms were decorated by Europe's foremost artists and craftsmen. King Adolf Frederik was the first king to move into the palace, in 1754. Today it is one of Stockholm's leading attractions. Thousands of visitors flock here every year to wander through its sumptuously furnished public rooms, such as the Hall of State, and explore its five museums.

Storkyrkan ②

Stockholm's 700-year-old cathedral is of tremendous national religious importance. It was from here that the Swedish reformer, Olaus Petri (1493–1552) disseminated his Lutheran message around the kingdom.

Originally, a village church was built on this site in the 13th century, probably by the city's founder, Birger Jarl. This was replaced in 1306 by the much bigger St Nicholas basilica. Over the centuries the basilica was altered; the interior was given a Gothic feel in the 15th century and a number of Baroque touches – including the pulpit – were added in the 17th century.

In 1743, the 66-m (216-ft) high tower was added. It has four bells, the largest of which weighs about 6 tonnes.

The cathedral houses some priceless treasures, including a silver altar, the "royal chairs" used by royalty on special occasions and a sculpture of St George and the Dragon, regarded as one of the finest late Gothic works of art in northern Europe.

Viking rune stone, Museum of National Antiquities

City Hall ③

Designed by the leading architect of the Swedish National Romantic style, Ragnar Östberg (1866–1945), Stadshuset contains the Council Chamber and 250 offices for city administrative staff. In the Golden Room, Byzantine-inspired wall mosaics contain 19 million pieces of gold leaf.

Kungsträdgården ④

In the 15th century this was the royal kitchen garden. Today the "King's Garden" is the city's oldest park and a popular meeting place for Stockholmers. There is something for everyone all year round here. In summer, concerts, food festivals and live street theatre provide entertainment, while in winter the central skating rink attracts adults and children alike.

The National Historical Museum ⑤

Opened in 1943, this museum initially made its name with its Viking exhibits, and its outstanding collections from the early Middle Ages. Many of the museum's gold treasures have been gathered together to form one of Stockholm's most remarkable sights, Guldrummet (the Gold Room), a 700-sq-m (7,500-sq-ft) underground vault built with some 250 tonnes of reinforced concrete to ensure security.

Nordic Museum ⑥
Resembling an extravagant Renaissance castle, the Nordic Museum portrays everyday life in Sweden from the 1520s to the present day. It was created by Artur Hazelius (1833–1901), the founder of Skansen Open Air Museum. In 1872, he started to collect objects that would remind future generations of the old Nordic farming culture.

The present building, designed by Isak Gustav Clason, was opened in 1907. Today the museum has more than one million exhibits on its four floors, ranging from luxury clothing to replicas of period homes. There is an exhibition on 20th-century Swedish interior design.

Rustic painted cupboard, Nordic Museum

Skansen Open Air Museum ⑦
Skansen opened in 1891 to show an increasingly industrialized society how people once lived. About 150 houses and farm buildings were assembled from all over Sweden, portraying the life of the peasants and landed gentry, as well as the *Sami* (Lapp) culture. The Town Quarter has original, wooden, urban dwellings brought here from around Stockholm to replicate a medium-sized 19th-century town. Modern glass-blowers, printers, potters and other craftsmen demonstrate traditional skills in restored workshops. A small zoo at the northern end of the museum houses bears, wolves and elks in natural-habitat enclosures, while the Aquarium houses an eclectic selection of rather more exotic creatures.

Vasa Museum ⑧
After a maiden voyage of just 1,300 m (4,265 ft) in calm weather, the 17th-century royal warship *Vasa* capsized in Stockholm's harbour on 10 August 1628, killing about 50 people. Guns were all that were salvaged from the vessel in the 1600s, and it was not until 1956 that marine archaeologist Anders Franzén found the ship after a persistent search.

It took five years to raise the ship from the sea floor, followed by a 17-year conservation programme to make the ship ready for public viewing. The hull was intact, but more than 13,500 pieces needed to be fitted together. *Vasa* has now been meticulously restored with more than 200 carved ornaments and 500 sculptures.

Modern Museum, Skeppsholmen

Skeppsholmen and Modern Museum ⑨
Once an imporant naval base, Skeppsholmen has been transformed into a centre for culture. Many of the naval buildings have been restored to hold a variety of museums and theatres, most importantly the Modern Museum. Built partly underground, the museum houses a magnificent collection of international and Swedish modern art. The building itself is highly acclaimed for its design.

Mariaberget ⑩
In 1759, a fire destroyed the wooden houses of Mariaberget, and the area was completely rebuilt. The result of this purposeful 18th-century town planning remains intact, and the character of the steep, winding streets and alleys has been well preserved. Towards the end of the 20th century, a conservation programme was implemented to safeguard the area's cultural heritage.

THE ARCHIPELAGO

To the east of Stockholm lies a beautiful archipelago consisting of more than 24,000 islands, rocks and skerries. Boat trips from Stockholm – often aboard traditional steamboats – take visitors out to the pine-covered islands with their red wooden houses. Here, visitors can wander through some breathtaking natural scenery, or hire boats or bikes to take them further afield. Some of the islands have beautiful, sandy beaches, which are popular with families.

Huvudskär in Stockholm's outer archipelago

Visby

Although Visby has a distinctly youthful ambience, especially in summer when its bars and restaurants are packed with young people, it still has a strong medieval feel, as ruined churches and converted warehouses cluster within the city wall. Capital of the island of Gotland, the city has existed at least since Viking times, but it was in the Middle Ages, when all Baltic trade routes met here, that it rose to economic prominence. Today tourism is an important source of income as visitors come to enjoy Gotland's beaches and lively summer atmosphere and to see the ample evidence of Visby's former wealth.

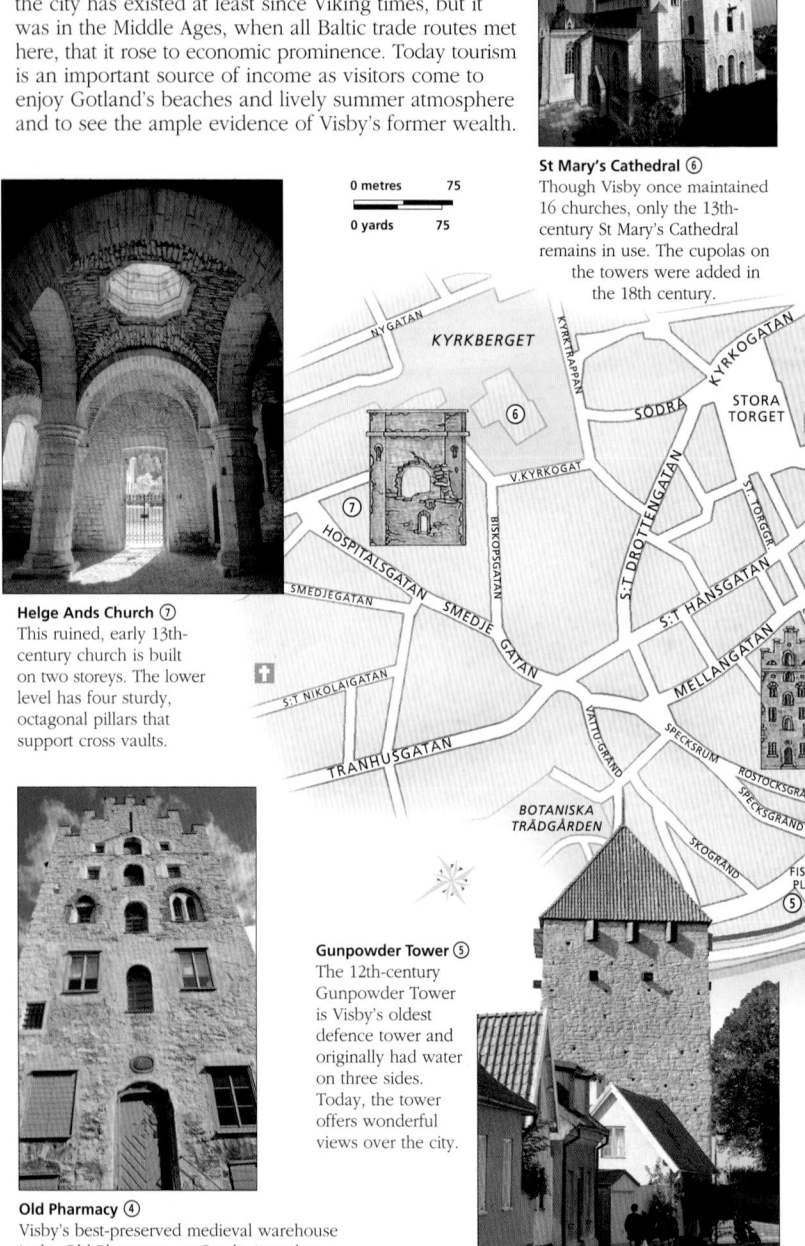

St Mary's Cathedral ⑥
Though Visby once maintained 16 churches, only the 13th-century St Mary's Cathedral remains in use. The cupolas on the towers were added in the 18th century.

Helge Ands Church ⑦
This ruined, early 13th-century church is built on two storeys. The lower level has four sturdy, octagonal pillars that support cross vaults.

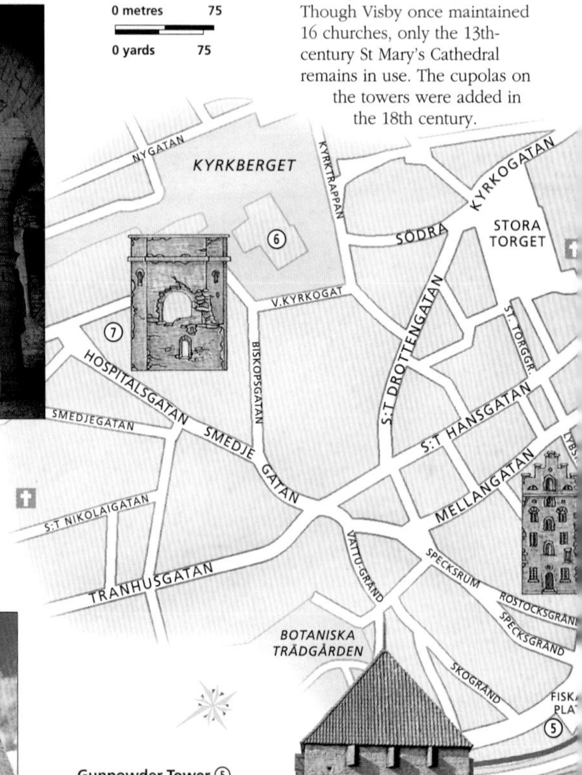

Old Pharmacy ④
Visby's best-preserved medieval warehouse is the Old Pharmacy, or Gamla Apoteket, a tall, narrow building with stepped gables.

Gunpowder Tower ⑤
The 12th-century Gunpowder Tower is Visby's oldest defence tower and originally had water on three sides. Today, the tower offers wonderful views over the city.

City Walls ③
Visby's 3.5-km (2-mile) long wall was built in about AD 1200, separating foreign traders from the local population. Up to 10 m (33 ft) high in places, it has 44 towers along its length.

Fornsal Museum and Natural History Museum ②
These two museums, next door to one another, cover 8,000 years of Gotland's history, as well as its flora and fauna.

Burmeister House ①
Built mainly from timber, this merchant's house dates from the 17th century. The top of the house held store-rooms, with the living quarters below.

ROUND GOTLAND RACE

Originally run in 1937, the Round Gotland Race has become one of the world's leading offshore races. The race starts from the Royal Swedish Yacht Club on Sandhamn, an island in the outer Stockholm archipelago. From here, boats set off on the 640-km (400-mile) course around Gotland. The race attracts hundreds of yachts every year, as well as thousands of spectators, who follow the start in private craft, or crowd the quays of Visby harbour to watch the competitors go by.

Visby harbour, Gotland

KEY SIGHTS

① Burmeister House
② Fornsal Museum and Natural History Museum ★
③ City Walls ★
④ Old Pharmacy
⑤ Gunpowder Tower
⑥ St Mary's Cathedral ★
⑦ Helge Ands Church

FACT FILE

TOURIST INFORMATION
Skeppsbron 4–6, Visby. ***Tel*** *(0498) 201 700.* ◯ *May–Aug: Mon–Fri to 5pm, Sat & Sun to 4pm (mid-Jun–mid-Aug: daily to 7pm); Sep–Apr: Mon–Fri to 4pm.*

MARKETS
Crafts Stora Torget; daily during summer.
Medieval market Held throughout the city; one week in early August.

LOCAL SPECIALITIES
Crafts
Ceramics, wool, lambskin, wood and glass.
Dishes
Flundra (freshly caught and smoked flounder).
Lamb dishes.
Saffranspanskaka (thick pancake made with saffron rice).
Drinks
Gotlandsdricka (home-brewed, slightly sweet beer. This varies from household to household and is never sold, but is commonly available at social events during the summer).

EXCURSIONS
Lummelundagrottarna 13 km (8 miles) N of Visby. Limestone caves with stalagmites and stalactites.
Lilla Karlsö and Stora Karlsö 27 km (16 miles) SW of Visby. Two islands off the coast of Gotland. Now nature reserves containing bird sanctuaries.
Burs 30 km (18 miles) S of Visby. Small town, set in rolling meadows, has an attractive 13th-century saddle church.
Fårö 54 km (34 miles) NE of Visby. A starkly beautiful island off the north coast of Gotland. Digerhuvud National Park has incredible limestone formations.

Finland summer cottage ▷

FINLAND

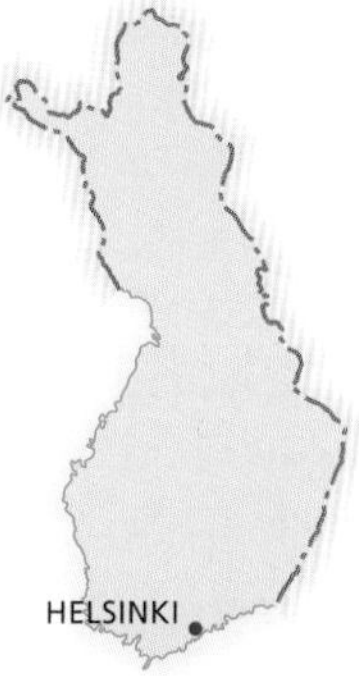

Helsinki

Finland was a province of Sweden from 1362 to 1807 and of Russia from 1807 to independence in 1917. Helsinki was founded by King Gustav Vasa of Sweden in 1550 to entice trade away from Tallinn *(see pp70–71)*, but it really flourished only after Suomenlinna Island Fortress was built in 1748. In 1812, Tsar Alexander I named it Finland's capital. Much of the elegant, Neo-Classical architecture, centred around Helsinki Cathedral, was built over the next 80 years. However, Helsinki is also renowned for its Romantic and Modernist buildings, such as the National Museum and Central Railway Station. In the 20th century, the Finns became world leaders in contemporary architecture, as reflected in Alvar Aalto's works and the ultra-modern Kiasma museum.

Central Railway Station ⑤
This striking fusion of National Romanticism and Functionalism, designed in pink granite by architect Eliel Saarinen (1873–1950), was built between 1905 and 1919.

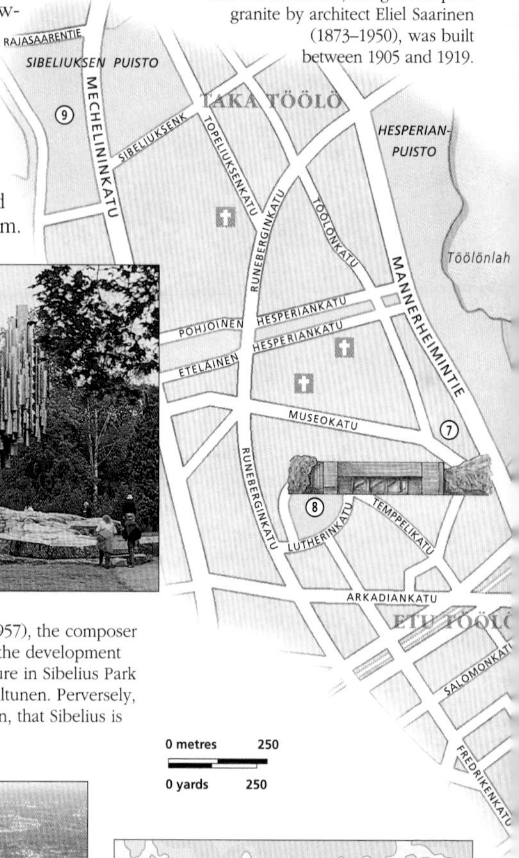

Sibelius Monument ⑨
Commemorating Jean Sibelius (1865–1957), the composer who played such an important part in the development of Finnish national identity, this sculpture in Sibelius Park was created in 1967 by sculptor Eila Hiltunen. Perversely, it imitates the one instrument, the organ, that Sibelius is reputed to have disliked intensely.

Suomenlinna Island Fortress ⑩
Founded in 1748, this is the biggest sea fortress in Scandinavia and is now a UNESCO World Heritage Site. The island offers visitors museums and cafés, as well as cobbled castle courtyards and marinas.

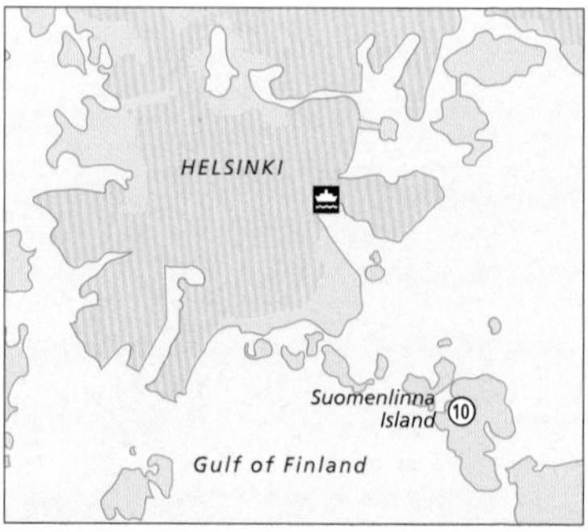

HELSINKI TO SUOMENLINNA ISLAND

Helsinki Cathedral ④
Completed in 1852, the gleaming, white, Lutheran cathedral with striking green cupolas is a much-loved landmark on Helsinki's skyline. The building's height is accentuated by its location at the top of a long, steep flight of steps.

Uspenski Cathedral ③
Embellished with green copper roofs and gold onion domes, the Orthodox cathedral is highly visible from the South Harbour's waterfront.

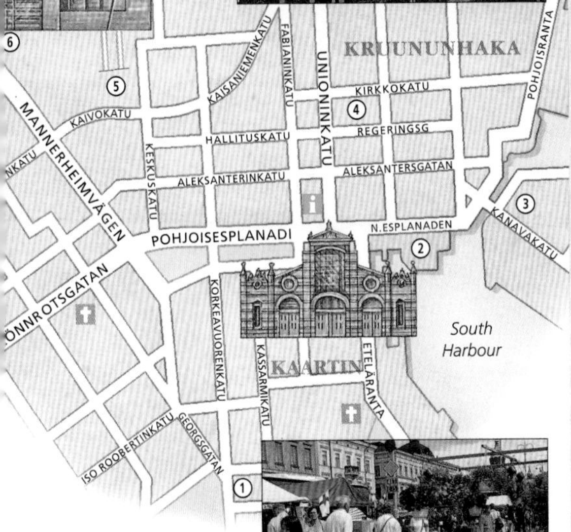

Market Square ②
This open-air market is at its best in summer when it is thronged with people enjoying coffee and snacks as well as buying produce.

KEY SIGHTS

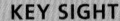

① Designmuseo
② Market Square
③ Uspenski Cathedral
④ Helsinki Cathedral
⑤ Central Railway Station
⑥ Kiasma, Museum of Contemporary Art
⑦ National Museum of Finland
⑧ Temppeliaukio Church ★
⑨ Sibelius Monument ★
⑩ Suomenlinna Island Fortress ★

FACT FILE

TOURIST INFORMATION

Pohjoisesplanadi 19. ***Tel** (09) 169 3757.* ☐ *May–Sep: Mon–Fri to 8pm, Sat & Sun to 6pm; Oct–Apr: Mon–Fri to 8pm, Sat & Sun to 4pm.*

MARKETS

Food & souvenirs Kauppatori (Market Square); Mon–Sat.

LOCAL SPECIALITIES

Crafts
Wooden items, glassware, ceramics, *ryijy* (rag rugs), sauna items, and *Sami* reindeer-skin products.
Dishes
Kesäkeitto (a seasonal summer vegetable soup).
Graavi lohi (marinated salmon).
Graavi kirjolohi (marinated trout).
Keitetyt ravut (crayfish with dill).
Lihamurekepiiras (meat loaf in sour-cream pastry).
Karjalanpaisti (Karelian mixed meat hotpot with allspice).
Vatkattu marjapuuro (whipped lingonberry pudding).
Drinks
Sima (lemon-flavoured mead).
Mesimarja (raspberry liqueur).
Karpalo (cranberry liqueur).
Koskenkorva (clear vodka).

EXCURSIONS

Järvenpää 38 km (24 miles) N of Helsinki. Former home of Sibelius and his wife, Aino, set in beautiful scenery. His grave is in the garden.
Porvoo 50 km (30 miles) E of Helsinki. Old coastal town, home of the Finnish national poet, Johan Ludwig Runeberg (1804–77). Sculpture gallery and museum.

ALVAR AALTO (1898–1976)

One of the 20th century's major architects, Alvar Aalto embraced the International Modern style, personalizing it with his love and understanding of materials and their properties. The Finnish forests inspired his wide use of wood and he invented bent plywood furniture. His most famous building is his last – Helsinki's Finlandia Hall, which comprises a concert hall (1971) and congress hall (1975). The harsh climate has meant that its Carrara marble façade has needed restoration.

Finlandia Hall, Alvar Aalto's masterpiece at Töölönlahti Bay

Exploring Helsinki

Central Helsinki occupies a peninsula indented with attractive inlets and harbours and the main sights are easily explored on foot. Many are near Market Square at the head of South Harbour, where cruise ships dock and from where excursion boats leave for Suomenlinna and other islands. Leading from the square is Esplanadi, which is full of designer shops. The main shopping street is Aleksanterinkatu, at the western end of which is Stockmann, Scandinavia's biggest department store. The Classically elegant Senate Square is also an easy stroll from Market Square.

Designmuseo ①

This museum's inspiring, very modern collection comprises items made in a wide variety of media, such as glass, pottery, textiles and timber, and covers decorative as well as industrial design. The 35,000 Finnish-designed objects are complemented by the best examples of international design. The museum is the oldest design museum in Scandinavia, established in 1873 as a teaching collection for students of the applied arts. It moved to its present premises in 1978. The museum shop has a selection of contemporary designer glass, ceramics, jewellery and books on Finnish design.

Market Square ②

In summer Finns enjoy sunning themselves in the cobbled Market Square (Kauppatori) overlooking the harbour, while eating sugar peas, strawberries and ice cream or drinking coffee. Finnish crafts stalls trade alongside fish, fruit and vegetable stalls, while farmers sell fresh produce (berries, new potatoes, dill) from boats. At one side is the blue-painted City Hall by the Neo-Classical architect Carl Ludwig Engel (1778–1840). A short walk away is the 19th-century red- and yellow-brick Old Market Hall containing a range of appetizing gourmet food shops.

Leading westwards from Market Square is the long, narrow Esplanadi Park, bordered by two pedestrian boulevards, also by Engel. At the market end is the bronze statue of a naked woman, *Havis Amanda* (1908), by Ville Vallgren. Although it is not known who she was, her famous statue has become a symbol of the city.

Old Market Hall, Market Square, full of specialist food shops

Uspenski Cathedral ③

Designed by A M Gornostayev and built in 1868, this red-brick Russian Orthodox cathedral is a flamboyant reminder of Finland's Russian era. Its lavish interior, resplendent with gold, silver, red and blue and with shadowy vaults resting on giant granite columns, forms a sharp contrast to the Lutheran austerity of Helsinki Cathedral. There is a splendid view over the heart of Helsinki from the terrace surrounding Uspenski Cathedral. Immediately around it is an area of old warehouses that have been converted into restaurants and shops.

Helsinki Cathedral ④

Designed by Carl Ludwig Engel, this Neo-Classical cathedral, formally named St Nicholas's Church, was built in the 1830s and 1840s. White Corinthian columns decorate the splendid exterior. Inside it has surprisingly little ornamentation apart from statues of the 16th-century Protestant reformers, Martin Luther, Philipp Melanchthon and Mikael Agricola, the last of whom translated the Bible into Finnish.

The cathedral dominates Senate Square, Engel's masterpiece commissioned by Finland's Russian rulers in the early 19th century. Viewed from the cathedral steps, the University of Helsinki stands on the right and the Council of State building on the left.

Central Railway Station ⑤

The architect Eliel Saarinen won the competition for the design of this remarkable building, blending the curves of National Romanticism with a rational plan and the rectangular lines of nascent Functionalism. It has a 48-m (160-ft) tall clocktower, and stern-faced, bemuscled statues by sculptor Emil Wikström clasp round lanterns and guard the station's exterior. The spacious interior features carved wooden fittings. Also noteworthy is the painting by Eero Järnefelt, which decorates the station's Eliel Restaurant.

Imposing giant sculptures at the Central Railway Station

Kiasma, Museum of Contemporary Art ⑥

This glass-and-metal-panelled building, controversially designed by American architect Steven Holl, was completed in 1998. He took Arctic light as his inspiration, the building's curved shapes maximizing the influx of natural light into the exhibition spaces. It was intended as a showcase for post-1960 art, but now also hosts contemporary art installations, drama and mixed media shows. Its interdisciplinary and international function is reflected in its name, as the Greek word *chiasma* means "crossing point".

National Museum of Finland ⑦

The building housing this museum is one of the most notable examples of Finnish National Romantic architecture, which featured irregular outlines, local materials and historical motifs. The museum illustrates the history of Finland from pre-historic times to the present, with exhibits enlivened by films, touch screens, costumes and room recreations. The striking and much-reproduced fresco by Akseli Gallen-Kallela (1865–1931) in the entrance hall depicts scenes from Finland's national epic, the *Kalevala*, compiled from folk poetry by Elias Lönnrot between 1835 and 1849.

Temppeliaukio Church ⑧

Built into a granite outcrop in the middle of a large square, this circular "Church in the Rock" is an astonishing piece of modern architecture. Consecrated in 1969, it is the work of architects Timo and Tuomo Suomalainen. The ceiling is an enormous, domed, copper disk, separated from the rough-surfaced rock walls by a ribbed ring of glass. As well as being a main visitor attraction, this popular Lutheran place of worship is also used for organ recitals and choral music.

Sibelius Monument ⑨

This stainless steel sculpture by Eila Hiltunen (b. 1922) stands on a rocky outcrop in a public park in Töölö, a prestigious

Temppeliaukio Church, blasted out of a granite outcrop

and affluent part of Helsinki. It was the winning design of a competition held to find a suitable monument to composer Jean Sibelius (1865–1957). It attracted much publicity, as tastes were then much divided between abstract and figurative art. As a compromise, a small bust of Sibelius was installed on the sculpture's rock base.

By drawing on many aspects of Finnishness in his music, especially landscape and folklore, Sibelius came to represent the emergent Finnish nationalism of the late 19th century.

Suomenlinna Island Fortress ⑩

The Swedes built this fortress between 1748 and 1772. Designed to defend the Finnish coast, it offered security to Helsinki's burghers and merchants and enabled the city to flourish. The fortress spans six islands and contains about 200 buildings, the majority of which date from the 18th century. Until the early 19th century, it had more residents than Helsinki. Today, 850 people still live on the islands, which are a 15-minute ferry ride from Market Square. Suomenlinna is Helsinki's main tourist attraction and offers outdoor picnic, walking and swimming areas, a visitor centre, cafés, restaurants, galleries and museums, including the popular doll and toy museum, and a historic submarine.

Kiasma, Museum of Contemporary Art, housing static and interactive displays

Peterhof palace outside St Petersburg, Russia ▷

RUSSIA

St Petersburg

Alexander Column

Determined to give his country a Baltic port, Peter the Great founded St Petersburg in the Neva delta in 1703. Over 40,000 peasants and Swedish prisoners of war died during building work in the fetid bogland, but in 1712 Peter declared the new city Russia's capital. Wishing to create a Western-style city, he employed Italian architects, whose sumptuous buildings set its elegant tone, even to this day. Among the city's prominent landmarks are the gilded dome of the cathedral of St Isaac, and the spire of SS Peter and Paul. Dvortsovaya Naberezhnaya is lined with stately palaces and Nevskiy Prospekt bustles with shops and cafés. A boat trip along St Petersburg's canals is a highlight of any visit.

The Hermitage ⑦
This vast museum includes the state rooms of the Winter Palace, the central section of whose river façade is seen above. It holds nearly three million exhibits, ranging from paintings to archaeological finds.

St Isaac's Cathedral ⑧
To support this colossal church's weight, thousands of piles had to be sunk into the marshy ground and 48 huge columns incorporated into the structure. It was designed in 1818 by Auguste de Montferrand and opened in 1858. In the Soviet era it was a museum of atheism.

Church on Spilled Blood ③
The visual impact of this late 19th-century church, built in flamboyant Russian Revival style, is created by the imaginative juxtaposition of interior and exterior materials.

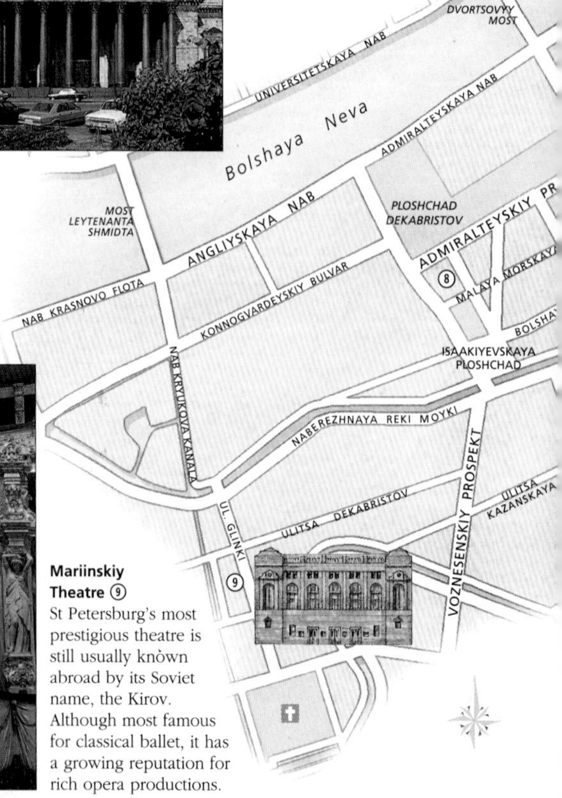

Mariinskiy Theatre ⑨
St Petersburg's most prestigious theatre is still usually known abroad by its Soviet name, the Kirov. Although most famous for classical ballet, it has a growing reputation for rich opera productions.

SS Peter and Paul Fortress ①
The founding of this fortress in 1703 by Peter the Great is considered to mark the founding of the city itself. The slim, gilded spire belongs to the SS Peter and Paul Cathedral, whose interior forms a magnificent setting for the tombs of the Romanov monarchs.

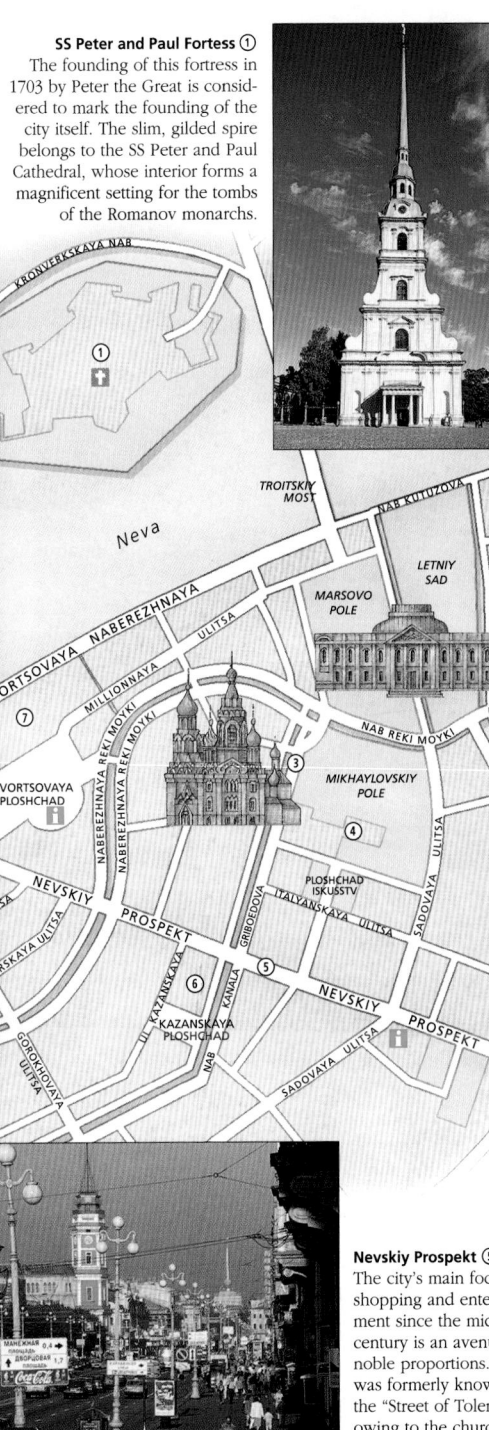

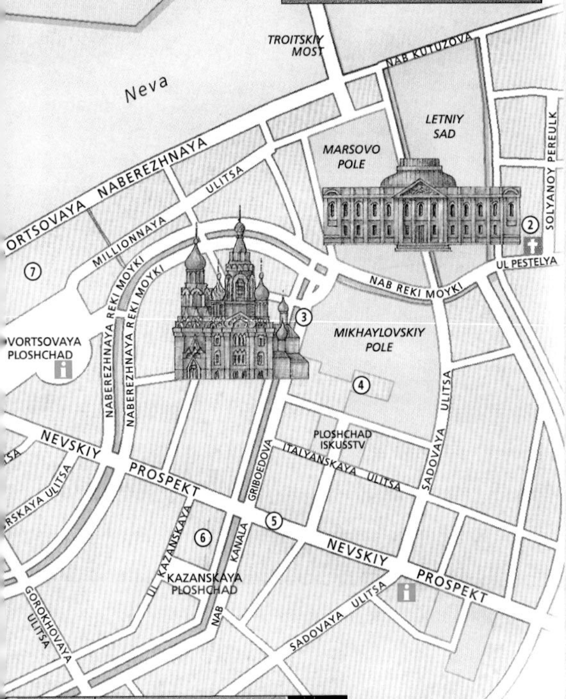

Nevskiy Prospekt ⑤
The city's main focus for shopping and entertainment since the mid-18th century is an avenue of noble proportions. It was formerly known as the "Street of Tolerance" owing to the churches of different denominations along it.

KEY SIGHTS

① SS Peter and Paul Fortress
② Stieglitz Museum
③ Church on Spilled Blood ★
④ Russian Museum
⑤ Nevskiy Prospekt
⑥ Cathedral of Our Lady of Kazan
⑦ The Hermitage ★ *(see pp64–7)*
⑧ St Isaac's Cathedral ★
⑨ Mariinskiy Theatre

FACT FILE

TOURIST INFORMATION

14, Sadovaya St. ***Tel*** *(812) 310 2822, (0812) 310 2231.*
Mon–Fri to 7pm, Sat to 6pm, Sun to 4pm.

MARKETS

Food Central Market, Kuznechnyy pereulok; daily.
Artworks and prints Vernisazh, Nevskiy prospekt 32–34; daily.
Souvenirs Kanal Griboedova (near Church on Spilled Blood); daily.

LOCAL SPECIALITIES

Crafts
Woodcarving, especially chess sets, toys and *matryoshka* dolls; *palekh* (miniature painting on papier-mâché boxes); woollen scarves.
Dishes
Ikra (black or red caviar).
Osetrina (salted/smoked sturgeon).
Rassolnik (soup with pickled cucumber and meat or fish).
Golubtsy (meat and rice in cabbage leaves with tomato sauce).
Morozhenoe (ice cream).
Drinks
Sankt-Petersburg (vodka). *Baltika, Nevskoye* and *Stepan Razin* (beers).
Kvass (made from fermented bread, currants and grain).

EXCURSIONS

Alexander Nevskiy Monastery 3 km (2 miles) SE of St Petersburg. Cathedral and famous cemeteries.
Tsarskoe Selo 25 km (16 miles) S of St Petersburg. Imperial palace.
Pavlosk 25 km (16 miles) S of St Petersburg. Palace and gardens.
Peterhof 30 km (19 miles) W of St Petersburg. Peter the Great's Palace with Grand Cascade.

Exploring St Petersburg
The city centre covers some of the more than 40 islands and many of the connecting bridges are adorned with sculptures and wrought iron. While SS Peter and Paul Fortress is on the northern bank of the Neva, most of the other famous sights are opposite, with the Hermitage on the grandiose southern waterfront. Stretching southeast from here is the great commercial street, Nevskiy Prospekt. Away to either side of it are the leafy Theatre and Arts squares with their stunning museums and other cultural institutions.

The Church on Spilled Blood, a memorial to Tsar Alexander II

SS Peter and Paul Fortress ①
This fortress was built in wood in 1703 and then replaced in stone by Domenico Trezzini. Its history is gruesome, as hundreds of forced labourers died on the job and it was later used to guard and torture political prisoners. Their cells are now open to visitors. In contrast is Trezzini's Baroque cathedral, illustrating Peter the Great's wish to turn his back on traditional Russian architecture. He used the spire for overseeing the construction of his city. The cathedral now houses the tombs of all the Tsars except Peter II and Ivan VI, as the remains of the last Tsar, Nicholas II, were brought here in 1998.

Stieglitz Museum ②
In 1876 the millionaire industrialist Baron Aleksandr Stieglitz founded the Central School of Industrial Design, training students by surrounding them with top-quality Western and Oriental works of art. In 1896 the collection was moved next door to this superb building designed by Maximilian Messmacher. The interior was decorated in national and period styles, echoing German and French Baroque and, above all, Italian Renaissance buildings. St Mark's in Venice *(see p217)*, the Raphael Rooms at the Vatican *(see p236)* and the Villa Madama in Rome were all copied. After serious damage during World War II, the school was revived to train craftsmen for the huge task of restoring the damaged city.

Tours are guided and among exhibits are opulent glassware, majolica and porcelain. There are also costumes made by Russian peasants in a room decorated in the style of medieval private apartments. Tours conclude in the Grand Exhibition Hall with its curving staircase of Italian marble and magnificent glass roof.

Dolls in Russian folk costume in the Terem Room, Stieglitz Museum

Church on Spilled Blood ③
This church was built on the spot where Tsar Alexander II was assassinated on 1 March 1881 by a revolutionary group. In 1883 his successor, Alexander III, held a competition for a permanent memorial. The winning design, in Russian Revival style, was by Alfred Parland and Ignatiy Malyshev. Building work finished in 1907.

On the exterior, jeweller's enamel covers the surface of the multi-coloured domes. The walls of the golden-domed bell tower are decorated with 144 mosaic coats of arms representing the towns, regions and provinces of the Russian empire. Mosaics on the main tympanum show scenes from the New Testament, while those in the *kokoshniki* gables either side of it portray saints.

Inside, more than 20 types of minerals, including jasper, rhodonite, porphyry and Italian marble, were lavished on the mosaics of the iconostasis, icon cases, canopy and floor.

Russian Museum ④

Standing in Arts Square, the Mikhaylovskiy Palace, built in the 1820s for Grand Duke Mikhail Pavlovich, is a fine Neo-Classical creation by Carlo Rossi. Nicholas II opened the museum here in 1898 to house Russian art. After the Russian Revolution, more works were brought here from private houses, palaces and churches. Avant-garde works of the 1910s–1930s, banned under Communism, re-emerged in the 1980s with *perestroika*.

Highlights of the collection include icons such as the 12th-century *Angel with the Golden Hair* and examples by the supreme master Andrey Rublev (c.1340–1430). There are also works by the great realist painter Ilya Repin (1844–1930), canvases by Symbolist Mikhail Vrubel (1856–1910), stage sets from the Ballets Russes and folk art.

The Russian Museum, displaying paintings by Russian artists

Nevskiy Prospekt ⑤

Russia's most famous street is also St Petersburg's main thoroughfare, laid out in the city's early days when it was called Great Perspective Road. It runs 4.5 km (3 miles) from Palace Square to the Alexander Nevskiy Monastery. The latter was founded in 1710 in honour of Alexander Nevskiy, Prince of Novgorod, who defeated the Swedes at the River Neva in 1240. Some of the best shops are around Gostinyy Dvor, the huge, 18th-century, arcaded shopping gallery. Nevskiy Prospekt also offers the Russian national library, plus many museums, churches, restaurants and cinemas.

Mural detail at Kazan Cathedral, a grandiose church built by Tsar Paul I

Cathedral of Our Lady of Kazan ⑥

This majestic church, designed by serf architect Andrey Voronikhin, was built between 1801 and 1811 to house the miracle-working icon of Our Lady of Kazan, which is said to have delivered Moscow from the Poles in 1612. The cathedral's impressive design, with an enormous arc of 96 Corinthian columns facing Nevskiy Prospekt, was inspired by St Peter's in Rome *(see pp234–5)*. The interior's most impressive features are the great, 80-m (262-ft) high dome and the massive, pink, Finnish granite columns with bronze capitals and bases. The north chancel holds the tomb of Field Marshal Mikhail Kutuzov, who skillfully masterminded the retreat from Moscow following the invasion of Napoleon's Grand Army in 1812, and was buried here with full military honours.

The Hermitage ①

See pp64–7.

St Isaac's Cathedral ⑧

Officially a museum, though services are held here on special occasions, this church is filled with 19th-century art. The iconostasis is framed by lapis lazuli and malachite columns, and the walls are faced with 14 coloured marbles and 43 other types of semi-precious stone. The painting on the ceiling (1847) is by Karl Bryullov. In front of the cathedral, in St Isaac's Square, is a statue of Peter the Great.

Mariinskiy Theatre ⑨

Named after Maria Alexandrovna, wife of Alexander II, this theatre was built in 1860 by Albert Kavos, architect of Moscow's Bolshoy. Between 1883 and 1896 Viktor Schröter added the ornamental detail to the façade. The dazzling blue and gold auditorium with twisted columns, atlantes, cherubs and cameos is original. The superb stage curtain by Aleksandr Golovin was added in 1914. Equally sumptous is the glittering foyer with mirrored doors.

THE RUSSIAN REVOLUTION IN ST PETERSBURG

After the 1917 February Revolution, which had led to the abdication of Tsar Nicholas II, the Provisional Government declared a political amnesty. Exiled revolutionaries such as Lenin and Trotsky arrived to set up an alternative government in St Petersburg, which became the cradle of the Russian Revolution. As soldiers deserted in droves from the battlefields of World War I, the leaders decided on an armed uprising. On 25 October the Winter Palace was stormed by Trotsky's Red Guard, leading to a three-year civil war between Bolsheviks (Reds) and Whites. The Tsar and his family, held prisoner in Tsarskoe Tselo palace, were murdered in 1918.

Bolshevik propaganda poster extolling the "Pacifist Army of Workers"

St Petersburg: The Hermitage ⑦

The Hermitage has an encyclopaedic collection of works of art occupying a grand ensemble of buildings. The most impressive part is Rastrelli's Baroque Winter Palace (1754–62), built as the winter residence of Tsarina Elizabeth. Its highlights are the Jordan Staircase, the Small Throne Room and the Malachite Room. Catherine the Great soon added the more intimate Small Hermitage, but in 1771 she commissioned the Large Hermitage to house her rapidly growing art collection. The theatre was completed in 1787. The New Hermitage was built between 1839 and 1851 in the reign of Nicholas I, who opened the New and Large Hermitages in 1852 as a public museum. Between 1918 and 1939, after the establishment of Soviet power, the Winter Palace was slowly incorporated into the Hermitage museum ensemble.

New Hermitage
Designed by German architect Leo von Klenze and integrated into the Large Hermitage, this is the only purpose-built museum space within the whole complex.

Court
Ministries These were located here until the 1880s.

Atlantes
Ten 5-m (16-ft) tall granite Atlantes hold up what was the public entrance to the Hermitage museum from 1852 until after the Revolution.

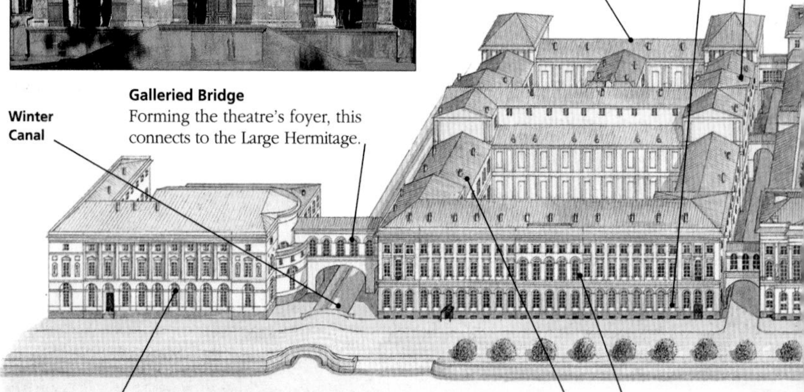

Winter Canal

Galleried Bridge
Forming the theatre's foyer, this connects to the Large Hermitage.

Theatre
This was designed by the Italian architect Giacomo Quarenghi. He was much admired by Catherine and spent the last 38 years of his life in St Petersburg.

Large Hermitage
Architect Yuriy Velten's extension was built to house Catherine the Great's paintings.

★ Raphael Loggias
Catherine was so impressed by engravings of Raphael's frescoes in the Vatican that in 1787 she commissioned copies to be made on canvas. Small alterations were made, such as replacing the Pope's coat of arms with the Romanov two-headed eagle.

Hanging Gardens
This unusual, raised garden is decorated with statues and fountains. During the 900-day Siege of Leningrad in World War II, when 670,000 citizens died, Hermitage curators grew vegetables here.

STAR SIGHTS

- ★ Raphael Loggias
- ★ Pavilion Hall
- ★ Winter Palace State Rooms

Winter Palace Façade
Rastrelli embellished the palace façades with 400 columns and 16 different window designs. Behind the first floor's central windows is the vast Nicholas Hall, which was used for balls of up to 5,000 guests.

Small Hermitage
Catherine used this annexe by Vallin de la Mothe and Yuriy Velten as a private retreat from the bustle of court.

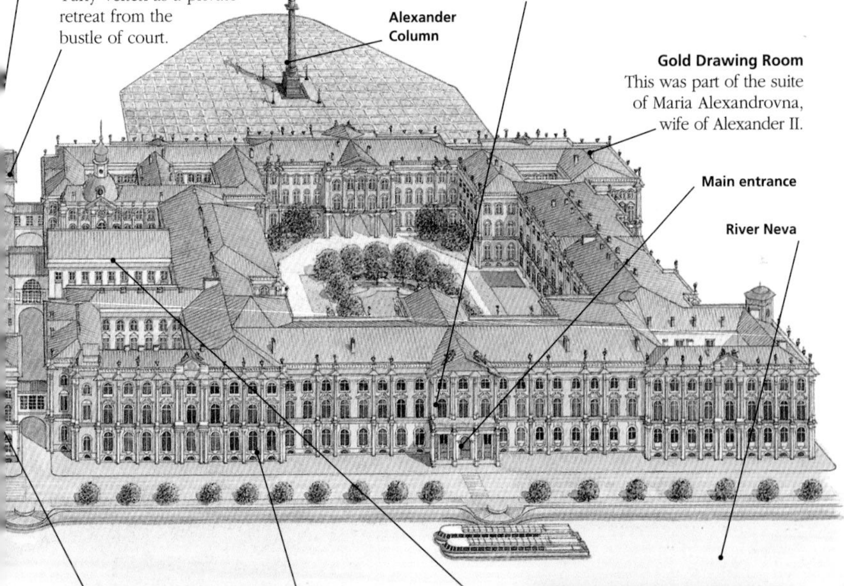

Gold Drawing Room
This was part of the suite of Maria Alexandrovna, wife of Alexander II.

Winter Palace
This was the official residence of the Imperial family until the 1917 Revolution.

★ Pavilion Hall
Built between 1850 and 1858, Andrey Stakenschneider's striking white marble and gold hall replaced Catherine's original interior. It houses the famous Peacock Clock, made in 1772 by the English clockmaker James Cox for Catherine's lover Prince Grigoriy Potemkin. He then presented it to her as a gift.

★ Winter Palace State Rooms
The tsars spared no expense in decorating rooms such as the Hall of St George, the former Throne Room. These rooms were not intended for private life, but were used for State ceremonies.

St Petersburg: The Hermitage Collections

Catherine the Great purchased some of Western Europe's best art collections between 1764 and 1774, acquiring over 2,500 paintings, 10,000 carved gems, 10,000 drawings and a vast amount of silver and porcelain, with which to adorn her palaces. None of her successors matched the quantity of her remarkable purchases. After the Revolution, the nationalization of both royal and private property brought more paintings and works of applied art, making the Hermitage one of the world's leading museums.

Litta Madonna (c.1491)
One of two works by Leonardo da Vinci in the museum, this masterpiece was admired by his contemporaries and was frequently copied.

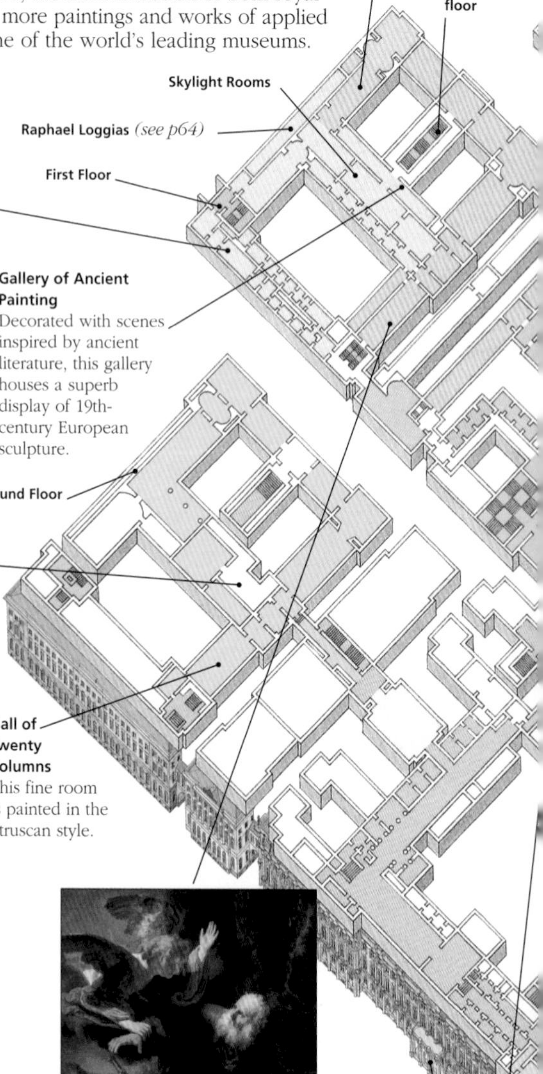

GALLERY GUIDE

Individual visitors enter via Palace Square then cross the main courtyard (group tours use other entrances by arrangement). It is a good idea to start with the Winter Palace state rooms on the first floor to get an overview of the museum. It is also advisable to concentrate on just one or two topics of interest. European art of the 19th and 20th centuries is best reached by either of the two staircases on the Palace Square side of the Winter Palace.

Abraham's Sacrifice (1635)
In the 1630s Rembrandt was painting religious scenes in a High Baroque style, using dramatic gestures rather than detail to convey his message. In this painting, Abraham is offering to sacrifice his son, Isaac. The Hermitage has one of the world's most outstanding collections of Rembrandt's work.

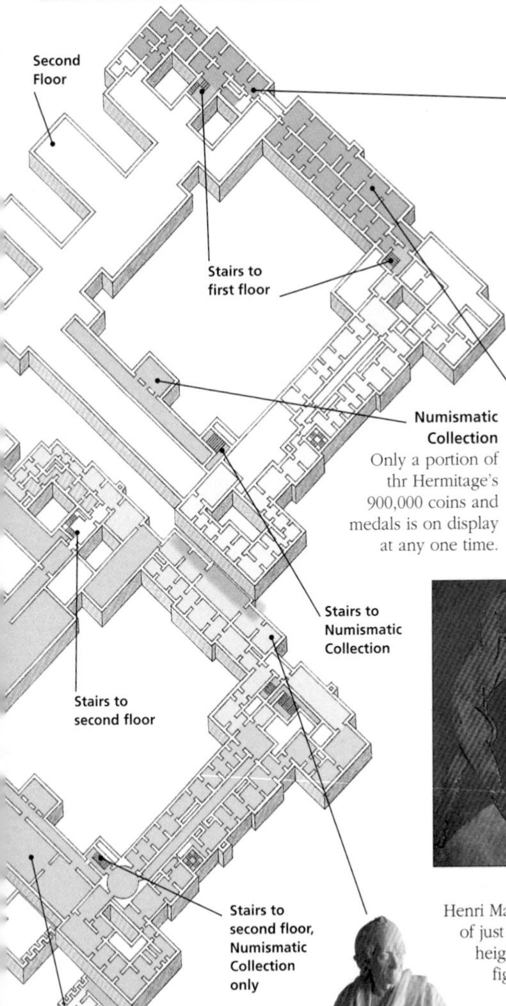

Numismatic Collection
Only a portion of thr Hermitage's 900,000 coins and medals is on display at any one time.

State Rooms
This section of the Winter Palace contains magnificent Russian and European *objets d'art*.

Ea Haere Ia Oe (1893)
This is one of the first works Paul Gauguin painted after he had left France for Tahiti. His desire to escape convention and artificiality found expression in his innovative use of primitive art as inspiration.

La Danse (1910)
Henri Matisse used bold shapes and strong tones of just three colours – blue, green and red – to heighten the drama and concentration of the figures, who are totally lost in their dance.

Voltaire (1781)
Catherine the Great corresponded with Voltaire for over 15 years and commissioned this marble statue of him from the French sculptor, Jean-Antoine Houdon. The French writer is dressed in the style of a Greek philosopher.

KEY TO FLOORPLAN

- **Prehistoric:** Rooms 11–24, 26, 33
- **Classical:** 102, 107–117, 121, 127–131
- **Oriental:** 34–47, 55–66, 69, 100, 351–371, 381–397
- **Russian:** 147–153, 155–189, 190–198, 204, 260, 269–271, 282, 304–307
- **Italian and Spanish:** 207–223, 226–242
- **Flemish, Dutch and German:** 243, 245–254, 258–259, 261–268
- **French and English:** 272–281, 283–287, 290–302
- **19th- and 20th-century European:** 314–325, 328–350
- **Temporary exhibition space**
- **Non-exhibition space**
- **No access**

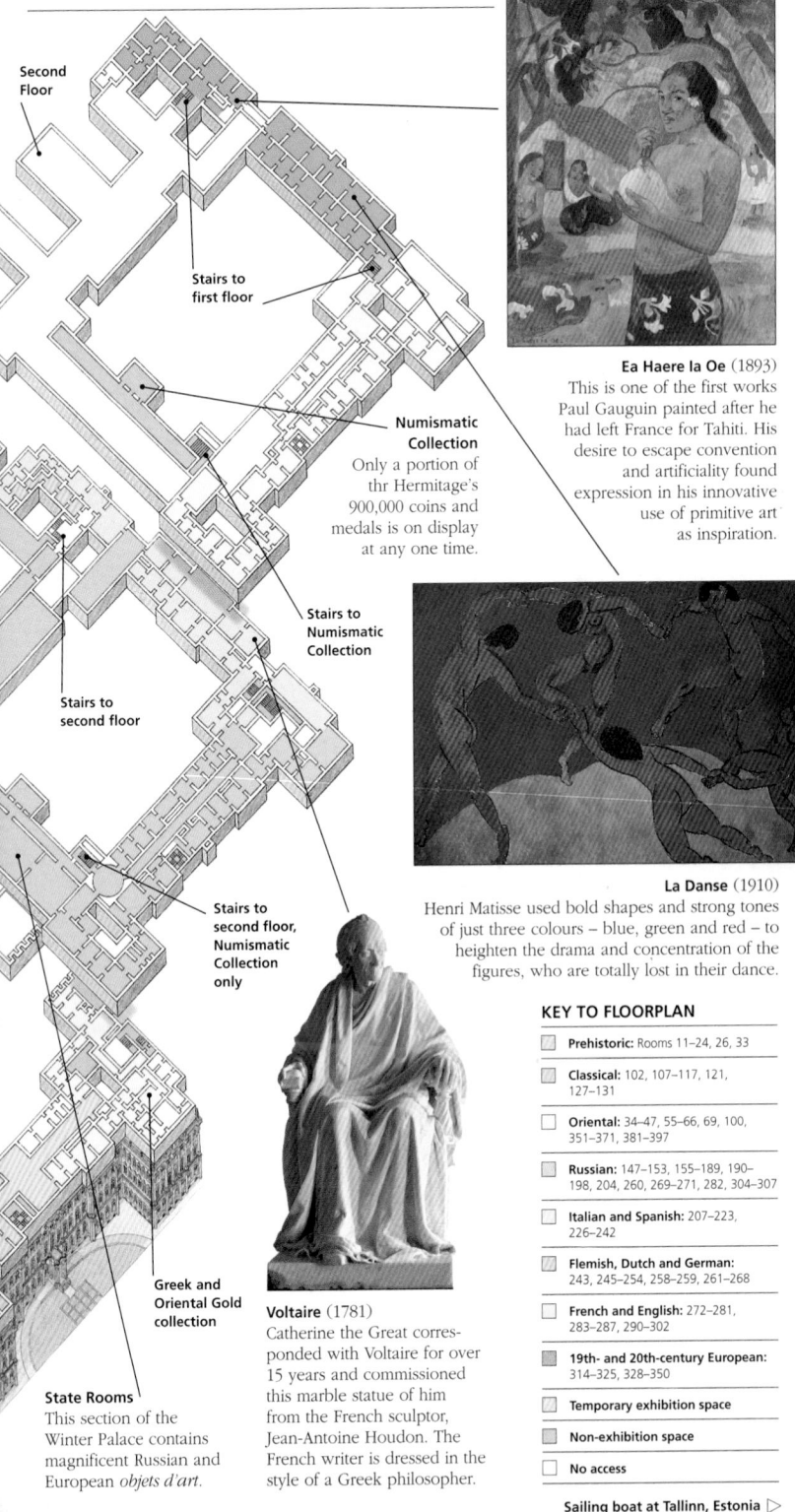

Sailing boat at Tallinn, Estonia ▷

ESTONIA AND LATVIA

TALLINN 70–71 • RIGA 72–73

Tallinn

Mosaic from the cathedral

Estonia is the most dynamic of the Baltic Republics, with Tallinn, its capital, facing Helsinki across the Gulf of Finland. Under foreign domination for most of its history – Tallinn means Danish town – and still showing the effects of decades of the harsh Soviet rule that ended in 1991, the old town inside its massive walls is embracing independence with alacrity. Bars and restaurants abound, the winding old cobblestone streets and squares ring with the sounds of open-air markets, brass bands, choirs and even string quartets. Largely closed to traffic, the old town offers numerous glimpses of tiny courtyards and winding stairs, as well as medieval carvings and Baroque monuments.

Dome Church ④
Atmospheric Toomkirik, dating from 1223, is the nation's oldest church. It was rebuilt in the 1600s and contains some fascinating tombs and a Baroque altar.

Toompea ⑤
Inhabited since prehistoric times, the upper Old City on Toompea Hill offers fine views from a number of viewing platforms. A treasured landmark, the 13th-century Toompea Castle now houses the Estonian Parliament.

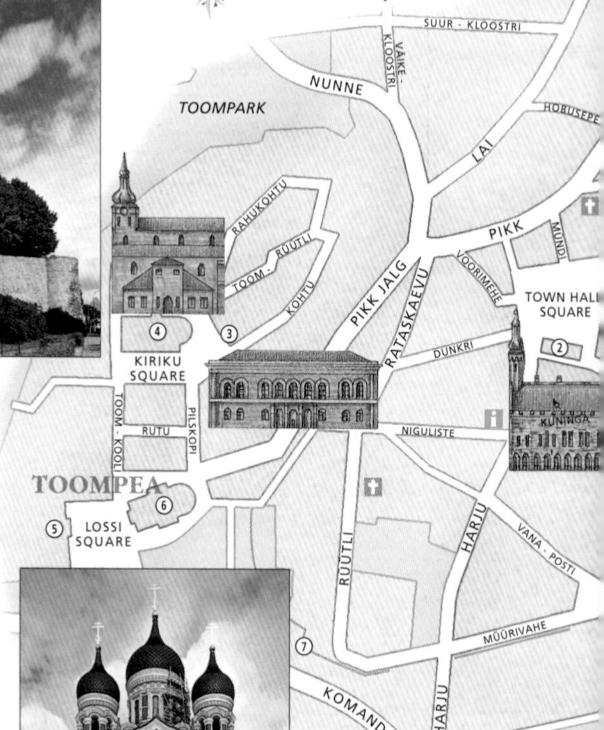

0 metres 100

0 yards 100

Art Museum of Estonia ③
Situated on Toompea Hill in the former Knighthood House, the Art Museum of Estonia was established in 1919. Its comprehensive collection of the best of Estonian art over the centuries is also the country's largest.

Alexander Nevskiy Cathedral ⑥
Some say the Czar purposely built this spectacular Russian Orthodox church, dating from 1900, on the grave of epic Estonian folk hero Kalev as part of his plan to dominate Estonia.

Fat Margaret Tower and Estonian Maritime Museum ①

Now housing a maritime museum with exhibits on the history of shipping and fishing, this massive early 16th-century bastion *Paks Margareeta* derives its name from a stout cannon in the tower. The building was a prison from 1830 to 1917.

Town Hall ②

The 13th-century Town Hall dominating the central square is a rare surviving Gothic town hall in Europe. Its spire offers superb panoramic views. The old city jail nearby houses the Photographic Museum showing 19th- and 20th-century works.

Kiek in de Kök Tower ⑦

This 15th-century watchtower, whose name means "Peep into the Kitchen", bears in its walls Russian cannonballs that supposedly lodged there during a 16th-century bombardment when the town was held by the Swedes. It houses a permanent exhibition of city history over six centuries, including unusual photographs and artifacts.

KEY SIGHTS

① Fat Margaret Tower and Estonian Maritime Museum ★

② Town Hall ★

③ Art Museum of Estonia

④ Dome Church

⑤ Toompea

⑥ Alexander Nevski Cathedral ★

⑦ Kiek in de Kök Tower

FACT FILE

TOURIST INFORMATION

Niguliste 2/ Kullassepa 4.
Tel *(372) 645 7777.* ◻ *May, Jun & Sep: Mon–Fri to 7pm (Sep: to 6pm), Sat & Sun to 5pm; Jul & Aug: Mon–Fri to 8pm, Sat & Sun to 6pm; Oct–Apr: Mon–Fri to 8pm, Sat to 3pm.*

MARKETS

Food Keskturg, Turu pöik 2; daily.
Crafts Katariina passage; daily.

LOCAL SPECIALITIES

Crafts

Leather goods, ceramics, wrought iron, amber work, jewellery, toy-making, glassware, national dress.

Dishes

Kartulid ja Sealiha (pork with potatoes). *Kotlet* (a type of hamburger with onions). *Sült* (jellied meat). *Kringel* (sweet bread with nuts and raisins).

Drinks

Saku (a brand of dark or light Estonian beer). *Gremi* (locally bottled brandy from Georgia). *Viru Valge* (local vodka).

EXCURSIONS

Kadriog Park and Palace 3 km (2 miles) E of Tallinn. The quiet haven of the park has ash and cherry trees, sculptures and fountains. The palace, Peter the Great's 18th-century "mini-Versailles" (though not finished in his lifetime) houses the museum of European art.

Rocca al Mare Open Air Museum 3 km (2 miles) NW of Tallinn. An exposition of mainly 19th-century Estonian rural life, including reconstructed thatched farmhouses, inns, churches, windmills and other buildings.

Riga

Sculpture from Dome Cathedral

Founded in the 1100s, Riga, the capital of Latvia, was occupied for centuries by Germany, Sweden, Poland and Russia. The port flourished through maritime trade and was once the biggest city in the Kingdom of Sweden. After a brief period of freedom from 1920 to 1940, Latvia came under first Nazi and then Soviet control. Independence was finally regained in 1991. Today Riga embraces Western culture and offers fine restaurants, bars, shops, and Internet cafés. The narrow, traffic-free streets of the old, walled city are a joy to explore.

Three Brothers ②
Comprising architectural styles from 15th-century Germanic to Baroque, these are the three oldest stone residential buildings in Riga. The Museum of Architecture at No. 19 contains original drawings, plans and photographs of buildings by Latvian architects.

Powder Tower and War Museum ③
The last 18th-century defence tower still standing contains a comprehensive museum of photos and memorabilia documenting military history and Latvia's suffering over the last 100 years of combat against wave after wave of invaders.

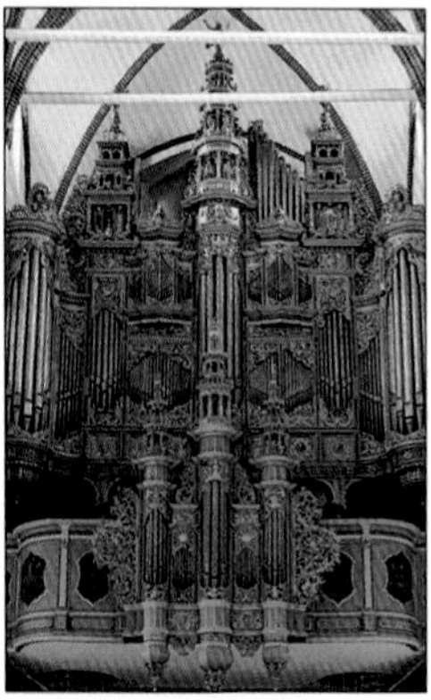

Dome Cathedral ⑦
The walls of this huge, red-brick cathedral are crammed with medieval plaques. One key feature is the 6,768-pipe organ, which is one of the largest in the world.

Museum of Decorative and Applied Arts ⑤
Formerly the 13th-century St George's church (the oldest stone church in Riga), this museum offers visitors examples of Latvian tapestries, porcelain, woodcuts, and more.

JUGENDSTIL ARCHITECTURE

Nearly half of central Riga's architecture is in the Art Noveau style (Jugendstil). A flourishing economy at the height of European Art Nouveau (1895–1915) meant that buildings could be built to reflect the age. Destruction of other cities during World War II has left Riga the largest surviving collection in this style, which is generally regarded as the finest in Europe. Mikhail Eisenstein was one of Riga's main Jugendstil architects.

Jugendstil detail on No. 10b Elizabetes Street

Elizabetes Street and Alberta Street ①
A superlative gallery of Jugendstil architecture may be seen at Nos. 2, 2a, 4, 6, 8 and 13 Alberta Street and Nos. 10a and 10b Elizabetes Street.

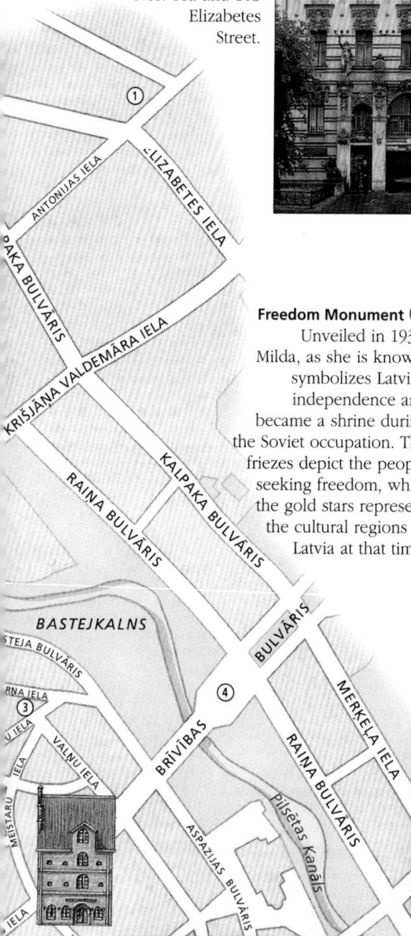

Freedom Monument ④
Unveiled in 1935, Milda, as she is known, symbolizes Latvian independence and became a shrine during the Soviet occupation. The friezes depict the people seeking freedom, while the gold stars represent the cultural regions of Latvia at that time.

St Peter's Church ⑥
Badly damaged during World War II, 13th-century St Peter's was rebuilt rather badly in Soviet style. A viewing platform around the spire affords fabulous 360° views over the entire city.

KEY SIGHTS

① Elizabetes Street and Alberta Street
② Three Brothers ★
③ Powder Tower and War Museum
④ Freedom Monument ★
⑤ Museum of Decorative and Applied Arts
⑥ St Peter's Church
⑦ Dome Cathedral ★

FACT FILE

TOURIST INFORMATION

Ratslaukums 6 (town hall square). ***Tel*** *(371) 703 7900.* ◯ *daily to 7pm.*

MARKETS

Food & general goods Central Market, Pragas 1; Tue–Sat to 6pm, Sun & Mon to 5pm.
General Vidzemes Market, Matisa 2; daily.

LOCAL SPECIALITIES

Crafts
Latvian linen, leather goods, wooden toys, Latvian and amber jewellery, Latvian folk costumes.
Dishes
Rupjmaize (dark rye bread). *Skaba putra* (cold barley soup with sour cream). *Piragi* (baked onion and bacon dumplings). *Cukas galerts* (cold pork in aspic). *Klingeris* (pretzel-shaped saffron pastry with almonds and raisins).
Drinks
Aldaris, Cesis and *Lacplesis* (beers). *Kristaldzidrais* (Latvian vodka). *Zverkavis* (a Latvian type of whisky). *Rigas Melnais Balzams* ("Black Balsam" is a dark, herbal liqueur often drunk with coffee or orange juice – blackcurrant in winter).

EXCURSIONS

Motor Museum 10 km (7 miles) E of Riga. Motor vehicles including vintage Rolls Royces and cars that belonged to Stalin and Brezhnev.
Salaspils 20 km (12 miles) SE of Riga. The concentration camp that existed here from 1941 to 1944 is now a memorial and museum.
Ethnographic Open Air Museum 10 km (7 miles) NE of Riga. Latvia's 18th- and 19th-century rural lifestyle is preserved here, on the shore of Lake Jugla.

Gdansk cityscape, Poland ▷

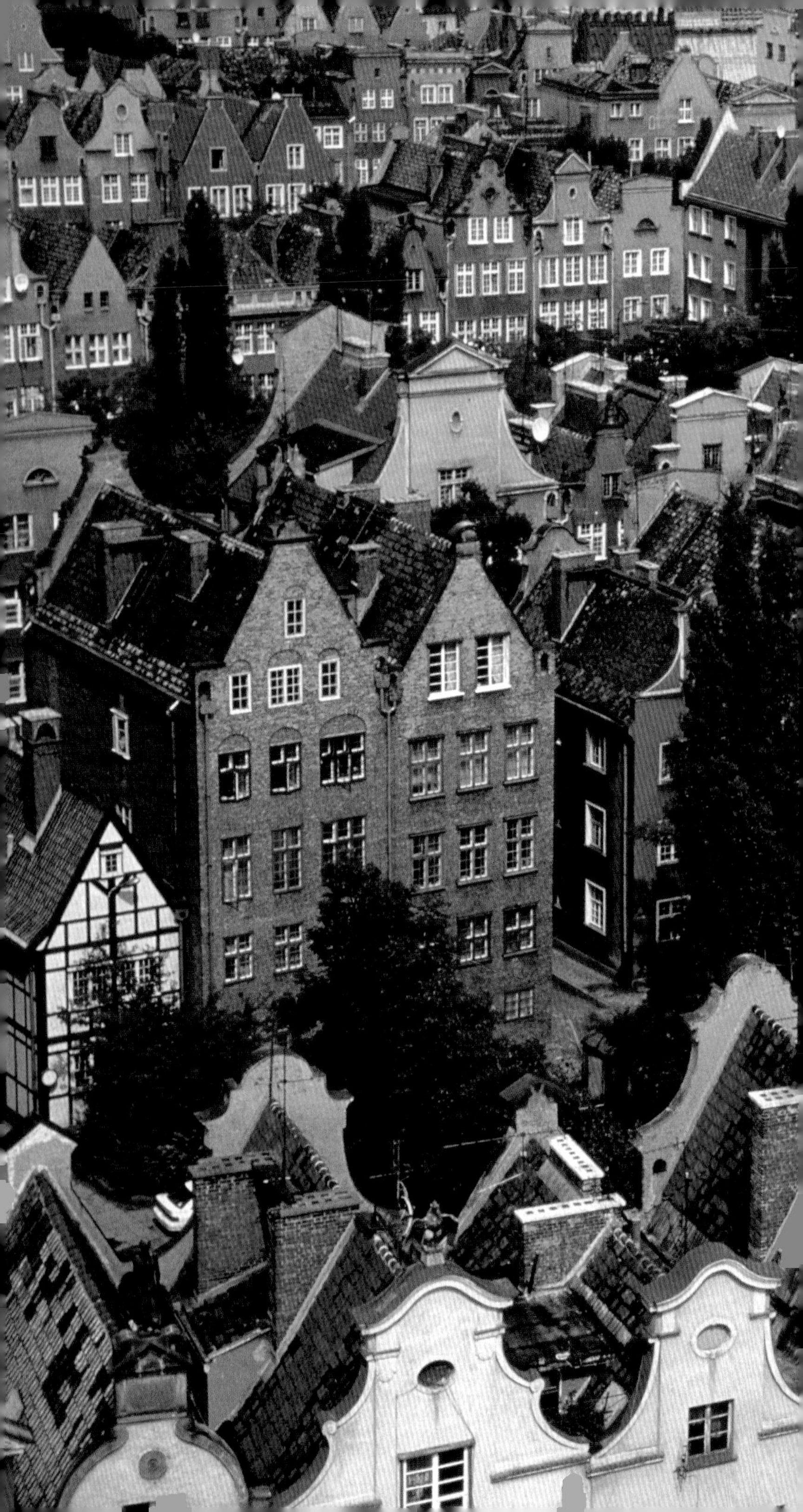

POLAND

Gdańsk (Gdynia)

Sited at the mouth of the Vistula, Gdańsk was ruled by the Teutonic Knights from 1308 to 1454, when it became the largest of the Hanseatic towns *(see p88)*, enriched by the export of timber and grain. It flourished under Polish rule from 1466 to 1793, was Prussian to 1920 and a Free City to 1939. The first shots of World War II were fired in Gdańsk and though the city was largely destroyed in the war, the centre has been fully restored. Today, the "Tri-City" consists of Gdańsk itself, Gdynia, the shipbuilding and port area, and Sopot, the beach resort. The finest street is the Royal Way, the most picturesque is Mariacka Street and Długie Pobneże (Long Quay) by Crane Gate is lively with cafés and shops.

Artus Court ⑤
This Gothic hall was the medieval city merchants' meeting place. Its 16th-century Renaissance tile stove is exceptional.

Main Town Hall ⑥
Finished in 1378, this is Gdańsk's finest Gothic building and houses the Museum of the History of Gdańsk. The Great Council Chamber has impressive allegorical frescoes.

Arsenal ①
This masterpiece of Dutch Mannerism was built between 1600 and 1609. The ground floor of the former weapons and ammunition store is today filled with shops. The building has a finely decorated façade.

Church of St Mary ②
Founded in 1343, but dating mainly from the 15th and 16th centuries, this is the largest brick church in the world. Visit its astronomical clock and many art treasures.

THE TEUTONIC KNIGHTS

The Knights were a German military religious order founded in Palestine in 1190 during the Third Crusade. They conquered the Baltic between 1229 and 1329, moving their headquarters to Malbork (then called Marienburg) in 1309, where they built this supreme example of a medieval brick castle. The Order still exists as a charitable body based in Vienna.

Malbork, the largest brick castle in Europe

National Museum ⑧
A wealth of artifacts, from wrought-iron grilles to sculpture and painting, fill this former Gothic Franciscan monastery. The highlight is Hans Memling's *Last Judgment* triptych (1471), made for the Church of St Mary.

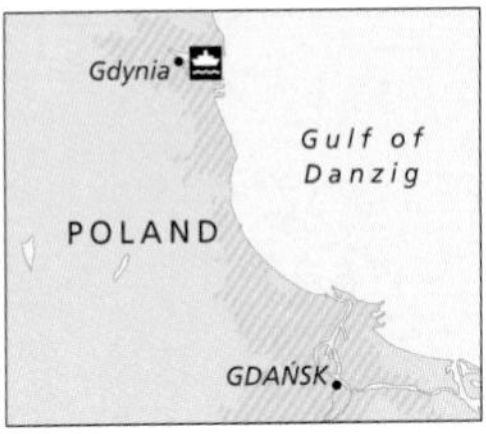

DISTANCE FROM PORT

22 km (14 miles) from city centre.

Mariacka Street ③
Considered Gdańsk's finest street, the picturesque houses, fronted by small terraces with sculptured stonework, have inspired writers and artists for centuries.

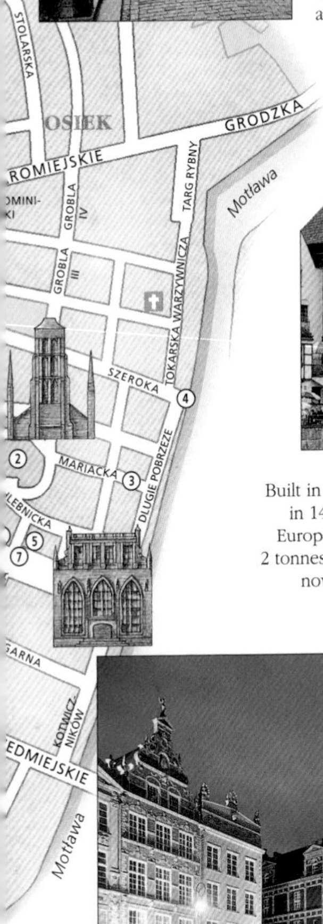

Gdańsk Crane ④
Built in the 14th century and renovated in 1444, this icon is one of Medieval Europe's largest structures. Able to lift 2 tonnes to a height of 27 m (90 ft), it is now part of the Maritime Museum.

Neptune Fountain ⑦
This fountain, with masterly ironwork (1633) and Flemish artist Peter Husen's bronze statue of Neptune (1615), has become a symbol of maritime Gdańsk. It stands on the Royal Way (Uliça Długa and Długi Targ), the parade route of Polish kings.

KEY SIGHTS

① Arsenal ★
② Church of St Mary ★
③ Mariacka Street
④ Gdańsk Crane
⑤ Artus Court
⑥ Main Town Hall ★
⑦ Neptune Fountain
⑧ National Museum

FACT FILE

TOURIST INFORMATION
ul. Dluga 45. ***Tel*** *(058) 301 91 51.* ◻ *Mon–Fri to 6pm, Sat & Sun to 4:30pm.*

MARKETS
Food Kupcy Dominikański 1; daily.

SHOPPING
Jewellery especially in Mariacka St.

LOCAL SPECIALITIES
Crafts
Carved and painted wooden objects; dolls in traditional costume.
Dishes
Rybonka (fish and noodle soup). *Polewka gdańska* (goulash soup). *Zylc* (pig's knuckle in aspic). *Kaczka po gdańsku* (duck cooked with oranges and orange liqueur). *Kruchy placek* (cherry or forest fruit pastries). *Makowiec* (poppy seed cake). *Sernik* (heavy cheese cake). *Piernik* (honey and sugar cake). *Pączek* (doughnuts with plum jam).
Drinks
Kaper, Gdańskie, Hevelius, Red Original (locally-brewed beers). *Goldwasser* (vodka liqueur containing tiny flakes of gold leaf).

EXCURSIONS
Shipyard Memorial Solidarności Square, Gdańsk. Monument to the 1970 dockyard strike casualties.
Westerplatte Monument 10 km (6 miles) N of Gdańsk. Commemorates outbreak here of World War II.
Oliwa 8 km (5 miles) NW of Gdańsk. Gothic Cathedral in lovely park. Famous organ recitals.
Malbork 56 km (35 miles) S of Gdańsk. Vast fortress. Museum has superb amber and armour exhibits.
Frombork 98 km (60 miles) E of Gdańsk. Copernicus's home town.

Tivoli Gardens in Copenhagen, Denmark ▷

DENMARK

Copenhagen

Although smaller than most capital cities, Copenhagen is every bit as busy, modern and cosmopolitan as its counterparts. The city grew out of the tiny fishing village of Havn, after Bishop Absalon built a castle to protect the harbour there in 1167. Benefiting from increasing trade, the settlement expanded, becoming known as København ("merchants' harbour"). In 1443, it became the Danish capital. Today, despite being the official residence of the Danish monarchy, the seat of government and the centre of media, trade and industry, the city remains remarkably relaxed and welcoming.

Round Tower ④
Built as an observatory in 1642 by Christian IV, the 35-m (115-ft) high Rundetårn (Round Tower) affords stunning views across the city.

Ny Carlsberg Glyptotek ⑩
Opened in 1897 by the brewer Carl Jacobsen, this gallery was created as a venue for bringing Classical art to ordinary people. It has fine collections of Ancient Egyptian, Greek and Roman sculptures and 19th-century European art. Its main attraction is a Mediterranean wintergarden, in which stands the Kai Nielsen sculpture, *Water Mother with Children* (1920).

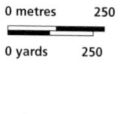

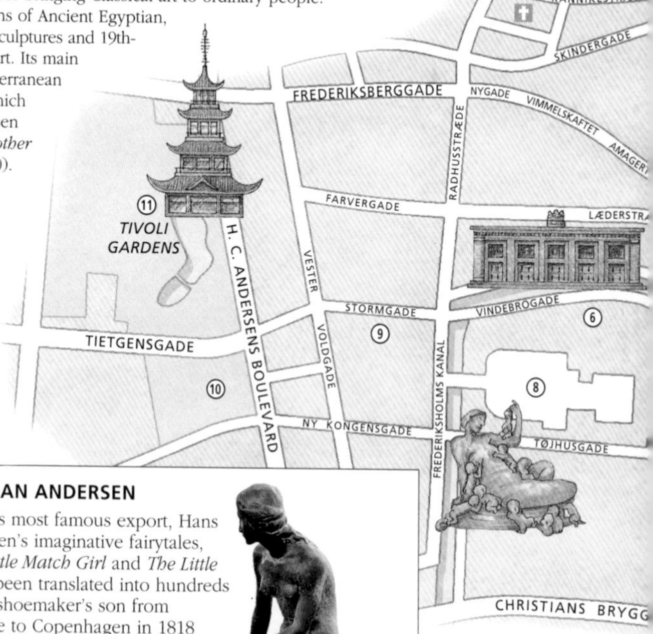

National Museum ⑨
This museum is devoted to Danish history from prehistoric to recent times, with a fine collection of Viking artifacts. Children can play in a replica viking ship in the Children's Museum.

HANS CHRISTIAN ANDERSEN

By far Denmark's most famous export, Hans Christian Andersen's imaginative fairytales, including *The Little Match Girl* and *The Little Mermaid,* have been translated into hundreds of languages. A shoemaker's son from Odense, he came to Copenhagen in 1818 aged just 14. Within a short time he had made a name for himself as a great storyteller and was courted by the aristocracy. He travelled extensively but always returned to Copenhagen, where he died in 1875.

Little Mermaid statue, Langelinie Pier

Christiansborg Palace ⑧
Built on the site of the fortress that marked the founding of Copenhagen in 1167, this 14th-century palace, rebuilt several times, has been the seat of the Danish parliament since 1918.

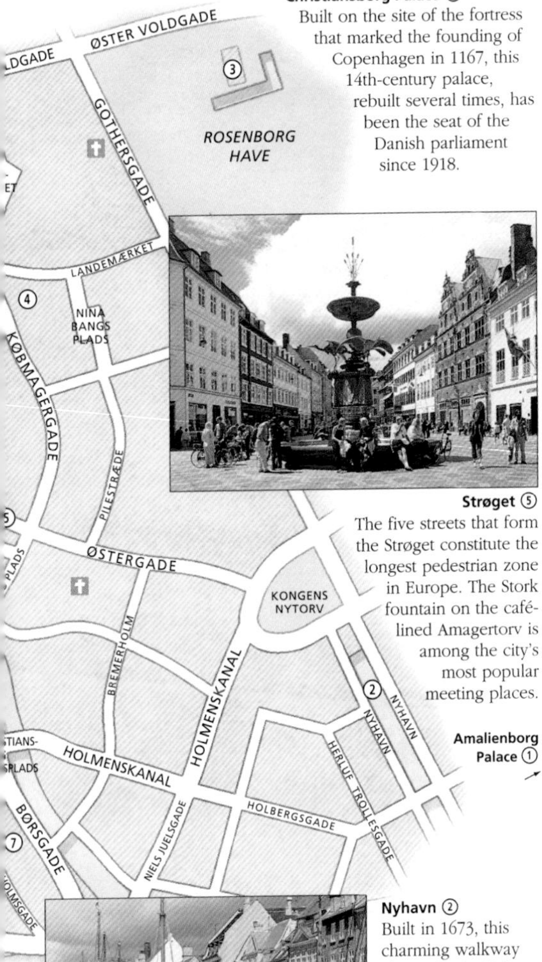

Strøget ⑤
The five streets that form the Strøget constitute the longest pedestrian zone in Europe. The Stork fountain on the café-lined Amagertorv is among the city's most popular meeting places.

Amalienborg Palace ①

Nyhavn ②
Built in 1673, this charming walkway alongside the Nyhavn canal is filled with market stalls. Its over-whelming choice of lively bars makes it an enjoyable place to sit and look out at the old sailing ships moored nearby.

KEY SIGHTS

① Amalienborg Palace ★
② Nyhavn
③ Rosenborg Palace ★
④ Round Tower
⑤ Strøget ★
⑥ Thorvaldsens Museum
⑦ Old Stock Exchange
⑧ Christiansborg Palace
⑨ National Museum
⑩ Ny Carlsberg Glyptotek
⑪ Tivoli Gardens ★
(see pp84–5)

FACT FILE

TOURIST INFORMATION

Vesterbrogade 4 A. ***Tel*** *70 22 24 42.* ◯ *Sep–Apr: Mon–Fri to 4:30pm, Sat to 1:30pm; May–Sep: to 8pm.*

MARKETS

Bric-à-brac Gammel Strand; summer: Fri & Sat. Israels Plads; summer: Sat.

SHOPPING

Royal Copenhagen porcelain and crystal, Georg Jensen silver at the Royal Copenhagen shopping complex on Amagertorv in Strøget, a famous shopping district.

LOCAL SPECIALITIES

Dishes
Smørrebrød (substantial open sandwich with toppings of fish, meat or vegetables).
Gravet laks (salmon marinated in sugar, salt, pepper and dill).
Pølser (bright red fried sausage).
Rødgrød med fløde (red fruit pudding with cream).
Sarah Bernhardt (marzipan cake).
Drinks
Aquavit (strong, spicy schnapps).

EXCURSIONS

Assistens Kirkegård
0.5 km (0.3 miles) N of Copenhagen. Massive cemetery containing graves of famous Danes, including philosopher Søren Kierkegaard and writer Hans Christian Andersen.
Carlsberg Brewery and Visitors Centre 1.5 km (1 mile) N of Copenhagen. Guided tours Tue–Sun.

Rosenborg Palace with its surrounding moat, imitating a fortification

Exploring Copenhagen
Originally founded on the site of a castle in the 11th century, Copenhagen grew by radiating outwards, so most of its historical and cultural sights are near the centre and within walking distance of each other. The centre of town, or Indre By, is a maze of often cobbled streets and alleyways, while to the south lies the main government administrative district. East of Amalienborg Palace lie the 16th-century Kastellet fortifications and beyond them Edward Eriksen's statue of the Little Mermaid *(see p80)* stares out to sea from Langelinie Pier.

Amalienborg Palace ①
Actually four identical Rococo palaces arranged symmetrically around a cobbled square with an imposing statue of Frederick V in the centre, Amalienborg has housed the Danish Royal Family since 1794. Two of the palaces still serve as Royal residences and while the present queen, Margrethe II, is in residence, a daily changing of the guard takes place in front of her home. The palace directly opposite is now a museum on the royal family and home to part of the Royal Collection, the bulk of which is held at Rosenborg Palace. The study of Christian IX (1818–1906) and the drawing room of his wife, Queen Louise, are filled with family presents and photographs, as well as a few delightful Fabergé pieces.

Guard outside Amalienborg Palace

Nyhavn ②
Until the 1970s, Nyhavn (New Harbour), a wide street divided in two by a narrow canal, was a district frequented mainly by sailors. Now antiques shops and restaurants have replaced all but one or two of the tattoo parlours, making Nyhavn a lively place to spend an hour or two enjoying a meal outdoors alongside the yachts moored on the canal. A number of the brightly painted town houses lining the canal date back to the 18th century. Denmark's famous writer Hans Christian Andersen lived, at various times, at Nos. 18, 20 and 67.

Rosenborg Palace ③
Christian IV originally built this palace as a two-storey summer residence between 1606 and 1607, and continued to rebuild and add to it over the next 30 years until the palace looked much as it does today. The interiors are particularly well preserved and its chambers, halls and ballrooms are filled with thousands of decorative objects, including amber chandeliers, life-sized silver lions, tapestries and thrones.

Two of the 24 rooms open to the public are stacked from floor to ceiling with porcelain and glassware. The "Porcelain Cabinet" includes examples from the famous Flora Danica dinner service for 100 guests, which was created by the Royal Copenhagen Porcelain factory between 1790 and 1803. Each piece is decorated with a different example of G C Oeder's work on Danish flowers and plants. The sumptuous glass room houses nearly 1,000 examples of old Venetian glass from the late 17th century, as well as glass from Bohemia, England, the Netherlands and Germany. Three rooms in the basement house the treasury, which holds the royal jewels.

Round Tower ④
Although only 35 m (115 ft) high, the Rundetårn has 209 m (686 ft) of spiral ramp that winds itself around the

inside of the tower seven and a half times. Built in 1642 by Christian IV as an observatory, the tower has for centuries offered magnificent views over the city to anyone willing to undertake the journey to the top. Not everyone has walked however; in 1716, Peter the Great rode up the ramp on horseback, and his wife, Yekatarina, made the journey in a two-wheeled carriage.

Strøget ⑤
Flanked by the squares of Gammeltorv and Nytorv, Strøget (pronounced "Stroy-et") Europe's longest pedestrian street. Stretching for 2 km (1 mile), it actually comprises five streets – Frederiksberggade, Nygade, Vimmelskaftet, Amagertorv and Østergade.

These streets are lined with Copenhagen's most exclusive shops, selling everything from designer-label clothing to the finest Danish porcelain and glass. A host of bustling cafés and restaurants offer shoppers a chance to rest and refuel, while cafés on Amagertorv's busy square offer views of the Stork Fountain and the red-brick Renaissance building of the Royal Copenhagen centre.

Thorvaldsens Museum ⑥
Built in 1848, this is Denmark's oldest museum. It houses the works of the country's most celebrated sculptor, Bertel Thorvaldsen (1770–1844). After completing his education in Denmark, Thorvaldsen lived for nearly 40 years in Rome, where he built up a world-wide reputation. Apart from his impressive sculptures, the museum also houses his private collection, including paintings by 19th-century European contemporaries.

Copenhagen's Old Stock Exchange with its gabled façade and twisted spire

Neo-Classical façade of Thorvaldsens Museum

Old Stock Exchange ⑦
Constructed between 1619 and 1640 by Christian IV, Denmark's "builder king", the Old Stock Exchange is an architectural masterpiece combining tiny windows, steep roofs and decorative gables. At the centre of the long, low building is a 54-m (177-ft) high tower, topped by a twisted spire representing four intertwined dragon's tails.

Pendant at the National Museum

Christiansborg Palace ⑧
Standing on its own island, Slotsholmen, and linked by a series of small bridges to Indre By, Christiansborg is the administrative centre of Denmark. Opened in 1916 as a royal palace, it houses not only the state parliament and government offices, but a number of museums and the underground ruins of Bishop Absalon's castle.

National Museum ⑨
Housed in an 18th-century former palace, the National Museum boasts extensive collections detailing the history of Denmark from prehistoric to modern times. Among the exhibits on Viking life, much of it from Jutland, are rune stones with inscriptions dating from around AD 1000, jewellery, treasure hoards, the contents of burial mounds, bones and even several bodies found preserved in peat bogs. A children's museum contains replicas of period clothing and information on how school life was 100 years ago.

Close by, and part of the museum, is a restored 19th-century Danish home with authentic interiors. Decorated panels, elaborately carved furniture and the characteristic profusion of paintings portray an upper-class household of the 1890s.

Ny Carlsberg Glyptotek ⑩
Copenhagen's most elegant art gallery was opened in 1897 by Carl Jacobsen, son of the founder of the Carlsberg Brewery. Housed in a large Neo-Classical building, the Glyptotek is best known for its Ancient art, in particular a magnificent collection of Etruscan pieces and one of Europe's finest collections of Roman portraits. The glass wing, opened in 1996, contains paintings by French Impressionists, while a number of rooms are dedicated to Danish sculpture and works by artists from Denmark's Golden Age of painting – the first half of the 19th century.

Tivoli Gardens ⑪
See pp84–5.

Copenhagen: Tivoli Gardens ⓫

Pierrot at the Pantomime Theatre

One of Copenhagen's greatest attractions, the Tivoli Gardens combine all the fun of fairground rides with fountains, fireworks, concerts, ballets, restaurants and cafés. Open during the summer and again at Christmas time, the Gardens have been carefully designed to seem bigger than their 12 acres. Every turn of the zig-zagging main avenue presents a new view to visitors strolling along it. After dusk, when the Gardens' footpaths are lit by more than 100,000 specially designed lamps, Tivoli's open-air theatres host *Commedia dell'Arte* plays and performances by international singers, acrobats and big bands. Every Wednesday and Saturday, at a quarter to midnight, a fireworks display lights up the night sky using fireworks produced in Tivoli's own factory.

Divan 2 is one of Tivoli's finest restaurants. It was established in 1843, when the gardens were originally opened.

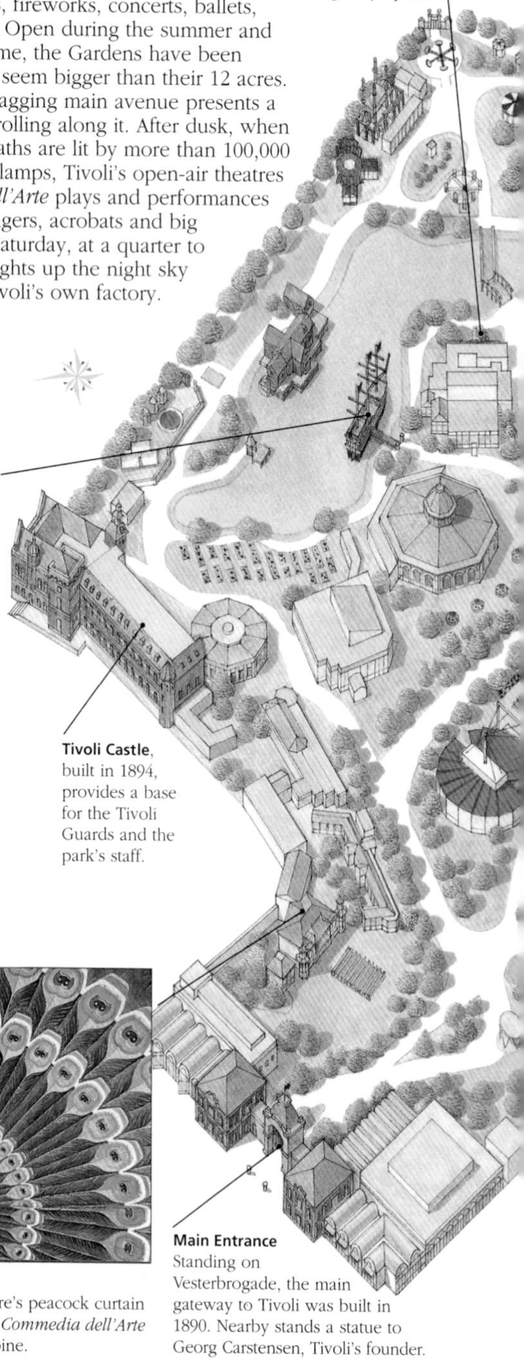

★ George III Frigate Ship
This 27-m (90-ft) long frigate, made in Jutland, is a replica of the Danish frigates dating from around 1700. Weighing some 100 tonnes, the ship is a popular restaurant at Tivoli.

Tivoli Castle, built in 1894, provides a base for the Tivoli Guards and the park's staff.

★ Pantomime Theatre
When the tail of the Pantomime Theatre's peacock curtain parts, audiences are introduced to the *Commedia dell'Arte* tales of Pierrot, Harlequin and Columbine.

Main Entrance
Standing on Vesterbrogade, the main gateway to Tivoli was built in 1890. Nearby stands a statue to Georg Carstensen, Tivoli's founder.

★ Chinese Pagoda
Dating from 1900, the Chinese Pagoda was built to a design by architect Knud Arne-Pedersen, Tivoli's director at the time. Standing four storeys high, it houses a restaurant serving Chinese and Danish food, and affords fine views over Tivoli's central lake. At night, the pagoda is lit by approximately 1,500 coloured lanterns.

STAR SIGHTS

- ★ George III Frigate Ship
- ★ Pantomime Theatre
- ★ Chinese Pagoda
- ★ Nimb

Concert Hall
Live music has always played an important part at Tivoli, and the Concert Hall was the main attraction when the gardens first opened in 1843. Seating 1,900 people, it presents a variety of classical-music concerts, often by internationally renowned artists.

★ Nimb
The Nimb building was erected in 1909, and holds a hotel and many restaurants. At night the roof and wall lights turn the building into a spectacular display of colour.

The Bubble Fountain was designed by the nuclear physicist Niels Bohr and built in 1961.

TIVOLI GARDENS GUARDS

On most Saturday and Sunday afternoons the boys of the Tivoli Guards march through the park, accompanied by their own band and a golden stagecoach bearing a child prince and princess. Originally founded in 1844 as a small group of 30 boys, the guards have grown to number more than 100, all aged between 9 and 16. The guards' uniform, which was introduced in 1872, usually comprises a red jacket, white trousers and a bearskin, though during the summer months a cooler blue uniform is often preferred.

The boys of the Tivoli Guards Band, sporting their lightweight blue uniforms

Marksburg Castle at Koblenz, Germany ▷

GERMANY

LÜBECK 88–89 • HAMBURG 90–93

Lübeck

Standing on an island surrounded by the canals and rivers of the Trave estuary, the city of Lübeck was originally founded in 1143. The city was founded for the second time in 1159 – by the Duke of Saxony, Henry the Lion – after the first settlement had burned down. The city grew quickly and within 100 years it had become the principal member of the powerful Hanseatic League. Although the city is no longer a major economic power, its magnificent churches and civic buildings testify to its former glory and the street layout of the Old Town still follows Henry the Lion's original plan. In 1987, UNESCO designated the Old Town a World Heritage Site.

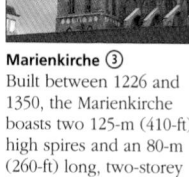

Marienkirche ③
Built between 1226 and 1350, the Marienkirche boasts two 125-m (410-ft) high spires and an 80-m (260-ft) long, two-storey central nave.

Rathaus ④
Lübeck's town hall, considered one of Germany's most beautiful, was built between the 13th and 15th centuries of red and black bricks. The north wing, with its impressive market façade, was constructed in 1435.

Holstentor ⑤
Constructed on swampy soil in 1464–78, the distinctive, round, turret-roofed towers of the Holstentor now lean rather alarmingly. Originally the city's gate, the building now houses the City History Museum.

St Annen Museum ⑥
Housed in the remains of a convent, the St Annen Museum has a collection of exhibits portraying the religious art and social history of Lübeck from the 13th to the 18th century.

HANSEATIC LEAGUE

In 1241, the towns of Lübeck and Hamburg *(see pp90–91)* formed a trading alliance. Driven by the need to protect their trading interests from political upheaval and pirates, cities from all over the Baltic, such as Novgorod and Visby *(see pp50–51)*, joined this alliance to form the Hanseatic League. For 400 years, the League was one of the most important political forces in Europe, as it organized and controlled trade by winning commercial privileges and monopolies. During the 16th century, however, internal divisions and the growth of nation states, such as England and the Netherlands, sent the League into decline. In 1669, the League held its last assembly, though it was never formally dissolved.

Seal of the citizens of Lübeck (1256)

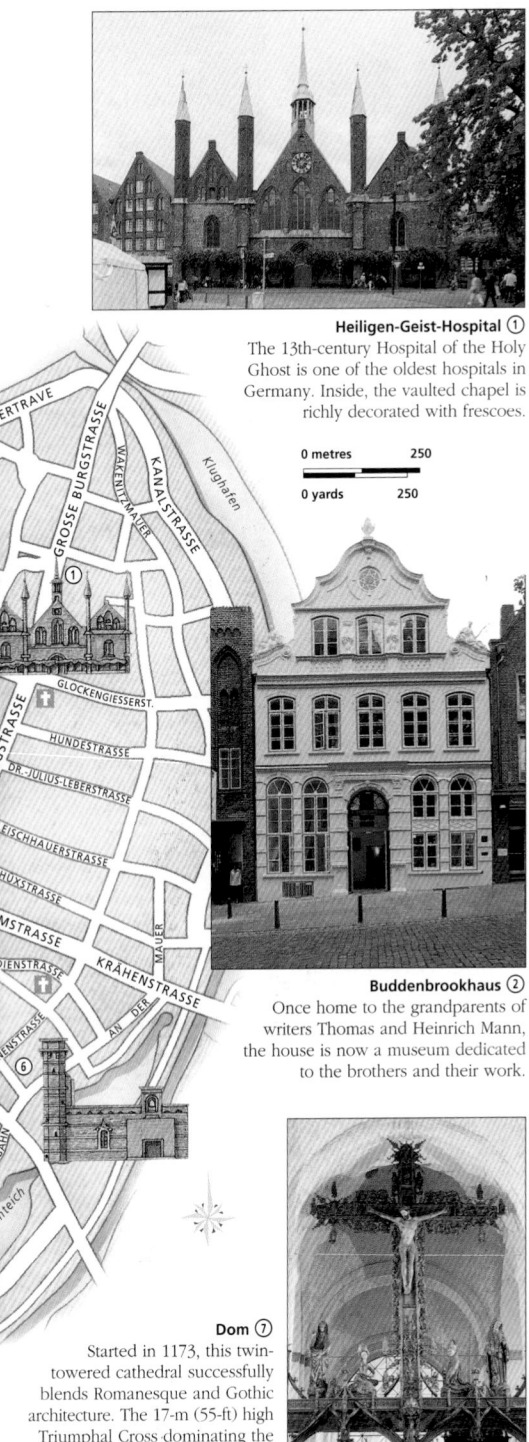

Heiligen-Geist-Hospital ①
The 13th-century Hospital of the Holy Ghost is one of the oldest hospitals in Germany. Inside, the vaulted chapel is richly decorated with frescoes.

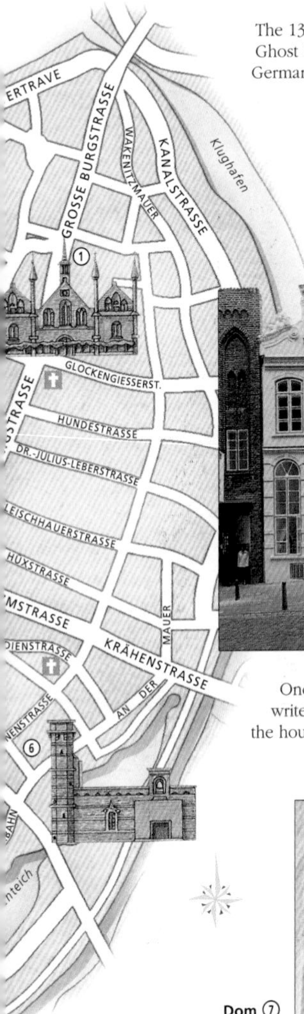

Buddenbrookhaus ②
Once home to the grandparents of writers Thomas and Heinrich Mann, the house is now a museum dedicated to the brothers and their work.

Dom ⑦
Started in 1173, this twin-towered cathedral successfully blends Romanesque and Gothic architecture. The 17-m (55-ft) high Triumphal Cross dominating the interior was created by the sculptor Berndt Notke in 1477.

KEY SIGHTS

① Heiligen-Geist-Hospital ★
② Buddenbrookhaus
③ Marienkirche ★
④ Rathaus
⑤ Holstentor ★
⑥ St Annen Museum
⑦ Dom

FACT FILE

TOURIST INFORMATION

Holstentor Platz. ***Tel*** *(0451) 889 97 00.* ◯ *Oct–May: Mon–Fri to 6pm, Sat to 3pm; Jun–Sep: Mon–Fri to 7pm, Sat to 3pm, Sun to 2pm.*

MARKETS

Crafts & antiques Hallenmarkt, near the train station; Sat.

LOCAL SPECIALITIES

Crafts
Candle-making, wickerwork, paper modelling.
Produce
Marzipan.
Dishes
Zander mit Radieschenpfannkuchen (fish with radish-filled pancakes). *Forelle mit Spargel* (trout served with asparagus). *Rote Grütze* (fruit-juice jelly with cream).
Drinks
Rotspon (a blend of red Burgundy wines).
Wittspon (a blend of white wines).

EXCURSIONS

Brodtener Steilufer 1.5 km (1 mile) N of Lübeck. A 4-km (2-mile) long cliff with a golf course and spectacular views over the sea.
Hansa Park 19 km (12 miles) NE of Lübeck. Family-oriented leisure park with a nautical theme, set on the coast near Sierksdorf.
Travemünde 20 km (12 miles) NE of Lübeck. Seaside town on the Baltic Sea with a casino and sandy beaches, ideal for watersports.
Ratzeburg 25 km (15 miles) SE of Lübeck. Lakeside town with a picturesque *altstadt* (old town) on a small island in a lake.
Graswarder Nature Reserve 52 km (31 miles) N of Lübeck. The breeding place of many sea and water birds. Tours in summer.

Hamburg

Detail from the Rathaus building

Germany's second-largest city, Hamburg was founded in the 9th century by the Holy Roman Emperor, Charlemagne. In 1189, the city was granted free trade rights, and Hamburg soon became an important port and a leading member of the Hanseatic League *(see p88)*. A fire in 1842 destroyed much of the city and the bombing raids of World War II again brought mass destruction, but the city's wealth always allowed it to recover quickly. Today, Hamburg is Germany's largest seaport and the media capital of the country.

Krameramtswohnungen ③
The last 17th-century buildings in Hamburg are these tiny houses that were retirement homes for storekeepers' widows. Most are now shops, but one has been kept in its original condition.

Fischmarkt ①
Between 5am and 9:30am on Sundays, Hamburg's fish market seethes with people either shopping or finishing off a long Saturday night. The best entertainment is provided by the fishmongers loudly hawking their wares.

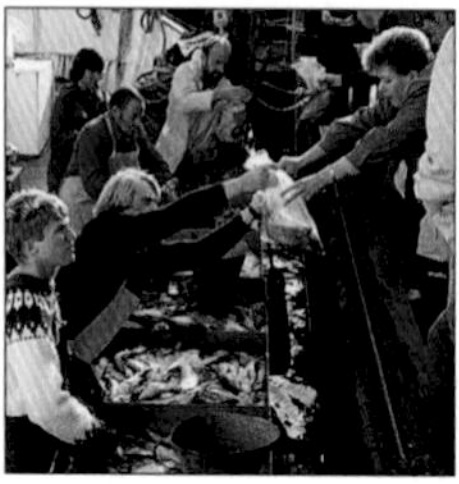

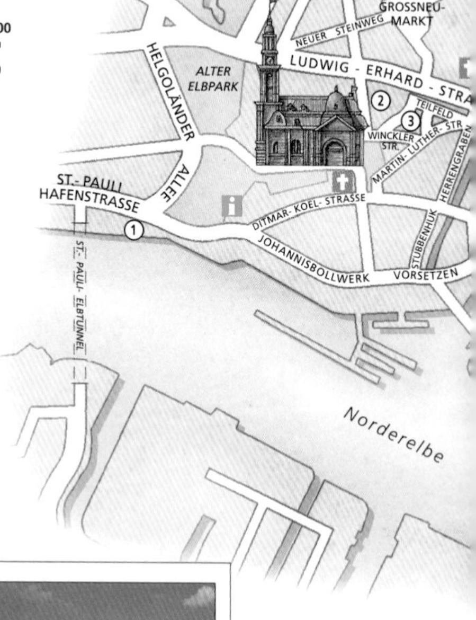

St Michaelis ②
The Lutheran interior of St Michaelis, built between 1648 and 1673, is designed to draw the eye to the pulpit. This famous church is Hamburg's city emblem.

HAMBURG PORT

Established during the 12th century, Hamburg's port ensured that for hundreds of years the city was one of the wealthiest in the world. In the 1880s, the establishment of a free port – where cargoes are exempt from customs formalities – led to the construction of the Speicherstadt, the largest self-contained warehouse complex in the world. Today, the port is still one of the largest in Europe, covering an area of 75 sq km (29 sq miles).

Hamburg harbour, with St Michaelis in the background

Rathaus ④
Hamburg's town hall, built between 1886 and 1897, is a massive Neo-Renaissance building. It still serves as the seat of the city's parliament, and most of its 647 rooms are lavishly decorated. The Great Hall is used for banquets and concerts.

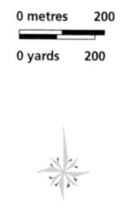

Kunsthalle ⑦
Hamburg's principal museum contains chronologically arranged collections of medieval to contemporary art. The New Wing, linked to the museum by an underground passage, houses the collection of contemporary art.

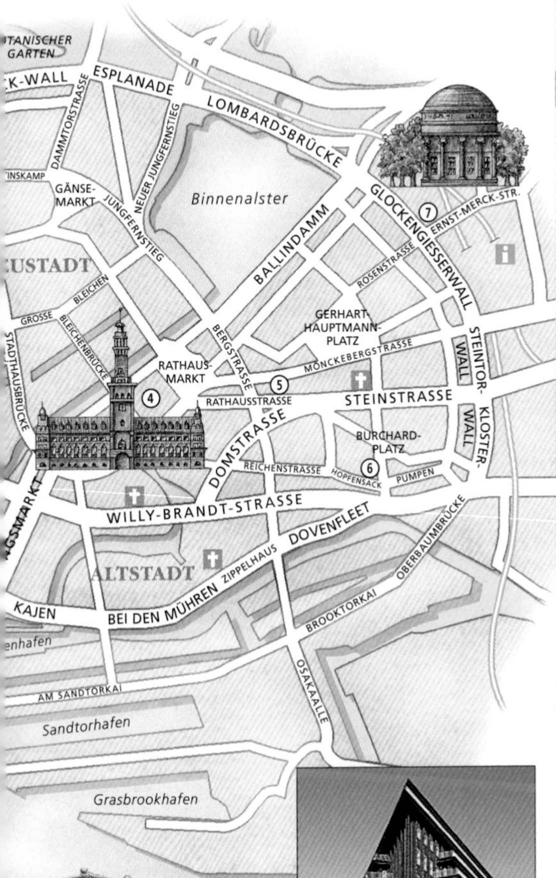

St Petri ⑤
Hamburg's oldest church, St Petri dates back to the 12th century. It was rebuilt twice – after the Great Fire of 1842 and again after World War II – and much of the architecture is now Neo-Gothic, though the church still boasts a 14th-century door knocker.

Chilehaus ⑥
Built in the early 1920s, this stark red-brick building was designed by the Expressionist architect Fritz Höger to resemble an ocean-going liner.

KEY SIGHTS

① Fischmarkt ★
② St Michaelis
③ Krameramtswohnungen
④ Rathaus
⑤ St Petri
⑥ Chilehaus ★
⑦ Kunsthalle ★
(see pp92–3)

FACT FILE

TOURIST INFORMATION

Central Station main entrance.
Tel *(040) 300 51 300.*
Mon–Sat to 9pm.

FESTIVALS

Hamburger Dom Heiligengeistfeld; late Mar, late Jul, early Nov.

MARKETS

Food Fischmarkt, Hafenstrasse; Sun am.

LOCAL SPECIALITIES

Produce
Herring, carp.
Dishes
Aalsuppe (a soup of plums, mixed vegetables and eels).
Labskaus (hash of potato, corned beef, onions, gherkins, herring, beetroot and fried egg).
Drinks
Holsten (lager).
Astra (lager).
Alsterwasser (lager and lemonade shandy).
Korn (a hot liqueur).
Lütt um lütt (beer fortified with schnapps).

EXCURSIONS

Oevelgönne 11 km (6.5 miles) W of Hamburg. Riverside suburb with old fishermen's houses. Museumshafen private museum has working antique boats. The Oevelgönner Seekiste (Sea Chest) displays maritime curiosities.
KZ-Gedenkstätte Neuengamme 18 km (11 miles) SE of Hamburg. WWII concentration camp that has been transformed into a museum and education centre.
Buxtehude 30 km (18 miles) W of Hamburg. Town on the River Este with a beautiful harbour in the Altstadt (Old Town) and some picturesque cafés and restaurants.

Hamburg: Kunsthalle ⑦

First opened to the public in 1869, the Hamburg Kunsthalle soon achieved worldwide recognition. The gallery's first director, Alfred Lichtwark, rediscovered some of the great Hamburg painters of the Medieval and Romantic periods, and nearly all of the 19th-century artist Philipp Otto Runge's works are now on display here. The gallery expanded rapidly, forcing it to change premises in 1919. In 1937, a Nazi crackdown on "degenerate art" resulted in the destruction of the modern department, but this has been rebuilt to become one of the best collections of contemporary art in Germany. To house it, a four-storey cubic extension with an underground link to the main gallery opened in 1997.

Sea of Ice (1823–4)
Caspar David Friedrich's dramatic work was probably inspired by an expedition to the North Pole by English explorer Edward William Parry.

★ Simeon and Hannah in the Temple (c. 1627)
Born in 1606 in Leiden, the Dutch artist Rembrandt Harmenszoon van Rijn made a name for himself from an early age. *Simeon and Hannah in the Temple*, painted when he was about 21 years old, shows the prophets Simeon and Hannah recognizing the infant Jesus as the Messiah, to the surprise of Mary and Joseph.

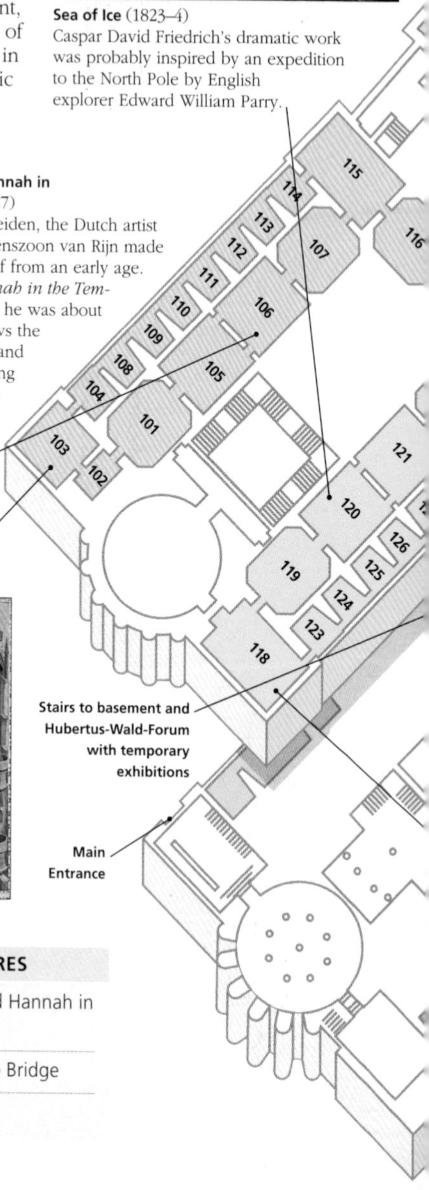

High Altar of St Peter's (1387)
Meister Bertram of Minden (c. 1330–1414) began working in Hamburg in 1373. He completed his major work, the *High Altar of St Peter's*, ten years later. Comprising 36 panels, the paintings depict the Creation, Old Testament stories and Christ's childhood.

STAR FEATURES

★ Simeon and Hannah in the Temple

★ Girls on the Bridge

★ Morning

GALLERY GUIDE

The focus of the museum is its collection of 19th-century German paintings, housed on the first floor of the main building, with the whole of Room 120 devoted to the works of Caspar David Friedrich. Also on this floor is the collection of Old Masters. The rest of the floor and the ground floor are taken up by early-20th-century paintings. The Gallery of Contemporary Art is housed in the extension.

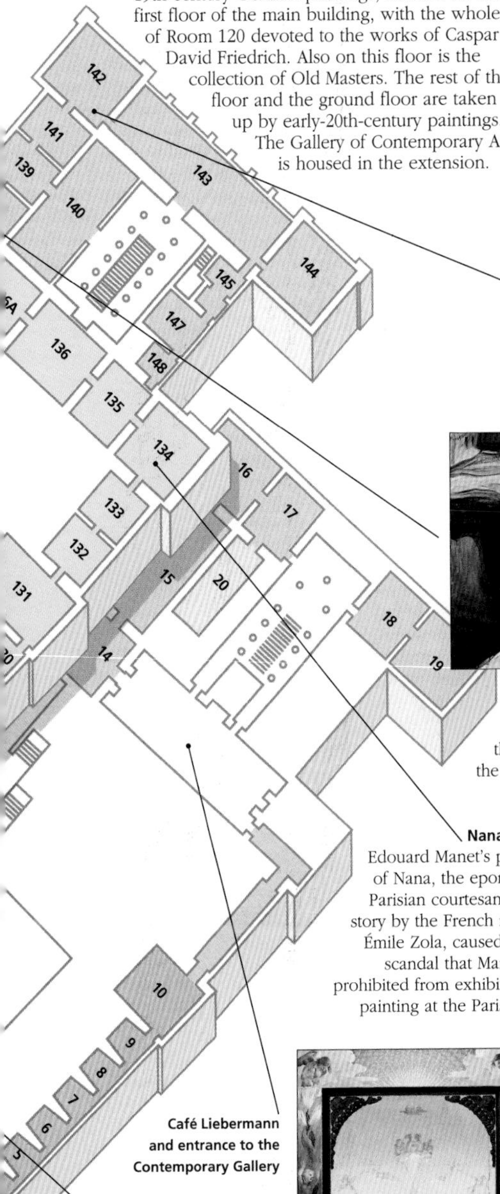

Self-portrait with Model (1910)
In 1926, 16 years after he first painted this picture, Ernst Ludwig Kirchner repainted certain sections to reinforce the distance between the model and the artist.

★ Girls on the Bridge (c. 1900)
This is one of six variations on a theme painted by Edvard Munch *(see p36)* in the early 1900s. He paid little attention to the landscape and focused on the relationships and tensions between the girls.

Nana (1877)
Edouard Manet's painting of Nana, the eponymous Parisian courtesan from a story by the French novelist Émile Zola, caused such a scandal that Manet was prohibited from exhibiting the painting at the Paris Salon.

Café Liebermann and entrance to the Contemporary Gallery

★ Morning (1808)
Philipp Otto Runge had intended his painting, *Morning*, to be one of a series of "Times of the Day", but he died, aged 33, before he could complete the others.

KEY

- Gallery of the Old Masters
- Gallery of the 19th Century
- Gallery of Classical Modernism
- Exhibition Gallery for drawings
- Art of Hamburg
- Non-exhibition space

Tulip fields in the Dutch countryside ▷

THE NETHERLANDS

Amsterdam

Founded as a fishing village in 1200, Amsterdam grew rich rapidly and its medieval wealth can be admired in the Gothic Oude Kerk. It became the region's chief trading city under the Habsburgs, but Dutch resistance to its Spanish ruler, Philip II, led to civil war. Amsterdam sided with Spain, but switched loyalties in 1578 to become the Protestant capital of the new Dutch Republic. The creation in 1602 of the Dutch East India Company (VOC) was the start of its 17th-century Golden Age, illustrated by the Koninklijk Paleis and paintings in the Rijksmuseum. The German occupation of World War II is symbolized by Anne Frank's house. Today, the city offers many high-quality museums, speciality beers and lively street life.

Koninklijk Paleis ②
Jacob van Campen's Neo-Classical Town Hall, built in the mid-17th century, became a royal palace in 1808 under Louis Napoleon. The finest room is the vast Burgerzaal, based on the assembly halls of Ancient Rome.

Jordaan ①
This area contains a mix of grand and workers' houses, the latter built in the 17th century to accommodate artisans whose industries were banned from the town centre. It is believed that Huguenot refugees called the area *jardin* (garden), later corrupted to Jordaan. This 18th-century staircase is in the Bartolotti house, one of the grander dwellings.

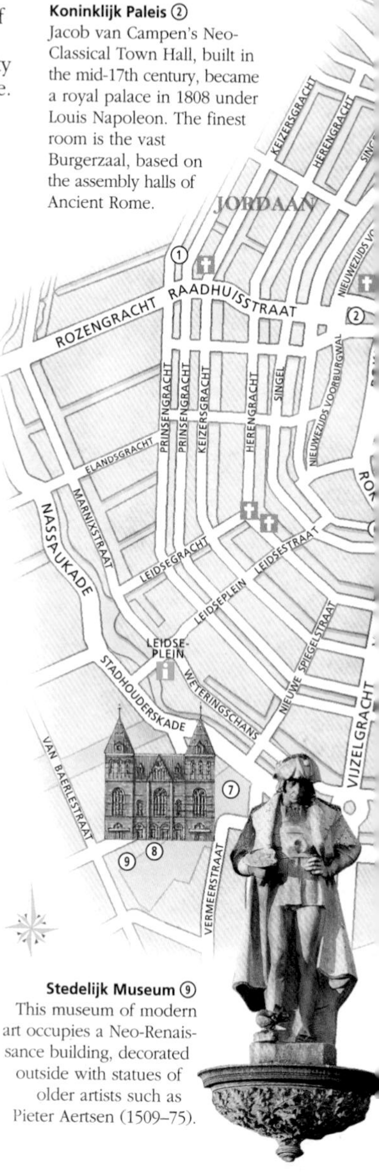

Stedelijk Museum ⑨
This museum of modern art occupies a Neo-Renaissance building, decorated outside with statues of older artists such as Pieter Aertsen (1509–75).

THE HISTORY OF THE CANALS

The Amstel was dammed in 1264 and the first canals (Oudezijds Voorburgwal and Grimburgwal) were cut in the 14th century on the city's eastern and southern borders. The Singel followed in the 15th century. Rapid population growth spurred city planner Hendrick Staets to quadruple Amsterdam's size in 1614. He built three new residential canals, Herengracht, Prinsengracht and Keizersgracht, together called the Grachtengordel (Canal Ring), protected by a fortified canal, Singelgracht. In the 1880s the oldest canals in the centre were filled in to provide easier access to the train station.

Houseboats on Brouwersgracht in the Jordaan

Oude Kerk ③
The oldest church in Amsterdam stands in the heart of the Oude Zijde (Old Side) – the eastern half of the city centre. The spire of the bell tower was added in 1566 and the 47-bell carillon in 1658.

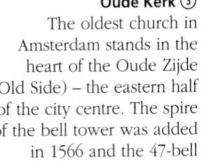

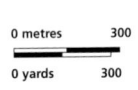

0 metres 300

0 yards 300

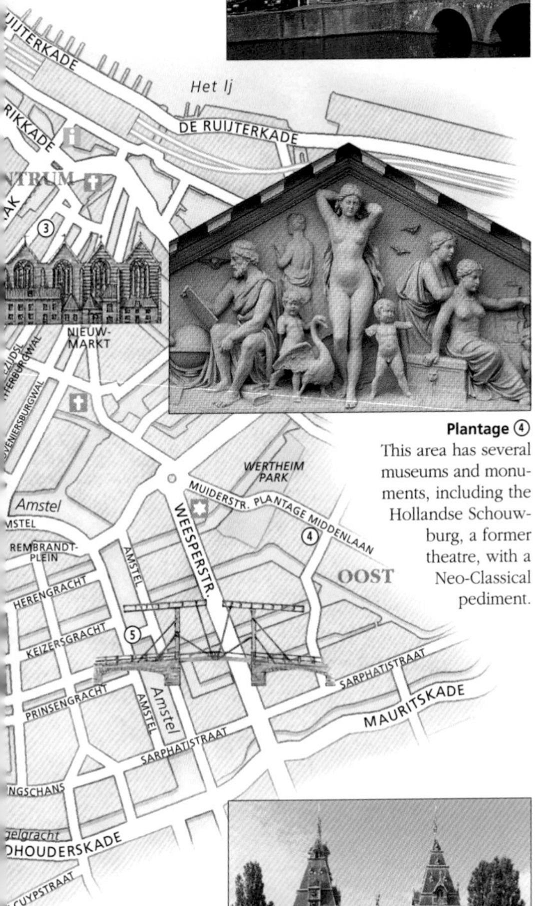

Plantage ④
This area has several museums and monuments, including the Hollandse Schouwburg, a former theatre, with a Neo-Classical pediment.

Rijksmuseum ⑦
Located in the Museum Quarter, a farming area until 1800, the nation's chief museum of Dutch art was built in Neo-Gothic style and houses a collection begun in the early 19th century.

KEY SIGHTS

① Jordaan ★ *(see pp98–9)*
② Koninklijk Paleis
③ Oude Kerk
④ Plantage
⑤ Magere Brug
⑥ Bloemenmarkt
⑦ Rijksmuseum ★ *(see pp102–3)*
⑧ Van Gogh Museum
⑨ Stedelijk Museum
⑩ Albert Cuypmarkt

FACT FILE

TOURIST INFORMATION

Leidseplein 1. ***Tel*** *900 400 40 40.*
daily to 5:30pm.

MARKETS

Food Albert Cuypmarkt, Albert Cuypstraat. Noordermarkt (Jordaan); Mon–Sat.
Flowers Bloemenmarkt, Singel; Mon–Sat.
Antiques Looier Kunst en Antiekcentrum, Elandsgracht 109; Sat–Thu pm.

SHOPPING

Diamonds In jewellery or unset.
Ceramics Genuine Delftware, miniature model canal houses.
Old maps & prints Amsterdam is historically famous for cartography.

LOCAL SPECIALITIES

Dishes
Erwtensoep (thick pea soup). *Bitterballen en frikadellen* (deep-fried meat balls with spicy rissoles). *Stamppot* (puréed potatoes, vegetables and smoked sausage). *Uitsmijter* (bread topped with cheese, ham and a fried egg).
Drinks
Jenever (a type of gin). *Columbus, Zatte, Amstel* (local beers).

EXCURSIONS

Zaanse Schans 13 km (8 miles) N of Amsterdam. Recreation of 17th-century life: shops, houses, artisans.
Delft 50 km (30 miles) SW of Amsterdam. Charming, 17th-century Old Town. Antique and modern hand-painted ceramics sold extensively. Tours of ceramics factories.

Amsterdam: Jordaan ①

West of the Grachtengordel *(see p96)*, the Jordaan still retains a network of narrow, characterful streets and delightful canals. Among the 17th-century workers' houses are dozens of quirky shops that are well worth a browse, selling anything from designer clothes to old sinks, and lively traditional cafés and bars that spill onto pavements. In contrast, a stroll along the Grachtengordel provides a glimpse into some of the city's grandest canal houses, including the Bartolotti House.

★ Anne Frank's House
For two years during the Nazi occupation, the Jewish Frank family and four others lived in a small upstairs apartment that was hidden behind a revolving bookcase.

Bloemgracht
This quiet, pretty canal was once a centre for makers of paint and dye.

★ Westerkerk
Rembrandt was buried in Hendrick de Keyser's huge, early 17th-century church, but the location of his grave is unknown. The Dutch monarchs, Queen Beatrix and Prince Claus, were married here in 1966.

Egelantiersgracht
Charming and tree-lined, this Jordaan canal is overlooked by an interesting mixture of old and new architecture. Pretty views are provided from its numerous bridges.

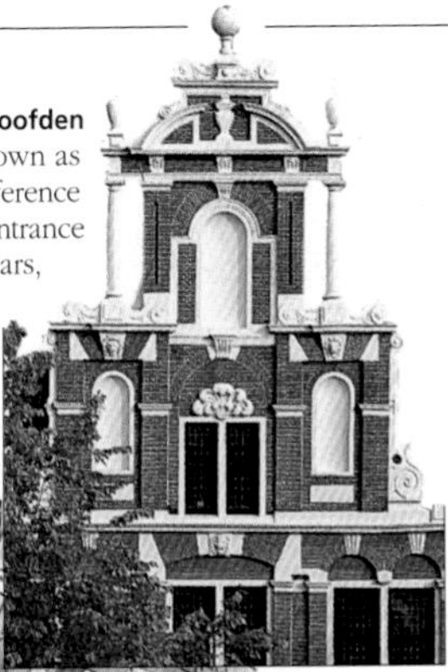

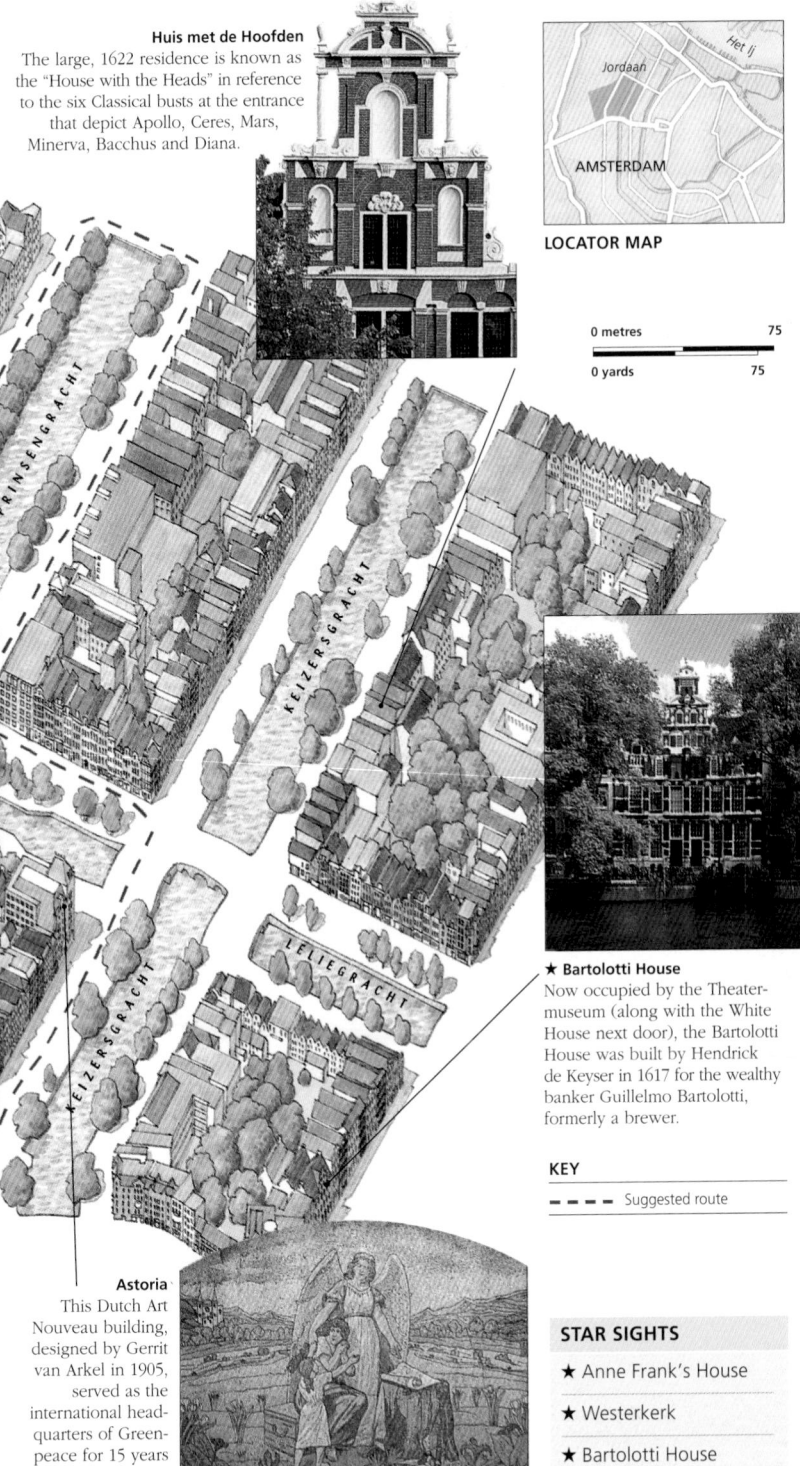

Huis met de Hoofden
The large, 1622 residence is known as the "House with the Heads" in reference to the six Classical busts at the entrance that depict Apollo, Ceres, Mars, Minerva, Bacchus and Diana.

LOCATOR MAP

0 metres 75
0 yards 75

★ Bartolotti House
Now occupied by the Theatermuseum (along with the White House next door), the Bartolotti House was built by Hendrick de Keyser in 1617 for the wealthy banker Guillelmo Bartolotti, formerly a brewer.

KEY

- - - - Suggested route

Astoria
This Dutch Art Nouveau building, designed by Gerrit van Arkel in 1905, served as the international headquarters of Greenpeace for 15 years from 1989.

STAR SIGHTS

★ Anne Frank's House

★ Westerkerk

★ Bartolotti House

Koninklijk Paleis, built to glorify the city and its government

Exploring Amsterdam

Leisurely walks or trips on a canal boat are the best way to take in the leafy atmosphere of the city's smaller canals, especially in the Jordaan district, and of the Plantage's parks. In the centre, the Oude Zijde and Nieuwe Zijde together form medieval Amsterdam. Around the Oude Kerk are the narrow lanes of the Red Light District, famous for prostitution since the 13th century. The main art museums are grouped conveniently close together.

Jordaan ①

See pp98–9.

Koninklijk Paleis ②

Still used occasionally by the Dutch royal family for official functions, this imposing building was designed as the town hall (Stadhuis). Work began on the vast, sandstone structure in 1648, the year in which the Treaty of Munster ended the 30 Year War with Spain and the Dutch Republic was recognized. The Neo-Classical design by Jacob van Campen (1595–1657) reflects the city's mood of confidence after the Dutch victory. The allegorical sculptures on the pediments are by Artus Quellien (1609–68) and the carillon by François Hemony, who also installed the carillon in the Oude Kerk.

The magnificence of the architecture is best appreciated in the Burgerzaal, which has a marble floor inlaid with maps of the eastern and western hemispheres, as well as the epic sculptures by Quellien. Most of the furniture dates from the early 19th century.

Oude Kerk ③

In the early 13th century, a wooden church stood here, but it was replaced in the 14th century by a Gothic single-aisled church. This grew into a basilica and became a gathering-place for traders and a refuge for the poor. Its paintings and statues were destroyed in the Alteration in 1578 (when Amsterdam changed sides in the civil war – *see p96*). However, the delicately-gilded ceiling and stained-glass windows survived. The oak-encased Great Organ by Christian Vater was added in 1724, since then little has changed. The tomb of Rembrandt's first wife, Saskia, is on the right of the organ.

Plantage ④

This area was once parkland, where 17th-century Amsterdammers spent their leisure time. From 1848, it became a graceful suburb with wide, tree-lined streets and painted, sandstone buildings. It is dominated by Artis, a complex that includes a planetarium, glass-houses, zoological and geological museums, a zoo with more than 5,000 species in a garden setting, an amphibarium and an excellent aquarium.

The area also has the superb national maritime museum (Nederlands Scheepvaart Museum), which has the world's largest collection of boats, including a replica of a Dutch East Indiaman. Hortus Botanicus is a fine botanical garden

Redeveloped former Dutch East India Company (VOC) warehouses along Entrepotdok in the Plantage district

Magere Brug over the River Amstel, a 20th-century replica of a 17th-century bridge

and Hollandse Schouwburg a former theatre that is now a memorial to the 104,000 Dutch Jewish victims of World War II. The 1725 De Gooyer Windmill is the most central of the city's six remaining windmills.

Magere Brug ⑤

Of Amsterdam's 1,400 or so bridges, Magere Brug (Skinny Bridge) is the best-known. The original drawbridge was built in about 1670. Tradition relates that it was named after two sisters named Mager, who lived on either side of the Amstel. However, it seems more likely that it acquired its name from its narrow *(mager)* design. The present bridge, built of African azobe wood, but in traditional double-leaf style, was installed in 1969. The mechanical drive was added in 1994.

Bloemenmarkt ⑥

This fragrant and beautiful-looking market is the last of Amsterdam's floating markets. In the past, nurserymen sailed up the Amstel and moored here to sell their goods directly from their boats. Today, the stalls of cut flowers and bedding plants are still floating, but are permanently moored.

Rijksmuseum ⑦

See pp102–3.

Van Gogh Museum ⑧

This large, stark museum, which opened in 1973, is based on a design by Gerrit Rietveld (1888–1964). He belonged to De Stijl, the Dutch artistic movement founded in 1917 that produced startlingly simple designs and whose works became icons of 20th-century Abstract art. A wing designed by Kisho Kurokawa opened in 1999.

The core of the Van Gogh collection comprises 200 paintings and 500 drawings amassed by Vincent's art-dealer brother, Theo, as well as 850 letters by Van Gogh to Theo, and selected works by his friends and contemporaries. Van Gogh began painting in 1880 and worked in the Netherlands for five years before moving to Paris, then Provence *(see p155)*. Paintings from these periods are on the first floor, while drawings and temporary exhibitions fill the museum's other areas.

Smoked fish at Albert Cuypmarkt

Stedelijk Museum ⑨

The City Museum was built to house a personal collection bequeathed to Amsterdam in 1855 by art connoisseur Sophia de Bruyn. In 1938, it became the national museum of modern art. While there are paintings by artists such as Picasso, Monet, Matisse, Mondrian and Cézanne, the emphasis is on post-1945 works. Exhibitions change constantly, with recent acquisitions reflecting the latest developments, not only in painting and sculpture, but also in printing, drawing, photography and video. The collection by artists of the Cobra movement, the group of Dutch and Scandinavian Expressionist artists formed in 1948, is excellent. The original building was completely restored and has been extended with a spectacular modern building. (**www**.stedelijk.nl).

Albert Cuypmarkt ⑩

Amsterdam's biggest street market, which runs along Albert Cuypstraat, began trading in 1904. The wide street, once a canal, is named after the Dutch landscape painter Albert Cuyp (1620–91). It is located in the Pijp district, originally built for workers.

Described by stall-holders as "the best-known market in Europe", it attracts some 20,000 visitors on weekdays and often twice as many on Saturdays. The goods on sale at the 325 stalls range from a variety of foodstuffs to cut flowers and clothes, and prices are among the lowest in Amsterdam.

***The Potato Eaters* (1885), Van Gogh's portrayal of Dutch peasant life**

Amsterdam: Rijksmuseum ⑦

The Rijksmuseum owns the world's best collection of Dutch art, assembled from the early years of the 19th century and put on show when the museum opened in 1885. If time is short, it is best to concentrate on the paintings of the Dutch Golden Age (17th century) by such masters as Rembrandt, Vermeer and Frans Hals. Other works span the medieval era to the 19th century and there is an excellent Asiatic section.

Winter Landscape with Skaters (1618)
Dutch painter Hendrick Avercamp specialized in intricate, icy winter scenes.

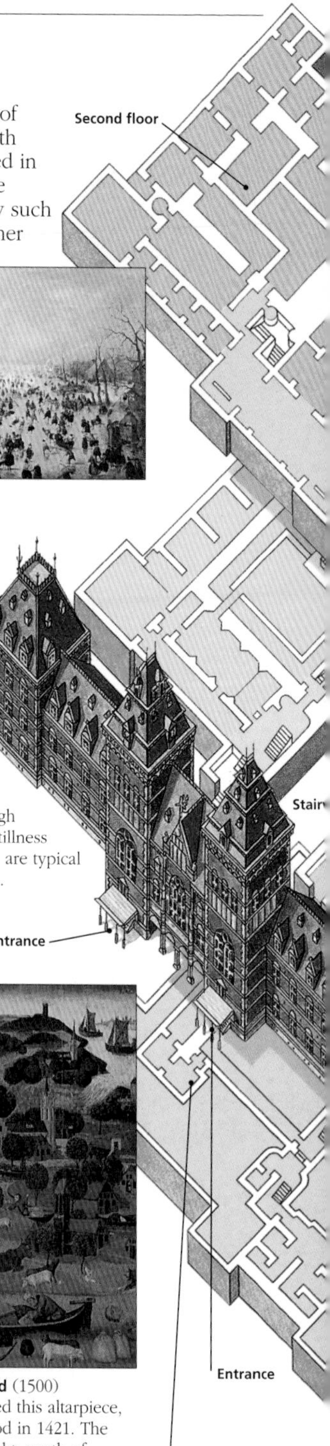

Neo-Gothic Façade
Built by P H J Cuypers (1827–1921), the red-brick museum has elaborate decoration, including coloured tiles.

★ The Kitchen Maid (1658)
The light falling through the window and the stillness of this domestic scene are typical of Jan Vermeer's work.

KEY TO FLOORPLAN

- Dutch history
- Dutch painting
- European painting
- Sculpture and decorative art
- Prints and drawings
- Asiatic art
- Temporary exhibitions
- Non-exhibition space

★ St Elizabeth's Day Flood (1500)
An unknown artist painted this altarpiece, showing a disastrous flood in 1421. The dykes protecting Dordrecht, south of Amsterdam, were breached and 22 villages were swept away by the flood water.

STAR FEATURES

★ St Elizabeth's Day Flood

★ The Night Watch by Rembrandt

★ The Kitchen Maid by Vermeer

★ The Night Watch (1642)
Long regarded as Rembrandt's most famous work and the showpiece of Dutch 17th-century art, this vast, dramatic canvas was commissioned as a group portrait of an Amsterdam militia company. The title was given to it in the 18th century, when dirty varnish had darkened the picture so much that it was wrongly assumed to be a night scene. The correct title is *The Militia Company of Captain Frans Banning Cocq and Lieutenant Willem von Ruytenburch*.

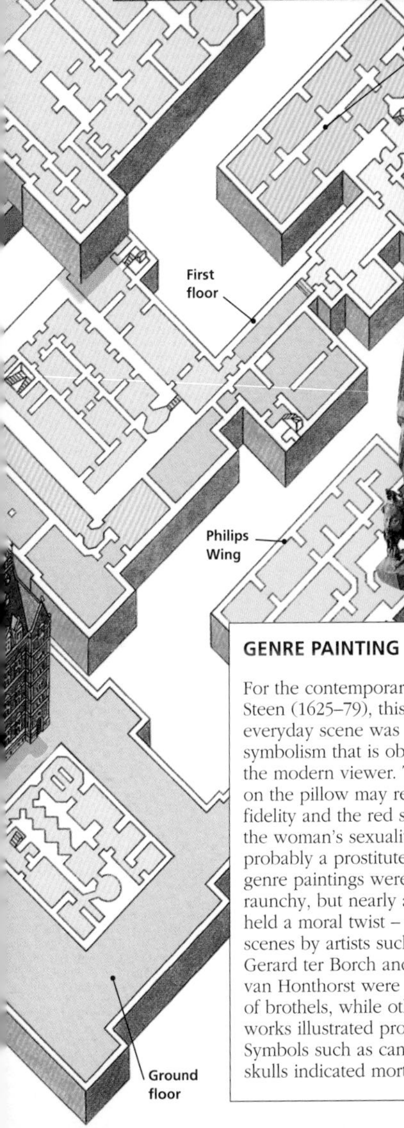

GALLERY GUIDE

There are entrances on either side of the driveway under the building – the left leads into the Dutch history section, the right to prints and drawings, sculpture and applied art. On the first floor there is a huge antechamber, with a shop and information desk. The entrance on the left here begins with 16th- to 19th-century painting. The museum offers a unique opportunity to view the masterpieces of the Golden Age. The highlights of the museum are on show in the refurbished Philips Wing.

St Barbara (c.1465)
This sculpture by the Master of Koudewater shows the saint stamping on her father, who had tried to stop her converting to Christianity.

GENRE PAINTING

For the contemporaries of Jan Steen (1625–79), this cosy everyday scene was full of symbolism that is obscure to the modern viewer. The dog on the pillow may represent fidelity and the red stockings the woman's sexuality; she is probably a prostitute. Such genre paintings were often raunchy, but nearly always held a moral twist – domestic scenes by artists such as Gerard ter Borch and Gerrit van Honthorst were symbolic of brothels, while other works illustrated proverbs. Symbols such as candles or skulls indicated mortality.

Jan Steen's *Woman at her Toilet*, painted in about 1660

Seven Sisters cliffs, England's East Sussex coast ▷

GREAT BRITAIN

Harwich

Façade detail of the Electric Palace Cinema

Since the Middle Ages, Harwich has been a bustling maritime centre and the town has featured prominently in Britain's naval history. Harwich ships and seamen played a major part in the defeat of the Spanish Armada in 1588, and, during the two world wars, Harwich served as an important naval base. The old quarter of this busy town still holds many reminders of its history, and buildings such as the Electric Palace Cinema – dating from 1911 and one of the oldest purpose-built cinemas in Britain – the Treadwheel Crane and the High and Low Lighthouses have been carefully preserved.

Treadwheel Crane
Situated on Harwich Green since 1932, this crane initially stood in the Naval yard. It dates back to 1667 and was used to lift naval goods until 1927. The crane was operated by men walking inside two parallel wheels – each 5 m (16 ft) in diameter and 1.5 m (4 ft) wide – spaced 1.5 m (4 ft) apart on a common axle. This was dangerous work as the crane had no braking system.

Low Lighthouse
Built in 1818, the High and Low Lighthouses were used to guide ships into port, captains lining one light above the other to get the right course. Today, the Low Lighthouse is a maritime museum.

Willy Lott's Cottage
This scene in Flatford has changed little since John Constable painted his most famous work, *The Haywain,* in 1821. At the time, the tenant of the cottage was Willy Lott, who worked at Flatford Mill on the other side of the millpond. Constable (1776–1837) was born in nearby East Bergholt, and the surrounding countryside, in particular the Stour River valley, provided the subject matter for a number of his paintings.

KEY SIGHTS

Electric Palace Cinema
High Lighthouse
Low Lighthouse ★
Treadwheel Crane

FACT FILE

TOURIST INFORMATION
Iconfield Park. ***Tel** (01255) 50 6139.* ◻ *Mon–Fri to 5pm, Sat & Sun to 4pm (winter: closed Sun).*

SHOPPING
Antiques Harwich Antique Centre, 19 Kings Quay Street.

LOCAL SPECIALITIES
Dishes
Whitebait (herring and sprat fry dipped in flour and fried).
Angels on horseback (oysters wrapped in bacon).
Oysters (eaten raw in their shells with lemon juice and Tabasco).

EXCURSIONS
Willy Lott's Cottage 25 km (17 miles) W of Harwich. This is the cottage featured in John Constable's *The Haywain*. Various art courses are now held in the mill.
Ipswich 40 km (25 miles) NW of Harwich. Suffolk's county town has 15th-century St Margaret's church and Christchurch Mansion, a Tudor house that boasts the best collection of Constable's paintings outside London.
Colchester 40 km (25 miles) W of Harwich. Britain's oldest recorded town and first Roman settlement, still featuring Roman walls and town gate. The Dutch Quarter still has tall 16th-century houses.

Southampton

For centuries Southampton has been a flourishing port. The *Mayflower* sailed from here to America in 1620, as did the *Titanic* at the start of its tragic voyage in 1912. The Maritime Museum has displays on both these ships, and others on the huge luxury liners that sailed from the port in the first half of the 20th century. At the head of the High Street stands the old city gate, Bargate, and walks can be taken around the city walls. Near the Westgate, the Tudor House Museum contains exhibits on Victorian and Edwardian life.

Bargate
Southampton's old city gate is the most elaborate medieval gate in England. Over the centuries Bargate has served as a tollgate, prison, guildhall and museum. It still has its 13th-century drum towers and is decorated with intricate, 17th-century armorial carvings.

New Forest
William I (the Conqueror)'s "new" forest is, despite the name, one of the few primeval oak woods in England, and was a popular hunting ground for Norman kings. Today this stretch of woodland is enjoyed by up to seven million visitors a year, who share it with the shaggy New Forest ponies, which are unique to the area, and over 1,500 fallow deer.

KEY SIGHTS

Bargate ★
Maritime Museum
Tudor House Museum

FACT FILE

TOURIST INFORMATION
9 Civic Centre Road. ***Tel** (02380) 833 333.* ▢ *Mon–Sat to 5:30pm.*

MARKETS
General Kingsland; Tue, Thu–Sat.

LOCAL SPECIALITIES
Dishes
Saxe-Coburg soup (creamy Brussels sprout soup with ham).

EXCURSIONS
Beaulieu 9 km (6 miles) SW of Southampton. Palace House, once the gatehouse of Beaulieu Abbey, now contains the National Motor Museum. There is an exhibition of monastic life in the abbey ruins.
New Forest 15 km (9 miles) SW of Southampton. Largest area of unenclosed land in southern England, covering 375 sq km (145 sq miles). It is home to deer and New Forest ponies.
Winchester 15 km (9 miles) N of Southampton. Small city, once the capital of the ancient kingdom of Wessex. The Norman cathedral contains a 12th-century black marble font. The Great Hall is all that remains of William I's castle.
Portsmouth 21 km (13 miles) SE of Southampton. Royal Naval Museum, hull of Henry VIII's favourite ship *Mary Rose* and Nelson's HMS *Victory*. The Spinnaker Tower, at 170 m (560 ft) tall, has stunning views of the city.

Winchester Cathedral
Building began on the cathedral in 1079. Much of the Norman architecture of this former Benedictine monastery remains despite continual modifications. The author Jane Austen's grave is situated in the cathedral's nave, at the end of which stand the oldest choir stalls in England, dating from around 1308. The Lady Chapel, which dates back to around 1500, was rebuilt by Elizabeth of York. The cathedral's library contains over 2,000 books, including the Winchester Bible, an exquisite work of 12th-century illumination.

London (Dover)

The largest city in Europe, London is home to about seven million people and covers 1,600 sq km (625 sq miles). It w as first founded by the Romans in the 1st century AD as an administrative centre and a trading port with Continental Europe. It has been the principal residence of British monarchs for 1,000 years, as well as being the centre of business and government. Although London is rich in historic buildings from all periods and has a diverse collection of museums, galleries and churches, it is an exciting contemporary city, packed with a vast array of theatres and shops.

South Bank ④
The site of London's main arts centre, the South Bank is also home to the London Eye, a vast wheel that offers spectacular views across London.

British Museum ⑥
Founded in 1753, the museum is extremely popular and attracts some five million visitors a year. The present building, constructed in the mid-19th century, contains treasures spanning thousands of years of world history. Items from prehistoric times, art from Ancient civilizations and Medieval, Renaissance and Modern artifacts are displayed. The architectural highlight is the modern glass-covered Great Court with the world-famous Reading Room at its centre.

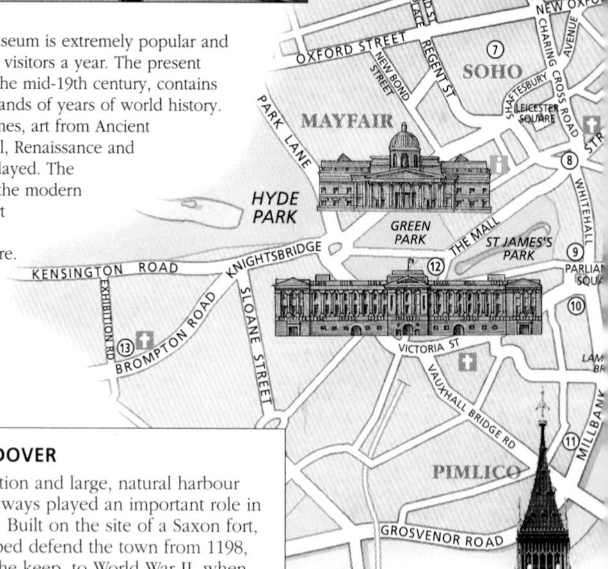

THE HISTORY OF DOVER

Dover's strategic position and large, natural harbour mean the town has always played an important role in the nation's defences. Built on the site of a Saxon fort, Dover Castle has helped defend the town from 1198, when Henry II built the keep, to World War II, when it was a command post for the Dunkirk evacuation. Today, Dover is the main port for cross-channel travel.

Dover Castle, defender of Britain for nearly 800 years

Whitehall and Westminster ⑨
This is the historical seat of both church and government, where the Houses of Parliament and Westminster Abbey face each other. Towering over them is the huge clock tower, commonly known as Big Ben.

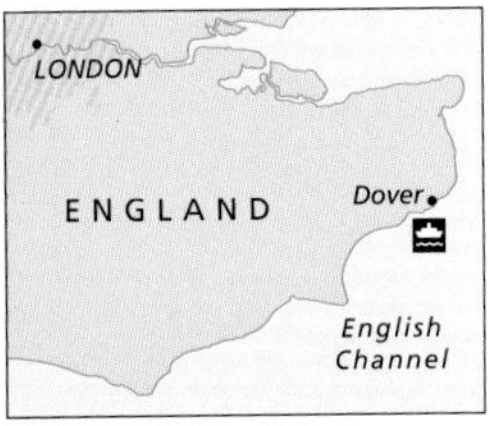

DISTANCE FROM PORT

128 km (80 miles) from city centre.

Covent Garden ⑤
Once famous as a vegetable market, Covent Garden's Piazza is now a busy shopping arcade, with cafés and street performers.

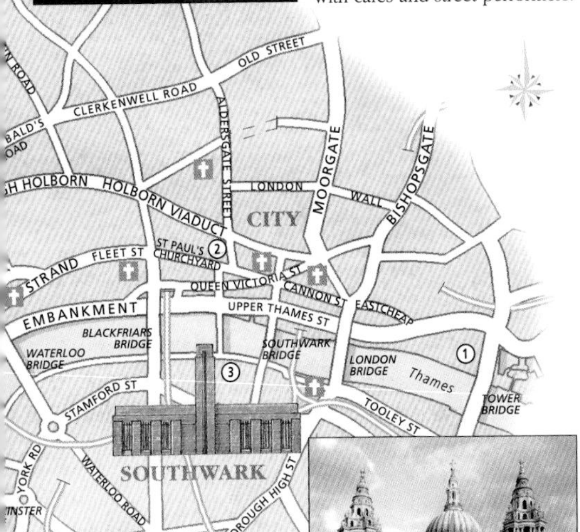

St Paul's Cathedral ②
Built after the fire of 1666, St Paul's still dominates the City skyline. The two side towers were added in 1707.

Tower of London ①
When it was finished, around 1097, the Tower of London's White Tower was the tallest building in London. A prison for much of its existence, the Tower of London is a popular attraction and houses the Crown Jewels.

KEY SIGHTS

① Tower of London ★ *(see pp112–13)*
② St Paul's Cathedral ★
③ Bankside
④ South Bank
⑤ Covent Garden
⑥ British Museum ★
⑦ Soho
⑧ National Gallery and Trafalgar Square ★
⑨ Whitehall and Westminster ★ *(see pp114–15)*
⑩ Westminster Abbey *(see pp116–17)* ★
⑪ Tate Britain
⑫ Buckingham Palace
⑬ Victoria and Albert Museum

FACT FILE

TOURIST INFORMATION

1 Regent St, SW1. ***Tel*** *(870) 1566 366.* *Mon–Fri to 6:30pm, Sat & Sun to 4pm (Jun–Oct: Sat to 5pm).*

MARKETS

Food Leadenhall Market, EC3; Mon–Fri.
Antiques Portobello Rd, W10; Sat.

SHOPPING

Designer clothes Many of the world's top designers have shops on and around Bond St, W1.
Books Chain stores rub shoulders with antiquarian bookshops on Charing Cross Rd, WC2.

LOCAL SPECIALITIES

Dishes
Fish 'n' chips (Fish dipped in batter and fried, traditionally served with a portion of chips).
Mixed grill (lamb chops, kidneys, sausages, steaks and gammon).
Drinks
London Dry Gin and tonic.

EXCURSIONS

Greenwich 10 km (6 miles) SE of central London. Home of *Cutty Sark*, Observatory and markets.
Hampton Court 20 km (12 miles) SW of central London. Home of Henry VIII, with gardens and maze.

Bankside's riverside walkway, with views over Tower Bridge

Exploring London

Though more spread out than in most European capitals, many of London's attractions are within walking distance of each other. The City itself covers little more than 2.5 sq km (1 sq mile) and the varied attractions of Bankside and the South Bank are on the opposite bank of the Thames. Just to the west, Westminster is the nation's political hub and site of the famous Abbey. To the north and west respectively, the upmarket residential areas of Bloomsbury and Kensington contain most of London's major museums.

Tower of London ①

See pp112–13.

St Paul's Cathedral ②

When the medieval cathedral of St Paul's was destroyed in the Great Fire of London (1666), Christopher Wren was asked to rebuild it. His original grand ideas were rejected by the authorities and today's watered-down plan was not finally agreed upon until 1675.

The interior of St Paul's is cool, beautifully ordered and extremely spacious. At its centre is the huge main dome, whose unusual acoustics cause whispers from the gallery to echo around it.

Wren was aided by some of the finest craftsmen of his day, and the carvings of Grinling Gibbons can be seen on the choir stalls, while the wrought ironwork of Jean Tijou can be found on the screens in the choir aisles.

Bankside ③

In the 1500s, Bankside's taverns, theatres and brothels attracted those looking for pleasures banned in the City. Then, in the 18th and 19th centuries, industrialization brought docks, factories and warehouses to the area. Today the docks are closed and Bankside has been redeveloped. A reconstruction of Shakespeare's Globe now stands a few hundred metres from the site of the original theatre, while the former Bankside Power Station has been transformed into the Tate Modern art gallery, which houses one of the world's premier collections of 20th-century art. Southwark Cathedral, which despite major alterations, still has medieval elements, is one of the few remnants of the area's historic past.

A walkway leading to the South Bank offers lovely views across the river, and links London's two most recent Thames crossings, Tower Bridge, built in 1894, and the "blade of light" Millennium footbridge, built in 2000.

South Bank ④

In 1951, this area, reduced to a wasteland during World War II, was chosen to host the Festival of Britain. The festival's only permanent building, the Royal Festival Hall, became the focal point of the South Bank arts centre, which includes the Royal National Theatre, the Hayward Gallery and the National Film Theatre. A little way upstream stands County Hall, home to the London Aquarium and the Saatchi Gallery. In front, the enormous wheel of the British Airways London Eye offers visitors a bird's eye view of the city.

Covent Garden ⑤

In the 1630s, Inigo Jones laid out the Piazza – London's first square – on the site of a former convent garden, and for a time it was one of the most fashionable residential areas of London. A market was established here in the mid-17th century and the first of a succession of theatres was built in 1732. Today Covent Garden is one of the city's liveliest districts, with stylish shops, open-air cafés and markets. The newly refurbished Royal Opera House nearby is one of the world's leading opera venues.

British Museum ⑥

Founded in the mid-18th century, the British Museum is the oldest public museum in the world. Its rich collection

The Millennium footbridge spanning the River Thames in front of the Tate Modern, Bankside

The stately façade of the National Gallery, viewed from the eastern side of Trafalgar Square

of artifacts was started by the physician Sir Hans Sloane (1660–1753). Over the years, Sloane's collection has been added to by purchases and gifts and now contains treasures from all over the world. Among these are the controversial Elgin Marbles from the Acropolis in Athens *(see pp312–15)*, the Sutton Hoo treasure hoard of an Anglo-Saxon king and the Rosetta Stone, the celebrated key to the Egyptian hieroglyphs.

Anglo-Saxon helmet, British Museum

Soho ⑦

Soho has been renowned for pleasures of the table, flesh and intellect since the area was first developed in the late 1800s. For its first hundred years, the area was one of London's most fashionable, and Soho residents of the time have gone down in history for their extravagant parties.

Today, the area is London's most famous gay district, and its many pubs, clubs and cafés also play host to the trendy media set. The myriad restaurants reflect the diversity of nationalities that have lived here over the centuries.

National Gallery and Trafalgar Square ⑧

London's main venue for rallies, Trafalgar Square was conceived by John Nash and constructed mainly during the 1830s. On the south side of the square, a 50-m (165-ft) high column, dating from 1842, commemorates Admiral Lord Nelson, Britain's most famous sea lord. The northern side is taken up by the façade of the National Gallery, built between 1834 and 1838 by William Wilkins. The gallery is London's principal art museum, with more than 2,300 paintings ranging from the Renaissance to the Impressionist period.

Whitehall and Westminster ⑨

See pp114–15.

Westminster Abbey ⑩

See pp116–17.

Tate Britain ⑪

Officially the national gallery of British art, the founding gallery of a series of Tates established around the country holds the largest collection of British art in the world. The gallery was founded in 1897 as a national gallery of British art by the sugar magnate Sir Henry Tate, who presented it with his own collection of mostly Victorian paintings. Next to it is the Clore Gallery, which houses the magnificent Turner Bequest featuring the works of J M W Turner, left to the nation by the artist himself.

Buckingham Palace ⑫

The headquarters of the British monarchy doubles as an office and a home, and is also used for ceremonial state occasions. About 300 people work here, including officers of the Royal Household. It is open to the public daily from July to September.

John Nash converted the original Buckingham House into a palace for George IV, who reigned from 1820 to 1830, but the first monarch to live at the palace was Queen Victoria. The east façade, the most famous view that faces the Mall, was added in 1913.

Victoria and Albert Museum ⑬

Founded in 1852 as a Museum of Manufactures, the V&A was renamed by Queen Victoria in memory of her late husband, Prince Albert. The 11 km (7 miles) of galleries contain one of the world's widest collections of fine and applied arts. Exhibits range from early Christian devotional objects to cutting-edge furniture design, and include sculptures, watercolours, jewellery, dresses, prints and musical instruments.

Scarlet Sunset (1833) by J M W Turner, part of Tate Britain's Turner Bequest

London: Tower of London ①

Soon after he became king in 1066, William the Conqueror constructed a fortress to guard the approach to London from the Thames Estuary. The White Tower, at the centre of the complex, was completed in 1097 and over the centuries other buildings and a perimeter wall were added. The Tower has served as a royal residence, armoury, treasury and most famously as a prison for enemies of the crown. Many were tortured and some died here, among them the "Princes in the Tower", the sons and heirs of Edward IV. Today the Tower is one of London's most popular sights. Its most celebrated residents are the "Beefeaters" and a colony of seven ravens, whose presence is protected by a legend that states that the kingdom will fall if ever they desert the Tower.

Beauchamp Tower
Many high-ranking prisoners were held here, often with their own retinues of servants. The tower was built by Edward I around 1281.

"Beefeaters"
Thirty-seven Yeoman Warders guard the Tower and live here. Their uniforms hark back to Tudor times.

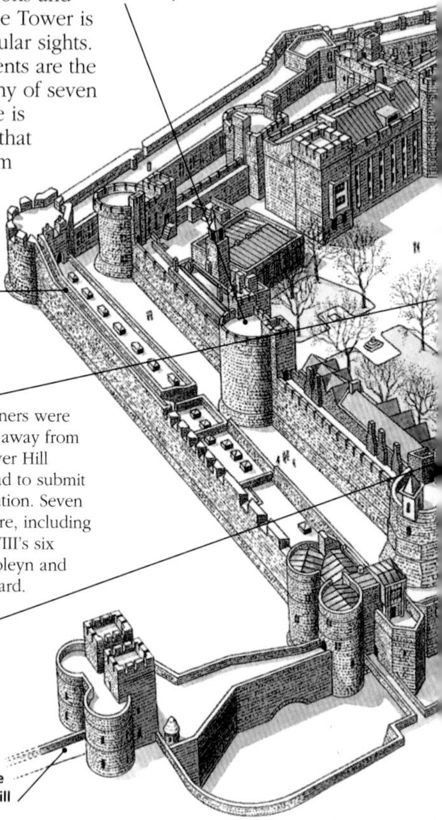

Outer wall
The wall was built in the 13th century.

Tower Green
Favoured prisoners were executed here, away from crowds on Tower Hill where many had to submit to public execution. Seven people died here, including two of Henry VIII's six wives, Anne Boleyn and Catherine Howard.

Main entrance from Tower Hill

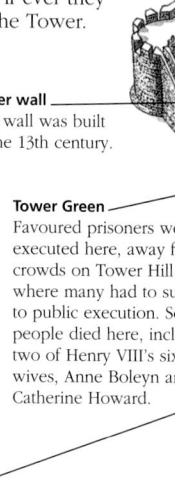

Queen's House
This Tudor building is the sovereign's official residence at the Tower.

THE CROWN JEWELS

The world's best-known collection of precious objects – now displayed in a splendid exhibition room – includes the priceless regalia of crowns, sceptres, orbs and swords used by the British Monarch at coronations and other state occasions. Most date from 1661, when Charles II commissioned replacements for regalia destroyed by Parliament after the execution of Charles I. Only a few older pieces survive. Most notable of these is the sapphire from what was reputed to be Edward the Confessor's ring, now incorporated into the Imperial State Crown. The crown was made for Queen Victoria in 1837 and has been used at every coronation since.

The Sovereign's Ring (1831)

The Sovereign's Orb (1661), a hollow gold sphere encrusted with jewels

★ Jewel House
Among the magnificent Crown Jewels is the Sceptre with the Cross (1660), which now contains the world's biggest diamond.

★ White Tower
The 27-m (90-ft) high White Tower gained its name when it was whitewashed in 1240, during the reign of Henry III.

STAR SIGHTS

- ★ Jewel House
- ★ White Tower
- ★ Chapel of St John

New Armouries
These were completed in 1664.

★ Chapel of St John
This beautiful Romanesque chapel, dating back to William the Conqueror, is a fine example of early Norman architecture.

Traitors' Gate
This riverside entrance to the Tower was used for prisoners brought by boat from trial in Westminster Hall – many of them on their way to die.

Bloody Tower
The young Edward V and his brother, depicted here by John Everett Millais (1829–96), were placed in the Bloody Tower by their uncle, Richard of Gloucester, after their father, Edward IV, died in 1483. The boys mysteriously disappeared, allowing Richard to be crowned Richard III later that year. In 1674, the skeletons of two children were found nearby.

London: Whitehall and Westminster ⑨

Celebrated for its rich diversity of architecture and its world-famous skyline, Whitehall and Westminster is where the visitor will discover the pomp and ceremony of London. It is here, at the historic seat of the government and the established church, that London matches the broad, stately avenues of Paris, Rome and Madrid. On weekdays, the tourists who flock to visit some of London's most famous sights are outnumbered by members of the civil service – the cogs of the governmental machine – whose offices dominate this most traditional of London's districts.

Earl Haig
The British World War I chief was sculpted by Alfred Hardiman in 1936.

Central Hall
This florid example of the Beaux Arts style was built in 1911 as a Methodist meeting hall. In 1946 the first General Assembly of the United Nations was held here.

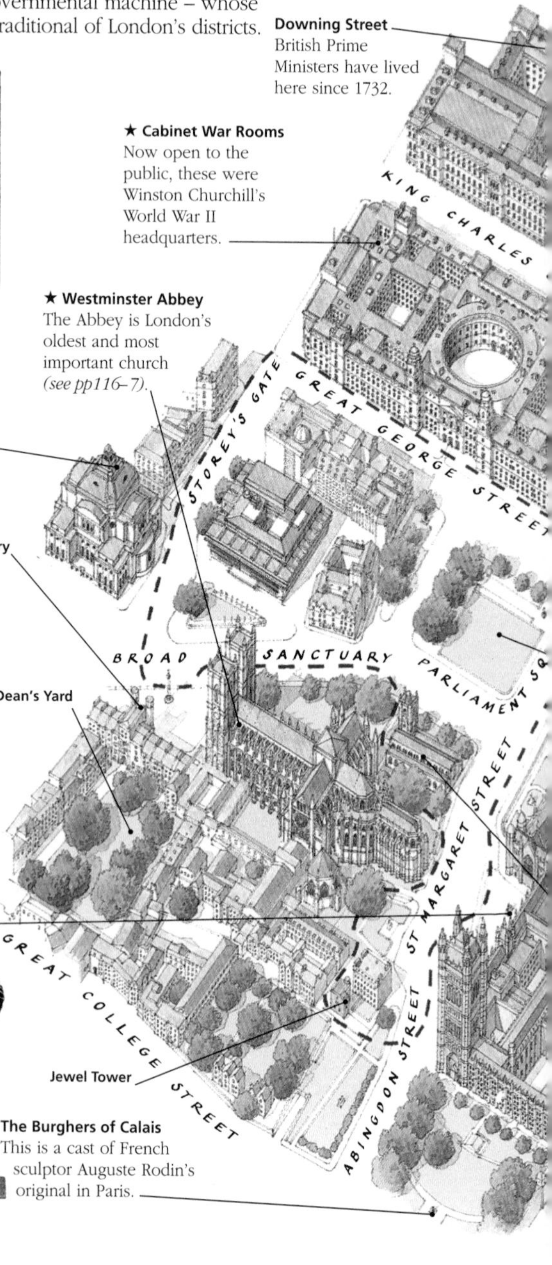

Downing Street
British Prime Ministers have lived here since 1732.

★ Cabinet War Rooms
Now open to the public, these were Winston Churchill's World War II headquarters.

★ Westminster Abbey
The Abbey is London's oldest and most important church *(see pp116–7)*.

The Sanctuary

Dean's Yard

Richard I's Statue
Carlo Marochetti's 1860 work depicts the 12th-century *Coeur de Lion*.

Jewel Tower

The Burghers of Calais
This is a cast of French sculptor Auguste Rodin's original in Paris.

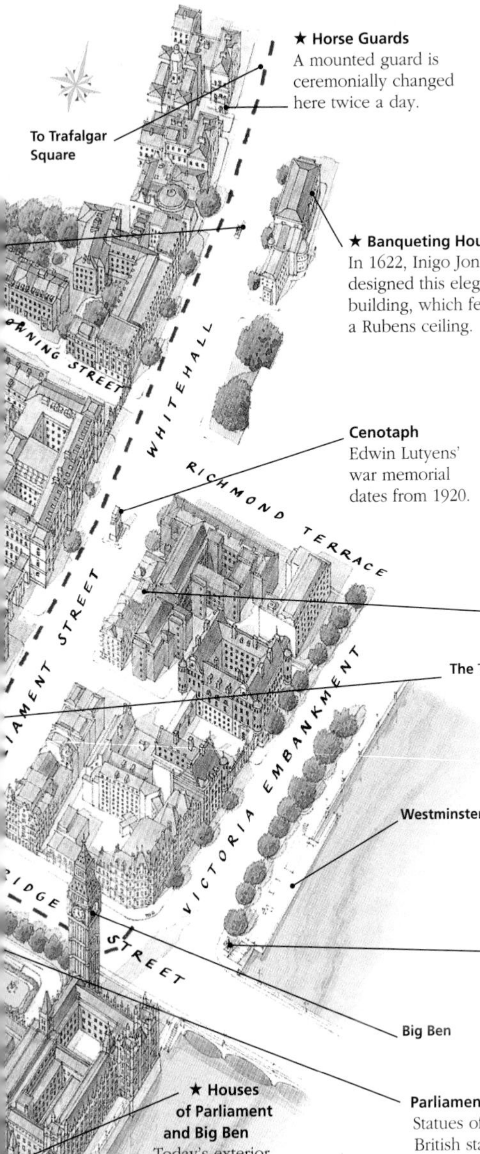

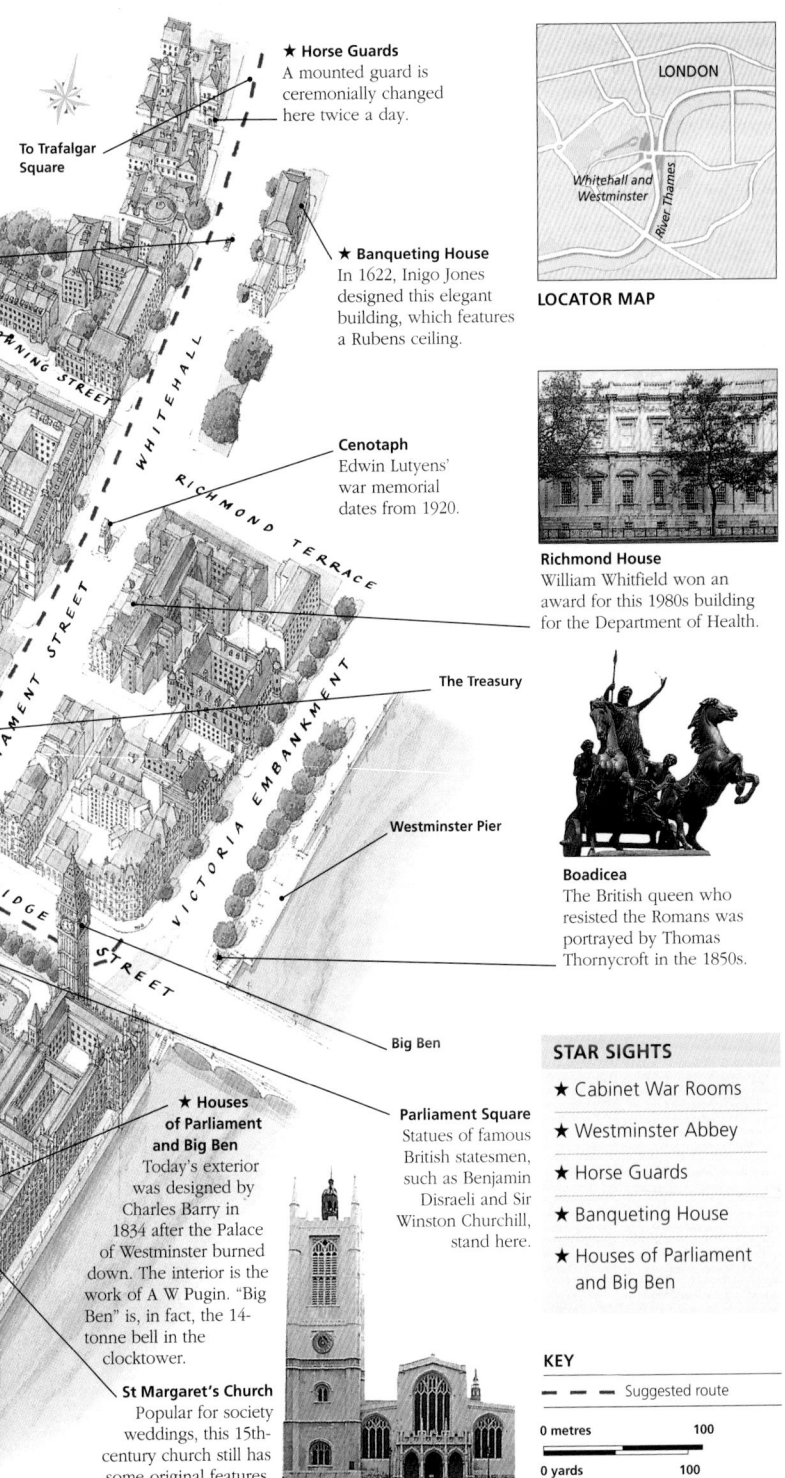

★ Horse Guards
A mounted guard is ceremonially changed here twice a day.

★ Banqueting House
In 1622, Inigo Jones designed this elegant building, which features a Rubens ceiling.

Cenotaph
Edwin Lutyens' war memorial dates from 1920.

The Treasury

Westminster Pier

Big Ben

★ Houses of Parliament and Big Ben
Today's exterior was designed by Charles Barry in 1834 after the Palace of Westminster burned down. The interior is the work of A W Pugin. "Big Ben" is, in fact, the 14-tonne bell in the clocktower.

Parliament Square
Statues of famous British statesmen, such as Benjamin Disraeli and Sir Winston Churchill, stand here.

St Margaret's Church
Popular for society weddings, this 15th-century church still has some original features.

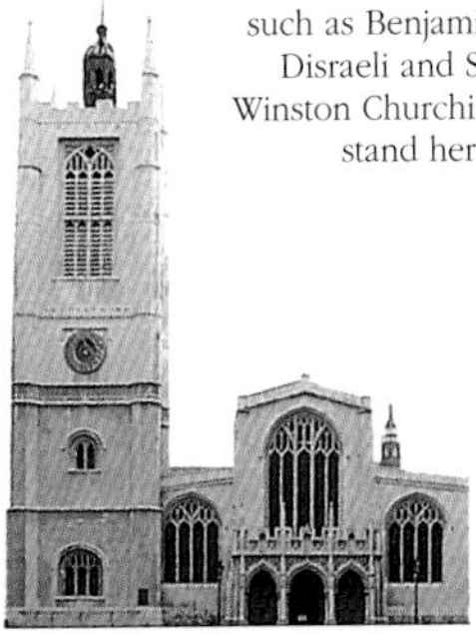

LOCATOR MAP

Richmond House
William Whitfield won an award for this 1980s building for the Department of Health.

Boadicea
The British queen who resisted the Romans was portrayed by Thomas Thornycroft in the 1850s.

STAR SIGHTS

- ★ Cabinet War Rooms
- ★ Westminster Abbey
- ★ Horse Guards
- ★ Banqueting House
- ★ Houses of Parliament and Big Ben

KEY

— — — Suggested route

0 metres 100

0 yards 100

London: Westminster Abbey ⑩

The abbey is famous as the resting-place of Britain's monarchs, and has been the setting for coronations and other pageants since the 13th century. It contains some glorious examples of medieval architecture and one of the most impressive collections of tombs and monuments in the world. Half national church, half national museum, Westminster Abbey is a popular attraction for both worshippers and tourists.

North Entrance
The stonework here, like this carving of a dragon, is Victorian.

★ Flying Buttresses
Massive flying buttresses help spread the great weight of the 31-m (102-ft) high roof of the nave.

★ West Front Towers
Until the 18th century, only the lower sections of these towers existed. The upper sections, built between 1734 and 1745, were designed by Sir Christopher Wren and Nicholas Hawksmoor, Wren's former clerk.

West Window
Completed in 1735, this depicts Abraham, Isaac, Jacob and 14 prophets.

West door

★ The Nave
Viewed from the west entrance, the soaring arches of the nave draw the eye past Edward Blore's choir screen to the windows of the apse.

Cloisters
Dating from the 13th and 14th centuries, the cloisters hold the the tombs of several medieval abbots.

★ Lady Chapel
The chapel, consecrated in 1512, has a superb vaulted ceiling and choir stalls dating from 1512. The tombs of Henry VII, who conceived the idea of building the chapel, and his queen can be found here.

STAR SIGHTS

- ★ Flying Buttresses
- ★ West Front Towers
- ★ The Nave
- ★ Lady Chapel
- ★ Chapter House

North Transept
Some of the Abbey's finest monuments can be found in three chapels on the east side of the transept.

St Edward's Chapel
Edward the Confessor's shrine and the tombs of many of England's monarchs are located in St Edward's Chapel.

★ Chapter House
This octagonal structure, built between 1245 and 1255, is worth seeing for its 13th-century tiles.

South Transept
Memorials to famous poets and writers stand here.

Abbey Museum

TIMELINE

1050 New Benedictine abbey church begun by Edward the Confessor

1376 Henry Yevele begins rebuilding the nave

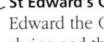

13th-century tile from the Chapter House

1838 Queen Victoria's coronation

1000 | 1200 | 1400 | 1600 | 1800 | 2000

1245 New church begun to the designs of Henry of Rheims

1269 Body of Edward the Confessor moved to the shrine in the abbey

1540 Monastery dissolved

1734 West towers begun

1953 Coronation of Elizabeth II in the abbey

Edinburgh (Leith)

Edinburgh bagpiper

With its striking medieval and Georgian districts, overlooked by the volcanic sill of Arthur's Seat to the south and Calton Hill to the north, Edinburgh is widely regarded as one of Europe's most handsome capitals. The city is famous for the arts, a pre-eminence reflected in its hosting every August of Britain's largest arts extravaganza, the Edinburgh Festival. An astonishing range of artistic and historical attractions and a renowned nightlife attract visitors here from all over the world.

National Museum of Scotland ⑤
Problems of space prevented Scottis antiquities such as this 9th-century Monymusk Reliquary from being ke in the Royal Museum, and resulted i the building of the Museum of Scotland next door.

Edinburgh Castle ①
Originally built in the 7th century, Edinburgh Castle has often been besieged and nearly completely destroyed on more than one occasion. The Castle has always risen again and attracts over one million visitors a year.

Scottish National Portrait Gallery ⑦
Portraits of famous Scots, including Robert Burns, and an exhibition on the royal house of Stuart can be seen on display in this gallery.

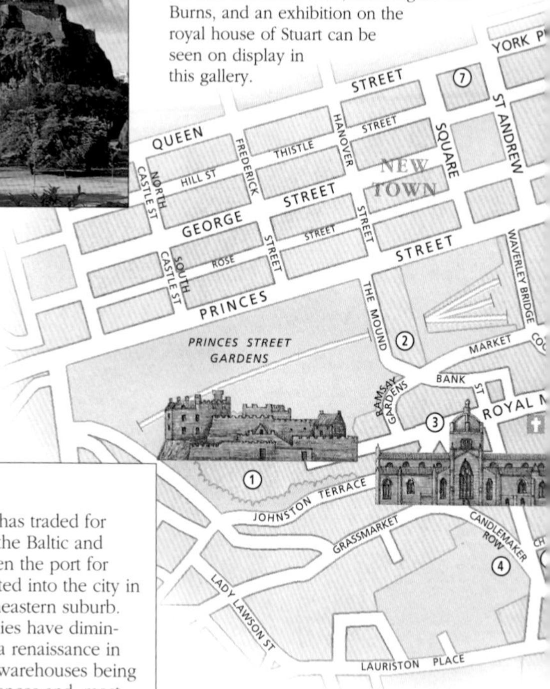

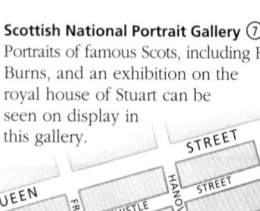

THE HISTORY OF LEITH

Leith is an historic port that has traded for centuries with Scandinavia, the Baltic and Holland, and has always been the port for Edinburgh. It was incorporated into the city in 1920 and now forms a northeastern suburb. Shipbuilding and port activities have diminished, but the city has seen a renaissance in other areas of activity, with warehouses being converted into offices, residences and, most notably, restaurants.

Leith Dock on the Firth of Forth, Edinburgh

Greyfriars Kirk ④
Completed in 1620, the church served as both a graveyard and prison for Protestant fighters during the 17th century. But it is most famous for its association with a dog, Bobby, who lived by his master's grave from 1858 to 1872.

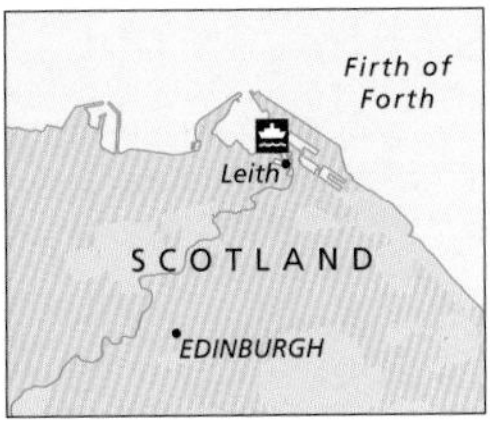

DISTANCE FROM PORT

3 km (2 miles) from city centre.

National Gallery of Scotland ②
One of the highlights of the National Gallery's Scottish works is Henry Raeburn's *Reverend Robert Walker Skating on Duddingston Loch* (c.1800).

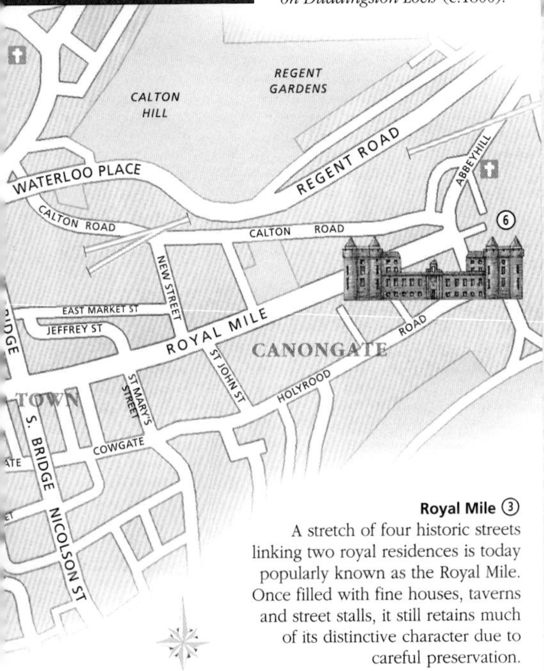

Royal Mile ③
A stretch of four historic streets linking two royal residences is today popularly known as the Royal Mile. Once filled with fine houses, taverns and street stalls, it still retains much of its distinctive character due to careful preservation.

The Palace of Holyroodhouse ⑥
Built by James IV in 1498, the Palace of Holyroodhouse has been the residence of many Scottish monarchs, including Mary, Queen of Scots. Bonnie Prince Charlie held court here in 1745. The palace now serves as the official Scottish residence of Queen Elizabeth II.

KEY SIGHTS

① Edinburgh Castle ★
(see pp120–21)

② National Gallery of Scotland ★

③ Royal Mile
(see pp122–3)

④ Greyfriars Kirk

⑤ National Museum of Scotland

⑥ The Palace of Holyroodhouse ★

⑦ Scottish National Portrait Gallery

KEY SIGHTS

TOURIST INFORMATION

3 Princes Street. ***Tel*** *0845 225 5121.* *Jul–Aug: daily to 8pm; spring & autumn: daily to 6pm; winter: daily to 5pm.*

MARKETS

Food Farmer's market, Castle Terrace; once a week (Jun–Dec).

SHOPPING

Traditional fashions Tailored kilts and knitwear can be purchased along the Royal Mile.

LOCAL SPECIALITIES

Crafts
Crystal, glassware and porcelain.

Dishes
Scotch broth (mutton or beef soup with pearl barley and vegetables).
Poached salmon (cooked whole).
Skirlie (fried oatmeal and onions).

Drinks
Glayva (whisky-based liqueur).
Ginger wine (raisin wine fortified with ginger).

EXCURSIONS

Rosslyn Chapel 10 km (7 miles) S of Edinburgh. Fascinating chapel dating from 1446.
Hopetoun House 20 km (12 miles) NW of Edinburgh. Stately home set in extensive parkland.
East Lothian Coast 20 km (12 miles) NE of Edinburgh. Dirleton and Tantallon castles are found in this windswept area. Attractive coastal walks.
Linlithgow Palace 29 km (17.5 miles) E of Edinburgh. One of Scotland's most visited ruins, dating back to the 14th century.

Edinburgh: Edinburgh Castle ①

Beam support in the Great Hall

Standing upon the basalt core of an extinct volcano, Edinburgh Castle is an assemblage of buildings dating from the 12th to the 20th century, which reflect its changing role as fortress, royal palace, military garrison and state prison. Though there is evidence of Bronze Age occupation of the site, the original fortress was built by the 6th-century Northumbrian king, Edwin, from whom the city takes its name. The castle was a favourite royal residence until James VI of Scotland also became king of England in 1603, after which he resided in England. After the Union of Parliaments in 1707, the Scottish regalia were walled up in the palace for over 100 years. The castle now holds the so-called Stone of Destiny, a relic of ancient Scottish kings, which was seized by the English and not returned until 1996.

★ Scottish Crown
Now on display in the palace, the crown was restyled by James V of Scotland in 1540.

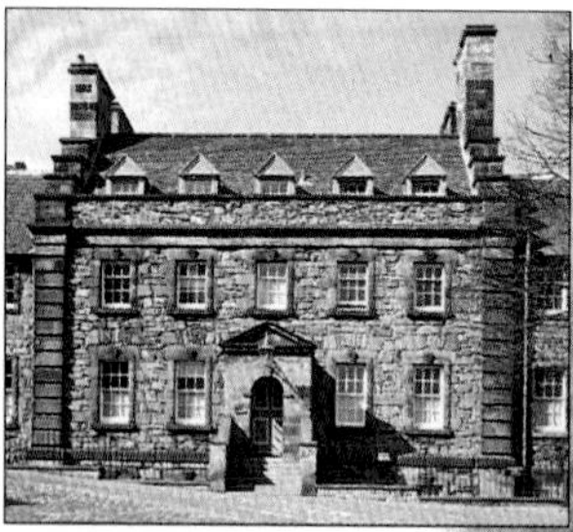

Governor's House
Complete with Flemish-style crow-stepped gables, this building was constructed for the governor in 1742 and now serves as the Officers' Mess for the castle garrison.

Vaults
The labyrinth of vaults underneath Edinburgh Castle served as a prison for foreign prisoners of war. This French graffiti, dating from 1780, recalls the many prisoners who were held in the vaults during the Napoleonic wars with France in the 18th and 19th centuries. Another prisoner, the 9th Earl of Argyll, was a staunch Protestant who supported the Duke of Monmouth in his attempt to seize the crown from James II of England. The rebellion failed and the Earl was captured and executed in 1685.

MONS MEG

Positioned outside St Margaret's Chapel, this siege gun (or bombard) was made in Belgium in 1449 for the Duke of Burgundy, who gave it to his nephew, James II of Scotland. Able to fire a stone cannonball 3.5 km (2 miles), it was used by James against the Douglas family in their stronghold of Threave Castle in 1455, and later by James IV against Norham Castle in England. After exploding during a salute to the Duke of York in 1682, it was kept in the Tower of London until it was returned in 1829.

STAR SIGHTS

- ★ Scottish Crown
- ★ Palace
- ★ Great Hall

Argyle Battery
This fortified wall commands a spectacular northern view of Edinburgh's New Town.

★ Palace
Mary, Queen of Scots gave birth to James VI in this 15th-century palace, which holds the Stone of Destiny and the Scottish Crown Jewels.

Esplanade
The annual Edinburgh Military Tattoo takes place here in August.

Half Moon Battery
Built in the 1570s, this served as a platform for the artillery defending the northeastern wing.

★ Great Hall
With its open-timber roof, the 15th-century hall was the meeting place of the Scottish parliament until 1639. Today it holds an interesting weaponry collection.

St Margaret's Chapel
This stained-glass window depicts Malcolm III's saintly queen, to whom the chapel is dedicated. Probably built by her son, David I, in the early 12th century, the chapel has survived numerous sieges and is the Castle's oldest building.

Edinburgh: Royal Mile ③

Eagle sign outside Gladstone's Land

The Royal Mile is a stretch of four ancient streets, from Castlehill to Canongate, which formed the main thoroughfare of medieval Edinburgh, linking the castle *(see pp120–21)* to the Palace of Holyroodhouse. Confined by the city wall, the "Old Town" grew upwards, with some tenements 20 storeys high. The city's medieval past is evident among the 66 alleys and closes off the main street.

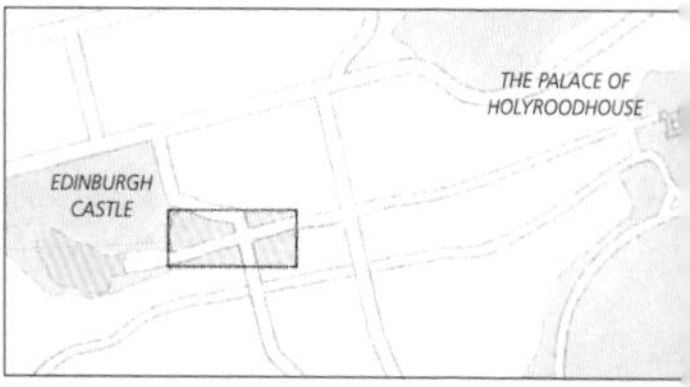

LOCATOR MAP

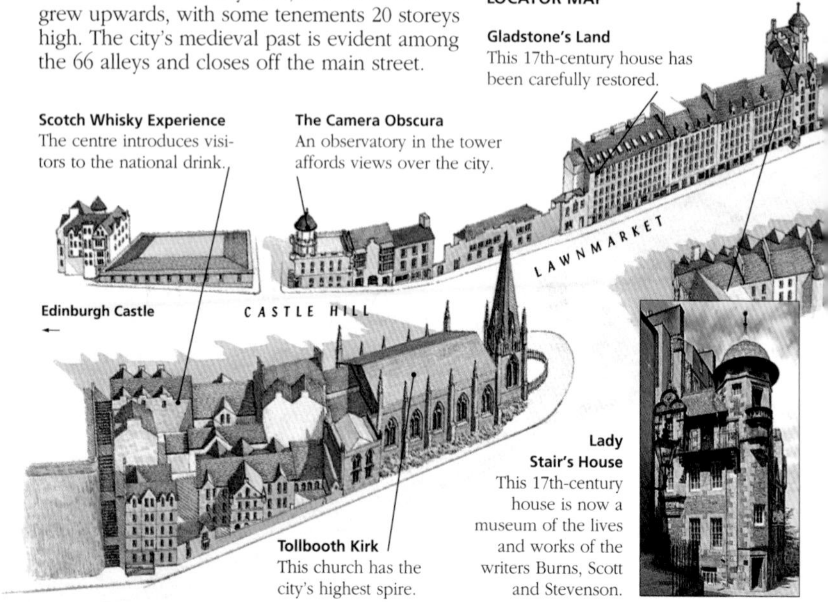

Gladstone's Land
This 17th-century house has been carefully restored.

Scotch Whisky Experience
The centre introduces visitors to the national drink.

The Camera Obscura
An observatory in the tower affords views over the city.

Lady Stair's House
This 17th-century house is now a museum of the lives and works of the writers Burns, Scott and Stevenson.

Tollbooth Kirk
This church has the city's highest spire.

Gladstone's Land

This restored merchant's house provides a realistic example of life in a typical Old Town house before overcrowding drove the rich residents northwest to the Georgian New Town. "Lands", as they were known, were tall, narrow buildings erected on small plots of land. The six-storey Gladstone's Land was named after Thomas Gledstanes, the merchant who built it in 1617. The house still has the original arcade booths on the street front and a painted ceiling with fine floral designs. Though it is extravagantly furnished, it also contains items that are a reminder of the less salubrious side of the old city, such as wooden overshoes that had to be worn in the dirty streets. The chest in the Painted Chamber is said to have been given by a Dutch sea captain to a Scottish merchant who saved him from a shipwreck. A similar house, named Morocco's Land, can be found further along the Royal Mile, on Canongate.

The bedroom of Gladstone's Land

Parliament House

Built in the 1630s, this Italianate building has been home to the Court of Session and the High Court since its original occupant, the Scottish Parliament, was dissolved after its union with the English Parliament in 1707. Scotland's parliament was finally re-established in 1999 with a building on Holyrood Road. Parliament House is worth seeing, as much for the spectacle of its gowned and wigged advocates as for the stained-glass window at the southern end of its Great Hall, commemorating the inauguration of the Court of Session by James V, in 1532.

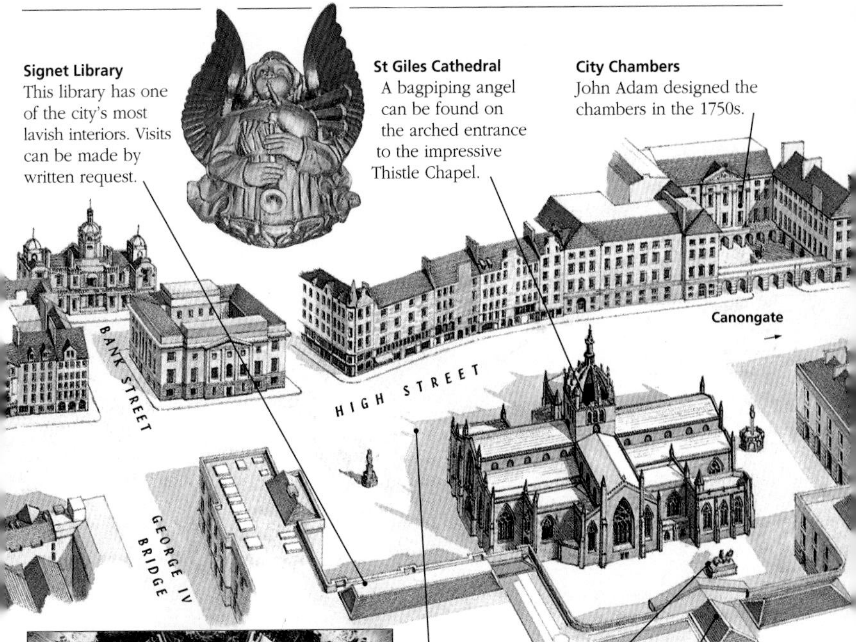

Signet Library
This library has one of the city's most lavish interiors. Visits can be made by written request.
St Giles Cathedral
A bagpiping angel can be found on the arched entrance to the impressive Thistle Chapel.
City Chambers
John Adam designed the chambers in the 1750s.
Canongate
BANK STREET
HIGH STREET
GEORGE IV BRIDGE
Charles II Statue
Heart of Midlothian
An arrangement of granite cobblestones is on the former site of the city jail.
Parliament House
Built in 1639, this was where the Scottish parliament convened until 1707.

Rib-vaulting in the Thistle Chapel, St Giles Cathedral

St Giles Cathedral

Properly known as the High Kirk (church) of Edinburgh, it is ironic that St Giles is popularly known as a cathedral. Though it was twice the seat of a bishop in the 17th century, it was from here that John Knox directed the Scottish Reformation with its emphasis on individual worship freed from the authority of bishops. A tablet marks the place where Jenny Geddes, a stallholder from a local market, scored a victory for the Protestant Covenanters by hurling her stool at a preacher reading from an English prayer book in 1637.

The Cathedral's Gothic exterior is dominated by a 15th-century tower, the only part to escape renovation in the 19th century. Inside, Sir Robert Lorimer's Thistle Chapel, built in 1911, can be seen. It features an elaborate rib-vaulted roof and carved heraldic canopies. The chapel honours the knights, past and present, of the Most Ancient and Most Noble Order of the Thistle. The carved royal pew in the Preston Aisle is used by Queen Elizabeth II when she is staying in Edinburgh.

EDINBURGH FESTIVAL

Every year, for five weeks in late summer, Edinburgh hosts one of the world's most important arts festivals, with every available space, from theatres to street corners, overflowing with international artists and performers. It has been held in Edinburgh since 1947 and brings together the best in contemporary theatre, music, dance and opera. The most popular event is the Edinburgh Tattoo. Held on the Castle Esplanade, it is a spectacle of Scottish infantry battalions marching to pipe bands from all over the world. The alternative Festival Fringe, involving some 600 companies, balances classic productions with a wide variety of innovative performances.

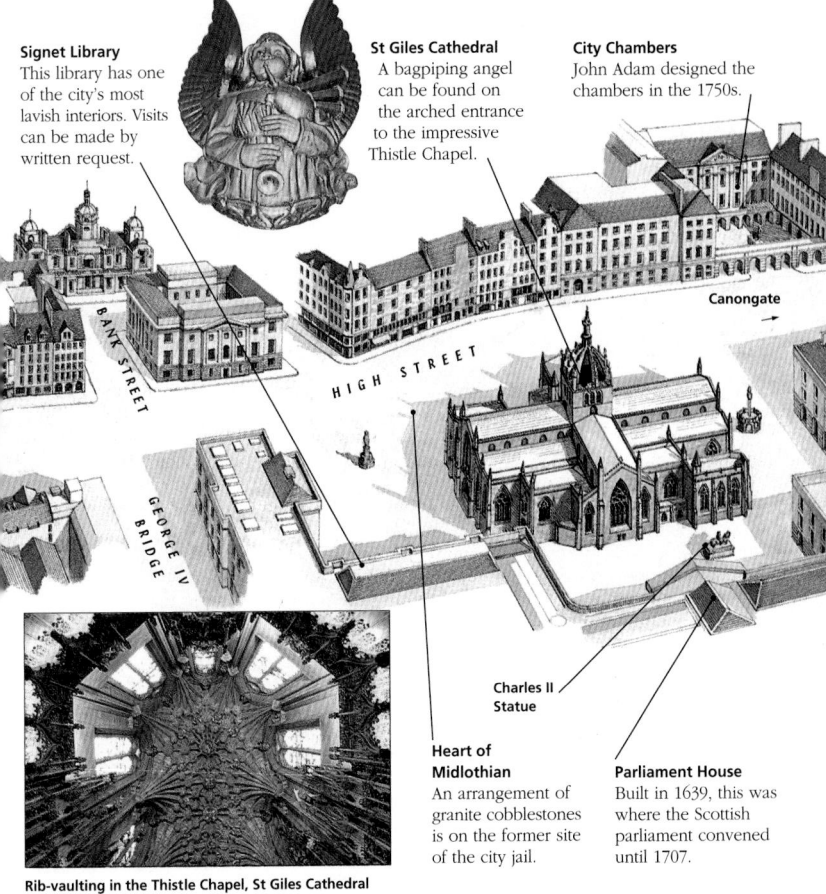

Street performer from the Edinburgh Festival Fringe

Glasgow (Greenock)

Glasgow shows audacity in everything from the profile of its new buildings to the range of designer clothes shops and the wit of its people. Originally a small salmon-fishing village, Glasgow really rose to prominence during the Industrial Revolution of the 19th century. By the 1970s, however, Glasgow was a city with a fading industrial history and little sense of direction. Since then much has changed. Recent years have seen the city embrace a glossy new image with refurbished buildings and a reputation for a vibrant nightlife.

Hunterian Museum and Art Gallery ①
The gallery houses Scotland's largest print collection and paintings by James McNeill Whistler (1834–1903).

Tenement House ③
More of a time capsule than a museum, this is an undisturbed record of life as it was in a modest Glasgow flat on a tenement estate in the early 20th century.

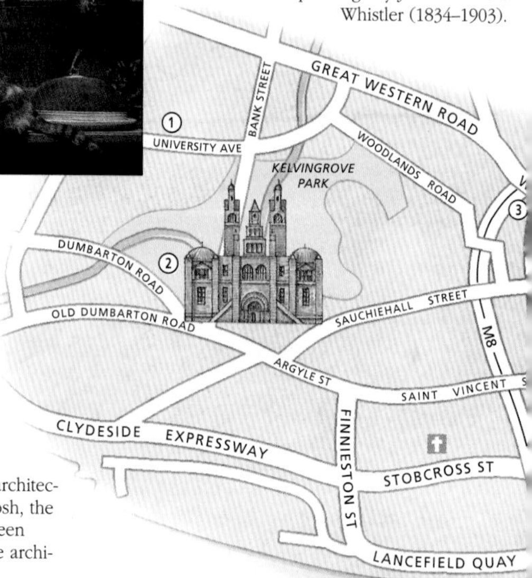

0 metres 750
0 yards 750

Glasgow School of Art ④
Widely considered to be the greatest architectural work of Charles Rennie Mackintosh, the Glasgow School of Art was built between 1897 and 1909. Every room echoes the architectural themes of the structure.

THE BURRELL COLLECTION

Given to the city in 1944 by the wealthy shipping owner Sir William Burrell (1861–1958), this internationally acclaimed collection is the star of Glasgow's renaissance, with artifacts of major importance in numerous fields of interest. The building that houses these pieces was purpose-built in 1983, and contains rooms devoted to tapestries, stained glass, sculpture and ancient civilizations.

The building housing the Burrell Collection

Willow Tea Room ⑤
Created by Charles Rennie Mackintosh in 1904 for celebrated restaurateur Miss Kate Cranston, this is the sole survivor of a series of delightful tea rooms.

Gallery of Modern Art ⑥
Offering a diverse selection of temporary exhibitions by local and international artists, the Gallery of Modern Art aims to review and address modern social issues. There is an Education and Access Studio in the attic, which also features talks by artists and a library and café in the basement.

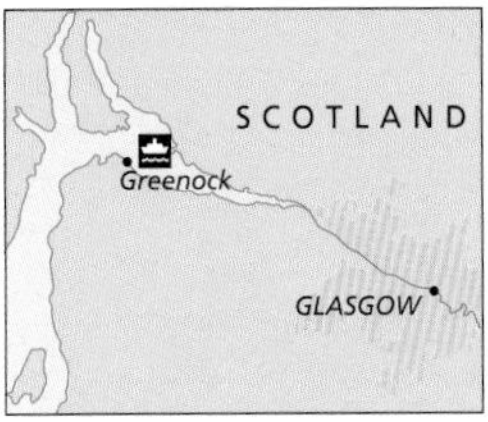

DISTANCE FROM PORT

40 km (25 miles) from city centre.

Glasgow Cathedral and Necropolis ⑦
This almost complete 13th-century church was built on the site of a chapel founded by St Mungo, Glasgow's patron saint. The necropolis is filled with monuments to the dead of Glasgow's merchant families.

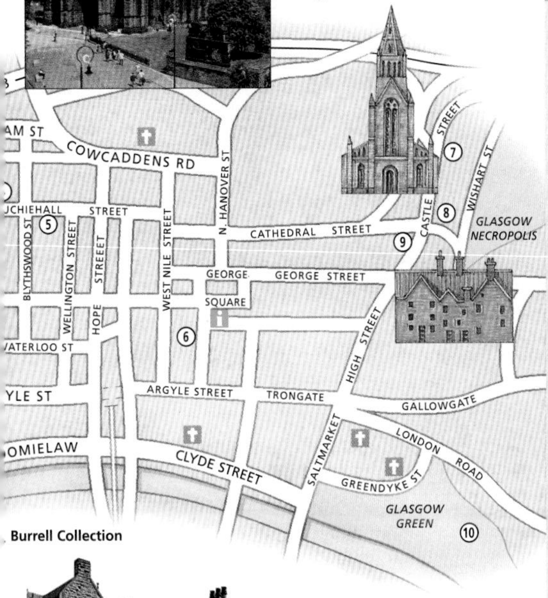

Provand's Lordship ⑨
Built as a canon's house in 1471, this is now Glasgow's oldest surviving house. Mary, Queen of Scots may have stayed here when she visited Glasgow in 1566 to see her cousin and husband, Lord Darnley.

KEY SIGHTS

① Hunterian Museum and Art Gallery
② Kelvingrove Art Gallery and Museum ★
③ Tenement House
④ Glasgow School of Art ★
⑤ Willow Tea Room
⑥ The Gallery of Modern Art
⑦ Glasgow Cathedral and Necropolis
⑧ St Mungo Museum of Religious Life and Art ★
⑨ Provand's Lordship
⑩ People's Palace

FACT FILE

TOURIST INFORMATION
11 George Square. ***Tel** (0141) 204 4400.* *Mar/Apr–early Jun: Mon–Sat 10am–6pm, Sun 10am–6pm; Jun & Sep: Mon–Sat 9am–7pm, Sun 10am–6pm; Jul & Aug: Mon–Sat 9am–8pm, Sun 10am–6pm; Oct–Mar/Apr: Mon–Sat 9am–6pm.*

MARKETS
General The Barras, between London Road and Gallowgate; Sat & Sun.

SHOPPING
Designer clothes In the heart of Glasgow, one square mile houses the most extraordinary collection of inspirational shopping, atmospheric cafés and fine restaurants.

LOCAL SPECIALITIES
Crafts
Jewellery, stained glass, tailoring.
Produce
Lanark Blue cheese.
Dishes
Haggis (spiced sheep's innards and oatmeal).
Drinks
Glengoyne (single malt whisky).
Irn-Bru (soft drink).

EXCURSIONS
Burrell Collection 3 km (2 miles) S of Glasgow city centre. A collection of important artworks.
Glengoyne Distillery 15 km (9 miles) N of Glasgow. An attractive distillery close to Loch Lomond.
New Lanark World Heritage Village 40 km (25 miles) SE of Glasgow. A beautifully preserved 200-year-old cotton mill village.

Kelvingrove Art Gallery and the Glasgow University buildings, seen from the south

Exploring Glasgow

Glasgow's industrial past and glossy image make it a city of contrasts. The city centre is a neat grid of streets running east to west and north to south on the northern bank of the River Clyde. This small area includes the main train stations and principal shopping facilities. Glasgow's chief galleries and museums can be found in the more affluent West End which prospered in the 19th century.

Hunterian Art Gallery ①

Named after Dr William Hunter (1718–83), the physician whose collection of paintings the gallery was built to house, the Hunterian Art Gallery contains Scotland's largest collection of prints. There are also works by a number of major European artists, including Rembrandt, dating back to the 16th century. A collection of work by the designer Charles Rennie Mackintosh is supplemented by a complete reconstruction of No. 6 Florentine Terrace, where he lived from 1906 to 1914.

A major collection of 19th- and 20th-century Scottish art includes work by William McTaggart (1835–1910), but by far the most famous collection is of work by the Paris-trained American painter, James McNeill Whistler (1834–1903), who influenced so many of the Glasgow School painters.

Kelvingrove Art Gallery and Museum ②

An imposing red sandstone building, Kelvingrove is Scotland's most popular gallery, housing a magnificent art collection and a superb collection of arms and armour. Following an extensive refurbishment completed in 2006, there are now an extra 3,000 objects on display. Exhibits have been chosen and grouped to reflect different aspects of the main collection. Kelvingrove's 17th-century Dutch and Flemish masters including Rembrandt can be seen, while 19th-century British artists include Turner and Constable. Scottish art and design is well represented with rooms dedicated to the Scottish Colourists and the late 19th-century Glasgow Style. Included here are two magnificent works by Charles Rennie Mackintosh; a fine Gesso panel and a 1904 writing cabinet.

Tenement House ③

Originally rented by Miss Agnes Toward, who lived here from 1911 to 1965, this modest Edwardian apartment-turned-museum remained largely unaltered during that time and, since Agnes apparently threw little away, the house has become a treasure trove of social history. In the parlour, used only on formal occasions, afternoon tea is laid out on a white lace cloth. The kitchen, with its coal-fired range and bed recess, is filled with the tools of a vanished era, such as a goffering-iron for ironing delicate lace, a washboard and a stone hot-water bottle.

Agnes's lavender water and medicines are still arranged in the bathroom, giving the feeling that she stepped out of the house 70 years ago and simply forgot to return.

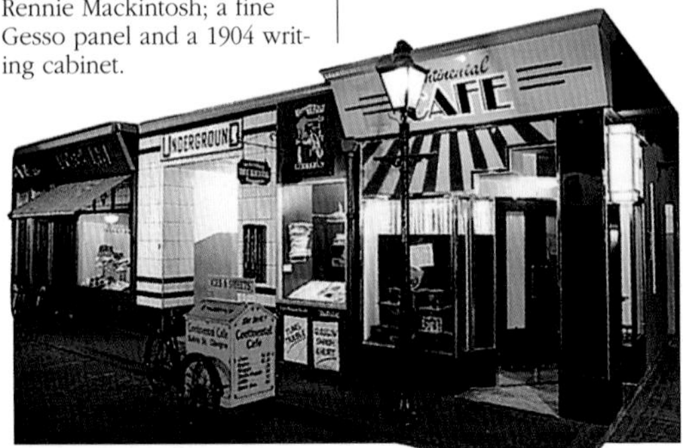

Museum of Transport's 1938 street, with its reconstructed Underground station

Glasgow School of Art ④

Due to financial constraints, Charles Rennie Mackintosh's Glasgow School of Art was built in two stages. The earlier, eastern half displays a severity of style, likened to a prison by a contemporary critic. The later, western half is characterized by a softer architectural style.Inside are the Furniture Gallery, Board Room and Library, this last being a masterpiece of spacial composition.

Willow Tea Room ⑤

Everything in this lively tearoom,from high-backed chairs to the tables and cutlery, was designed by Charles Rennie Mackintosh. In particular, the Room de Luxe sparkles with eccentricity, with striking mauve and silver furniture, coloured glass and a flamboyant leaded door.

Exterior of the Glasgow School of Art, Mackintosh's masterpiece

Gallery of Modern Art ⑥

Originally built in 1755 as the country retreat for one of Glasgow's 'Tobacco Lords,' this Neo-Classical building houses contemporary art by both local and international artists. The gallery also hosts temporary exhibitions. The permanent collection consists of pieces by Scottish artists Ken Currie and John Bellany placed alongside Warhol's and Hockney's. The Gallery of Modern Art is committed to making contemporary art accessible to everyone and throughout the year presents a variety of events and projects.

Glasgow Cathedral and Necropolis ⑦

One of the few cathedrals to escape destruction during the Scottish Reformation by adapting itself to Protestant worship, Glasgow Cathedral is built on two levels. The crypt contains the tomb of St Mungo, a 6th-century bishop. The Blacader Aisle, which is reputed to have been built over a cemetery blessed by St Ninian, has a ceiling thick with decorative bosses.

Behind the cathedral, a likeness of the Protestant reformer John Knox surveys the city from his Doric pillar overlooking the Victorian cemetery, or necropolis, with its crumbling monuments.

Exterior detail from the St Mungo Museum

St Mungo Museum of Religious Life and Art ⑧

Although it has the appearance of a centuries-old fortified house, the St Mungo Museum of Religious Life and Art was actually completed in 1993. This fascinating museum explores the importance of religion throughout the world. The top floor tells the story of the country's religion from a non-denominational perspective. The other floors are given over to works of art, including religious artifacts and artworks such as burial discs from Neolithic China, contemporary paintings by Aboriginal Australians and some excellent Scottish stained glass from the early part of the 20th century.

Provand's Lordship ⑨

Built in 1471 as a home for the Lord of Provan, this three-storeyed building now serves as a museum. Its low ceilings and austere wooden furniture create a vivid impression of life in a wealthy 15th-century household. At the back lies a tranquil, medieval garden.

People's Palace ⑩

This Victorian sandstone structure was built in 1898 to house a cultural museum for the people of Glasgow's East End. It has everything from temperance tracts to trade-union banners, suffragette posters to the comedian Billy Connolly's banana-shaped boots, thus providing a social history of the city from the 12th century to the present day.

CHARLES RENNIE MACKINTOSH

Glasgow's most celebrated designer, Mackintosh (1868–1928) entered the Glasgow School of Art at the age of 16. After graduating, he gained fame as an architect and interior designer. His use of straight lines and flowing curves appealed to avant-garde artists in Vienna and, after exhibiting there in 1900, he gained a world-wide following. In the same year, he submitted plans for a House for an Art Lover to a magazine competition. The plans lay unused until a Mackintosh enthusiast initiated building in Glasgow in 1989.

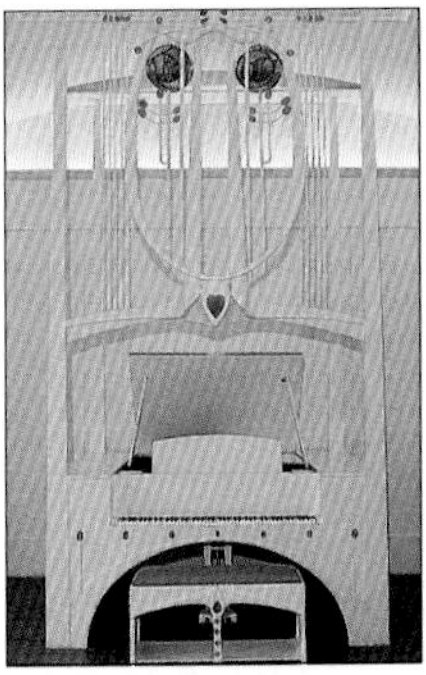

Piano in the Music Room, House for an Art Lover

Scotch Whisky

Whisky has long been a part of the Scottish way of life. Distilled in Scotland for centuries, it was once highly regarded as a cure for a variety of diseases. All malt whiskies are produced using much the same process, but the environment, maturity and storage of the whisky have such a strong bearing on its character that every one is a different experience. There is no "best" malt whisky – some are suited to drinking at bedtime, others as an aperitif. All the distilleries named below produce highly rated Single Malt Scotch Whiskies, a title that is revered by true whisky connoisseurs.

A 1920s steam wagon transporting The Glenlivet to the nearby railways

Talisker is an individualistic malt with an extremely hot, peppery, powerful flavour that is guaranteed to warm the toes.

Glenmorangie is the biggest selling single malt in Scotland, with a light, flowery taste and strong perfume.

Lochnagar is reputed to have been a favourite with Queen Victoria, who visited this distillery located near Balmoral. This is a sweet whisky with overtones of sherry.

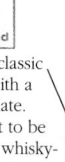

Lagavulin is a classic Islay whisky with a dry, smoky palate. Islay is thought to be the best of the whisky-producing islands.

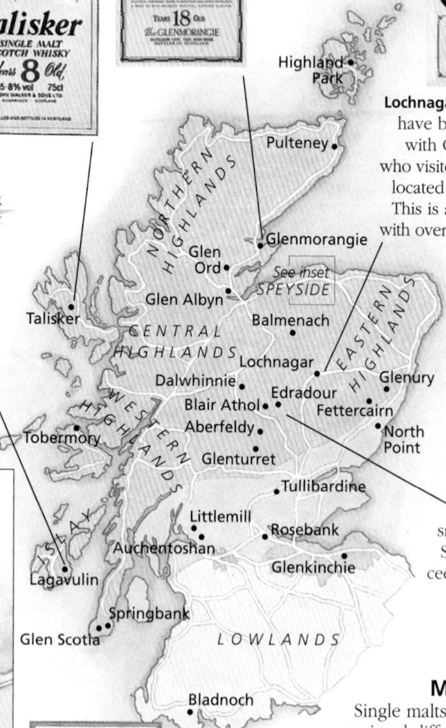

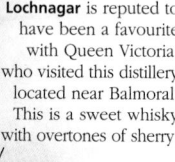

Edradour is th smallest distillery i Scotland but it suc ceeds in producing deliciously minty creamy whisky

SPEYSIDE WHISKIES

The region of Speyside, where barley is widely grown, is the setting for over half of Scotland's malt whisky distilleries.

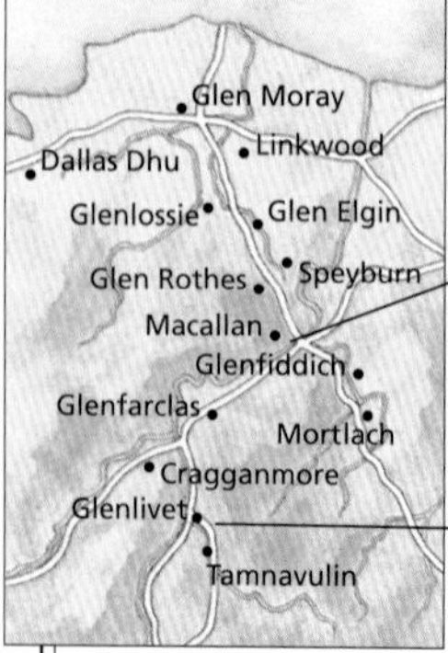

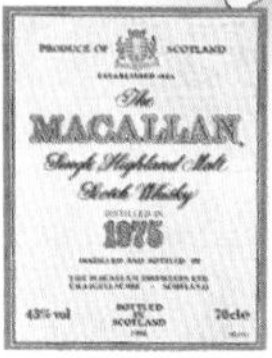

The Macallan is widely acknowledged as being the "Rolls Royce of Single Malts". Aged in sherry casks, it has a full flavour.

The Glenlivet is the most famous of the Speyside malts, distilled since 1880.

MALT REGION

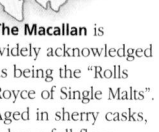

Single malts vary according regional differences in the pe and stream water used. Th map illustrates the divisio of the traditional whisk distilling regions in Scotlan Each whisky has subtle b recognizable regional flavo characteristic

KEY

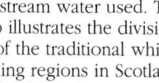

- Single malt distilleries

HOW WHISKY IS MADE

Traditionally made from just barley, yeast and stream water, Scottish whisky (from the Gaelic *usquebaugh*, or the "water of life") takes a little over three weeks to produce, though it must be given at least three years to mature. Maturation usually takes place in oak casks, often in barrels previously used for sherry. The art of blending was pioneered in Edinburgh in the 1860s.

Barley grass

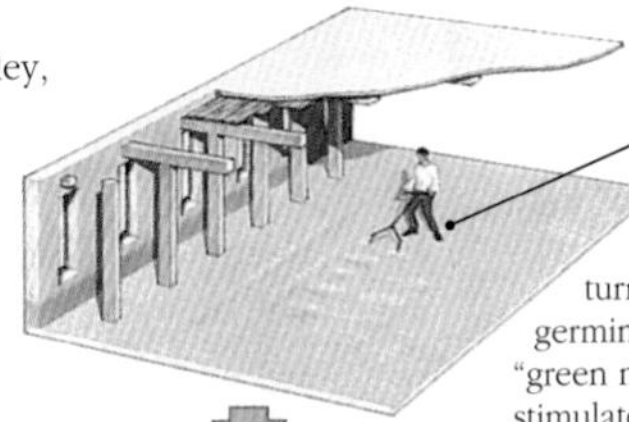

1 The first stage is malting. Barley is soaked in water and spread on the malting floor. Regular turning helps the grain to germinate, producing a "green malt". Germination stimulates the production of enzymes that turn the starches into fermentable sugars.

2 Drying of the barley halts germination after 12 days of malting. This is done over a peat fire in a pagoda-shaped malt-kiln. The smoke gives flavour to the malt and eventually to the mature whisky. The malt is gleaned of germinated roots and then milled.

3 Mashing of the ground malt, or "grist", occurs in a large vat known as a "mash tun", which holds an enormous quantity of hot water. The malt is soaked and begins to dissolve, producing a sugary solution called "wort", which can then be extracted for fermentation.

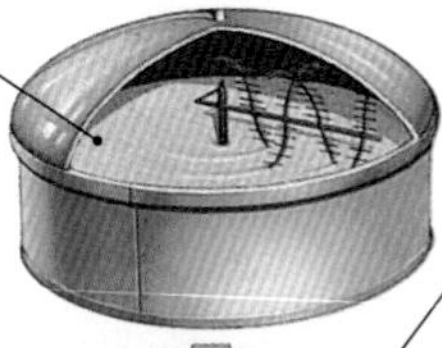

4 Fermentation occurs when yeast is added to the cooled wort in wooden vats, or "washbacks". The mixture is stirred for several hours as the yeast turns the sugar into alcohol, producing a clear liquid called "wash".

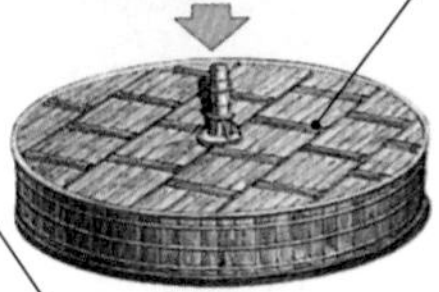

5 Distillation involves boiling the wash twice so that the alcohol vaporizes and condenses. In copper "pot stills", the wash is distilled – first in the "wash still", then in the "spirit still". Now purified, with an alcohol content of 57 per cent, the result is young whisky.

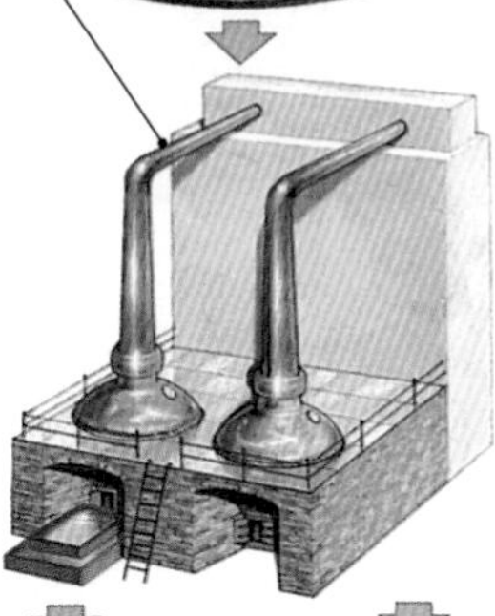

Traditional drinking vessels, or quaichs, made of silver

6 Maturation is the final process. The whisky mellows in oak casks for a legal minimum of three years. Premium brands give the whisky a 10- to 15-year maturation, though some are given up to 50 years.

Blended whiskies are made from a mixture of up to 50 different single malts.

Single malts are made in one distillery, from pure barley malt that is never blended.

IRELAND

Dublin

Detail from the Custom House

Many people are lured to Dublin to savour the ambience of a city that produced such great literary figures as James Joyce, Oscar Wilde and Samuel Beckett. The city was founded by the Vikings in the 10th century, though the area had been inhabited some 8,000 years earlier, and remained a small town until the 17th century, when Protestant refugees from all over Europe began to flock to Dublin. Since Ireland's independence from Britain in 1922, Dublin has become the political, economic and cultural centre of the country, offering a wealth of attractions for visitors.

Christ Church Cathedral ⑧
Built by Dublin's Anglo-Norman conquerors between 1172 and 1220, the cathedral stands on high ground above the River Liffey. The building was extensively restored in the 1870s.

Dublin Castle ⑦
St Patrick's Hall is part of the suite of luxury State Apartments housed on the upper floors of the southern side of this castle. Today the rooms are used for functions of national importance, such as presidential inaugurations.

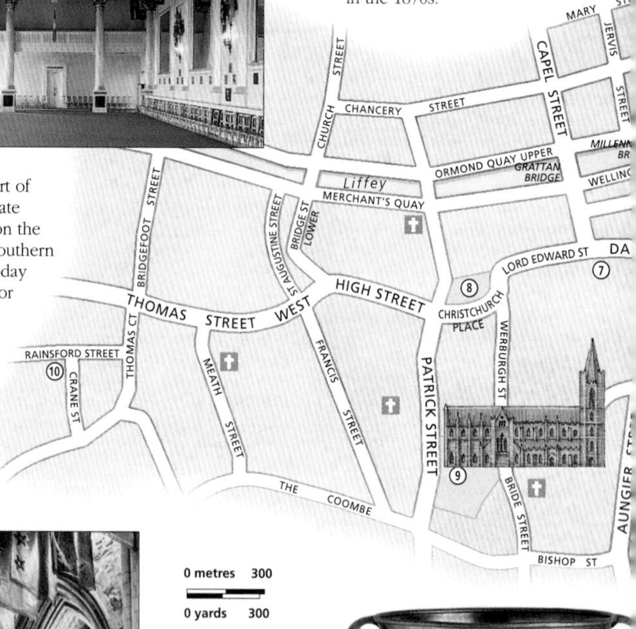

St Patrick's Cathedral ⑨
As well as a spectacular choir featuring banners and stalls decorated with the insignia of the Knights of St Patrick, the cathedral also has Ireland's largest and most powerful organ. There are also memorials to Dean Jonathan Swift and some prominent Anglo-Irish families.

National Museum ③
Dating from the Stone Age to the 20th century, the museum's artifacts include the Ardagh Chalice (c. AD 800), a Celtic Christian relic.

Trinity College ④
Since its founding in 1592, the college has had many famous students. Attractions include the 9th-century *Book of Kells*, and Pomodoro's *Sphere within Sphere* (1982).

Temple Bar ⑥
This popular arts and entertainment district occupies a maze of narrow, cobbled streets between Dame Street and the River Liffey.

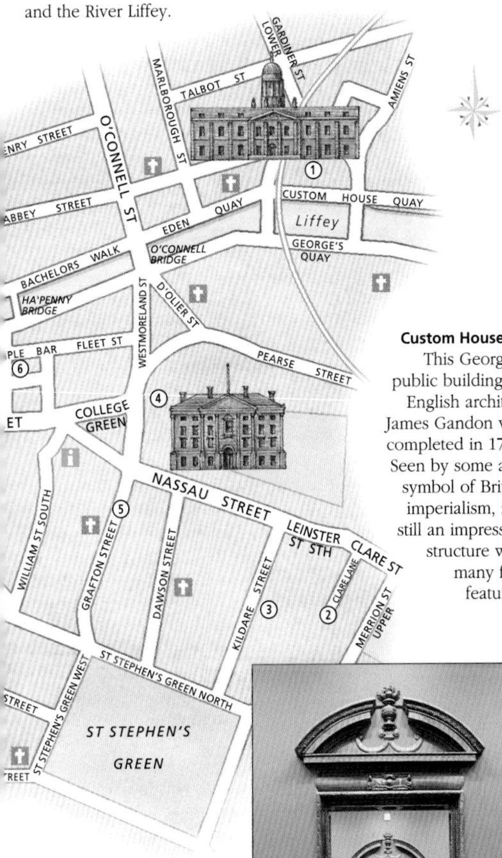

Custom House ①
This Georgian public building by English architect James Gandon was completed in 1791. Seen by some as a symbol of British imperialism, it is still an impressive structure with many fine features.

National Gallery ②
Opened to the public in 1864, this purpose-built gallery holds an eclectic collection that is particularly strong on Irish and Italian art. Its most prized painting is *The Taking of Christ* (1602) by Caravaggio.

KEY SIGHTS

① Custom House
② National Gallery ★
③ National Museum ★
④ Trinity College ★
(see pp136–7)
⑤ Grafton Street
⑥ Temple Bar
⑦ Dublin Castle
⑧ Christ Church Cathedral
⑨ St Patrick's Cathedral
⑩ Guinness Storehouse

FACT FILE

TOURIST INFORMATION

Suffolk Street. ***Tel*** *from UK: 0800 039 7000, 353 605 7700; from Ireland: 1 850 230 330*
Mon–Sat 9am–5:30pm; Sun 10:30am–3pm.

MARKETS

Antiques Francis Street; daily. **Food & flowers** Moore St; Mon–Fri. **Food, crafts, books & fashion** Temple Bar market; Sat.

LOCAL SPECIALITIES

Crafts
Crystal (Waterford, Tyrone, Jerpoint), ceramics (Royal Tara China, Belleek Pottery), linen, jewellery, Donegal tweed, *Bodhrán* drums and beaters.
Produce
St Killian, Carrigaline, Cashel Blue and *Durrus* cheeses.
Dishes
Dublin coddle (chopped sausages and ham or bacon in stock with potatoes and onions). *Irish stew* (thick casserole made with lamb or mutton). *Porter cake* (classic Irish cake with dried fruit and stout). *Mussel soup* (mussels in creamy fish stock flavoured with herbs).
Drinks
Guinness (smooth, black, malty stout with a distinctive white head). *Irish whiskey* (including Jameson, Old Bushmills and Power and Son).

EXCURSIONS

Powerscourt 22 km (13 miles) S of Dublin. Ireland's finest ornamental gardens set at the foot of Great Sugar Loaf Mountain.
Castletown House 40 km (24 miles) W of Dublin. Impressive 18th-century Palladian stately home.

Illuminated façade of the Custom House, reflected in the River Liffey

Exploring Dublin

Although it is a fairly small city, Dublin offers a wealth of attractions that draw in millions of visitors each year. The heart of the modern city lies just to the south of the River Liffey, around College Green. Many of Dublin's more up-market shops and restaurants are on Grafton Street and Trinity College, the National Gallery and the National Museum can be found nearby. Further west, not far from Dublin Castle, is the Temple Bar area, which is considered the trendiest part of town. North of the river, the Abbey and Gate theatres act as cultural magnets.

Custom House ①

This majestic building was designed as the custom house by the English architect James Gandon. However, nine years after its completion it was rendered nearly obsolete, when the 1800 Act of Union moved the custom and excise business to London. In 1921, supporters of the political party Sinn Fein celebrated an election victory by setting fire to what they saw as a symbol of British imperialism, causing extensive damage. It was not until 1991 that the renovated building was reopened as government offices.

The main façade consists of pavilions at each end with a Doric portico at its centre. The arms of Ireland crown the two pavilions and a series of allegorical heads by Dublin sculptor Edward Smyth form the keystones of arches and entrances. The heads depict Ireland's main rivers and the Atlantic Ocean. A statue of Commerce stands on top of the central copper dome.

National Gallery ②

This purpose-built gallery was opened to the public in 1864. It houses many excellent exhibits, which have entered the collection largely due to a number of generous bequests, such as the Milltown collection of works of art from Russborough House. Playwright George Bernard Shaw was also a benefactor, leaving a third of his estate to the gallery.

An additional wing was added to the gallery which has over 700 works on display. The outstanding collection of Western European art ranges from the Middle Ages to the present day with the most important gathering of Irish art in the world. Although the emphasis is on Irish landscape art and portraits, including Jack Yeats' *For the Road*, every major school of European painting is well represented, with works by Goya, El Greco, Vermeer, Titian and Monet. The light-flooded Millennium Wing concentrates on modern Irish art and showcases major travelling shows.

National Museum ③

The National Museum of Ireland was built in the 1880s to Sir Thomas Deane's design. Its domed rotunda has marbled pillars and a mosaic floor depicting the signs of the zodiac. The Treasury houses priceless items such as the Broighter gold boat, while an exhibition of Ireland's Bronze Age gold contains some beautiful jewellery. Other exhibitions include a display of Viking artifacts and "The Road to Independence", which covers Ireland's history between 1900 and 1921. Many of the collections have now moved to the museum's annexe at Collins Barracks.

Trinity College ④

See pp136–7.

Grafton Street ⑤

The spine of Dublin's most popular shopping district runs from Trinity College to the St Stephen's Green Shopping Centre. At the northern end is Jean Rynhart's 1988 bronze statue of Molly Malone, the celebrated street trader from

For the Road **by Jack Yeats (1871–1957), National Gallery, Dublin**

St Patrick's Cathedral with Minot's Tower

the traditional Irish folk song. This busy pedestrianized stretch boasts a wide variety of shops, including Brown Thomas, one of Dublin's most elegant department stores, which sells designer clothes and exclusive perfumes.

Grafton Street's most famous landmark is Bewley's Oriental Café at No. 78. Although not the oldest branch of this 150-year-old Dublin institution, this is Bewley's most popular location and a favourite meeting point for Dubliners and visitors alike.

On many of the side streets off Grafton Street there are numerous pubs providing an alternative to Bewley's. Among them is Davy Byrne's, which has been frequented by Dublin's literati for years.

Temple Bar ⑥

The cobbled streets between Dame Street and the Liffey are named after Sir William Temple, who acquired the land in the early 1600s. The term "bar" meant a riverside path. Home to a number of small businesses during the 1800s, the area later went into decline until the early 1960s, when the land was bought up with plans to build a new bus station. Artists and record, clothing and book shops took the cheap short-term leases offered in the meantime and stayed on when the plans were scrapped. Temple Bar prospered, and today it is an exciting place, with bars, restaurants, shops and galleries, including the Irish Film Centre, the Gallery of Photography and the National Photographic Archive.

Dublin Castle ⑦

For seven centuries Dublin Castle was a symbol of English rule, ever since the Anglo-Normans built a fortress here in the 13th century. Nothing remains of the original structure except the much modified Record Tower. After a fire in 1684, the Surveyor-General, Sir William Robinson, laid down the plans for the castle in its present form. In the castle's Upper Yard are the State Apartments, including St Patrick's Hall, which served as home to the British-appointed Viceroys of Ireland.

Christ Church Cathedral ⑧

Archbishop Laurence O'Toole and Richard de Clare (better known as Strongbow), the Anglo-Norman conqueror of Dublin, instigated the building of Christ Church Cathedral in 1172. By the 19th century it was in a state of disrepair, but was remodelled by architect George Street in the 1870s. The 20-m (68-ft) high nave houses a medieval lectern and Strongbow's monument. The crypt contains tombs which were previously housed in the cathedral.

St Patrick's Cathedral ⑨

Ireland's largest church was founded beside a well where St Patrick is said to have baptized converts in around AD 450. The original wooden chapel was rebuilt in stone by Archbishop John Comyn in 1192. Today, St Patrick's is the national cathedral of the Protestant Church of Ireland.

Much of the 91-m (300-ft) long building dates back to the 13th century. The interior is dotted with busts, monuments and brasses, including memorials to the harpist Turlough O'Carolan (1670–1738) and the writer Jonathan Swift (1667–1745).

Memorial to Turlough O'Carolan in St Patrick's Cathedral

At the western end is a tower, restored by Archbishop Minot in 1370, now known as Minot's Tower.

Guinness Storehouse ⑩

This Guinness exhibition is housed in a 19th-century warehouse, which was used for storing bales of hops until the 1950s. A self-guided tour takes the visitor through 200 years of brewing this famous stout, showing how production has changed since Arthur Guinness began in December 1759.

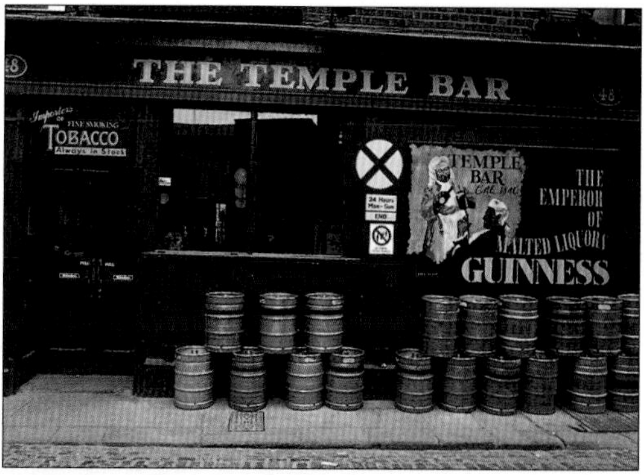

The Temple Bar public house, Temple Bar, Dublin

Dublin: Trinity College ④

Trinity College coat of arms

Trinity college was founded in 1592 by Queen Elizabeth I on the site of an Augustinian monastery. Originally a Protestant college, it was not until the 1970s that Catholics started entering the university. Among the many famous students to attend the college were playwrights Oliver Goldsmith and Samuel Beckett, and political writer Edmund Burke. Trinity's lawns and cobbled quads provide a pleasant haven in the heart of the city. The major attractions are the Old Library and the *Book of Kells*, housed in the Treasury.

★ Campanile
The 30-m (98-ft) bell tower, built in 1853 by Sir Charles Lanyon, provides a focal point for the cobblestoned Parliament Square.

Chapel
Dating from 1798, this is the only chapel in the Republic to be shared by all denominations. The painted window above the altar dates from 1867.

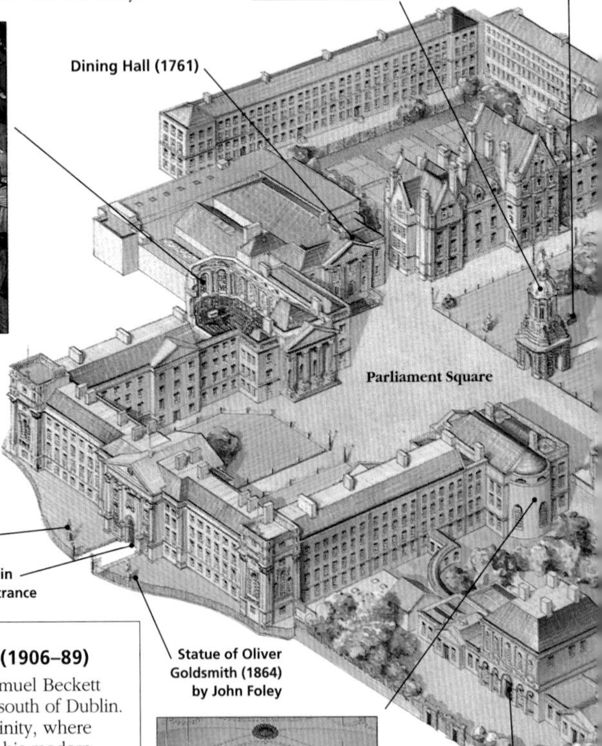

Reclining Connected Forms (1969) by Henry Moore

Dining Hall (1761)

Parliament Square

Statue of Edmund Burke (1868) by John Foley

Main entrance

Statue of Oliver Goldsmith (1864) by John Foley

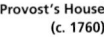

Provost's House (c. 1760)

SAMUEL BECKETT (1906–89)

Nobel prizewinner Samuel Beckett was born at Foxrock, south of Dublin. In 1923 he entered Trinity, where he was placed first in his modern literature class. He was also a keen member of the college cricket team. Forsaking Ireland, Beckett moved to France in the early 1930s. Many of his works such as *Waiting for Godot* (1951) were written first in French, and then later translated, by Beckett, into English.

★ Examination Hall
Completed in 1791 to a design by Sir William Chambers, this single-vaulted chamber features a gilded oak chandelier and ornate ceilings by Michael Stapleton.

Library Square
The red-brick building (known as the Rubrics) on the eastern side of Library Square was built around 1700 and is the oldest surviving part of the college.

STAR SIGHTS

- ★ Campanile
- ★ Examination Hall
- ★ Treasury
- ★ Old Library

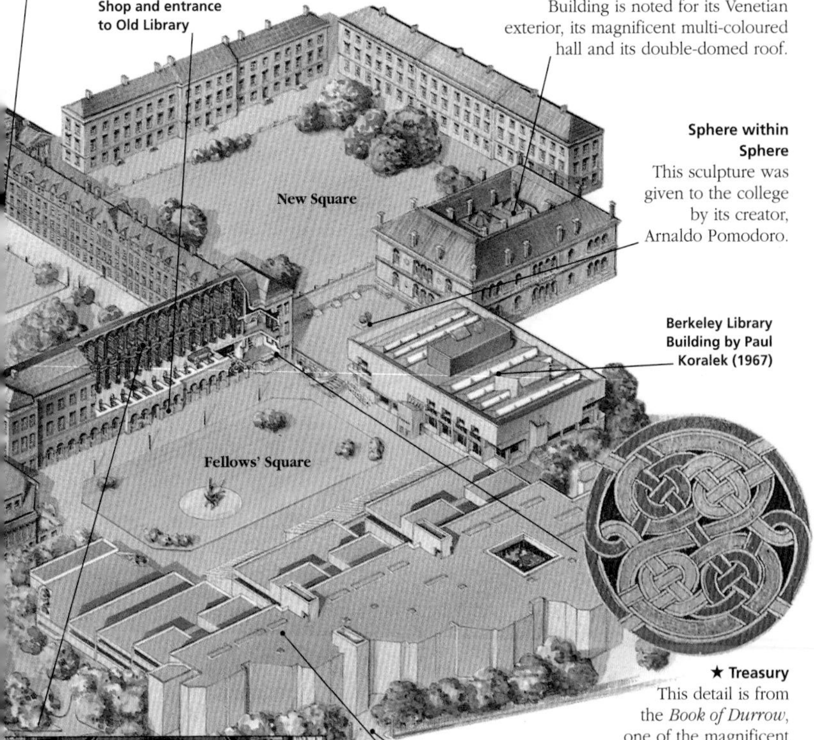

Shop and entrance to Old Library

Museum Building
Completed in 1857, the Museum Building is noted for its Venetian exterior, its magnificent multi-coloured hall and its double-domed roof.

Sphere within Sphere
This sculpture was given to the college by its creator, Arnaldo Pomodoro.

Berkeley Library Building by Paul Koralek (1967)

★ Treasury
This detail is from the *Book of Durrow*, one of the magnificent illuminated manuscripts housed in the Treasury. The celebrated *Book of Kells* is also housed here.

Entrance from Nassau Street

Douglas Hyde Gallery
Built in the 1970s, this gallery houses temporary art exhibitions.

★ Old Library
Built in 1732, the Old Library's spectacular Long Room measures 64 m (210 ft) from end to end. It houses 200,000 antiquarian texts, marble busts of scholars and the oldest surviving harp in Ireland.

Typical landscape of Provence, France ▷

FRANCE

Cherbourg
Le Havre
PARIS
FRANCE
Bordeaux
Aix-en-Provence
Nice
MONACO
Monte-Carlo
Arles
Cannes
Marseille
St-Tropez
Corsica
Ajaccio

Paris (Le Havre)

The Seine flows through the heart of Paris and many of the city's great buildings are either along its banks or close to it. Paris sprang from a village on the Ile de la Cité, which was inhabited by the Parisii tribe and which the Romans conquered in 55 BC. The latter expanded onto the Left Bank and, after marshes were drained in medieval times, the city grew outwards during the Renaissance and Baroque eras. Napoleon endowed it with monuments, but it was Baron Haussmann's grand transformation in the 1800s that gave Paris its great, tree-lined boulevards. A renovation plan initiated in 1962 restored historic buildings and gave Paris spectacular new landmarks and museums.

Sacré-Coeur ①
Though completed in 1914, the consecration of this vast Roman Catholic basilica was delayed until 1918.

Eiffel Tower ④
A two-tiered lighting system shows off this 10,100-tonne symbol of Paris to better effect than ever before.

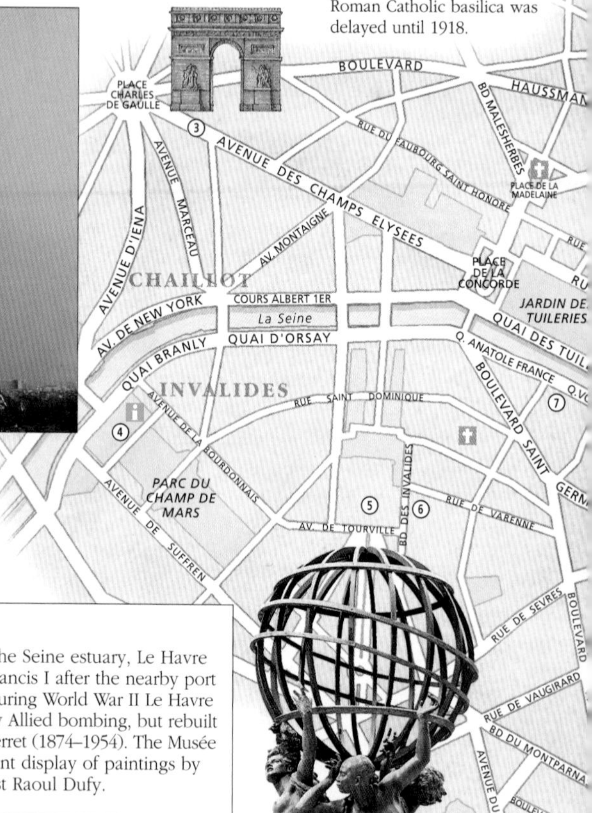

LE HAVRE

Sited at the mouth of the Seine estuary, Le Havre was built in 1517 by Francis I after the nearby port of Harfleur silted up. During World War II Le Havre was almost flattened by Allied bombing, but rebuilt to designs by August Perret (1874–1954). The Musée Malraux has an excellent display of paintings by the Le Havre-born artist Raoul Dufy.

Le Havre's busy commercial port at the mouth of the Seine

Musée d'Orsay ⑦
This showcase of Art Nouveau and Impressionist art includes the *Four Quarters of the World* by Jean-Baptiste Carpeaux

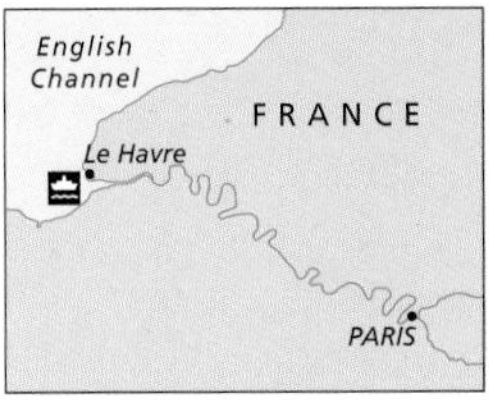

DISTANCE FROM PORT

200 km (125 miles) from city centre.

Musée du Louvre ⑨
The celebrated Greek *Winged Victory of Samothrace*, dating from around 200 BC, is among the Louvre's fabulous collection of antiquities.

Pompidou Centre ⑪
A riotous jumble of glass and steel, this gallery of 20th-century and contemporary art is Paris' top tourist attraction.

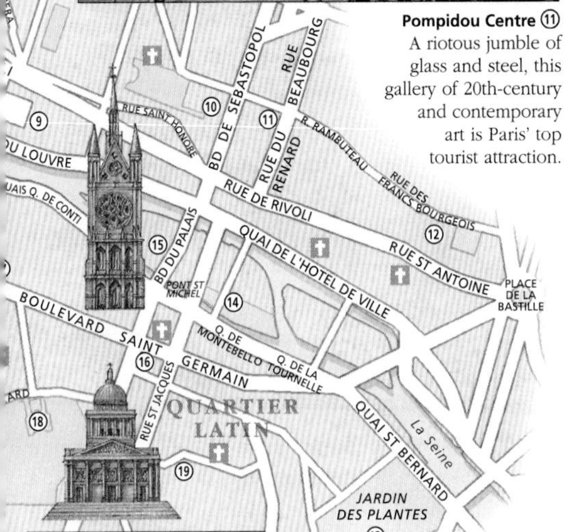

Notre-Dame ⑭
Notable among the features of the west façade are the rose window and the left-hand Portal of the Virgin, with its 13th-century statues.

KEY SIGHTS

① Sacré-Coeur
② Opéra de Paris Garnier
③ Champs-Elysées ★
④ Eiffel Tower ★
(see p147)
⑤ Invalides
⑥ Musée Rodin
⑦ Musée d'Orsay ★
⑧ Jardin des Tuileries
⑨ Musée du Louvre ★
(see pp144–6)
⑩ Forum des Halles
⑪ Pompidou Centre
⑫ Le Marais
⑬ Jardin des Plantes Quarter
⑭ Notre-Dame ★
⑮ Sainte-Chapelle
⑯ Musée National du Moyen Âge
⑰ St-Germain-des-Prés
⑱ Palais du Luxembourg
⑲ Panthéon
⑳ Cimetière du Montparnasse

FACT FILE

TOURIST INFORMATION

Main Tourist Office: 25 Rue Pyramides, 75001.

MARKET

Flowers Place de la Madeleine; Mon–Sat. **Food** Rue de Buci and Rue de Bretagne; Mon–Sat & Sun am.

SHOPPING

Prêt-à-porter fashion Boulevard St Germain and Rue du Four.
Quality jewellery Boucheron, Cartier, Daniel Swarowski, Mauboussin, Harry Winston and couture houses.
Porcelain & crystal Rue du Paradis.

LOCAL SPECIALITIES

Dishes
Homard persillé (lobster terrine).
Drinks
Sirops à l'eau (flavoured syrups).

EXCURSIONS

Versailles 10 km (6 miles) W of Paris. Colossal palace of Louis XIV.
Disneyland Paris 32 km (20 miles) E of Paris. Family theme park.

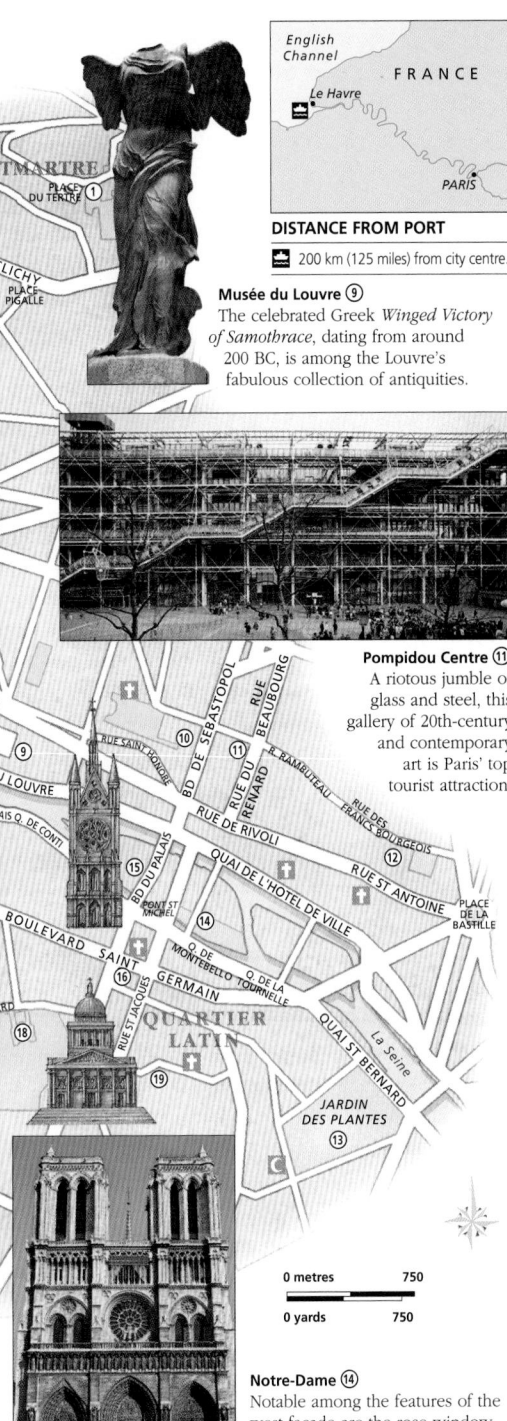

Exploring Paris

The historic heart of the city, with the great Gothic sights of Notre-Dame and the Sainte-Chapelle, is the Ile de la Cité between the Seine's left and right banks. On the *Rive Droite* (right bank) is Le Marais, a fascinating area of mansions, fashionable galleries, boutiques and the Place des Vosges, the city's loveliest square. Close by are the modern Pompidou and Les Halles complexes, crowded with art lovers and shoppers. Further west is the Louvre and luxury shopping around Avenue Montaigne and Rue du Faubourg St Honoré.

The *Rive Gauche* (left bank) has the café-filled Latin Quarter, the monumental Invalides area and the Eiffel Tower.

Montmartre, the historic artists' area to the north, still retains a village atmosphere.

Crowds flocking to the shops, cafés and cinemas of the Champs-Elysées

Sacré-Coeur ①

This Neo-Romanesque church stands at the top of the hill of Montmartre, its huge dome and bell tower dominating the area's tiny squares and winding streets. In 1870, at the outbreak of the Franco-Prussian war, businessmen Alexandre Legentil and Rohault de Fleury vowed to build a basilica to the Sacred Heart of Christ if Paris were saved from invasion. Paris did survive a long siege, and building work on a great church began to a design by Paul Abadie in 1875.

The result has never been considered particularly graceful, but the basilica is vast and impressive. The tower contains an 18.5-tonne bell, one of the heaviest in the world. The Byzantine-style mosaic of Christ, of 1912 to 1922, in the chancel is by Luc Olivier Merson. The bronze portico doors depict scenes of the life of Christ.

Opéra de Paris Garnier ②

Sometimes compared to a giant wedding cake, this extravagant building was designed in 1862 by Charles Garnier for Napoleon III. The Prussian War and the 1871 uprising delayed the opening until 1875.

The interior is famous for the Grand Staircase made of white Carrara marble with a balustrade of red and green marble. It is lit by a huge chandelier and rises to the Grand Foyer, which has a mosaic-encrusted ceiling. The five-tiered auditorium is a riot of gold leaf, red velvet and plaster cherubs, with a ceiling painted by Marc Chagall in 1964. Though operatic productions are now shared with the Opéra de Paris Bastille, the Opéra Garnier is still the home of ballet in Paris.

The Opéra Garnier, a mix of styles from Neo-Classical to Neo-Baroque

Champs-Elysées ③

Paris's most famous thoroughfare was laid out in 1667 by Louis XIV's landscape gardener, André Le Nôtre. He extended the royal view from the Tuileries by creating a tree-lined avenue. It was named The Elysian Fields and has been France's "triumphal way" since the homecoming of Napoleon's body from St Helena in 1840. The later addition of cafés and restaurants transformed it into a world-famous boulevard.

At the western end is the Arc de Triomphe, built after Napoleon's victory in 1805 at the Battle of Austerlitz. The top of the arch offers a fine view of the 12 radiating boulevards by Baron Haussmann *(see p140)*. Beneath it is the Tomb of the Unknown Soldier. At the eastern end of the Champs-Elysées are formal gardens and two exhibition halls built in 1900: the Grand Palais and the Petit Palais, with city art collections.

Le déjeuner sur l'herbe (1863) by Edouard Manet at the Musée d'Orsay

Eiffel Tower ④
See p147.

Invalides ⑤
The imposing Hôtel des Invalides, designed by Libéral Bruand, was built in the 1670s by Louis XIV to house 6,000 wounded and homeless veterans. At its centre lies the huge, golden-roofed Dôme Church designed by Jules Hardouin-Mansart as the king's private chapel. It later became a French military memorial after Napoleon's remains were brought to the crypt in 1861. The soldiers' church is the starkly Classical St-Louis-des-Invalides, also by Bruand. Ongoing refurbishment may mean sections are closed.

The Hôtel houses the Musée de l'Armée, one of the most comprehensive museums of military history in the world, and the Musée de l'Ordre de la Libération, devoted to the Free French of World War II.

Musée Rodin ⑥
Auguste Rodin (1840–1917), regarded as one of the greatest French sculptors, lived and worked in this building, the Hôtel Biron, from 1908 until his death. In return for his state-owned apartment and studio, he left his work to the nation and it is now exhibited here.

Some of Rodin's most celebrated sculptures are on view in the beautiful rose garden: *The Burghers of Calais, The Thinker, The Gates of Hell* and *Balzac*. The indoor exhibits span Rodin's entire career. Highlights include *The Kiss* and *Eve*.

The Thinker (c.1880) by Rodin

Musée d'Orsay ⑦
Victor Laloux's superb mainline railway station was designed for the 1900 Universal Exhibition. In 1986, 47 years after it had closed as a station, it reopened as a museum. It shows the rich diversity of visual art from 1848 to 1914 and explains the era's social, political and technological context, including the history of cinematography. The ground floor has works to 1870, with styles such as Neo-Classical (Ingres's *La Source*), Romantic (Delacroix's *Tiger Hunt*) and Realist (Manet's *Le déjeuner sur l'herbe*). The central aisle has sculpture illustrating the eclecticism of the mid-19th century. The middle level features Art Nouveau, decorative arts and architecture. Among the Impressionist paintings on the top floor are Monet's *Rouen Cathedral* and Renoir's *Dancing at the Moulin de la Galette*. Post-Impressionist art includes Van Gogh's *Eglise d'Auvers*, Seurat's pointillist *Le Cirque*, Gauguin's colourful Symbolist work and Toulouse-Lautrec's depictions of Parisian women. Matisse's *Luxe, Calme et Volupté* is a highlight of the post-1900 display.

Jardin des Tuileries ⑧
These formal gardens once belonged to the old Palais des Tuileries, which was destroyed by Communard rebels in 1871. They are Paris's oldest public gardens, created by Catherine de Médicis in the 16th century and laid out in Classical style in the 17th by André Le Nôtre. His formal avenues, terraces and topiary were later softened with lime and chestnut trees. At the eastern end, in the adjoining Jardin du Carrousel *(see p144)*, are bronze nudes by Aristide Maillol (1861–1944).

The gardens' western end is formed by the huge Place de la Concorde. It was laid out in 1763 and was the site of the guillotine during the French Revolution. The 3,300-year-old obelisk is from the Temple of Rameses II in Luxor.

Musée du Louvre ⑨
See pp144–6.

Forum des Halles ⑩
This modern complex, known more simply as Les Halles, was built in 1979, amid much controversy, on the site of Paris's former meat, fruit and vegetable market. The present underground levels 2 and 3 are occupied by an array of shops, from small boutiques to megastores. Above ground there are well-tended gardens, pergolas and mini-pavilions. Also outside are the palm-shaped, glass-and-metal buildings that house the Pavillon des Arts and Maison de la Poésie, cultural centres for contemporary art and poetry.

Paris: Musée du Louvre ⑨

The Musée du Louvre, containing one of the most important art collections in the world, has a history dating back to medieval times. It was first built as a fortress in 1190 by King Philippe-Auguste to protect Paris against Viking raids. The base of two towers can be seen in underground excavations. François I initiated its transformation into a Renaissance palace in 1527 and four more centuries of kings and emperors improved and enlarged it. The Arc de Triomphe du Carrousel celebrates Napoleon's victories in 1805. Owing to the vast size of the Louvre's collection, it is useful to set a few viewing priorities before starting.

Arc de Triomphe du Carrousel completed in 180

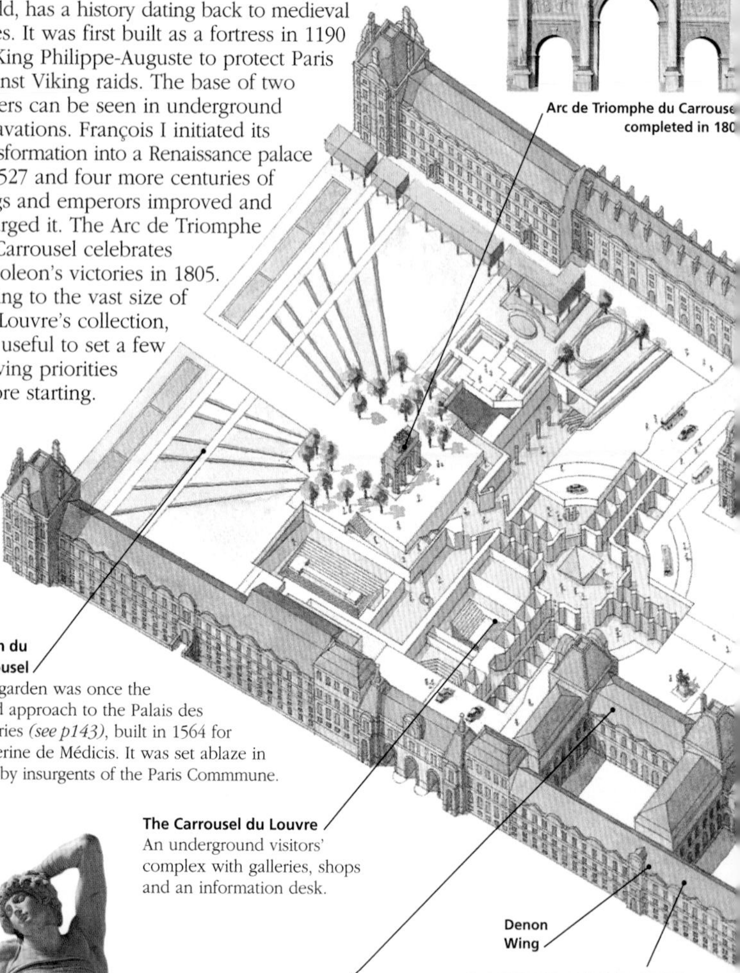

Jardin du Carrousel
This garden was once the grand approach to the Palais des Tuileries *(see p143)*, built in 1564 for Catherine de Médicis. It was set ablaze in 1871 by insurgents of the Paris Commmune.

The Carrousel du Louvre
An underground visitors' complex with galleries, shops and an information desk.

Denon Wing

Dying Slave
Michelangelo sculpted this work between 1513 and 1520 as part of a group of statues for the base of the tomb of Pope Julius II (1503–13) in Rome. The statue was given instead to Henri II in 1550.

★ Mona Lisa
Leonardo da Vinci painted this small portrait of a Florentine noblewoman in about 1504. In 1515 he brought it with him to France, where he lived for three years until his death. It was regarded as the prototype of the Renaissance portrait.

The Lacemaker
In this exquisite work painted in about 1665, Jan Vermeer gives viewers a glimpse of everyday domestic life in Holland.

STAR FEATURES

- ★ Mona Lisa
- ★ Pyramid Entrance
- ★ Venus de Milo

Cour Marly
This glass-roofed area protects the famous sculptures of wild horses by Guillaume Coustou. They were made for Louis XIV's palace of Marly in 1745. In 1795, they were moved to the Place de la Concorde, where replicas now stand.

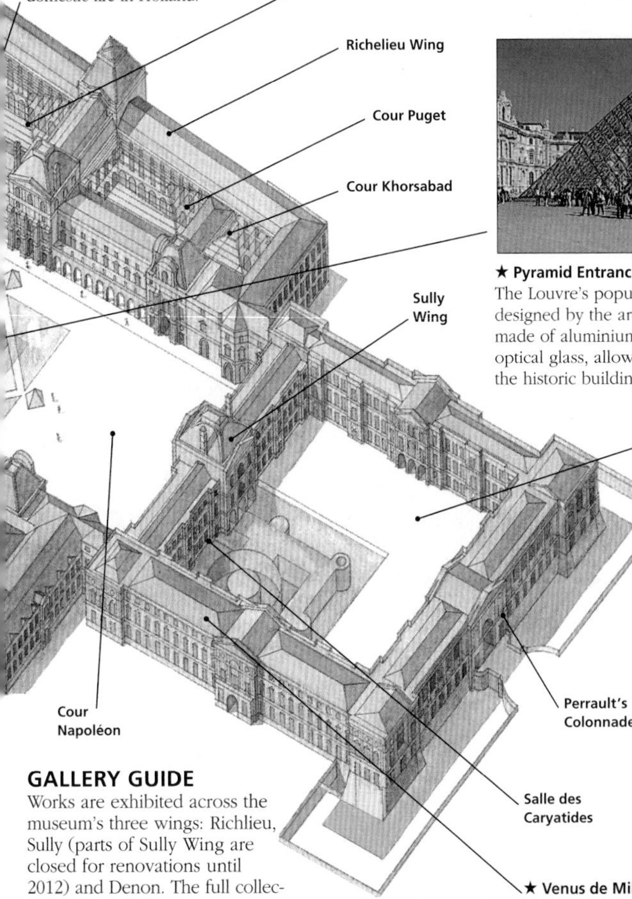

★ Pyramid Entrance
The Louvre's popular main entrance, designed by the architect I M Pei, is made of aluminium and low-reflection optical glass, allowing visitors to see the historic buildings through it.

GALLERY GUIDE

Works are exhibited across the museum's three wings: Richlieu, Sully (parts of Sully Wing are closed for renovations until 2012) and Denon. The full collection of European paintings (1400–1848) is mostly by French artists. The Oriental, Egyptian, Greek, Etruscan and Roman departments feature many new acquisitions and rare treasures.

★ Venus de Milo
Found in 1820 on the Greek island of Mílos, this ideal of feminine beauty was made in the Hellenistic Age at the end of the 2nd century BC. A plinth found with her was inscribed "Andros of Antioch on the Menander", an otherwise unknown artist.

Paris: Exploring the Louvre

The galleries are best approached from the main reception area under the Glass Pyramid. From here, corridors radiate out to each of the wings of the museum. Paintings and sculpture are arranged by country of origin; the 8,000 *objets d'art* are mainly organized thematically.

The Fortune Teller (c.1594) by Caravaggio

EUROPEAN PAINTING: 1200 TO 1850

Outstanding in the French section is the 1455 *Villeneuve-les-Avignon Pietà* by Enguerrand Quarton and works by 18th-century masters of melancholy, Watteau, and of frivolity, J H Fragonard. Dutch Flemish, German and English painting is well represented and includes Van Eyck's *Madonna of the Chancellor Rolin* (c. 1435). Other highlights are Bosch's satirical *Ship of Fools* (1500) and Dürer's *Self-portrait* (1493). Among the 1200–1800 Italian collection are works by early masters such as Giotto, Cimabue and Fra Angelico, as well as several works by Leonardo da Vinci and Caravaggio.

EUROPEAN SCULPTURE: 1100 TO 1850

There are many early Flemish and German masterpieces to admire, such as Tilman Riemenschneider's *Virgin of the Annunciation* (late 15th-century) and Adrian de Vries's long-limbed *Mercury and Psyche* of 1593, made for Rudoph II in Prague. Among French Romanesque works is the unusual tomb of the Burgundian official Philippe Pot with eight hooded mourners. Works by French sculptor Pierre Puget (1620–94) stand in the Cour Puget and include his *Milo of Crotona*, the Greek athlete who was caught in a cleft in a tree stump and eaten by a lion. The celebrated wild horses of Marly *(see p145)* stand among other French masterpieces, such as Jean Antoine Houdon's 19th-century busts of famous men.

Italian sculpture includes splendid exhibits such as Michelangelo's *Slaves* and Benvenuto Cellini's *Nymph*.

ORIENTAL, EGYPTIAN, GREEK, ETRUSCAN AND ROMAN ANTIQUITIES

The Louvre's collection of antiquities ranges from the Neolithic era to the fall of the Roman Empire. Mesopotamian art includes one of the world's oldest legal documents: a black basalt block bearing the code of Babylonia's King Hammurabi, dated about 1700 BC. There is an impressive reconstruction of part of the palace of the Assyrian king, Sargon II (722–705 BC), and a large Egyptian section. A special crypt is dedicated to the god Osiris.

The collection of Greek and Roman fragments is vast. These include the famous *Venus de Milo (see p145)* and *Winged Victory of Samothrace (see p141)*. There is an interesting display of Greek and Roman glassware of the 6th century BC. Also of note are a Roman bronze head of the emperor Hadrian and an Etruscan terracotta sarcophagus of a couple seated as if at a feast.

Tomb of Philippe Pot by Antoine le Moiturier

OBJETS D'ART

This eclectic section displays precious items such as silver, jewellery, clocks, watches, snuffboxes, carved ivory and Limoges enamel. Decorative objects include glassware, porcelain, majolica, tapestries and furniture. There are also scientific instruments and armour.

Treasures from the Abbey of St Denis, where French kings were crowned, include a 1st-century serpentine plate with a 9th-century border of gold and precious stones. The French Crown Jewels include the coronation crowns of Louis XV and Napoleon. The Régent, one of the most celebrated diamonds in existence, was worn by Louis XV at his coronation in 1715.

The *Hunts of Maximilian* are a remarkable series of tapestries made in 1530 for Emperor Charles V. The large collection of French furniture is displayed by period or in rooms devoted to distinguished donations. There are pieces, for example, by André-Charles Boulle, cabinet-maker to Louis XIV.

Paris: Eiffel Tower ④

The Eiffel Tower from the Trocadero

Built to impress visitors to the Universal Exhibition of 1889, the Eiffel Tower (Tour Eiffel) was intended as a temporary addition to the Paris skyline. Designed by Gustave Eiffel, it was fiercely decried by 19th-century aesthetes – the author Guy de Maupassant lunched there so that he did not have to see it. It was the world's tallest building until 1931, when New York's Empire State building was completed.

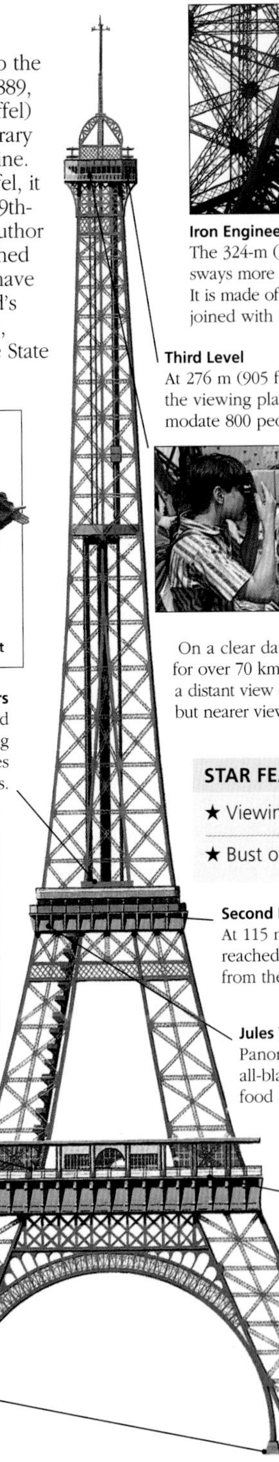

Iron Engineering
The 324-m (1,063-ft) tower never sways more than 7 cm (3 inches). It is made of 15,000 pig-iron struts joined with 2.5 million rivets.

Third Level
At 276 m (905 ft) above the ground, the viewing platform can accommodate 800 people at a time.

★ Viewing Gallery
On a clear day it is possible to see for over 70 km (43 miles), including a distant view of Chartres Cathedral, but nearer views are just as thrilling.

DARING FEATS

The tower has inspired many crazy stunts. It has been climbed by mountaineers, cycled down by a journalist and, in 1912, a Parisian tailor named Reichelt attempted to fly from it in a cape – with fatal results.

Stuntman Reichelt

Double-decker Elevators
In busy periods the elevators' limited capacity means that there can be long waits. Queuing for the lifts requires patience and a good head for heights.

STAR FEATURES

★ Viewing Gallery

★ Bust of Eiffel

Second Level
At 115 m (376 ft), this is reached by lift or 359 steps from the first level.

Cineiffel
This small audio-visual museum tells the history of the tower through a short film. It includes footage of famous people's visits.

Jules Verne Restaurant
Panoramic views, sleek all-black decor and superb food reward diners here, in one of the best restaurants in Paris.

★ Bust of Gustave Eiffel
This honorific bust by Antoine Bourdelle was placed under the tower in 1929. Eiffel had also been honoured in 1889 with the Légion d'Honneur.

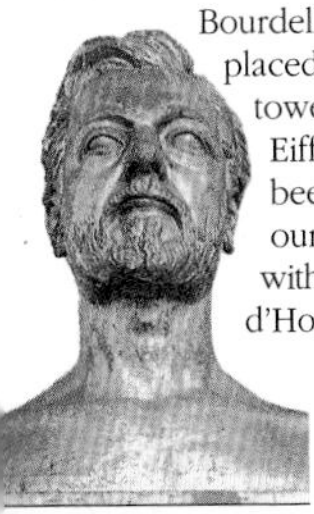

First Level
At 57 m (187 ft) high, this can be reached by lift or by climbing the 360 steps. There is a post office here.

Gargoyles on Notre-Dame's Galerie des Chimères, which runs across the top ledge of the cathedral's façade, just below the twin towers

Pompidou Centre ⑪
The Pompidou, which opened in 1977, is in effect a building turned inside out: the massive steel struts that make up its skeleton and the service ducts are all on the outside. Air-conditioning ducts are blue, water green, electricty yellow and those through which people move (such as escalator shafts) are red. The idea of architects Richard Rogers, Renzo Piano and Gianfranco Franchini was to show the public how a building works.

Permanent exhibits represent schools such as Fauvism, Cubism and Surrealism, including works by Matisse, Picasso, Chagall, Miró and Pollock, as well as many contemporary artists. The Atelier Brancusi recreates the workshop of Paris based Romanian artist Constantin Brancusi (1876–1957).

Le Marais ⑫
Once a marsh *(marais)*, this district saw its heyday in the 17th century, when fashionable society built sumptuous *hôtels* (mansions) here. Its most famous square is the beautiful Place des Vosges, with Victor Hugo's home at No. 6. The area was declared a national monument in 1962 and many buildings have been restored, some as museums. The Musée Picasso, home of the world's largest collection of his works, was the palatial home of a salt-tax collector. The vast Musée Carnavalet is devoted to the history of Paris, with the *objets d'art* set in rich, period rooms. Close by is the high-tech, 1989 Opéra de Paris Bastille.

Jardin des Plantes Quarter ⑬
This was once a quiet area containing monastic gardens and Louis XIII's medicinal herb garden. The latter, planted in 1626, was opened to the public in 1640 as the Jardin des Plantes and, under the direction of the great naturalist Buffon (1707–88), became a leading botanical garden. It has a remarkable alpine collection.

Paris's Roman past is evident nearby in the ruins of the 2nd-century AD Arènes de Lutèce amphitheatre. Rue Mouffetard was a major Roman street; today it has several street markets and many of its present buildings are 17th- and 18th-century, some shops still have very old painted signs. Also close by is the Manufacture des Gobelins, the still-functioning, 17th-century tapestry factory, and the Institut du Monde Arabe showing Arab decorative arts in a stunning, modern building.

Place des Vosges in the Marais – elegant in its perfect symmetry

Notre-Dame ⑭
This majestic, Gothic cathedral on the Ile de la Cité stands on the site of a Roman temple. The first stone was laid in 1163 by Pope Alexander III. When the building was completed in 1330, it was 130 m (430 ft) long and featured spectacular flying buttresses. The south tower holds the famous Emmanuel bell, and the 387 steps of the north tower can be climbed for a view of the famed gargoyles.

During the Revolution, Notre-Dame was ransacked, renamed the Temple of Reason, then used as a wine store. In 1804 Napoleon restored religion and had himself crowned Emperor here. Restoration was begun in 1841 by Viollet le Duc, who added the spire and gargoyles. Treasures inside include the statue of the Virgin and Child known as Our Lady of Paris, and the polychrome chancel screen, both 14th-century, and Nicolas Coustou's *Pietà* of 1723 behind the high altar.

Sainte-Chapelle ⑮
Ethereal and magical, this chapel is a unique architectural masterpiece. It was built in 1248 by Louis IX to hold relics, including Christ's purported Crown of Thorns. The windows of the king and courtier's upper chapel portray more than 1,000 biblical scenes in a kaleidoscope of red, gold, blue and green. The great rose window of 1485 illustrates the the Apocalypse. The sombre but richly-coloured lower chapel was for commoners.

Musée National du Moyen Âge ⑯

This museum offers a combination of Gallo-Roman ruins incorporated into a mansion completed in 1498 for the Abbot of Cluny in Burgundy. It has a superlative collection of medieval art. Highlights include the Golden Rose of Basel made by goldsmith Minucchio da Siena in 1330 for Pope John XXII. The Gallery of Kings displays 28 stone heads of the Kings of Judah carved in 1220. Visitors can also see the six celebrated *Lady and the Unicorn* tapestries woven in *millefleurs* style in the late 15th century.

St-Germain-des-Prés ⑰

Originating in 542 as a basilica to shelter holy relics, this is the oldest church in Paris. Rebuilt, it became a Benedictine abbey in the 11th century, but burned down in 1794. One of the three original towers survived, and the rest of the church was restored in the 19th century. The interior styles are an interesting juxtaposition of 6th-century marble columns, Romanesque arches and Gothic vaulting. Famous tombs here include that of the 17th-century philosopher René Descartes.

Palais du Luxembourg ⑱

Now the home of the French Senate, this palace was built for Marie de Médicis, widow of Henri IV. It was designed by Salomon de Brosse in the style of the Palazzo Pitti *(see p222)* in her native Florence. When it was finished in 1631, Marie had been banished from Paris, but it remained a royal palace until the Revolution. It was a prison briefly and, in World War II, a Luftwaffe headquarters. The Musée du Luxembourg in the east wing is closed until 2012.

Jardin du Luxembourg – the gardens of the adjacent palace

Panthéon ⑲

Grateful to have survived a serious illness in 1744, Louis XV had architect Jacques-Germain Soufflot design a great church to honour St Geneviève, patron saint of Paris. The façade was inspired by the Pantheon in Rome *(see p239)*. The building was completed in 1790 during the Revolution and redesignated to hold the tombs of France's heroes. Napoleon returned it to the Church in 1806 and commissioned the dome's fresco *The Glorification of St Geneviève*. However, it was reconfirmed as a civic pantheon in 1885. In the crypt are the tombs of Voltaire, Zola and Rousseau, among others.

Cimetière du Montparnasse ⑳

Napoleon planned this cemetery outside the city walls to replace the congested ones inside Paris. It opened in 1824. Among the famous at rest here are Simone de Beauvoir, Jean-Paul Sartre, Jean Seberg, Man Ray, Charles Baudelaire, and Samuel Beckett. There are many fine sculptures, some by artists buried here. The central statue is Horace Daillion's *Angel of Eternal Sleep* (1902).

THE PALACE OF VERSAILLES

The present palace, started by Louis XIV in 1668, grew around Louis XIII's hunting lodge. Architect Louis Le Vau built the first section, arranging his buildings around what is now called the Marble Courtyard. From 1678, Jules Hardouin-Mansart added huge, new wings and the famous Hall of Mirrors, as well as the Royal Chapel, with its distinctive Baroque murals. Charles Le Brun designed the state apartments and André Le Nôtre the gardens. Versailles was by then the largest palace in Europe, capable of housing 20,000 people. The Opera House was completed in 1770, in time for the marriage of the future Louis XVI and Marie-Antoinette. Once in residence, Marie-Antoinette favoured the Petit Trianon, a small château in the grounds, and a series of thatched cottages there, built to allow her to play-act the life of a shepherdess.

One of the many pools in Versailles' magnificent formal gardens, overlooked by the state apartments

Cherbourg

Calvados apple brandy

Cherbourg has been a port and naval base since the mid-19th century and its harbours are still used by the French navy. Place Général de Gaulle in the town centre is a ten-minute walk from the port. From here it is a short stroll to the Parc Emmanuel Liais, home of an attractive botanical garden and the Musée d'Histoire Naturelle. Fort du Roule, built in 1854 and situated on a hilltop above the town, can only be reached on foot and is about twenty minutes walk. Its Musée de la Libération documents the D-Day invasion and France's liberation from German occupation. The D-Day landing beaches are east of Cherbourg.

Cherbourg Town Centre
Activity is focused on the flower-filled market square and surrounding streets. The Musée Thomas-Henry houses a collection of fine art, including some 17th-century Flemish works. There are also portraits by Jean-François Millet (1814–75), who is more famously known, however, for his rustic landscapes. Millet was born in the neighbouring village of Gréville-Hague.

Rugged cliffs west of Cherbourg on the Cotentin Peninsula

D-Day Landing Beaches
East of Cherbourg are the beaches used for the D-Day landings of World War II, the Allied invasion of occupied France that began in the early hours of 6 June 1944. British, Canadian and Free French troops landed on Gold, Juno and Sword beaches and US troops on Utah and Omaha beaches. The remnants of Mulberry Harbour, the floating harbour towed across from England onto which supplies were unloaded, can be seen at Arromanches-les-Bains.

The remains of Mulberry Harbour used by Allied forces in World War II

KEY SIGHTS

Fort du Roule and Musée de la Libération ★

Musée Thomas-Henry

Parc Emmanuel Liais

FACT FILE

TOURIST INFORMATION

2 quai Alexandre III. ***Tel*** *(02) 33 93 52 02.* ☐ *Mon–Sat to 6pm (Jun–Sep: to 6:30pm; Jul & Aug: Sun to 12:30pm).*

MARKETS

Food & clothes Place Général de Gaulle; Thu to 3pm.

LOCAL SPECIALITIES

Crafts
Lace, pottery, umbrellas.
Dishes
Camembert and *Pont l'Evèque* (creamy cheeses).
Livarot (a pungent cheese).
Fruits de mer (varied seafood).
Rillettes (a paste of pork or goose seasoned with herbs).
Tarte tatin (caramelized apple tart).
Drinks
Jus de pomme (apple juice). *Cidre* (cider). *Calvados* (apple brandy). *Benedictine* (herbal liqueur).

EXCURSIONS

Cotentin Peninsula Just W of Cherbourg. Impressive cliff scenery.
D-Day Landing Beaches 50 km (30 miles) E of Cherbourg. British, US and German war cemeteries.
Bayeux 78 km (47 miles) SE of Cherbourg. Cathedral city. Home of the 11th-century Bayeux Tapestry.

Bordeaux

Sited near the mouth of the River Garonne, Bordeaux has exported wine since Roman times, but it was under English rule (1154–1453) that merchants began making huge fortunes from wine sales to England. Along the city's waterfront are grand Classical façades and the Esplanade des Quinconces, a vast, leafy space with fountains and statues created in the mid-19th century. Just east of the Esplanade is the CAPC, a gallery of modern art in a renovated warehouse. Bordeaux's liveliest area is around the Cours de l'Intendance, Allées de Tourny and Cours Clémenceau, full of fashionable shops and cafés, while the adjacent Rue Ste-Catherine is the main shopping street. Other sights include the Cathédrale St-André, Basilique St-Michel, with a huge hexagonal belfry, and the Musée des Beaux Arts, which has fine paintings.

Grand Théâtre
Built between 1773 and 1780 by Victor Louis, this theatre is a masterpiece of Neo-Classical style, crowned by 12 statues of the muses. The auditorium is renowned for its extraordinary acoustics. The main staircase was later imitated by Garnier for his Paris Opéra *(see p142)*.

Porte de la Grosse Cloche
Spanning the Cours Victor Hugo on the western edge of old Bordeaux, between the cathedral and the river, is this city gate. It was built between the 13th and 15th centuries and contains a clock dating from 1759 with a great bell. Further up the street is the Musée d'Aquitaine, which illustrates the region's history.

KEY SIGHTS

Basilique St-Michel
CAPC
Cathédrale St-André
Esplanade des Quinconces ★
Grand Théâtre ★
Musée d'Aquitaine
Musée des Beaux Arts
Place de la Bourse
Porte de la Grosse Cloche

FACT FILE

TOURIST INFORMATION

12 Cours du 30 juillet. ***Tel*** *(05) 56 00 66 00.* ◯ *summer: Mon–Sat to 7pm (Jul & Aug to 7:30pm), Sun to 6:30pm; winter: Mon–Sat to 6:30pm, Sun to 4:30pm.*

MARKETS

Food Pl des Capucins; Tue–Sun am.

LOCAL SPECIALITIES

Crafts
Wine paraphernalia, porcelain.
Produce
Fine wines. The main wine regions of Bordeaux are: *Barsac, Blaye, Bourg, Cérons, Graves, Médoc, Pessac-Léognan, Pomerol, St Emilion, Sauternes, Entre-Deux-Mers.*
Dishes
Huîtres (oysters).
Entrecôte à la bordelaise (grilled steak with red wine sauce).
Canelés (sweet griddled pastries).

EXCURSIONS

Wine châteaux Many can be visited for tasting and buying. Call the Tourist Office for information.

Place de la Bourse, an elegant 18th-century square, open on one side to the River Garonne

The Wines of France

Picker's hod

Winemaking in France dates back to the Iron Age, although it was the Romans who disseminated the culture of the vine and the practice of winemaking throughout the country. The range, quality and reputation of the fine wines of Bordeaux, Burgundy, the Rhône and Champagne in particular have made them role models the world over. France's everyday wines can be highly enjoyable, too, with plenty of good-value wines now emerging from the southern regions, including much-improved Provençal rosés.

Traditional vineyard cultivation

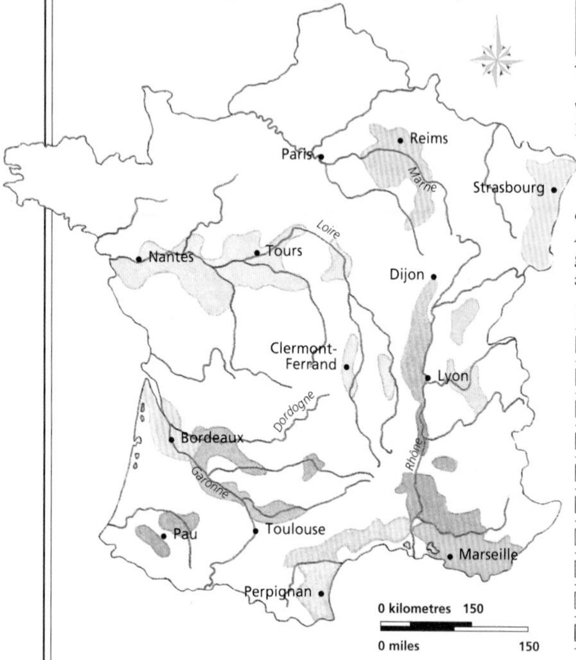

Wine Regions
Each of the 10 principal wine-producing regions has its own identity, based on grape varieties, climate and *terroir* (land). *Appellation contrôlée* laws guarantee a wine's origins and production methods.

KEY

- Bordeaux
- Burgundy
- Champagne
- Alsace
- Loire
- Provence
- Jura and Savoie
- The Southwest
- Languedoc-Roussillon
- Rhône

HOW TO READ A WINE LABEL

Even the simplest label will identify the wine and provide a key to its quality. It will bear the name of the wine and its producer, its vintage, if there is one, and whether it comes from a strictly defined area *(appellation contrôlée* or *VDQS)* or is a more general *vin de pays* or *vin de table*. It may also have a regional grading, as with the *crus classés* in Bordeaux. The shape and colour of the bottle is also a guide to the kind of wine it contains. Green glass is often used since this helps to protect the wine from light.

The property or producer

Château-bottled, rather than a blend from a merchant or grower's co-operative.

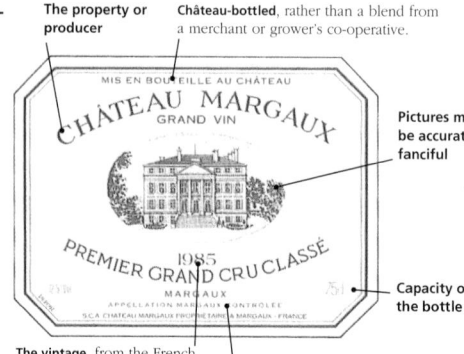

Pictures may be accurate or fanciful

Capacity of the bottle

The vintage, from the French word *vendange*, or harvest.

The wine's *appellation contrôlée*

HOW WINE IS MADE

Wine is the product of the juice of freshly picked grapes, after natural or cultured yeasts have converted the grape sugars into alcohol during the fermentation process. The yeasts, or lees, are normally filtered out before bottling.

Old wine press

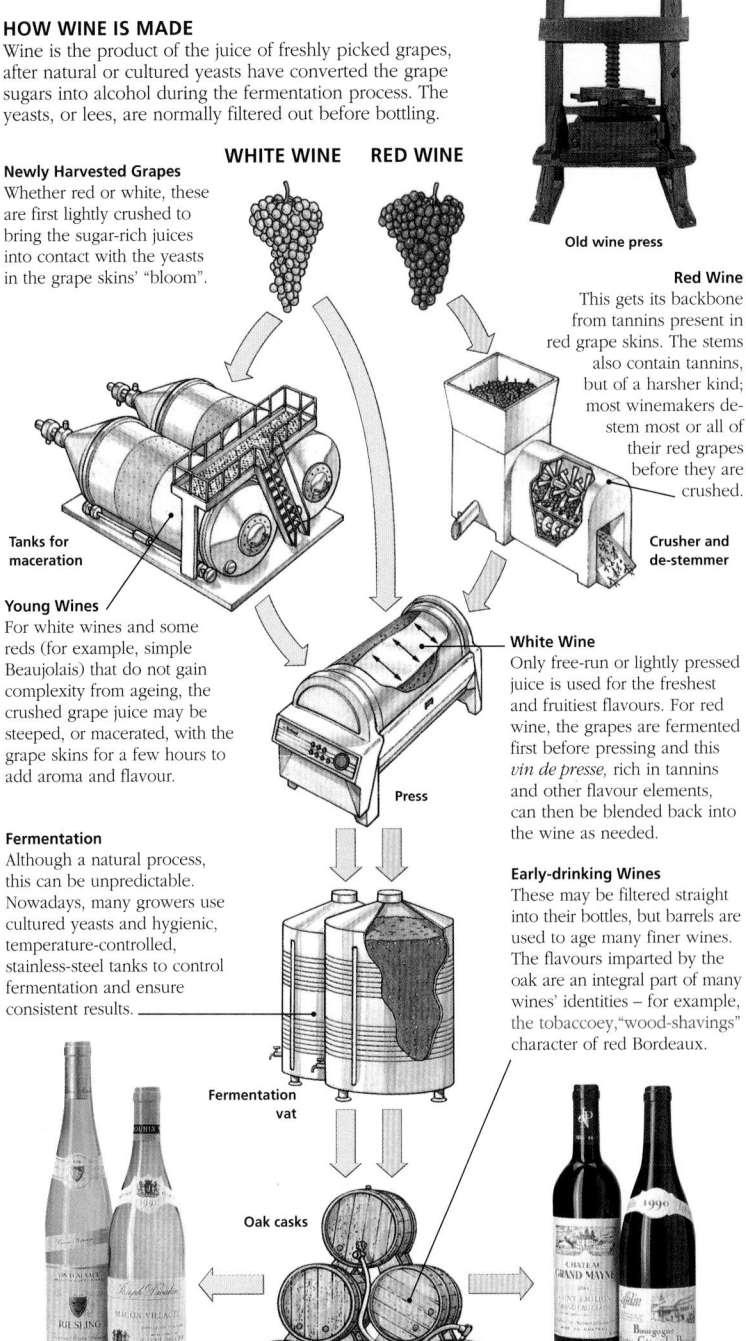

WHITE WINE **RED WINE**

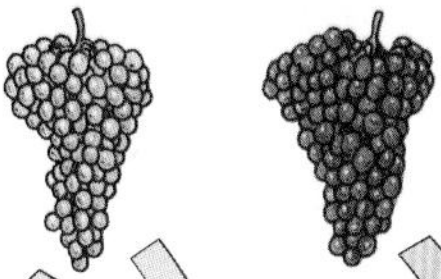

Newly Harvested Grapes
Whether red or white, these are first lightly crushed to bring the sugar-rich juices into contact with the yeasts in the grape skins' "bloom".

Red Wine
This gets its backbone from tannins present in red grape skins. The stems also contain tannins, but of a harsher kind; most winemakers de-stem most or all of their red grapes before they are crushed.

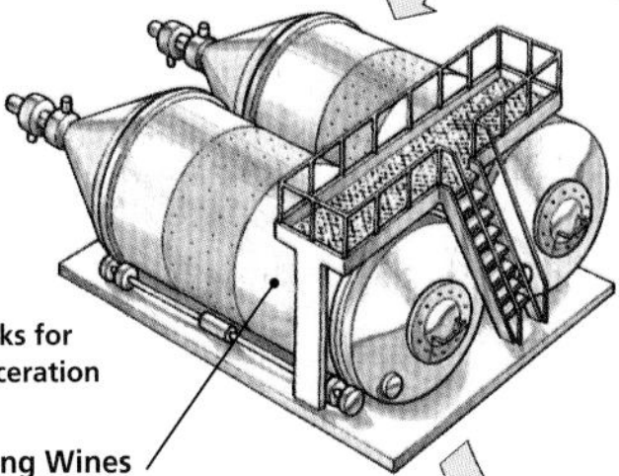

Tanks for maceration

Crusher and de-stemmer

Young Wines
For white wines and some reds (for example, simple Beaujolais) that do not gain complexity from ageing, the crushed grape juice may be steeped, or macerated, with the grape skins for a few hours to add aroma and flavour.

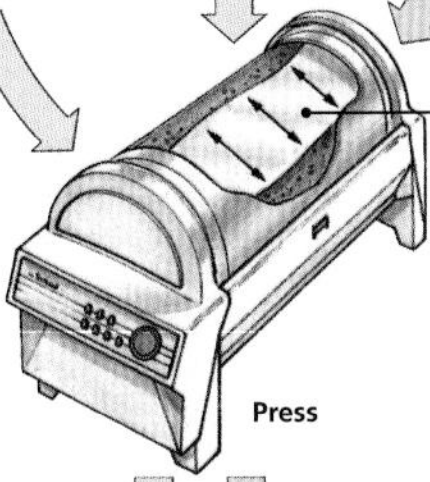

Press

White Wine
Only free-run or lightly pressed juice is used for the freshest and fruitiest flavours. For red wine, the grapes are fermented first before pressing and this *vin de presse,* rich in tannins and other flavour elements, can then be blended back into the wine as needed.

Fermentation
Although a natural process, this can be unpredictable. Nowadays, many growers use cultured yeasts and hygienic, temperature-controlled, stainless-steel tanks to control fermentation and ensure consistent results.

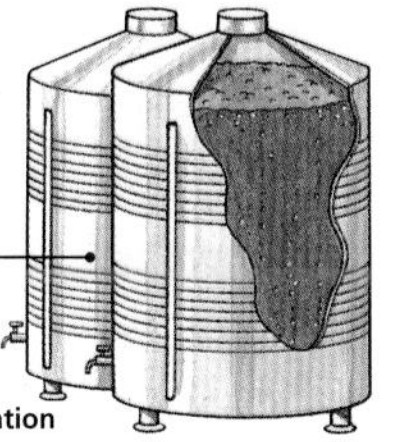

Fermentation vat

Early-drinking Wines
These may be filtered straight into their bottles, but barrels are used to age many finer wines. The flavours imparted by the oak are an integral part of many wines' identities – for example, the tobaccoey,"wood-shavings" character of red Bordeaux.

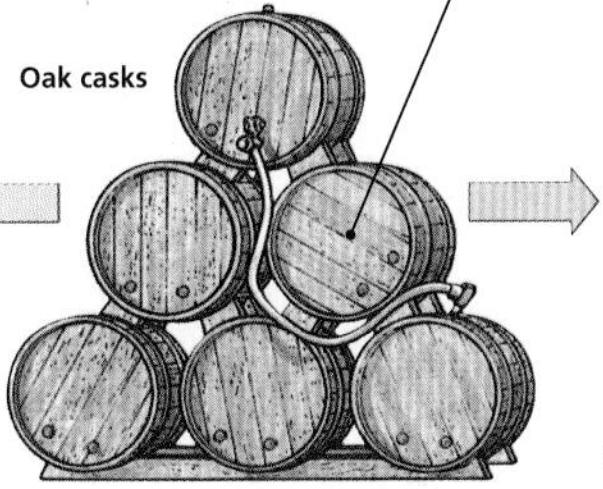

Oak casks

Different shades of glass identify the wine regions

Bottle shapes typical of red Bordeaux (left) and Burgundy

Marseille

Marseille is France's largest commercial and naval port and its oldest major city, founded by the Greeks in 600 BC. It became a focus for Oriental trade and its mix of cultures was so varied that author Alexandre Dumas called it "the meeting place of the entire world". At its centre are the Vieux Port and the old town, full of quiet squares, stepped streets and 18th-century houses. In contrast, leading away from the port is the bustling boulevard of La Canebière. Among the city's churches is the Neo-Byzantine Cathédrale de la Major of 1893. Its finest building is the Vieille Charité hospice of 1694 and its most elegant house (1873) is now the Musée Grobet-Labadié.

Vieux Port
The Old Harbour lies to the south of the commercial docks and between the guardian forts of St-Jean (1447 and 1664) and St-Nicolas (1665). High above it, with superb views of the city, is Notre-Dame-de-la-Garde, another 19th-century Neo-Byzantine extravaganza. It is presided over by a golden Madonna on top of the bell tower.

Basilique St-Victor
Marseille's most impressive religious building is this fortified abbey church founded in the 5th century and rebuilt between the 11th and 14th. It has a warren of crypts, some of them dating from the 5th century. Here were found pagan and early Christian sarcophagi, including that of St Victor, who was martyred in the 3rd century.

KEY SIGHTS

- Basilique St-Victor ★
- Cathédrale de la Major
- Musée Grobet-Labadié
- Notre-Dame-de-la-Garde
- Palais Longchamps
- Vieille Charité ★
- Vieux Port ★

FACT FILE

TOURIST INFORMATION

4 La Canebière. ***Tel** (04) 91 13 89 00.* ◯ *Mon–Sat to 7pm, Sun to 5pm.*

MARKETS

Fish Prom du Grand Large; daily am.

LOCAL SPECIALITIES

Crafts
Pottery, *savon de Marseille* (soap).
Dishes
Bouillabaisse (fish soup).
Moules marinières (mussels).
Drinks
Dry white wines from Cassis. Red wines from Bandol. Rosé wines from the Côtes de Provence region. *Pastis* (aniseed spirit aperitif).

EXCURSIONS

Château d'If 2 km (1 mile) W of Marseille. Island fortress (1524), famous as the prison of Dumas' fictional Count of Monte Cristo.
Cassis 25 km (16 miles) E of Marseille. Attractive fishing port.

The Palais Longchamps, a 19th-century folly housing the Musée des Beaux-Arts and d'Histoire Naturelle

Arles (Marseille)

Carved capital, St-Trophime

Near the apex of the Rhône delta, Arles was the capital of the three Roman Gauls (France, Spain and Britain). It has some superb remains of that period, both outdoors and in the Musée de l'Arles Antique. From then until the late Middle Ages, the Alyscamps (Elysian Fields) were among the Western world's largest cemeteries. Today, an avenue of marble tombs remains. St-Trophime, with exquisitely sculptured cloisters, is one of the best Romanesque churches in Provence. The Musée Arlaten (closed until 2013), exhibits Provençal folklore and the Musée Réattu, modern art. To the south of Arles are the wetlands of the Camargue, famous for their wild horses, flamingoes and the gypsy pilgrimage church of Les Stes-Maries-de-la-Mer.

Arènes

This oval amphitheatre is the most impressive of Arles' Roman buildings and the biggest in Roman Gaul, measuring 136 m (446 ft) by 107 m (351 ft). It could seat 21,000. The three towers were added in medieval times, when the interior was filled with shops and dwellings. These were cleared in the 1800s. Now Provençal- and Spanish-style bullfights are held here. Nearby are the remains of the Théâtre Antique, a 12,000-seat Roman theatre, and the baths of a Constantinian palace.

***L'Arlésienne* by Van Gogh (1888)**

VAN GOGH IN ARLES

In February 1888, Vincent Van Gogh (1853–90) moved to Arles and painted more than 200 canvases in his 15 months here, but the town has none of his work. In belated appreciation of this lonely artist, the Hôtel-Dieu has been turned into L'Espace Van Gogh, with a library and exhibition space. Several sites are evocative of him, however. The Café Van Gogh in the Place du Forum has been renovated to look as it did in his *Café du Soir* (1888). Van Gogh was joined in Arles by Gauguin, and it was a quarrel between them that induced the crisis during which Van Gogh cut off part of his ear. In 1889 he took himself to an asylum at St Rémy near Arles, but committed suicide the next year.

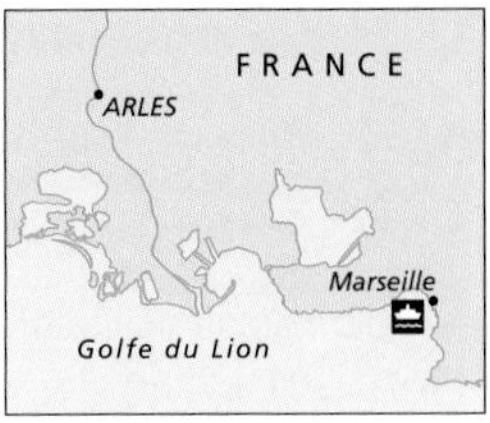

DISTANCE FROM PORT

60 km (37 miles) from city centre.

KEY SIGHTS

Alyscamps

Arènes ★

Musée Arlaten

Musée de l'Arles Antique

Musée Réattu

St-Trophime ★

Théâtre Antique

FACT FILE

TOURIST INFORMATION

Blvd des Lices. ***Tel*** *(04) 90 18 41 20.*

Oct–Mar: Mon–Sat to 4:45pm, Sun to 2:30pm; Apr–Sep: daily to 6:45pm.

MARKETS

General Blvd des Lices; Sat am.

LOCAL SPECIALITIES

Produce

Dried herbs, printed cotton textiles.

Dishes

Daube de boeuf (beef casserole). *Brandade de morue* (salt-cod pâté).

Drinks

Costières de Nîmes (local wines).

EXCURSIONS

Camargue 26 km (10 miles) S of Arles. Wetland nature reserve.

Musée Arlaten, in a grand mansion

Aix-en-Provence (Marseille)

Atalante, Pavillon de Vendôme

Founded by the Romans, Aix grew to be the medieval capital of Provence and a centre of learning. Today, it remains a city for students' and has many cosmopolitan venues to explore. Aix is often called the "city of a thousand fountains" for its many fine, 18th-century examples. In the Old Town is the Cathédrale St-Sauveur with a 4th-century baptistry. Aix's museums include the Musée des Tapisseries (tapestries), Musée Estienne de St Jean (folklore), Atelier Cézanne, the artist's house, Pavillon de Vendôme, a grand 17th-century house and Musée Granet (fine art and archaeology).

Hôtel de Ville
Aix's town hall occupies a Baroque mansion built between 1655 and 1670 by the Parisian architect Pierre Pavillon. It has a particularly fine courtyard. In the square in front is a flower market and an 18th-century fountain, with bearded stone heads spouting spring water. The clock tower beside the Hôtel was built in the 16th century on medieval foundations and carries an astronomical striking clock installed in 1661.

Cézanne's studio, filled with his furniture and personal belongings

Cours Mirabeau
This is Aix's most elegant street. Along its length are 17th- and 18th-century mansions on one side and cafés and shops on the other. Its plane trees shade three of the city's loveliest fountains. The moss-covered one, installed in 1734, spouts water at 34°C from thermal springs known to the Romans. A Roman bath, the Thermes Sextius, and an 18th-century spa complex lie a little way west of the cathedral.

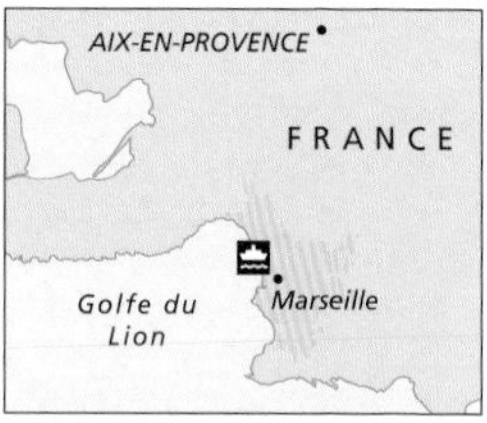

DISTANCE FROM PORT

30 km (19 miles) from city centre.

KEY SIGHTS

Atelier Paul-Cézanne
Cathédrale St-Sauveur ★
Cours Mirabeau ★
Hôtel de Ville
Musée Granet
Musée des Tapisseries
Musée Estienne de St Jean
Pavillon de Vendôme

FACT FILE

TOURIST INFORMATION
2 place du Général de Gaulle.
Tel *(04) 42 16 11 61.* *Oct–May: daily to 7pm; Jun–Sep: daily to 8pm (Jul & Aug: to 9pm).*

MARKETS
Flowers Place de la mairie; Tue, Thu & Sat am.
Food Place des Prêcheurs; Tue, Thu & Sat am.

LOCAL SPECIALITIES
Crafts
Santons (Christmas crib figures).
Dishes
Truffles.
Soupe au pistou (vegetable and bean soup with basil).
Gigot d'agneau (leg of lamb).
Calissons (almond-paste sweets).
Drinks
Coteaux d'Aix-en-Provence (local red, white and rosé wines).
Diablo (fruit syrup with lemonade).

EXCURSIONS
Montagne Ste-Victoire 15 km (9 miles) E of Aix. The mountain that inspired Cézanne.
Abbaye de Silvacane 24 km (14 miles) W of Aix. Monastery.
Salon-de-Provence 32 km (20 miles) W of Aix. Nostradamus's adopted home town.
Luberon 33 km (14 miles) N of Aix. Limestone mountain national park.

St-Tropez

Bust of St Torpès in the parish church

Shot in St-Tropez, Brigitte Bardot's 1956 film *And God Created Woman* and her decision to live here changed the fortunes of the fishing village, turning it into a playground for gilded youth. Mass tourism followed, with visitors more interested in spotting a celebrity than visiting the historic sights. Today there are many more luxury yachts than fishing boats in the harbour. St-Tropez was badly bombed in World War II, but the old town behind the waterfront was rebuilt in original style. Its main features are the 19th-century Eglise de St-Tropez, named after the Roman Christian martyr, St Torpès, and the Place des Lices, lively with cafés, *boules* players and the Harley-Davidson set. The 16th-century citadel east of town has an interesting naval museum.

Musée de l'Annonciade
This innovative gallery has stunning Post-Impressionist art, including *Open Window* (1926) by Charles Camoin.

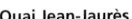

Quai Jean-Jaurès
Ever since Paul Signac came to St-Tropez in 1892, the attractively painted houses and packed cafés along the quay have enticed visitors and inspired other painters such as Matisse and Bonnard.

KEY SIGHTS

Citadelle and Musée Naval
Eglise de St-Tropez
Musée de l'Annonciade ★
Old Town

FACT FILE

TOURIST INFORMATION

Quai Jean-Jaurès. ***Tel*** *(08) 92 68 48 28.* *Nov–Mar: daily to 6pm; Apr–Oct: daily to 7pm (Jul & Aug: to 8pm).*

MARKETS

Fish Place aux Herbes; Tue–Sun am. **General** Pl. des Lices; Tue & Sat am.

LOCAL SPECIALITIES

Produce
Marrons glacés (candied chestnuts).
Tarte Tropézienne (cream cake).
Dishes
Courgettes farcies (courgettes filled with vegetables).*Bavette à l'échalotte* (beef with shallots).
Filet de chapon farci (stuffed fish).
Drinks
Domaine Gavoty and *Domaine St-André-de-Figuière* (red wines).
Ch. La Gordonne and *Domaine de la Croix* (rosé wines).

EXCURSIONS

Fréjus 20 km (12 miles) NE of St-Tropez. Oldest Roman city in Gaul.
Port-Grimaud 10 km (6 miles) W of St-Tropez. Modern resort.

Castle ruins above the old village of Grimaud, from which there are good views of Port-Grimaud and the coast

Nice: Old Town

A dense network of alleys, narrow buildings and pastel, Italianate façades make up the Old Town of Nice. Its streets contain many fine 17th-century Italianate churches, among them St-François-de-Paule, behind the Opéra, and l'Eglise du Jésus in the Rue Droite. The seafront is taken up by Les Ponchettes, which was Nice's chief promenade before the Promenade des Anglais was built further west in the 1820s. The hills overlooking the Old Town are occupied by the Cimiez district, where there is a museum to Henri Matisse (1869–1954) who spent 38 years in Nice.

★ Cathédrale Ste-Réparate
Built in 1650 by the Nice architect J-A Guiberto, this Baroque church has lavish plasterwork, a fine dome of glazed tiles and an 18th-century tower.

Palais de Justice
This imposing building was inaugurated on 17 October 1892, replacing the smaller quarters used before Nice became part of France in 1860. Nice had belonged to the House of Savoy (with a few brief interruptions) since 1388.

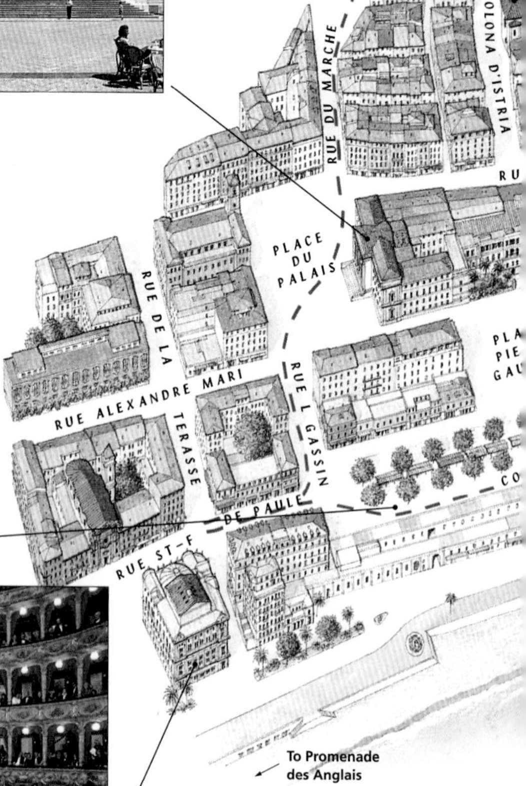

★ Cours Saleya
Busy in the day with an enticing vegetable and flower market, this street is also lively in the evening.

Opera House
The ornate and sumptuous Opéra de Nice was designed by Charles Garnier *(see p142)* and was completed in 1887.

Chapelle de la Miséricorde
This 1740 Baroque church has a fine Rococo interior. Highlights include the two altarpieces of the Virgin by Louis Bréa and Jean Miraihet.

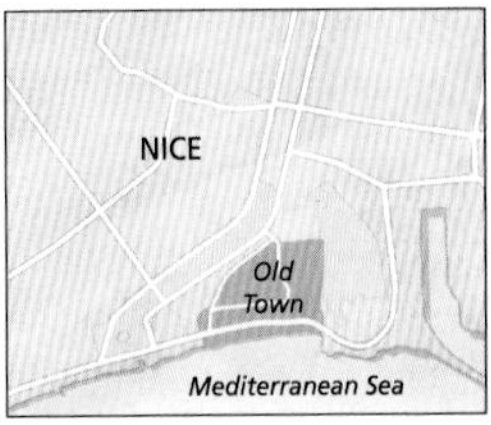

LOCATOR MAP

★ Palais Lascaris
The staircase of this elegant, 17th-century palace is flanked by 18th-century statues of Mars and Venus; the trompe l'oeil ceiling is by Genoese artists. An 18th-century pharmacy has been recreated on the ground floor.

0 metres 100

0 yards 100

KEY

— — — Suggested route

Les Ponchettes
One of Nice's most unusual architectural features is the row of low white buildings along the sea-front. Once used by fishermen, they are now a mix of galleries and ethnic restaurants.

STAR FEATURES

★ Cathédrale Ste-Réparate

★ Cours Saleya

★ Palais Lascaris

Cannes

Lord Brougham, British Lord Chancellor, put Cannes on the map in 1834 when he built a villa here after being entranced by the mild climate of the then fishing village. Today, it has become a resort of the rich and famous, busy all year round and renowned for its festivals. With its casinos, fairs, beach, boat and street life, there is plenty to do, even though it lacks great museums and monuments. Its heart is the Bay of Cannes and the palm-fringed, seafront Boulevard de la Croisette. Behind the Vieux Port (Old Port), small streets wind up to Le Suquet district, site of the Roman town of Canoïs Castrum, with the 1648 church of Notre-Dame de l'Espérance and the ethnographic Musée de la Castre in a 12th-century castle.

Carlton Hotel and Cannes Beach
This grand hotel was built in 1911 by architect Henri Ruhl, and the original Rococo-style dining room still survives. The twin black cupolas are said to be modelled on the breasts of La Belle Otéro, a half-gypsy courtesan. Most hotels in Cannes have their own beaches, to which a small charge is normally made for entry.

Boulevard de la Croisette
Cannes' famous beach-side boulevard, though noisy with traffic in summer, is bordered by luxury boutiques and hotels such as the Carlton. At its eastern end is one of Cannes' two gaming houses, the Casino Croisette, open all year round. At the western end is the summertime Palm Beach Casino.

KEY SIGHTS

Boulevard de la Croisette
Carlton Hotel ★
Musée de la Castre
Notre-Dame de l'Espérance

FACT FILE

TOURIST INFORMATION
Palais des Festivals, 1 Blvd de la Croisette. ***Tel*** *(04) 92 99 84 22.*
Jul & Aug: daily to 8pm; Sep–Jun: daily to 7pm.

MARKETS
General Rue du Marché Forville; Tue–Sun am.

LOCAL SPECIALITIES
Crafts
Perfumes from Grasse, hand-blown glassware from Biot, orange-flower water and pottery from Vallauris.
Dishes
Daurade royale (sea bream). *Estouffade d'agneau* (braised lamb). *Beignets de fleurs de courgettes* (deep fried courgette flowers).

EXCURSIONS
Vallauris 4 km (2 miles) NE of Cannes. Many potters' studios.
Iles de Lérins 5 km (3 miles) S of Cannes. Abbey, chapels and a fort.
Biot 11 km (7 miles) N of Cannes. Glassworks revived by Picasso.
Grasse 15 km (9 miles) NW of Cannes. Centre of perfume-making.
St-Paul-de-Vence 19 km (11 miles) NE of Cannes. Medieval hilltop village with celebrated modern art gallery, the Fondation Maeght.

THE CANNES FILM FESTIVAL

The first Cannes Film Festival took place in 1946 and, for almost 20 years, it remained a small and exclusive affair, attended mainly by artists and celebrities who lived or were staying on the coast. The arrival of the "starlet", especially Brigitte Bardot, in the mid-1950s marked the change from artistic event to media circus, but Cannes remains the international marketplace for film-makers and distributors, with the *Palme d'Or* prize conferring high status on its winner. The festival is held every May in the huge Palais des Festivals, which opened in 1982. In the nearby Allée des Stars handprints in the concrete pavement immortalize film celebrities.

Roman Polanski handprint

Monaco and Monte-Carlo

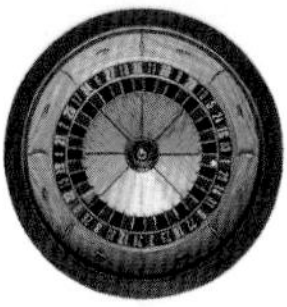

Roulette wheel for a game at the Casino

The dramatic heights of Monte-Carlo are the best-known area of the principality of Monaco. The land was bought from the Genoese in 1309 by the Grimaldis, who remain the world's oldest ruling family. From the harbour it is only a ten-minute stroll to Monte-Carlo's famous Grand Casino. A further 20-minute walk takes visitors to the Old Town. Here a miniature tourist train runs every 20 minutes from the splendid Musée Océanographique and takes in the main sights in a 35-minute round trip. The 16th-century Palais du Prince (open in summer), home of Prince Rainier III, features priceless furniture and magnificent frescoes. The beautiful, 19th-century Neo-Romanesque Cathédrale holds the tombs of Princess Grace and Prince Rainier, who died at the age of 81 in 2005 after a reign of 55 years.

Palace *Carabinier*
Guarded by sentries, the Palais du Prince may be visited daily from April to October.

Grand Casino
Monte-Carlo's most famous building was built in 1878 by Paris Opéra architect Charles Garnier *(see p142)*. The terrace offers superb views over Monaco and the coast. Monte-Carlo is named after Charles III, who opened the first casino here in 1865 to save himself from bankruptcy.

KEY SIGHTS

Cathédrale
Grand Casino
Jardin Exotique ★
Musée Océanographique ★
Palais du Prince ★

FACT FILE

TOURIST INFORMATION

2a Boulevard des Moulins, Monte-Carlo ***Tel** (92) 16 61 16.*
Mon–Sat to 7pm, Sun am.

MARKETS

Food Place d'Armes, Monte-Carlo; daily am.

LOCAL SPECIALITIES

Crafts
Colourful, printed fabrics, Vallauris pottery, Biot glassware, lavender bags, *santons* (painted terracotta figures), tableware and decorative items in carved wood.
Dishes
Bouillabaisse (fish soup). *Loup grillé au fenouil* (grilled sea bass with fennel). *Bar à La Monégasque* (baked sea bass with potatoes and tomatoes). *Socca* (savoury chick pea pancake). *Barbagilian* (deep fried swiss chard). *Tarte au citron* (lemon tart).
Drinks
Pastis (an aniseed-flavoured aperitif). *Tisanes* (flower and herb infusions).

EXCURSIONS

Menton 7 km (4 miles) NE of Monaco. Old resort town.
Cap Ferrat 8 km (5 miles) SW of Monaco. The fine Musée Ephrusssi de Rothschild can be visited.

Monte-Carlo seen from the village of La Turbie – one of the best views on the French Riviera

Corsica

Spartium junceum

Known as "The Scented Isle", Corsica's main appeal is its scenery of herb-filled maquis *(see pp206–7)*, mountains, forests and idyllic beaches. For 200 years to the 1200s, Corsica belonged to Pisa *(see pp220–21)*; it then fell to the Genoese, who sold it to France in 1769. The main ports are the capital, Ajaccio, and Bastia, which has an attractive Old Port and a Genoese citadel. Bastia's Chapelle St-Croix has a *Black Christ* fished from the sea in 1428 and its church of Ste-Marie has a *Virgin* made of a tonne of silver. Calvi is a smaller military port and holiday resort. Bonifacio in the south is sited on a peninsula, with a citadel above a fine harbour.

The Vieux Port (Old Port) of Bastia, full of Italianate buildings

Statue of Napoleon, Ajaccio
Napoleon Bonaparte was born in Ajaccio in 1769. Visitors can also see his birthplace, Maison Bonaparte, and the Cathédrale Notre-Dame de la Miséricorde, where he was baptized. The Musée Fesch has a superb collection of art looted by Napoleon's uncle, Cardinal Fesch, during the Italian campaign. There are works by Botticelli, Veronese and Titian.

KEY SIGHTS

Ajaccio ★
Bastia ★
Bonifacio
Calvi

FACT FILE

TOURIST INFORMATION

3 boulevard du Roi Jérôme, Ajaccio. ***Tel*** *(04) 95 51 53 03.* *Nov–Mar: Mon–Fri to 6pm, Sat to 5pm; Apr–Oct: Mon–Sat to 7pm, Sun to 1pm (Jul & Aug: Mon–Sat to 8pm, Sun to 7pm).*

MARKETS

Food Square Campinchi, Ajaccio; Tue–Sun (clothes Sat & Sun); Pl. de l'Hôtel de Ville, Bastia; Tue–Sun am.

LOCAL SPECIALITIES

Crafts Knives, pottery.
Dishes
Aziminu (fish stew). *Anciulatta* (onion pasty). *Figatellu* (wood-grilled liver sausage). *Tianu* (wild boar stew). *Brocciu* (goats'/ewes' milk cheese). *Fiadone* (lemon and *brocciu* cake). *Inugliatta* (anis and wine pancake).
Drinks
Cap Corse (sweet or dry white wines or the similarly named liqueur). *Patrimonio* (red and white wines). Mandarin, myrtle, chestnut and strawberry-tree fruit liqueurs.

EXCURSION

Filitosa 70 km (44 miles) S of Ajaccio. Life-sized, granite warriors between 3,000 and 4,000 years old.

Bonifacio's 12th-century citadel, headquarters of the French Foreign Legion from 1963 to 1983

◁ **Fisherman outside one of the houses in Bastia, on Corsica's northeastern coast**

PORTUGAL

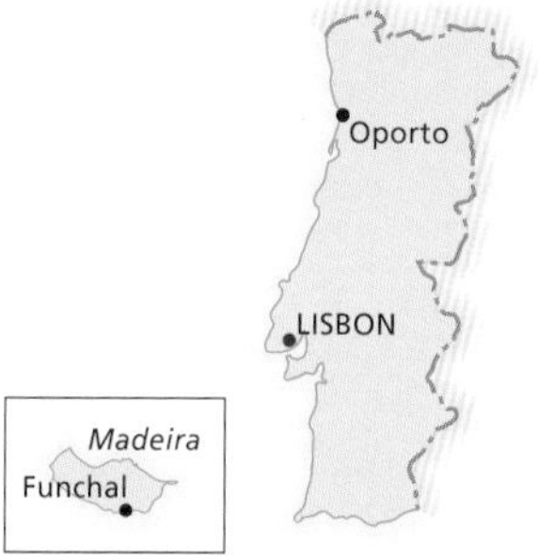
Oporto
LISBON
Madeira
Funchal

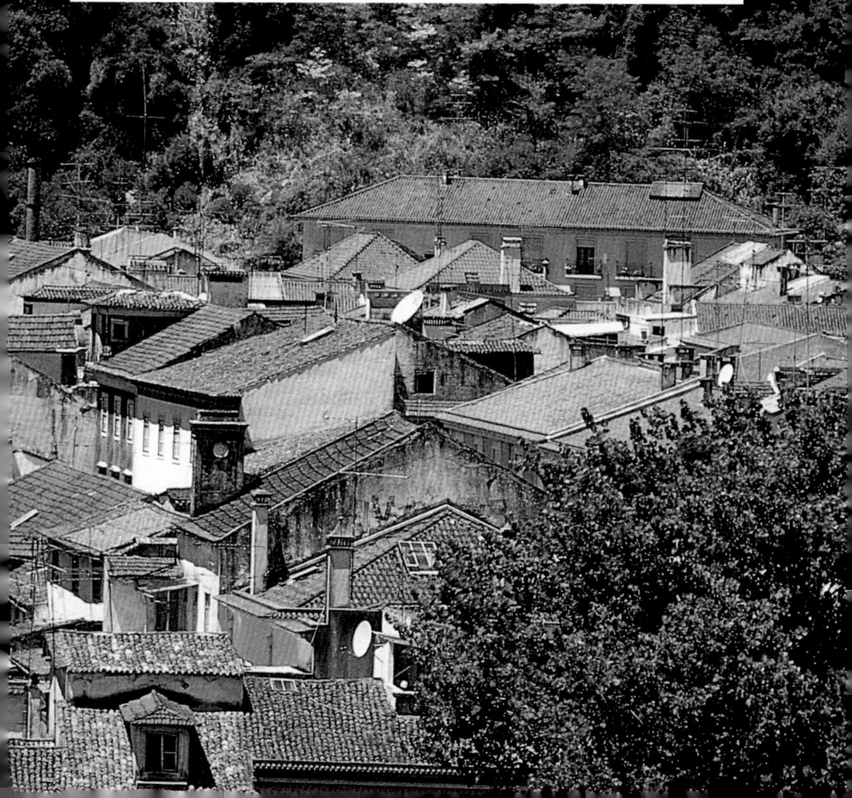

Oporto

Ever since the Romans built a fort here, where their trading route crossed the Douro, Oporto has prospered from commerce. Quick to expel the Moors in the 11th century and to profit from provisioning crusaders en route to the Holy Land, Oporto took advantage of the wealth generated by Portugal's maritime discoveries in the 15th and 16th centuries. Loss of the lucrative spice trade to the Dutch was compensated for in 1703, when an agreement with England created a new market for the wines of the Dourp valley. Still a thriving industrial centre and Portugal's second largest city, Oporto combines commercial hubbub with unpretentious charm.

Igreja dos Clérigos ④
Built in the 18th century by Niccolò Nasoni, this church's imposing tower is still one of Portugal's tallest buildings.

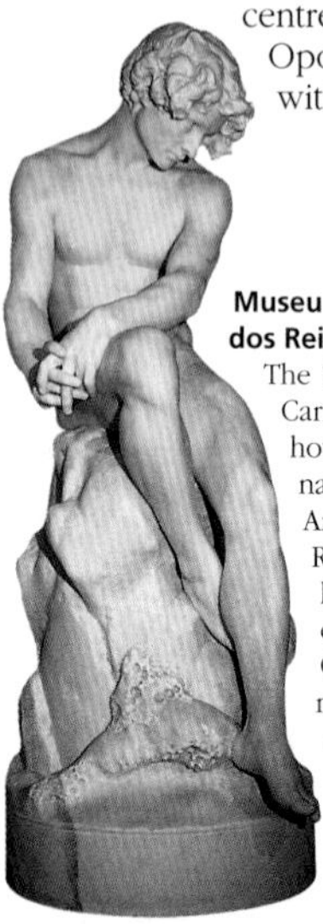

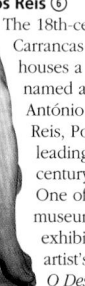

Museu Soares dos Reis ⑥
The 18th-century Carrancas Palace houses a museum named after António Soares dos Reis, Portugal's leading 19th-century sculptor. One of the museum's star exhibits is the artist's own *O Desterrado*.

São Francisco ⑤
The ornate 18th-century interior of this 14th-century church comprises over 200 kg (450 lb) of gold. It is wrought into cherubs, garlands and animals on the high altar, columns and pillars.

THE STORY OF PORT

Port was "discovered" in the 17th century when British merchants doctored wine from the Douro valley with brandy to stop it from turning sour in transit. It was found that the stronger and sweeter the wine, the better the flavour it acquired. Today, the majority of port production takes place in Vila Nova de Gaia on the south side of the Douro. More than 50 companies, many still under British control, are based here, blending and ageing most of the world's supply of port.

Port barges at Vila Nova de Gaia

◁ **Templar fortress of Covento de Cristo overlooking the town of Tomar, Portugal**

São Bento Station ③
Oporto's central railway station was completed in 1916. Inside, a feast of *azulejo* tiles by Jorge Colaço depicts early modes of transport, rural festivities and historic scenes.

Igreja Românica de Cedofeita ⑦
Constructed in Romanesque style in the 12th century, this little church is the oldest in the city.

Sé ②
Repeated modification has left this cathedral with a wide variety of architectural styles. An 18th-century staircase links two floors of Gothic cloister, which are decorated with Biblical scenes.

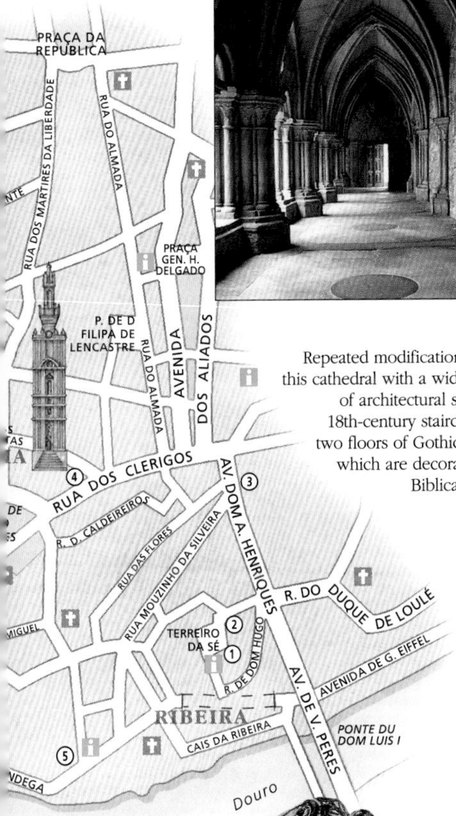

Casa-Museu Guerra Junqueiro ①
This lovely 18th-century Baroque building was once the home of the 19th-century poet and Republican activist, Guerra Junqueiro. Now it is a museum housing his private collection.

KEY SIGHTS

① Casa-Museu Guerra Junqueiro
② Sé ★
③ São Bento Station ★
④ Igreja dos Clérigos
⑤ São Francisco
⑥ Museu Soares dos Reis
⑦ Igreja Românica de Cedofeita

FACT FILE

TOURIST INFORMATION
Rua Clube dos Fenianos 25.
Tel *(2) 23 39 34 72.* ◯ *daily to 5:30pm, (Jun–Sep: daily to 7pm)*

MARKETS
Food & household goods
Bolhão market, between Rua de Santa Catarina and Rua Sá da Bandeira; Mon–Sat.

FESTIVALS
Festas da Cidade 2nd half of Jun.
São João de Porto 23–24 Jun.

SHOPPING
Silver Rua das Flores is traditionally the street for silversmiths.
Shoes The shoe trade is centred around Rua 31 de Janeiro.

LOCAL SPECIALITIES
Dishes
Caldo verde (kale soup).
Linguíça (smoked tongue sausages).
Pastéis de bacalhau (salt-cod cakes).
Queijo da Serra (soft cheese).
Cozido á portuguesa (meats, sausages and vegetables served in their own broth).
Truta de Barroso (local trout stuffed with ham).
Bacalhau à Gomes de Sá (layers of salt-cod, potato and onion).
Bola (bread layered with meat).
Sopa dorada (sponge cake with ground almonds and egg yolk).
Drinks
Bagaceira or *bagaço* (brandy made from grape skins).
Port (wine blended with brandy).
Ginginha (spirit made from cherries).

EXCURSION
Vila Nova de Gaia, 1km (0.6 mile) S of Oporto. Most port companies have their lodges here.

Lisbon

Portugal's capital, a city of about one million people, sits on the north bank of the Tagus estuary, 17 km (10 miles) from the Atlantic. The central area of Baixa was devastated by the earthquake of 1755, and today's carefully planned grid of elegant streets is essentially an 18th-century creation. To either side, the narrow streets and hills of the Alfama and Bairro Alto districts provide interesting walks and wonderful views. To the west, at the mouth of the Tejo, lies Belém. From here, during the 15th and 16th centuries, ships set out into the unknown world, and impressive buildings such as the Mosteiro dos Jerónimos still bear testimony to Portugal's days as a forcible maritime power.

Igreja do Carmo ⑤
The graceful skeletal arches of this Carmelite church, once the largest in Lisbon, stand as a reminder of the earthquake of 1755.

Mosteiro dos Jerónimos ①
Much of this magnificent 16th-century monastery, with its ornate south portal, is in the style of architecture known as Manueline, after King Manuel I, who commissioned the building.

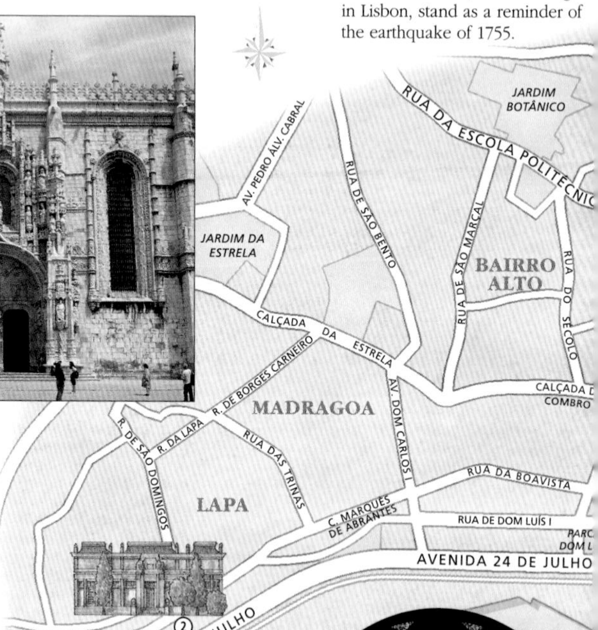

São Roque ④
Opulent mosaics adorn the Baroque Capela de São João inside the 16th-century church of São Roque. Commissioned in 1742, the chapel was first built in Rome and blessed by the Pope, before being dismantled and shipped to Lisbon.

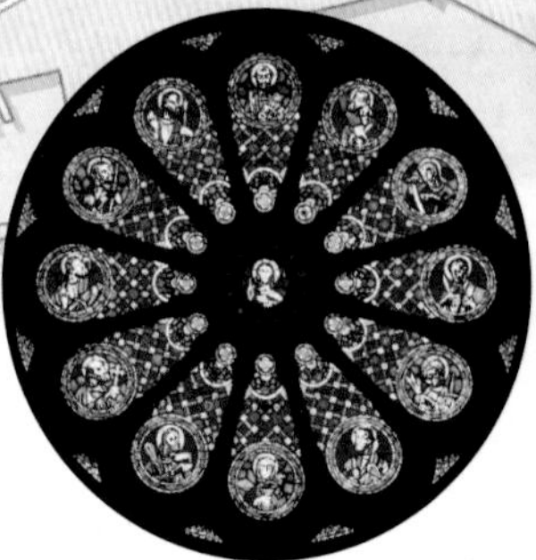

Sé ⑧
Lisbon's greatly restored cathedral is a solidly built Romanesque building lit by a beautiful rose window. The relics of St Vincent, the city's patron saint, are on display in the treasury.

Elevador de Santa Justa ⑥
This wrought-iron lift was built at the beginning of the 20th century by French architect Raoul Mesnier du Ponsard. Passengers can travel to the top of the tower for superb views of the city. The walkway linking the lift with the nearby Igreja do Carmo is currently closed for renovations.

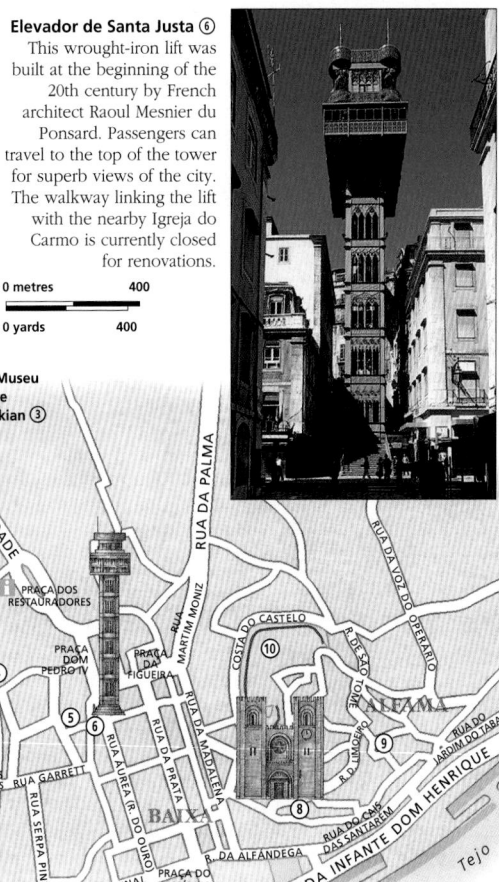

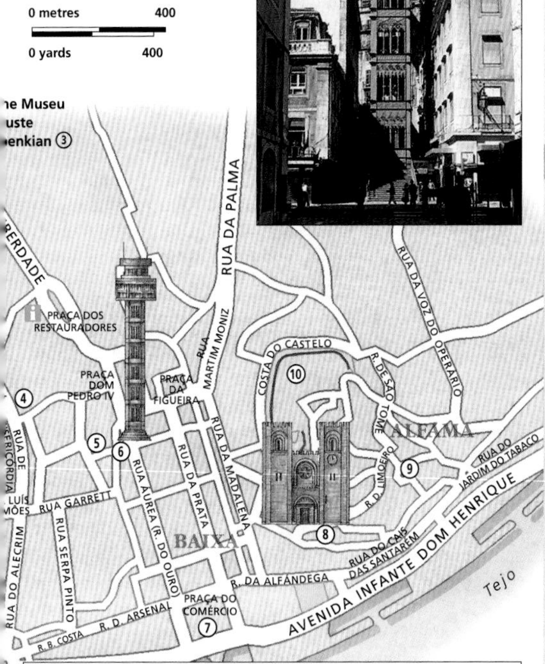

LISBON'S GREAT EARTHQUAKE

On All Saints' Day 1755, a huge earthquake struck Lisbon, reducing most of it to rubble. More than 20 churches collapsed, crushing worshippers inside, and soon fires started by church candles were sweeping the city. Fleeing the flames, many people took to the Tagus in boats, but they were shipwrecked by huge waves that flooded the low-lying areas. In all, the earthquake did incalculable damage to Lisbon, the scars of which can still be seen.

An engraving of Lisbon's earthquake of 1755

KEY SIGHTS

① Mosteiro dos Jerónimos ★
② Museu Nacional de Arte Antiga
③ Museu Calouste Gulbenkian
④ São Roque
⑤ Igreja do Carmo
⑥ Elevador de Santa Justa
⑦ Praça do Comércio
⑧ Sé
⑨ Alfama ★ *(see pp170–71)*
⑩ Castelo de São Jorge ★

FACT FILE

TOURIST INFORMATION

Rua do Arsenal, 15. ***Tel** (21) 031 27 00.* ☐ *daily to 8pm.*

MARKETS

Flea Market Feira da Ladra, Campo de Santa Clara, Alfama; Tue & Sat am.

LOCAL SPECIALITIES

Crafts
Vista Alegre (fine porcelain tableware), *azulejos* (glazed tiles), *artesanato* (a variety of regional crafts such as lace, wool, and silver and gold items), *gravuras* (prints sold in bookshops).

Dishes
Açorda de marisco (shellfish soup).
Porco à alentejana (pork and clams).
Queijo da Serra (hard cheese).
Sardinhas assadas (charcoal-grilled sardines).

Drinks
Medronho (liqueur made from the fruit of the strawberry tree).
Aguardente (brandy).
Bucelas (dry white wine produced just northwest of Lisbon).

EXCURSIONS

Museu Nacional do Azulejo
2km (1.2 miles) NE of Lisbon. The cloisters of the Convento da Madre de Deus provide a stunning setting for the National Tile Museum. Decorative panels, individual tiles and photographs trace the evolution of tile-making.
Sintra 20km (12 miles) NW of Lisbon. Once a favourite summer retreat for the kings of Portugal; now a World Heritage site.

Lisbon: Alfama ⑨

A fascinating quarter at any time of the day, the Alfama district looks stunning when drenched in early morning sunshine as locals go about their lives. Many African immigrants have settled here and several venues play music from Mozambique and the Cape Verde Islands. The quarter is characterized by its steep streets and steps, and a walk around the maze of winding alleyways reveals crumbling churches, picturesque corners and shady terraces. Visitors can enjoy panoramic views such as those from Miradouro de Santa Luzia and Largo das Portas do Sol.

Largo das Portas do Sol
Today café tables overlook the Alfama, but Portas do Sol was once one of the entrance gates to the old city.

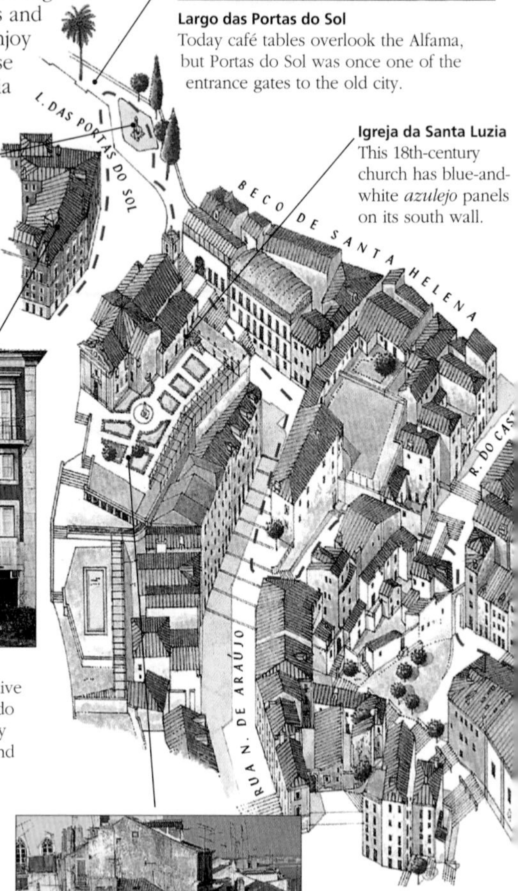

Statue of St Vincent
A modern statue of St Vincent holding the emblem of Lisbon, a boat with two ravens, stands in Largo das Portas do Sol.

Igreja da Santa Luzia
This 18th-century church has blue-and-white *azulejo* panels on its south wall.

★ Museu de Artes Decorativas
Established as a museum of decorative arts in 1953 by the banker Ricardo do Espírito Santo Silva, the 17th-century Palácio Azurara houses fine 17th- and 18th-century Portuguese furniture, textiles, silver and ceramics.

KEY

- - - - Suggested route

0 metres 25

0 yards 25

★ Miradouro de Santa Luzia
The view from the bougainvillea-clad terrace by the church of Santa Luzia spans the tiled roof tops of the Alfama. This is a pleasant place to rest after a walk around the area's steep streets.

STAR SIGHTS

★ Museu de Artes Decorativas

★ Miradouro de Santa Luzia

Beco dos Cruzes
Like most of the alleyways (*becos*) that snake their way through the Alfama, Beco dos Cruzes is a steep cobbled street. Locals often hang washing between the tightly packed houses.

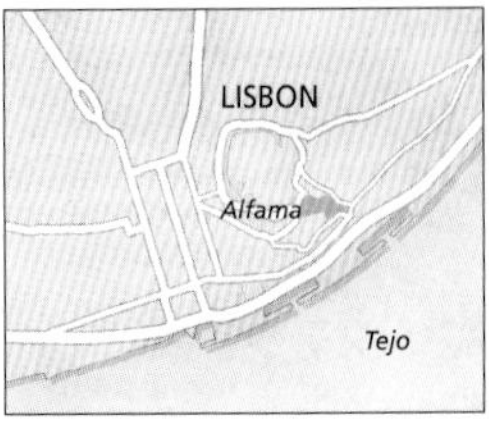

LOCATOR MAP

Rua de São Pedro
In the early mornings, *varinas* bring the catch of the day to this lively fish market, which offers a wide variety of fish, including *peixe espada* (scabbard fish).

Largo do Chafariz de Dentro
This square takes its name from the 17th-century fountain *(chafariz)* that was originally placed within *(dentro)* rather than outside the 14th-century walls.

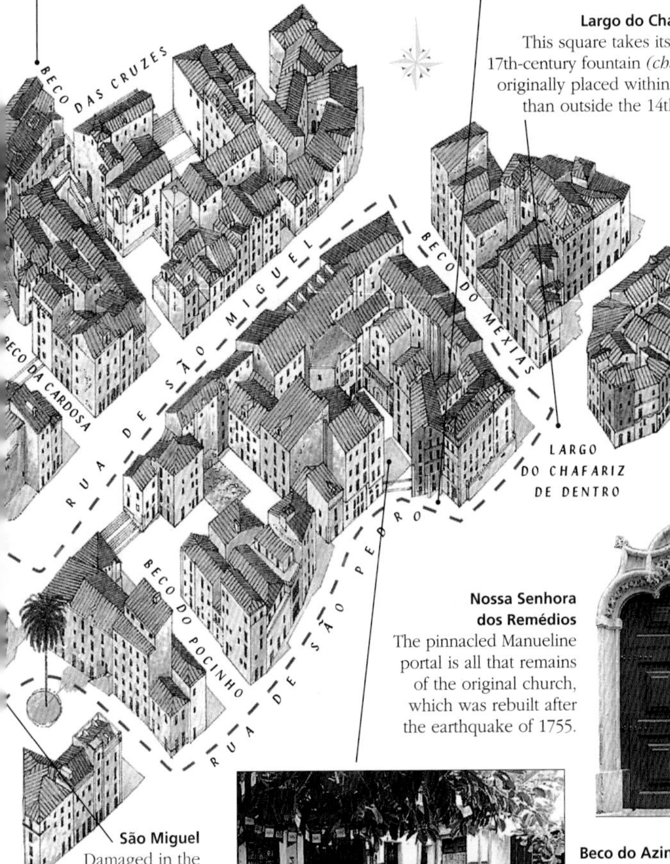

Nossa Senhora dos Remédios
The pinnacled Manueline portal is all that remains of the original church, which was rebuilt after the earthquake of 1755.

São Miguel
Damaged in the 1755 earthquake, the rebuilt church of São Miguel retains a few of its earlier features, including a fine ceiling of Brazilian jacaranda wood.

Beco do Azinhal
Hidden in Alfama's labyrinth of alleyways, popular restaurants spill out onto open-air patios. The *Lautasco*, found here, serves excellent traditional food.

Exploring Lisbon

An attractive city, Lisbon is a pleasure to explore, and walking can be one of the best ways to see it. However, it is also hilly, and even the fittest of sightseers will soon tire. The trams, buses and lifts (*elevadores*) provide welcome respite for the foot-weary visitor, and offer some excellent views of the city.

Mosteiro dos Jerónimos ①

Commissioned by Manuel I in 1501, this monastery was financed largely by "pepper money", the profits made from the spice trade. The monastery was entrusted to the Order of St Jerome (Hieronymites) until 1834, when all religious orders were disbanded.

The Monastery of St Jerome is the culmination of Manueline architecture, and is far more elaborately decorated than the prevailing Gothic style. A highlight is the cloister, with its richly decorated arches and balustrades. A wing built in a similar style in 1850 houses Lisbon's Museu Nacional de Arqueologia.

Museu Nacional de Arte Antiga ②

The national art collection of Portugal is housed in a 17th-century palace that was built for the counts of Alvor. In 1770, it was acquired by the Marquês de Pombal and remained in the possession of his family for over a century. The museum was inaugurated in 1884 and houses the largest collection of paintings in

Stall holder selling fruit and vegetables

Portugal. Particularly strong on Portuguese early religious work, it also contains works by artists such as Dürer, Bosch and Raphael. In 1940, an annex was built on the site of the St Albert Carmelite monastery, which had been destroyed in the 1755 earthquake *(see p169)*. All that survived was the chapel, now part of the museum.

Museu Calouste Gulbenkian ③

Housing oil magnate Calouste Gulbenkian's unique and wide-ranging collection of art, the museum is one of the finest in Europe. The exhibits, which span over 4,000 years from ancient Egyptian statuettes, through translucent Islamic glassware, to Art Nouveau brooches, are displayed in spacious and well-lit galleries, laid out both chronologically and geographically with many overlooking the gardens or courtyards. Rooms 1–6 are dedicated to Classical and Oriental art and rooms 7–17 house European painting, sculpture, furniture, silverware and jewellery. Highlights include Rembrandt's *Portrait of an Old Man* (1645) and a fine marble statue of *Diana*, goddess of the hunt by the French sculptor Jean-Antoine Houdon.

São Roque ④

Behind São Roque's austere façade is a remarkably rich interior. The Renaissance church was founded in the late 1500s by the Jesuit order, then at the peak of its power. In 1742 the Chapel of St John the Baptist was commissioned by João V from Italian architects Luigi Vanvitelli and Nicola Salvi, the latter the designer of the Trevi Fountain in Rome *(see p232)*. Constructed and richly embellished, the chapel was given the Pope's blessing in the church of Sant'Antonio dei Portoghesi in Rome before being dismantled and taken to Lisbon on three ships.

Among the many tiles in the church, the oldest and most interesting are those in the third chapel on the right, dating from the mid-16th century, and dedicated to São Roque (St Roch), protector against the plague. Other noteworthy features of the church include the *trompe l'oeil* ceiling, showing scenes of the Apocalypse. The sacristy features a coffered ceiling and painted panels depicting the life of the 16th-century Jesuit missionary, St Francis Xavier.

Igreja do Carmo ⑤

Devastated by the earthquake of 1755, Gothic ruins are all that remains of this Carmelite church built on a slope overlooking the Baixa district. Founded in the late 14th century by Nuno Álvares Pereira, the church was at one time the biggest in Lisbon. Now the nave stands open to the sky, roses grow

Detail from Bosch's *The Temptations of St Antony* triptych, c.1500

Marble steps leading to the Praça do Comércio from the Tejo (Tagus)

up its ancient pillars, pigeons perch on the ruined arches and cats wander among the scattered statuary.

The chancel is now an archaeological museum with a small collection of sarcophagi, statuary, ceramics and mosaics. There are also finds from the Americas, including ancient mummies.

Elevador de Santa Justa ⑥

Also known as the Elevador do Carmo, this Neo-Gothic lift was built at the beginning of the 20th century and is one of the more eccentric features of the Baixa. Two wood-panelled cabins with brass fittings ferry passengers up and down a gothic-style tower embellished with delicate filigree. The very top of the tower, reached by a tight spiral staircase, is given over to café tables. The high vantage point commands splendid views of the grid pattern of the Baixa district, the castle on the opposite hill, and the Igreja do Carmo.

Praça do Comércio ⑦

More commonly known by the locals as *Terreiro do Paço* (Palace Terrace), this huge open space was the site of the royal palace for 400 years. After the first palace was destroyed in 1755, a new palace of arcaded buildings, later converted into government offices, was built around three sides of the square. A statue of King José I, ruler at the time of the savage earthquake, stands in front of the triumphal arch that dominates the north side of the square.

The best view of the square – and the marble steps that once conveyed royalty and ambassadors up to it – is from the Tagus. A ferry can be taken from Lisbon to Cacilhas on the southern bank.

Sé ⑧

In 1150, three years after he recaptured Lisbon from the Moors, Afonso I built a cathedral for the first bishop of Lisbon, on the site of the old mosque. *Sé* is short for *Sedes Episcopalis*, the seat (or see) of a bishop. Repeatedly devastated by earthquakes, and renovated over the centuries, today's cathedral blends a variety of architectural styles. The façade, with twin castellated belltowers and a splendid rose window, and the nave are Romanesque. The chapels and the cloister, which has elegant double arches and some finely carved capitals, are Gothic.

The sacristy houses the cathedral's treasury, which contains a varied collection of silver, statuary, ecclesiastical robes, illustrated manuscripts and a selection of relics associated with St Vincent.

Alfama ⑨

See pp170–71.

Castelo de São Jorge ⑩

Originally built by the Moors, the castle has been, at various times, a royal residence, a theatre, a prison and an arms depot. After the 1755 earthquake, the ramparts remained `in ruins until they were renovated in 1938. The castle may not be authentic, but the gardens and the narrow streets of the Santa Cruz district within the walls afford a pleasant stroll and the views are the finest in Lisbon.

View across the city to the Castelo de São Jorge from Miradouro de São Pedro de Alcântara

Madeira: Funchal

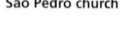

Tiling on Palácio do Governo Regional, Avenida M. Arriaga

The deep natural harbour of Madeira's capital, Funchal, attracted early settlers in the 15th century. The historic core of the capital still overlooks the harbour and boasts fine government buildings and stately 18th-century houses with shady courtyards, iron balconies and carved black basalt doorways. Visitors have justly called Funchal a "little Lisbon" because of the town's steep cobbled streets and overall air of grandeur.

Igreja do Colégio
This church, founded by the Jesuits in 1574, has a plain ex or, contrasting with the interi richly decorated high altar, fra by carved, gilded wood.

Rua da Carreira and Rua do Surdo
These streets feature many of their original, elegant houses.

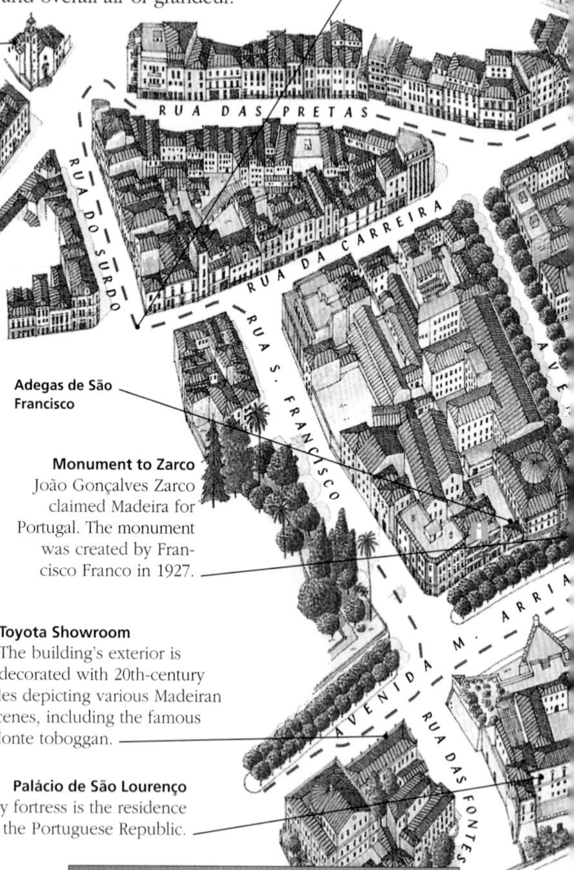

São Pedro church

Museu Municipal
This former mansion houses an aquarium and is a favourite with children.

Adegas de São Francisco

Monument to Zarco
João Gonçalves Zarco claimed Madeira for Portugal. The monument was created by Francisco Franco in 1927.

Toyota Showroom
The building's exterior is decorated with 20th-century tiles depicting various Madeiran scenes, including the famous Monte toboggan.

Palácio de São Lourenço
This 16th-century fortress is the residence of the Minister of the Portuguese Republic.

0 metres 50
0 yards 50

Yacht Marina
Lined with seafood restaurants, the yacht marina on Avenida do Mar (otherwise known as Avenida das Comunidades Madeirenses) is ideal for a relaxing stroll. The sea wall around the marina offers good views of the ocean.

Avenida do Mar

Câmara Municipal
Funchal's city hall is an imposing 18th-century mansion. The fountain in its courtyard depicts Leda and the Swan. Inside, a small museum traces the history of Funchal in photographs.

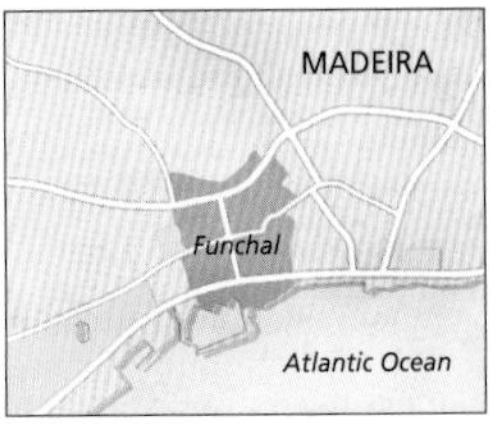

LOCATOR MAP

Museu de Arte Sacra
Flemish paintings and wooden statues are among the religious treasures in this museum.

★ Praça do Município
Contrasting black and white stones pave the attractive municipal square. The Câmara Municipal is on the northeastern side of the square.

Rua do Aljube
In the street that runs along the north side of the Sé, flower sellers in their traditional costumes offer a colourful array of exotic flowers.

Palácio do Governo Regional

★ Sé
São Tiago (St James) is one of many gilded figures that adorn the choir stalls in Funchal's 15th-century cathedral.

KEY

- - - - Suggested route

STAR SIGHTS

★ Praça do Municipio

★ Sé

Whitewashed houses with red-tiled roofs in Montefrío, near Granada, Spain ▷

SPAIN

A Coruña
Bilbao
Vigo
Barcelona
MADRID
Menorca
Maó
Palma de Mallorca
Mallorca
Ibiza
Jerez de la Frontera
Seville
Granada
Málaga
Cádiz
Gibraltar
THE CANARY ISLANDS
La Palma
Fuerteventura
Santa Cruz de Tenerife
Tenerife
Las Palmas de Gran Canaria
Gran Canaria

Bilbao

Bilbao (Bilbo in Basque) has been one of Spain's main industrial cities since the 19th century and is its leading commercial port. Innovative urban regeneration has produced some stunning modern buildings on derelict industrial sites, notably the titanium-clad Guggenheim Museum. In contrast, the *casco viejo* (old town), around the Cathedral, dates from the 14th century and is full of characterful bars. Visitors will eat well in Bilbao, as the Basque Country is renowned for its cuisine.

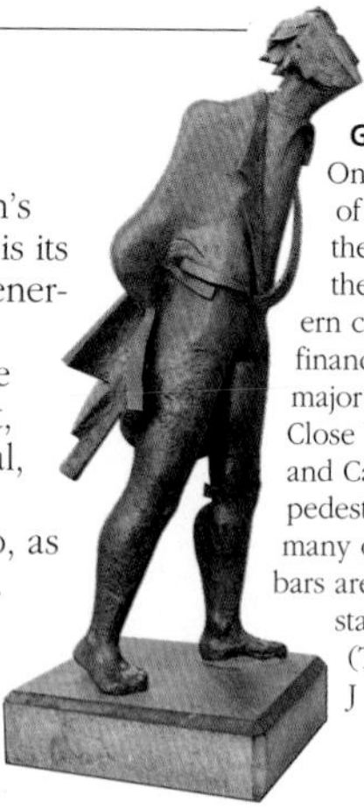

Gran Vía ③
Once the main street of 19th-century Bilbao, the Gran Vía is still at the heart of the modern city, comprising the financial district and a major shopping area. Close by are Calle Arbieto and Calle Diputación, pedestrian streets where many of Bilbao's finest bars are found. This 1997 statue *El Paseante* (The Stroller) is by J T Gómez Nazabal.

Museo Guggenheim Bilbao ①
Part of New York's Solomon R Guggenheim Foundation, this remarkable titanium, glass and limestone building by North American architect Frank Gehry opened in 1997. The collection represents an intriguingly broad spectrum of modern and contemporary art.

Museo de Bellas Artes ②
The fine art on display here includes 15th- and 16th-century Catalan European masterpieces plus modern works by renowned artists including Francis Bacon, Paul Cézanne, Eduardo Chillida and Paul Gauguin.

Mercado de la Ribera ⑦
A spectacular selection of fish, meat, fruit and vegetables is sold here. Said to be Europe's largest covered market, La Ribera was built in 1929, although there has been a tradition of holding markets on this site since medieval times.

Museo Vasco ⑤
Housed in a 16th-century monastery, this museum devoted to Basque archaeology, ethnography and history was opened to the public in 1921 and is one of the most important museums in the Basque Country. It has displays of Basque art, folk artifacts and photographs of traditional Basque life. In the cloister is the *Idol of Mikeldi*, an animal-like carving dating from the 3rd to the 2nd century BC, which represents a love of nature.

Catedral de Santiago ⑥
The origins of this Gothic cathedral predate the foundation of Bilbao. Its location was once the site of a church dedicated to St James, which was built for pilgrims on their way to Santiago de Compostela *(see p180)*.

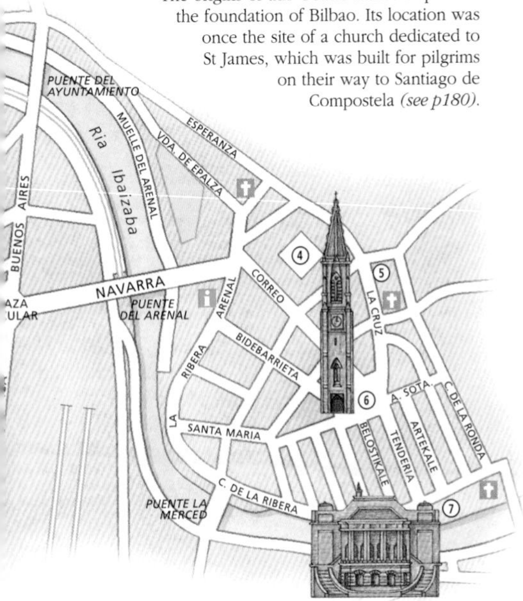

Plaza Nueva ④
This closed, Neo-Classical square with its 64 arches supported by Doric columns was built in 1851. The Basque Language Academy is housed here. Not far away, opposite the Teatro Arriaga, is the Café Boulevard, one of Bilbao's most famous literary rendezvous.

KEY SIGHTS

① Museo Guggenheim Bilbao ★
② Museo de Bellas Artes
③ Gran Vía ★
④ Plaza Nueva
⑤ Museo Vasco
⑥ Catedral de Santiago
⑦ Mercado de la Ribera

FACT FILE

TOURIST INFORMATION

Plaza Ensanche 11. ***Tel*** *944 710 301.* ☐ *Mon–Fri to 7:30pm.*

MARKETS

Food Mercado de la Ribera; Mon–Sat am.

SHOPPING

Designer clothes Many international designers have shops in the Gran Vía and adjacent streets.

LOCAL SPECIALITIES

Crafts
Wrought iron, equipment for *pelota* (the Basque national game).
Dishes
Porrusalda (cod and leek soup).
Bacalao a la vizcaína (salt-cod with a sweet pepper and chilli sauce).
Txangurro relleno (spider crab au gratin).
Angulas (elvers cooked in oil, garlic and chilli).
Chipirones/calamares en su tinta (squid in their ink).
Idiazábal (smoked cheese).
Canutillos de Bilbao (pastry rolls filled with custard).
Drinks
Txakolí (the local wine, mostly white, fruity, sharp and young).
Rioja (not produced locally, but still the area's most popular wine).

EXCURSIONS

Getxo 15 km (9 miles) NW of Bilbao. Small port on Río Nervión.
Castillo de Butrón 18 km (11 miles) N of Bilbao. Castle and park.
Gernika-Lumo 30 km (19 miles) E of Bilbao. Its bombing by the Nazis in 1937 was depicted by Picasso in his *Guernica* (now in Madrid).

A Coruña

This busy port was probably originally founded by the Phoenicians. In AD 60 it was taken by the Romans, whose lighthouse, the Torre de Hércules, still survives. A Coruña's Old Town lies on a promontory and is encircled by 13th-century walls. Its narrow streets contain the city's most attractive square, Plazuela de las Bárbaras, and the Romanesque churches of Santa María and Santiago, the latter with a Baroque tower and 19th-century rose window. The newer town on the isthmus has a beach on one side and the city's large port on the other. The latter is flanked by the elegant Avenida de la Marina, famous for its 19th-century, glazed balconies, and the café-filled Plaza María Pita. The port is protected by a well-preserved 16th-century fort, the Castillo de San Antón.

Avenida de la Marina
The tall houses facing the port along this renowned promenade all have façades entirely composed of the glassed-in balconies typical of Galicia. For this reason, A Coruña is known as the City of Glass.

KEY SIGHTS

- Avenida de la Marina ★
- Castillo de San Antón
- Colegiata de Santa María
- Iglesia de Santiago
- Plazuela de las Bárbaras
- Torre de Hércules ★

FACT FILE

TOURIST INFORMATION

Dársena de la Marina. **Tel** *981 221 822.* ◯ *Mon–Sat to 7pm, Sun to 2pm.*

MARKETS

Medieval fair Ciudad Vieja (Old Town); last two weeks of July.

LOCAL SPECIALITIES

Crafts
Ceramics from El Castro nearby.

Dishes
Caldeirada (fish and potato stew).
Lacón con grelos (pork with sweet cabbage and *chorizo* sausage).
Empanada (a flat cod or tuna pie).
Tetilla (local soft, salty cheese).

EXCURSION

Santiago de Compostela
80 km (50 miles) S of A Coruña. Magnificent cathedral and old town.

Torre de Hércules
This lighthouse on the northern tip of the city peninsula has been continuously in use since it was built in the 2nd century AD. The Roman tower was given its square outer skin in 1791. There are fine views from the top.

SANTIAGO DE COMPOSTELA

In the Middle Ages, Santiago de Compostela was Christendom's third most important place of pilgrimage after Jerusalem and Rome. Half a million pilgrims a year used to come and pray at the shrine of St James (Santiago) from all over Europe, most of them arriving along the 'French Route', the main way over the Pyrenees via Roncesvalles. According to legend, the body of Christ's apostle James was brought to Galicia. In 813 the relics were supposedly discovered at Santiago de Compostela, where a church was built by Alfonso II. The present building, however, dates from the 11th to 12th centuries. Though the exterior was remodelled and given a richly-sculptured Baroque façade, the medieval interior has survived almost intact. The carved Pórtico da Gloria (west door) is one of the wonders of Christian art. Around the cathedral is a splendid ensemble of narrow streets, old squares and historic, granite buildings.

High altar, Santiago Cathedral

Vigo

Galicia's largest town is also the biggest fishing port in Spain and derives its name from its Roman name, Vicus Spacorum. It lies on one of the four large rias that make up the Rias Baixas – Galicia's beautiful western coast. Here, the landscape is hilly and pine-covered, the beaches are beautiful and the climate is much milder than on the wilder coast to the north. In the 16th and 17th centuries, Vigo's importance as a port of entry for New World treasures attracted the attention of the English, who raided it in 1585, 1589 and 1702. Vigo is not noted for its historic buildings, but its oldest part near the port is full of character and fine tapas bars. Named the Barrio del Berbés, it was the sailors' and fishermen's quarter and its Calle de la Pescadería is famous for its oyster stalls. Museo Quiñones de León exhibits paintings and local archaeology.

Bronze sculpture by Manuel Oliveira in Vigo's Praza de España
This large bronze sculpture dominating the Praza de España was installed in the early 1990s. It is by self-taught, local artist Manuel Oliveira. He became fascinated by the wild horses of Galicia early in his life and developed an incredible talent for portraying them in sculpture.

KEY SIGHTS

Calle de la Pescadería ★
Praza de España
Museo Quiñones de León

FACT FILE

TOURIST INFORMATION

Calle Teófilo Llorente 5.
Tel *986 22 47 57.* *Mon–Sat to 7pm (Jul–Aug daily).*

MARKETS

General Mercadillo A Pedra; daily.
Fish, meat & vegetables Mercado del Berbés; Mon–Sat am.

LOCAL SPECIALITIES

Dishes
Ostras (oysters). *Arroz de vieiras* (rice with shellfish). *Tarta de yema* (sweet cake made with egg yolk).
Drinks
Ribeiro (slightly sparkling wine, often served in porcelain cups).

EXCURSIONS

Illas Cíes 12 km (8 miles) from Vigo. Uninhabited, nature reserve islands at the mouth of Vigo's ria.
Baiona 25 km (15 miles) SW of Vigo. Galicia's best summer resort.
Pontevedra 25 km (15 miles) NE of Vigo. Delightful old town at the head of the next ria. The Museo de Pontevedra has superb Celtic Bronze Age treasures.

Calle de la Pescadería
Vigo's ria is famous for its mussel and oyster beds. In this street near the port oysters are sold from slabs made of the local granite. The stallholders open oysters for customers, who then take them to local bars to eat with lemon and accompanying drinks. The street is also called La Pedra ("The Stone").

Vigo's Suspension Bridge and Ria
Vigo, though a busy commercial town, occupies a very attractive setting near the mouth of a deep ria spanned by a high suspension bridge and surrounded by wooded hills. A magnificent panorama over Vigo and its bay can be seen from the town's hilltop viewpoint in the Parque del Castro.

Gran Canaria

Farmer and donkey

Gran Canaria's beaches have made it the most popular of the Canary Islands with holidaymakers, and the high-rise Playa del Inglés-Maspalomas complex is one of Spain's biggest resorts. The island, however, also offers a surprising range of scenery. There are miles of wind-sculpted sand dunes behind Maspalomas in the sunny south; lush banana and citrus fruit plantations in the cloudier northwest around Agaete; the huge Caldera de la Bandama, an impressive volcanic crater, in the northeast; and spectacular mountain scenery in the interior. A visit to the Pico de las Nieves mountain at 1,949 m (6,394 ft) and the basalt rock formations of Roque Nublo will reward with fabulous views on a clear day. Las Palmas, the capital and port, is the Canaries' largest city. It has faded somewhat since its heyday in the golden era of cruising *(see pp12–13)*, but has an attractive old quarter around the cathedral.

Casa de Colón, Las Palmas de Gran Canaria

This mansion dates from the end of the 15th century and was the residence of the island's Spanish governors. Columbus is reputed to have stayed here in 1492. The building now houses a museum displaying objects, paintings and maps related to his voyages.

The sand dunes at Maspalomas, between hectic Playa del Inglés and a golf course, now a nature reserve protected from further development

KEY SIGHTS

Agaete

Caldera de la Bandama

Dunas de Maspalomas ★

Las Palmas de Gran Canaria

Puerto Rico

Roque Nublo ★

FACT FILE

TOURIST INFORMATION

Calle León y Castillo 17, Las Palmas. ***Tel** 928 21 96 00.*

Mon–Fri to 3pm.

MARKETS

Food & general Plaza del Mercado, Mercado del Puerto in Calle Albareda and Mercado Central in Calle Galicia, Las Palmas; daily am.

LOCAL SPECIALITIES

Crafts

Pottery, knives, baskets, embroidery.

Dishes

Potaje de berros (watercress stew). *Sama frita con mojo verde* (fried fish in garlic and coriander sauce). *Bienmesabe* (an almond dessert). *Flor de guía* (a soft sheep's cheese).

Drinks

Ron (local white or dark rum).

Puerto Rico

This popular resort clings to the steep, rocky and barren shoreline west of Maspalomas. Although overdeveloped with apartment complexes, it has an attractive beach created from a crescent of imported sand and excellent water sports facilities. Puerto Rico enjoys the best sunshine record in Spain.

Tenerife

Dragon Tree (*Dracena draco*)

In the language of its aboriginal Guanche inhabitants, Tenerife means "Snowy Mountain" after its most striking feature and Spain's highest peak, the Mount Teide volcano. The island is the largest of the Canaries, damp and lushly vegetated in the north, sunny and arid in the south. Both the national park of Mount Teide and the Montes de Anaga, north of the capital Santa Cruz, abound with a wide variety of birds and plants. The Canaries' most unusual plant, and symbol of the island, is the dragon tree, which grows no rings, making specimens' ages a mystery. Some, such as the famous one at Icod de los Vinos, may be thousands of years old. La Orotava is an attractive historic town centred around the Baroque Iglesia de Nuestra Señora de la Concepción, and Puerto de la Cruz is the oldest resort. The latter's botanical gardens were founded in 1788 with specimens from Spain's overseas colonies.

Parque Nacional del Teide
The wild, mineral-tinted scenery surrounding the volcanoes of Pico del Teide (dormant) and Pico Viejo, (which last erupted in the 18th century), is now a protected area. 180,000 years ago a much larger cone collapsed leaving behind the 16-km (10-mile) wide caldera of Las Cañadas and the smaller volcano, Mount Teide, rising above it. From the plateau of Las Cañadas, visitors can take an eight-minute cable car ride to within 160 m (525 ft) of El Teide's summit.

Plaza de los Patos, Santa Cruz de Tenerife
The focus of Tenerife's capital is Plaza de España with some fine, historic buildings, but there are also small, pretty squares, such as the one above, embellished with a colourful pavement and tiled benches.

KEY SIGHTS

La Orotava
Montes de Anaga
Parque Nacional del Teide ★
Puerto de la Cruz
Santa Cruz de Tenerife ★

FACT FILE

TOURIST INFORMATION
Plaza de España, Santa Cruz de Tenerife. ***Tel*** *922 23 95 92.*
Mon–Fri to 6pm (Jul–Sep: to 5pm), Sat to 1pm (Jul–Sep: to noon).

MARKETS
Food & flea Mercado de África, Santa Cruz de Tenerife; daily am.

LOCAL SPECIALITIES
Crafts
Embroidery, ceramics, woodcarving.
Dishes
Conejo en salmorejo (rabbit and tomato stew).
Papas arrugadas (small, unskinned potatoes boiled in very salty water).
Puchero (saffron-flavoured vegetable and meat stew).
Drinks
Tacoronte-Acentejo (local red and white wines).

Lago Martiánez Lido, Puerto de la Cruz
This beautiful lido was designed by the Lanzarote architect César Manrique (1920–92), who campaigned for traditional, environmentally friendly development. It has sea-water pools, palms and fountains, compensating for the lack of good beaches nearby.

Cádiz

Cádiz can lay claim to being Europe's oldest city. Legend names Hercules as its founder, though history credits the Phoenicians with establishing the town of Gadir in 1100 BC. It later thrived under the Carthaginians, faded slowly to obscurity under the Romans and Moors, but rose to prosperity again after the Christian Reconquest of 1262. Today, Cádiz is a busy port, with an historic city centre crammed onto a peninsula at the end of a narrow isthmus. In surprising contrast to the tightly-packed houses are the well-tended gardens and open squares on the northern and western seafronts and the vast, spacious cathedral, with its eye-catching, yellow-tiled dome, on the southern seafront. The church of San Felipe Neri (1719) is where Spain's first liberal constitution was proclaimed in 1812, while the Museo de Cádiz displays archaeology, paintings and puppets made for Andalusian village fiestas.

KEY SIGHTS

Catedral Nueva ★

Museo de Cádiz

Oratorio de San Felipe Neri

Seafront gardens ★

FACT FILE

TOURIST INFORMATION

Paseo de Canalejas s/n.
Tel *956 241 001.*
Mon–Fri to 6:30pm (Jul–Aug: to 7pm), Sat & Sun to 5pm.

MARKETS

Food Mercado Central, Plaza de las Flores; Mon–Sat am.

LOCAL SPECIALITIES

Dishes

Fideos con caballa or cazón (thin noodles with mackerel or dogfish).
Pan de Cádiz (marzipan sweets).

Drinks

Jerez and *Manzanilla* (sherries).

EXCURSIONS

El Puerto de Santamaría 20 km (12 miles) NE of Cádiz. Main sherry exporting port. *Bodegas* to visit.
Medina Sidonia 40 km (25 miles) E of Cádiz. White hilltop town.

Singers at Cádiz's *Carnaval*, mainland Spain's biggest pre-Lent carnival

Cádiz Old Town

The Old Town, rising uphill behind the cathedral, is full of narrow, dilapidated alleys criss-crossing at right angles, the walls often decorated with religious tile paintings. Lack of space on the peninsula meant that the white, Moorish-style houses were built tall and the squares tiny.

CATEDRAL NUEVA

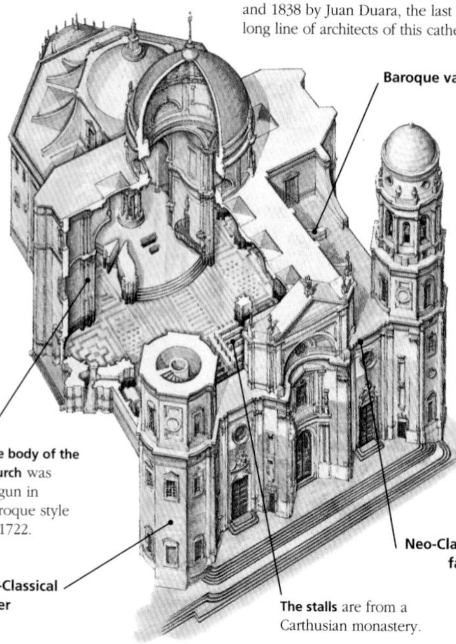

The cupola was built between 1812 and 1838 by Juan Duara, the last in a long line of architects of this cathedral.

Baroque vaults

The body of the church was begun in Baroque style in 1722.

Neo-Classical façade

Neo-Classical tower

The stalls are from a Carthusian monastery.

Jerez de la Frontera (Cádiz)

Fino **from Jerez**

The capital of sherry production is surrounded by chalky countryside blanketed with vines in neat rows. The foundations of the modern sherry trade were laid by British merchants who settled here, reflected in the Anglo-Spanish names over several *bodega* (cellar) entrances. A tour of a *bodega*, through cellars piled high with *soleras*, will enable visitors to distinguish between sherry types – *fino* (dry), *amontillado* (aged in a barrel, either dry or slightly sweet), *oloroso* (rich in colour and taste and sometimes sweetened) and *dulce* (cream – dark and sweet). The city tourist office can provide details of the tours available. Jerez also has a famous equestrian school in a fine building by Charles Garnier *(see p142)*, and there is a magnificent clock museum, the Palacio del Tiempo, containing one of Europe's largest collection of timepieces. The Palacio de Penmartín houses the Andalusian Flamenco Centre and offers exhibitions and audiovisual shows of traditional local music and dance. There is a partially restored, 11th-century *alcázar* (fortress) and the Catedral del Salvador is notable for the painting *The Sleeping Girl* by Francisco de Zurbarán (1598–1664).

A sherry *solera*
Fortified with pure grape spirit, young wine from the top cask is blended with older wine from the lower barrels. The *solera* system thus ensures that the quality of bottled sherry is consistent.

DISTANCE FROM PORT

35 km (22 miles) from city centre.

KEY SIGHTS

Alcázar

Catedral del Salvador

Palacio del Tiempo

Palacio de Penmartín

Real Escuela Andaluza de Arte Ecuestre ★

Sherry *bodegas* ★

FACT FILE

TOURIST INFORMATION

Alameda Cristina s/n, Claustros de Sto. Domingo. ***Tel*** *956 33 88 74.* *Mon–Fri to 6:30pm (Jun–Sep: to 7pm), Sat & Sun to 2:30pm (Jul–Aug: to 4pm).*

MARKETS

Food Calle Doña Blanca; Mon–Sat am.

LOCAL SPECIALITIES

Dishes

Langostino (lobster). *Berza* (cabbage stew). *Riñones al jerez* (kidneys in sherry). *Bienmesabe* (dogfish with vinegar and cumin). *Tocino de cielo* (baked egg sweet).

Drinks

Jerez and *Manzanilla* (sherries).

EXCURSION

Sanlúcar de Barrameda 30 km (19 miles) NW of Jerez. Famous for *Manzanilla*, a dry, light sherry.

Real Escuela Andaluza de Arte Ecuestre
This world-famous school of equestrian art was established in 1973. At midday on Thursdays (also Tuesdays, March to October and Fridays, July to October) there are displays of exquisite dressage, pageantry and carriage driving. In the mornings, visitors can watch horses being trained.

Seville (Cádiz)

Tile roundel from the Triana district

The capital of Andalusia, Seville has a rich cultural heritage. In 12th-century Moorish Spain it was the capital of the Almohads from Morocco, and both the famous Giralda (cathedral bell tower) and Torre del Oro are from this era. After the Christian Reconquest of 1492, Seville was granted a monopoly on trade with the New World and became one of Europe's richest ports, acquiring some splendid Renaissance and Baroque buildings. The historic district of Santa Cruz is a delightful maze of whitewashed, narrow streets surrounding the awe-inspiring cathedral. Close by is Calle de las Sierpes, Seville's most popular shopping street.

Triana ⑧
Once the quarter of bullfighters and flamenco dancers, Triana retains a traditional character and is famous for its potteries, ceramics shops, bars and flower-filled streets.

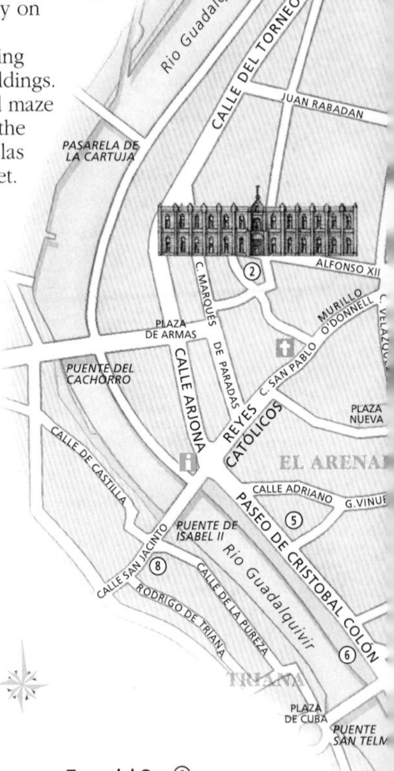

Museo de Bellas Artes ②
Set in a former convent built around three patios (1612), this is one of Spain's best art galleries. It shows paintings and sculpture from the medieval to modern period, focusing on the work of Seville School artists such as Murillo, Juan de Valdés and Zurbarán.

Plaza de Toros de la Maestranza ⑤
Spain's most famous bullring was completed in 1881 and seats 14,000 spectators. Visitors can see the matadors' chapel and picadors' stables, and a museum displays costumes, portraits and posters. The last scene of Bizet's opera *Carmen* is set here.

Torre del Oro ⑥
In Moorish Seville the Tower of Gold, built in 1220, was part of the city fortifications. It served as a lookout, with a defensive chain stretched across the river to a twin tower opposite.

Basílica de la Macarena ①
Dating from 1949, this church houses the much-loved image of the Virgen de la Macarena. Her magnificent processional finery is in the Treasury.

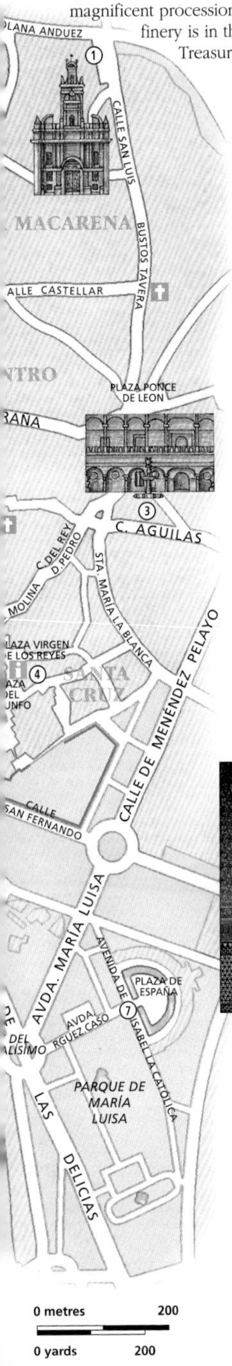

DISTANCE FROM PORT

120 km (75 miles) from city centre.

Casa de Pilatos ③
This 16th-century palace of the Dukes of Medinaceli was thought to resemble Pontius Pilate's house in Jerusalem. Its collection of Roman sculptures includes *Leda and the Swan*.

Santa Cruz ④
The old Jewish quarter, with its maze of white alleyways, is Seville's most picturesque district and contains many of the city's famous sights. In the Reales Alcázares visitors can see this sumptuous Ambassadors' Hall.

Plaza de España & Parque María Luisa ⑦
The huge semi-circular plaza was the centrepiece for the 1929 Ibero-American Exposition. The attractive park was landscaped as a leafy setting for its pavilions.

KEY SIGHTS

① Basílica de la Macarena
② Museo de Bellas Artes ★
③ Casa de Pilatos
④ Santa Cruz ★ *(see pp188–9)*
⑤ Plaza de Toros de la Maestranza
⑥ Torre del Oro
⑦ Plaza de España & Parque María Luisa
⑧ Triana

FACT FILE

TOURIST INFORMATION

Avenida de la Constitución 21. ***Tel*** *95 478 75 78.* *Mon–Fri to 7:30pm, Sat & Sun to 3pm.*

MARKETS

Food Plaza del Altozano in Triana & Calle Pastor y Landero; both Mon–Sat am.
Flea Alameda de Hércules; Sun am.

LOCAL SPECIALITIES

Crafts
Ceramics (sold city-wide, but especially in Triana), traditional flamenco fans, embroidered shawls, ruffled dresses, mantillas and Cordoban hats, blue Seville glassware made by La Trinidad glass factory.
Dishes
Aceitunas (olives. The Seville region is renowned for its olives).
Gazpacho (cold tomato soup).
Jamón serrano (cured mountain ham, notably from Jabugo).
Pescado frito (fried fish).
Soldaditos de pavia (salt-fish strips).
Cocido andaluz (chick pea stew).
Pato con aceituna (duck and olives).
Rabo de toro (braised bull's tail).
Ternera a la sevillana (a beef dish).
Yemas de San Leandro (baked egg-yoke cakes).
Drinks
Los Palacios and *Aljarafe* (red wines of Seville province).
Mosto (a semi-dry aperitif wine).

EXCURSION

Itálica 8 km (5 miles) NW of Seville. Archaeological site of one Spain's oldest Roman cities, founded in 206 BC. Birthplace of Emperors Trajan & Hadrian.

Seville: Santa Cruz ④

Window grille, Santa Cruz

The maze of narrow streets east of the Moorish Real Alcázar and the great Gothic cathedral, resting place of Christopher Columbus, represents Seville at its most romantic. Picturesque alleys lead to tiny, hidden plazas and give glimpses into patios embellished with painted ceramic tiles and flowers. Once a Jewish ghetto, its restored buildings, with characteristic wrought-iron window grilles, are now a harmonious mix of up-market homes and tourist accommodation. Good tapas bars and restaurants keep the area buzzing well into the small hours.

Plaza Virgen de los Reyes
Horse-drawn carriages line this plaza, which has an early 20th-century fountain by José Lafita.

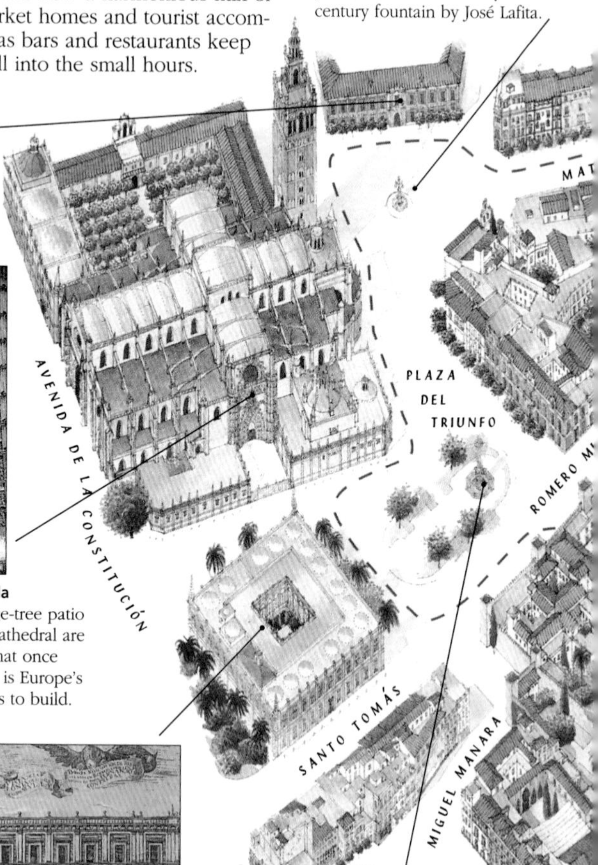

Palacio Arzobispal
This 18th-century Archbishop's Palace is still used by Seville's clergy.

★ Cathedral and La Giralda
The bell tower and orange-tree patio of Seville's 15th-century cathedral are a legacy of the mosque that once stood here. The cathedral is Europe's largest and took 100 years to build.

Archivo de Indias
Built in the 16th century as a merchants' exchange, the Archive of the Indies now houses a vast collection of letters, maps and drawings relating to the Spanish colonization of the Americas.

Plaza del Triunfo
A Baroque column celebrates the city's survival of the great earthquake of 1755. Opposite is this modern statue of the Immaculate Conception.

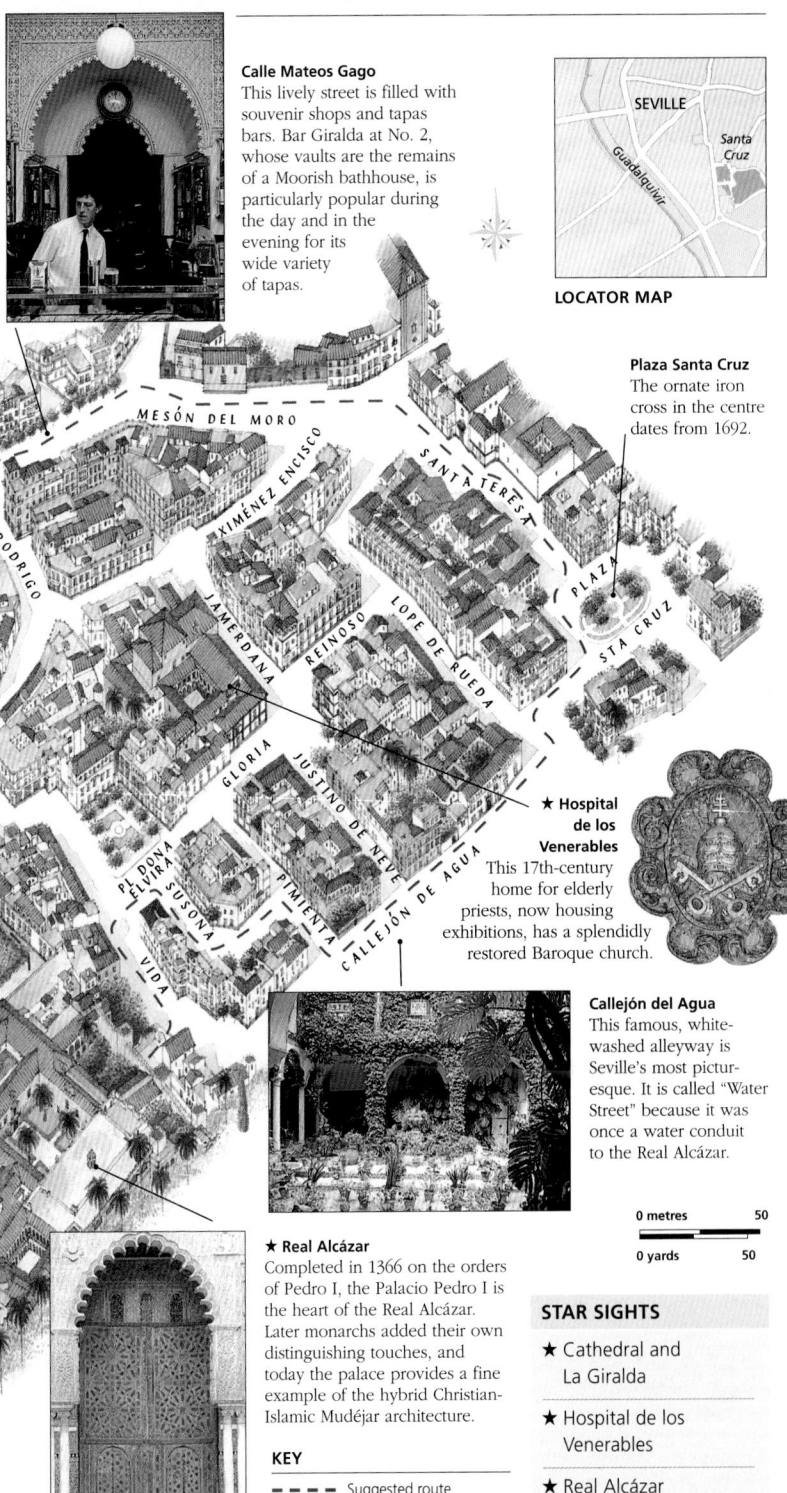

Calle Mateos Gago
This lively street is filled with souvenir shops and tapas bars. Bar Giralda at No. 2, whose vaults are the remains of a Moorish bathhouse, is particularly popular during the day and in the evening for its wide variety of tapas.

LOCATOR MAP

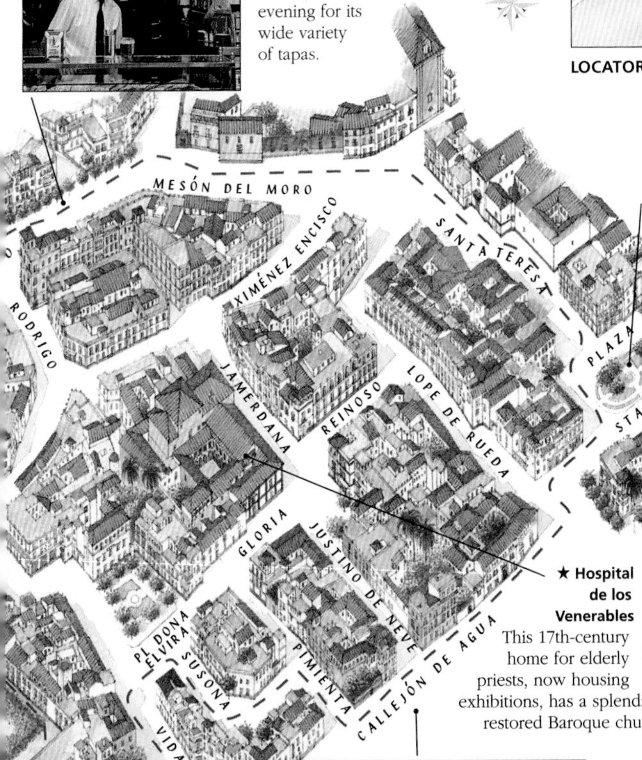

Plaza Santa Cruz
The ornate iron cross in the centre dates from 1692.

★ Hospital de los Venerables
This 17th-century home for elderly priests, now housing exhibitions, has a splendidly restored Baroque church.

Callejón del Agua
This famous, white-washed alleyway is Seville's most pictur-esque. It is called "Water Street" because it was once a water conduit to the Real Alcázar.

0 metres 50

0 yards 50

★ Real Alcázar
Completed in 1366 on the orders of Pedro I, the Palacio Pedro I is the heart of the Real Alcázar. Later monarchs added their own distinguishing touches, and today the palace provides a fine example of the hybrid Christian-Islamic Mudéjar architecture.

KEY

- - - - Suggested route

STAR SIGHTS

★ Cathedral and La Giralda

★ Hospital de los Venerables

★ Real Alcázar

Flamenco, the Soul of Andalusia

Seville feria poster of 1953

More than just a dance, flamenco is a forceful artistic expression of the joys and sorrows of life. Although it has interpreters worldwide, it is a uniquely Andalusian art form, traditionally performed by gypsies. There are many styles of *cante* (song) from different parts of Andalusia, but no strict choreography – dancers improvise from basic movements, following the rhythm of the guitar and their feelings. Flamenco was neglected in the 1960s and 1970s, but serious interest has once again returned. There has been a revival in traditional styles and the development of exciting new forms.

Sevillanas, a style of folk dance that strongly influenced flamenco, are danced by Andalusians in their bars and homes.

The origins of flamenco are hard to trace. Gypsies may have been the main creators of the art, mixing their own Indian-influenced culture with existing Moorish and Andalusian folklore, and with Jewish and Christian music. There were gypsies in Andalusia by the early Middle Ages, but only in the 18th century did flamenco begin to develop into its present form.

At a *tablao* (flamenco club) there will be at least four people on stage, including the hand clapper.

THE SPANISH GUITAR

Classical guitar

The guitar has a major role in flamenco, traditionally accompanying the singer. The flamenco guitar developed from the modern classical guitar, which evolved in Spain in the 19th century. Flamenco guitars have a lighter, shallower construction and a thickened plate below the soundhole used to tap rhythms. Today, flamenco guitarists often perform solo. One of the greatest, Paco de Lucía, began by accompanying singers and dancers before making his debut as a soloist in 1968. His inventive style, which today combines traditional playing with Latin, jazz and rock elements, has influenced many musicians outside the realm of flamenco, such as Raimundo Amador, who plays flamenco-blues.

Master guitarist Paco de Lucía

Singing is an integral part of flamenco and the singer often performs solo. Camarón de la Isla (1952–92), a gypsy born near Cádiz, was among the most famous 20th-century *cantaores* (flamenco singers). He began as a singer of expressive *cante jondo* (literally, "deep song"), from which he developed his own, rock-influenced style. He has inspired many singers.

WHERE TO ENJOY FLAMENCO

In Seville, the Barrio de Santa Cruz *(see pp188–9)* has good *tablaos* and, in Granada, Sacromonte's caves are an exciting venue. Most of the leading performers, however, are based in Madrid.

La Chana was a *bailaora* (female dancer) renowned for her fiery and forceful movements. Cristina Hoyos, another dancer famous for her highly polished personal style, leads her own flamenco dance company, which has enjoyed world-wide acclaim since the 1980s.

The proud yet graceful posture of the *bailaora* is suggestive of a restrained passion.

A harsh, vibrating voice is typical of the singer.

Traditional polka-dot dress

The *bailaor* (male dancer) plays a less important role than the *bailaora*. However, many have achieved fame, including Antonio Canales. He has introduced a new beat through his original foot movements.

THE FLAMENCO TABLAO

These days it is rare to come across spontaneous dancing at a *tablao,* but if dancers and singers are inspired, an impressive show usually results. Artists performing with *duende* ("magic spirit") will hear appreciative *olés* from the audience.

FLAMENCO RHYTHM

The unmistakable rhythm of flamenco is created by the guitar. Just as important, however, is the beat created by hand-clapping and by the dancer's feet in high-heeled shoes. The *bailaoras* may also beat a rhythm with castanets; Lucero Tena (born in 1939) became famous for her solos on castanets. Graceful hand movements are used to express the dancer's feelings of the moment – whether pain, sorrow or happiness. Like the movements of the rest of the body, they are not choreographed and styles vary from person to person.

Castanets made of wood

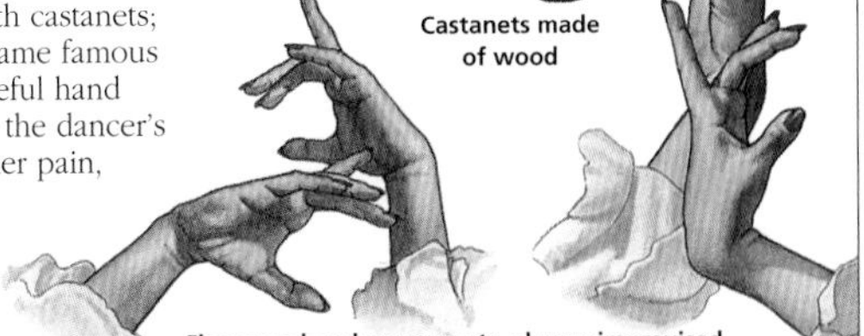

Flamenco hand movements, always improvised

Gibraltar

Gibraltarian Barbary ape

Native Gibraltarians are descendents of Britons, Spaniards, Genoese Jews and Portuguese who remained after the Great Siege (1779–83), when Spain attempted, unsuccessfully, to recapture the Rock. Britain had seized Gibraltar during the War of the Spanish Succession in 1704 and been granted it "in perpetuity" by the Treaty of Utrecht nine years later. As the gateway to the Mediterranean, the Rock was essential to Britain in colonial times, and the treaty is still invoked in response to Spanish claims to Gibraltar. Each year, around 4 million people stream across the frontier at La Línea to visit this speck of England bolted onto Andalusia. Pubs, pints of ale, fish and chips, pounds sterling and bobbies on the beat all contrast with Spain. Most visitors are Spaniards, who cross the border to go shopping.

Keep ③
The lower part of this Moorish castle, built in the 8th century, is still used to house Gibraltar's prison population.

Great Siege Tunnels ②
Soldiers' barracks and storerooms fill 50 km (31 miles) of tunnels.

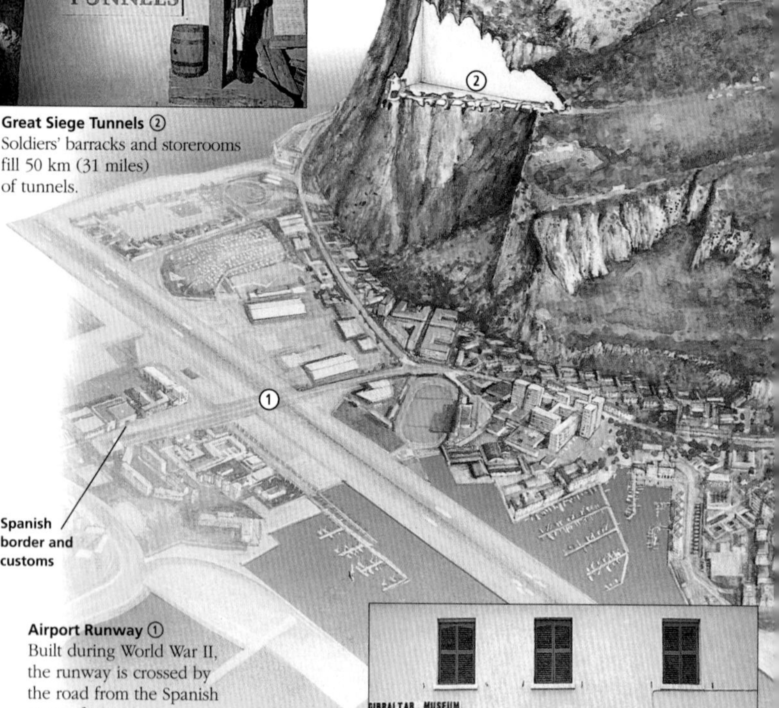

Airport Runway ①
Built during World War II, the runway is crossed by the road from the Spanish town of La Línea.

Gibraltar Museum ④
Built on the site of Moorish baths, this museum houses an exhibition of Gibraltar's history under British rule. The Moors occupied the Rock from AD 711 to 1462.

St Michael's Cave ⑦
During World War II these caves served as a bomb-proof military hospital. These days, classical concerts are held here, taking advantage of the good acoustics. Beyond the main cave are smaller caves with stalactites.

KEY SIGHTS

① Airport Runway
② Great Siege Tunnels ★
③ Keep
④ Gibraltar Museum
⑤ Cable Car
⑥ Apes' Den
⑦ One-hundred-ton Gun
⑧ Europa Point
⑨ St Michael's Cave ★

FACT FILE

TOURIST INFORMATION

Duke of Kent House, Cathedral Square. ***Tel*** *350 200 450 00.*
Mon–Sat to 5:30pm.

SHOPPING

Wines, spirits, perfume, tobacco and inexpensive ceramics.

LOCAL SPECIALITIES

Dishes
The food offered is conventionally British, with roast beef, fish and chips, baked beans and deep-fried scampi featuring on most menus.
Drinks
British pubs are the most common drinking establishment.

EXCURSIONS

The border with Spain is open, but delays are frequent. Visitors to Spain will need passports.

Apes' Den ⑥
This is the home of Gibraltar's tailless apes. Legend has it that the British will keep the Rock only as long as the apes remain.

Europa Point ⑨
Gibraltar's southernmost tip looks out to North Africa.

One-hundred-ton Gun ⑧
Installed here in 1884, it took two hours to load this gun. It could fire shells weighing 910 kg (2,000 lb).

Cable Car ④
A cable car runs from here to the top of the Rock; at 450 m (1,475 ft), it is often shrouded in mist.

Alhambra (Málaga)

A magical use of space, light, water and decoration characterises this most sensual piece of architecture located in the east of Granada city. Built under the Nasrid dynasty (1238–1492) by three of its rulers, it represents their idea of paradise on Earth, and was created to belie an image of waning power. Modest materials were used (tiles, plaster and timber), but they were superbly worked. Although the Alhambra suffered from decay and pillage, including an attempt by Napoleon's troops to blow it up, the building has undergone extensive restoration and the delicate craftsmanship still dazzles the eye.

★ Salón de Embajadores
The ceiling of this sumptuous throne room, built between 1334 and 1354, represents the seven heavens of the Muslim cosmos.

★ Patio de Arrayanes
Set amid myrtle hedges and graceful arcades, this pool reflects light into the surrounding halls.

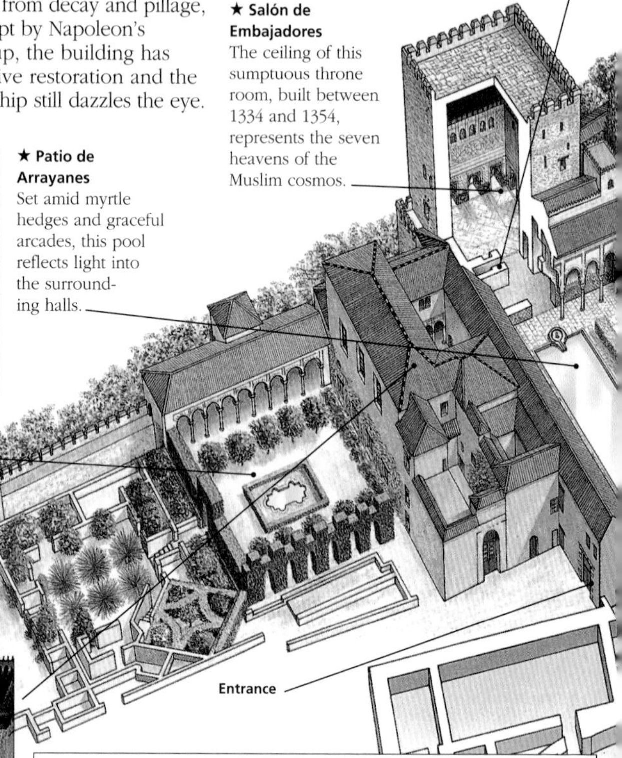

Patio del Mexuar
The Mexuar, or council chamber, completed in 1365, was where the sultan listened to the petitions of his subjects and held meetings with his ministers. It was converted to a chapel after the Reconquest.

PLAN OF THE ALHAMBRA

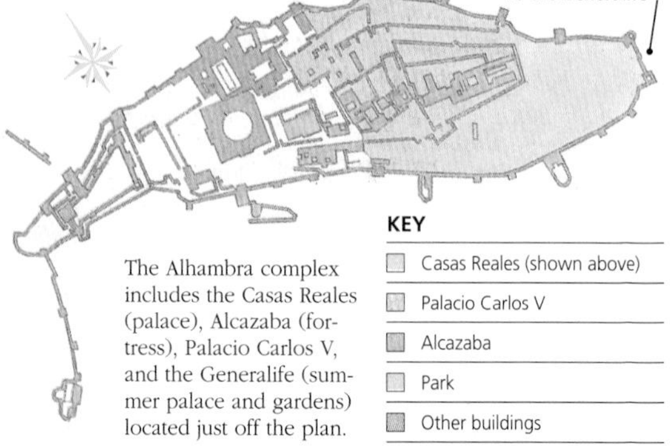

The Alhambra complex includes the Casas Reales (palace), Alcazaba (fortress), Palacio Carlos V, and the Generalife (summer palace and gardens) located just off the plan.

KEY

- Casas Reales (shown above)
- Palacio Carlos V
- Alcazaba
- Park
- Other buildings

Palacio del Partal
A tower and its pavilion, with a five-arched portico, are all that remain of the Palacio del Partal, the Alhambra's oldest palace.

DISTANCE FROM PORT

128 km (80 miles) from city centre.

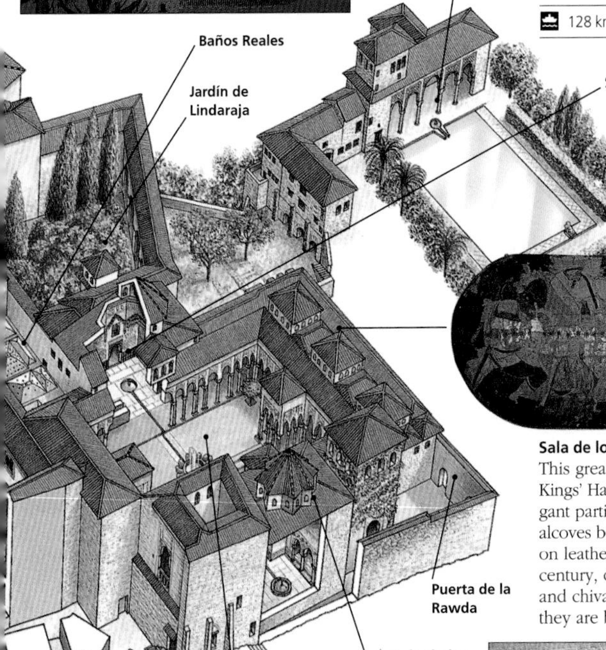

Baños Reales

Jardín de Lindaraja

Sala de las Dos Hermanas
With its honeycomb dome, the Hall of the Two Sisters is a superb example of Spanish Islamic architecture.

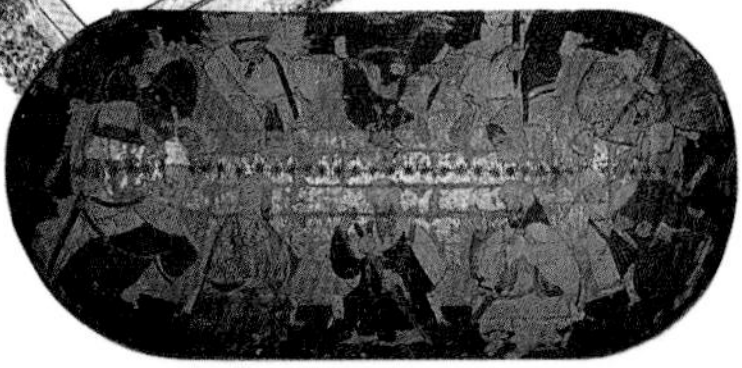

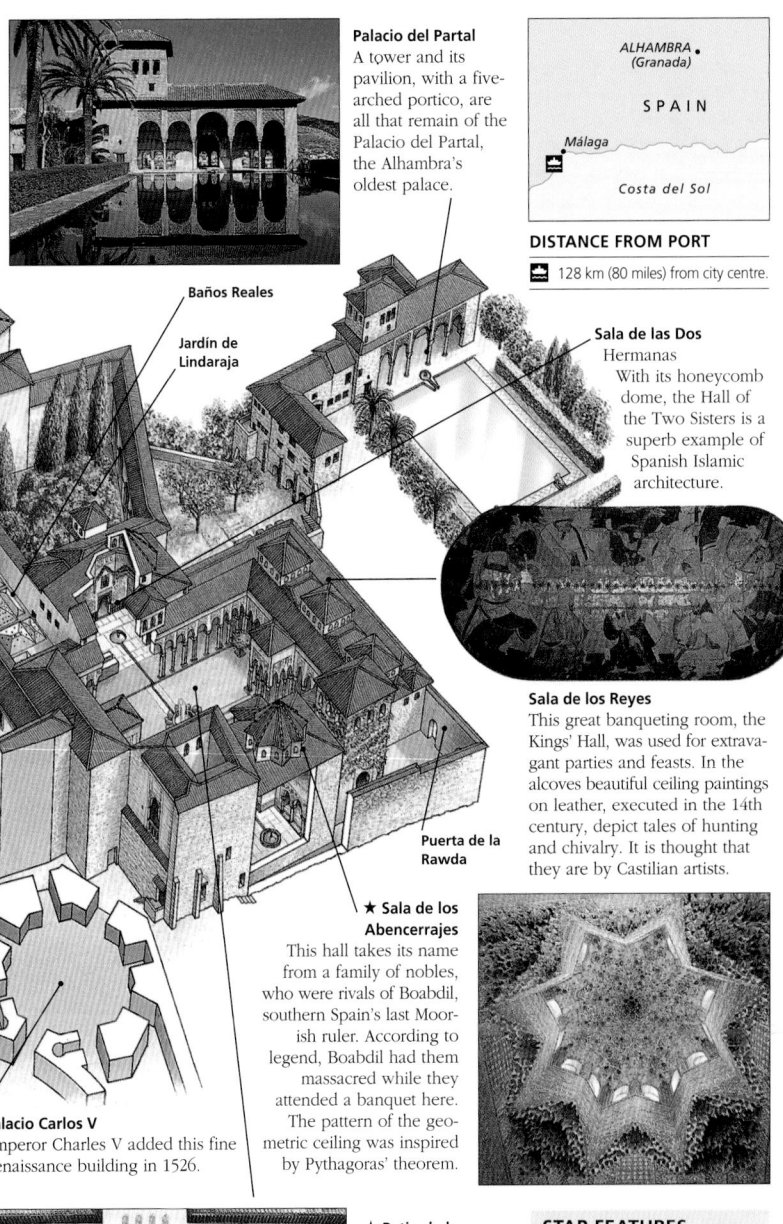

Sala de los Reyes
This great banqueting room, the Kings' Hall, was used for extravagant parties and feasts. In the alcoves beautiful ceiling paintings on leather, executed in the 14th century, depict tales of hunting and chivalry. It is thought that they are by Castilian artists.

Puerta de la Rawda

★ Sala de los Abencerrajes
This hall takes its name from a family of nobles, who were rivals of Boabdil, southern Spain's last Moorish ruler. According to legend, Boabdil had them massacred while they attended a banquet here. The pattern of the geometric ceiling was inspired by Pythagoras' theorem.

alacio Carlos V
mperor Charles V added this fine enaissance building in 1526.

★ Patio de los Leones
Built by Muhammad V, this patio is lined by arcades supported by 124 slender marble columns – each one with a differently carved capital. At its centre a fountain rests on 12 marble lions.

STAR FEATURES

- ★ Salón de Embajadores
- ★ Patio de Arrayanes
- ★ Sala de los Abencerrajes
- ★ Patio de los Leones

Málaga

Façade detail, Málaga cathedral

Since Phoenician times (when it was known as Malaca) Málaga has been a busy commercial port. It flourished especially in the 19th century, when sweet *málaga* wine was one of Europe's favourite drinks until phylloxera ravaged the area's vineyards in 1876. Now *málaga* is again a popular dessert wine. The city's most interesting sight is the Moorish Alcazaba, behind which are the ruins of another Moorish castle, the 14th-century Castillo de Gibralfaro. The old town radiates from the cathedral, which was begun in 1508 and is a bizarre mix of styles. The Museo de Picasso, in the Palacio de los Condes de Buenavista, has over 200 works by the native artist. The Picasso Foundation exhibits another collection in the house where he was born, the Casa Natal. To the east, Nerja is an attractively situated resort, famous for its cave paintings.

KEY SIGHTS

Alcazaba ★
Casa Natal de Picasso
Castillo de Gibralfaro
Cathedral
Museo de Picasso

FACT FILE

TOURIST INFORMATION

Plaza de la Marina,11. ***Tel*** *95 212 20 20.* ☐ *Nov–Mar: daily to 6pm; Apr–Oct: Mon–Fri to 7pm, Sat & Sun to 7pm.*

MARKETS

Food Atarazanas; Mon–Sat am.

LOCAL SPECIALITIES

Dishes

Boquerones en vinagre (small marinated fish).
Rabo de toro a la Rondeña (braised bull's tail stew).

Drinks

Málaga (very sweet dessert wine).
Moscatel (sweet dessert wine).

EXCURSIONS

Nerja 35 km (22 miles) E of Málaga. Resort and prehistoric caves.
Montes de Málaga 15 km (9 miles) N of Málaga. Nature reserve.

Nerja
This well-established resort lies on a cliff above a sandy cove at the foot of the beautiful Sierra de Almijara. There are sweeping views from the restaurant-lined promontory, called the Balcón de Europa. East of town are the Cuevas de Nerja; vast caverns with 20,000-year-old wall paintings.

Alcazaba
This vast fortress was built between the 8th and 11th centuries on the site of a Roman town. There is a partially excavated Roman amphitheatre just outside the entrance. The remains of Moorish walls can be seen, but the real attraction is the fascinating Museo Arqueológico, housing Moorish, Roman and Phoenician artifacts.

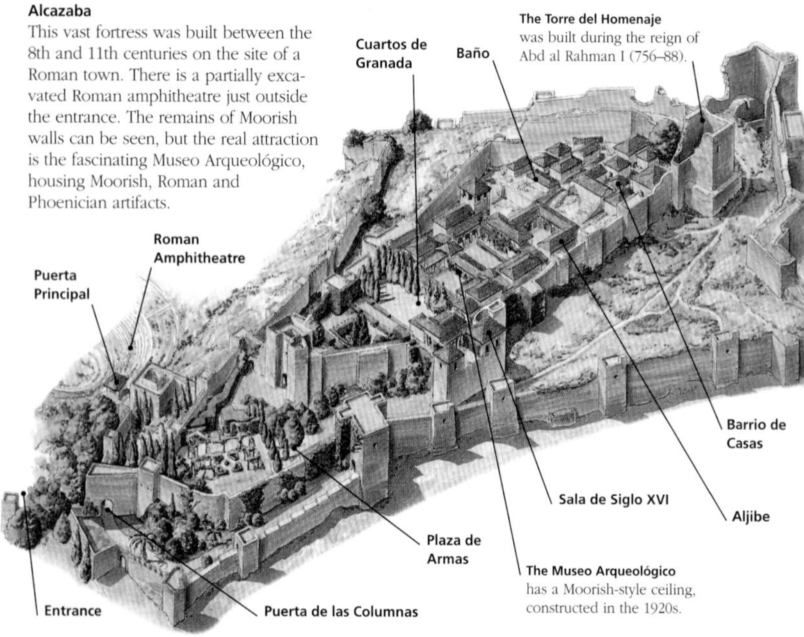

Ibiza

Ibizan shepherdess

This small island, the nearest of the Balearics to the Spanish mainland, was untouched by tourism until the 1960s, when it began to appear in Europe's holiday brochures. Its modern reputation for wild nightlife is justified – Ibiza town has a greater concentration of clubs and discos than anywhere else in Europe. However, the island has not completely lost its character. The countryside, particularly in the north, is a patchwork of groves of olive, fig and almond trees and wooded hills, and the coast is indented by innumerable rocky coves. In the south, flamingos populate the salt flats. The cathedral in the capital Ibiza, or Eivissa (a dialect of Catalan is spoken in all the Balearics), dates from the arrival of the Catalans on the islands in the 13th century. Two notable 16th-century monuments are the Portal de ses Taules, a gateway in the old city wall, and the Església de Santo Domingo with Baroque frescoed walls and ceiling. Sant Antoni, the second town, is now a lively resort, while Santa Eulària has retained more of its old centre intact.

KEY SIGHTS

Cathedral

Església de Santo Domingo ★

Ibiza Old Town

Ses Salines

Santa Eulària

FACT FILE

TOURIST INFORMATION

Calle Antonio Riquer 2, Andenes del Puerto, Ibiza. ***Tel*** *971 191 951.*
Jun–Sep: Mon–Sat to 8pm; Oct–May: Mon–Fri to 1:30pm, Sat to 2pm.

MARKETS

Food Es Canar, Santa Eulària; Wed am. Les Dàlies, Sant Carles; Sat am.

LOCAL SPECIALITIES

Crafts

Embroidery, jewellery, ceramics.

Dishes

Burrida de ratjada (skate with almonds).

Guisat de marisc (seafood hotpot).

Sofrit de pagès (meat stew).

Flaó (a cheese pastry dessert).

Graixonera (a doughy cake).

Orelletes (anis-flavoured buns).

Drinks

Herbes eivissenques (herbal liqueur).

Santa Eulària
This 16th-century, whitewashed church with a pretty, covered courtyard stands among the houses of the old quarter of Santa Eulària d'es Riu. The town was built on top of a little hill, because this site was more easily defended than the seashore below. Adjacent to the church is the Museu Etnològic, a folk museum in a renovated farmhouse. Old photographs show how drastically Ibiza has changed over the last 50 years.

Sa Penya District of Ibiza Town
The old quarter of Ibiza is a miniature citadel guarding the mouth of the almost circular bay. It is crowned by the cathedral, built in Catalan Gothic style in the 13th century with 18th-century additions.

Ses Salines
Before the arrival of mass tourism, salt production was Ibiza's main industry, mostly from the salt flats of Ses Salines in the southeast of the island. Salt is still produced today, with most of it being exported to Scandinavia for salting fish. The salt flats are also an important refuge for many birds, including flamingos.

Mallorca

Mallorca is often likened to a continent rather than simply an island. Its varied nature never fails to astonish, whether in landscape, culture or pure entertainment. The fertile central plains produce cereal and fruit crops, with vineyards around Binissalem, while the Tramuntana region in the north is ruggedly mountainous. Mallorca's mild climate and lovely beaches have made it a foremost package holiday destination. Among the many who have fallen in love with the island's climate and landscape are the 19th-century writer George Sand and composer Frédéric Chopin, who stayed at the monastery of Valldemossa. Author Robert Graves settled in Deià, today still an artists' colony, drawn like many others by the west coast's enchanting scenery, dotted with splendid viewpoints. On the east coast, the sea has hollowed out the vast caverns of the Coves del Drac and Coves d'Artà. Palma, the capital, is in the south. In the old town, its great cathedral, with one of the world's widest naves, was built by the Catalan-Aragonese kings, who ousted the Moors in 1229.

Cloisters of the Convent de Santo Domingo in Pollença
This convent contains the town museum, exhibiting local archaeology, and holds a music festival every August. Pollença is one of the island's most popular tourist spots, but retains a picturesque appearance in its ochre-coloured houses and winding streets. Its fine churches include the 18th-century Nostra Senyora dels Àngels.

Deià
This village lies on Mallorca's spectacular west coast. Crowded in summer, it has been colonized by artists and writers since the English poet and novelist Robert Graves (1895–1985) came here in 1929.

KEY SIGHTS

Coves d'Artá and Coves del Drac ★

Deià

Palma de Mallorca Cathedral and Old Town ★

Pollença

Valldemossa

FACT FILE

TOURIST INFORMATION

Plaça de la Reina 2, Palma de Mallorca. ***Tel*** *971 173 990.*
Mon–Fri to 8pm, Sat to 2pm.

MARKETS

Food Mercat Olivar, Palma de Mallorca; daily am.

LOCAL SPECIALITIES

Crafts
Embroidery, carved olive wood, wrought iron, glassware.

Dishes
Huevos a la sollerica (fried eggs, *sobrassada* sausage and pea sauce).
Tumbet (pepper, tomato and potato casserole).
Ensaimada (sweet spiral yeast bun).

Drinks
Palo (an almond liqueur).

Palma Cathedral
Locally called Sa Seu, this vast, superbly sited building is one of the most breathtaking in Spain. It was begun in the 14th century and the vaulting was completed in 1587. In the 19th century, Gaudí *(see p200)* remodelled the interior and designed the highly original, wrought-iron canopy above the altar.

Menorca

Local gin

Menorca is the Balearic island furthest from the mainland. Its coastline is, arguably, more unspoiled than any other in Spain. The countryside remains largely green and pleasant with cows roaming the fields, which are divided by characteristic stone walls. The northern half of the island is more hilly and wilder than the southern half. The two main towns, Maó, the capital, in the east and Ciutadella in the west, are filled with historic buildings and beautiful squares. Ciutadella's Plaça des Born is one of Spain's most impressive squares, containing aristocratic mansions with Italianate façades. Menorca differs from its neighbours in having come under British rule from 1713 to 1782, and this era is interestingly reflected in Maó's Georgian-influenced architecture. Menorca also has abundant reminders of its more distant history in its estimated 1,600 Bronze Age sites – so many that the island has been described as an open-air museum. There are tower-like *talaiots, navetas* built in the shape of upturned boats and *taulas*, which consist of two slabs of rock placed in a "T".

Cala Turqueta
This is one of the many attractive coves cut in the white limestone of the island's southern coast. The northern coast is characterized by darker rocks eroded into cliffs and more sharply indented with rias.

Trepucó
Menorca is exceptionally rich in prehistoric remains and the majority of the sites are the work of the Talaiotic people of 2,000–1,000 BC. The *talaiots* are the huge stone towers of the Bronze Age villages.

KEY SIGHTS

Cala Turqueta
Plaça des Born and Ciutadella Old Town ★
Maó Harbour and Town
Trepucó ★

FACT FILE

TOURIST INFORMATION
Moll de Llevant 2. ***Tel*** *902 929 015.* ◯ *daily to 6pm.*

MARKETS
Crafts & local delicacies Ferreries; Sat am. Mercadal; Fri evening.
Food El Carme, Maó; Mon–Sat.

SHOPPING
Leather goods & jewellery
Found all over the island.

LOCAL SPECIALITIES
Dishes
Mahonesa (mayonnaise, reputedly invented in Maó. Popular with fish).
Caldereta de llagosta (lobster, garlic, tomato and pepper casserole).
Ternellas (stuffed sheep's intestines).
Formatge de Maó (local cheese).
Drinks
Ginebra (highly perfumed local gin).

Maó Harbour and Town
The capital has an exceptionally fine harbour. The quietly elegant town rising behind it was occupied by the British three times in the 18th century, leaving a legacy of sobre Georgian town houses. A charming vegetable market is held in the 18th-century Església del Carme's cloister.

Barcelona

Christopher Columbus

Barcelona, one of the Mediterranean's busiest ports, is more than the capital of Catalonia. In culture, commerce and sports it not only rivals Madrid, but also considers itself on a par with the greatest European cities. The success of the 1992 Olympic Games confirmed this to the world. Although there are plenty of fine, historical monuments in the Barri Gòtic (Gothic Quarter), Barcelona is best known for the scores of buildings of the *Modernista* movement, the immensely imaginative Catalan variant of Art Nouveau spear-headed by Antoni Gaudí. Barcelona continues to sizzle with creativity, with bars, public parks and outdoor sculpture all displaying bold contemporary design. From the renovated Port Vell (Old Port), thronged with cafés, it is a pleasant stroll up the lively Rambla to the medieval heart of the old town, with its narrow, traffic-free streets.

Palau de la Música Catalana ⑦
Designed by Lluís Domènech i Montaner and completed in 1908, this concert hall with a glorious stained glass dome is a jewel of *Modernista* architecture.

La Rambla ④
Alive at all hours of the day and night, this wide avenue flanks the whole of Barcelona's historic centre.

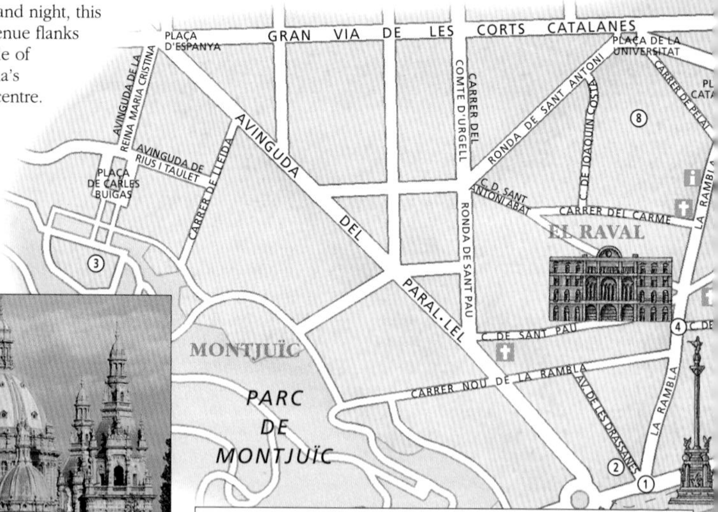

Museu Nacional d'Art de Catalunya ③
Housed in the main building of the 1929 International Exhibition is Europe's finest collection of Romanesque frescoes and a stunning display of Gothic art.

GAUDÍ'S BARCELONA

Gaudí studied at Barcelona's School of Architecture and built his first house in the city in 1888. He went on to design or collaborate on designs for almost every known media, creating furnishings as well as buildings. His greatest contributions to Barcelona are the Sagrada Família, Casa Milà and Casa Batlló. Casa Milà, completed in 1910, has a façade of white undressed stone and not a single straight wall inside.

Façade of Casa Milà on Passeig de Gràcia

grada Família ⑩
udí's unfinished masterpiece, gun in 1882 and still under nstruction, rises above the eets of the Eixample, the 19th-ntury expansion of the city.

sseig de Gràcia ⑨
e Eixample's elegant ain avenue is a showcase *Modernista* buildings, cluding Gaudí's Casa là and Casa Batlló, and omènech i Montaner's sa Lleó Morera.

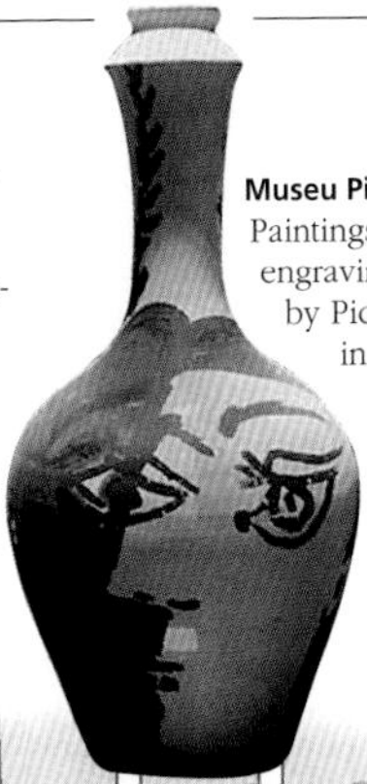

Museu Picasso ⑥
Paintings, drawings, engravings and ceramics by Picasso are housed in several adjacent medieval palaces in the Barri Gòtic. There are exceptional examples of his early work.

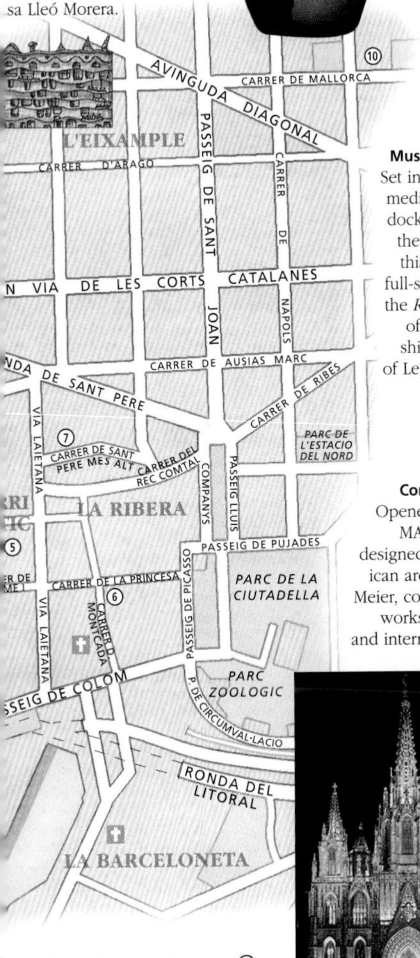

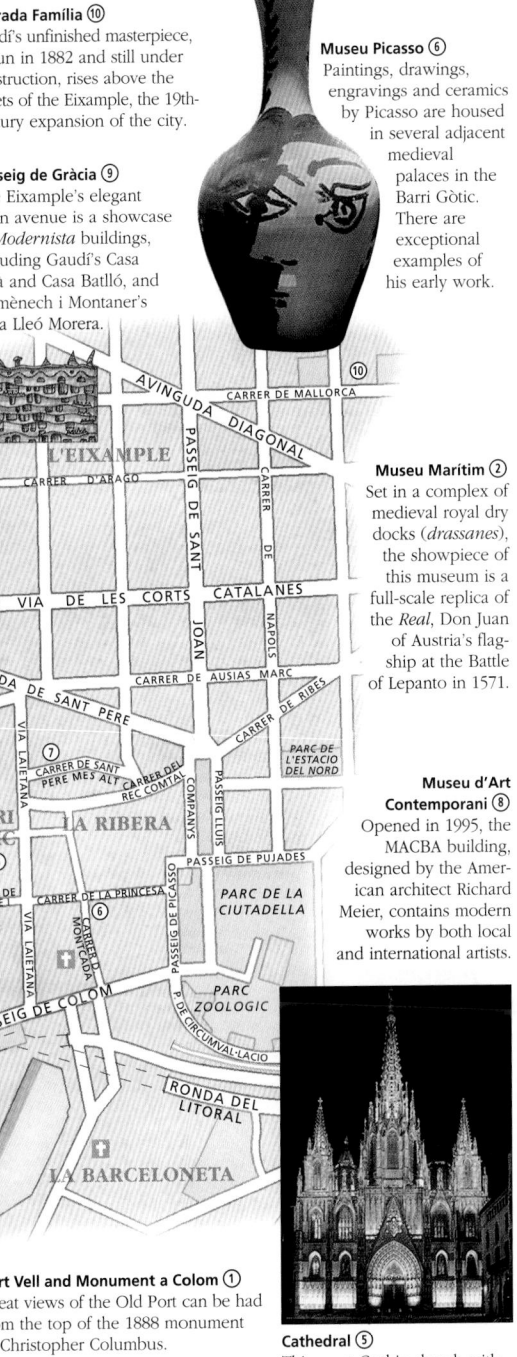

Museu Marítim ②
Set in a complex of medieval royal dry docks (*drassanes*), the showpiece of this museum is a full-scale replica of the *Real*, Don Juan of Austria's flagship at the Battle of Lepanto in 1571.

Museu d'Art Contemporani ⑧
Opened in 1995, the MACBA building, designed by the American architect Richard Meier, contains modern works by both local and international artists.

Cathedral ⑤
This great Gothic church with its beautiful cloister was begun in 1298. The façade and spires were completed between 1889 and 1913 to plans dated 1408.

ort Vell and Monument a Colom ①
reat views of the Old Port can be had om the top of the 1888 monument Christopher Columbus.

0 metres 500
0 yards 500

KEY SIGHTS

① Port Vell and Monument a Colom
② Museu Marítim
③ Museu Nacional d'Art de Catalunya
④ La Rambla ★ *(see pp202–3)*
⑤ Cathedral
⑥ Museu Picasso
⑦ Palau de la Musica Catalana
⑧ Museu d'Art Contemporani
⑨ Passeig de Gràcia
⑩ Sagrada Família ★ *(see pp204–5)*

FACT FILE

TOURIST INFORMATION
Plaça de Catalunya, subterrani.
Tel *932 85 38 34.* ◻ *daily to 9pm.*

MARKETS
Food La Boqueria, La Rambla; Mon–Sat.
Antiques Plaça Nova; Thu am.
Coins, stamps & books Plaça Reial; Sun am.

SHOPPING
Fashion Leather shoes, handbags and Spanish designer clothes.
Antiques Many shops in the Barri Gòtic, such as in Carrer de la Palla.

LOCAL SPECIALITIES
Crafts
Catalan ceramics.
Dishes
Botifarra, fuet, bulls, llonganisseta (all varieties of sausage).
Amanida catalana (mixed salad).
Esqueixada (salt-cod salad).
Arròs negre (rice with squid).
Graellada de marisc (grilled seafood with garlic mayonnaise).
Crema catalana (egg custard).
Drinks
Cava (Catalan sparkling wine).
Penedès, Costers del Segre, Tarragona (good, red, Catalan wines).

EXCURSIONS
Montserrat 55 km (35 miles) N of Barcelona. Benedictine monastery in spectacular mountain setting.
Poblet 120 km (75 miles) NW of Barcelona. Fine Gothic monastery.

Barcelona: La Rambla ④

The historic 2-km avenue of La Rambla, leading to the Port Vell (Old Port), is busy around the clock, especially in the evenings and at weekends. Newsstands, caged bird and flower stalls, tarot readers, musicians and mime artists throng the wide, tree-shaded central walkway. Among its famous buildings are the Liceu, the second biggest opera house in Europe, which reopened, fully restored, in 1999 after being gutted by fire, and La Boqueria food market, one of the best in Europe, with towering, artistically arranged piles of fruit and vegetables at the front and fish and meat at the back. Some grand mansions also grace La Rambla, interspersed with shops and hotels.

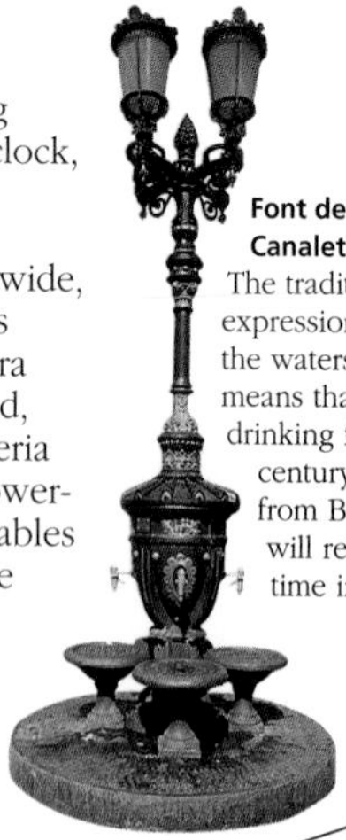

Font de Canaletes
The traditional expression "to drink the waters of Canaletes" means that anyone drinking from this 19th-century fountain is from Barcelona, or will return at some time in their life.

Palau de la Virreina
In 1771, Philip V's viceroy *(virrei)* to Peru used his New World wealth to build this Classical-Baroque palace, the city's largest private mansion. He died four years after its completion, leaving it to his widow, the *virreina*.

★ Mercat de Sant Josep
Popularly known as "La Boqueria", this is the city's most colourful food market. It was designed in the 1840s as an open-air space, but was given its iron-framed building in the early 20th century.

★ Gran Teatre del Liceu
Barcelona's opera house was first inaugurated in 1847, but had to be rebuilt after fires in 1861 and 1994. The latest rebuilding recreated the red and gold "jewel box" decor of the auditorium, but also incorporated much-improved facilities.

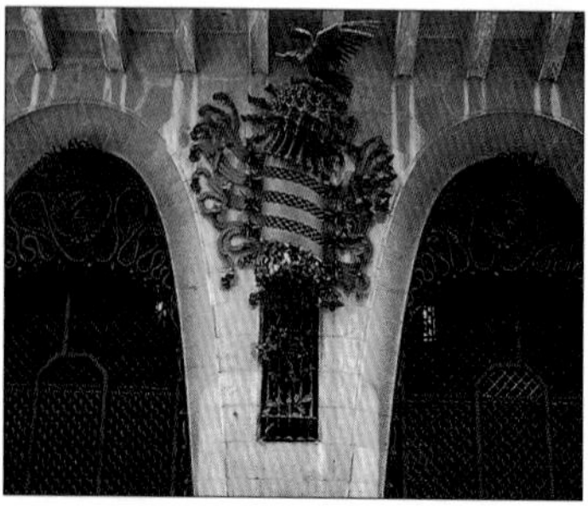

★ Palau Güell
This was Gaudí's first major building in the city centre and established his reputation for outstanding, original architecture. It was built in 1889 for the industrialist Count Eusebi Güell.

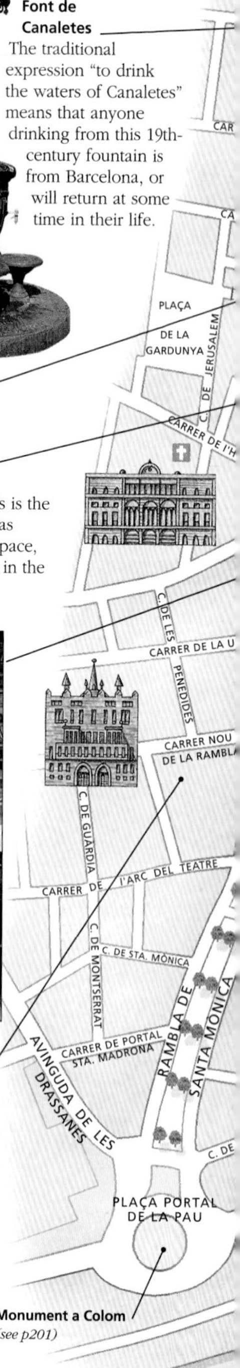

0 metres 100
0 yards 100

Monument a Colom
(see p201)

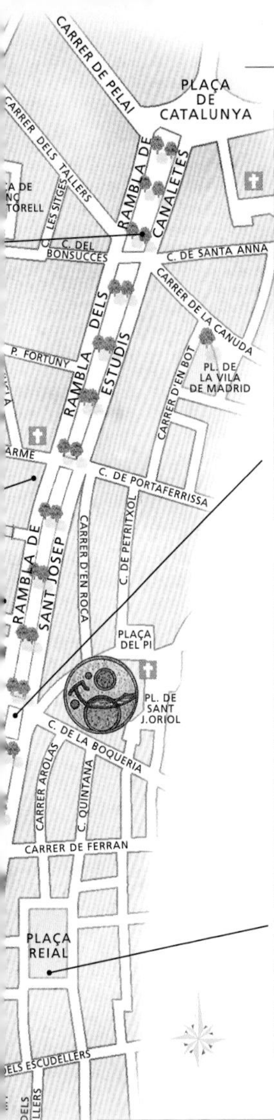

STAR SIGHTS

★ Mercat de Sant Josep

★ Gran Teatre del Liceu

★ Palau Güell

★ Plaça Reial

Plaça de la Boqueria
This square features a mosaic pavement designed in 1976 by Joan Miró (1893–1983) and an Art Deco dragon designed for a former umbrella shop.

★ Plaça Reial
Barcelona's most formal square, Plaça Reial was built in the 1850s after a design by Francesc Molina, who drew his inspiration from the typical Castilian *plaza mayor* (main town square). Renovation of the yellow façades and flagstones has restored its original elegance. The lampposts were designed by Antoni Gaudí *(see p200)*. On Sundays the square is occupied by a coin, stamp and book market.

The monument to Columbus at the bottom of the tree-lined Rambla

THE HISTORY OF LA RAMBLA

The name of this long avenue, leading from the Plaça de Catalunya, Barcelona's central square, to the statue of Columbus on the seafront, comes from the Arabic *ramla*, meaning the dried-up bed of a seasonal river. Barcelona's 13th-century city wall followed the left bank of one such river that flowed from the Collserola Hills. Convents, monasteries and the university were built on the opposite bank in the 16th century, outside the city wall, and are today remembered in the names of the five consecutive Ramblas that make up the great avenue. As time passed, the riverbed was gradually filled in. In the 1770s, the old city wall was torn down, grand houses began to be built, trees planted and La Rambla became a fashionable place along which to stroll. In 1835 an outbreak of anticlerical arson, and expropriations of church land just afterwards, swept away La Rambla's last convents.

Barcelona: Sagrada Família ④

Naturalistic carving

Europe's most unconventional church, the Temple Expiatori de la Sagrada Família is an emblem of a city that is well-known for its individualism. Crammed with symbolism inspired by nature, it is the greatest work of Antoni Gaudí (1852–1926). In 1883, a year after work had begun on a Neo-Gothic church on the site, the task of completing it was given to Gaudí, who changed everything, extemporizing as he went along. It became his life's work and he lived like a recluse on the site for 16 years. He is buried in the crypt. At his death only one tower on the Nativity façade had been completed, but work resumed after the Civil War and several more have since been finished to his original plans. Work continues today, financed by public subscription.

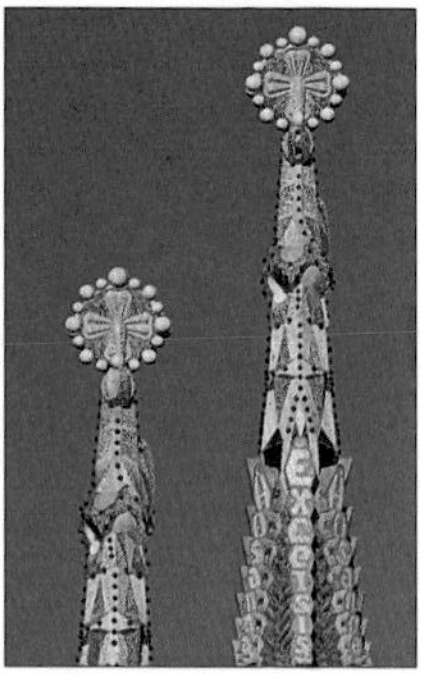

Bell Towers
Eight of the 12 spires, one for each Apostle, have been built. Each is topped by Venetian mosaics.

THE FINISHED CHURCH

Gaudí's initial ambitions have been scaled down over the years, but the design for the completion of the building remains impressive. Still to come is the central tower, which will be encircled by four large towers representing the Evangelists. Four towers on the Glory (south) façade will match the existing four on the Passion (west) and Nativity (east) façades. An ambulatory – like an inside-out cloister – will run round the outside of the building.

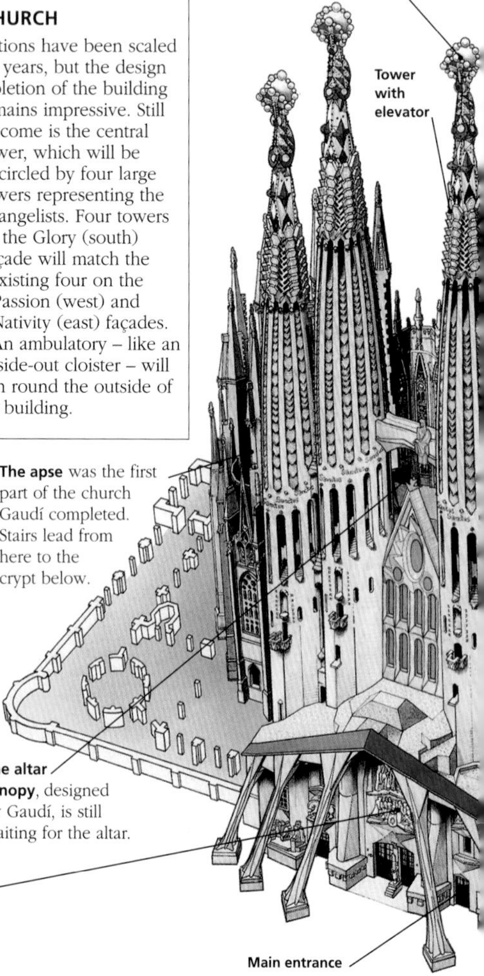

Tower with elevator

The apse was the first part of the church Gaudí completed. Stairs lead from here to the crypt below.

The altar canopy, designed by Gaudí, is still waiting for the altar.

Main entrance

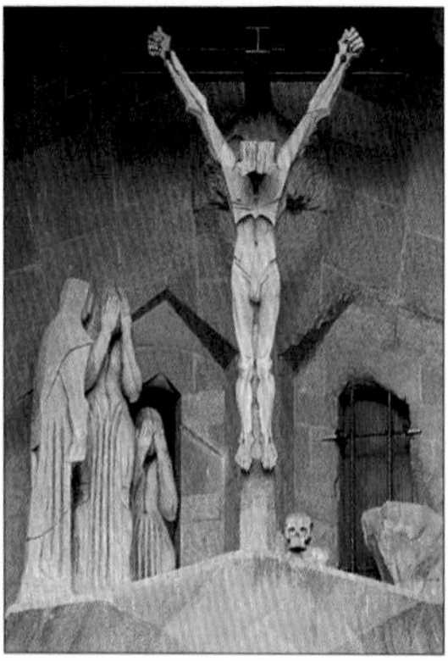

★ Passion Façade
This bleak, controversial façade with angular and often sinister figures is by Barcelona-born Josep Maria Subirachs. Rather than follow Gaudí's plans, he has created an entirely new design.

Spiral Staircases
There are 370 steep steps in each tower. Majestic views reward those who venture to the top of the towers via the elevator.

STAR FEATURES

★ Passion Façade

★ Nativity Façade

★ Crypt

Tower with elevator

★ Nativity Façade
This section of Gaudí's church, finished in 1904, has doorways that represent Faith, Hope and Charity. Scenes of the Nativity and Christ's childhood are embellished with symbolism: the cypress tree at the pinnacle of the arch symbolizes the Church and on it, white doves represent the congregation.

★ Crypt
The crypt, in which Gaudí is buried, was built by the original architect, Francesc de Paula Villar i Lozano, in 1882 and is where services are held. At the apex of the central vault is a lovely sculpture of the Annunciation. The lower floor contains a small museum, tracing the careers of both architects and the church's history.

Nave
In the nave, which is still under construction, a forest of fluted pillars will support four galleries above the side aisles, while skylights let in natural light.

Glory Façade
This façade, still under construction, will depict humankind gaining glory through redemption. The virtues, sins, purgatory, sacraments, the Last Judgment, and the Holy Trinity will all be symbolized in stone.

Mediterranean Flora & Fauna

Common Poppy

The Mediterranean climate has favoured the evolution of a diverse flora and fauna that is distinct from that of much of the rest of Europe. Characterized by long, hot summers and cool, damp, but virtually frost-free winters, it is rich in evergreen trees and shrubs, such as holm oaks, olives and Aleppo pines. Many spring annuals, bulbs and orchids are adapted to the highly seasonal rains, which fall between autumn and early spring. Most growth and flowering occurs then, when moisture levels allow, and many become dormant during the dry summer months. Nectar-rich, very colourful and fragrant with many aromatic herbs, the flora attracts a wealth of bees, butterflies and cicadas, which in turn provide a source of food for diverse reptiles and birds.

Spanish broom bears its bright yellow blooms in spring. It is characteristic of the *matollar* landscape of Spain's eastern Mediterranean coast.

COASTAL LANDSCAPE

Tough, aromatic, evergreen shrubs are characteristic of the coastal flora. Although the littoral appears barren in high summer, it is very colourful in spring when spangled with the flowers of bulbs, orchids and shrubs. Loggerhead turtles may come ashore to lay their eggs on deserted, sandy beaches.

MAQUIS AND GARRIGUE

Maquis is typically a dense community of evergreen shrubs and small trees, including tree heathers *(Erica arborea)* and strawberry trees *(Arbutus unedo)*. The more open garrigue is characterized by aromatic shrubs such as lavenders, rosemary, thyme and cistus, with spring-flowering bulbs and orchids.

The sea lily is a bulbous plant with very fragrant, showy, white flowers. *Pancratium illyricum* (left) grows in Sardinia and Corsica; the sea daffodil, *Pancratium maritimum,* lines coastal sands all round the Mediterranean and blooms in summer.

Aromatic lavenders, such as this bold *Lavandula stoechas*, are an important component of the low scrubby vegetation of the garrigue, lending scent and colour in spring and early summer.

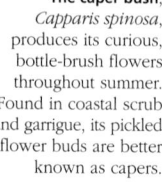

The caper bush, *Capparis spinosa*, produces its curious, bottle-brush flowers throughout summer. Found in coastal scrub and garrigue, its pickled flower buds are better known as capers.

The green lizard is one of several species that live around the Mediterranean. It prefers the cover of dense vegetation, but is often seen skittering away when disturbed while basking in the sun.

WILD BIRDLIFE IN THE MEDITERRANEAN REGION

Swifts are common in villages and towns, while in wilder, stony and sandy habitats the crested lark sings its reedy song. Many warblers are summer visitors; some, such as the Dartford warbler, are permanent residents of marshy habitats. The little egret is a striking inhabitant of coastal waters; on higher ground, gliding predators such as the black kite and buzzard are common.

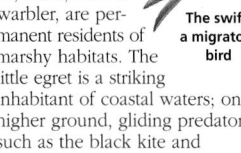

The swift, a migratory bird

Dartford warbler, with cocked tail

WILDFLOWERS OF THE MEDITERRANEAN REGION

The flora of the Mediterranean is extremely rich and diverse, and is dominated by evergreen trees and shrubs, usually with tough, leathery leaves that enable them to survive the hot, dry summers. Frosts are rare and most rainfall occurs in spring and autumn, the moisture resulting in two distinct flushes of bloom; the most prolific of these is in spring, with a later, lesser one in autumn. Many of the native wildflowers will appear familiar, because they are commonly grown as ornamentals in the gardens of more northern European regions.

Wild gladiolus grows in dry, sun-baked areas. Some seven species can be found.

Cyclamen are often found in shady areas beneath trees and shrubs. There are both spring- and autumn-blooming species.

Orchids are spring highlights. The Greek spider orchid (above) grows on mainland Greece, Crete and the Aegean islands.

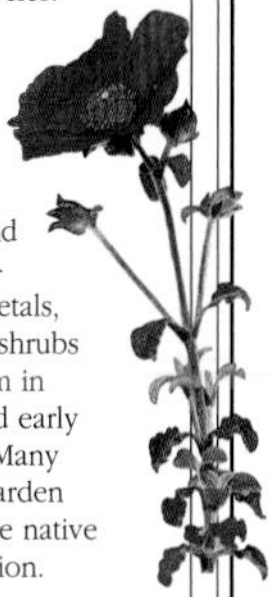

Cistus, with bright anthers and crumpled-looking petals, are small shrubs that bloom in spring and early summer. Many familiar garden species are native to the region.

TYPICAL TREES OF THE MEDITERRANEAN

The elegant, slender outline of the Italian cypress, *Cupressus sempervirens*, can be seen throughout the Mediterranean. It is a highly decorative tree and is often found in gardens and cemeteries. In the wild it grows on stony hill slopes. It produces rot-resistant timber, which was formerly used in construction.

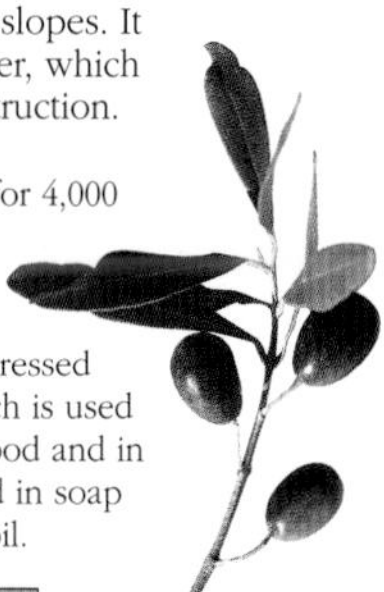

Olives have been cultivated for 4,000 years. The fruit is picked either unripe (green) or ripe (black) and then cured for eating. Ripe olives are also pressed for olive oil, the best of which is used as salad oil, for preserving food and in cosmetics. Inferior oil is used in soap and lubricants and as lamp oil.

Olive trees are slow-growing, drought-resistant and extremely long-lived evergreens, which can grow up to 10 m (33 ft) tall. They bear tiny, fragrant white flowers in the late summer.

Orange trees are extensively cultivated in the warmer parts of the Mediterranean. The fruits can take up to a year to mature.

Florence's Duomo, Italy ▷

ITALY

Venice
Genoa
Portofino
Pisa
Florence
Livorno
Siena
Civitavecchia
ROME
Naples
Sardinia
Capri
Pompeii
Cagliari
Palermo
Sicily
Messina

Sardinia

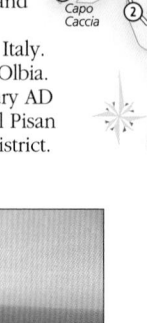

Sardinian basketwork

Sardinia is most famous for its translucent seas and the luxury holiday resorts on the Costa Smeralda. However, the entire coastline is picturesque, with isolated coves, coral strands and long, sandy beaches, spectacular cliffs and flamingo-filled marshes. Inland are rolling uplands and the rugged Gennargentu Mountains. The dominant feature of the island is the 7,000 *nuraghes*, conical structures built between 1800 and 300 BC by the Nuraghic people, about whom almost nothing is known. Sardinia was settled by the Phoenicians in around 1000 BC, after whom the Romans, the Pisans and Genoese, and then the Aragonese held sway before it was passed to the House of Savoy and united with Italy.

The main ports are Cagliari, Porto Torres and Olbia. Cagliari, the capital, is notable for its 2nd-century AD rock-cut Roman amphitheatre and the medieval Pisan and Spanish architecture in its high Castello district.

Porto Torres ④
This modern port's most famous sight is San Gavino, one of the island's most important Romanesque churches.

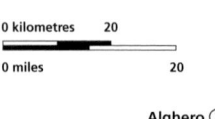

Capo Caccia ③
Towering above the sea, this promontory offers wonderful views of Alghero and provides a habitat for herring gulls, peregrine falcons and rare griffon vultures. Near the lighthouse, 656 steps lead to Neptune's Grotto, whose 2.5 km (1.5 miles) of caverns can be seen by guided tour.

Alghero ②
Populated by settlers from Barcelona and Valencia in the 14th century, this lively port is the most Spanish of all Sardinian towns in terms of architecture and culture.

The old town centre, a maze of narrow, cobbled streets within the ancient fortified quarter, can be easily explored on foot.

Maddalena Archipelago ⑤
The archipelago is noted for its rich bird life, and only two of its seven main islands are inhabited. Caprera holds the tomb and former home of Garibaldi.

Porto Cervo ⑥
At the heart of the Costa Smeralda, Porto Cervo is a resort for the seriously wealthy. Its marina is one of the best in Europe.

Costa Smeralda ⑦
The Emerald Coast is a beautiful stretch of coast-line, developed in the late 1950s by a consortium of magnates into one of the world's most opulent holiday resorts.

Cagliari ①
For visitors arriving by sea, the first view of the city is of elegant, arcaded Via Roma. Behind it is the old Marina district, full of trattorias and craft and antiques shops.

KEY SIGHTS

① Cagliari ★
② Alghero
③ Capo Caccia
④ Porto Torres
⑤ Maddalena Archipelago
⑥ Porto Cervo
⑦ Costa Smeralda ★

FACT FILE

TOURIST INFORMATION

Piazza Matteotti 9, Cagliari.
Tel *070 66 92 55.* *daily to 8pm.*

MARKETS (CAGLIARI)

Food & handicrafts Sapori di Sardegna, Vico dei Mille 1; daily.
Antiques Piazza del Carmine; 1st, 2nd, 4th & 5th Sun of each month. Piazza Giovanni XXIII; 3rd Sun of each month (except Jul & Aug).

LOCAL SPECIALITIES

Crafts
Table linen, lace, *pibbiones* (embroidered fabrics), hand-woven rugs and baskets, ceramics, cork, leatherwork, wrought-iron and carved wood, filigree jewellery. Look for the ISOLA (Sardinian Institute of Handicrafts) sign.
Dishes
Culurgiones (large ravioli). *Aragosta alla catalana* (lobster in vinaigrette). *Stufato di capretto* (kid casserole). *Pecorino* (sheep's milk cheese). *Carasau* and *coccoi* (breads). *Pardulas*, also known as *casadinas* (fresh cheese pastries).
Drinks
Vernaccia, Vermentino and *Semidano* (white wines).
Cannonau, Monica di Sardegna and *Anghelu Ruju* (red wines).
Cannonau, Vernaccia, Malvasia, Moscato and *Nasco* (dessert wines).
Mirto (myrtle liqueur).

EXCURSIONS

Santissima Trinità di Saccargia 35 km (22 miles) SE of Porto Torres. The most famous Romanesque church in Sardinia. Frescoes.
Valle della Luna 85 km (55 miles) NE of Porto Torres. Valley with amazing rock formations.
Su Nuraxi 60 km (37 miles) N of Cagliari. The largest Nuraghic site.
Tharros 115 km (70 miles) S of Alghero. Ruins of a large Punic city.

Genoa

A 19th-century stone lion on the steps of the Duomo

Genoa, birthplace of Christopher Columbus, is Italy's most important commercial port. It became a prominent sea power in the 10th century, and in 1339 Simon Boccanegra was elected its first doge. In the 16th century, the doge Andrea Doria and rich merchants proved astute patrons of the arts. The historic centre is famous for its *carruggi* (old, narrow streets), as well as the grand *palazzi* along the Renaissance Via Balbi and 16th-century Via Garibaldi. Near the Porta Soprana is a house where Columbus may have lived. The regeneration of Genoa's port has given the city some remarkable architecture, such as Renzo Piano's Bigo, built in 1992.

The Bigo, a sculptural structure incorporating a revolving sightseeing lift

San Lorenzo
Genoa's cathedral, with its black-and-white striped Gothic façade, is a blend of architectural styles, from 12th-century Romanesque to 17th-century Baroque. Highlights are the gilded nave ceiling painted with scenes of San Lorenzo's martyrdom (1624), the chapel of St John the Baptist with a 13th-century sarcophagus that once held the saint's remains, and the Treasury.

The Palazzo Reale
This palace on Via Balbi and the Palazzo Bianco and Palazzo Rosso on Via Garibaldi together house some of Genoa's finest works of art.

KEY SITES

Bigo
Casa di Colombo (Columbus Family House)
Palazzo Bianco ★
Palazzo Reale
Palazzo Rosso ★
Porta Soprana
San Lorenzo ★

FACT FILE

TOURIST INFORMATION
Via Garibaldi 12R.
Tel *105 57 29 03.*
daily to 6:30pm.

MARKETS
Food Mercato Orientale, Via XX Settembre; Mon–Sat to 7:30pm.

LOCAL SPECIALITIES
Crafts
Filigree from Campoligure, glassware from Altare, majolica and other ceramics from Albisola near Savona further east along the Ligurian coast.
Dishes
Farinata (flat snack-bread made of chickpea flour and oil).
Trofie alla Genovese (pasta with pesto sauce. Genoa is the city of origin of this famous sauce).
Pansotti con sugo di noci (spinach- and egg-filled pasta with a sauce of nuts, garlic and ricotta cheese).
Cima (a veal and vegetable dish).
Frutta candita (candied fruits, sometimes chocolate-coated).
Pandolce (a light cake made with orange-flower water).
Drinks
Red wines produced from local grape varieties, such as *Rossese* and *Ormeasco*.
White wines produced from local grape varieties, such as *Pigato* and *Vermentino*.

EXCURSIONS
Pegli 10 km (6 miles) W of Genoa. Romantic gardens at the 19th-century Villa Durazzo-Pallavicini. Naval museum in the 16th-century Villa Doria.
Nervi 8 km (5 miles) E of Genoa. Passeggiata Anita Garibaldi seaside promenade. Landscaped park at Villa Gropallo and rose garden at adjoining Villa Grimaldi.

Portofino

The picturesque setting of this former fishing village and its natural deep-water harbour, called Portus Delphinus in Roman times, have made it Italy's most exclusive resort, crammed with the yachts of the wealthy. It occupies a narrow inlet at the end of a peninsula on Liguria's Riviera di Levante – the attractive, rocky coastline stretching east from Genoa and dotted with other popular holiday resorts. The entire Portofino peninsula, the northern half covered in pine, olive, eucalyptus and chestnut trees and the southern half in *macchia* (Mediterranean scrub, *see pp206–7*), is a protected natural park. No cars are allowed into Portofino village. A footpath leads from the village to the church and 15th-century fortress of San Giorgio and, beyond them, to the lighthouse at Punto Portofino – the tip of the peninsula. Another path leads to the medieval abbey of San Fruttuoso. Its church dates from 984, but the abbey was built by the Doria family in the 13th century. The tower was added in the 16th-century.

Church of San Giorgio Set high above the village, this church dates from 1154. It contains relics reputed to be those of St George, the dragon-slayer, brought here by the Crusaders.

Characteristic Façade Old houses, painted in tones of red and ochre and with traditional green shutters, cluster around the harbour, contrasting with white, luxury motor yachts.

KEY SIGHTS

Church of San Giorgio

Harbour ★

Punta di Portofino and lighthouse

FACT FILE

TOURIST INFORMATION

Via Roma 35. ***Tel** 0185 26 90 24.*
Apr–Sep: daily to 7:30pm; Oct–Mar: Tue–Sun to 4:30pm.

MARKETS

Food Piazza Caprera, Santa Margherita Ligure; Mon–Sat am.

SHOPPING

Designer clothes Most exclusive designers have shops in Portofino.

LOCAL SPECIALITIES

Crafts Bobbin lace.

Dishes

Frisceu di baccalà (salt-cod fritters).

Torta pasqualina (chard pie).

Frisceu (lettuce or onion fritters).

Panissa (pan-fried slices of chick-pea- or chestnut-meal dough).

Paciugo (fresh cherry ice cream).

Drinks

Sciacchetra (red wine from the Cinque Terre region).

EXCURSIONS

Abbazia di San Fruttuoso 30 mins by boat or a 2-hr walk NW of Portofino village. Historic abbey.

Santa Margherita Ligure 5 km (3 miles) N of Portofino. Elegant resort.

Rapallo 13 km (8 miles) N of Portofino. Elegant resort.

Portofino harbour and village on the edge of an attractive peninsula, now a protected natural park

Venice

Venice was founded in the 1st century AD by the Veneti seeking shelter from Goth attack. It was a world power from the 12th to the 14th century and controlled Mediterranean trade into the 17th. The Grand Canal is a showcase of its history, with nearly every *palazzo* bearing the name of a once-grand family. At the heart of the city are the Piazza and Basilica of San Marco and the Palazzo Ducale (Doge's Palace). From here, most sights can be reached on foot.

Rialto Bridge ⑦
The Rialto Bridge was built across the Grand Canal in 1591 in what was then the main business area of the city. It was named after the ancient commercial seat of Venice where the first inhabitants settled.

Santa Maria Gloriosa dei Frari ⑥
This vast Gothic edifice, built by Franciscan friars between 1250 and 1338, is a rich repository of Venetian painting and sculpture.

Scuola Grande di San Rocco ⑤
Built from 1515 to 1549 to honour St Roch, the Scuola was a charitable institution for the sick. The walls and ceilings are decorated with a remarkable cycle of paintings by Tintoretto.

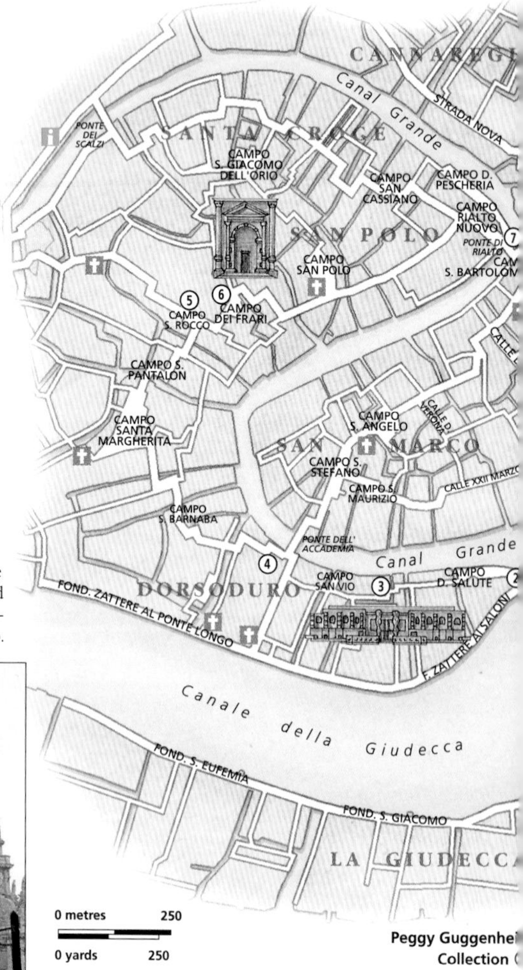

Santa Maria della Salute ②
Built to commemorate the end of the 1630 plague, this monumental Baroque church is one of Venice's most imposing buildings.

Peggy Guggenhei Collection (
This famous collection paintings and sculptur representing influenti modern art movements w installed in the Palaz Venier dei Leoni in 195

Piazza San Marco ⑧
St Mark's 98-m (323-ft) high campanile soars above the glorious façade of the great basilica and the piazza's busy cafés and graceful porticoes. From the top of the tower there is a great view of the piazza and also out over Venice to the Alps.

Palazzo Ducale ⑩
The colonnaded Palazzo Ducale is a triumph of Gothic architecture. It was once the Republic's seat of power and home to the doge and his family. New doges were crowned with the *zogia*, or dogal cap, at the top of the Giants' Staircase *(see p218)*.

St Mark's Basilica ⑨
Gleaming with gold mosaics, this oriental extravaganza is a blend of Byzantine and Western influences. Its greatest treasure is the Pala d'Oro, a gem-set gold altarpiece from the 10th century.

Accademia ④
This matchless collection of paintings provides a complete spectrum of the Venetian school. It spans five centuries and includes Veneziano's *Coronation of the Virgin* (1325).

San Giorgio Maggiore ①
The church and monastery on this island were built between 1559 and 1580 by Andrea Palladio. The church houses works of art; the monastery is a cultural and exhibition centre.

THE VENETIAN CARNIVAL

The Venetian gift for intrigue comes into its own during Carnival, a vibrant, playful festival preceding the abstinence of Lent. Masks and costume play a key role in this anonymous world, in which social divisions disappear. The tradition began in the 11th century and reached its peak of popularity and outrageousness in the 18th century. After a period of decline, it was revived in 1979.

Modern Carnival revellers

KEY SIGHTS

① San Giorgio Maggiore
② Santa Maria della Salute
③ Peggy Guggenheim Collection
④ Accademia ★
⑤ Scuola Grande di San Rocco
⑥ Santa Maria Gloriosa dei Frari
⑦ Rialto Bridge
⑧ Piazza San Marco ★ *(see pp216–17)*
⑨ St Mark's Basilica ★
⑩ Palazzo Ducale ★ *(see pp218–19)*

FACT FILE

TOURIST INFORMATION

Piazza San Marco 71f. ***Tel*** *041 52 98 740.* ◯ *daily to 3:30pm.*

MARKETS

Fruit & vegetables Erberia, Rialto; Mon–Sat am.
Fish Pescheria, Rialto; Tue–Sat am.

LOCAL SPECIALITIES

Crafts
Glassware, marbled paper sold in sheets or as decorated stationery, Burano lace table linen and lingerie, Carnival masks.
Dishes
Brodo di pesce (Venetian fish soup).
Baccalà mantecato (paste of dried salt-cod, olive oil, parsley and garlic).
Sardine in saor (sweet and sour sardines).
Risi e bisi (pea and bacon risotto).
Fegato alla veneziana (calf's liver and onions).
Drinks
Valpolicella (red wine from the Veneto region, notably *Recioto* varieties – rich, sweet and strong).
Prosecco (sparkling white wine).
Bellini (*Prosecco* with peach juice).

EXCURSIONS

Islands in Venice's lagoon:
Murano Centre of glass-making since 1291. Good glass museum.
Burano Lace and linen stalls and lively fish trattorias.
Torcello Cathedral of Santa Maria dell'Assunta with splendid mosaics. Byzantine church of Santa Fosca.

Venice: Piazza San Marco ⑧

Lion of St Mark

Throughout its long history Venice's Piazza San Marco has witnessed pageants, processions, political activities and countless carnival festivities. Tourists flock here in their thousands, for the Piazza's eastern end is dominated by two of the city's most important and historical sights – St Mark's Basilica and the Palazzo Ducale. These magnificent buildings complement the Campanile, Museo Correr and Torre dell'Orologio, not to mention the gardens of the Giardinetti Reali, open-air orchestras, elegant cafés – notably Quadri and Florian's – and stylish boutiques. Close to the waters of the lagoon, the Piazza is one of the first points to suffer at *acqua alta* (high tide). People can then be seen traversing the duckboards that are set up to crisscross the flooded square.

Bacino Orseolo
Named after the 10th-century doge, Pietro Orseolo, this is a customary mooring place for gondolas.

Caffè Quadri
This was favoured by Austrian occupying troops (1815–66).

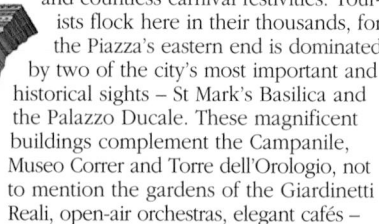

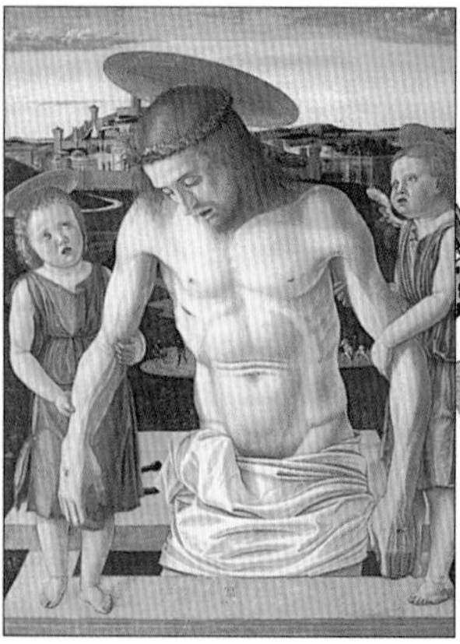

Museo Correr
Giovanni Bellini's *Pietà* (1455–60) is one of many Renaissance masterpieces in the second-floor picture gallery. Galleries on other floors cover the history of the city.

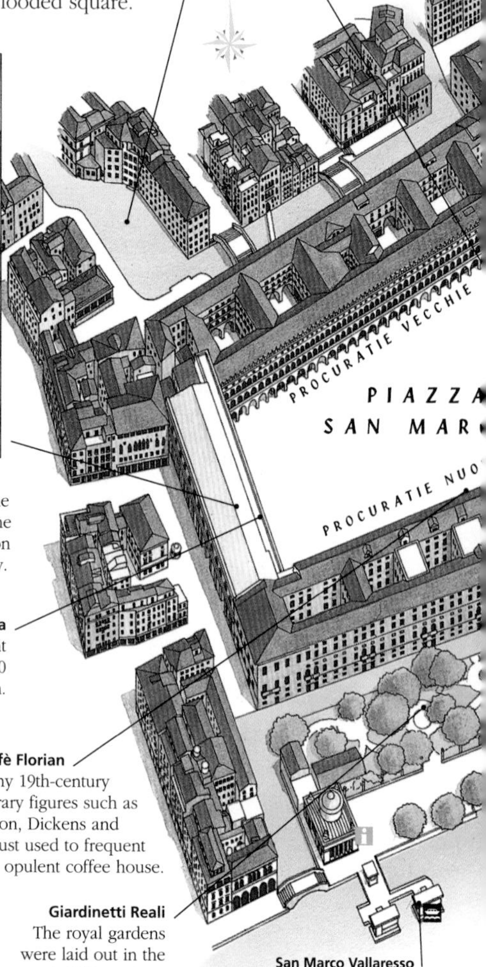

Ala Napoleonica
This is the square's most recent side, built by Napoleon in 1810 to create a new ballroom.

0 metres 75

0 yards 75

Caffè Florian
Many 19th-century literary figures such as Byron, Dickens and Proust used to frequent this opulent coffee house.

Giardinetti Reali
The royal gardens were laid out in the early 19th century.

San Marco Vallaresso

STAR SIGHTS

- ★ St Mark's Basilica
- ★ Palazzo Ducale
- ★ Campanile

Torre dell'Orologio
The Madonna on the 15th-century clock tower is greeted during Epiphany and Ascension Week by clockwork figures of the Magi.

LOCATOR MAP

Piazzetta dei Leoncini
The square was named after the pair of porphyry lions that stand here.

★ St Mark's Basilica
Built over centuries from the 11th century, St Mark's was the doge's private chapel until it became the city's cathedral in 1807.

★ Palazzo Ducale
Once the Republic's seat of power and home to its rulers, the Doge's Palace *(see pp218–19)* is a triumph of Gothic architecture.

★ Campanile
Today's tower of 1912 replaced the 16th-century one that collapsed in 1902. The top provides spectacular views of the city.

Museo Archeologico
The museum's Classical sculptures had a strong influence on Venetian Renaissance artists.

Columns of San Marco and San Teodoro
The columns marked the main entrance to Venice when the city could be reached only by sea.

San Marco Giardinetti

The Zecca
Work on this fine building started in 1537. It was the city mint until 1870 and gave its name to the *zecchino* or Venetian ducat.

Libreria Sansoviniana
The ornate vaulting of the magnificent, 16th-century library stairway is decorated with frescoes and gilded stucco.

Venice: Palazzo Ducale ⑩

The Palazzo Ducale (Doge's Palace) was the official residence of each Venetian ruler (doge), as well as Venice's seat of government and justice. It was founded in the 9th century as a fortified castle, but fire destroyed this and several subsequent buildings. The present palace owes its external appearance to the building work of the 14th and early 15th centuries. To create their airy Gothic masterpiece, the Venetians broke with tradition by perching the bulk of the pink Verona marble palace on a lace-like loggia and portico of Istrian stone. For centuries, this was the city's only building to be entitled *palazzo*; the rest were merely called *Ca'* (*Casa*, or house).

★ Giants' Staircase
This 15th-century staircase by Antonio Rizzo is crowned by Sansovino's statues of Mars and Neptune, symbols of Venice's power.

Arco Foscari
Copies of Antonio Rizzo's statues of *Adam and Eve* (1480s) adorn this fine arch.

★ Porta della Carta
This 15th-century Gothic gate was once the main entrance to the palace. From it, a vaulted passageway leads to the Arco Foscari, a glorious, pinnacled, triumphal arch, and the internal courtyard.

★ Sala del Maggior Consiglio
This vast hall was used as a meeting place for members of Venice's Great Council. Tintoretto's huge *Paradise* of 1590 fills the end wall.

Sala dello Scudo
The walls of this room, once part of the doge's private apartments, are covered with maps of the world. In the centre of the room are two giant 18th-century globes.

STAR FEATURES

★ Giants' Staircase

★ Porta della Carta

★ Sala del Maggior Consiglio

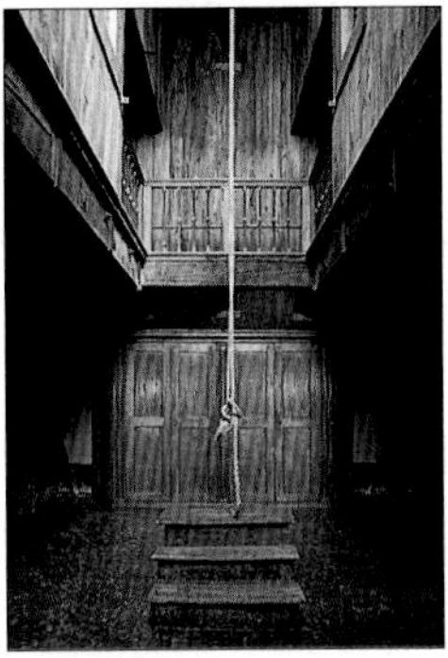

Torture Chamber
The interrogation of state prisoners took place here. Suspects were hung by their wrists from a cord in the centre of the room.

Sala delle Quattro Porte

Sala del Consiglio dei Dieci

Drunkenness of Noah
This early 15th-century sculpture, symbolic of the frailty of man, is set on the corner of the palace.

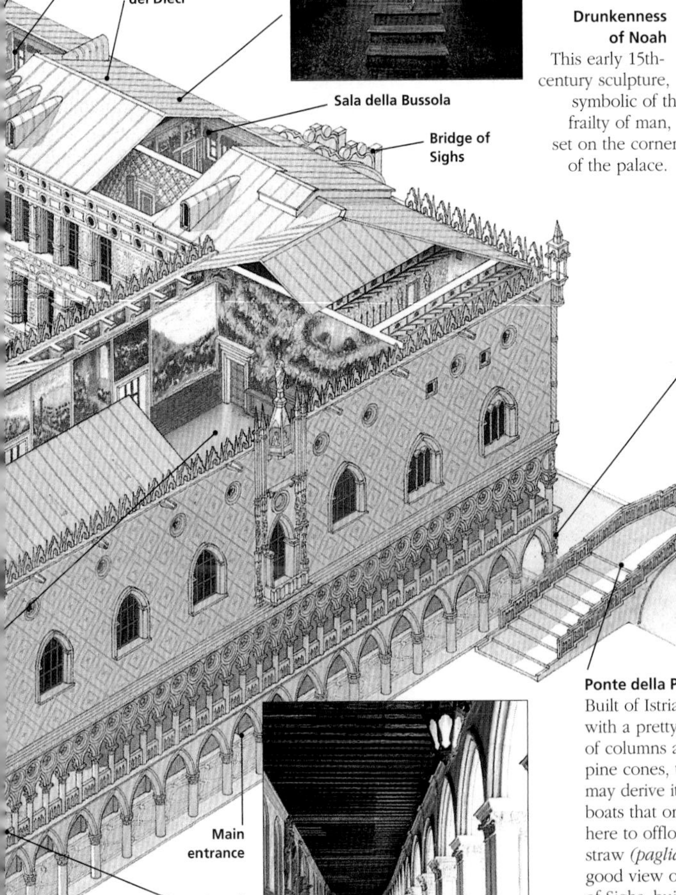

Sala della Bussola

Bridge of Sighs

Main entrance

Ponte della Paglia
Built of Istrian stone with a pretty balustrade of columns and sculpted pine cones, this bridge may derive its name from boats that once moored here to offload bales of straw *(paglia)*. It offers a good view of the Bridge of Sighs, built in 1600 to link the Palazzo Ducale to the new prisons.

Loggia
Each arch of the ground level portico supports two arches of the elegant loggia, which commands beautiful views of Venice's lagoon.

Pisa (Livorno)

From the 11th to the 13th centuries, Pisa's navy ensured the city's dominance in the western Mediterranean. Trade with Spain and North Africa led to a scientific and cultural revolution and remarkable architectural development. This can be seen in the Duomo and other religious buildings on the Campo dei Miracoli (Field of Miracles), which blend Romanesque colonnading, Gothic pinnacles and Moorish marble inlay techniques. Piazza dei Cavalieri, in Pisa's ancient centre, is the most attractive square and the colonnaded Borgo Stretto has elegant shops. Stately 16th-century *palazzi* flank both banks of the Arno.

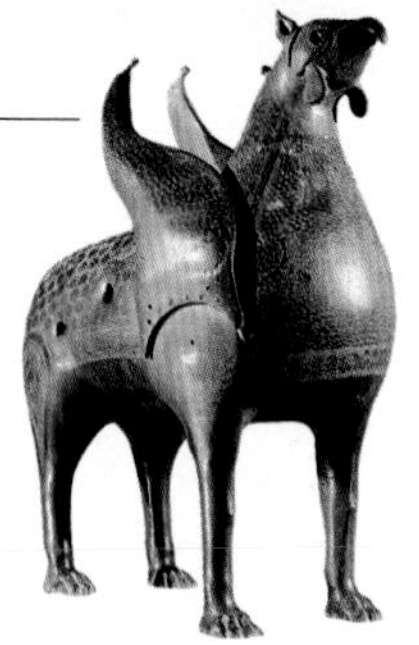

Museo dell'Opera del Duomo ④
A 10th-century Islamic bronze hippogriff is among the exhibits showing how both Islam and Classical Rome influenced medieval Pisan architects.

Duomo, Baptistry and Campo Santo ②
Carrara marble was used extensively in the decoration of the cathedral buildings and the cloister-enclosed Campo Santo cemetery.

LEANING TOWER ②

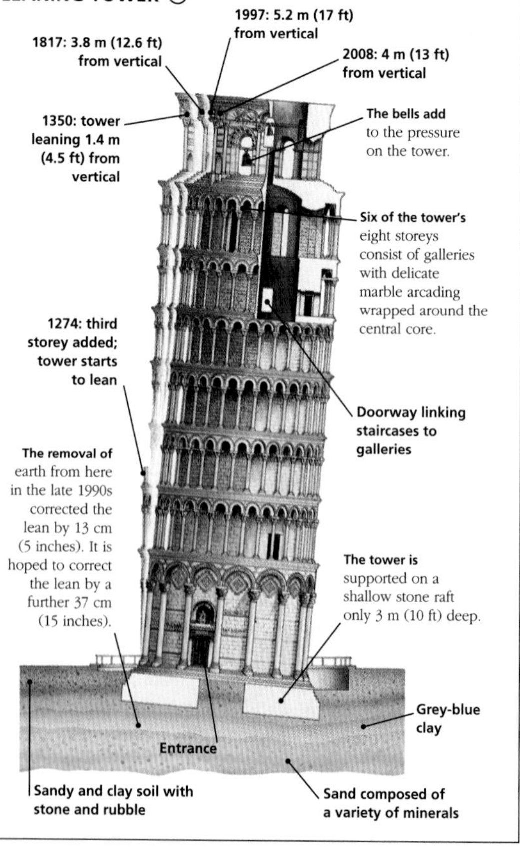

Museo delle Sinopie ③
Sketches from the frescoes that decorated the Campo Santo are preserved here. The frescoes themselves were destroyed in 1944.

Piazza dei Cavalieri ⑤
A statue of Cosimo I, crowned first Grand Duke of Tuscany in 1570, stands in this Renaissance square.

DISTANCE FROM PORT

22 km (14 miles) from city centre.

Museo Nazionale di San Matteo ⑥
Set in a medieval monastery, this museum displays Pisan painting and sculpture from the 12th to the 17th centuries.

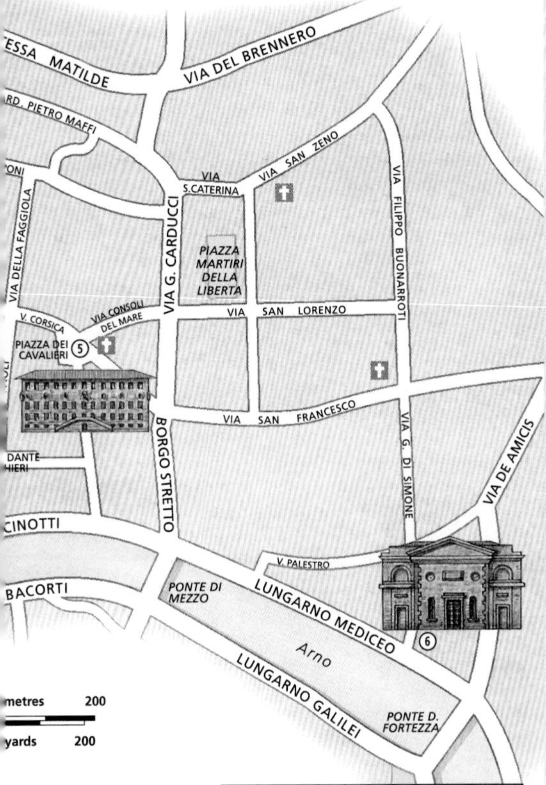

Santa Maria della Spina ⑦
Gothic pinnacles and niches sheltering statues of the apostles and saints decorate the roof of this tiny church. It was built in 1230 and from 1333 has housed a thorn *(spina)* said to be from Christ's Crown of Thorns.

KEY SIGHTS

① Leaning Tower ★
② Duomo, Baptistry and Campo Santo ★
③ Museo delle Sinopie
④ Museo dell'Opera del Duomo
⑤ Piazza dei Cavalieri
⑥ Museo Nazionale di San Matteo
⑦ Santa Maria della Spina

FACT FILE

TOURIST INFORMATION

Piazza Arcivescovado 8. ***Tel** 050 56 04 64;* Piazza Vittorio Emanuele 16. ***Tel** 050 422 91.*
Jul & Aug: Mon–Fri to 7pm (Sep–Jun: to 6pm), Sat to 1:30pm.

MARKETS

Food Piazza delle Vettovaglie; Mon–Sat am.
Clothes & household goods Via del Brennero; Wed & Sat am.
Antiques Streets around Piazza dei Cavalieri; 2nd Sat & Sun of each month (except Jul & Aug).

LOCAL SPECIALITIES

Crafts
Carved alabaster from Volterra, wooden furniture, marquetry and carvings from Ponsacco and Cascina, shoes and leather goods from San Miniato and Santa Croce sull'Arno, ceramics from Montopoli in Val d'Arno.
Produce
Truffles, notably from San Miniato. Monti Pisani virgin olive oil.
Dishes
Zuppa alla pisana (vegetable soup).
Pasta e ceci (pasta with chickpeas).
Anguille con piselli (eels with peas).
Trippa alla pisana (tripe casserole).
Cée alla salvia (eels with sage).
Bordatino (cabbage soup).
Drinks
Local wines, including *Chianti delle Colline Pisane, Bianco Pisano di San Torpé, Colli dell'Etruria Centrale* and *Montescudaio.*

EXCURSION

San Piero a Grado 6 km (4 miles) SW of Pisa. A very early 11th-century church built on the spot where St Peter is believed to have first set foot in Italy in AD 42.

Florence (Livorno)

As an independent city state, Florence became one of Italy's leading powers in the 13th century, first as a republic, then, until 1737, under the banking dynasty of the Medici. Its cosmopolitan society and wealth attracted artists and architects, who filled it with some of Italy's greatest Renaissance works. Historic Florence is compact and most of the great sights are accessible on foot. Many of the most famous, including the Duomo, Uffizi art gallery and statue-filled Piazza della Signoria, cluster in its western half. The eastern half, while similarly rich in *palazzi*, is also the place to shop. Across the river in the quieter Oltrarno district is the Medici's vast Palazzo Pitti.

Santa Maria Novella ①
Behind the Renaissance façade is a Gothic interior with superb frescoes by Masaccio and Uccello and a glorious Spanish chapel.

Ponte Vecchio ⑦
Florence's oldest surviving bridge was designed by Giotto's pupil Taddeo Gaddi and built in 1345. Its picturesque shops have been occupied by goldsmiths and jewellers since 1593.

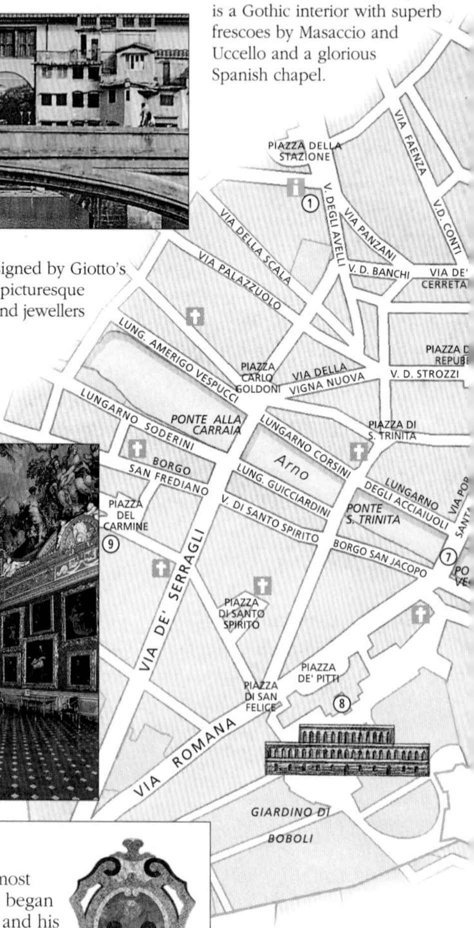

San Lorenzo ②
This parish church of the Medici was built in 1419 by Brunelleschi. Michelangelo's plans for the façade were never executed.

Palazzo Pitti ⑧
Originally built for the banker Luca Pitti, this enormous palace was bought by the Medici in 1550 and became their main residence. The richly decorated rooms display countless Medici family treasures.

THE MEDICI OF FLORENCE

The Medici held power in the city almost continuously from 1434 to 1743. Rule began discreetly with Cosimo il Vecchio: he and his descendents directed Florentine policy with popular support without ever being voted into office, but later generations gained titles and power and ruled by force. While two became pope, Leo X (1513) and Clement VII (1523), the most famous Medici was the poet and statesman Lorenzo the Magnificent (1449–92).

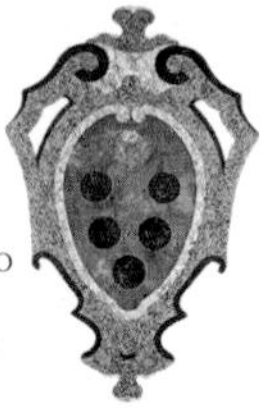

Medici coat of arms, San Lorenzo

Brancacci Chapel ⑨
Frescoed by Masolino, Masaccio and Filippino Lippi between 1424 and 1480, this famous chapel of the church of Santa Maria del Carmine celebrates the life of St Peter.

DISTANCE FROM PORT

85 km (53 miles) from city centre.

Piazza della Signoria ⑤
A copy of Michelangelo's *David* stands beneath the clock tower of the square's Palazzo Vecchio, Florence's town hall. The original is in the Galleria dell'Accademia.

Duomo, Campanile and Baptistry ③
Richly decorated with coloured marble inside and outside, this is Europe's fourth largest church. The 13th-century Baptistry is famous for its great doors *(see p226)*.

Santa Croce ④
The Gothic church of Santa Croce contains the tombs and monuments of many famous Florentines, among them Galileo, Michelangelo and Machiavelli.

Uffizi ⑥
Italy's greatest art gal-
lery was built between
560 and 1580 as offices
(uffici) for the Medici
duke, Cosimo I *(see p221)*. His successor,
Francesco I, used the
op storey to display the
Medici art treasures;
the paintings have re-
nained here ever since.

KEY SIGHTS

① Santa Maria Novella
② San Lorenzo
③ Duomo, Campanile and Baptistry *(see pp226–7)* ★
④ Santa Croce
⑤ Piazza della Signoria
⑥ Uffizi ★
⑦ Ponte Vecchio
⑧ Palazzo Pitti ★
⑨ Brancacci Chapel

FACT FILE

TOURIST INFORMATION
Via Cavour 1r. ***Tel*** *055 29 08 32.* *Mon–Sat to 6:30pm, Sun to 1:30pm.*

MARKETS
Food Mercato Centrale, Via dell'Ariento; Mon–Sat am.
General Piazza San Lorenzo; daily to 7:30pm.
Leather goods & souvenirs Mercato Nuovo, Via Calimala; daily to 7:30pm.

SHOPPING
Fashion shoes & bags Especially around Piazza di Santa Croce.
Designer clothes In Via della Vigna Nuova & Via de' Tornabuoni.
Jewellery Fine gold & silver.

LOCAL SPECIALITIES
Crafts
Embroidery and leather goods.
Dishes
Ribollita (thick vegetable soup).
Bruschetta (savoury-topped toast).
Pappardelle alla lepre (pasta in a rich hare sauce).
Bistecca alla fiorentina (steak grilled with herbs).
Cantucci (whole-almond biscuits).
Drinks
Chianti Classico and *Rufinah*, *Brunello di Montalcino* and *Rosso di Montalcino* (all good varieties of the classic Tuscan wine).
Galestro (a Tuscan white wine).
Vin santo (a dessert wine).

EXCURSION
Piazzale Michelangelo 2 km (1 mile) E of centre. A fabulous viewpoint overlooking Florence. Nearby is San Miniato al Monte, a very beautiful Romanesque church.

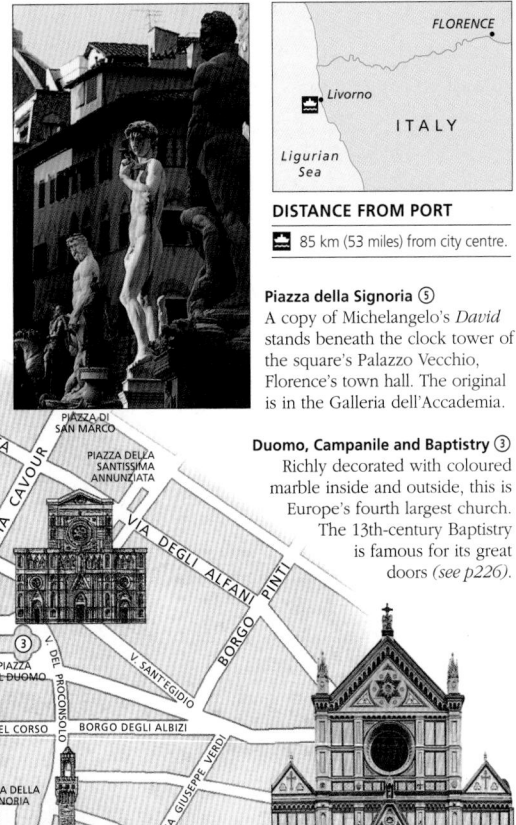

Florence: Around the Duomo

Statue on the façade of Orsanmichele

Much of Florence was rebuilt during the Renaissance, but the eastern part of the city retains a distinctly medieval feel. With its maze of tiny alleyways, it would still be recognizable to Dante (1265–1321) and his beloved, Beatrice Portinari. Dante's house, the Casa di Dante, still stands near the Badia Fiorentina, one of the city's oldest churches, founded in 978. He would also recognize the gaunt outlines of the Bargello, across the road from the Badia, and the Baptistry. One of the oldest streets is the Borgo degli Albizi. Now lined with Renaissance *palazzi,* it follows the line of the ancient Roman road to Rome.

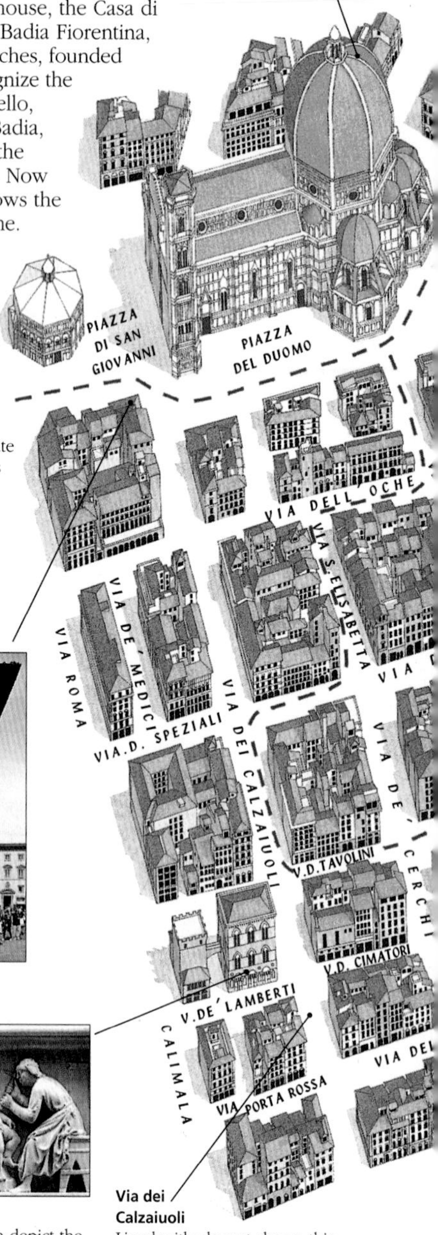

Dome
Brunelleschi designed the Duomo's great dome to dwarf the buildings of ancient Greece and Rome.

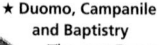

★ Duomo, Campanile and Baptistry
The vast Duomo holds up to 20,000 people. It is elegantly partnered by Giotto's campanile and the Baptistry, whose doors demonstrate the artistic ideas that led to the Renaissance.

Loggia del Bigallo
This was built in 1358 for the Misericordia, a charitable organization founded in the 13th century. During the 15th century, abandoned children were displayed here for three days. If their parents did not claim them, they were then sent to foster homes.

★ Orsanmichele
The carvings on the walls of this Gothic church depict the activities and patron saints of the city's trade guilds, such as the Masons and Carpenters.

Via dei Calzaiuoli
Lined with elegant shops, this street is the focus of the *passeggiata*, the traditional evening stroll.

★ Museo dell'Opera del Duomo
Works removed from the Duomo, Campanile and Baptistry, such as this panel by Verrocchio, are displayed in this museum.

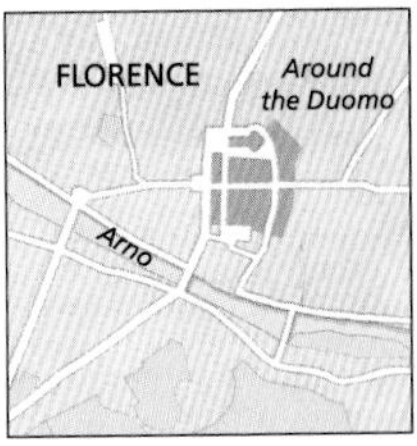

LOCATOR MAP

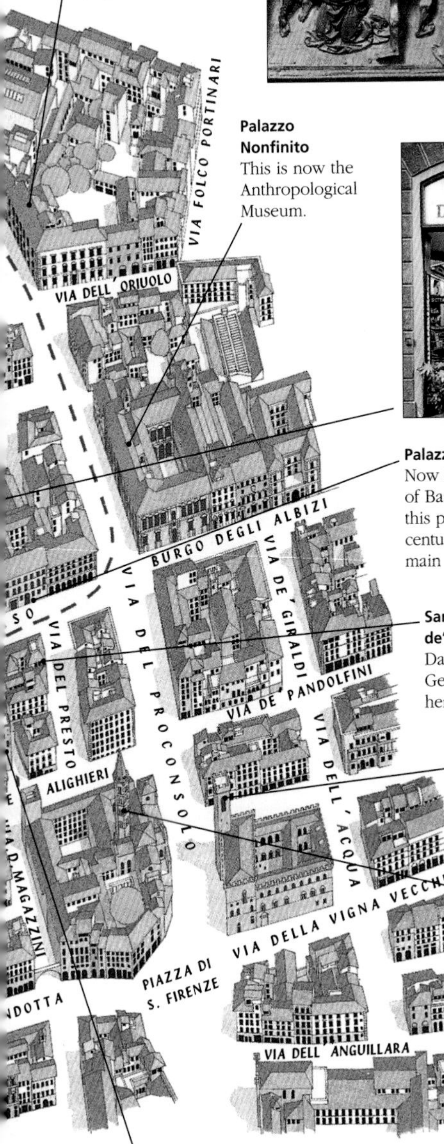

Palazzo Nonfinito
This is now the Anthropological Museum.

Pegna
This mini-supermarket tucked away in the Via dello Studio sells a range of gourmet treats including chocolate, honey, wine, balsamic vinegar and olive oil.

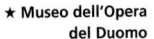

Palazzo Salviati
Now the head office of Banca Toscana, this palazzo has 14th-century frescoes in the main banking hall.

Santa Margherita de' Cerchi
Dante married Gemma Donati here in 1285.

★ Bargello
Formerly the town hall, this building now houses applied arts and sculpture, such as this figure by Bartolomeo Ammannati (1511–92).

Badia Fiorentina
The bell of this abbey regulated daily life in medieval Florence.

Casa di Dante
This medieval house is reputedly the birthplace of the great poet Dante.

KEY

– – – Suggested route

0 metres 100

0 yards 100

STAR SIGHTS

- ★ Duomo, Campanile and Baptistry
- ★ Orsanmichele
- ★ Museo dell'Opera del Duomo
- ★ Bargello

Florence: Duomo, Campanile and Baptistry ③

Set in the heart of Florence, Santa Maria del Fiore – the Duomo, or cathedral – dominates the city with its huge dome. Its sheer size was typical of Florentine determination to lead in all things and, to this day, no other building stands taller in the city. The Baptistry is one of Florence's oldest buildings, dating perhaps to the 4th century. The celebrated North and East doors were commissioned from Lorenzo Ghiberti in 1401 to mark Florence's deliverance from the plague. The Campanile was designed by Giotto in 1334.

Campanile
At 85 m (276 ft), the Campanile is 6 m (20 ft) shorter than the dome. It is clad in white, green and pink Tuscan marble.

★ Baptistry Ceiling
The colourful mosaics date from the 12th and 13th centuries. A lively portrayal of the Last Judgment can be seen in the apse above the large, octagonal font where many famous Florentines, including Dante, were baptized.

Neo-Gothic Façade
Though echoing the style of Giotto's marble Campanile, the façade was only added between 1871 and 1887.

Terracotta Panels
The bas-reliefs are by Andrea Pisano.

East Doors of the Baptistry
Dubbed the "Gate of Paradise" by Michelangelo, the doors' sculptured bronze panels show Ghiberti's mastery of perspective.

Steps to Santa Reparata
The crypt contains the remains of the 4th-century church of Santa Reparata, demolished in 1296 to make way for the cathedral.

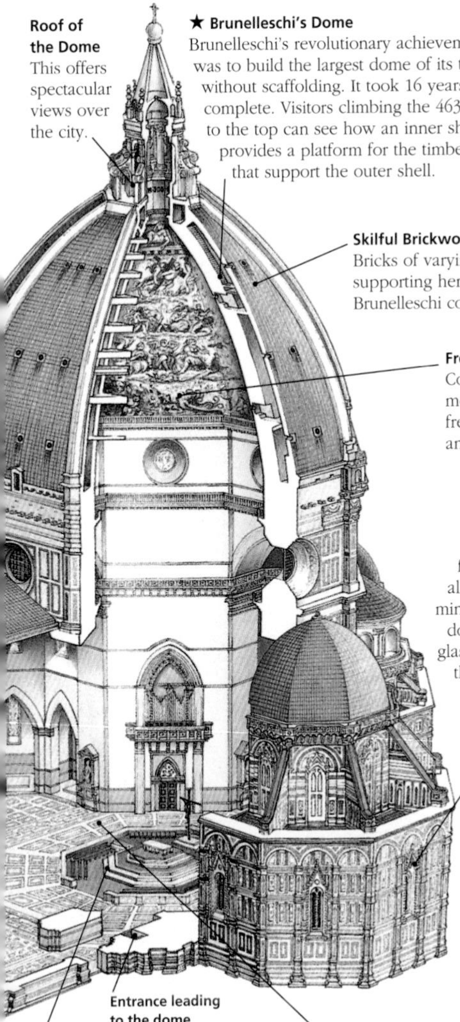

Roof of the Dome
This offers spectacular views over the city.

★ Brunelleschi's Dome
Brunelleschi's revolutionary achievement was to build the largest dome of its time without scaffolding. It took 16 years to complete. Visitors climbing the 463 steps to the top can see how an inner shell provides a platform for the timbers that support the outer shell.

STAR FEATURES

- ★ Baptistry
- ★ Brunelleschi's Dome

Skilful Brickwork
Bricks of varying size were set in a self-supporting herringbone pattern, a technique Brunelleschi copied from the Pantheon in Rome.

Frescoes of the Last Judgment
Contrasting with the similarly inspired mosaics in the Baptistry are these frescoes painted by Giorgio Vasari and Federico Zuccari in the 1570s.

Chapels at the East End
The three apses house five chapels each and all are crowned by a miniature copy of the dome. The stained-glass windows in the apses were designed by Lorenzo Ghiberti.

Entrance leading to the dome

Marble Sanctuary
Surrounding the High Altar, this was decorated by Baccio Bandinelli.

Marble Pavement
The view from the dome shows that the 16th-century marble pavement is laid out as a maze.

TIMELINE

Panel from South Doors

- **4th–5th centuries** The Baptistry and Santa Reparata church built
- **897** First documented record of the Baptistry
- **11th–13th centuries** Baptistry reclad in green and white marble
- **1209** Zodiac pavement laid in Baptistry
- **1271** *The Last Judgment* completed on Baptistry ceiling
- **1296** Arnolfo di Cambio begins the new cathedral on the site of Santa Reparata
- **1338** Andrea Pisano's South Doors added
- **1359** Giotto's Campanile completed
- **1403–24** Ghiberti's North Doors added
- **1425–52** Ghiberti's East Doors, the "Gate of Paradise", added
- **1436** Dome completed
- **1887** Long-delayed completion of the cathedral façade

400 | 600 | 800 | 1000 | 1200 | 1400 | 1600 | 1800

Siena (Livorno)

Unicorn *contrada* symbol

The principal sights of Siena are found in the network of narrow streets and alleys around the fan-shaped Piazza del Campo. Scarcely any street is level, as Siena, like Rome, is built on seven hills. This adds to the pleasure of exploring: one minute the city is laid out to view before you and the next you are in a warren of medieval houses. Packed into Siena are the 17 *contrade* (parishes) whose animal symbols are everywhere on carvings, plaques and car stickers.

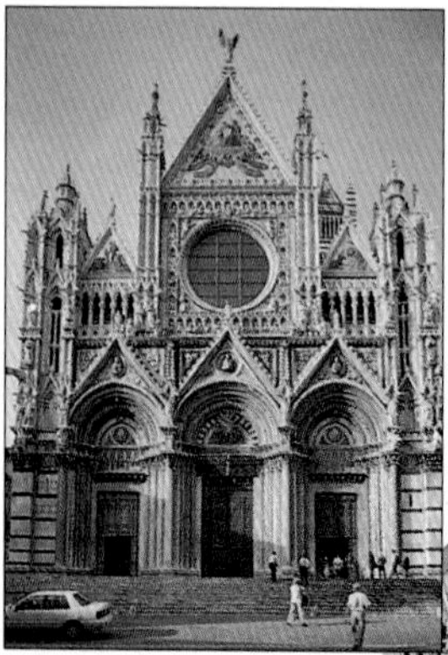

★ Duomo
Had the nave been completed, this grand church (1136-1382) with a splendid marble façade would have been the largest in Christendom.

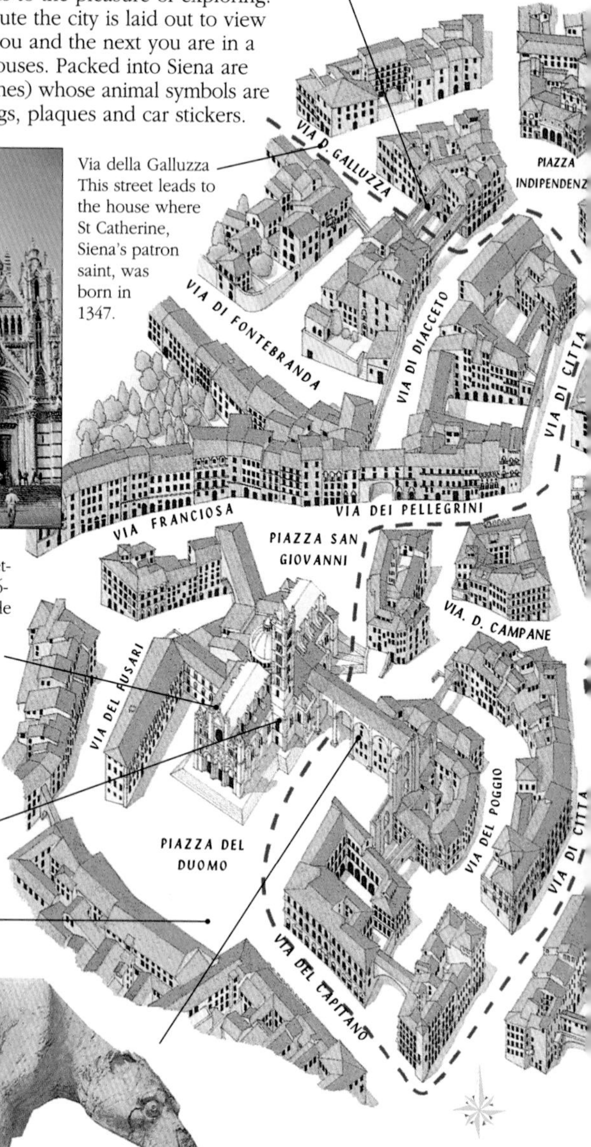

Aerial bridges and corridors
These picturesque structures linking buildings on opposite sides of the streets are characteristic of Siena.

Via della Galluzza
This street leads to the house where St Catherine, Siena's patron saint, was born in 1347.

Campanile
Each tier of the bell-tower (1313) has one window fewer than the floor above.

Piazza del Duomo
Antique shops line the nearby streets.

Museo dell'Opera del Duomo
Statues of a wolf suckling Remus abound; legend tells that his son Senius founded the city of Siena.

KEY

– – – Suggested route

0 metres 300

0 yards 300

Loggia della Mercanzia
Built in 1417, the arcade is where Siena's merchants and money dealers carried out their business.

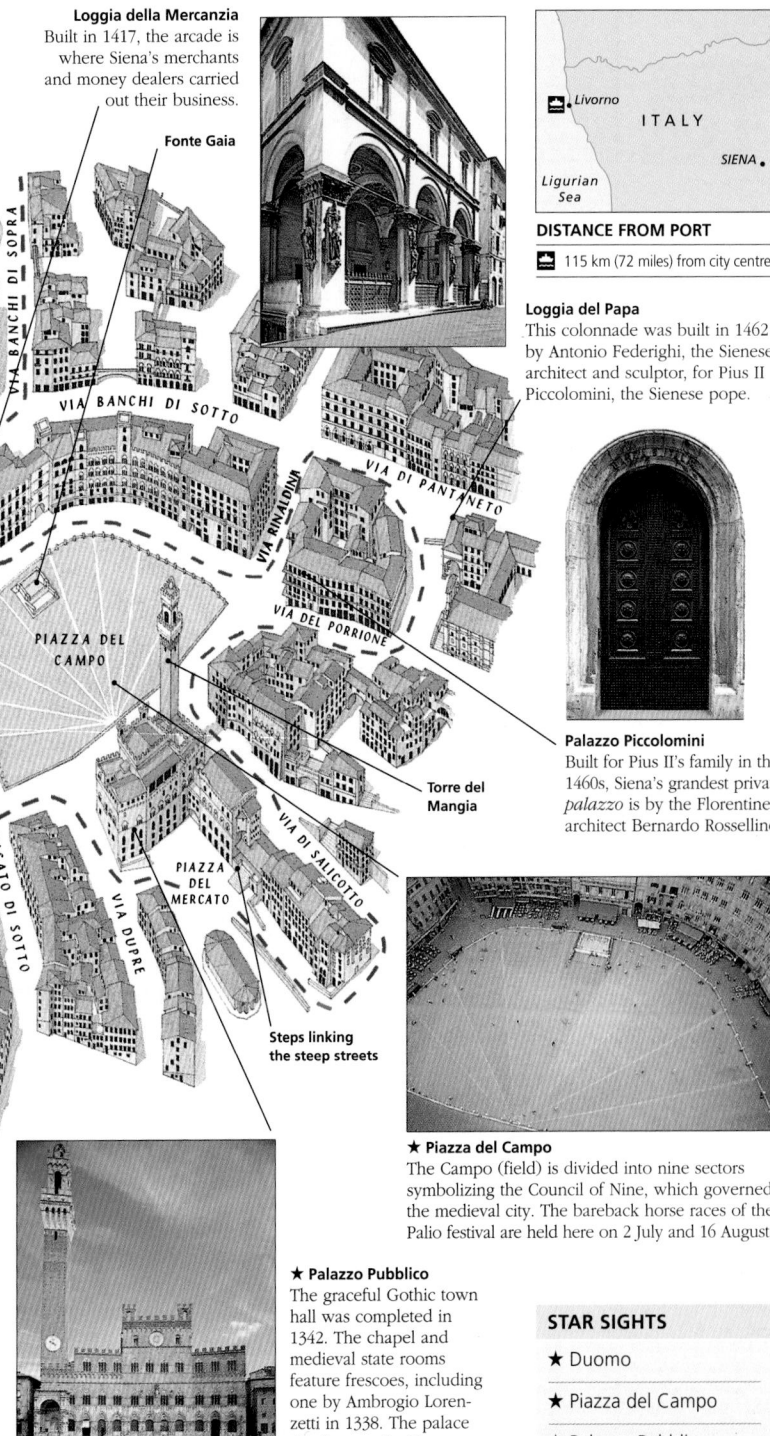

DISTANCE FROM PORT

115 km (72 miles) from city centre.

Fonte Gaia

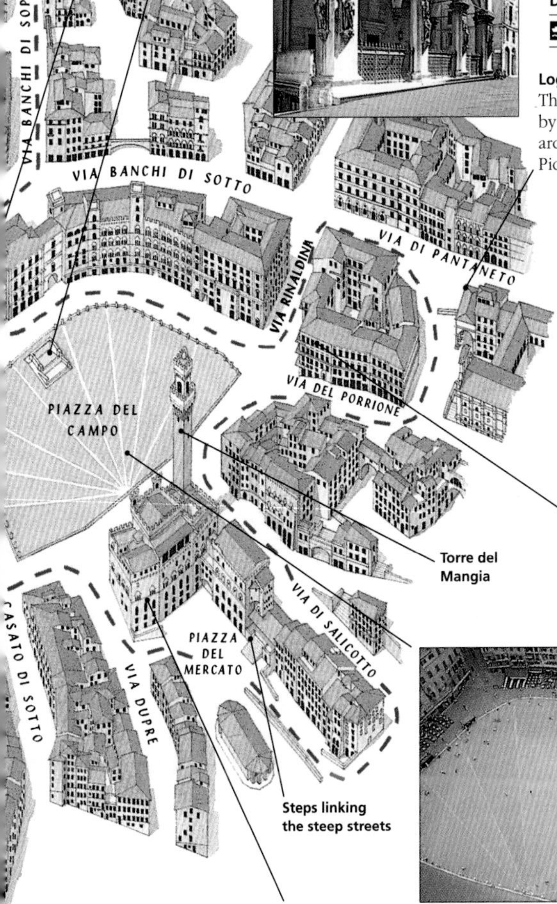

Loggia del Papa
This colonnade was built in 1462 by Antonio Federighi, the Sienese architect and sculptor, for Pius II Piccolomini, the Sienese pope.

Palazzo Piccolomini
Built for Pius II's family in the 1460s, Siena's grandest private *palazzo* is by the Florentine architect Bernardo Rossellino.

Torre del Mangia

Steps linking the steep streets

★ Piazza del Campo
The Campo (field) is divided into nine sectors symbolizing the Council of Nine, which governed the medieval city. The bareback horse races of the Palio festival are held here on 2 July and 16 August.

★ Palazzo Pubblico
The graceful Gothic town hall was completed in 1342. The chapel and medieval state rooms feature frescoes, including one by Ambrogio Lorenzetti in 1338. The palace also houses the Museo Civico (City Museum).

STAR SIGHTS

- ★ Duomo
- ★ Piazza del Campo
- ★ Palazzo Pubblico

Rome (Civitavecchia)

She-wolf with twins Romulus and Remus

Legend says that Romulus founded Rome in 753 BC and archaeology also dates the first settlement to around that time. After 300 years as a kingdom, it was governed for 500 years as a Republic. This, in turn, was superseded by the Roman Empire, which endured from 27 BC to AD 395. Imperial Rome became the centre of the Christian world when, in AD 313, Constantine granted freedom of worship to Christians. After many centuries of decline the city rose to new dominance in the Renaissance and Baroque periods, when artists and architects flocked to work for the papacy. Although steeped in history, today's Rome is a vibrant city that successfully juxtaposes its ancient and modern identities.

Castel Sant'Angelo ③
This grim fortress was built as Emperor Hadrian's mausoleum and was later enlarged as a papal fortress. The rooftop offers splendid views of Rome.

St Peter's Basilica ①
Michelangelo designed the majestic dome – the tallest in the world – of this magnificent 16th-century basilica. The interior is sumptuously decorated in different types of marble.

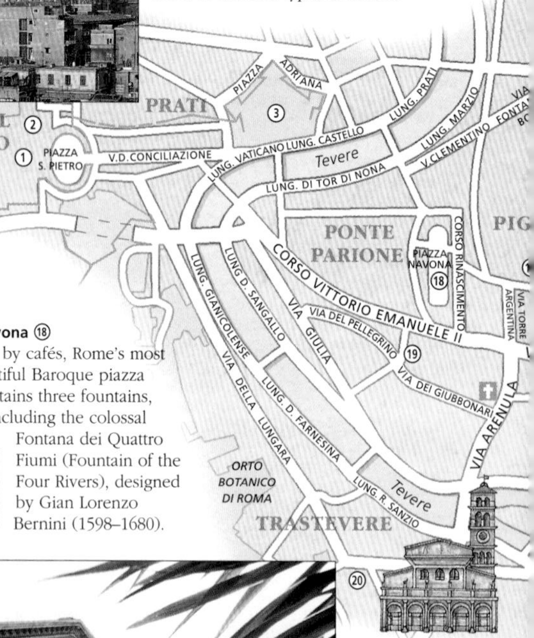

Piazza Navona ⑱
Flanked by cafés, Rome's most beautiful Baroque piazza contains three fountains, including the colossal Fontana dei Quattro Fiumi (Fountain of the Four Rivers), designed by Gian Lorenzo Bernini (1598–1680).

Vatican Museums ②
Four centuries of papal patronage and connoisseurship have resulted in one of the world's greatest collections of Classical and Renaissance art, displayed in equally magnificent buildings.

0 metres 600

0 yards 600

Pantheon ⑰
Completed in AD 118, the "Temple of All the Gods" is a marvel of Roman engineering and Rome's only Classical building to have survived in its entirety.

DISTANCE FROM PORT

85 km (53 miles) from city centre.

Piazza di Spagna and Spanish Steps ⑤
Most attractive when the azaleas are in bloom, this long flight of steps from the piazza to Trinità dei Monti is in one of Rome's most exclusive shopping areas.

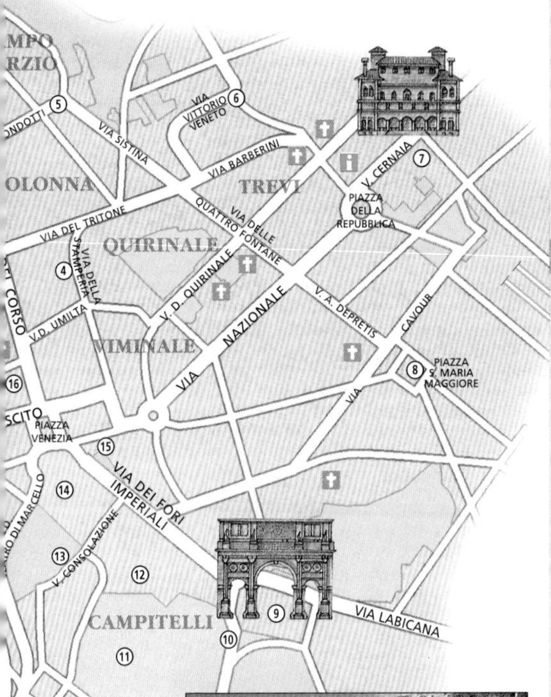

Colosseum ⑨
Commissioned by Emperor Vespasian to provide free public entertainment for 55,000 spectators, this 1st-century AD amphitheatre is the largest ever built in the Roman world.

KEY SIGHTS

① St Peter's Basilica ★ (see pp234–5)

② Vatican Museums ★ (see pp236–7)

③ Castel Sant'Angelo

④ Trevi Fountain

⑤ Piazza di Spagna and Spanish Steps

⑥ Via Veneto

⑦ Museo Nazionale Romano

⑧ Santa Maria Maggiore

⑨ Colosseum ★

⑩ Arch of Constantine

⑪ Palatine

⑫ Roman Forum

⑬ Capitoline Museums

⑭ Santa Maria in Aracoeli

⑮ Trajan's Column

⑯ Palazzo Doria Pamphilj

⑰ Pantheon ★

⑱ Piazza Navona

⑲ Campo de' Fiori

⑳ Santa Maria in Trastevere

FACT FILE

TOURIST INFORMATION

APT, Via Parigi 11. ***Tel*** *06 48 89 91.*
Mon–Sat to 7pm.

MARKETS

Food Piazza Campo de' Fiori, Via Andrea Doria & Piazza Testaccio; Mon–Sat am.
Prints & books Largo della Fontanella de Borghese; Mon–Sat am.

LOCAL SPECIALITIES

Dishes
Spaghetti alla carbonara (spaghetti with bacon, egg and cream).
Risotto alla romana (rice with liver, Marsala and pecorino cheese).
Crostata di ricotta (cheesecake).
Drinks
Frascati, Colli Albani, Castelli Romani, Marino, Velletri (white wines).

EXCURSIONS

Catacombs of San Callisto & San Sebastiano Via Appia Antica, Rome.
Ostia Antica 25 km (16 miles) SW of Rome. Rome's 2nd-century port.
Hadrian's Villa 25 km (16 miles) E of Rome. Vast 2nd-century site.
Villa d'Este Tivoli, 32 km (20 miles) E of Rome. Renaissance gardens.

The Trevi Fountain, Rome's grandest and best-known fountain, almost fills the small Piazza di Trevi

Exploring Rome

Much of Rome's *centro storico* (historic centre) lies in a bend of the Tiber and its attractive, narrow, cobbled streets are best explored on foot. The Vatican is just across the river. The major Classical remains are in and near the Forum, and a first sight of them from the top of the Capitoline is an unforgettable experience. Rome has some of the world's loveliest fountains, richest museums and many churches, which all form a part of its vast historic wealth.

St Peter's Basilica ①

See pp234–5.

Vatican Museums ②

See pp236–7.

Castel Sant'Angelo ③

This fortress takes its name from the rooftop statue of the Archangel Michael. Beginning life in AD 139 as Emperor Hadrian's mausoleum, it later served as part of the Aurelian city walls, as a medieval prison and as a papal residence in times of political unrest. It is now a museum where dank dungeons and fine apartments of Renaissance popes reveal the castle's history.

Trevi Fountain ④

Nicola Salvi's theatrical design for Rome's largest and most famous fountain was completed in 1762. It features Oceanus flanked by two Tritons, one trying to master an unruly sea-horse, the other leading a quieter beast, to symbolize the contrasting moods of the sea.

The site originally marked the terminal of the Aqua Virgo aqueduct, built in 19 BC by Augustus's right-hand man and son-in-law, Agrippa, to bring water to Rome's new baths. One of the upper reliefs shows a young girl, Trivia, after whom the fountain may have been named. She is said to have first shown the spring, 22 km (14 miles) from the city, to thirsty Roman soldiers.

Piazza di Spagna and Spanish Steps ⑤

Rome's most famous square is named after the Palazzo di Spagna, the 17th-century Spanish Embassy to the Holy See. In the 18th and 19th centuries the area was full of hotels for aristocrats doing the Grand Tour, as well as lodgings for artists, writers and composers. The English poet John Keats died in 1821 in the pink house at the foot of Spanish

VATICAN CITY

The Vatican was established as a sovereign state under the Lateran Treaty of 1929 and is ruled by the pope, Europe's only absolute monarch. About 1,000 people live here and the city has its own post office, banks, currency, radio station, judicial system and daily newspaper, *l'Osservatore Romano*. The papal audience chamber, seating 12,000 people, was opened in 1971.

Coat of arms of Pope Urban VIII Barberini

Although papal domiciles had existed next to the old St Peter's *(see p234)*, the popes' official residence from the 4th century to 1309 (when they left for Avignon) was the Lateran Palace in the south of Rome. The Vatican took its place on their return in 1377 and the current buildings all date from after that time.

Steps. This dramatic flight was built in the 1720s by the French owners of the church of Trinità dei Monti at the top. The obelisk there is an ancient Roman imitation of Egyptian ones.

Via Condotti, at the bottom of the steps, gleams with Italy's top designer clothes stores.

Via Veneto ⑥

This elegant street was laid out in 1879 in the great building boom of Rome's first years as the capital of Italy. Its upper section is lined with late 19th-century hotels and canopied pavement cafés. At its lower end, close to Piazza Barberini, is Santa Maria della Concezione, an unassuming Baroque church whose crypt is decorated with the skeletons of 4,000 Capuchin monks. Overlooking the piazza opposite Via Veneto is the Palazzo Barberini, built by Pope Urban VIII in the 1630s. It has sumptuous rooms and a dazzling ceiling fresco by Pietro da Cortona.

The onset of autumn in elegant, 19th-century Via Veneto

Museo Nazionale Romano ⑦

Founded in 1889, this museum holds most of the antiquities found in Rome since 1870, as well as pre-existing collections, and is one of the world's leading museums of Classical art. It is housed in five buildings. The three described here are very close together and offer an excellent, high-quality selection of the museum's holdings.

The 19th-century Palazzo Massimo has impeccably arranged galleries on four floors. They display Roman coins and jewellery, exquisite frescoes and mosaics and an impressive collection of statuary. This includes sculptured portraits (notably the famous statue of Emperor Augustus found in Via Labicana), funerary stelae and figures of athletes and actors. The frescoes excavated at the Renaissance Villa Farnesina are exceptional examples of Roman painting.

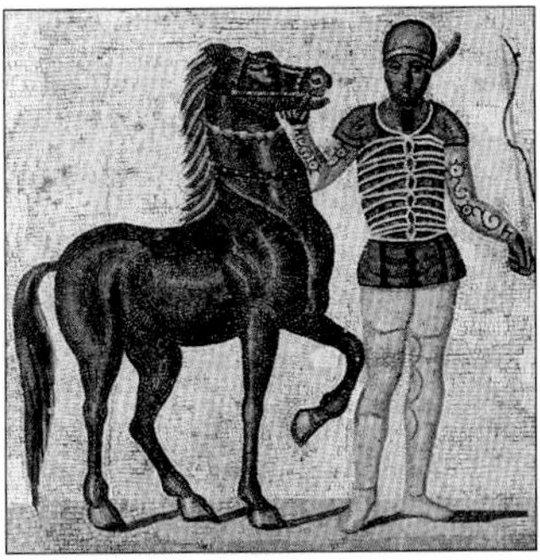

One of the Quattro Aurighe mosaics, Palazzo Massimo alle Terme, Museo Nazionale Romano

The Aula Ottagona nearby is among the best preserved of Diocletian's buildings, with a vault second only in size to the Pantheon's. It exhibits decorations from Roman baths. The adjacent Baths of Diocletian has an array of Roman statues. The two other branches, the Palazzo Altemps and Crypta Balbi, are in the *centro storico*.

Santa Maria Maggiore ⑧

Of all the great Roman basilicas, Santa Maria Maggiore has the most successful blend of different architectural styles. It was founded in AD 420 and completed by Pope Sixtus III between 432 and 440 – the colonnaded triple nave is part of the original building. The Cosmatesque marble floor and delightful Romanesque bell tower with blue ceramic roundels are medieval. The coffered ceiling is Renaissance and was a gift of Pope Alexander VI Borgia at the end of the 15th century. It is said to have been gilded with the first gold to have been brought from the New World by Columbus. The church's twin domes and imposing front and rear façades are Baroque. The mosaics are Santa Maria's most famous feature; the Biblical scenes in the nave and the mosaics on the triumphal arch are all 5th century. The mosaics of the Virgin in the apse and of Christ enthroned in the loggia are 13th-century, as is the tomb (1299) of Cardinal Rodriguez, which has superb Cosmatesque marblework.

Colosseum ⑨

Rome's greatest amphitheatre was commissioned by Emperor Vespasian in AD 72 and built on the marshy site of a lake in the grounds of Nero's palace, the Domus Aurea. It was completed in AD 80 by his son, Titus, who organized a 100-day-long inaugural extravaganza. From then on, deadly gladiatorial combats and wild animal fights were staged free of charge by the emperor and wealthy citizens for public entertainment. The amphitheatre was built to a practical design, with 80 numbered entrance arches, allowing easy access to 55,000 spectators who were seated according to rank within ten minutes.

First recorded in the 11th century, the name "Colosseum" probably derived from the Colossus of Nero, a huge gilt statue that once stood outside.

Glorious 13th-century mosaic of the Coronation of the Virgin, church of Santa Maria Maggiore

Rome: St Peter's Basilica ①

Rome's sumptuous, marble-clad basilica of St Peter, Catholicism's most sacred shrine, draws pilgrims and tourists from all over the world. It holds hundreds of precious works of art, some salvaged from the 4th-century church built by Emperor Constantine, others commissioned from Renaissance and Baroque artists. The dominant tone is set by Bernini, who created the baldacchino twisting up below Michelangelo's huge dome. He also designed the cathedra in the apse. The throne is supported by the figures of four saints and contains fragments once thought to be relics of the chair from which St Peter delivered his first sermon.

★ Dome of St Peter's
Michelangelo designed the 136.5-m (448-ft) high dome, but it was not completed in his lifetime.

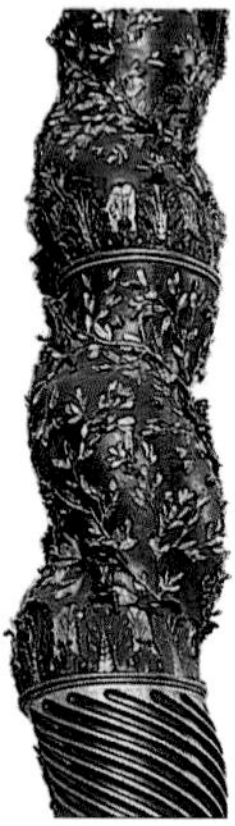

★ Baldacchino
Commissioned by Pope Urban VIII Barberini in 1624, Bernini's extravagant Baroque canopy stands over St Peter's tomb. The four massive columns, decorated with Barberini bees, are made of bronze stripped from the portico of the Pantheon *(see p239)*.

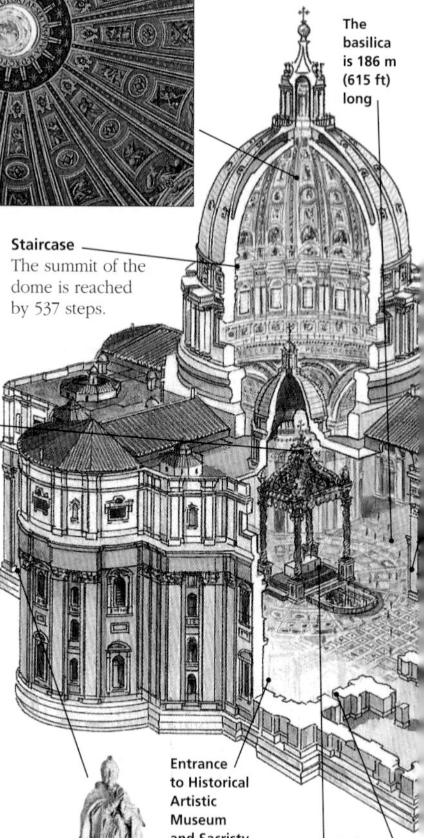

The basilica is 186 m (615 ft) long

Staircase
The summit of the dome is reached by 537 steps.

Entrance to Historical Artistic Museum and Sacristy

Stairs to the dome

Papal Altar
This stands over the crypt where St Peter is reputed to have been buried.

Monument to Pope Alexander VII
Bernini's last work in St Peter's was finished in 1678 and shows the Chigi pope among the allegorical figures of Truth, Justice, Charity and Prudence.

HISTORICAL PLAN OF ST PETER'S BASILICA

St Peter was buried in AD 64 in Rome in a necropolis near the site of his crucifixion in the Circus of Nero. In AD 324 Constantine constructed a basilica over the tomb. The old church was rebuilt in the 15th century, and various architects developed the existing structure throughout the 16th and 17th centuries. The new church was inaugurated in 1626.

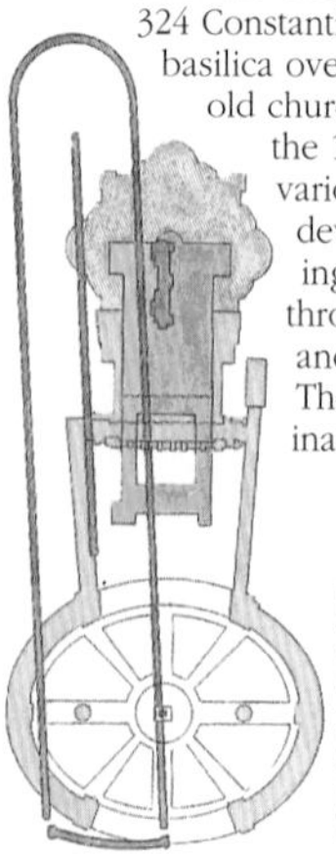

KEY
- Circus of Nero
- Constantinian
- Renaissance
- Baroque

Grottoes
This fragment of a 13th-century mosaic by Giotto, salvaged from the old basilica, is now in the Grottoes, where many popes are buried.

STAR FEATURES

★ Dome of St Peter's

★ Baldacchino

Michelangelo's *Pietà*
Protected by glass since an attack in 1972, the *Pietà* was created in 1499 when Michelangelo was only 25.

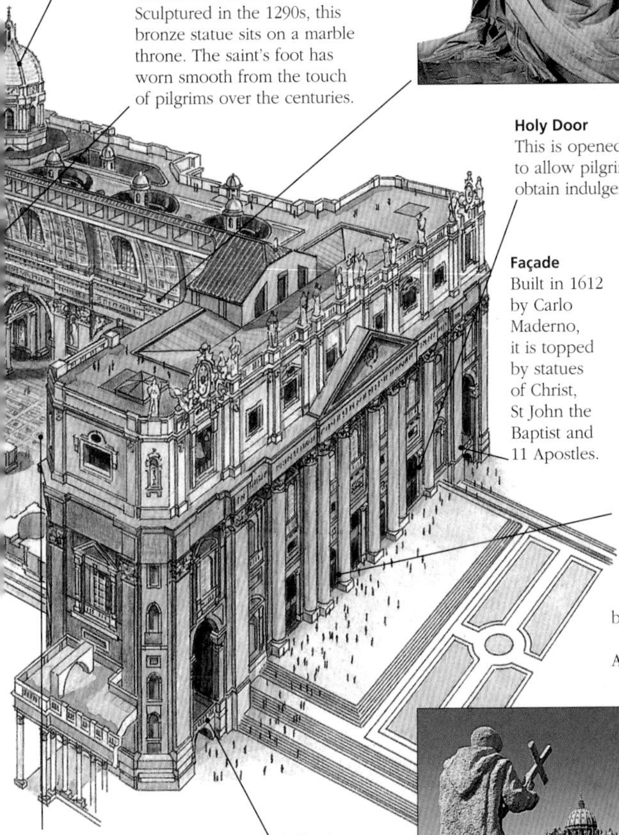

Two minor cupolas by Vignola (1507–73)

Arnolfo di Cambio's *St Peter*
Sculptured in the 1290s, this bronze statue sits on a marble throne. The saint's foot has worn smooth from the touch of pilgrims over the centuries.

Holy Door
This is opened only in Holy Years to allow pilgrims entering here to obtain indulgences.

Façade
Built in 1612 by Carlo Maderno, it is topped by statues of Christ, St John the Baptist and 11 Apostles.

Filarete Door
The door panels came from the old basilica and were decorated between 1439 and 1445 with biblical reliefs by Antonio Averulino (also known as Filarete).

Nave Floor Markings
These show how other churches compare in length with St Peter's.

Atrium by Carlo Maderno

Piazza San Pietro
On Sundays, religious festivals and special occasions such as canonizations, the pope blesses the crowds from a balcony.

Rome: Vatican Museums ②

These vast buildings were originally the palaces of Renaissance popes, such as Julius II, Innocent VIII and Sixtus IV, but in the 18th century became a showcase for the papacy's priceless works of art. Visitors today have to follow a one-way system. Be sure to conserve energy for the Sistine Chapel and Raphael Rooms, which are 30 to 40 minutes' walk from the entrance.

EGYPTIAN AND ASSYRIAN ART

The wide-ranging Egyptian collection contains finds from 19th- and 20th-century excavations in Egypt, as well as statues that were brought to Rome in Imperial times. There are also Roman imitations of Egyptian sculpture. The Assyrian Room is decorated with reliefs from the palaces of the Kings of Nineveh.

ETRUSCAN AND ITALIC ART

This collection comprises artifacts from pre-Roman civilizations in Villanoviani and Etrusci from Neolithic times to the 1st century BC, when they were absorbed into the Roman state. Chief among the Etruscan exhibits are objects from the Regolini-Galassi tomb in the necropolis of Cerveteri, one of the greatest Etruscan cities.

GREEK AND ROMAN ART

The greater part of the Vatican Museums is dedicated to Greek and Roman art. Mosaics are displayed on walls and floors, exhibits line corridors and famous sculptures decorate the main courtyards. The prize pieces form the nucleus of the Pio-Clemente Museum – the sculptures in the pavilions around its Octagonal Courtyard are among the greatest achievements of Western art. The superb *Laocoön*, sculpted by three artists from Rhodes, had been known from a description by Pliny the Elder and was found near the ruins of Nero's palace in 1506. The smaller Chiaramonti Museum has a striking colossal head of the goddess Athene. The Gregorian Profane Museum charts the evolution of Roman art from reliance on Greek style to a recognizably Roman style. The Greek Vase Room offers a complete view of this art form.

LOCATION OF THE MUSEUMS' MAIN SECTIONS

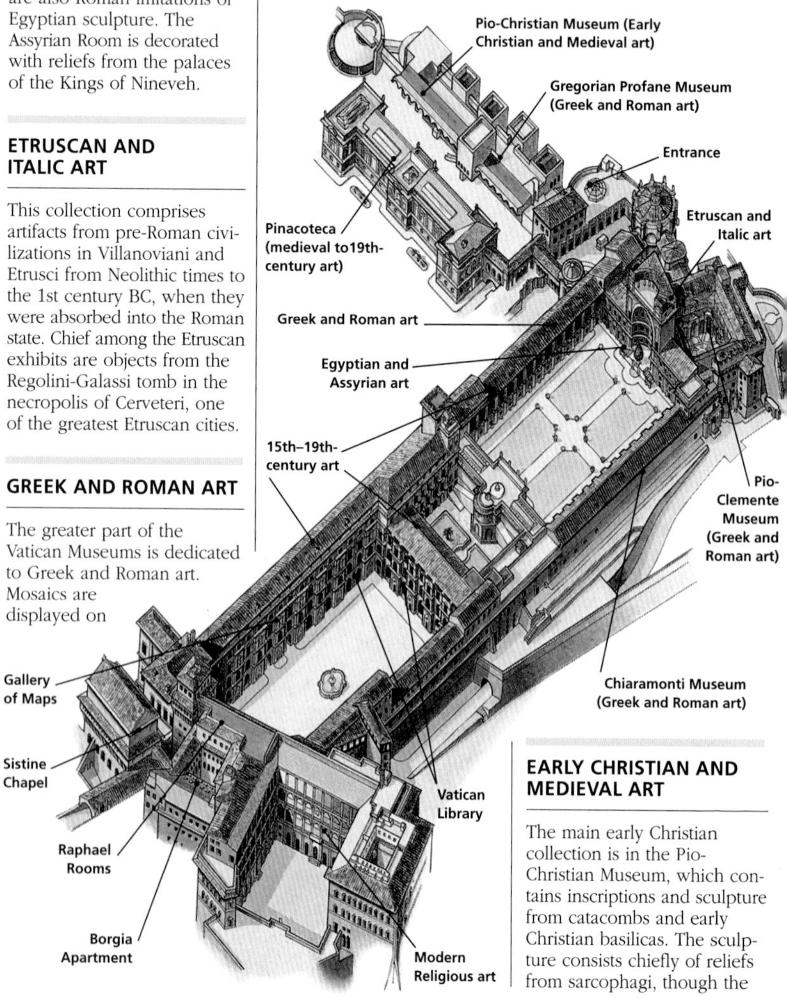

EARLY CHRISTIAN AND MEDIEVAL ART

The main early Christian collection is in the Pio-Christian Museum, which contains inscriptions and sculpture from catacombs and early Christian basilicas. The sculpture consists chiefly of reliefs from sarcophagi, though the

Detail from Giotto's *Stefaneschi Triptych*

most striking work is a 4th-century sculpture of the Good Shepherd. Its interest lies in the way it blends Biblical imagery with pagan mythology. The first two rooms of the Pinacoteca display late medieval art, in particular painted altarpieces. The outstanding work is Giotto's *Stefaneschi Triptych* of about 1300 from the main altar of old St Peter's. It shows Jacopo Stefaneschi offering the triptych to St Peter.

15TH- TO 19TH-CENTURY ART

The Pinacoteca has many important Renaissance works. Highlights of the 15th century include Leonardo da Vinci's unfinished *St Jerome* and a *Pietà* by Giovanni Bellini. Works of the 16th century include a *Transfiguration*, the *Madonna of Foligno* and eight tapestry cartoons by Raphael, a *Deposition* by Caravaggio, *St Helen* by Veronese and an altarpiece by Titian. Many Renaissance popes were connoisseurs of the arts, considering it their duty to sponsor the leading goldsmiths, painters and sculptors. The galleries around the Cortile del Belvedere were decorated by great artists between the 16th and 19th centuries. The Gallery of Tapestries has hangings woven in Brussels to designs by students of Raphael, while the apartment of Pope Pius V has 15th-century Flemish hangings. The Gallery of Maps is frescoed with 16th-century maps of ancient and contemporary Italy.

Of note near the Raphael Rooms are the Room of the Chiaroscuri and Pope Nicholas V's private chapel, the latter frescoed by Fra Angelico between 1447 and 1451. The Borgia Apartment was decorated in the 1490s by Pinturicchio and his pupils for Pope Alexander VI Borgia.

MODERN RELIGIOUS ART

Modern artists exhibited in the Vatican Museums face daunting competition from the great works of the past. Few modern works are displayed conspicuously, the exception being Giuseppe Momo's spiral staircase of 1932 at the main entrance, and Giò Pomodoro's abstract sculpture, standing in the middle of the Cortile della Pigna.

Sala dei Misteri in the Borgia Apartment, richly decorated with frescoes by Pinturicchio

In 1973, a contemporary art collection was opened in the Borgia Apartment by Pope Paul VI. It comprises more than 800 exhibits by artists from all over the world in a great variety of media, showing many contrasting approaches to religious subjects. Painters include Edvard Munch, Georges Braque, Paul Klee and Graham Sutherland. There are projects for church decoration by Matisse, Luigi Fontana and Emilio Greco, and ceramics by Picasso.

Detail of a sibyl of the Greek Oracle of Delphi, Sistine Chapel

RAPHAEL ROOMS AND SISTINE CHAPEL

Pope Julius II commissioned Raphael to decorate four rooms of his private apartments in 1503. The frescoes quickly established the young artist's reputation, but Raphael died in 1520 before they were finished. The rooms of Heliodorus and of the Segnatura are by Raphael himself, while the other two rooms are largely by his pupils.

Michelangelo frescoed the ceiling of the Sistine Chapel for Pope Julius between 1508 and 1512. Recent restoration has revealed the vibrancy of the original colours. The central panels depict the Creation and the Fall and around them are other biblical subjects. The Classical Sibyls are said to have foretold the birth of Christ. The walls were frescoed in the 15th century. On the side walls, the 12 paintings of events in the lives of Christ and Moses are by artists including Ghirlandaio, Botticelli, Perugino and Signorelli. Michelangelo completed the walls between 1534 and 1541 and added the great altar fresco, *The Last Judgment*.

Courtyard garden of the House of the Vestal Virgins in the Forum

Arch of Constantine ⑩
Dedicated in AD 315, 15 years before Constantine moved the Empire's capital to Byzantium, this triumphal arch is one of Imperial Rome's last monuments. It celebrated Constantine's defeat of his co-emperor, Maxentius, in AD 312 at the Battle of the Milvian Bridge. Constantine attributed his victory to a vision of the Holy Cross, but there is nothing Christian about the arch: most of the medallions, reliefs and statues were taken from earlier pagan monuments. There are statues of Dacian prisoners, reused from Trajan's Forum, and reliefs of Marcus Aurelius, including one where he distributes bread to the poor. Inside the arch are reliefs of Trajan's victory over the Dacians. These are probably by the artist who worked on Trajan's Column.

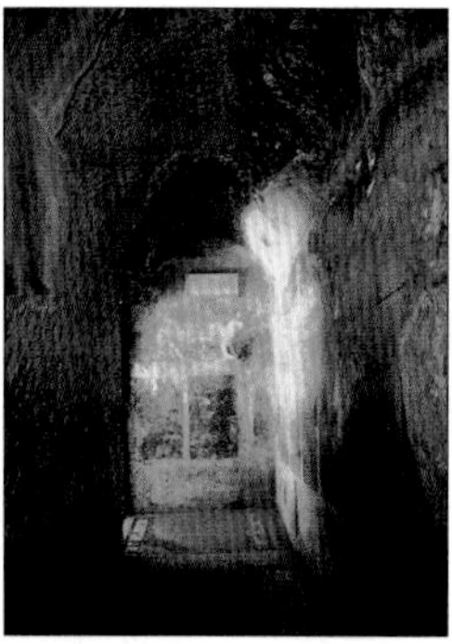

House of Livia on the Palatine

Palatine ⑪
The Palatine Hill, overlooking the Forum, is where Romulus is said to have founded Rome. It was also the residence of Roman emperors for 400 years. The most extensive ruins are the two wings of Domitian's huge palace: the Domus Augustana (private apartments) and Domus Flavia (public rooms). Adjacent to the former are giant arches that once supported the palace of Septimius Severus *(see pp264–5)*. The House of Livia is where Augustus and his wife, Livia, probably lived, and the Cryptoporticus is a series of underground corridors built by Nero. There is also a Stadium and a Temple to Cybele, a fertility goddess.

Roman Forum ⑫
The Forum was the centre of political, judicial and commercial life in ancient Rome. Legal cases were heard in the basilicas, and the huge arches of the Basilica of Constantine give an idea of the scale of these public buildings. The main street, clearly visible among the ruins, was the Via Sacra (Sacred Way), the route followed by processions up to the Capitol to give thanks at the Temple of Jupiter. The best preserved monument is the Arch of Septimius Severus. The Temple of Vesta, beside the House of the Vestal Virgins, was one of Rome's most sacred shrines.

Capitoline Museums ⑬
A magnificent collection of paintings and Classical sculptures is displayed in two palaces on the summit of the Capitoline Hill, the centre of the Roman World. These, the beautiful piazza between them and the Cordonata, a broad flight of steps leading up to it, were all designed by Michelangelo.

The Palazzo Nuovo became the world's first public museum in 1734 when Pope Clement XII Corsini decreed that its collection of statues should be freely accessible. Today, the two floors of galleries are still devoted chiefly to sculpture. Most of the finest works are Roman copies of Greek masterpieces and include the *Discobolus* (Discus-thrower) and *Dying Galatian*. The Palazzo dei Conservatori has more Classical statues in the first-floor rooms, remarkable for their 16th- and 17th-century decoration. Here can be seen the 5th-century BC Etruscan bronze of the She-wolf of Rome *(see p230)*. The upper art galleries include works by Veronese, Tintoretto, Van Dyck, Rubens and Titian.

Esquiline Venus, Capitoline Museums

Santa Maria in Aracoeli ⑭
The 124 marble steps leading up to the church were completed in 1348, some say in thanks for the passing of the Black Death, but probably to celebrate the Holy Year, 1350. There is a street-level entrance at the back. The church dates from at least the 6th century and stands on the site of the Temple of Juno on the northern summit of the Capitoline. The 22 columns were taken from ancient buildings; the inscription on the third one to the left reads: *a cubiculo Augustorum* (from the bedroom of the emperors). The gilded ceiling, with naval motifs, commemorates the Papal–Spanish defeat of the Turks at the Battle of Lepanto in 1571. The frescoes of the life of St Bernadino of Siena in the first chapel to the right were painted in the 1480s by Pinturicchio.

Trajan's Column ⑮

This superbly sculptured monument dominates the ruins of Trajan's Forum, which was built to commemorate his conquest of Dacia (present-day Romania) in AD 106. The forum was a vast, colonnaded, open space flanked by two great libraries, between which the column originally stood. Scenes of the Dacian campaigns in AD 101–2 and 105–6 spiral up the 30-m high stem. The minutely detailed reliefs were designed to be seen from viewing platforms on the libraries and consequently are difficult to interpret from the ground. Behind the column are the buildings of Trajan's Markets, which are being restored.

Detail from Trajan's Column

Palazzo Doria Pamphilj ⑯

The oldest parts of this great *palazzo* in the heart of Rome date back to 1435. The porticoed Corso courtyard is 16th-century. When the Pamphilj family took over in 1647, they built a new wing, a chapel and a theatre. The gallery above this courtyard and the Via del Corso façade are in the decorative, 18th-century *barocchetto* style, which came to dominate the building.

The family art collection has over 400 paintings dating from the 15th to the 18th centuries. They include a famous portrait of Pope Innocent X Pamphilj by Velázquez, and works by Titian, Caravaggio, Lorenzo Lotto, Guercino and Claude Lorrain. The opulent private apartments retain many original furnishings, including Brussels and Gobelins tapestries.

The portico of the Pantheon, supported by huge granite columns

Pantheon ⑰

The Pantheon is the most extraordinary and best-preserved ancient building in Rome. This marvel of Roman engineering, built between AD 118 and 125, was designed by Emperor Hadrian to replace a rectangular temple built by Agrippa between 27 and 25 BC. The portico incorporates elements of that early temple.

Only from inside can the scale and beauty of the vast hemispherical dome be appreciated. It was cast by pouring concrete over a temporary wooden framework. The hole at the top, the *oculus*, lets in the only light to illuminate the marble interior, much of which is Roman. Today, the Pantheon houses tombs, including those of Raphael and Italian kings.

Piazza Navona ⑱

Rome's most beautiful Baroque piazza follows the shape of a 1st-century stadium built by Domitian for athletic contests. Its present appearance dates from the 17th century when Pope Innocent X commissioned the church of Sant'Agnese in Agone, a new family palace, the Palazzo Pamphilj, next door and the central Fontana dei Quattro Fiumi (Fountain of the Four Rivers), Bernini's magnificent fountain. Its four figures symbolize the rivers Plate, Ganges, Danube and Nile. The piazza's other fountains, the Fontana de Nettuno (of Neptune) and Fontana del Moro (of the Moor) are 16th-century.

Campo de' Fiori ⑲

The "Field of Flowers" was one of the liveliest piazzas of medieval and Renaissance Rome, surrounded by inns for pilgrims and other travellers. Cardinals and nobles mingled with foreigners and fishmongers in the market, and Caravaggio killed his opponent after losing a game of tennis in the piazza. This was also an official place of execution: the hooded statue in the centre is of the philosopher Giordano Bruno, burnt at the stake here in 1600 for suggesting that the earth moved round the sun. Today's market, trattorias, shops and bars still make the piazza an animated hub of activity.

Santa Maria in Trastevere ⑳

Set in Rome's picturesque old quarter of Trastevere, this was probably the city's first place of Christian worship and was founded, according to legend, by Pope Callixtus I in the 3rd century. It became a focus of devotion to the Virgin, as reflected in the many images of her in the remarkable mosaics. The present church and the mosaics date from the 12th and 13th centuries. Those on the façade and in the apse are particularly beautiful. The oldest is a 7th-century icon above the altar in the Cappella Altemps.

Mosaic of the Coronation of the Virgin, Santa Maria in Trastevere

Naples

Naples lies in a beautiful bay dominated by Mount Vesuvius. Its name derives from the ancient Greeks' settlement, Neapolis, but its golden age was as the capital of the medieval Angevin and Aragonese kingdoms. The historic centre is easily explored on foot. Its main axes are Via Toledo (also called Via Roma), running north from the Palazzo Reale to Piazza Dante, and a long, narrow street known as *Spacca-napoli* (split Naples). The latter's central sections (named Via Benedetto Croce and Via San Biagio dei Librai) have been likened to an open-air museum for their many fine buildings.

Museo Archeologico Nazionale ①
This museum is one of the world's most important. It has been receiving the treasures of Pompeii, Herculaneum and other towns of Campania since 1790, and also houses the fabulous Farnese collection of Classical sculpture. There is an Egyptian collection in the basement.

Santa Chiara ⑤
Restoration after World War II uncovered the church's austere Provençal-Gothic structure. The adjacent convent's cloister was redesigned by Vaccaro in 1742 to incorporate painted majolica tiles.

Castel Nuovo ⑥
This fortress was built by Alfonso V of Aragon, who in 1443 became Alfonso I, King of Naples and Sicily. The triumphal entrance arch is a masterpiece of the early Renaissance. Only the Capella Palatina remains of the original castle built for Charles of Anjou in 1280.

Palazzo Reale ⑦
Begun by Domenico Fontana for the Spanish Viceroys in 1600 and expanded and embellished by subsequent residents, Naples' royal palace has great halls filled with furniture, tapestries, paintings and porcelain. The 19th-century statues in the façade depict the dynasties of Naples. A large part of the building is now occupied by the Biblioteca Nazionale, which has papyrus scripts from Erculano.

San Lorenzo Maggiore ③
This mainly 14th-century Franciscan church has an 18th-century façade. For Naples, it is a rare Gothic edifice. Excavations in the cloister have revealed the remains of a Roman Basilica.

Duomo di San Gennaro ②
The early 14th-century Duomo lies behind a mostly 19th-century façade. San Gennaro, the patron saint of Naples, was martyred in AD 305. His tomb is in the Cappella Carafa, built in 1506, and his relics are kept in the adjacent museum.

0 metres 250

0 yards 250

San Gregorio Armeno ④
This is the church of a Benedictine convent and one of Naples' most important religious sites. It has a sumptuous Baroque interior with frescoes (1671–84) by the prolific Neapolitan painter Luca Giordano.

The attractive Bay of Naples overlooked by Mount Vesuvius

KEY SIGHTS

① Museo Archeologico Nazionale ★
② Duomo di San Gennaro
③ San Lorenzo Maggiore
④ San Gregorio Armeno ★
⑤ Santa Chiara
⑥ Castel Nuovo
⑦ Palazzo Reale

FACT FILE

TOURIST INFORMATION

Piazza del Gesù Nuovo.
***Tel** 081 551 27 01.* ☐ *Mon–Sat to 7:30pm, Sun to 2:30pm.*

MARKETS

Food Mercatino della Pignasecca near Piazza Carità; Mon–Sat (closed Thu pm). Torretta, Via Mergellina; Mon–Sat am.
Antiques Via Francesco Caracciolo; monthly on penultimate Sat & Sun.

SHOPPING

Antiques Many shops selling quality antiques and bric-à-brac.
Capodimonte porcelain.

LOCAL SPECIALITIES

Crafts
Nativity crib figures (especially around Via San Gregorio Armeno), traditional Neapolitan masks.
Dishes
Pizza (first created in Naples).
Pizza napolitana (wafer-thin basil, garlic, tomato and anchovy pizza).
Sartù di riso (moulded rice with savoury garnishes).
Pasta e fagioli (pasta and beans).
Sfogliatelle (sweet pastry filled with ricotta cheese and candied fruit).
Drinks
Lacryma Christi (white wine from the slopes of Mount Vesuvius).
Greco di Tufo (regional white wine).
Limoncello (a lemon liqueur).

EXCURSIONS

Museo Nazionale di Capodimonte in NW of Naples. Superb paintings in a former royal palace. Large park.
Certosa di San Martino in SE of Naples. Museum of Neapolitan art and history in a former monastery.
Caserta 40 km (25 miles) N of Naples. A grandiose royal palace.

Pompeii (Naples)

An earthquake in AD 62, which shook Pompeii and damaged many buildings, was merely a prelude to the tragic day in AD 79 when Mount Vesuvius erupted, burying the town in 3 m (10 ft) of pumice and ash. Although it was discovered in the 16th century, serious excavation began only in 1748, revealing a city frozen in time. In some buildings, paintings and sculpture have survived and graffiti is still visible on street walls.

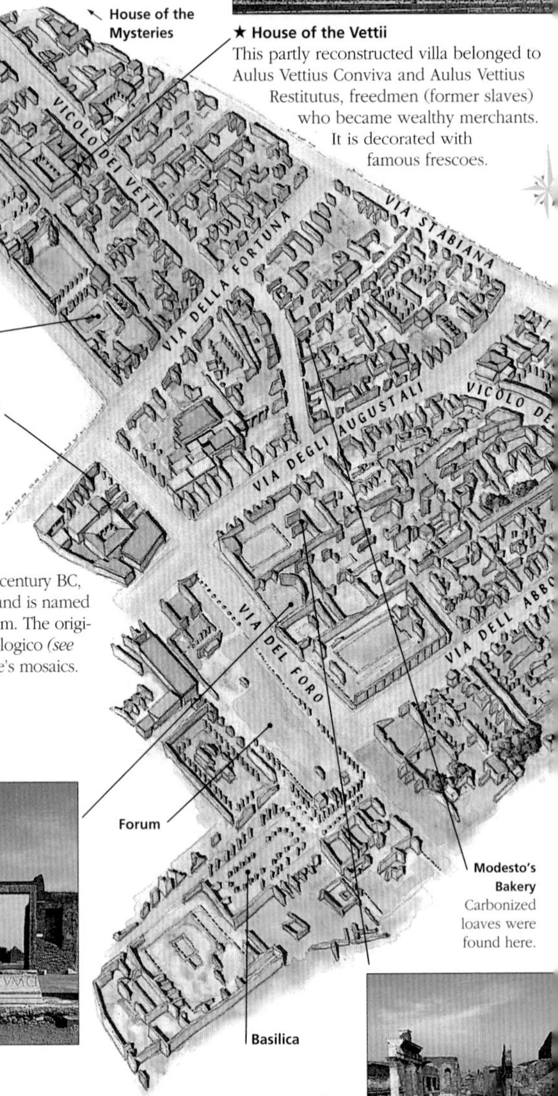

House of the Mysteries

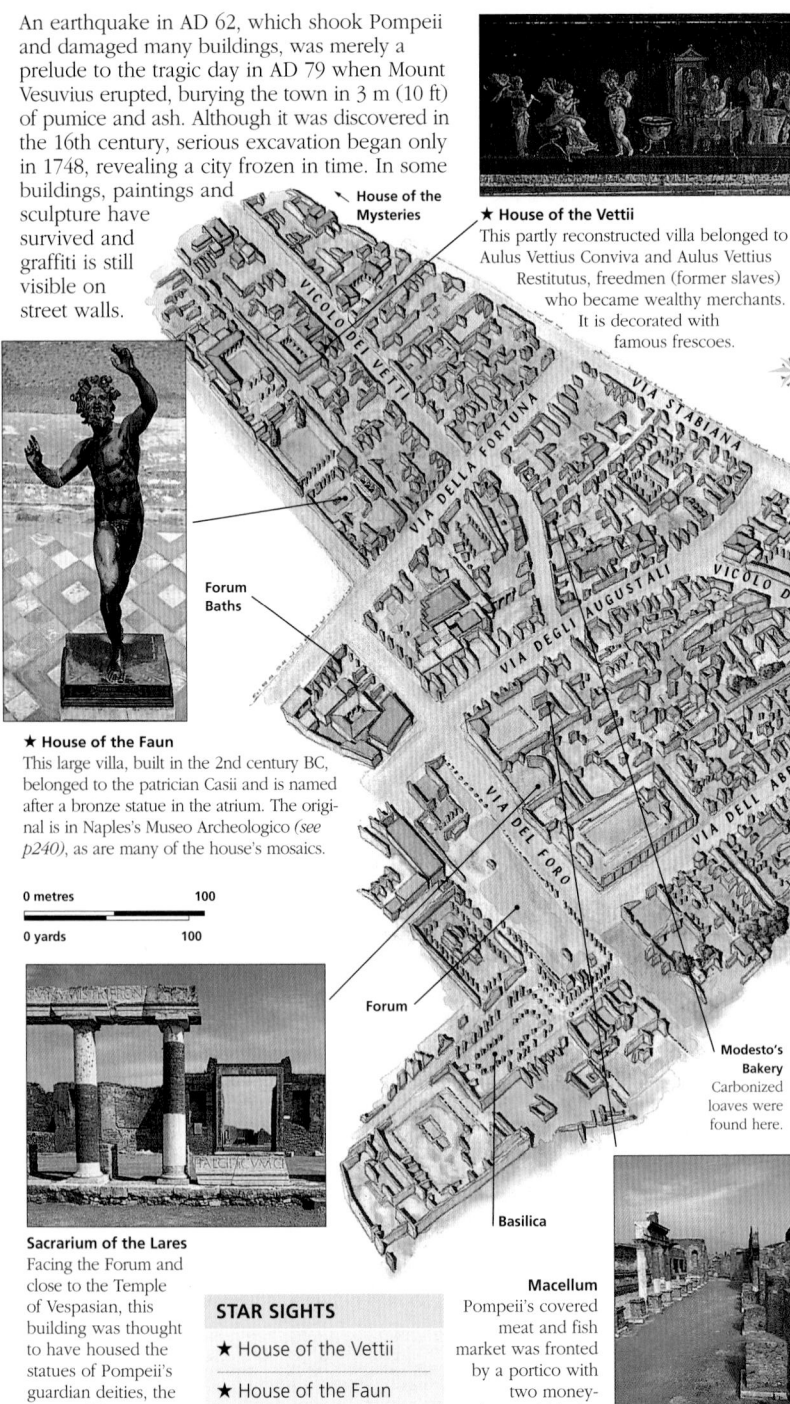

★ House of the Vettii
This partly reconstructed villa belonged to Aulus Vettius Conviva and Aulus Vettius Restitutus, freedmen (former slaves) who became wealthy merchants. It is decorated with famous frescoes.

Forum Baths

★ House of the Faun
This large villa, built in the 2nd century BC, belonged to the patrician Casii and is named after a bronze statue in the atrium. The original is in Naples's Museo Archeologico *(see p240)*, as are many of the house's mosaics.

0 metres 100

0 yards 100

Forum

Modesto's Bakery
Carbonized loaves were found here.

Sacrarium of the Lares
Facing the Forum and close to the Temple of Vespasian, this building was thought to have housed the statues of Pompeii's guardian deities, the Lares Publici.

Basilica

Macellum
Pompeii's covered meat and fish market was fronted by a portico with two money-changers' kiosks.

STAR SIGHTS

- ★ House of the Vettii
- ★ House of the Faun

PLAN OF POMPEII

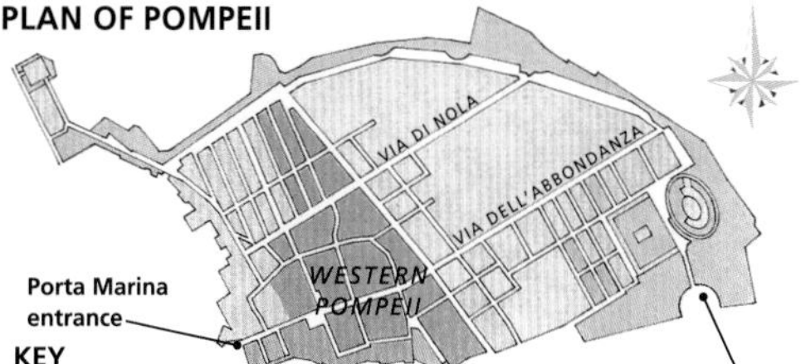

KEY

Area illustrated below

DISTANCE FROM PORT

30 km (19 miles) from site.

WESTERN POMPEII

This detailed illustration is of the fully excavated western area, where the most impressive and remarkably intact Roman ruins are located. There are several large patrician villas in the eastern section, as wealthy residents built their homes outside the town centre. However, much of eastern Pompeii awaits excavation.

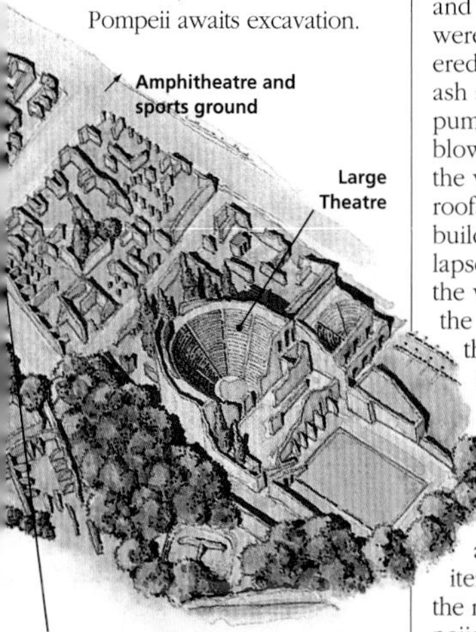

★ Via dell'Abbondanza
This was one of the original and most important roads through the city. Along it stood fine private homes and many shops and inns.

VESUVIUS AND THE CAMPANIAN TOWNS

Nearly 2,000 years after the eruption of Mount Vesuvius, the Roman towns in its shadow are still being released from the petrification that engulfed them. Both Pompeii and Stabiae (Castellammare di Stabia), to the south-east of Naples and Vesuvius, were smothered by hot ash and pumice-stone, blown there by the wind. The roofs of the buildings collapsed under the weight of the volcanic detritus. To the west, Herculaneum (Ercolano) vanished under a sea of mud. A large number of its buildings have survived, their roofs intact, and many domestic items were preserved by the mud. About 2,000 Pompeiians perished, although few, if any, of the residents of Herculaneum died.

In AD 79 Pliny the Elder, the Roman soldier, writer and naturalist, was the commander of a fleet stationed off Misenum (present-day Miseno, west of Naples) and with his nephew, Pliny the Younger, observed the eruption from afar. Eager to see this natural catastrophe closer to hand, Pliny the Elder proceeded to Stabiae, but was overcome by fumes and died. Based on reports by survivors, Pliny the Younger related the first hours of the eruption and his uncle's death in great detail in two letters to the Roman historian, Tacitus.

Pompeiian vase, Museo Nazionale Archeologico

Much of our knowledge of the daily lives of the ancient Romans derives from the excavations of Pompeii and Herculaneum. Most of the artifacts from them, as well as from Stabiae, have been moved to the Museo Archeologico Nazionale in Naples *(see p240)*, contributing to one of the world's most outstanding and fascinating archaeological collections.

Mount Vesuvius has not erupted since 1944, and today interested visitors are quite safe to reach it by train or car. There is so much to see at Pompeii that you will probably need a day to explore it.

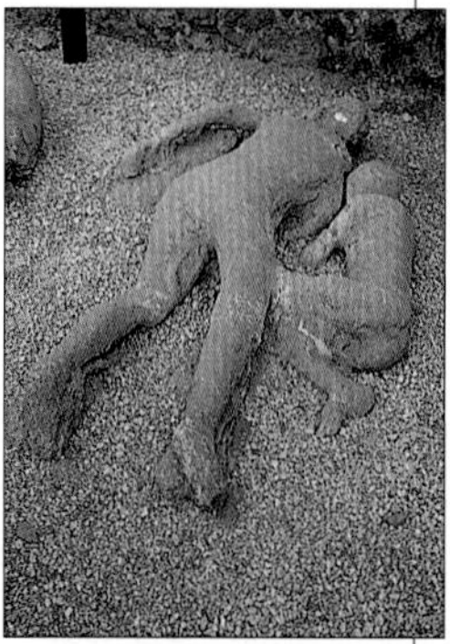

Casts of a dying mother and child in the museum in Naples

Capri

Excursion taxi

With idyllic views and almost constant sunshine, Capri lies just off the southern tip of the Bay of Naples. Its first illustrious residents were the Roman emperors Augustus and Tiberius (27 BC–AD 37). For ten years, Tiberius ruled Rome from Capri and the ruins of his luxurious villa can still be seen today. Despite this noble history, the island saw few visitors until the 19th century, when the German poet August Kopisch found the Grotta Azzurra, which was known to locals but not to travellers on the Grand Tour. Tourism began to flourish and Capri became the haunt of foreign politicians, artists and intellectuals, among them Oscar Wilde and Alexandre Dumas. Today, despite year-round crowds, it still retains its attractiveness.

Marina Grande ①
Capri's main harbour is a colourful village with seafood restaurants. When Tiberius first arrived, the island was accessible only from a small beach here. A funicular now takes visitors to central Capri.

Rocky Beaches
Sunloungers are set up among the rocks on this island beach.

Grotta Azzurra ⑨
The "Blue Grotto" owes its name to the intense blue of the water inside it, caused by light refraction.

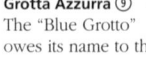

Anacapri ⑧
On the slopes of Monte Solaro, Anacapri is the island's second town. Its church of San Michele, built in 1719, has an extraordinary majolica floor depicting the expulsion of Adam and Eve from Paradise. The beautiful Villa San Michele, built by Swedish physician and philanthropist Axel Munthe (1857–1949), contains his collection of art and sculpture.

Villa Jovis ②
The largest of Capri's Roman villas, this retreat built by Emperor Tiberius stands on the mountain named after him. Excavations have revealed baths, apartments, cisterns, a possible observatory and the "balcony", a high-level walk with panoramic views.

Giardini di Augusto ⑤
Built on the ruins of an imperial villa, these beautiful gardens once belonged to Friedrich Alfred Krupp. He later donated them to the island and they were renamed in honour of Emperor Augustus.

I Faraglioni ③
Capri's most striking offshore rocks soar up to 109 m (360 ft) out of the sea.

Certosa di San Giacomo ④
This former Charterhouse with two cloisters was founded in 1371. Part of it is a museum with mystic paintings by German theosophist Karl W Diefenbach (1851–1913).

KEY SIGHTS

① Marina Grande
② Villa Jovis
③ I Faraglioni
④ Certosa di San Giacomo
⑤ Giardini di Augusto
⑥ La Piazzetta ★
⑦ Via Krupp
⑧ Anacapri
⑨ Grotta Azzurra ★

FACT FILE

TOURIST INFORMATION
Piazza Umberto I.
***Tel** 081 837 06 86.*
summer: daily to 8:30pm; winter: Mon–Sat to 6:15pm.

MARKETS
Food Capri (Marina Grande); Mon–Sat am. Anacapri; Mon, Wed & Fri am.
Clothes Anacapri; Thu am.

SHOPPING
Clothes Designer fashions.
Perfumes Locally made specialities.
Art and antiques Many galleries.
Food Traditional delicatessens.

LOCAL SPECIALITIES
Dishes
Ravioli alla Caprese (pasta stuffed with local *caciotta* cheese).
Drinks
Limoncello (a lemon liqueur).

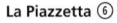

Via Krupp ⑦
Commissioned by the German industrialist Friedrich Alfred Krupp in 1900 to connect Hotel Quisisana with the Marina Piccola, this famous road makes a vertiginous descent towards the sea in a series of hairpin bends.

La Piazzetta ⑥
At the heart of the island's main town of Capri is the famous *Piazzetta*, officially Piazza Umberto I, but better known as "the salon of the world". It is the island's most popular meeting place, its café tables often packed late into the night. The piazza is surrounded by twisting medieval streets and overlooked by the Baroque dome of Santo Stefano, the former cathedral, and a clock tower that may once have been the bell tower.

Palermo

The Trinacria, ancient symbol of Sicily

Sicily's capital lies in the Conca d'Oro (Golden Shell), a natural amphitheatre below Monte Pellegrino. Palermo flourished from 831 to 1072 under Arab rule and its Arabic past is most apparent in the Vucciria, the medieval casbah-style market in the Kalsa. This old Arab quarter later became the Norman fishermen's district, and it is for its Norman architecture that Palermo is most famous. The originally 12th-century Duomo stands on Corso Vittorio Emanuele, the main street, which is full of impressive buildings and elegant stores. The city also has many fine Baroque buildings.

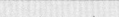

Cappella Palatina
This jewel of Norman architecture was built between 1132 and 1140 by Roger II, founder of the Norman Kingdom of Sicily in 1130. The central dome and apse have wonderful Byzantine-style mosaics and the nave's ceiling is intricately coffered and painted in Arab style. The chapel was part of the Palazzo dei Normanni (Norman royal palace), now the Sicilian parliament building.

Fontana Pretoria
Tuscan sculptor Francesco Camilliani originally designed this beautiful fountain in the 1550s for the garden of a Florentine villa. When it was acquired instead by the Palermitan Senate, it became known as the "Fountain of Shame" because of its statues of nude figures.

San Giovanni degli Eremiti
Standing on the site of a mosque, this church was built for Roger II between 1132 and 1148. Arab-Norman craftsmen reused part of the mosque in their structure and an oriental influence is evident in the cubic forms, red domes and filigreed windows. Between the church (now deconsecrated) and other remains of the mosque is a ruined 13th-century monastery cloister in a pretty, tree-shaded garden.

KEY SIGHTS

Cappella Palatina ★
Duomo ★
Fontana Pretoria
Palazzo dei Normanni
San Giovanni degli Eremiti
Vucciria

FACT FILE

TOURIST INFORMATION
Piazza Castelnuova 34. ***Tel*** *091 605 83 51.* ☐ *Mon–Sat to 7pm, Sun to 1pm.*

MARKETS
Food & general goods Vucciria, Via Roma & Piazza Ballarò; all daily.
Antiques near Porta Uzeda; daily.

LOCAL SPECIALITIES
Crafts
Traditional wooden puppets.
Dishes
Bottarga (salted tuna roe).
Involtini di pesce (swordfish with raisin and pine nut stuffing).
Caponata (aubergine/egg plant stew with capers and olives).
Pasta con le sarde (pasta with sardines, fennel and raisins).
Cassata (ice cream of ricotta cheese and candied fruit on sponge cake).
Drinks
Duca di Salaparuta (local red wine).
Marsala (fortified sweet wine from Marsala, drunk all over Sicily).

EXCURSIONS
Monreale Cathedral 9 km (6 miles) SW of Palermo. Sicily's greatest Norman sight. Mosaics.
Segesta 85 km (53 miles) SW of Palermo. Greek temple from 5th century BC; 3rd-century BC theatre.

Messina

Although Messina was almost completely destroyed by an earthquake in 1908 and heavily bombed in 1943, some historic buildings were rebuilt and the Museo Regionale holds many treasures, including works by Caravaggio. The Duomo dates from 1160 to 1197 and its campanile houses the world's largest astronomical clock, built in 1933. The beautiful church of Santissima Annunziata dei Catalani displays the typical ecelcticism of 12th-century Norman architecture, with rich decoration.

Mount Etna
Said by the Romans to be the forge of Vulcan, god of fire, Etna is Europe's largest active volcano. Visitors can take trips up to the eerie lunar landscape of solidified lava and black rock at 2,700 m (8,900 ft).

Fontana d'Orione
Designed by Fra Giovanni Angelo Montorsoli in 1547, this is the finest 16th-century fountain in Sicily. The reclining statues represent the rivers Nile, Ebro, Tiber and Camaro (the last of which fed the fountain). He also designed the Fontana di Nettuno (1557) in the Piazza Unità d'Italia.

The 2nd-century remains of Taormina's magnificently situated theatre, originally built by the Greeks with a seating capacity for 5,000 spectators.

KEY SIGHTS

Duomo
Fontana d'Orione ★
Museo Regionale
Santissima Annunziata dei Catalani ★

FACT FILE

TOURIST INFORMATION

Via dei Mille 272. ***Tel** 090 293 52 92.* ☐ *Mon–Wed to 6pm, Thu & Fri am.*

MARKETS

Food Viale Giostra, Viale Europa & Via Catania; all Mon–Sat am.
Clothes Viale Giostra; Tue & Fri am.
Flea market Orso Corbino; Sun am.

LOCAL SPECIALITIES

Crafts
Ceramics.
Dishes
Pesce spada (swordfish).
Pesce stocco a ghiotta (stockfish in tomato, caper and celery sauce).
Pasta 'ncaciata (pasta with meat balls, sausage, cheese and eggs).
Maccheroni alla Norma (pasta with tomatoes and aubergine/egg plant).
Calamari in umido (squid in tomato sauce).
Gamberi fritti (fried prawns).
Cannoli (ricotta-stuffed pastries).
Pignolata (fried dough with honey and chocolate or lemon cream).
Torroncini (almond nougat).
Marzipan fruits and a great variety of other sweets.
Drinks
Granita (creamy ice with lemon, coffee or almond flavouring).
Corvo and *Colomba palatino* (local red and white wines).
Donnafugata and *Regaleali* (local wines, both in red and white styles).
Amaro Averna (a bitter liqueur).
Strega (a bitter liqueur).

EXCURSIONS

Taormina 50 km (30 miles) S of Messina. A splendidly-sited historic city. Famous for its Greek theatre, begun in the 3rd century BC and rebuilt by the Romans.
Mount Etna summit 100 km (60 miles) SW of Messina. The beautiful scenery can be admired from the roads and the Circum-etnea Railway that circle Etna's base. The climb to the summit should only be made with a guide.

Fishing boats, Malta ▷

PISCES

MALTA

VALLETTA 250–251

Valletta

Malta's capital has the largest and best naturally protected harbour in the Mediterranean. After the Knights of St John had narrowly managed to beat off the Turks during the Great Siege of 1565, Grand Master Jean de la Valette ordered massive fortifications and the creation of a fully planned city on virgin ground. The streets were laid out as a grid to allow cooling sea breezes to blow through them unimpeded. Today it remains a remarkably unspoilt historic city with splendid Renaissance buildings, including the Knights' *auberges* (inns) and palatial cathedral, and a large proportion of Baroque buildings. The main shopping street is Republic Street, flanked by houses with characteristic Maltese balconies.

Auberge de Castille, Léon et Portugal ②
Now the prime minister's office, this inn was built in the Renaissance era by the Spanish and Portuguese Knights. The Baroque façade was added in 1744.

Upper Barraca Gardens ①
These were originally the private gardens of the Italian Knights. They offer magnificent views across the Grand Harbour to the Cottonera, the conglomeration of towns and fortifications opposite. Vittoriosa Birgu, behind Fort St Angelo on the central promontory there, was the Knights' first capital on Malta.

National Museum of Archaeology ③
Housed in the French Knights' Auberge de Provence, this has displays of Maltese Neolithic, Phoenician, Punic and Roman artifacts. Most fascinating are the figurines and large stone sculptures from the islands' prehistoric temples.

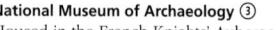

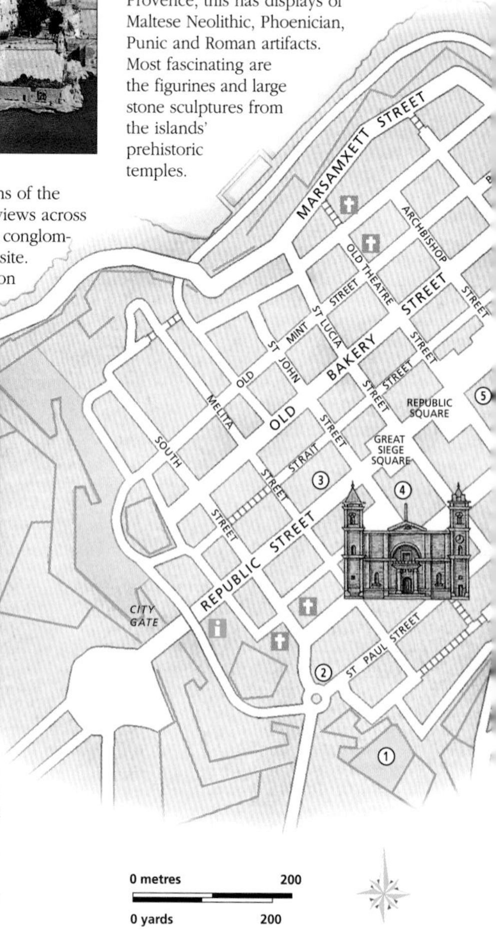

Grand Master's Palace ⑤
Built in 1580 to a design by the Maltese architect Gerolamo Cassar, who drew the plans for so many of Valletta's important buildings, the residence of the Knights' Grand Masters is now the President's Palace. The state rooms and Armoury may be visited. The latter has exceptional suits of armour from the 16th to 18th centuries, including one gold-plated example.

Casa Rocca Piccola ⑥
The dining room (above), library, chapel and several other rooms of the home of the 9th Marquis of Piro can be visited. They provide an evocative insight into the past lifestyle of Malta's aristocracy.

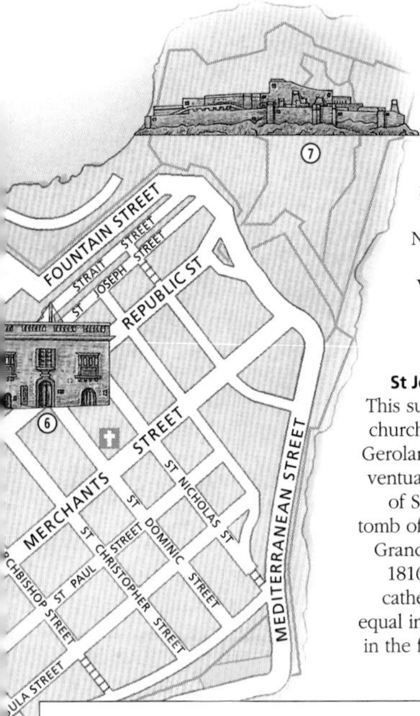

Fort St Elmo ⑦
Built in 1552 to ward off the Turks, the fort famously resisted their Great Siege of 1565. One of the halls houses the National War Museum, which is strong on World War II material.

St John's Co-Cathedral ④
This sumptuously decorated church was built in 1577 by Gerolamo Cassar as the conventual church of the Order of St John. It contains the tomb of many of the Knights' Grand Masters (leaders). In 1816 the Pope raised it to cathedral status to make it equal in rank to the cathedral in the former capital, Mdina.

THE KNIGHTS OF ST JOHN

The Order was founded in Jerusalem in the 11th century to care for sick pilgrims, but soon gained a military role in the Crusades against Islam. In 1530 the Knights, who all came from Europe's noblest and richest families, were given Malta as a headquarters by Holy Roman Emperor Charles V. They were divided into eight Langues ("tongues"), Auvergne, Provence, France, Aragon, Castile, England, Germany and Italy, symbolized by the eight points of the Maltese cross. In 1798 they were expelled from Malta by Napoleon and re-founded as a humanitarian order in Rome in the 19th century.

Grand Master Jean de la Valette

KEY SIGHTS

① Upper Barracca Gardens
② Auberge de Castille, Léon et Portugal
③ National Museum of Archaeology
④ St John's Co-Cathedral ★
⑤ Grand Master's Palace
⑥ Casa Rocca Piccola ★
⑦ Fort St Elmo

FACT FILE

TOURIST INFORMATION

1 City Arcades, City Gate.
Tel *(22) 91 54 40.* ◯ *Mon–Sat to 5:30pm, Sun to 1pm.*

MARKETS

Food Market Hall, Merchant Street; Mon–Sat.

LOCAL SPECIALITIES

Crafts
Ceramics, glassware, wrought-iron goods, embroidery and lace.
Dishes
Aljotta (fish soup with garlic). *Bzar ahdar mimli* (peppers stuffed with meat, olives and capers). *Hobz biz-zejt* (bread topped with tomatoes, capers and spices). *Stuffat tal-fenek* (rabbit braised with tomatoes and red wine). *Torta tal-lampuka* (fried lampuka fish baked in pastry).
Drinks
Kinnie (a soft drink).
Cisk, Blue Label, Hop Leaf, Clipper (local beers).
Marsovin Cabernet Sauvignon, Verdala, Green Label (local wines).

EXCURSIONS

Tarxien 6 km (4 miles) S of Valletta. Malta's finest Megalithic temples.
Marsaxlokk 8 km (5 miles) S of Valletta. Colourful fishing port.
Mdina 12 km (7 miles) SW of Valletta. Malta's former capital. An historic, walled cathedral city.
Mellieha 16 km (10 miles) NW of Valletta. Hilltop town with cave dwellings. Long, sandy beaches.
Blue Lagoon On Comino Island, 25 km (16 miles) NW of Valletta. Good swimming in translucent waters.
Gozo Island 28 km (17 miles) NW of Valletta. The capital Victoria has an impressive Citadel. Nearby are the Megalithic Ggantija Temples.

Berber village, Morocco ▷

NORTH AFRICA

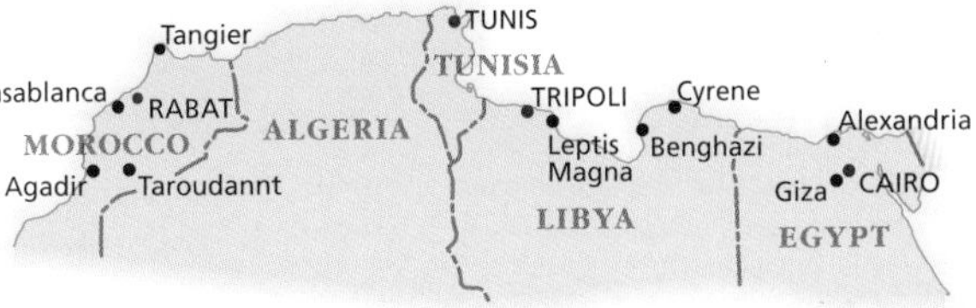

Morocco: Agadir

Intricate Berber jewellery

Agadir, the regional capital of the South, draws thousands of visitors a year. Its gentle climate together with its sheltered beach and hotels make it Morocco's second tourist city after Marrakech. Agadir's modern centre, the Nouveau Talborj, was built south of the old city after a terrible earthquake razed the area in the 1960s. In the heart of the city is the Vallée des Oiseaux, a park containing aviaries with exotic birds and a small zoo. The hilltop ruins of the Kasbah offer stunning views of Agadir and the bay, alive with the customary souk and cafés. Arts and crafts of the Saharan nomads, with costumes and jewellery, are well represented in the Musée du Patrimoine Amazigh.

Agadir Beach
South of the city, this fine sand beach stretching 9 km (6 miles), is Agadir's main attraction, offering some of the safest swimming off Morocco's Atlantic coast. The city enjoys 300 days of sunshine a year. Sailboards, jet-skis and water scooters can be hired and rides, on horses or camels, are also on offer. Cafés, hotels and restaurants line the beach.

Imouzzer des Ida-Outanane
The spectacular drive to the village of Immouzer twists up a dramatic valley through banana plantations and olive groves. Its chief sight is the waterfall with fascinating rock formations surrounded by palm trees. Visitors can also take a mule ride through the peaceful countryside, sit at a quiet café or buy honey, the local speciality.

Tafraoute
In a valley lush with date palms, this small, prosperous town lies in the Anti-Atlas Mountains. Its pink and ochre-painted houses harmonize with the awe-inspiring landscape, where deep-red volcanic rocks, extruded in ancient eruptions, tower upwards in contorted cliffs and peaks.

KEY SIGHTS

Beach ★
Musée Bert Flint
Old Kasbah
Souk
Vallée des Oiseaux ★

FACT FILE

TOURIST INFORMATION
Im Iguenouan. Av. Mohamed V.
Tel *(028) 84 63 77.*
daily to 6pm.

MARKETS
Souvenirs Rue Chayr el Hamra Mohammed ben Brahim; daily.

LOCAL SPECIALITIES
Crafts
Enamelled silver jewellery.
Dishes
Harira (chick pea and mutton soup).
Couscous (steamed semolina).
Brochettes (mutton or liver kebabs).
Tagine (spicy fish or meat stew).
Pastilla (flaky-pastry pigeon pie).
Drinks
Nègre (a black variety of mint tea).

EXCURSIONS
Immouzer des Ida-Outanane 61 km (38 miles) N of Agadir. A beautiful mountain village with dramatic waterfalls.
Tafraoute 150 km (90 miles) SE of Agadir. Small town in a strikingly colourful landscape of villages set around a valley of date palms.
Essaouira 180 km (110 miles) N of Agadir. The location for Orson Welles' 1952 film *Othello*, this enchanting blue- and white-painted enclave has long been a haven for artists and freethinkers.

Morocco: Taroudannt (Agadir)

Taroudannt lies within splendid, crenellated, ochre walls that were first built in the 11th century, though today's walls date from the 16th and 18th centuries. The town is, as it always has been, the chief market town of the fertile Sous valley and has lost little of its traditional charm. Life centres on the labyrinthine Arab and Berber Souks where everything from antiques to soap is sold. A plethora of shops makes it one of the best places in Morocco to buy carpets, old pots, traditional cloaks and reed and leather woven mats made by desert tribes. The walls are best viewed from the horse-drawn *calèches* that stop outside the Palais Salam Hotel. Outside the ramparts is a tannery selling goat-skin and camel-hide sandals, lambskin rugs, leather bags, belts and slippers.

Berber Souk
Vegetables on sale in the souk are always fabulously fresh. People buy supplies daily, often directly from local farmers who have harvested the produce only hours before. Bargaining takes place not just over expensive carpets, but over every last carrot.

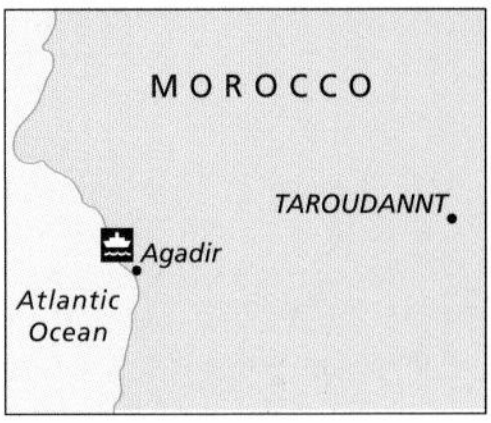

DISTANCE FROM PORT

81 km (50 miles) from town centre.

KEY SIGHTS

Berber Souk ★
Arab Souk ★
Palais Salam Hotel
Tanneries
Walls ★

FACT FILE

TOURIST INFORMATION

No tourist office. See Agadir.

MARKETS

Food Bab el Khemis; Thu & Sun.

LOCAL SPECIALITIES

Crafts
Woven mats, fine woven cloaks.
Dishes
Kefta (spicy mutton meatballs).
Merguez (spicy sausages).
Drinks
Thé à la menthe (sweet green mint tea).

EXCURSIONS

Kasbah de Freïja 8 km (5 miles) E of Taroudannt. Ruins of a palace and small *koubba* (domed tomb).
Tioute 35 km (21 miles) SE of Taroudannt. Pre-19th-century kasbah, damaged in 1960 earthquake, and ruins of an old Jewish quarter.
Amagour Crater 40 km (24 miles) S of Taroudannt. Extinct volcano. Weird natural rock formations include bridges, tunnels and caverns.

Palais Salam Hotel
This fine, picturesque hotel was the 19th-century palace of the pasha (governor) of Taroudannt. Its walls of traditional, sun-baked mud bricks provide a spectacular backdrop for the palm trees and *mihrab*-shaped swimming pool.

Morocco: Casablanca

One of the largest cities in Africa, Casablanca is the economic capital of Morocco and its most westernized city. The site has been used as a trading port since around 500 BC, but it was only during the French protectorate (from 1912 to 1956) that the city assumed its pivotal role in the Moroccan economy. Side by side with the modernity of its wide, straight avenues and high-rise office blocks, the millennial face of Morocco can still be found in the Old Medina, and there are some fine examples of Moorish colonial architecture to be admired. The last king, Hassan II, left a memorial to his reign on the shoreline – the largest mosque outside Saudia Arabia, with a 200-m (656-ft) high minaret.

Old Medina ②
These narrow alleyways give a taste of how Moroccan life has been for centuries. The sea-facing cannons at the 19th-century Skala fortifications are remnants of the reign of Sidi Mohammed Ben Abdullah.

Great Mosque of Hassan II ①
Perched beside the sea, this mosque was built entirely with donations from the people of Morocco. Occasionally, the roof of the vast prayer hall slides open so that worshippers can pray directly beneath the heavens.

CASABLANCA – THE MOVIE

Although Casablanca is the setting, and indeed the title, of one of Hollywood's most romantic movies, the connection with the city ends there. Not a single frame of the film was shot in Morocco, let alone Casablanca. Yet in 1942, the year of its release, the World War II Casablanca landings of British and US troops on this coast not only liberated Morocco from French Vichy control but also gave a tremendous boost to the film. After almost 60 years *Casablanca*, starring Humphrey Bogart and Ingrid Bergman (though originally cast with Ronald Reagan and Ann Sheridan), still captures the imagination of thousands.

Film poster

Cathédrale du Sacré-Coeur ⑤
Designed by Paul Tornon in 1930, this deconsecrated church with its gargoyles and buttresses deliberately borrow elements of *zellij* (tile mosaic, *see p271)* design in its intricate stained-glass windows.

Central Market ③
Housed in a wonderful Moorish courtyard, the central arcades burgeon with cut flowers, fresh vegetables, pyramids of oranges and other fruits and all the cornucopia of the ocean.

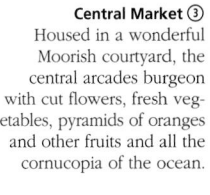

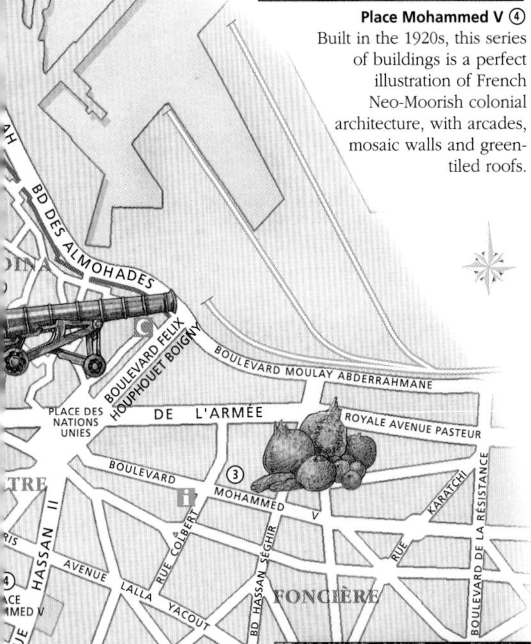

Place Mohammed V ④
Built in the 1920s, this series of buildings is a perfect illustration of French Neo-Moorish colonial architecture, with arcades, mosaic walls and green-tiled roofs.

Notre-Dame-de-Lourdes ⑥
Completed in 1956, the year the French left Morocco, this church still holds services for the small French and expatriate population that remains in Casablanca.

New Medina ⑦
Shopping for souvenirs is delightful in this French-built copy of an 18th-century Moroccan quarter, which is filled with bazaars and craft shops.

KEY SIGHTS

① Great Mosque of Hassan II ★
② Old Medina ★
③ Central Market ★
④ Place Mohammed V
⑤ Cathédrale du Sacré-Coeur
⑥ Notre-Dame-de-Lourdes
⑦ New Medina

FACT FILE

TOURIST INFORMATION

55, Rue Omar Slaoui. ***Tel*** *(02) 227 11 77.* ◯ *daily to 6pm.*

MARKETS

Food & flowers Boulevard Mohammed V; daily.
Antiques & ornaments Rue Mustapha el-Maami; daily.

LOCAL SPECIALITIES

Crafts
Leatherwork, Mediouna carpets, *zellij* mosaic items.
Dishes
Harira and *khobz* (mutton and pulse soup with traditional flat bread). *Couscous* (steamed semolina). *Baghrir* (thick pancakes with honey).
Drinks
Gris de Boulaouane (rosé wine from just south of the city).

EXCURSIONS

Sidi-Abd-er-Rahmane 5 km (3 miles) W of Casablanca. Cluster of shrines on a promontory. Non-Muslims are forbidden on the promontory, but the sunset views from the shore are spectacular.
Mohammedia 28 km (17 miles) N of Casablanca. A popular resort with a racecourse, casino, golf course, marina and beaches.
Azemmour 80 km (50 miles) S of Casablanca. Pleasant little town surrounded by 14th-century ramparts. Little to see within the town itself, but the view from the other side of the river is one of the most picturesque in Morocco.
Rabat 87 km (54 miles) NE of Casablanca. Capital of Morocco. The main sights include the 12th-century, unfinished but finely carved minaret, known as the Tour Hassan, and the Chellah, a walled necropolis where sacred eels are thought to cure infertility.

Morocco: Tangier

Water seller, Grand Socco

Overlooking the Straits of Gibraltar, the ancient port of Tangier was founded by the Berbers before 1000 BC, and it is the oldest continually inhabited city in Morocco. Spread over the foothills of the Rif mountains, it is a city vibrant with Eastern colour. The nucleus is the vast, labyrinthine Medina, the market quarter, which pulsates with noise and vitality. From their workshops in back alleys, craftsmen make traditional goods for busy shops and stalls in the crowded streets. Yet behind wrought-iron railings the visitor will see cool fountains, mosques and tranquil courts decorated with mosaics. Despite its unification with Morocco in 1956, Tangier remains a rich melting pot of cultures and religions, where the spires of Christian churches contrast interestingly with the minarets of Muslim mosques.

Dar el Makhzen ①
Built within the Kasbah in the 17th century, the palace housed sultans with their wives, harems and entourages until 1912. Now it is a museum of Moroccan arts.

The city of Tangier, rising above the port

Kasbah ②
The Kasbah, built in Roman times, was where the sultans once held court. This ancient citadel is separated from its alleys by sturdy fortress walls and four massive stone gateways. Inside there are palaces, a treasury house, law courts and an old prison.

Grand Socco ⑥
Traders from the Rif mountains, to the south-east of Tangier, come to barter their goods at this busy main square at the heart of the city. The official name of the square is Place du 9 Avril 1947, which commemorates a visit by Sultan Mohammed V on that date.

Rue es Siaghin ⑤
The Medina's main artery, Rue es Siaghin, offers a staggering array of merchandise; shop owners along the street offer passersby mint tea in a bid to persuade them to buy.

THE INTERNATIONAL ERA

Orson Welles, once a familiar sight on the streets of Tangier

From 1932 until its incorporation into Morocco in 1956, Tangier was an international zone, tax free and under the control of a committee of 30 foreign nations. The international era was characterized by financial fraud, espionage, large-scale smuggling, liberal sexual licence and profligacy by wealthy tax exiles, such as Barbara Hutton, the heiress of the Woolworth fortune, who at one time was among the world's richest women. Celebrities such as the French artist Henri Matisse, American "Beat" novelist Jack Kerouac and esteemed American film director and actor Orson Welles added colour to the international scene.

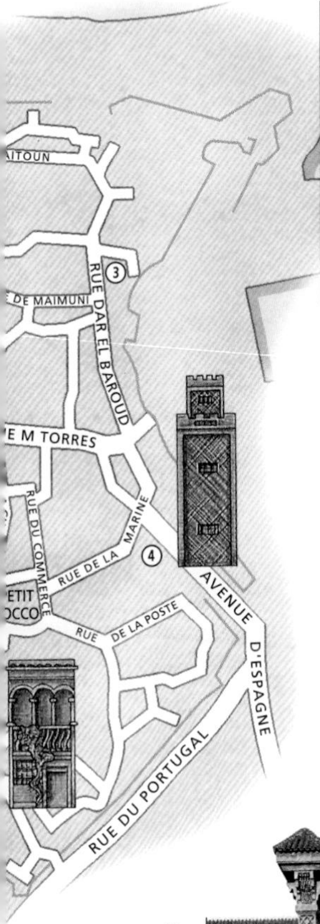

Hôtel Continental ③
Numerous intrigues have been played out at this 19th-century hotel, which sits at the edge of the old Medina and overlooks the port. Today it is a fine place to sit and drink tea.

0 metres 250
0 yards 250

American Legation ⑦
This former palace, a gift from Sultan Moulay Slimane in 1821, was the United States' first diplomatic mission and remained the American Embassy until 1961. It now houses an art museum.

Grand Mosque ④
Green and white inarets rise above this nassive edifice built in the 17th century. An xquisitely carved gateway suggests more reasures within; however non-Muslims may not enter the mosque.

KEY SIGHTS

① Dar el Makhzen ★
② Kasbah ★
③ Hôtel Continental
④ Grand Mosque ★
⑤ Rue es Siaghin
⑥ Grand Socco
⑦ American Legation

FACT FILE

TOURIST INFORMATION

29 boulevard Pasteur. ***Tel** (039) 94 80 50.* ◻ *daily to 6pm.*

MARKETS

General goods Rue es Siaghin; daily (closed Fri pm).
Grand Socco Place du 9 Avril 1947; daily (closed Fri pm).

LOCAL SPECIALITIES

Crafts
Pottery copying ancient geometric motifs, carpets.
Dishes
Chorba Belhout (fish stew with tomatoes, ginger, saffron and sweet and hot red peppers).
Harira (thick bean soup, flavoured with mutton or chicken, lemon and tarragon).
Samak mahshi (any large, white fish stuffed with rice, pine nuts and almonds, served with a tamarind sauce).
Cornes de gazelle (croissant-like pastries filled with honey and almonds).
Drinks
Orange pressé (freshly-squeezed orange juice, with a little grapefruit or lemon added).
Thé à la menthe (mint tea).

EXCURSIONS

Grottoes of Hercules 10 km (6 miles) W of Tangier. According to classical mythology, Hercules *(see p331)* rested here after finishing his labours.
Tétouan 47 km (30 miles) E of Tangier. Medina within fortified walls, with a royal palace in the centre. Archaeological Museum and Museum of Moroccan Arts.
Chechaouèn 84 km (52 miles) SE of Tangier. Founded in 15th century by Moulay Ali Ben Rachid. Kasbah Museum and Great Mosque of Jamaa el Kebir.

Tunisia: Tunis

One of the Mediterranean's best-kept secrets, the old, white, hill town of Tunis dates back to the 8th century Arab conquest. During the French colonial period of 1881 to 1956, a rational grid of streets was added to the snaking alleyways of the old Medina, and the city is now the thriving political and economic capital of Tunisia. Avenue Habib Bourguiba offers a leisurely stroll, where pavement cafés compete for business and shade is provided by a sculptural avenue of ficus trees. In the Medina, however, all is frantic activity; the sounds of metalworkers, perfumers, hat-makers in their narrow booths and salesmen in the carpet bazaars are punctured from time to time by the cry of the *muezzin* as he calls the faithful to prayer.

Medina ⑥
The best of Tunis's shopping lies in and around Rue Jamaa ez Zitouna. Tunisian antiques can be bought here at No. 45, while turned and carved olive wood is available from Rue des Tamis.

Bardo Museum ⑦
Just outside the city centre, the Bardo Museum holds a breathtaking collection of Roman mosaics, including this fine portrait of the Roman poet Virgil, flanked by Clio and Melpomene, the Muses of History and Tragedy.

Souk des Chéchias ⑤
In a sedate quarter of the Medina, craftsmen make the traditional felt *chechia* hats in much the same way as they have for centuries.

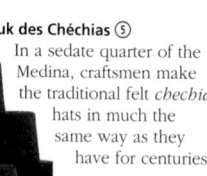

Zitouna Mosque ④
Built in the 9th century, the Zitouna (Olive Tree) Mosque is Tunis's spiritual centre and provides a welcome place of calm in the middle of the hectic Medina. It is said to be built over a temple to the ancient goddess Athena.

THE ANCIENT CITY OF CARTHAGE

The 2nd-century AD Antonine Baths.

The Romans invaded the Phoenician city of Carthage in 146 BC and razed it to the ground, only to rebuild it as the most important city in their North African empire. Just around the bay from Tunis itself, the ruins are largely built over by prosperous modern villas, but there are fascinating glimpses of the ancient city to be had at the Antonine Baths, the Punic Harbour and the Tophet, not to mention the National Museum of Carthage on the hill. Virgil's *Aeneid* describes the tragic love affair between Dido, Queen of Carthage, and the eponymous Aeneas.

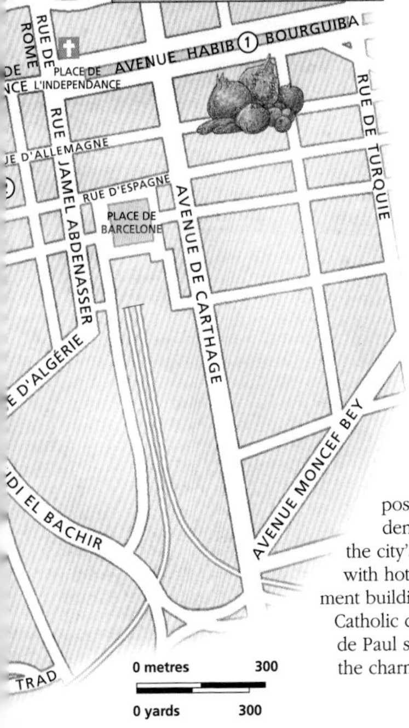

Museum of Dar Ben Abdallah ③
The pleasure is as much in the beautiful tiled courtyard of this stately 18th-century town house as in the exhibits themselves, which show Tunisian domestic traditions, textiles, furniture and jewellery.

Central Market ②
This is the place to overhear mouth-watering recipes traded from stall-holder to housewife over fresh wild mushrooms, marinated olives and piles of fresh seasonal fruit, vegetables and seafood.

Avenue Habib Bourguiba ①
Named after Tunisia's post-independence president (in power 1957–87), the city's main street is dotted with hotels, cafés and government buildings. The 19th-century Catholic cathedral of St Vincent de Paul stands almost opposite the charming Art-Deco theatre.

KEY SIGHTS

① Avenue Habib Bourguiba
② Central Market
③ Museum of Dar Ben Abdallah
④ Zitouna Mosque ★
⑤ Souk des Chéchias
⑥ Medina ★
⑦ Bardo Museum ★

FACT FILE

TOURIST INFORMATION

1 Ave Mohammed V.
Tel *(071) 341077. ◻ daily to 5:45pm (Jul & Aug: to 6:30pm).*

MARKETS

Aromatic oils & spices Souk el-Attarine; daily.

LOCAL SPECIALITIES

Crafts
Bakhnoug (fine embroidered veils).
Chechia (foldable felt hats).
Dishes
Couscous (wheat grain with meat, vegetables and a spicy sauce).
Mechouia (appetizer of peppers, tomatoes and onions, mixed with lemon, tuna and egg).
Brik (fried pastry parcels of minced tuna or vegetables and egg).
Bouza (sorghum and hazlenut cake).
Drinks
Thé à la menthe (mint tea).
Château Mornag (red wine).
Muscat de Kelibia (white wine).
Gris de Tunisie (rosé wine).

EXCURSIONS

Carthage 16 km (10 miles) E of Tunis. Ruins of the important ancient city first settled by the Phoenicians in around 725 BC.
Sidi bou Said 18 km (11 miles) NE of Tunis. A radiantly pretty village beyond Carthage. Highlights include Ennajma Ezzahra Palace and the many cafés.
La Marsa 20 km (13 miles) N of Tunis. Elegant holiday resort for Tunis's middle classes with chic architecture along the beachfront.
Kerkouane 120 km (72 miles) NE of Tunis. Excavated ruins of a 6th-century Punic town, destroyed by the Romans around the same period as Carthage. There is also an archaeological museum.

Libya: Tripoli

Though Libya's government offices moved to the new city of Sirte in 1998, Tripoli, the political centre for four centuries, is still the economic capital and heart of the country. It looks out over a large, sheltered harbour and has a medieval medina (old town). Within it are the Roman arch of Marcus Aurelius built in the 2nd century AD, the Gurgi Mosque, founded in 1833, with a beautiful, tiled prayer hall, the Karamanli House Museum illustrating 19th- and 20th-century upper-bourgeois life, and the covered souk, which is best visited mid-morning or just before dusk. The Al-Saray Museum has a breathtaking collection of archaeological treasures. The ruins of Roman Sabratha are about an hour's drive from Tripoli.

Medina
It is traditional throughout the Muslim world for houses to be built facing onto a central courtyard, with no external windows and only a door giving onto the outside world. Often there was a room off the entrance hall where male visitors could be entertained without entering the female realm beyond. Here, in courtyards such as this and in the surrounding rooms, women cooked, ate, slept and chatted.

A view across the seafront and port of Tripoli

KEY SIGHTS

Arch of Marcus Aurelius

Gurgi Mosque ★

Al-Saray Museum ★

Karamanli House Museum

Medina

FACT FILE

TOURIST INFORMATION

Libya Tourism Investment and Promotion Board, Tripoli.
Tel *(021) 340 5112.*
◯ *Mon–Thu & Sat to 2:30pm.*

MARKETS

General Covered Souk, off Green Square, Medina; daily.

LOCAL SPECIALITIES

Crafts
Silver jewellery, Hand of Fatima talismans, leather sandals, waistcoats.

Dishes
Sherba (spiced soup). *Haraymi* (marinated fish in tomato and herb sauce). *Maghli* (fried marinated chicken). *Salata mashwia* (puréed vegetables). *Torshi* (spicy mashed potatoes). *Gharaiba* (almond cake).

Drinks
Tea (with mint leaves or peanuts).

EXCURSIONS

Sabratha 67 km (40 miles) W of Tripoli. Impressive remains of a Roman port city, then called Sabrata.

Al-Khums 97 km (60 miles) E of Tripoli. Coastal town with good beaches and public gardens.

Misratah 200 km (120 miles) E of Tripoli. Arabic Old Town; European- and Turkish-influenced New Town.

Sabratha
Sabratha's incredible late 2nd-century AD Roman theatre, the largest in North Africa, was excavated in the 1930s, and has been a World Heritage Site since 1982. In its heyday the theatre could seat 5,000 spectators watching a repertory of comedy, farce, mime and tragedy. On the stage wall is a frieze depicting mythological figures and actors. The three storeys of columns supporting the backdrop are made from marble imported from all over the Mediterranean.

Libya: Cyrene (Benghazi)

Decorated columns

Greek Colonists founded the hilltop town of Cyrene in 630 BC on the advice of the oracle at Delphi and named it after Kurana, the guardian nymph of the new town's life-giving spring. Cyrene then dominated life in eastern Libya for 1,000 years. In 323 BC, under the Ptolemies of Egypt, it became the capital of the local confederation of Greek colonies known as the Pentapolis, but fell to the Romans in about 75 BC. During the Arab invasions in the 7th century AD, Cyrene went into decline, surviving only as a farming village until archaeologists revealed its treasures in the 1920s. Its focal point was the Sanctuary of Apollo, built in honour of the god's oracle at Delphi. The Agora, the 5th-century BC Greek Temple of Zeus, the 2nd-century AD Roman House of Jason Magnus, with some good mosaics, and the large hillside Necropolis are the other most notable remains.

Naval Monument
In Cyrene's central Agora (public square), a winged figure of Victory stands on the prow of a sculpted Ancient Greek battleship, probably commemorating a 3rd-century BC sea victory by the city. The nearby altars would have been used for roasting whole animals as offerings to the gods. Cyrene's founder, King Battus, is thought to be buried nearby.

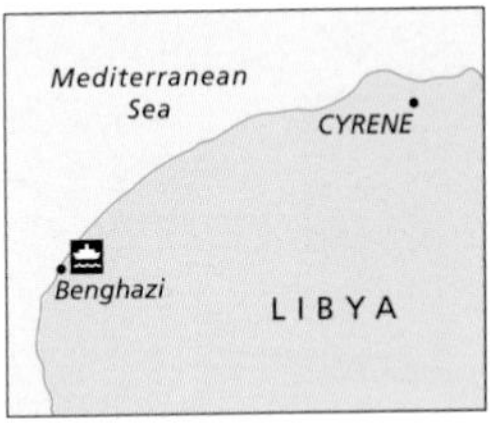

DISTANCE FROM PORT

200 km (124 miles) from site.

KEY SIGHTS

Agora ★

House of Jason Magnus

Necropolis

Roman Forum

Sanctuary of Apollo ★

Temple of Zeus

FACT FILE

TOURIST INFORMATION

No tourist office. See Tripoli.

LOCAL SPECIALITIES

Dishes

Tabahij (aubergine/eggplant and courgette in spicy tomato sauce). *Filfil harr makshi bil hoot* (jalapeño peppers stuffed with fish).

EXCURSIONS

Apollonia 20 km (12 miles) N of Cyrene. Former port to the city of Cyrene and, renamed Sousa, the 4th- to 7th-century AD provincial capital. Partially-excavated ruins include 1st-century theatre and baths.

Slonta 30 km (18 miles) SW of Cyrene. Only known ruins of pre-Islamic native Libyan settlement. Excavated temple, and figurines on display outside.

Derna 75 km (45 miles) E of Cyrene. A traditional settlement with a picturesque town centre, good beaches and small harbour. Shoreline caves once used by early Christians who feared persecution.

Sanctuary of Apollo
Among the city's earliest monuments, but rebuilt in the 4th century BC and 2nd AD, this vast temple complex became a pilgrimage centre where people performed ritual ablutions and sacrifices. Huge Roman baths, sections of which are still visible, were later built over part of it.

Libya: Leptis Magna (Tripoli)

Column detail, Severan Basilica

One of the world's greatest ruined cities, and a World Heritage Site since 1982, Leptis Magna attests to the prosperity and status of the Roman empire in North Africa. Leptis was particularly fortunate in AD 193 when Septimius Severus, a native of the city, became emperor of Rome. During his reign the population grew to some 70,000, and magnificent buildings were raised to glorify his name. Attacks by nomadic tribes led eventually to the city's abandonment, and it was subsequently engulfed by sand dunes.

Market
Once surrounded by arcades and centred on two beautiful kiosks, this grand trading place was endowed by one wealthy citizen, Annobal Rufus, in 9 to 8 BC.

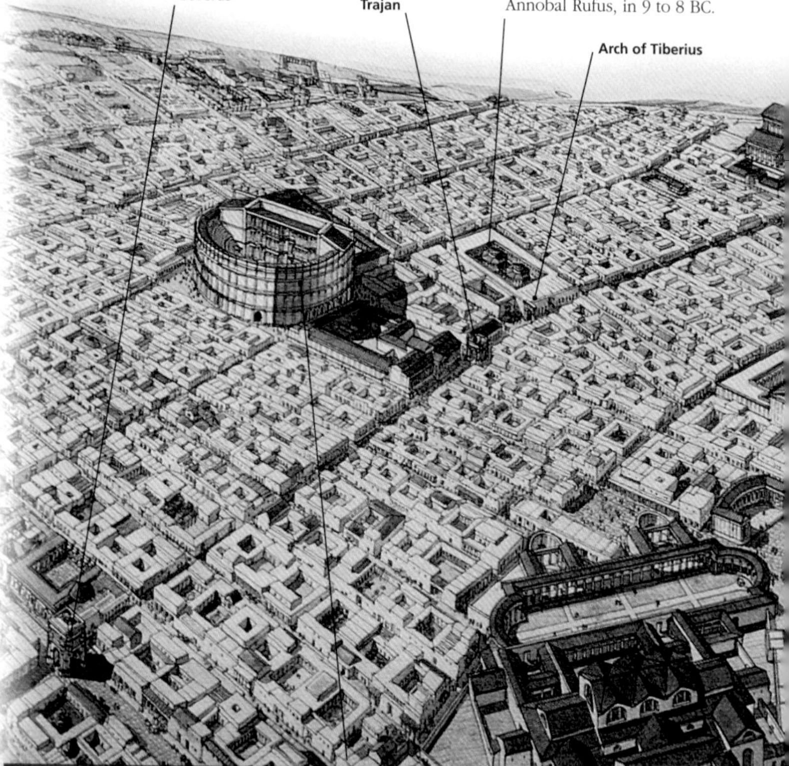

★ Theatre
Like the market, this vast structure was given to the city by Annobal Rufus. The lowest, wider stone steps would have held chairs for distinguished visitors. From the top, the panoramic view of the ancient city is magnificent.

★ Severan Basilica
Begun during the reign of Septimius to house the law courts, this massive double-apsed building was turned into a church by Justinian (AD 483–565), though part of it appears to have served as a synagogue from the 5th century AD.

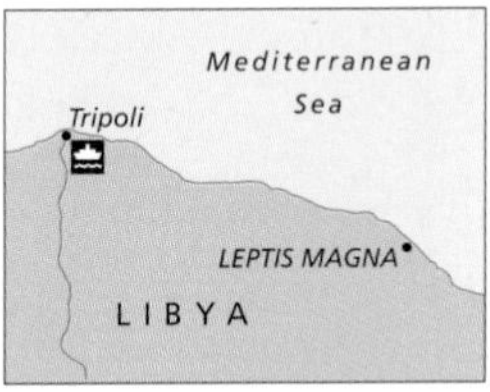

DISTANCE FROM PORT

122 km (76 miles) from site.

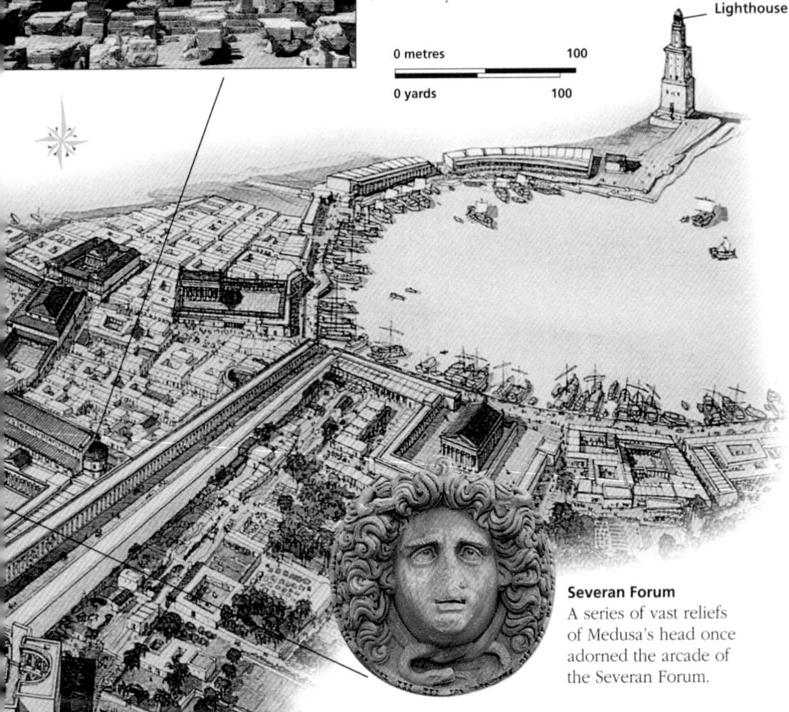

Severan Forum
A series of vast reliefs of Medusa's head once adorned the arcade of the Severan Forum.

RECONSTRUCTION OF LEPTIS MAGNA

This shows magnificent buildings erected during the reigns of successive emperors. In 2005 mosaics dating from the 2nd century were found here.

Hadrian's Baths
This baths complex includes and an outdoor sports ground *(palaestra)*, hot and warm baths *(caldarium and tepidarium)*, once heated by underfloor fires, and a huge cold bath *(frigidarium)* with two plunge pools, one still containing water.

STAR FEATURES

★ Theatre

★ Severan Basilica

Egypt: Alexandria

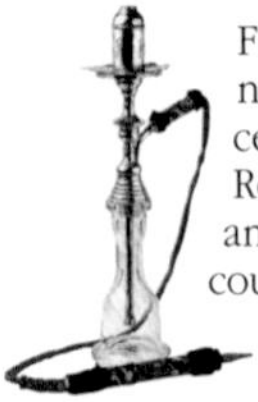

Narghile (bubble pipe)

Founded by Alexander the Great in 331 BC, for nearly a millennium this great seaport was a centre of learning and commerce second only to Rome. It was home to the world's greatest library and the fabulous Pharos, a towering lighthouse counted as one of the Seven Wonders of the Ancient World. Cleopatra, Queen of Egypt, held court here, where she was romanced by Marc Antony. Sadly, Classical Alexandria is long buried, but it has provided the foundations for a modern city where 19th-century Greek and Italian influences still echo in some fine architecture and in the names attached to countless old-world cafés and patisseries.

Fortress of Qaitbey ①
This 15th-century fortress occupies the site of the ancient Pharos. The base of the fortress walls reveals some of the giant blocks that remain of the legendary lighthouse.

El-Mursi Abul Abbas Mosque ②
Little more than half a century old, this building is constructed over the tomb of a 13th-century Andalusian saint – the city's patron saint of fishermen. The square beside the mosque is one of the most vibrant locales in Alexandria.

Souk ③
Souk in Arabic means market or bazaar; Alexandria's central souk is one block in from the seafront and stretches over 1 km (0.6 mile). It has sections devoted to everything from herbalists to carpet-sellers, and from fruit and vegetables to gold and silver jewellery.

Catacombs of Kom el-Shoqafa ⑧
In this series of Roman-era burial chambers sunk deep below the surface, intriguing reliefs merge pharaonic deities and Roman mythology. Nearby is a 27-m (89-ft) high, free-standing column dating from AD 297, commonly known as Pompey's Pillar.

Corniche ④
Alexandria's finest feature is a 2-km (1-mile) wide arc bordering the Eastern Harbour. It is graced by some gorgeous 19th-century architecture, most notably the Cecil Hotel (now a Sofitel), where former guests have included Somerset Maugham and Sir Winston Churchill.

liotheca Alexandrina ⑤
signed by Norwegian architects, s striking piece of 21st-century chitecture has an enormous disc-aped glass roof set at an gle like a rising sun. e circular exterior the main library etched with aracters m a babel languages.

Graeco-Roman Museum ⑥
Packed with statuary and artifacts relating to the city's Classical past, the museum has marble busts of the city's founder, Alexander, and several impressive, large mosaics.

CLEOPATRA'S PALACE

Towards the end of the 1990s a French-Egyptian team of underwater archaeologists announced the discovery of the palace where Cleopatra died more than 2,000 years ago. Long submerged under the water, this beautifully preserved sphinx, as well as pavements and columns from ancient Alexandria's royal quarter, have been found.

Sphinx found near Cleopatra's Palace

Kom al-Dikka ⑦
This 2nd-century Roman theatre was discovered in 1965 and is in an excellent state of preservation. Beside it are the exposed mosaic floors of a Roman-era villa.

KEY SIGHTS

① Fortress of Qaitbey
② El-Mursi Abul Abbas Mosque ★
③ Souk ★
④ Corniche
⑤ Bibliotheca Alexandrina ★
⑥ Graeco-Roman Museum ★
⑦ Kom al-Dikka
⑧ Catacombs of Kom esh-Shoqafa

FACT FILE

TOURIST INFORMATION
El Raml Square.
Tel (03) 485 1556. ◻ *daily to 6pm (summer: to 8pm).*

MARKETS
Antiques Rue Attarine; daily.

LOCAL SPECIALITIES
Crafts
Brass, copper, carpets, leather, *mashrabiya* (wooden lattice window covers), *narghile* (bubble pipes).
Dishes
Falafel (deep-fried chickpea balls).
Kushari (rice, macaroni, lentils and onions served with a hot sauce).
Om ali (creamy cold rice with raisins and coconut).
Drinks
Karkaday (soft drink brewed from hibiscus leaves).
Tamarhindi (liquorice soft drink).

EXCURSIONS
Abu Qir 24 km (15 miles) E of Alexandria. Famous as the site of Nelson's defeat of the French fleet at the Battle of the Nile in 1798. Underwater excavations have found artifacts from some of the sunken French ships.
El-Alamein 105 km (65 miles) W of Alexandria. Site of the famous World War II battle, the Commonwealth War Cemetery here has graves of 7,367 Allied soldiers and a memorial listing the names of 11,000 men who were never found. A German cemetery with 4,280 graves is 4 km (2.5 miles) further west. The Italian cemetery is another 3 km (2 miles) further to the west.

Egypt: Pyramids of Giza (Alexandria)

Nearly 5,000 years ago, Giza became the royal burial ground (or necropolis) for Memphis, then capital of Egypt. In less than 100 years, three pyramid complexes were completed, each intended as a tomb. After a king's death, his body was brought by boat to the valley temple for preparation before being taken up the causeway and buried under the pyramid. For many years afterwards priests made daily offerings to the dead god-king in the adjacent mortuary temple. The Giza tombs are part of a belt of almost 100 pyramids that stretch from the outskirts of Cairo south across the desert to the oasis of Fayoum.

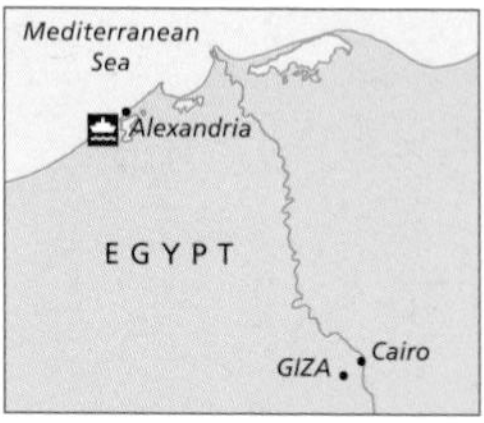

DISTANCE FROM PORT

180 km (112 miles) from site.

Pyramids of Giza
Three successive generations built these monumental structures during the 4th Dynasty of the Old Kingdom (2686–2181 BC).

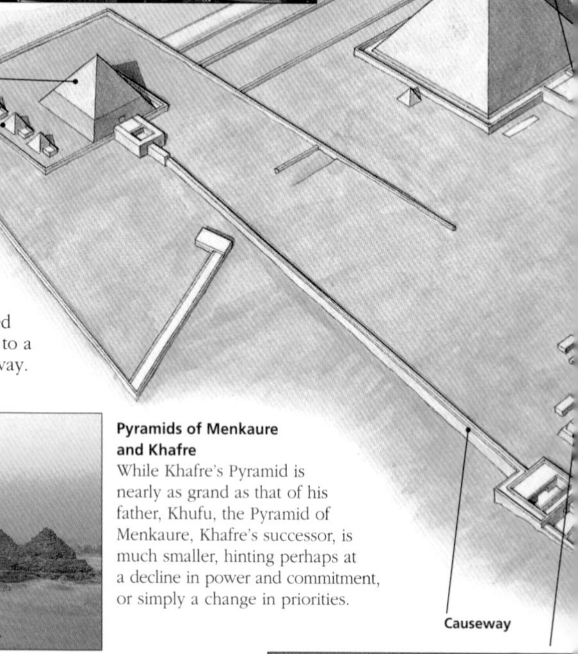

GIZA PLATEAU RECONSTRUCTION

As well as the main pyramid and various satellite pyramids, the standard complex included a mortuary temple joined to a valley temple by a causeway.

Pyramids of Menkaure and Khafre
While Khafre's Pyramid is nearly as grand as that of his father, Khufu, the Pyramid of Menkaure, Khafre's successor, is much smaller, hinting perhaps at a decline in power and commitment, or simply a change in priorities.

Tomb of Khentkawes
This large but rarely visited building was the last major tomb built at Giza. Queen Khentkawes, daughter of Menkaure, probably gave birth to the new dynasty that moved its necropolis south to Abu Sir.

STAR SIGHTS

★ Great Pyramid

★ Sphinx

CAIRO, CITY OF 1,000 MINARETS

Known as the "City of 1,000 Minarets", Cairo bristles with medieval Islamic architecture, but its history is considerably older. The site was a camp for the builders of the pyramids, and a settlement took root when the Romans fortified the area. Nestled on the fertile Nile Delta, the city blossomed under various Arab dynasties (640–1516) on wealth generated by taxing merchant ships, but its fortunes turned with the opening of alternative routes to the East. Returned to the Egyptians in 1952 for the first time since 525 BC, Cairo is rich in culture and history, and home to some of the world's oldest churches, synagogues and mosques.

Cairo's skyline, a mixture of modern and medieval Islamic styles, seen at dawn

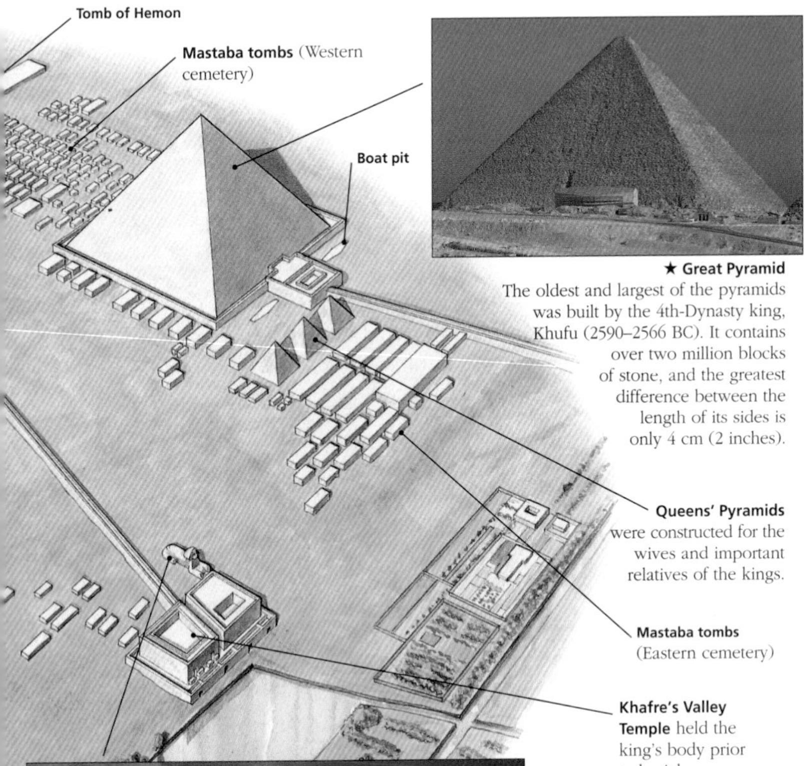

★ Great Pyramid
The oldest and largest of the pyramids was built by the 4th-Dynasty king, Khufu (2590–2566 BC). It contains over two million blocks of stone, and the greatest difference between the length of its sides is only 4 cm (2 inches).

Queens' Pyramids were constructed for the wives and important relatives of the kings.

Mastaba tombs (Eastern cemetery)

Khafre's Valley Temple held the king's body prior to burial.

★ Sphinx
Guardian of the Giza Plateau, the leonine Sphinx is known to the Arabs as *Abu al-Hol*, the "father of terror". Archaeologists date it to 2500 BC, making it the earliest known sculpture of ancient Egypt. A royal headdress frames what could be the likeness of King Khafre.

North African Crafts

There is a vibrant tradition of handicrafts from the Nile to the Atlantic. Ceramic pots, tooled leatherwork, carpets, jewellery and fine woodwork cascade from the counters and shelves of souks in all the main towns. With workshops scattered among the shops, it is easy to watch craftsmen and women at work, much as they have been for hundreds of years. Ever since the Arab conquest of North Africa in the 8th century, the decorative arts have been influenced by the non-figurative traditions of Islamic art. Islam forbids the representation of the human form, so geometric and calligraphic patterns proliferate on carpets and kaftans, with occasional symbolic representations of animals. In Morocco and Tunisia the most popular forms of jewellery are headbands, pendants, brooches, breast ornaments and a characteristic triangular brooch.

Inside a Souk
Craftsmen are still grouped by trade as they have been since medieval times.

Making a Carpet
As densely knotted as their Persian cousins, North African carpets take many months to make.

Small pictograms of birds and antelope are often found on carpets.

A central lozenge is typically Moroccan and is said to symbolize the earth.

Dyes were traditionally made from natural pigments – orange from henna leaves, red from madder root, blue from the indigo plant – and they harmonized well with their surroundings.

CARPETS AND RUGS

Carpet-making is the one craft presided over by women. Because each tuft of wool is individually knotted, carpets can be more expensive than *kilims* (rugs), which are woven on a loom. There are thousands of designs, with each tribe, and in some places each family, following its own time-honoured traditions.

Engravers at work in a souk

METAL ENGRAVING

The tell-tale tap, tap, tap of metal on metal can be heard in most North African souks. Geometric patterns attain their dizziest heights on the large metal tabletops and trays that are engraved by hand throughout the region. Circular patterns are often said to be representations of the cosmos, although designs with camels and palm trees specially engraved for tourists are just as likely to be found today. In many souks craftsmen will inscribe people's name on items such as plates, cups and ashtrays.

Detail of hand engraving

Pottery
Potters' quarters are located on the edge of towns to prevent the spread of fire from the kilns. Here sophisticated pots and plates are thrown on electric wheels, while in the countryside pots are made by hand. Each country has towns that specialize in ceramics, such as Nabeul in Tunisia and Safi in Morocco.

POTS AND TILES

Tiles have always played an important role in interior decoration, in friezes and as panels on walls and floors. They vary from the floral panels produced in areas where the Andalusian influence is strong, to those of the more geometric Islamic tradition. Highly decorative plates are common, but some potters continue to make the same pots as their forefathers, using comparatively limited natural glazes.

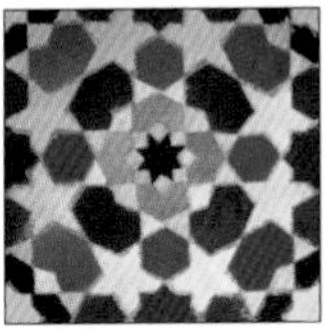

A geometric *zellij* panel from Morocco

Pot with a traditional glaze

Colourful Moroccan plates in many designs and sizes

Massed display of leather slippers in Morocco

JEWELLERY

For centuries Berber women have been adorned, particularly on their wedding day, by tiers of heavy silver jewellery. Silver was traditionally mined in small quantities all over North Africa, but most of the seams are now worked out. Gold came from the other side of the Sahara, in camel caravans, but was only for the rich. Fashions change, however, and even rural women now crave the gold and gemstones that were traditionally worn by city dwellers.

Gold Jewellery
Jewellery design reflects many influences. This pendant earring of granulated gold is based on a lavish Ancient Egyptian model.

Berber Women
Before a festival or wedding, a Berber woman takes a bath in the communal hammam *(see p288)*, then henna is applied to hands, feet and face. Finally, jewellery gives a distinctive finish to the costume.

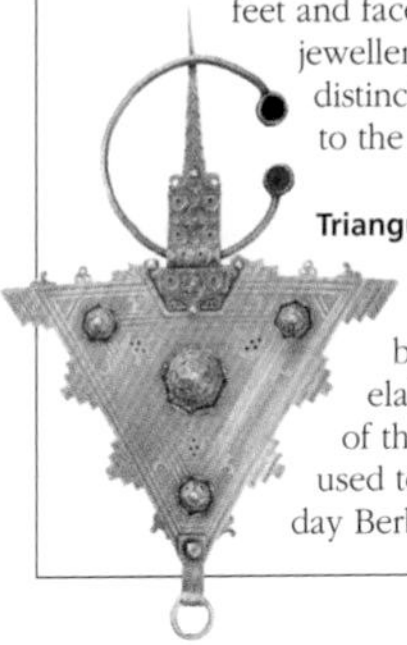

Triangular Brooch
This curious, enamelled brooch is an elaborate version of the brooches used to fasten every day Berber dresses.

LEATHER GOODS

Using the skin of everything from camels to foxes, tanners treat and dye hides in courtyard tanneries, spreading them out on river banks or roof-tops to dry. Highly coloured flip-flops are characteristic of the Saharan tribes of Libya, while in Morocco the pointed *babouches*, (leather slippers) are ubiquitous. Beautifully worked wallets and leather-bound notebooks are also widely available.

ISRAEL

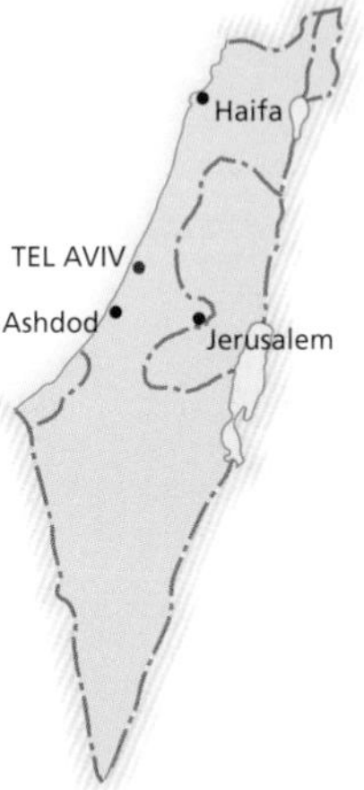

JERUSALEM 274–275 • HAIFA 276–277

Jerusalem (Ashdod)

A Jewish menorah

With a history stretching back over 3,000 years, Jerusalem contains the holiest sites of Jews (the Western Wall) and Christians (Christ's Tomb in the Byzantine Church of the Holy Sepulchre), and the third most important Muslim site (the Haram esh-Sharif). The Mount of Olives offers a very fine view of the Old City, whose four architecturally distinct quarters, Jewish, Muslim, Christian and Armenian, reflect Jerusalem's multicultural past and present. The greatest sight is the Haram esh-Sharif, built on top of the remains of the Jews' First Temple (Solomon's Temple) and Second Temple, destroyed by invaders in 539 BC and AD 70 respectively.

Via Dolorosa ⑤
Tradition says this was the route walked by Christ from his trial to Calvary. Above is the third of the 14 Stations of the Cross along it. Each represents one event in the story.

Church of the Holy Sepulchre ⑥
A church has stood here over what is believed to be the site of Christ's crucifixion and burial since AD 335. This marble slab and altar mark his tomb.

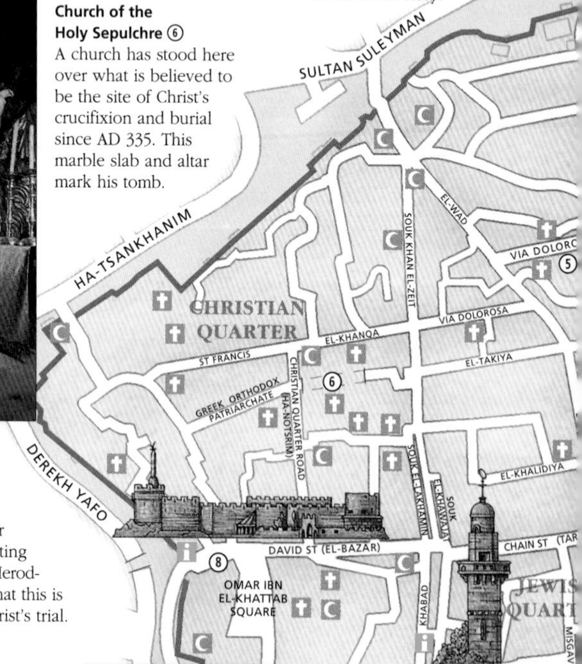

Citadel ⑧
This 14th-century fortress houses the Tower of David Museum illustrating the history of Jerusalem. Herodian foundations suggest that this is the most likely site of Christ's trial.

Hurva Square ⑦
Full of cafés, this is the heart of th Jewish Quarter. The evocative arc here belonged to a synagogue des troyed in the 1948 Arab-Israeli Wa

MOUNT OF OLIVES

At the bottom of this hill, rich in Christian sites, are the Garden and Cave of Gethsemane where Christ prayed before his arrest, and where Judas betrayed him, and the underground church sheltering the Tomb of the Virgin. At the top is the Mosque of the Ascension. Sacred to Muslims and Christians, it is the supposed site of Christ's Ascension. The Church of the Paternoster covers a grotto where Christ is believed to have taught the Disciples the Lord's Prayer.

Church of the Paternoster on the Mount of Olives

Haram esh-Sharif ②
At the centre of this Islamic religious complex is the celebrated, golden-roofed Dome of the Rock, completed in AD 691.

DISTANCE FROM PORT

75 km (47 miles) from city centre.

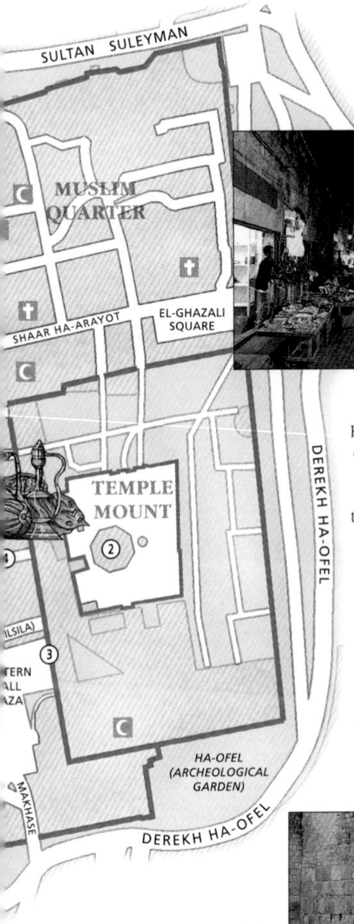

Cotton Merchants' Market ④
Known in Arabic as Souk el-Qattanin, and possibly the most atmospheric street in the Old City, this 12th-century covered market with 50 softly-lit shops was built by the Crusaders.

Western Wall ③
This wall and the plaza beside it, which acts as a huge, open-air synagogue, became the Jews' chief place of pilgrimage because it was the only part of the ruins of the Second Temple to which, under Ottoman rule (1516–1831), they were allowed access.

KEY SIGHTS

① Mount of Olives ★
② Haram esh-Sharif ★
③ Western Wall ★
④ Cotton Merchants' Market
⑤ Via Dolorosa
⑥ Church of the Holy Sepulchre ★
⑦ Hurva Square
⑧ Citadel

FACT FILE

TOURIST INFORMATION

Jaffa Gate Entrance, Old City.
***Tel** (02) 627 6429.*
Sat–Thu to 5pm, Sun to 1pm.

MARKETS

Brass and copperware El-Wad Road; daily.
Religious items & Palestinian rugs Christian Quarter Road; daily.
Judaica Cardo; Sun–Fri.
Leather goods Muristan; daily.
Souvenirs David Street; daily.

LOCAL SPECIALITIES

Crafts
Candles, copperware, brassware.
Dishes
Tabbouleh (bulgar wheat salad). *Jerusalem mixed grill* (spiced chicken livers, hearts, lights and other offal served with pitta bread). *Mussakhan* (a Palestinian dish of roast chicken, onions and sumac). *Challah* (sweet plaited bread for the Jewish Sabbath and holy days).
Drinks
Taybeh (a light beer). *Shai naana* (Arabic tea with fresh mint leaves). *Tkoa* and *Hebron* (wines from the Judaean hills around Jerusalem).

EXCURSIONS

Bethlehem 8 km (5 miles) S of Jerusalem. Church of the Nativity built over the Grotto of the Nativity where Christ is said to have been born. Surviving 4th-century nave walls and floor mosaics.
Herodion 20 km (12 miles) S of Jerusalem. Ruins of a fortified palace (c.20 BC) of Herod the Great.
Dead Sea & Qumran 50 km (30 miles) E of Jerusalem. Spectacular desert scenery. Qumran is where the 1st-century Dead Sea Scrolls were found in 1947.

Haifa

Lying at the foot of Mount Carmel, Haifa was a small trading port for most of its history. In the late 19th century it became important as a refuge for Jewish immigrants, and from 1918 to 1948 was under British rule during their occupation of Palestine. Now Haifa is Israel's third largest city and its chief industrial centre. Behind the busy port and the older, somewhat dilapidated districts, the newer, wealthier areas with gleaming shopping centres are built on the mountain's steep slopes. These are also the setting for the Stella Maris Monastery and the immaculately kept Baha'i Temple and gardens. The glass-capsuled cable car offers an easy way up to them from Bat Galim. Haifa's much-visited biblical sight, Elijah's Cave, is nearby.

Bat Galim and Cable Car ⑧
The main attraction of the Bat Galim district is the seafront promenade with outdoor cafés, restaurants and diving and surfing clubs. From here, the glass bubbles of the cable car climb up to the peak of Mount Carmel.

Wadi Nisnas ①
Located close to Haifa, Wadi Nisnas was traditionally a densely populated Arab quarter. A stroll around its streets reveals bustling markets and attractive, if rather neglected, Arab architecture.

Stella Maris Carmelite Monastery ⑤
The Carmelite order, founded nearby in 1150, dedicated this monastery on the slopes of Mount Carmel to the Virgin Mary. The ceiling painting shows Elijah and the chariot of fire.

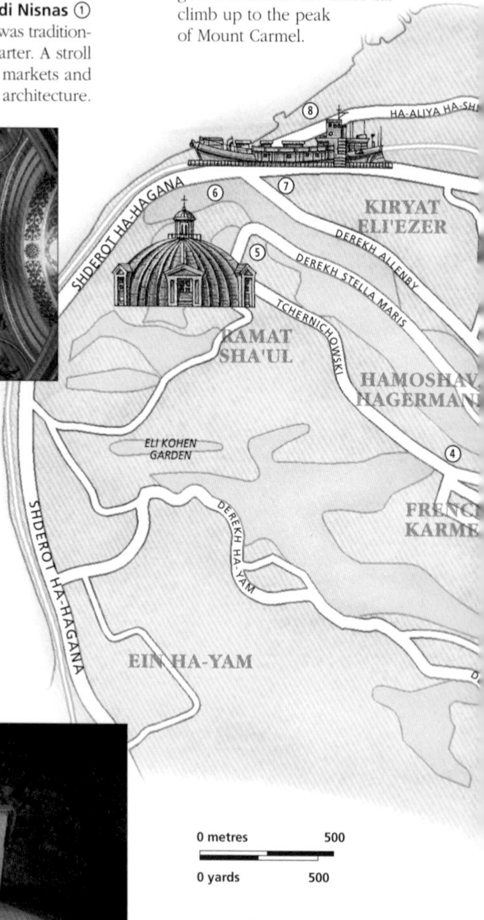

Clandestine Immigration and Navy Museum ⑦
Built around a real refugee boat, this museum tells the story of Jewish attempts to reach Palestine through the British blockade of the 1930s and 1940s.

Elijah's Cave ⑥
Below the Carmelite Monastery is the cave where, according to the Bible's First Book of Kings, Elijah is said to have hidden from King Ahab and Queen Jezebel after killing the prophets of Baal on Mount Carmel.

Ursula Malbin Sculpture Garden ④
Twenty-two bronze figures of children, donated by the contemporary Haifa sculptor Ursula Malbin, stand in this well-tended garden. Its pathways offer wide-ranging views over the bay.

Mané Katz Museum ②
This is the former home of the Jewish Expressionist painter Mané Katz (1894–1962), who lived and worked in Paris before emigrating to Haifa. Visitors can see changing exhibitions either of paintings by him, such as the *Three Rabbis* (c.1955) shown here, or of his collection of sculptures and judaica.

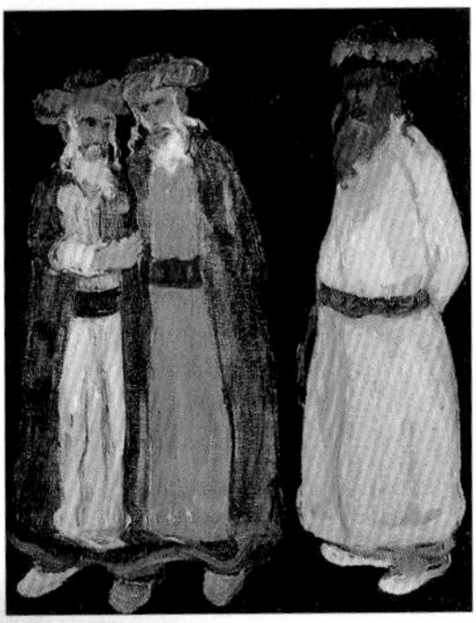

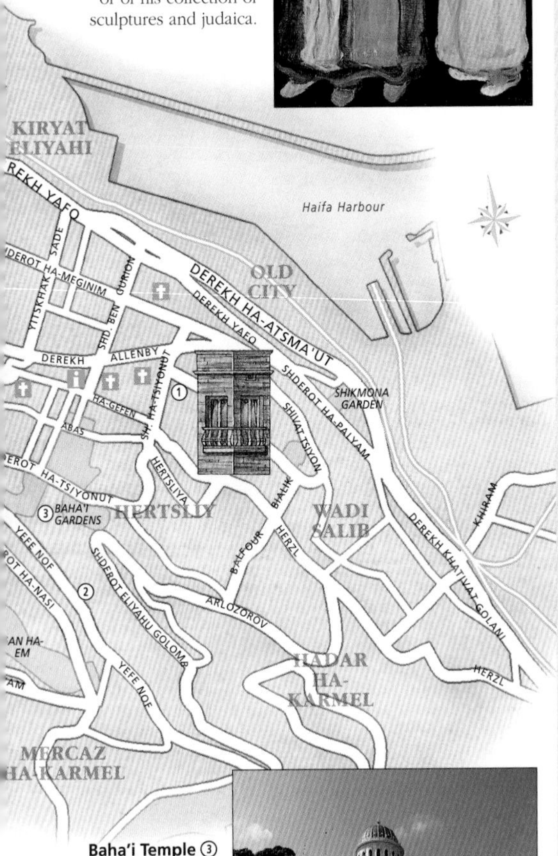

Baha'i Temple ③
Set in a beautifully-kept hillside park, Haifa's most striking landmark is this impressive, golden-domed shrine. It is the headquarters of the Baha'i faith.

KEY SIGHTS

① Wadi Nisnas
② Mané Katz Museum
③ Baha'i Temple ★
④ Ursula Malbin Sculpture Garden
⑤ Stella Maris Carmelite Monastery
⑥ Elijah's Cave
⑦ Clandestine Immigration and Navy Museum ★
⑧ Bat Galim and Cable Car

FACT FILE

TOURIST INFORMATION

48 Ben Gurion Avenue. ***Tel** (04) 853 56 06.* ◯ *Sun–Thu to 5pm; Fri to 1pm, Sat & public hols to 3pm.*

MARKETS

Food & souvenirs Daliyat El-Carmel; daily.

LOCAL SPECIALITIES

Crafts
Hand-made soap, jewellery and glassware.

Dishes
Falafel (deep-fried chickpea balls).
Shawarma (spit-grilled, pressed lamb with pitta bread and salad).
Konafa (pistachios in crisp pastry).

Drinks
Carmel wines from Mount Carmel.

EXCURSIONS

Acre 18 km (11 miles) N of Haifa. Ancient Crusader city, rebuilt by the Ottomans in the 16th century.
Nazareth 33 km (20 miles) SE of Haifa. Site of the Annunciation and childhood of Jesus. Basilica of the Annunciation, built in 1939.
Megiddo 35 km (22 miles) SE of Haifa. Excavated site of successive hilltop cities dating from the 3rd millennium to the 7th century BC. Biblical site of Armageddon, where the New Testament says the final battle between Good and Evil will take place at the end of the world.
Caesarea 43 km (26 miles) S of Haifa. Major archaeological site. Remains of Herod the Great's palace, and of a Roman theatre, hippodrome and aqueduct.
Sea of Galilee 50 km (30 miles) E of Haifa. Historical and religious sites and lakeside holiday resorts.

Biblical Sites of the Holy Land

Many of the stories recounted in the Old Testament are located in Egypt, Sinai and the "Land of Canaan", which corresponds roughly to present-day Israel. By contrast, the life of Jesus, as narrated by the gospels, was played out in a relatively small arena; he was born in Bethlehem, grew up in Nazareth and the crucifixion, resurrection and ascension all took place in Jerusalem. Both Testaments provide geographical details of the places they describe, and the modest scale of many of these stands in poignant contrast to the events that occurred in them. Archaeological evidence confirms many, but not all, of the Biblical sites of today.

The Destruction of Sodom ①
When Sodom was destroyed by God, only Lot and his family were spared, but his wife looked back and was turned into a pillar of salt.

The Death of Moses ②
Moses is said to have seen the Promised Land from the summit of Mount Nebo and died in the same place. Christian tradition identifies Mount Nebo as being just southwest of modern-day Amman. As the Bible states, the whereabouts of Moses' tomb is unknown (Deuteronomy 34: 1–7).

Joshua Conquers Jericho ③
The Old Testament story tells how the walls of Jericho fell to the blast of horns (Joshua 6). This ancient oasis was the first city conquered by the Israelites, led by Joshua, after they emerged from their 40 years in the wilderness.

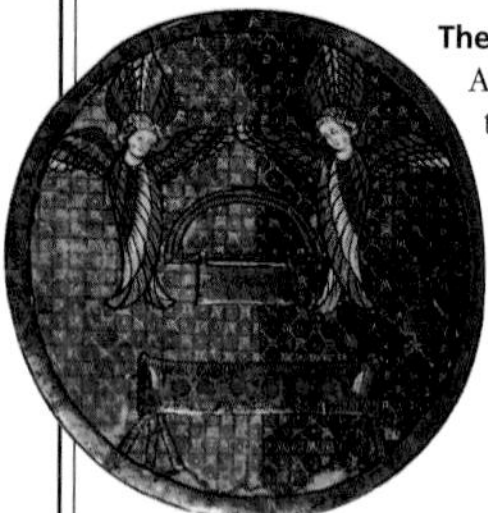

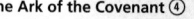

The Ark of the Covenant ④
At Shiloh the Jews built the first temple, and in it they placed the Ark of the Covenant. This 13th-century illumination shows the Ark, which contained the Ten Commandments, being carried by a pair of angels.

David Defeats Goliath ⑤
As the champion of the Israelites during the reign of King Saul, David defeated Goliath and routed the Philistines (I Samuel 17). The site of the battle is given as the Ha-Ela Valley, northwest of Hebron.

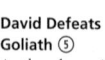

Elijah and the Prophets of Baal ⑥
Elijah challenged the prophets of the Canaanite god Baal (left). When sacrifices were made only Elijah's offering burst into flames, proving who the true God was (I Kings 18). The traditional site of this event is Mount Carmel, at Haifa *(see pp276–7)*.

The Annunciation (7)
At Nazareth Mary was visited by the angel Gabriel and told of her forthcoming child (Luke 1: 26–38). The episode is commemorated by the Basilica of the Annunciation.

The Birth of Jesus (8)
Jesus was born in a manger in Bethlehem and an angel appeared to shepherds in nearby fields telling them of the birth (Luke 2: 1–20). A church was first built on the site in the 4th century and a star marks the alleged site of the Nativity.

The Baptism of Christ (9)
John the Baptist preached the coming of the Messiah and recognized Jesus as the "Lamb of God" (Matthew 3). The site, also known as Qasr el Yehud, lies east of Jericho on the Jordanian border and is considered to be the most likely place for Jesus' baptism. Although it is situated in a military zone, it is nevertheless still accessible daily.

The Temptations (10)
Following his baptism, Jesus was tempted by the Devil to break his 40-day fast (Matthew 4: 1–11). The Greek Orthodox Monastery of the Temptation on Mount Quarntal marks the site of the supposed encounter.

The Multiplication of the Loaves and Fishes (11)
The gospels locate this famous miracle of the "feeding of the 5,000" (Matthew 15: 32–39) on the shores of the Sea of Galilee. It is commemorated in a church at Tabkha, where this mosaic lies in front of the altar. It shows a basket of bread flanked by fish.

The Sermon on the Mount (12)
This longest of Jesus' sermons begins with the Beatitudes: "Blessed are the meek for they shall inherit the earth…" (Matthew 5 –7). Tradition has it delivered at Tabkha, where the Church of the Beatitudes stands today.

Harbour at Sidon, Saida, Lebanon ▷

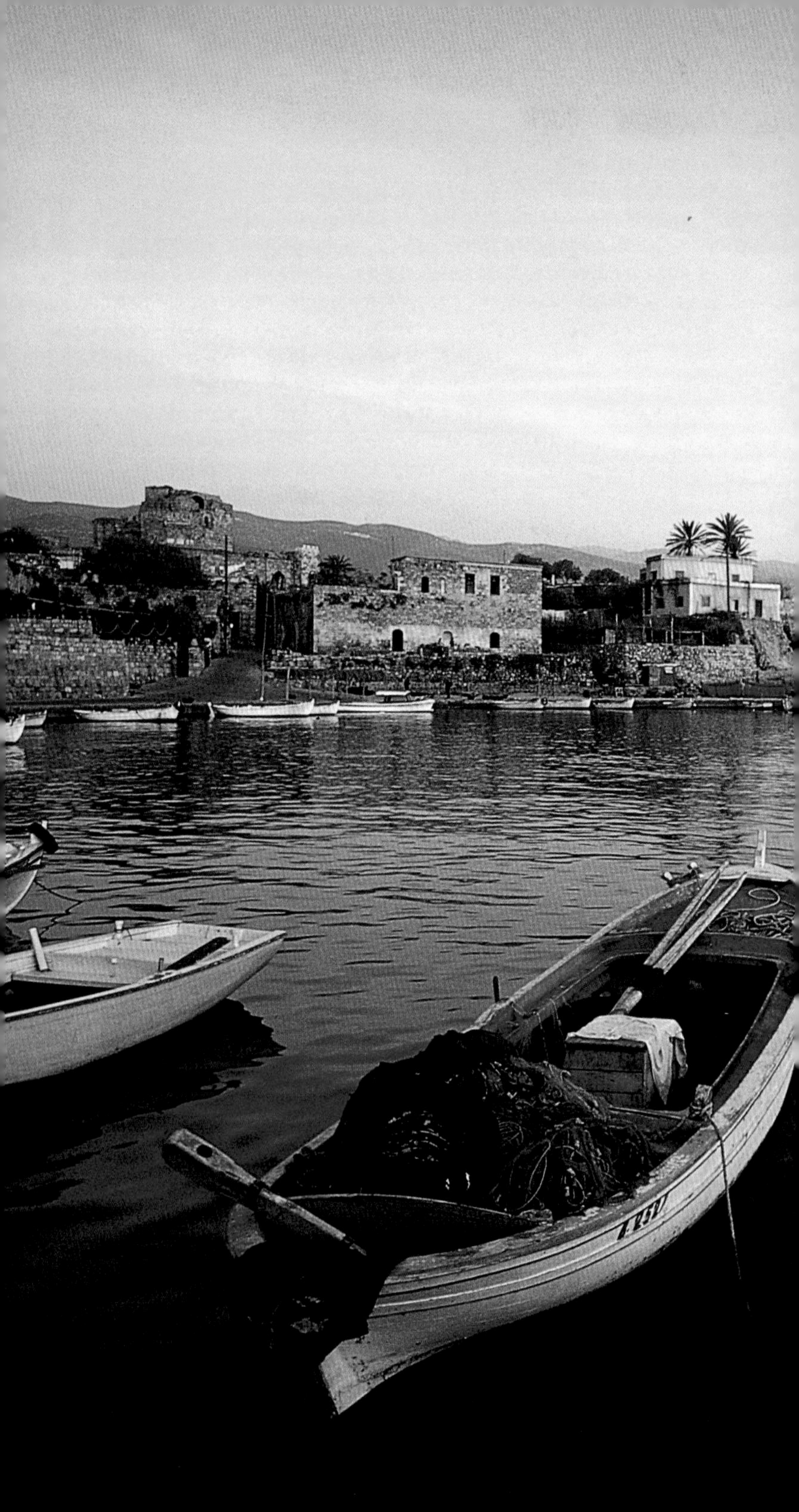

LEBANON

Beirut

Bread seller on the Corniche

Berytus, as Beirut was originally known, was a modest port during Phoenician times (around 2000 BC) and grew in importance under the Romans. With the arrival of Islam and the Arabs it experienced a long period of decline, a trend that only became reversed as recently as the 19th century, when the city gained importance as a trading centre and gateway to the region. Its port became the largest on the eastern Mediterranean and Beirut became a major commercial centre, with a reputation for hedonism that saw the city nicknamed the "Paris of the East". Civil War in the 1970s and 1980s changed the city's image to one of bullets, bombs and hostage taking. The flourishing cosmopolitan capital of chic shops, restaurants and nightclubs that emerged is still threatened by ongoing conflicts.

Corniche ③
Officially called Avenue de Paris, the Corniche is Beirut's grand seafront avenue. It is a favourite spot for late afternoon and weekend promenades where push-cart peddlers sell iced cactus fruit and *kaak*, a crisp bread with sesame seeds and thyme.

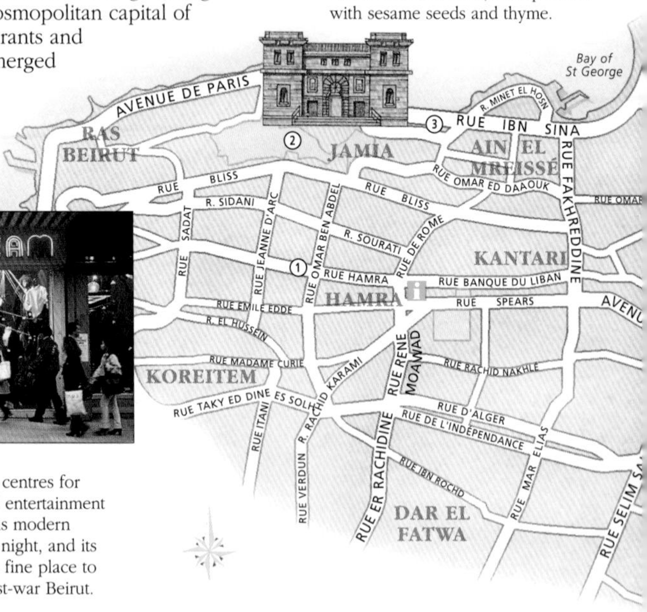

Hamra ①
One of Beirut's main centres for shopping, dining and entertainment is on Rue Hamra. This modern area is busy day and night, and its pavement cafés are a fine place to observe the new, post-war Beirut.

CIVIL WAR IN BEIRUT

Downtown restoration in Beirut

Beirut suffered terribly during Lebanon's 16-year war fought between Christians and Muslims, also with Syrian and Israeli involvement. The city was split into Christian East Beirut and Muslim West Beirut, with a no man's land, known as the Green Line, running directly through the old city centre. Whole neighbourhoods were destroyed, including the central district, which was the scene of some of the worst fighting. Further military conflict jeopardised the massive redevelopment projects under way in the central district. The last Syrian troops withdrew from Beirut on 26 April 2005 and diplomatic relations were established between the two countries on 15 October 2008.

0 metres 500
0 yards 500

American University in Beirut ②
The Middle East's most prestigious university has an extensive site overlooking the Mediterranean. There is a small archaeological museum on the campus with a collection of some 12,000 objects dating predominantly from prehistory, but covering periods to the Islamic era.

Central Beirut ④
Beirut's central district was devastated during the Civil War and faces further destruction in ongoing conflicts, despite undergoing one of the largest urban redevelopment programmes in the world.

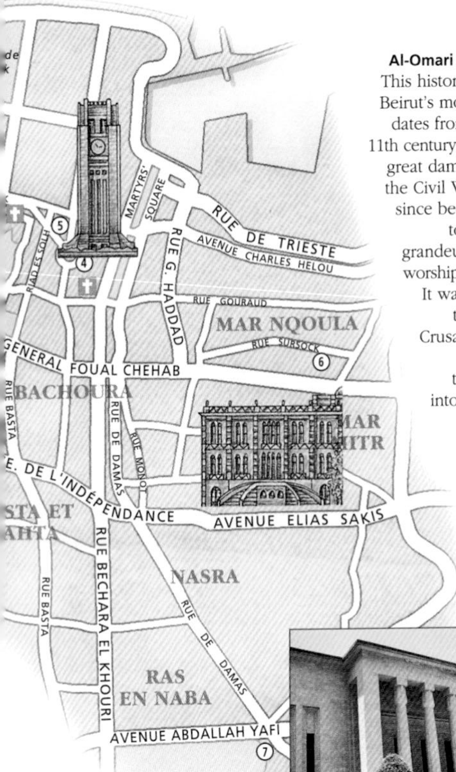

Al-Omari Mosque ⑤
This historic mosque, Beirut's most striking, dates from the early 11th century. It suffered great damage during the Civil War but has since been restored to its former grandeur, allowing worship to resume. It was originally the site of a Crusader church and later transformed into a mosque.

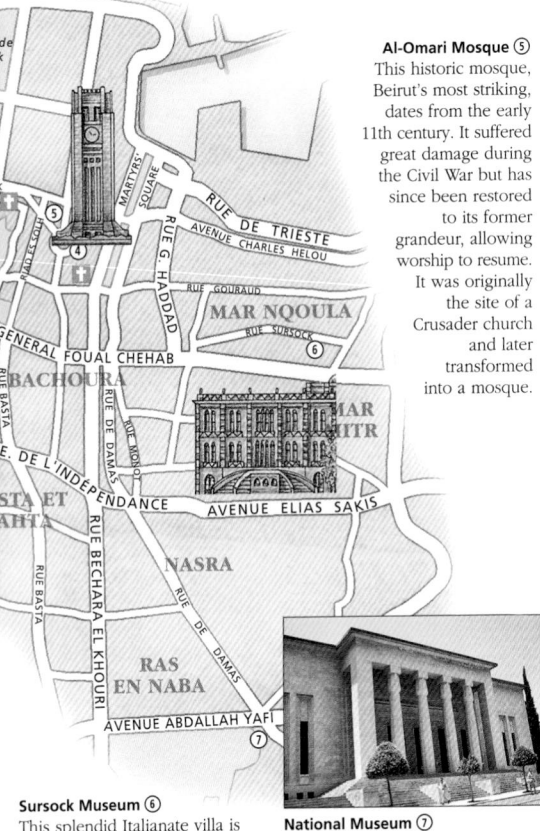

Sursock Museum ⑥
This splendid Italianate villa is the former home of the Sursock family. The permanent collection includes Japanese engravings and numerous works of Islamic art. The museum's main function, however, is to provide a venue for the work of contemporary Lebanese artists.

National Museum ⑦
The collection that survived Lebanon's Civil War includes archaeological pieces from the Bronze Age and Phoenician eras, but is particularly strong on Byzantine and Roman remains, with some fine statuary and beautiful, large mosaics.

KEY SIGHTS

① Hamra
② American University in Beirut
③ Corniche ★
④ Central Beirut ★
⑤ Al-Omari Mosque
⑥ Sursock Museum
⑦ National Museum ★

FACT FILE

TOURIST INFORMATION
Rue Banque du Liban. ***Tel*** *(01) 340 940.* ☐ *Mon–Sat to 2pm.*

LOCAL SPECIALITIES
Dishes
Babaghanouj (baked aubergine/eggplant purée mixed with chopped tomato and onion).
Kibbeh (deep-fried minced lamb and pine nuts in bulgar wheat).
Labneh (cheesy yoghurt dip flavoured with mint or garlic).
Loubieh (French bean salad with tomato and onions).
Mashi (vine leaves stuffed with spiced rice and minced meat).
Tabbouleh (bulgar wheat, parsley and tomato salad).
Baklava (layered filo pastry with crushed nuts and pistachios drenched in syrup).
Drinks
Araq (aniseed spirit).
Qahwa (bitter, gritty coffee, sometimes flavoured with cardamom).

EXCURSIONS
Jeitta Grotto 15km (9 miles) NE of Beirut. Stunning stalactite and stalagmite-filled cave complex fashioned by millions of years of erosion. There is a boat ride through the lower caverns.
Byblos (Jbail) 40km (25 miles) N of Beirut. Ancient temples, Roman colonnades and a Crusader castle in a gorgeous coastal setting.
Beit Eddine 48 km (30 miles) SE of Beirut. 19th-century Italianate mountain palace with marvellous views and a collection of 5th- and 6th-century mosaics.
Sidon (Saida) 50km (31 miles) S of Beirut. Historic port city with picturesque old city of bazaars and Islamic architecture, and a Crusader castle on an island.

Baalbek (Beirut)

Rainwater spout, Temple of Jupiter

The temples here form the best preserved Classical architectural ensemble in the Middle East, and the area was designated a World Heritage Site in 1984. Although Phoenician in origin, the site as seen today is Roman, begun during the reign of Augustus (27 BC–AD 17). Such was the scale of the project that it took ten generations to complete. The Temple of Jupiter surpassed in size and grandeur anything else ever built in the Roman Empire. Ultimately, however, Christianity triumphed over the pagan gods and Baalbek fell out of use. It was used as a fortress by the Arabs from AD 636, raided by Mongol hordes in the 13th and 14th centuries and abandoned in the 16th century.

The grandiose architecture of Baalbek, set off by an impressive mountain backdrop

★ Temple of Jupiter
Only six columns remain to convey the massive scale of this building. Each is 2.5 m (8 ft) in diameter and 22 m (72 ft) high, the equivalent of a six-storey apartment block.

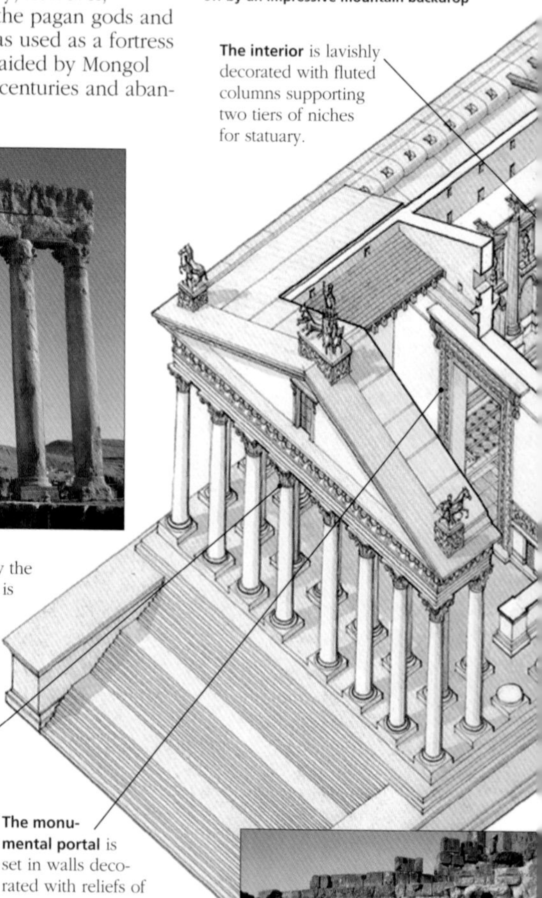

The interior is lavishly decorated with fluted columns supporting two tiers of niches for statuary.

The Corinthian columns of the peristyle (colonnade) still support the enormous cornice stones and huge triangular pediment.

The monumental portal is set in walls decorated with reliefs of vines, grapes and other Bacchanalian motifs.

★ Hexagonal Court
Acting as a vestibule to the Temple of Jupiter, this court's central area was open to the sky and decorated with a mosaic floor. It was surrounded by a covered arcade.

STAR SIGHTS

- ★ Temple of Jupiter
- ★ Hexagonal Court
- ★ Temple of Bacchus
- ★ Great Court

★ Temple of Bacchus
Although generally assumed to have been dedicated to Dionysus, the Graeco-Roman god of wine and drinking, because of its vine decoration, some archaeologists believe it was a temple to the sun.

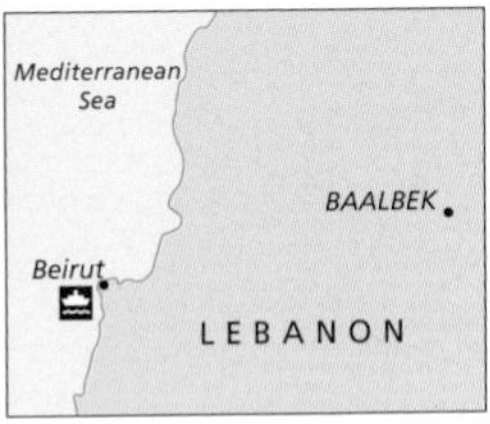

DISTANCE FROM PORT

80 km (50 miles) from Baalbek.

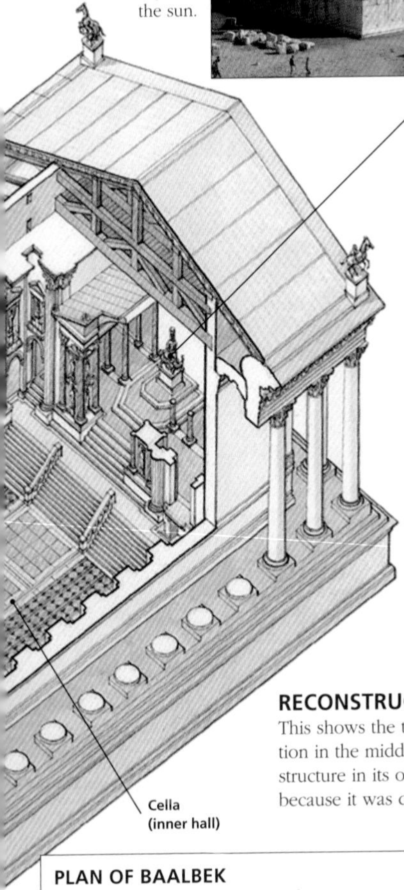

The statue of the dedicatory god would have stood here, at the temple's western end, approached by a flight of stairs.

★ Great Court
This huge, colonnaded area is where sacrifices and dances took place to the fertility god, Baal, the Semitic forerunner of Jupiter. At the centre is a large sacrificial altar flanked by decorated ablution pools.

RECONSTRUCTION OF THE TEMPLE OF BACCHUS

This shows the temple as it would have been after its completion in the middle of the 2nd century AD. Although a huge structure in its own right, it was known as the "small temple" because it was dwarfed by the adjacent Temple of Jupiter.

Cella (inner hall)

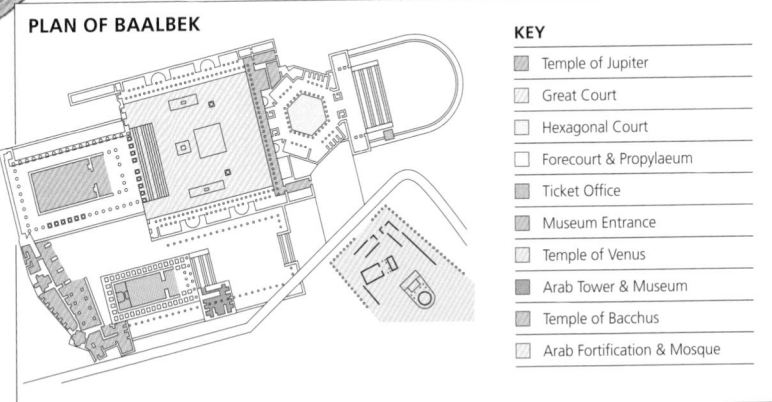

PLAN OF BAALBEK

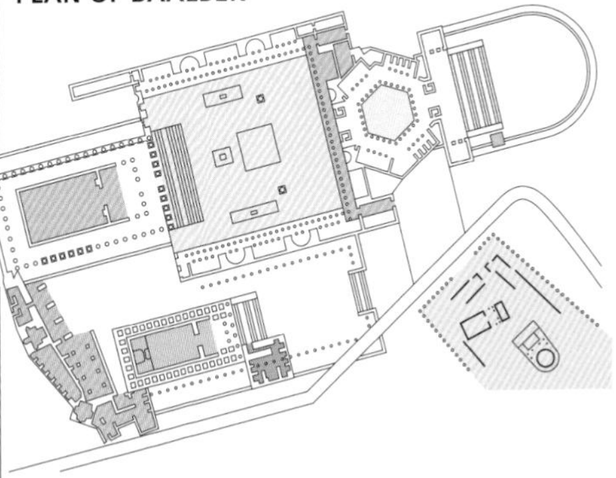

KEY

- Temple of Jupiter
- Great Court
- Hexagonal Court
- Forecourt & Propylaeum
- Ticket Office
- Museum Entrance
- Temple of Venus
- Arab Tower & Museum
- Temple of Bacchus
- Arab Fortification & Mosque

Chiite Mosque, Damascus, Syria ▷

SYRIA

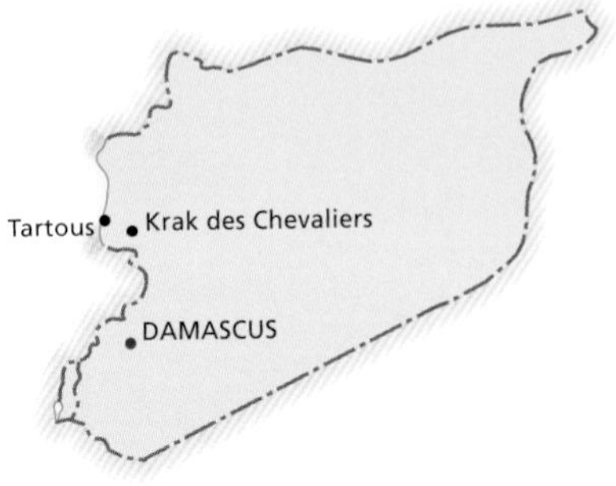
Tartous
Krak des Chevaliers
DAMASCUS

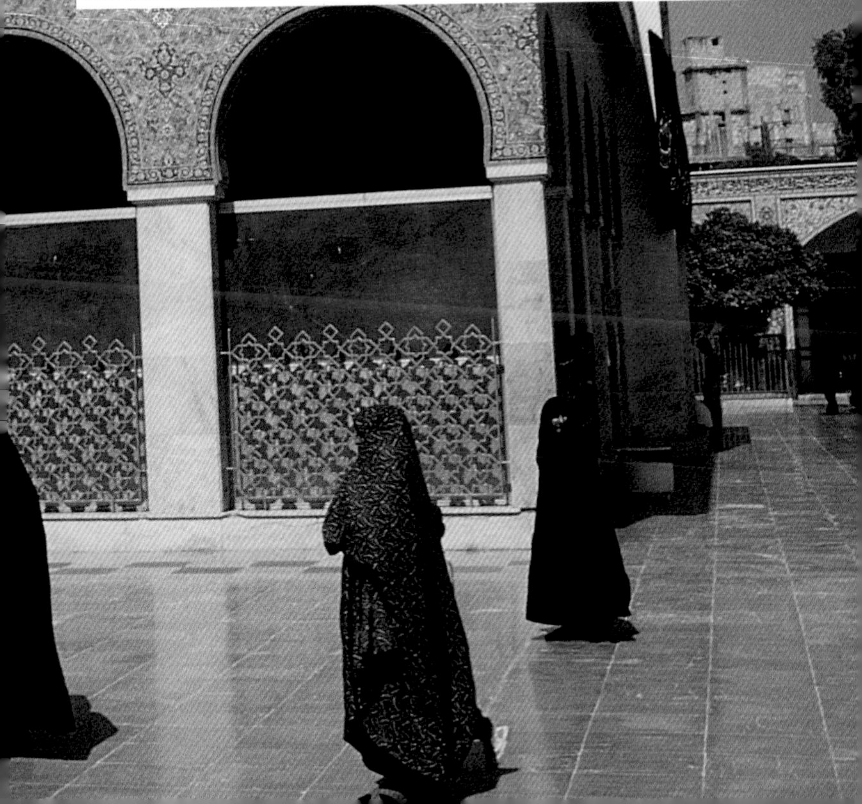

Damascus (Tartous)

Detail from Umayyad Mosque

Damascus claims to be the oldest continuously inhabited city in the world, and it certainly has plenty to show for its past. The Old City's main street is referred to in the Bible and Roman remains underpin the fine Umayyad Mosque, itself one of the oldest Islamic places of worship. Narrow alleys are filled with medieval gateways that open onto mosques, palaces and mausoleums, but best of all is the oriental bazaar, with its countless shops trading everything from perfumes and spices to wedding dresses and prayer mats. Numerous street-side coffeehouses, full of patrons smoking waterpipes, offer a break from the heat of the city, and meals can be eaten in style at a number of former merchant houses that now serve excellent local cuisine.

National Museum ①
Syria has a vast wealth of archaeological history, having been occupied by Phoenicians, Persians, Greeks, Romans and crusading European armies. The collection here includes a reconstructed tomb from Palmyra, a 2nd-century painted synagogue and Mesopotamian artifacts from the ancient city of Mari, including distinctive statuettes (with fur skirts and lively black eyes) that are as old as Egypt's Pyramids.

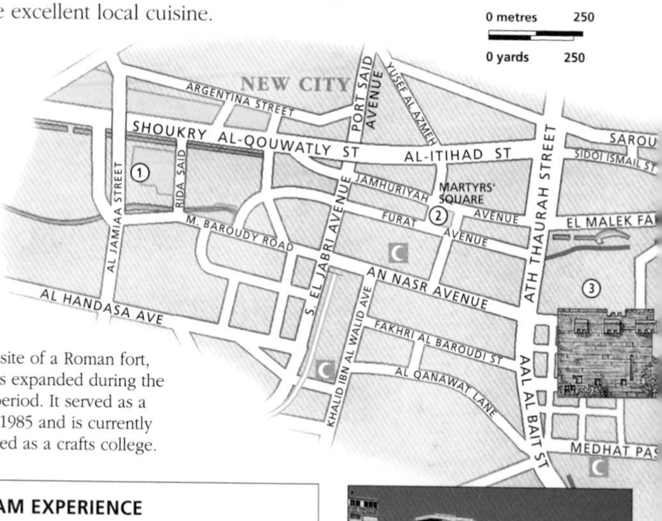

Citadel ③
Originally the site of a Roman fort, the Citadel was expanded during the early Islamic period. It served as a barracks until 1985 and is currently being developed as a crafts college.

THE HAMMAM EXPERIENCE

Known in the West as a 'Turkish Bath,' the hammam in Damascus is as much a social institution as a way of getting clean. The complete experience involves steaming in a sauna-like 'hot room' for a good half an hour before being scrubbed with a camel-hair mitten. The next stage involves a healthy massage and a lengthy period spent relaxing and sipping tea, swathed and turbaned in towels. The whole process takes a couple of hours, and it is best enjoyed in company, the way the locals do it. Most hammams are a men-only affair, but some baths are occasionally open to women.

Hammam Nureddin, the finest bath in Damascus

Martyrs' Square ②
Formerly the hub of 19th-century Damascus, Martyrs' Square is relatively rundown today, though it remains busy, with plenty of shops and a small vegetable market. The Telegraph Column commemorates the completion of the first telegraph line to Mecca.

Umayyad Mosque ④
The Umayyad Mosque has walls covered with gold and green mosaics and a tomb supposedly containing the head of John the Baptist. It is one of the city's most beautiful mosques.

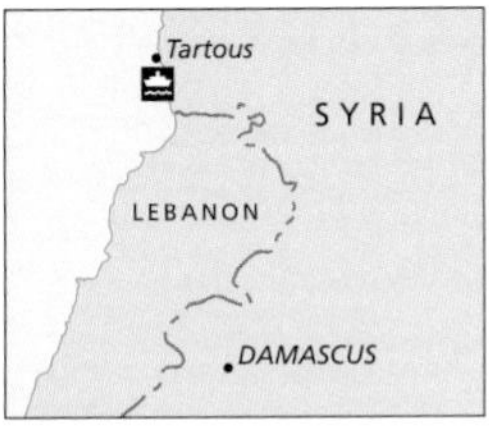

DISTANCE FROM PORT

200 km (124 miles) from city centre.

Azem Palace ⑤
Built in 1749, the palace is a perfect example of the highly decorative and geometric Damascene style of architecture.

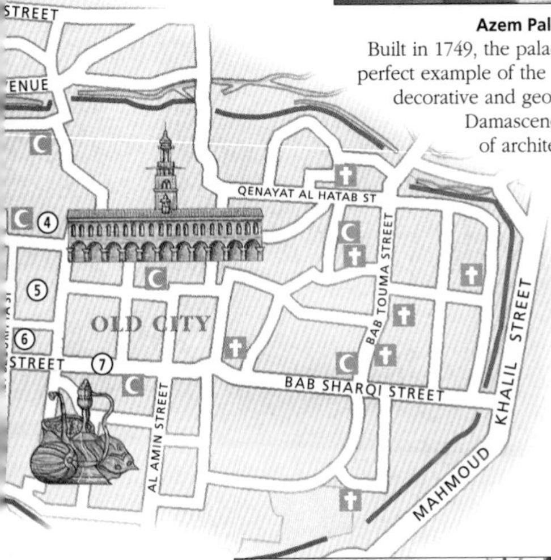

Hammam Nureddin ⑥
Founded in the mid-12th century, this is the grandest of the city's hammams and the oldest example of its kind in Damascus.

Straight Street ⑦
The main axis of Roman and medieval Damascus, Straight Street is a mile-long stretch of shops and stalls selling clothing, textiles, spices, coffee, crafts and carpets.

KEY SIGHTS

① National Museum ★
② Martyrs' Square
③ Citadel
④ Umayyad Mosque ★
⑤ Azem Palace ★
⑥ Hammam Nureddin
⑦ Straight Street

FACT FILE

TOURIST INFORMATION

29 Mai Avenue. ***Tel*** *(011) 221 0122.* *Sat–Thu to 7pm.*

MARKETS

Grand Bazaar
Old City; Sat–Thu to 9pm (Oct–Mar: to 8pm).

HAMMAMS

Hammam Nureddin
Hassan Kharet Bzouriyya St; daily to 11pm.
Hammam al-Qaimariyya
North of Sharia Qaimariyya; daily to 5pm. Open to women.

LOCAL SPECIALITIES

Crafts
Steel and copper trays inlaid with gold and silver wire, wooden boxes and chessboards decorated with mother-of-pearl, Damascene tablecloths with geometrical designs, *Galabiyyas* (long, loose cotton robes), *Arghileh* (bubblepipes).
Dishes
Baklava (layered pastry filled with nuts and soaked in honey).
Kebab halebi (minced lamb grilled on a skewer served in a heavy tomato sauce).
Koubeh (lamb with bulgur wheat).
Makhlouba (rice mixed with chopped aubergine/eggplant, diced lamb or chicken, almonds and walnuts).
Drinks
Araq (aniseed liqueur).
Aseer (freshly squeezed fruit juice).

EXCURSIONS

Bosra 150 km (93 miles) S of Damascus. Roman amphitheatre and Arab fortress.
Palmyra 300 km (186 miles) NE of Damascus. Some of the finest Roman ruins in the Middle East.

Krak des Chevaliers (Tartous)

One of the finest castles in the world, Krak des Chevaliers was built in the middle of the 12th century by the Crusaders. Having captured Jerusalem *(see pp274–5)* and the Holy Land from the Muslims, they required strong bases from which to defend their newly won territories. The largest of a string of such fortresses, Krak des Chevaliers withstood countless attacks and sieges, but the Crusaders abandoned it after their defeat at the hands of the Arabs in 1271. Villagers settled within the walls and remained there until the 1930s, when the castle was cleared and restored.

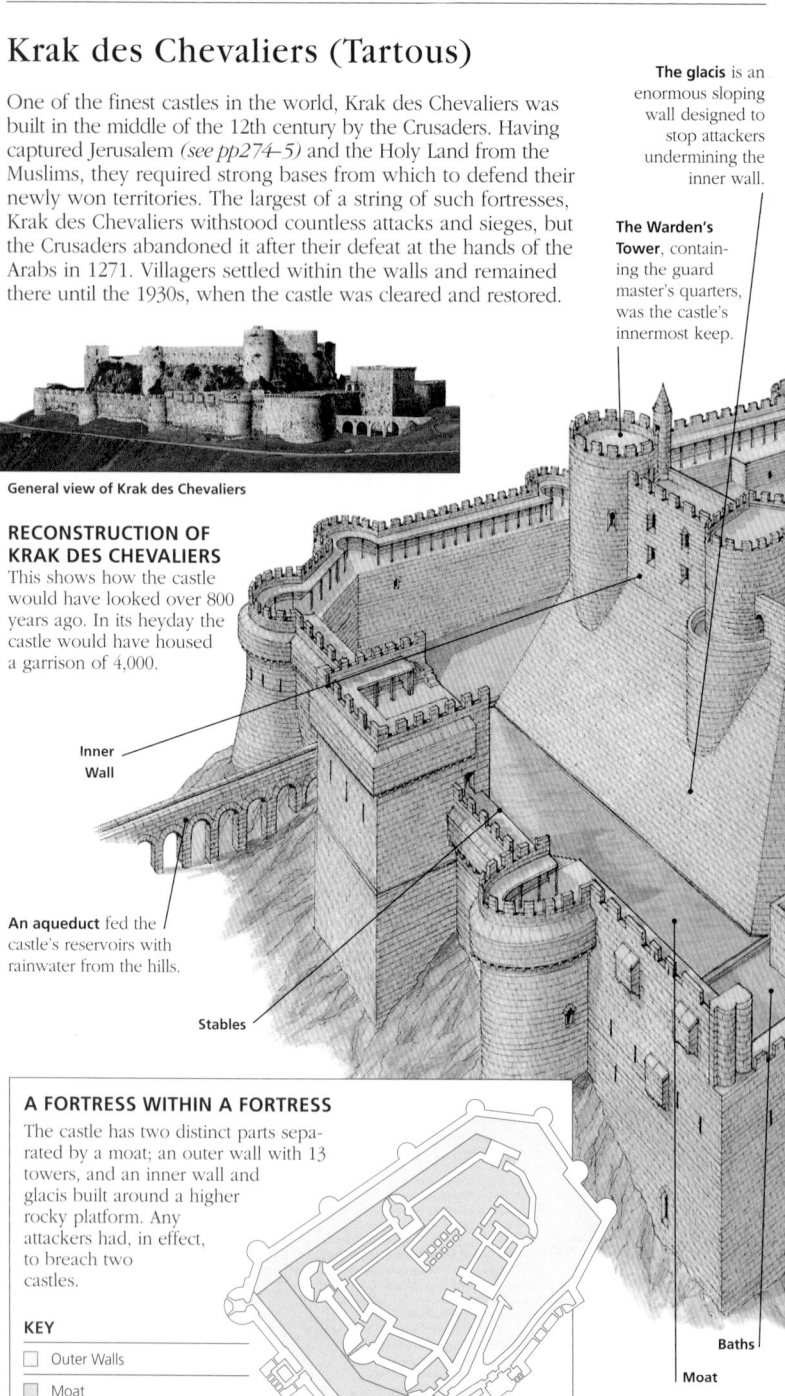

General view of Krak des Chevaliers

RECONSTRUCTION OF KRAK DES CHEVALIERS

This shows how the castle would have looked over 800 years ago. In its heyday the castle would have housed a garrison of 4,000.

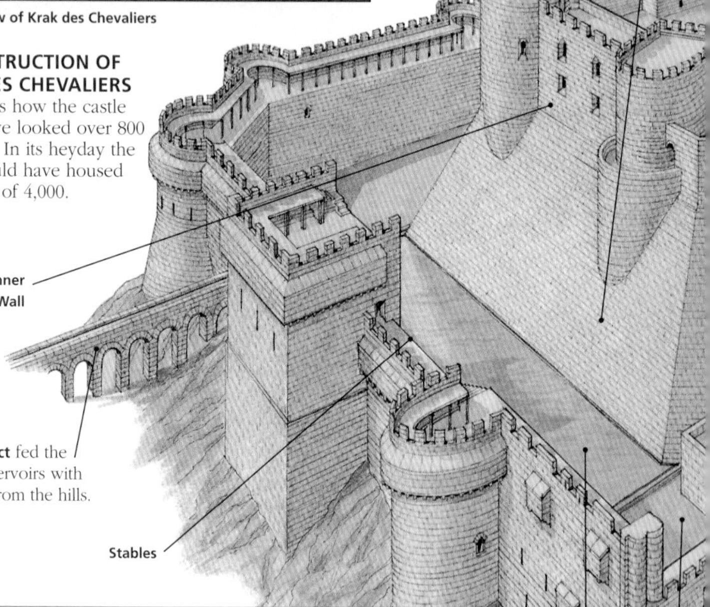
The glacis is an enormous sloping wall designed to stop attackers undermining the inner wall.
The Warden's Tower, containing the guard master's quarters, was the castle's innermost keep.
Inner Wall
An aqueduct fed the castle's reservoirs with rainwater from the hills.
Stables
Baths
Moat

A FORTRESS WITHIN A FORTRESS

The castle has two distinct parts separated by a moat; an outer wall with 13 towers, and an inner wall and glacis built around a higher rocky platform. Any attackers had, in effect, to breach two castles.

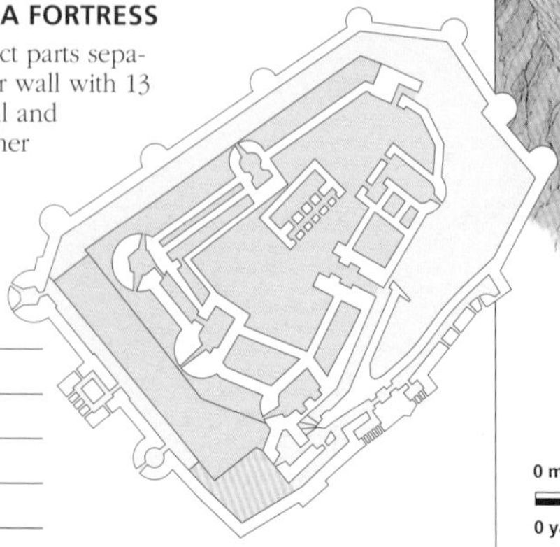

KEY

- Outer Walls
- Moat
- Inner Walls
- Baths

0 metres 100

0 yards 100

★ Tower of the King's Daughter The northern face of this tower has a large projecting gallery from which rocks could be hurled if the outer wall was breached. At ground level the tower is decorated with three blind arches.

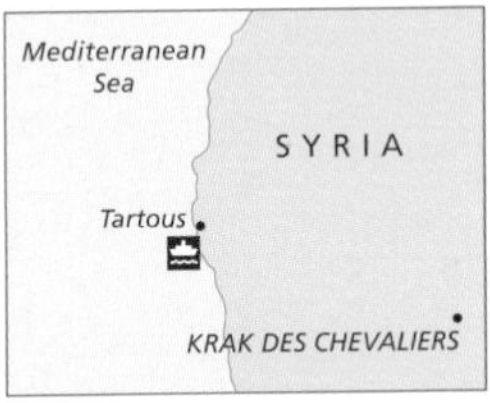

DISTANCE FROM PORT

50 km (31 miles) from site.

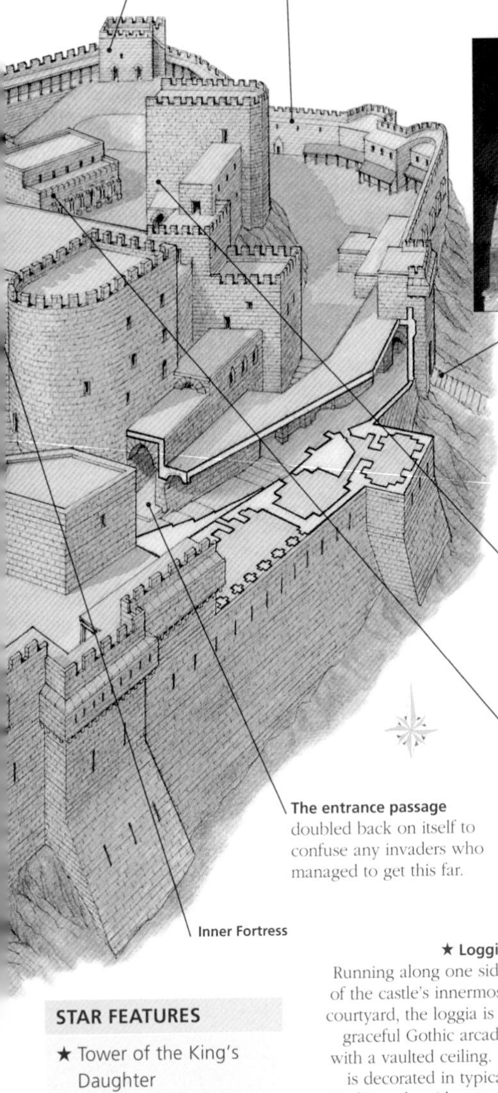

Outer wall

★ Main Entranceway A long, stepped passage leads from the site of the former drawbridge to the upper castle. Small ceiling apertures throw light into the corridor, though they were also designed for pouring boiling oil over invaders. The passageways are high and wide enough to allow for mounted riders.

The chapel was built by the Crusaders and later converted into a mosque after the Muslim conquest. Its Islamic *minbar* (pulpit) can still be seen.

The entrance passage doubled back on itself to confuse any invaders who managed to get this far.

Inner Fortress

★ Loggia Running along one side of the castle's innermost courtyard, the loggia is a graceful Gothic arcade with a vaulted ceiling. It is decorated in typical Gothic style with carved floral motifs and animals. Beyond the loggia is the Great Hall, which functioned as a refectory.

STAR FEATURES

- ★ Tower of the King's Daughter
- ★ Main Entranceway
- ★ Loggia

Süleymaniye Mosque in Istanbul, Turkey ▷

TURKEY

The Bosphorus
Istanbul
ANKARA
Izmir
Ephesus
Kuşadası
Bodrum

Bodrum

A fishing village until the early 1970s, Bodrum is built on the ruins of ancient Halicarnassus. It is now Turkey's liveliest resort, attracting poets, singers, artists and package tourists. Its perfect harbour was colonized by Greeks in the 11th century BC and the city later flourished under Persian rule. It was here that the historian Herodotus (484–420 BC) was born, but Halicarnassus's greatest glory was under Mausolus, who ruled on behalf of the Persians from 377 to 353 BC. His tomb, one of the Seven Wonders of the Ancient World, was so well-known that it bequeathed the word "mausoleum". Originally a temple-like structure decorated with reliefs and statuary on a massive base, only the foundations and a few pieces of sculpture now remain. After the brief tenure of the Knights of St John *(see p251)*, who founded the Castle of St Peter in 1404, the city sank into obscurity. Today, the sheltered anchorage is busy with yachts and locally-built *gulets* used by seafaring holidaymakers.

Castle of St Peter

Built by the Knights Hospitaller in 1402, the castle, also known as the Petronium, has altered little since Sultan Süleyman the Magnificent expelled the Knights of St John in 1522. The co-existence of ancient history and a pellucid sea has allowed Bodrum to specialize in underwater archaeology. Among the artifacts in the castle's museum are Mycenaean amphorae, gold medallions, copper ingots, the hull of a Byzantine ship and a large quantity of fine ancient glass, all excavated from the sea floor.

Ancient Theatre

The theatre was begun by Mausolus; the Romans enlarged it to seat an audience of 13,000. It has been restored for use during the summer months and gives a magnificent view over the town and harbour.

KEY SIGHTS

Ancient Theatre

Castle of St Peter ★

Harbour ★

Mausoleum of Halicarnassus

FACT FILE

TOURIST INFORMATION

Baris Meydanı 48. ***Tel*** *(252) 316 1091.* ◯ *Jun–Oct: daily to 6pm; Nov–May: daily to 5pm.*

MARKETS

Textiles Market Place; Tue.

Food & souvenirs Market Pl; Fri.

LOCAL SPECIALITIES

Crafts

Kilim slippers, natural sponge.

Dishes

Lamb Shawarma (lamb cooked on a spit).

Kefal (charcoal-grilled grey mullet with rocket salad).

Börek (rich, layered pastry filled with cheese).

Drinks

Efes (the local lager).

Doluca Rosé (a local rosé wine).

EXCURSIONS

Gümüşlük 18 km (11 miles) W of Bodrum. Village along the harbour.

Milas Labryanda 60 km (37 miles) NE of Bodrum. 4th-century BC sacred site high in hills. Views.

Harbour

The view of Bodrum's attractive natural harbour is enhanced by elegant *gulets*. Based on the design of traditional sponge-fishing boats, these are chartered by people holidaying off the unspoiled but inaccessible coastline.

Izmir

In the 1st century BC the Greek historian Strabo described Roman Smyrna as the most beautiful city in Ionia. The same cannot be said for its modern equivalent, Izmir. During the Ottoman period *(see p298)* its large Greek, Armenian, Italian, Spanish and Sephardic Jewish communities made it seem a foreign enclave within Turkey. After World War I, Greece was given a mandate over the Izmir region, but when a Greek army pushed further inland Turkish reprisal was swift. Over three days in September 1922, three-quarters of old Izmir burned to the ground and, with it, the tolerance of Greeks and Turks for one another. Today the city is a commercial and industrial metropolis and Turkey's second port. Most of the main sights, including the Archaeological and Ethnographic museums and the frenetic bazaar quarter, are near leafy, waterside Konak Meydanı (Square). There is a superb view from the Kadifekale (Velvet Castle). Uphill from the Roman Agora is a district of pre-1922 wooden houses, which gives an idea of what was lost in the great fire.

KEY SIGHTS

Archaeological Museum ★
Caravanserai
Ethnographic Museum ★
Kadifekale
Old City Bazaar
Roman Agora

FACT FILE

TOURIST INFORMATION

Regional Directorate of Tourism, Akdeniz Mah. 1344 ***Tel*** *(232) 483 5117.* ◻ *Apr–Oct: daily to 6:30pm; Nov–Mar: daily to 4pm.*

MARKETS

General Old City Bazaar; daily.

LOCAL SPECIALITIES

Dishes

Izmir Köfte (meat balls with fried peppers, tomatoes and potatoes).
Imam Bayildi (aubergine/eggplant stuffed with onion and tomato).

Drinks

Ayran (drinking yoghurt).
Raki (aniseed-flavoured spirit).

EXCURSIONS

Pergamon 120 km (75 miles) N of Izmir. 2nd-century BC capital of Eumenes II. Acropolis and theatre.
Çeşme 80 km (50 miles) W of Izmir. Pleasant seaside town.

Old City Bazaar
Izmir's bazaar quarter occupies an entire district. The stalls of each trade are grouped together, with clothing and jewellery around Anafartalar Caddesi and leather goods the speciality of Fevzipaşa Bulvarı. While exploring, visitors will stumble upon the food market, selling mounds of mouth-wateringly fresh vegetables, fruits, nuts and spices.

Caravanserai
This handsome late 16th-century building, known as Kizlarağasi, was built to house visiting merchants. They were given rooms on the first floor, while their pack animals were stabled on the ground floor.

Pergamon
Among the impressive ruins of this wealthy Greek and Roman city are those of the partly reconstructed Trajan Temple. It was built by Emperor Hadrian (AD 117–138) in honour of his predecessor, Trajan.

Ephesus (Kuşadası)

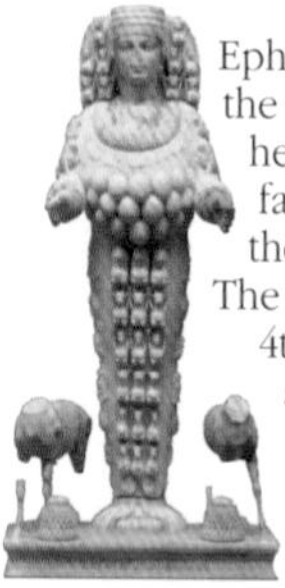

Statue of Artemis, 2nd century AD

Ephesus is one of the greatest ruined cities in the western world. A Greek city was first built here in about 1000 BC and very soon rose to fame as a centre for the worship of Cybele, the Anatolian Mother Goddess. The city we see today was founded in the 4th century BC by Alexander the Great's successor, Lysimachus. But it was under the Romans that Ephesus became the chief port on the Aegean, with a population of around 250,000. Most of the surviving structures date from this period. As the harbour silted up the city declined, but played an important part in the establishment of Christianity. Two great Councils of the early Church were held here, in AD 431 and 449. It is said that the Virgin Mary spent her last years nearby and that St John the Evangelist came from Pátmos *(see p318)* to look after her.

★ Library of Celsus
This was built between AD 117 and 125 by Gaius Julius Aquila as a memorial to his father, Gaius Julius Celsus Polemaeanus, governor of the Roman province of Asia, of which Ephesus was the capital. The library housed some 12,000 scrolls, which perished during the Goths' sack of the city in AD 262. Plaster copies of statues representing the intellectual virtues (Wisdom, Goodness, Thought and Knowledge) adorn the niches.

Private Houses
Life in these affluent mansions was much like that on the mainland of Roman Italy. The houses are finely decorated with mosaics, frescoes and courtyards with fountains.

Street of Curetes
On either side of this paved street are public latrines, a row of ten small shops, a brothel, three impressive tombs, fountains, monument bases and side streets to smart houses.

STAR FEATURES

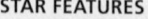

- ★ Library of Celsus
- ★ Theatre
- ★ Temple of Hadrian

Ruined buildings flanking a street in the ancient city of Ephesus

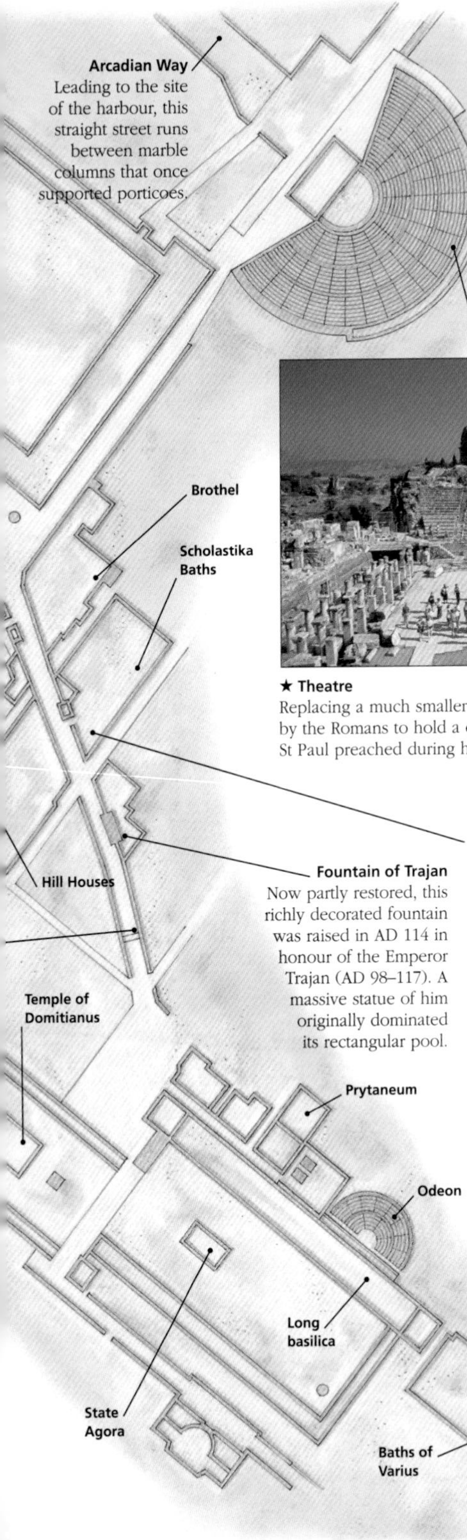

Arcadian Way
Leading to the site of the harbour, this straight street runs between marble columns that once supported porticoes.

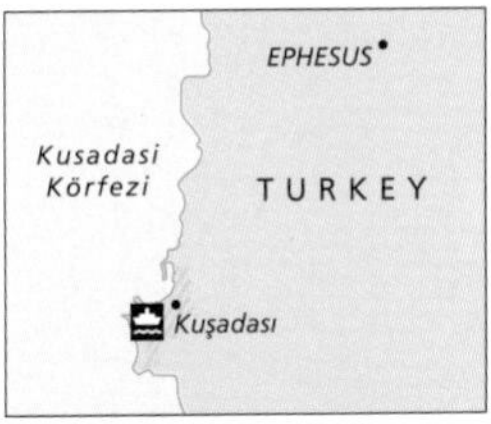

DISTANCE FROM PORT

12 km (8 miles) from city centre.

★ Theatre
Replacing a much smaller Greek theatre, this massive structure was built by the Romans to hold a capacity audience of 24,000. It was here that St Paul preached during his stay in Ephesus between AD 53 and 55.

Fountain of Trajan
Now partly restored, this richly decorated fountain was raised in AD 114 in honour of the Emperor Trajan (AD 98–117). A massive statue of him originally dominated its rectangular pool.

★ Temple of Hadrian
Dedicated in AD 118, this temple was rebuilt in the 4th century, when much of the decoration was replaced with 3rd-century carving. The head sculpted on the keystone of the arch represents Tyche, the guardian of the fortune of the city.

Istanbul

Ceramics sold in the Grand Bazaar

Istanbul was founded by the Greeks in about 676 BC as Byzantion and renamed Byzantium in AD 64 when it was conquered by the Romans. The Byzantine era lasted from AD 330, when Emperor Constantine made it his capital, until 1453 when the Ottomans, under Sultan Mehmet II, seized it. This was the first time the city walls had been breached since their completion in 422, but much of their impressive length remains. The sultanate was finally abolished by Atatürk in 1922.

Istanbul's most famous monuments – Haghia Sophia, the Blue Mosque, Topkapı Palace and the Archaeological Museum – are all close together, while the Süleymaniye Mosque is in the Bazaar Quarter, near the Grand Bazaar.

Süleymaniye Mosque ⑦
Istanbul's main mosque was built in the 1550s for Süleyman the Magnificent. Around it are its former bathhouse, kitchen, schools, caravanserai and hospital, which cared for 1,000 poor people daily.

Grand Bazaar ⑥
Established in the 1450s, hundreds of booth-like shops crowd a labyrinth of streets covered by painted vaults. The complex is surrounded by a wall pierced by several gateways.

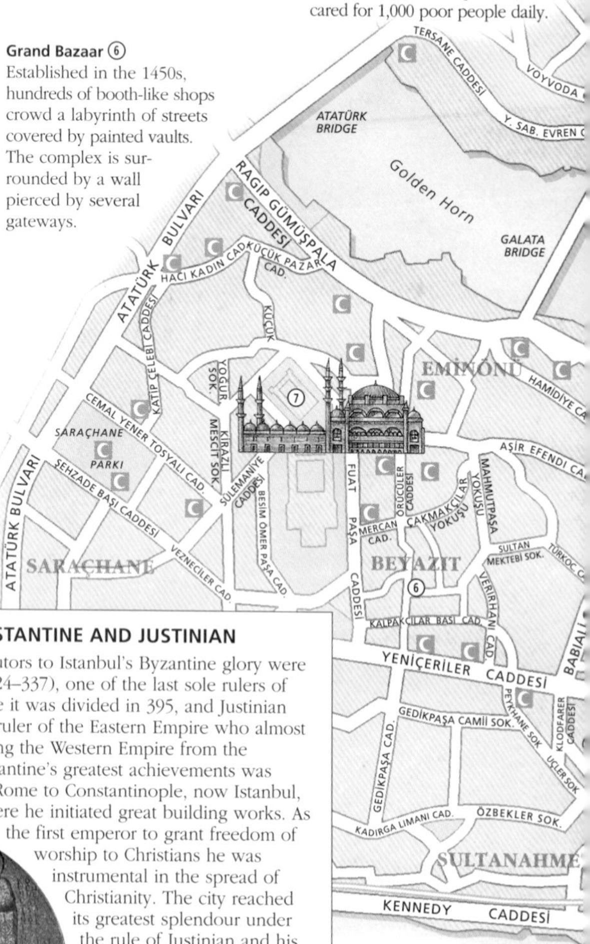

THE EMPERORS CONSTANTINE AND JUSTINIAN

The two greatest contributors to Istanbul's Byzantine glory were Constantine the Great (324–337), one of the last sole rulers of the Roman Empire before it was divided in 395, and Justinian (527–565), the powerful ruler of the Eastern Empire who almost succeeded in reconquering the Western Empire from the barbarians. One of Constantine's greatest achievements was moving his capital from Rome to Constantinople, now Istanbul, where he initiated great building works. As the first emperor to grant freedom of worship to Christians he was instrumental in the spread of Christianity. The city reached its greatest splendour under the rule of Justinian and his influential wife, Theodora.

Virgin and Child with Constantine and Justinian, Haghia Sophia

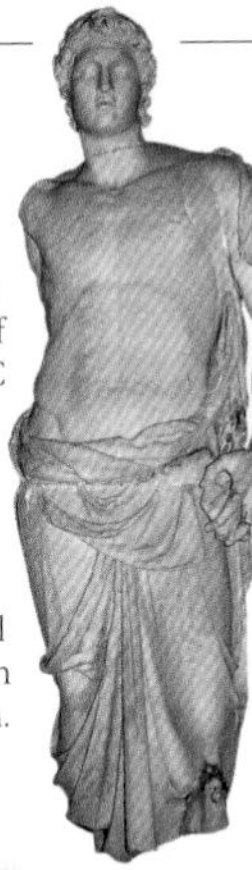

Archaeological Museum ②
This vast collection spans 5,000 years, from figurines of the Mother Goddess of the 3rd millennium BC to 19th-century Turkish pottery. It has one of the world's richest Classical collections. Visitors should not miss the breathtaking sarcophagi from the royal necropolis at Sidon in Lebanon.

Topkapi Palace ①
For 400 years from 1465 the Ottoman sultans ruled their empire from this vast palace. Its art collection, jewel-filled treasury, opulent rooms (many decorated with znik tiles), and leafy courtyards are indisputable highlights of a visit to Istanbul.

Haghia Sophia ③
Inaugurated by the Christian emperor Justinian and converted to a mosque in the 1400s, this vast building is famous for its Byzantine-era mosaics.

Blue Mosque ④
Taking its name from the mainly blue/znik tiles decorating the interior, this mosque with six minarets was built between 1609 and 1616.

Museum of Turkish and Islamic Arts ⑤
Displaying more than 40,000 items, this museum in an early 16th-century palace is famed for its collection of carpets. An ethnographic section focuses on nomadic life.

KEY SIGHTS

① Topkapı Palace ★ *(see pp302–3)*
② Archaeological Museum
③ Haghia Sophia ★ *(see p301)*
④ Blue Mosque ★ *(see p300)*
⑤ Museum of Turkish and Islamic Arts *(see p300)*
⑥ Grand Bazaar
⑦ Süleymaniye Mosque

FACT FILE

TOURIST INFORMATION
Divanyolu Caddesı 3, Sultanahmet. ***Tel*** *(0212) 518 18 02.* ◯ *daily to 5pm.*

MARKETS
General Grand Bazaar, Çarşikapı Caddesı, Beyazıt; Mon–Sat.
Spices Spice Bazaar, Cami Meydanı Sok; Mon–Sat.
Carpets & crafts Cavalry Bazaar (Arasta Çarşi), Torun Sok; Mon–Sat.

LOCAL SPECIALITIES
Crafts
Traditional Istanbul miniatures inspired by museum originals, blue-and-white striped glass from Paşabahçe, gold, silver and semi-precious stone jewellery, blue glass-eye pendants, carpets and kilims from western Turkey's 13 carpet-weaving areas, copperware.
Dishes
Midye dolması (rice-filled mussels).
Balik bugulama (steamed fish stew).
Drinks
Raki (an anise-flavoured spirit).
Sahlep (a hot orchid-root drink).
Türk Kahvesi (Turkish coffee).

EXCURSIONS
Princes' Islands 16 km (10 miles) SE of Istanbul. Pine-forested islands. Büyükada has elegant, 19th-century houses. Motor vehicles are banned.
Edirne 225 km (140 miles) NW of Istanbul. Its Selimiye Mosque is the finest Ottoman mosque in Turkey.
Dardanelles 255 km (160 miles) SW of Istanbul. Gallipoli Peninsula has a national park, World War I cemeteries and memorials.

Istanbul: Sultanahmet Square

Two of Istanbul's most venerable monuments, the Blue Mosque and Haghia Sophia, face each other across Sultanahmet Square (Sultanahmet Meydani), next to the 3rd-century Roman Hippodrome. Also in this fascinating historic quarter are several museums, including the Museum of Turkish and Islamic Arts and the Mosaics Museum. The latter was created by roofing over mosaics that once paved the floors of the Byzantine rulers' Great Palace, now all that remain of this medieval palace. No less colourful are the cries of the *simit* (bagel) hawkers and restaurant waiters, and the chatter of children selling postcards.

Tomb of Sultan Ahmet
Stunning 17th-century znik tiles adorn the final resting place of Ahmet I. The building forms part of the outer complex of the Blue Mosque.

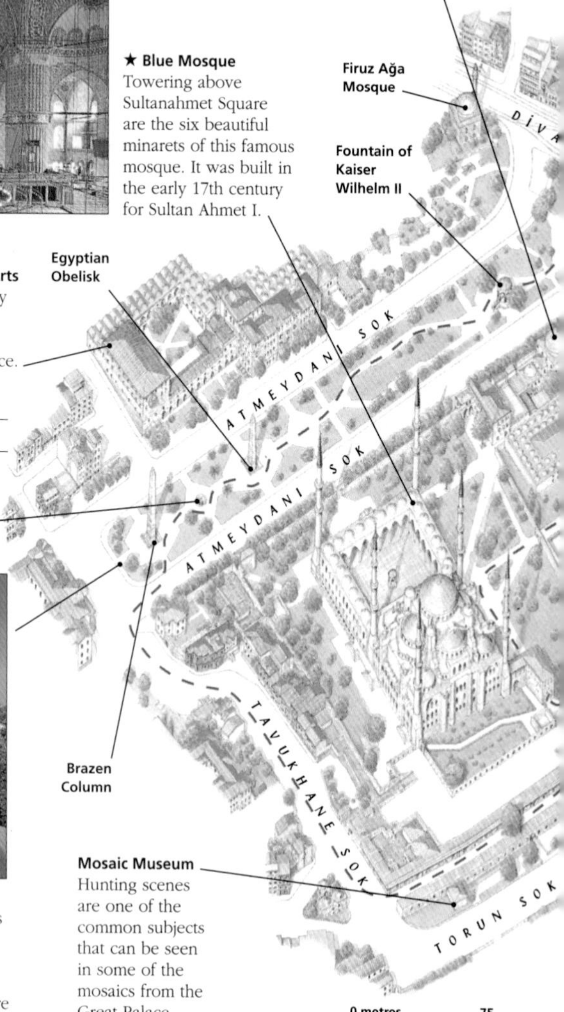

★ Blue Mosque
Towering above Sultanahmet Square are the six beautiful minarets of this famous mosque. It was built in the early 17th century for Sultan Ahmet I.

Firuz Ağa Mosque

Fountain of Kaiser Wilhelm II

Egyptian Obelisk

Museum of Turkish and Islamic Arts
Rugs and yurts, the tents used by Turkey's nomadic peoples, are included in this impressive collection in Ibrahim Pasha Palace.

KEY

– – – Suggested route

Serpentine Column

Brazen Column

Hippodrome
This stadium was the city's focus for more than 1,000 years. Only a few sections remain, such as the central line of monuments. Today, the road around the square almost directly follows the line of the ancient chariot-racing track.

Mosaic Museum
Hunting scenes are one of the common subjects that can be seen in some of the mosaics from the Great Palace.

★ Basilica Cistern
This marble head of Medusa is one of two Classical column bases found in the Basilica Cistern. The cavernous, pillared and vaulted cistern was laid out in AD 532 to serve the Great Palace with water.

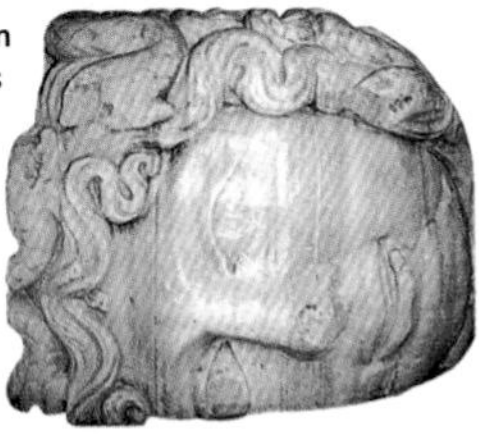

LOCATOR MAP

Stone pilaster
This is all that survives of the Milion, a triumphal gateway from which distances in the Byzantine Empire were measured.

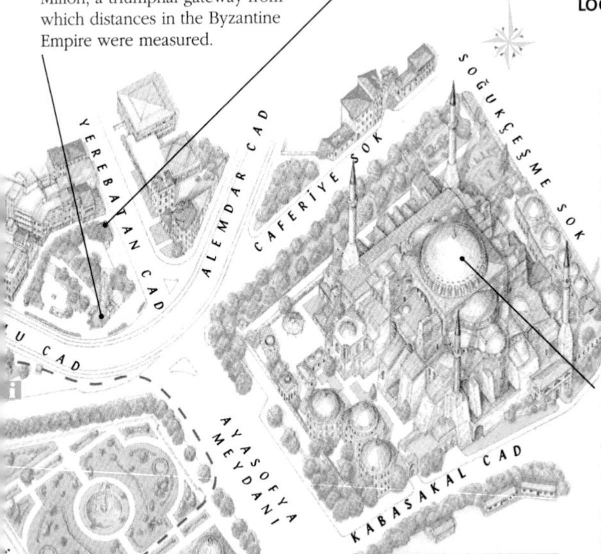

★ Haghia Sophia
The supreme church of Byzantium is more than 1,400 years old and has survived in a remarkably good state. Inside it are several glorious, figurative mosaics, some dating back to the 9th century.

Baths of Roxelana
Koca Mimar Sinan (c.1491–1588), architect to Süleyman the Magnificent, built these beautiful baths for use by the congregation of Haghia Sophia. The baths are named after the Sultan's chief wife.

Istanbul Crafts Centre
Visitors have a rare opportunity here to observe Turkish craftsmen practising a range of traditional skills.

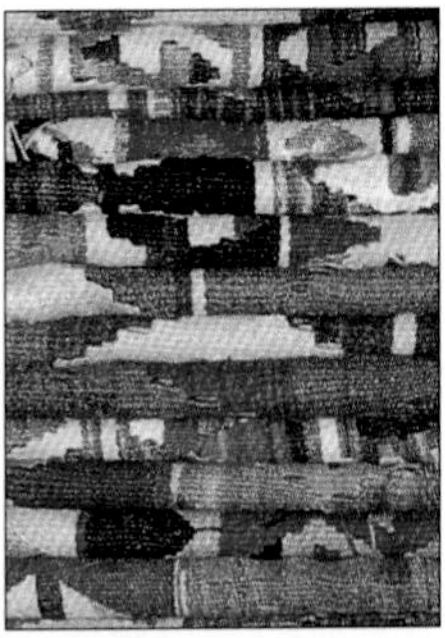

Cavalry Bazaar (Arasta Çarşi)
The two rows of shops along either side of this lane reflect the bazaar's origins as Ottoman stables that flanked a long stable yard. Carpets are the main items touted, although jewellery and other handicrafts are also sold.

STAR SIGHTS

- ★ Blue Mosque
- ★ Basilica Cistern
- ★ Haghia Sophia

Istanbul: Topkapı Palace ①

Süleyman I's *tuğra* over the main gate

Between 1459 and 1465, shortly after his conquest of Byzantine Constantinople, Mehmet II *(see p298)* built Topkap¡ Palace to live in. It was conceived as a series of pavilions contained by four huge courtyards, a stone version of the tented encampments from which the nomadic Ottomans had emerged. Initially, the palace served as the seat of government and contained a school in which civil servants and soldiers were trained. In the 16th century, however, the officials were moved to the grand vizier's offices of the Sublime Porte nearby. Sultan Abdül Mecit I left Topkap¡ in 1853 in favour of Dolmabahçe Palace further along the Bosphorus *(see pp304–7)* in the east of the city. In 1924 the sultans' treasures were nationalized and Topkap¡ was opened to the public as a museum.

★ Harem

The labyrinth of brilliantly tiled rooms where the sultan's wives, children and concubines (slaves from the empire) lived can be visited on a guided tour.

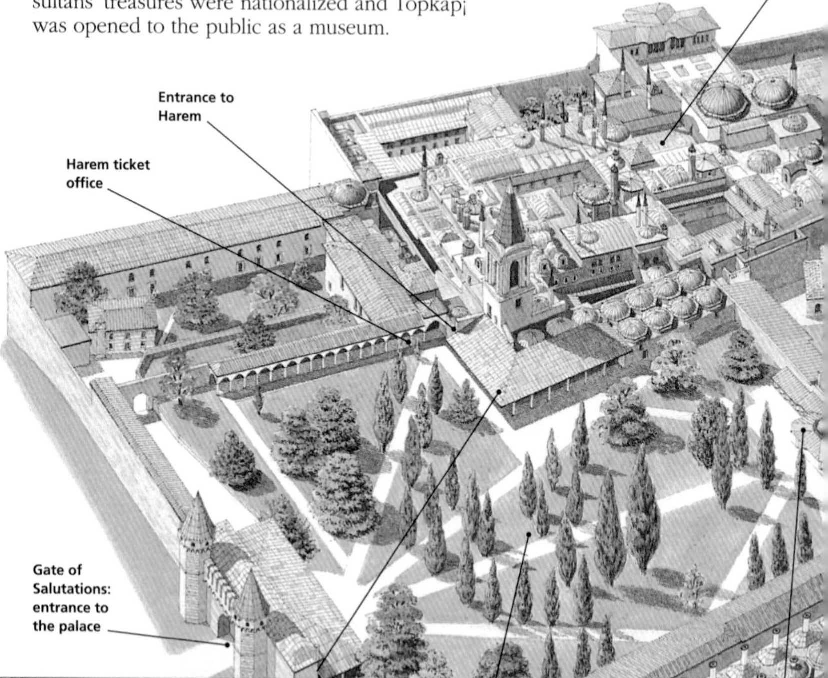

Divan

The viziers of the imperial council met in this chamber, sometimes watched covertly by the sultan.

Gate of Felicity

This is also called the Gate of the White Eunuchs.

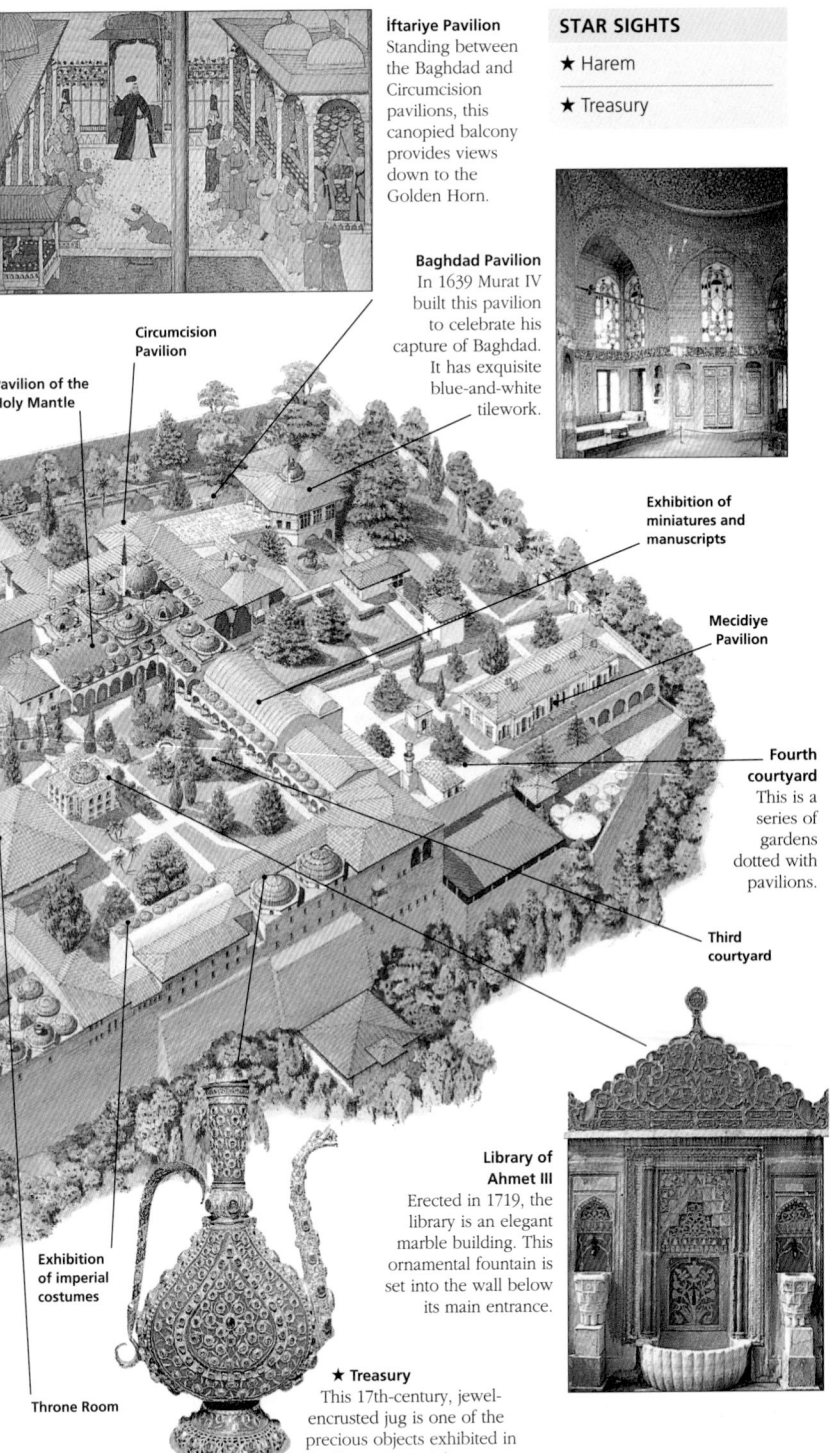

İftariye Pavilion
Standing between the Baghdad and Circumcision pavilions, this canopied balcony provides views down to the Golden Horn.

STAR SIGHTS

★ Harem

★ Treasury

Baghdad Pavilion
In 1639 Murat IV built this pavilion to celebrate his capture of Baghdad. It has exquisite blue-and-white tilework.

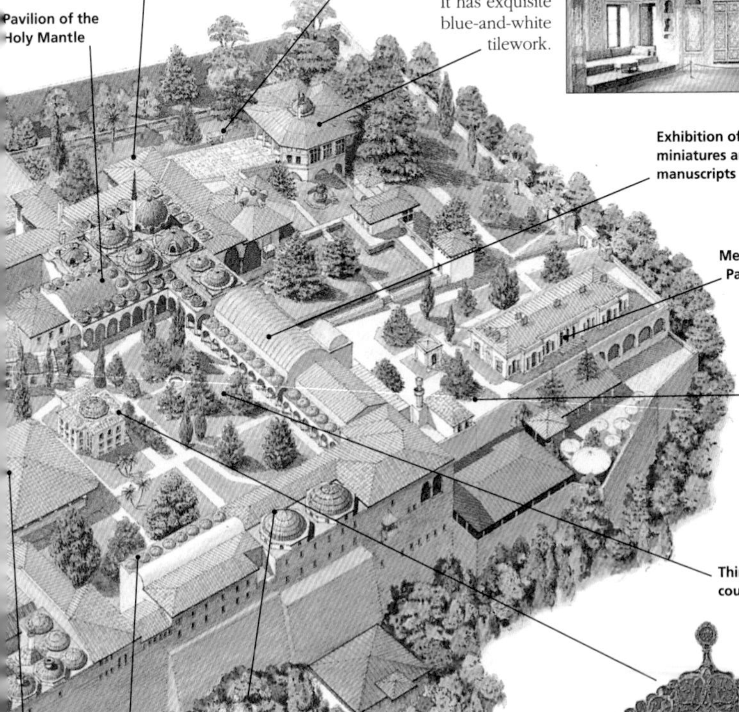

Fourth courtyard
This is a series of gardens dotted with pavilions.

Library of Ahmet III
Erected in 1719, the library is an elegant marble building. This ornamental fountain is set into the wall below its main entrance.

★ Treasury
This 17th-century, jewel-encrusted jug is one of the precious objects exhibited in the former imperial treasury.

The Bosphorus

Ceremonial gate, Çırağan Palace

Stretching for 30 km (19 miles) between the Sea of Marmara and the Black Sea, the Bosphorus separates the continents of Europe and Asia. For much of its length, its shores are lined with wooden waterside villas known as *yalıs*, graceful mosques, such as the 16th-century skele Mosque, and opulent 19th-century palaces. The southern end of the Bosphorus is dominated by Istanbul *(see pp298–9)*, the tranquil former palace gardens of Yildiz Park contrasting with bustling suburbs such as the former fishing village of Ortaköy, which nestles at the foot of the Bosphorus Bridge. Completed in 1973, this 1,560-m (5,120-ft) long suspension bridge was the first to span the straits.

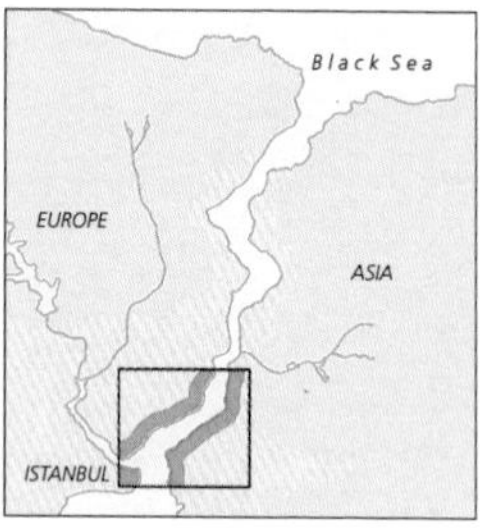

LOCATOR MAP

Dolmabahçe Palace
Situated on what was once a bay, this opulent 19th-century palace has a series of ornate gates along the waterfront. These were used by the sultan to enter the palace from his imperial barge.

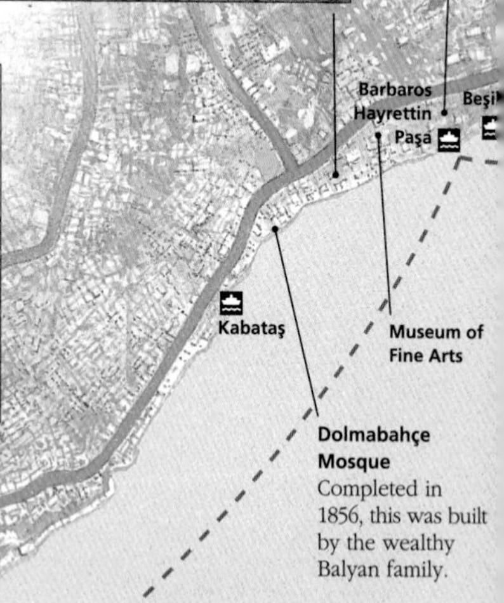

The Bosphorus Trip
Laden with sightseers, the Turkish Maritime Lines (TDİ) ferry travels up the Bosphorus two to three times daily. The trip affords superb views of the city, including Suleymaniye Mosque *(see p298)*.

Dolmabahçe Mosque
Completed in 1856, this was built by the wealthy Balyan family.

Leander's Tower
One of Istanbul's landmarks, this 18th-century tower stands on its own small island. The tower is open to the public.

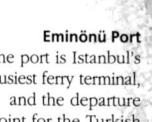

Eminönü Port
The port is Istanbul's busiest ferry terminal, and the departure point for the Turkish Maritime Lines ferry.

See pages 306–7

Arnavutköy
Galatasaray Island
Çengelköy
Ortaköy
Yıldız Park
Bosphorus Bridge
Beylerbeyi
Fethi Ahmet Paşa Yalı
Kuzguncuk
İskele Mosque
Üsküdar
rem
0 metres 750
0 yards 750
KEY
Motorway
Main road
Other road
Built-up area
Ferry boarding point
Route of Bosphorus trip
Yalı
Viewpoint

Fishing on the Bosphorus
Mackerel, mullet, *hamsi* (similar to anchovy) and sardine all attract the myriad fishing vessels – from large trawlers to tiny rowing boats – that ply the Bosphorus.

Ortaköy Mosque
Sultan Abdül Mecit I ordered the construction of this Baroque mosque, with its tympanum arches and corner turrets. It was built in 1855 by Garabet Amira and Nigoğayos Balyan.

Galatasaray Island
The island is a private sports complex.

Sadullah Paşa Yalı
Painted red-brown like many old *yalıs*, this was built in 1783.

Çırağan Palace
Dating from 1874, the palace was destroyed by a fire in 1910. It was rebuilt in 1990 as a luxury hotel.

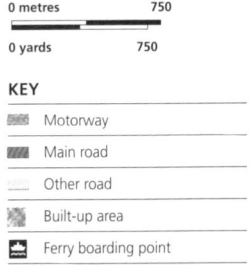

Beylerbeyi Palace
This elegant marble fountain adorns one of the principal atriums of the 19th-century Beylerbeyi Palace.

Şemsi Paşa Mosque
Built in 1580, this is one of the smallest mosques commissioned by a grand vizier. The circular windows are an allusion to Iemsi Paßa, whose name derives from the Arabic word for "sun".

The Middle Bosphorus

Paşabahçe glass vase

North of Arnavutköy, the outskirts of Istanbul give way to attractive towns and villages, such as Bebek. This is one of the most fashionable villages of the Bosphorus, famous for its marzipan and the bars and cafés lining its waterfront. The Bosphorus flows fast and deep as the channel reaches its narrowest point – 700 m (2,300 ft) across – on the approach to the Fatih Sultan Mehmet suspension bridge. The fortresses of Europe and Asia face each other across the water near here. Several elegant *yalıs* are also found in this part of the strait, particularly in the region around the Küçüksu and Göksu Rivers, known to Europeans as the Sweet Waters of Asia. The marble-fronted Küçüksu Palace has one of the loveliest façades on the shores of the Bosphorus.

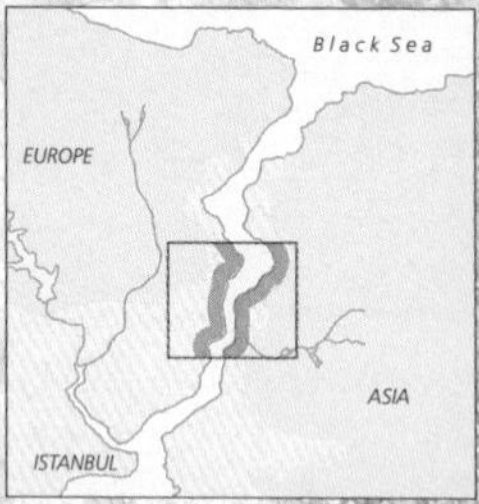

LOCATOR MAP

İstinye Bay
This huge natural bay, the largest inlet on the Bosphorus, has been used as a harbour for centuries. A fish market is held along the quay every morning.

Emirgan Park
Situated above the charming village of Emirgan, this park is famous for its tulips in the spring. The grounds contain pleasant cafés and 19th-century pavilions.

Bosphorus University
One of the most prestigious in Turkey, the university enjoys spectacular views over the Bosphorus.

Fortress of Europe
Situated at the narrowest point on the Bosphorus, this fortress was built by Mehmet II in 1452, as a prelude to his invasion of Constantinople. Open air performances are now staged here.

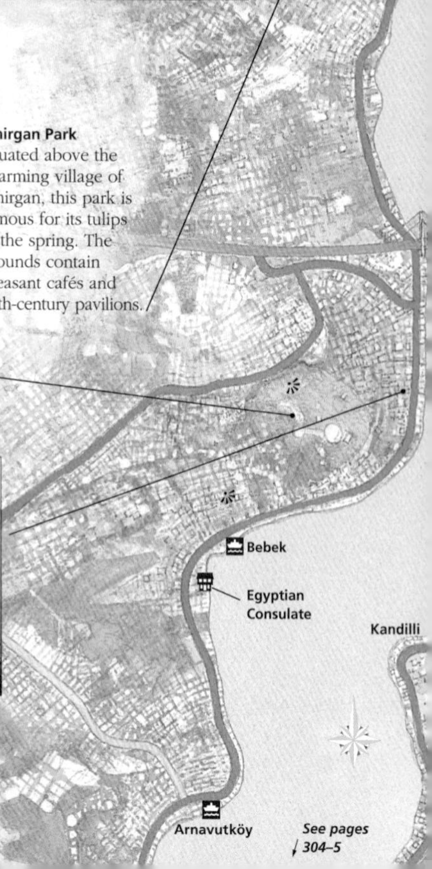

See pages 304–5

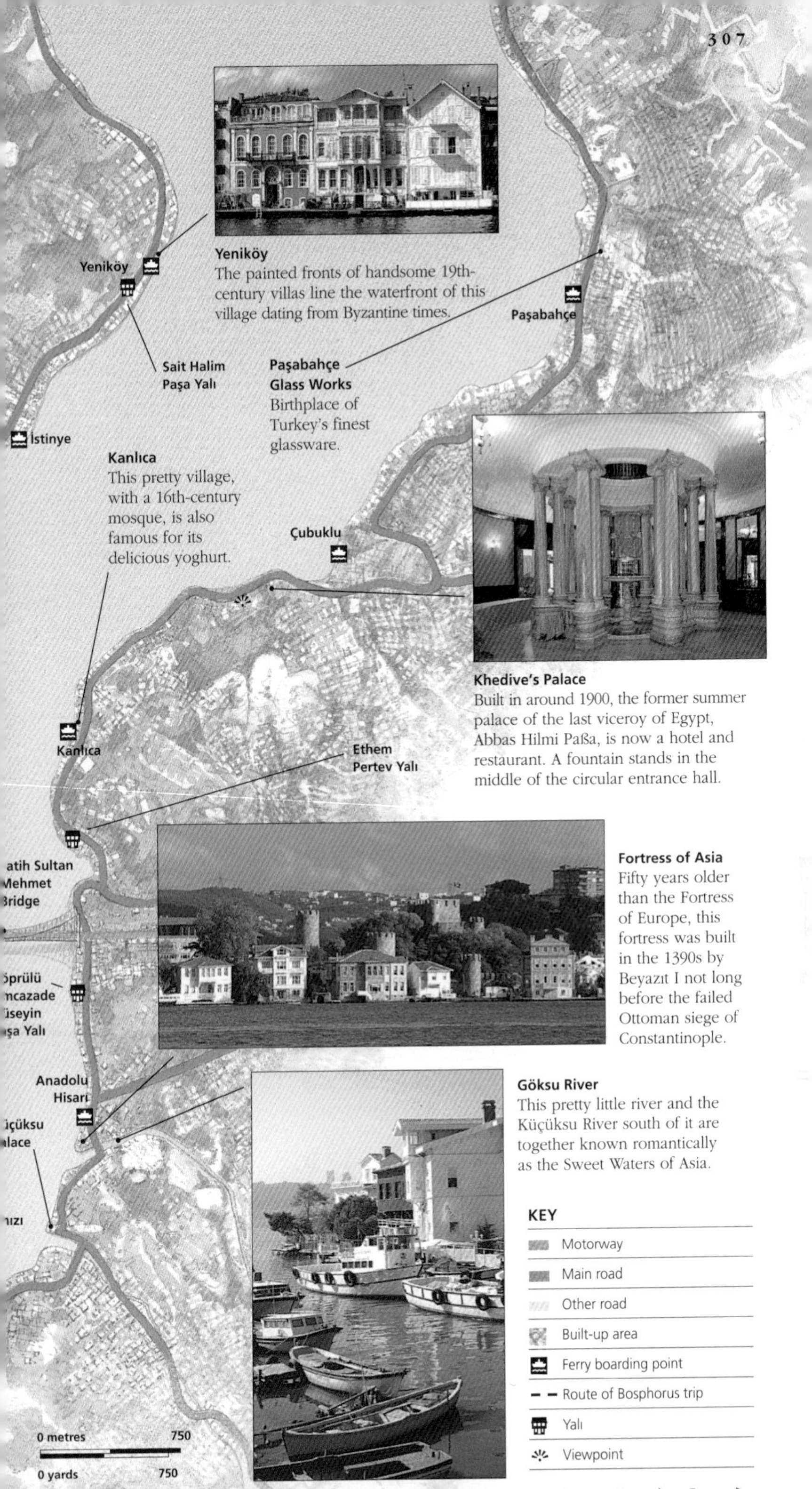

Yeniköy
The painted fronts of handsome 19th-century villas line the waterfront of this village dating from Byzantine times.

Paşabahçe Glass Works
Birthplace of Turkey's finest glassware.

Kanlıca
This pretty village, with a 16th-century mosque, is also famous for its delicious yoghurt.

Khedive's Palace
Built in around 1900, the former summer palace of the last viceroy of Egypt, Abbas Hilmi Paßa, is now a hotel and restaurant. A fountain stands in the middle of the circular entrance hall.

Fortress of Asia
Fifty years older than the Fortress of Europe, this fortress was built in the 1390s by Beyazıt I not long before the failed Ottoman siege of Constantinople.

Göksu River
This pretty little river and the Küçüksu River south of it are together known romantically as the Sweet Waters of Asia.

KEY

- Motorway
- Main road
- Other road
- Built-up area
- Ferry boarding point
- Route of Bosphorus trip
- Yalı
- Viewpoint

Cliff-top whitewashed windmills overlooking the sea at Olympos, Karpathos, Greece ▷

GREECE
AND CYPRUS

Athens (Piraeus)

Athens has been a city for 3,500 years, but its greatest glory was during the Classical period of ancient Greece, from which so many buildings and artifacts still survive. The 5th century BC in particular was a golden age, when the great democratic leader Perikles oversaw the building of the Acropolis *(see pp312–15)*. Within the Byzantine Empire and under Ottoman rule, Athens lost importance, becoming little more than a village. It returned to prominence in 1834, when it was made the capital of a newly independent Greece. Today, it is a busy, modern metropolitan centre.

Kerameikós ②
This ancient cemetery has been a burial ground since the 12th century BC. Most of the graves remaining today are along the Street of Tombs.

Agora ③
From 600 BC, this was the political heart of Athens. The Stoa of Attalos was reconstructed in the 1950s on its original, 2nd-century BC foundations. It now houses the Agora Museum.

Tower of the Winds ⑤
Built in the 2nd century BC, the 12-m (40-ft) high tower was originally designed as a water clock, including sundials and a compass. Constructed by the Syrian Andronikos Kyrrhestes, it features allegorical reliefs of the relevant winds on each of its sides.

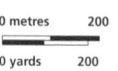

0 metres 200
0 yards 200

Acropolis ④
The rock of the Acropolis has always dominated Athens. For over 2,000 years, the imposing ruins of the Parthenon – built on the orders of Perikles – have provided a notable landmark for the city.

THE HISTORY OF ANCIENT ATHENS

The area around the Acropolis has been occupied for more than 7,000 years, but it was not until around 800 BC that Athens emerged as a city state. The city grew in power and influence, and by 450 BC it led the Western World in philosophy, writing, theatre and the arts. An extravagant building programme, initiated by the great leader and statesman Perikles (495–429 BC), gave rise to some of its most impressive buildings. In 388 BC the city was defeated by Philip of Macedon, but continued to flourish under Macedonian and, later, Roman rule. With the decline of the Roman Empire, however, the influence of Athens dwindled.

Perikles, who initiated the building of the Parthenon

lational rchaeological luseum ①
)ne of the world's inest archaeological nuseums, this iouses artifacts lating from the Neolithic period to ζoman times.

'o the National rchaeological luseum ①

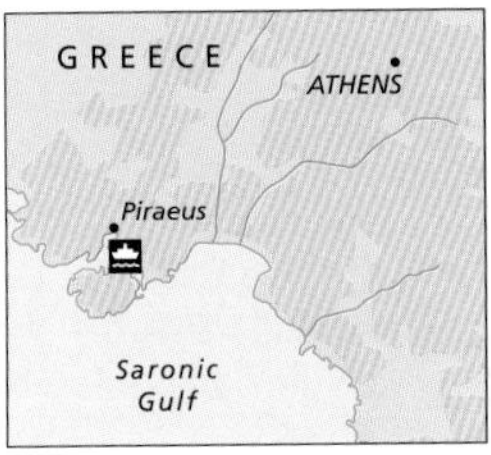

DISTANCE FROM PORT

10 km (6 miles) from city centre.

Museum of Cycladic Art ⑧
This striking building of marble and glass, opened in 1986, houses the finest collection of Cycladic art in the world. Particularly notable are the female figurines.

Benáki Museum ⑦
Formed from a private collection, the museum contains an eclectic array of art, costumes and handicrafts.

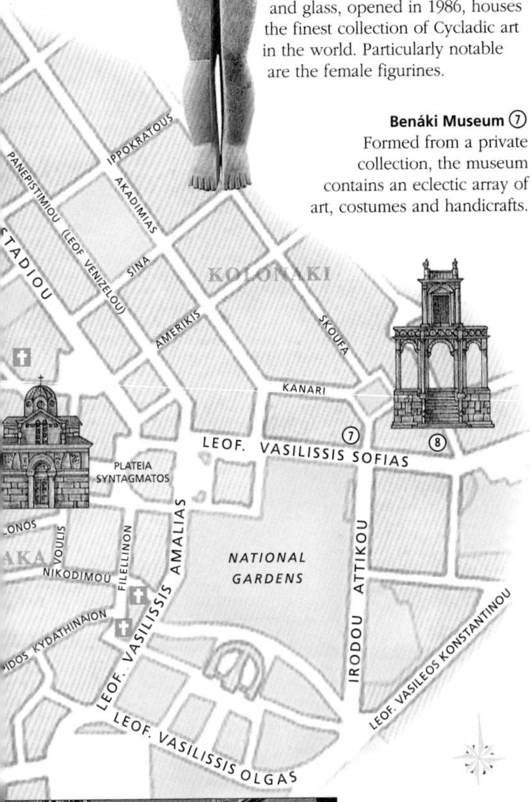

Panagía Gorgeopíkoös ⑥
Affectionately known as Mikrí Mitrópoli (Little Cathedral), this church is one of the best-preserved Byzantine buildings in Athens. Built entirely from Pentelic marble, its walls include carved reliefs taken from Classical buildings.

KEY SIGHTS

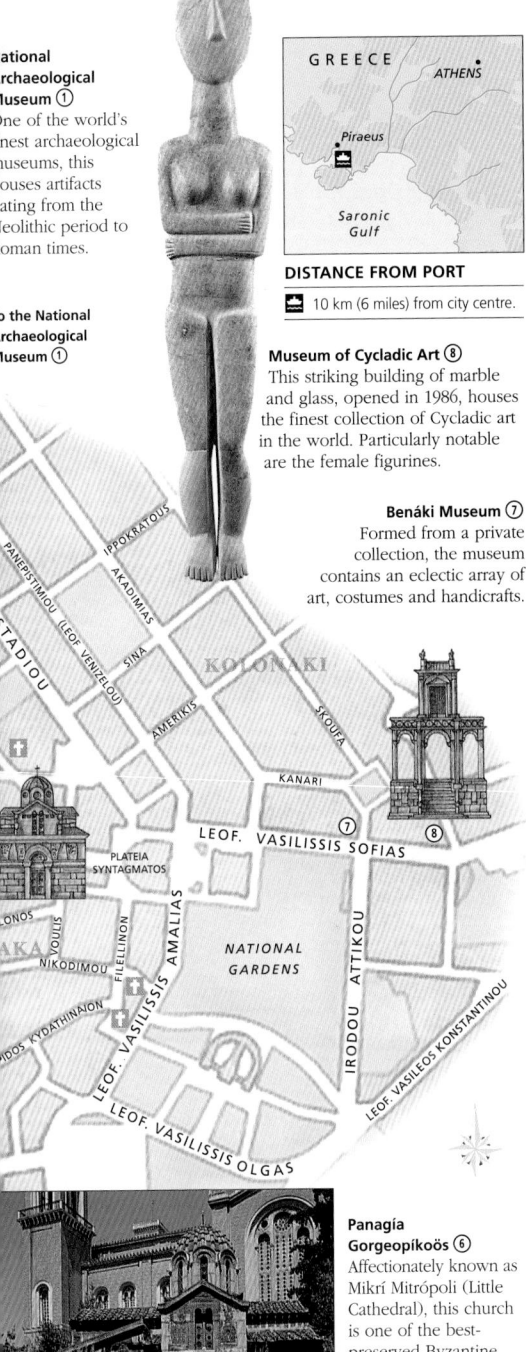

① National Archaeological Museum ★
② Kerameikós
③ Agora
④ Acropolis ★ *(see pp312–15)*
⑤ Tower of the Winds
⑥ Panagía Gorgeopíkoös
⑦ Benáki Museum
⑧ Museum of Cycladic Art ★

FACT FILE

TOURIST INFORMATION
7 Tsoha Street. ***Tel*** *(210) 870 70 70.* *Mon–Fri to 3pm*; summer: to 2:30pm.

MARKETS
Bric-à-brac Monastiraki Flea Market, Pandrossou Street; Sun.
Food Central Market, Athinas Street; daily.
Fruit & vegetables Xenokrátous, Kolonáki; Fri.

SHOPPING
Leather goods Bargain hunters should head for Mitropóleos, Ermou, Aiólou and nearby streets.
Jewellery World-class jewellers can be found along Stadíou and Panepistimíou.

LOCAL SPECIALITIES
Crafts
Hand-painted icons, jewellery, pottery, sandals.
Dishes
Sparángia kai agináres (artichoke hearts and asparagus).
Souvlákia (grilled pieces of pork and lamb).
Kotópoulo riganáto (Spit-roast chicken with oregano).
Pastéli (honey-sesame candy).
Drinks
Ouzo (aniseed-flavoured spirit).
Salépi (made from sesame seeds).
Retsina (wine flavoured with resin).

EXCURSIONS
Monastery of Dafne 10 km (6 miles) NW of Athens. 5th-century monastery with outstanding Byzantine mosaics.
Ancient Eleusis 22 km (14 miles) NW of Athens. Ruins of an ancient religious centre.

Athens: Acropolis ④

In the mid-5th century BC, Perikles persuaded the Athenians to begin a grand programme of new building work in Athens that has come to represent the political and cultural achievements of Greece. The most impressive building took place on the Acropolis. Here, a massive gateway led to the top of the rock, on which stood three temples in contrasting styles. The Theatre of Dionysos on the southern slope was developed further in the 4th century BC, and the Theatre of Herodes Atticus added some 400 years later.

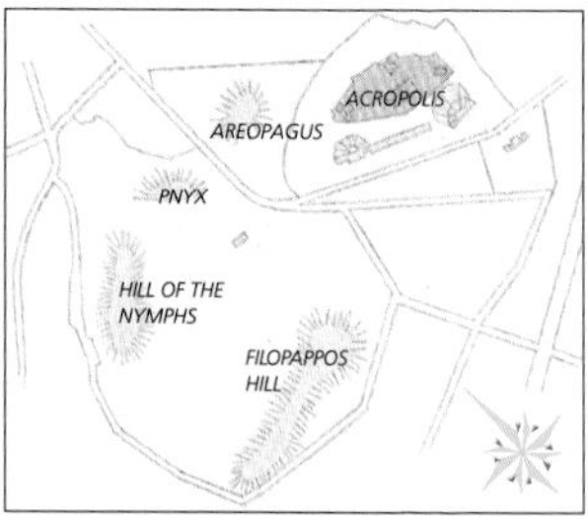

LOCATOR MAP

★ Porch of the Caryatids
Statues of women were used in place of columns on the south porch of the Erechtheion. The originals, four of which can be seen in the Acropolis Museum, have now been replaced by casts.

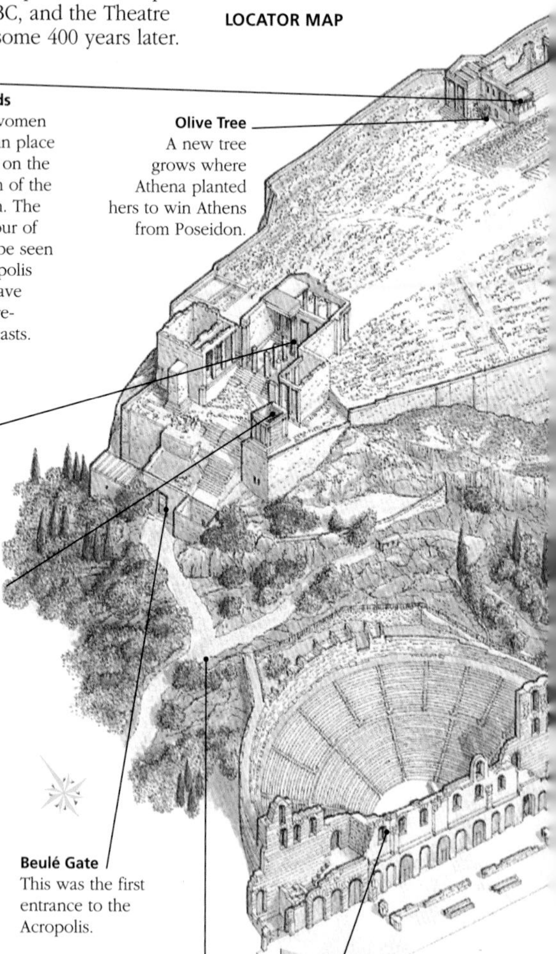

Olive Tree
A new tree grows where Athena planted hers to win Athens from Poseidon.

The Propylaia
Built in 437–432 BC, the Propylaia formed a new entrance to the Acropolis.

★ Temple of Athena Nike
A temple to Athena of Victory stands on the west side of the Propylaia. Built in 426–421 BC it was positioned so that it would overlook the vulnerable right side – soldiers carried their shields on their left arms – of anyone ascending.

Beulé Gate
This was the first entrance to the Acropolis.

Pathway to Acropolis from ticket office

Theatre of Herodes Atticus
Also known as the Odeion of Herodes Atticus, this superb theatre was originally built in AD 161 and was covered by a roof made from cedar. It was restored in 1955 for the Athens Festival, and is used today for outdoor plays and concerts.

★ Parthenon
Although few sculptures are left on this famous temple to Athena, some can still be admired in the Acropolis Museum.

STAR SIGHTS

- ★ Parthenon
- ★ Porch of the Caryatids
- ★ Temple of Athena Nike

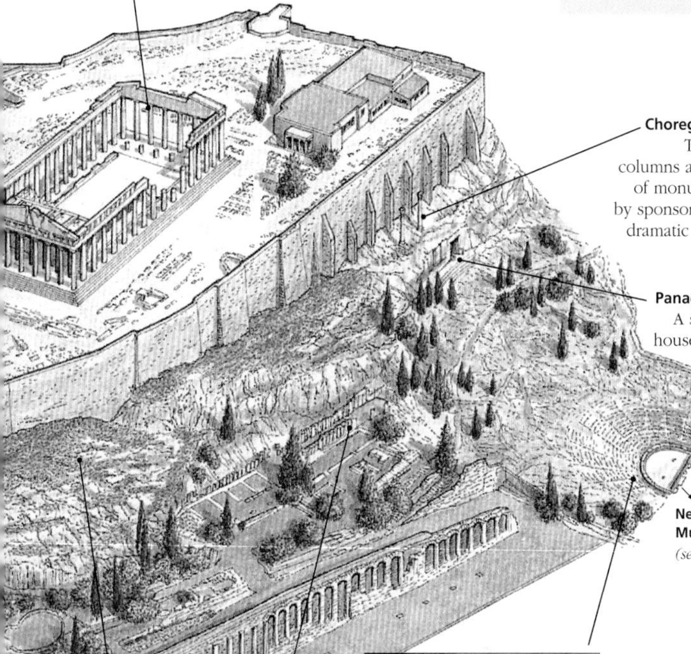

Choregic Monuments
Two Corinthian columns are the remains of monuments erected by sponsors of successful dramatic performances.

Panagía i Spiliótissa
A small chapel is housed in a cave in the Acropolis.

New Acropolis Museum
(see p315)

Shrine of Asklepios

Stoa of Eumenes

The Acropolis Rock
Easy to defend, this site has been occupied for nearly 5,000 years.

Theatre of Dionysos
Greek tragedy was born at this theatre. Initially a modest earth-and-wood structure, it was rebuilt and expanded in the 4th century BC, sporting figures such as this one of the satyr Silenus.

TIMELINE

3000 BC First settlement on the Acropolis during Neolithic period

480 BC All buildings of Archaic period destroyed by the Persians

AD 51 St Paul delivers sermon on Areopagus Hill

AD 267 Germanic Heruli tribe destroy Acropolis

St Paul

3000 BC | **2000 BC** | **1000 BC** | **AD 1** | **AD 1000**

1200 BC Cyclopean wall built to replace original ramparts

510 BC Delphic Oracle declares Acropolis a holy place of the gods, banning habitation by mortals

447–432 BC Construction of the Parthenon under Perikles

Perikles (495–429 BC)

AD 1687 Parthenon damaged by Venetians

AD 1987 Restoration of the Erechtheion completed

Athens: Exploring the Acropolis

Relief of *Mourning Athena*

Once through the first entrance, the Beulé Gate, straight ahead is the Propylaia, the grand entrance to the temple complex. Before going through, it is worth exploring the Temple of Athena Nike on the right. Beyond the Propylaia, dominating the top of the rock, are the Erechtheion and the Parthenon. Built as an expression of the glory of ancient Athens, the Parthenon remains the city's emblem to this day. From here, or anywhere on top of the Acropolis, there are stunning views across the city. Since 1975, access to all the temple precincts has been banned to prevent further damage.

View of the Acropolis from the southwest

Beulé Gate

The gate is named after the French archaeologist Ernest Beulé who discovered it in 1852. It was built in AD 267 after the raid of the Heruli, a Germanic people, as part of the Roman Acropolis fortifications. It incorporates stones used to build the choregic monument of Nikias, which was situated near the Stoa of Eumenes. Parts of the original monument's dedication are still visible over the architrave. There is also an inscription identifying a Roman, Flavius Septimius Marcellinus, as donor of the gateway. In 1686, when the Turks destroyed the Temple of Athena Nike, they used the marble to build a bastion for artillery over the gate.

Temple of Athena Nike

This small temple was built from 426 to 421 BC to commemorate Athens' victories over the Persians. The temple frieze has representative scenes from the Battle of Plataea (479 BC). Designed by Kallikrates, the temple stands on a 9.5-m (31-ft) high platform. It has been used as an observation post and ancient shrine to the goddess of Victory, Athena Nike, of whom there is a remarkable sculpture on the balustrade. Legend records the temple site as the place from which King Aegeus threw himself into the sea, believing that his son Theseus had been killed in Crete by the Minotaur.

The eastern end of the Erechtheion

Built of Pentelic marble, the temple has four 4-m (13-ft) high Ionic columns at each portico end. It was reconstructed between 1834 and 1838, after being destroyed in 1686 by the Turks. In 1935, it was again dismantled and reconstructed according to information resulting from extensive research.

Propylaia

Work began on this enormous entrance to the Acropolis in 437 BC. Although the outbreak of the Peloponnesian War in 432 BC curtailed its completion, its architect Mnesikles created a building admired throughout the ancient world. The Propylaia comprises a rectangular central building divided by a wall into two porticoes. These were punctuated by five entrance doors, rows of Ionic and Doric columns and a vestibule with a blue-coffered ceiling decorated with gold stars. Two wings flank the main building. The north wing was home to the *pinakothíki*, an art gallery.

During its chequered history – later as archbishop's residence, Frankish palace and Turkish fortress and armoury – parts of the building have been accidentally destroyed; it even suffered the misfortune of being struck by lightning in 1645 and, later, the explosion of the Turkish gunpowder store.

Erechtheion

Built between 421 and 406 BC, the Erechtheion is situated on the most sacred site of the Acropolis. It is said to be where Poseidon left his trident marks in a rock and Athena's olive tree sprouted in their battle for possession of the city. Named after Erechtheus, one of the mythical kings of Athens, the temple was a sanctuary to both Athena and Erechtheus-Poseidon.

Famed for its elegant and extremely ornate Ionic architecture and caryatid columns in the shape of women, this extraordinary monument is built on several levels. The large rectangular cella was divided into three rooms, one of which contained the holy statue of Athena Polias. The cella was bounded by north, east and south porticoes. The south is the Porch of the Caryatids, the maiden statues that are now in the Acropolis Museum.

The Erechtheion complex has been used for a range of purposes, including a harem for the wives of the Turkish *disdar* (commander) in 1463. It was almost completely destroyed by a Turkish shell in 1827 during the War of Independence. restoration has caused heated disputes: holes have been filled with new marble, and copies have been made to replace original features that have been removed to the safety of the museum.

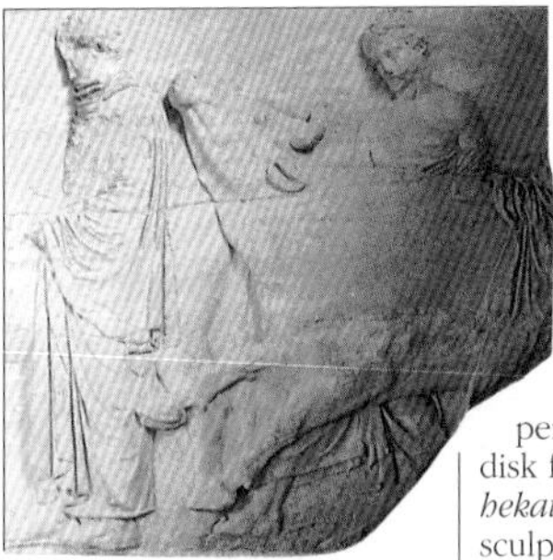

A youth leading a cow to sacrifice, from the Parthenon's north frieze

Acropolis Museum

Built below the level of the Parthenon, the Acropolis Museum lies in the south-east corner of the site. The Museum's collection is devoted to finds from the Acropolis. Treasures include fine statues from the 5th century BC and well-preserved segments of the Parthenon frieze. The museum also features a glass-floored gallery, which offers visitors the opportunity to observe on-going excavations in progress.

The collection begins on the ground floor gallery which displays archaeological finds from the sanctuaries and settlements that developed around the Acropolis. Of particular note are the vases and spindle whorls from the sanctuary of Nymphe and artefacts from the temple of Dyonysos Eleuthereus, which offer valuable insight into the ceremonies and traditions of ancient Greece.

The Archaic Gallery, on the first floor, is ordered chronologically starting with fragments of pediment statues dating from the 6th century BC. A scale model from the Mycenaean Period illustrates the significance of the Acropolis as a seat of political power and its use as a residential area. Exhibits from later periods, including a bronze disk from a temple roof and *hekatompedon* pediment sculptures show the change of status, of the Acropolis, into a religious centre. To the south side of the gallery is an impressive array of free-standing sculptures that date from the 5th-century BC and include depictions of young women (*korai*) and horse riders (*ippeis*).

The Parthenon gallery on the third floor offers stunning views over the surrounding area. On display, among other exhibits, is a well-preserved *metope* from the south side of the Parthenon, showing the battle between the Lapiths and centaurs. The remaining parts of the Parthenon frieze depict a *Panathenaic* procession including *apobates* (slaves riding the chariot horses), the *thallophoroi* (bearers of the olive branches) and a sacrificial cow.

The exhibition concludes by returning to a first floor gallery, which displays Roman copies of classical masterpieces.

The *Moschophoros* (Calf-Bearer), a sculpture from the Archaic period

THE ELGIN MARBLES

These famous sculptures, also called the Parthenon Marbles, are held in the British Museum in London. They were acquired by Lord Elgin between 1801 and 1803 from the occupying Turkish authorities. He sold them to the British nation for £35,000 in 1816. There is great controversy surrounding the Marbles. While some argue that they are more carefully preserved in the British Museum, the Greek government does not accept the legality of the sale and many believe they belong in Athens. A famous supporter of this cause was the Greek actress and politician, Melína Merkoúri.

The newly arrived Elgin Marbles at the British Museum, in a painting by A Archer

Corinth

Mosaic of Bacchus (Dionysos) in Acrocorinth

The ancient Greek city of Corinth – destroyed and rebuilt by the Romans – owed its prosperity to its position on the isthmus linking the Peloponnese to the Greek mainland. Under the patronage of the Roman emperors, the city grew to a population of 750,000 and acquired a reputation for licentious living. The modern town of Corinth – moved and repeatedly rebuilt after successive earthquakes – has little to attract the visitor, but the nearby ruins of the ancient city provide a striking testament to past glory. The remains of theatres, temples and public buildings draw visitors in their thousands to marvel at the Temple of Apollo and wander along the marble-paved Lechaion Way, the road that linked the city with the port of Lechaion. Above the ancient city, the fortified mountain of Acrocorinth affords magnificent views of the area. This was one of medieval Greece's most important fortresses, and the ruins of mosques, churches and towers scattered around the mountain serve as reminders of the various conquering nations that have occupied it.

KEY SIGHTS

Acrocorinth ★

Corinth Canal

Temple of Apollo ★

FACT FILE

TOURIST INFORMATION

Tourist Police, Ermou 51.
Tel (27410) 23282.
daily to 2pm.

LOCAL SPECIALITIES

Crafts
Thick cotton sweaters.
Produce
Olives, olive oil, currants.
Dishes
Stifado (beef with pearl onions).
Bardouniotiko (chicken stuffed with cheese, olives and walnuts).
Arni souvla (lamb on the spit).
Kokorétsi (offal on the spit).
Drinks
Mavrodaphne (dark, sweet wine).

EXCURSIONS

Heraion of Perachóra 15 km (9 miles) NW of Corinth. Ruins of 8th-century BC religious centre.
Ancient Neméa 28 km (17 miles) SW of town. Ruins of ancient Corinth with temple to Zeus dating from 4th century BC.

Acrocorinth
The mountain of Acrocorinth has been held and refortified by every occupying power in Greece since Roman times. Entry to the fortifications is through three gateways from different eras – Turkish, Frankish and Byzantine.

Corinth Canal
Plans to build a canal cutting through the 6-km (4-mile) wide isthmus near Corinth have existed since Roman times. However, it was not until the late 19th century that the 23-m (75-ft) wide waterway was completed.

Temple of Apollo
Built in 550 BC, this is among the most striking structures in Ancient Corinth. It was one of the few buildings preserved by the Romans when they rebuilt the site in 46 BC, having destroyed it 100 years earlier. Little now remains of the temple, apart from this cluster of Doric columns.

Mýkonos

Pétros the Pelican, the island mascot

Sandy beaches, a dynamic nightlife and plenty of sunshine have made this small, barren island one of the most favoured in the Cyclades. Tourism is the main source of income for the island. The first tourists began to arrive in the 1950s on their way to see the archaeological wonders on the island of Delos, and today Mýkonos's own charms have made it a hugely popular destination in its own right. The island's main town is the supreme example of a Cycladic village, built in a maze of narrow lanes to defy the wind and pirate raids. A tangle of dazzling, white alleys runs between cube-shaped houses up to Kástro, the oldest part of town, where the excellent Folk Museum is built on part of an ancient castle wall. Down by the water's edge at Little Venice (officially known as Alefkándra), the balconies of the houses jut out over the sea.

KEY SIGHTS

Folk Museum ★
Little Venice ★
Mýkonos Harbour
Panagía Paraportianí
Platýs Gialós beach

FACT FILE

TOURIST INFORMATION
Tourist Police, Municipality Building. *Tel (22890) 22482.* *daily to 10pm.*

FESTIVALS
Fishermen's festival (30 Jun).

LOCAL SPECIALITIES
Crafts
Jewellery, woven goods.
Produce
Kopanistí (cheese).
Dishes
Mykonic Mostra (a type of rusk with tomatoes and cheese).

EXCURSION
Delos 8-km (5-mile) boat trip from Mýkonos town. Tiny island with ruins of ancient religious centre – one of Greece's most important archaeological sites.

Mýkonos Harbour
The island's small but busy harbour is a popular destination for cruise ships. Taxi boats set off from here for the neighbouring island of Delos, taking visitors to see the ruins of what was once a major religious centre and thriving commercial port.

Platýs Gialós Beach
One of Mýkonos's best beaches, Platýs Gialós, lies 3 km (2 miles) south of Mýkonos town. Boasting water sports and a long sweep of sand, this is the main family beach on the island.

Panagía Paraportianí
So named because it was built on the site of the postern gate *(parapórti)* of a medieval fortress, this small, asymmetrical church consists of four chapels built at ground level, with another above. The earliest part of the church dates from 1425, while the rest was built in the 16th and 17th centuries.

Pátmos

Votive offerings from pilgrims to Pátmos

Quieter and more peaceful than many of the other Greek islands, Pátmos has managed to profit from tourism without losing its identity. The island is considered sacred by both Orthodox and Western Christians, as it was here that St John the Divine, writer of the book of Revelations, was exiled by the Roman emperor Domitian in AD 95. Nearly a thousand years later, a monastery to the saint was founded near present-day Chora, and grew to be one of the wealthiest and most influential in Greece. Today the monastery is the first place most tourists visit, after docking at the port of Skála. Pátmos has plenty to surprise and delight, from excellent beaches and a sophisticated nightlife to the historical treasures of Chora, such as the convent of Zoödóchou Pigís with its beautiful frescoes and peaceful gardens and the folk museum at the Venetian-style Simantiris House.

Skála
Curled around a wide, sheltered bay, Skála, the island's port and main town, provides a docking point for the many ferries, yachts and cruise ships that bring visitors to Pátmos. Exclusive gift shops and boutiques give the town a stylish, upmarket feel.

Holy Cave of the Apocalypse
Inside the church of Agía Anna is the cave in which St John lived and worked while he was on the island. The cave contains the rock on which the book of Revelations was written and an indentation where the saint is said to have rested his head.

KEY SIGHTS

Holy Cave of the Apocalypse
Monastery of St John ★
Simantiris House
Skála
Zoödóchou Pigís

FACT FILE

TOURIST INFORMATION
Skala Patmou. ***Tel** (22470) 31158.*
Sep–Jun: Mon–Fri to 2:30pm; Jul & Aug: daily to 9pm.

FESTIVALS
Niptír at the Monastery of St John (Maundy Thursday).
Panagía Kámpos (15 Aug).

LOCAL SPECIALITIES
Crafts
Hand-made jewellery, embroidery, hand-woven fabric.
Dishes
Pougia (sweets).
Melitzanes me revithia (aubergine/eggplant and chickpea casserole).

EXCURSION
Kámpos 5 km (3 miles) N of Skála. Settlement with beautiful Church of the Annunciation.

Monastery of St John
Founded in 1088 by the Blessed Christodoulos, this hilltop monastery is one of the wealthiest and most influential in Greece, and an important place of worship for Orthodox and Western Christians. From the cobbled main courtyard, doors lead off to rooms containing a wealth of religious treasures.

Santoríni

Rock carving in Ancient Thira

The name Santoríni was given to this island by the Venetians who arrived in the 13th century and named it after their patron saint, Saint Irene. The island was once part of a larger island called Strogyle, which was ripped apart in about 1450 BC by a massive earthquake and volcanic eruption about four times the size of Krakatoa. A huge volume of lava buried the town of Akrotíri, and the rush of water filling the caldera left by the explosion caused a huge wave that devastated Minoan Crete. In the 9th century BC, the Dorians, extending their empire from mainland Greece, settled on the crescent-shaped remains of the island calling their colony Thíra and establishing a capital on the headland of Mésa Vounó. Today's Santoríni is a stunning island, with its picturesque white villages clinging to volcanic cliffs above black-sand beaches. The island's capital, Firá, perches above the caldera, and the town's hotels and bars afford magnificent views, especially at sunset. Outside Firá, interesting archaeological sites, local wineries and small volcanic islands all wait to be explored.

Akrotíri
Some 3,500 years of burial under volcanic ash has preserved much of this former Minoan outpost on the southwestern tip of the island. Excavations have unearthed beautiful frescoes, as well as houses dating from the 16th century BC, many still containing huge storage jars.

Firá
Founded in the 18th century, when islanders moved from the Venetian capital of Skáros, Firá was rebuilt after it was devastated by an earthquake in 1956. Narrow, cobbled streets thread their way between characteristic domed churches and whitewashed houses.

KEY SIGHTS

Akrotíri ★
Ancient Thíra
Firá

FACT FILE

TOURIST INFORMATION
Pelican Travel, Central Square, Firá. ***Tel** (22860) 22220.* *daily to 9:30pm.*

FESTIVALS
Classical music, Firá (Aug–Sep).

LOCAL SPECIALITIES
Crafts
Pottery.
Produce
Kapari (spice).
Dishes
Pseftoketédes (fried balls of tomato, onion and bread).
Melitinia (cheese and honey pies).
Drinks
Visanto (sweet white wine).
Nichteri (dry white wine).

EXCURSION
Palaiá Kaméni 6-km (3-miles) boat trip from Firá. Small island with springs in which visitors can take a hot mud bath.

Ancient Thíra
Commanding the rocky headland of Mésa Vounó, the ruins of this ancient city date back as far as the 9th century BC. Here the remains of temples, private houses, an early Christian basilica and a theatre overlook the sea some 370 m (1,215 ft) below.

Rhodes: Rhodes Old Town

The town of Rhodes has been inhabited for more than 2,400 years. A city was first built here in 408 BC, and when the Knights of St John arrived in 1309 they built their citadel over these ancient remains. The Knights' medieval citadel, dominated by the towers of the Palace of the Grand Masters, forms the centre of the Old Town; the new town lies beyond the original walls. Of the walls' 11 gates, Koskinoú (St John's) gate, which leads into the Bourg quarter, has the best view of the city's defences. The Old Town is now a World Heritage Site.

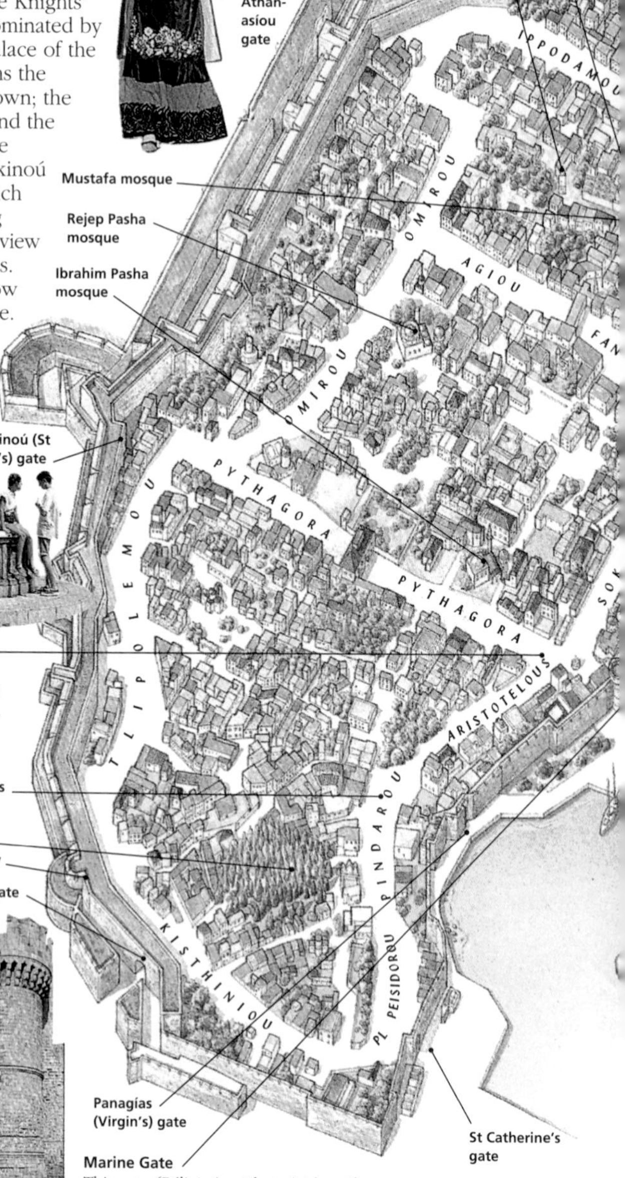

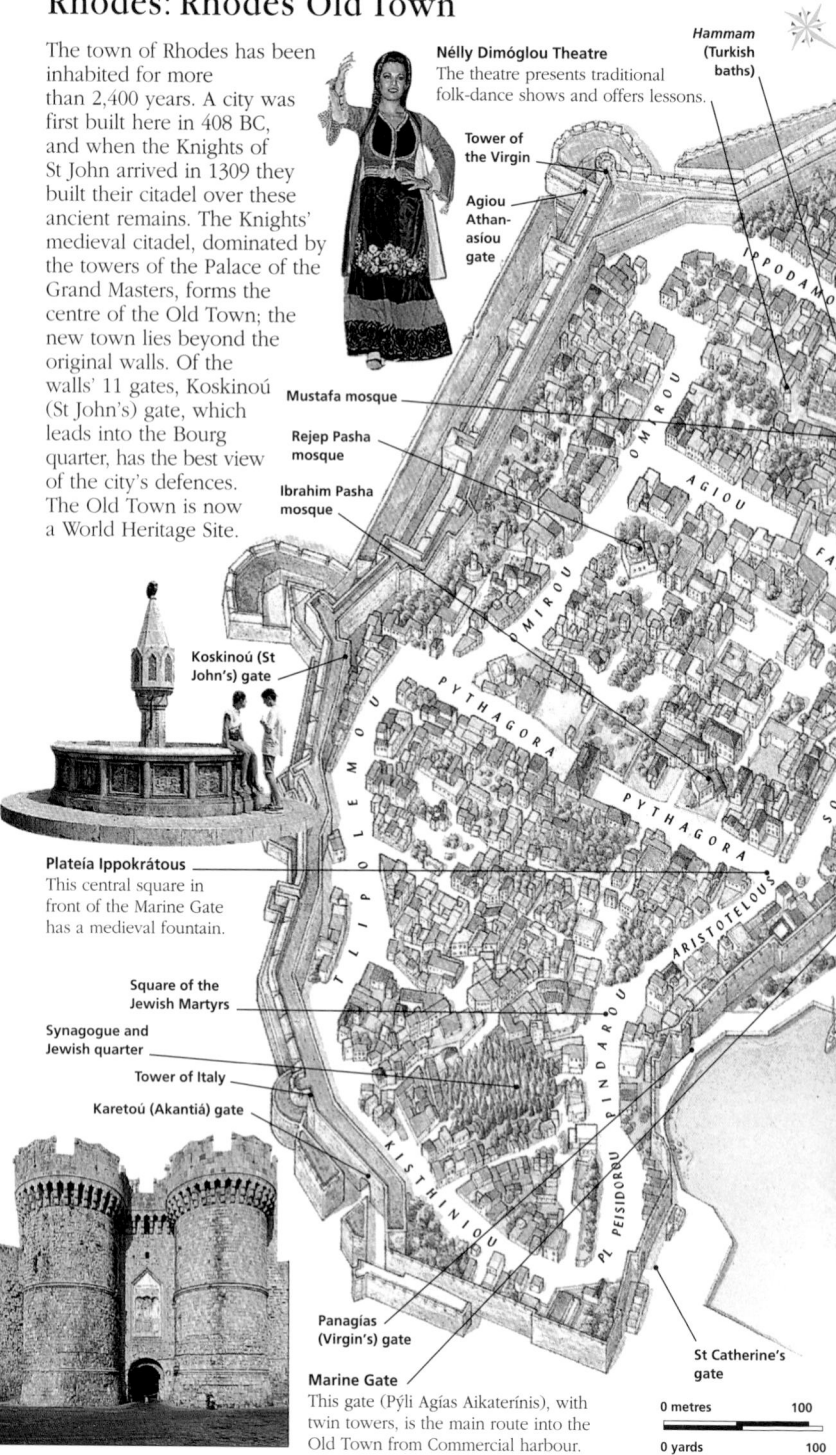

Nélly Dimóglou Theatre
The theatre presents traditional folk-dance shows and offers lessons.

Plateía Ippokrátous
This central square in front of the Marine Gate has a medieval fountain.

Marine Gate
This gate (Pýli Agías Aikaterínis), with twin towers, is the main route into the Old Town from Commercial harbour.

Mosque of Süleyman
First built in 1523, the mosque commemorates Süleyman's conquest of Rhodes.

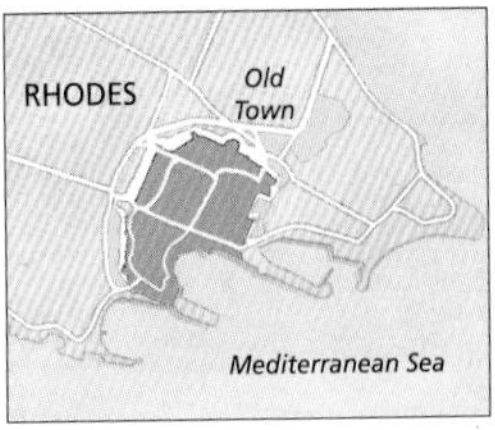

LOCATOR MAP

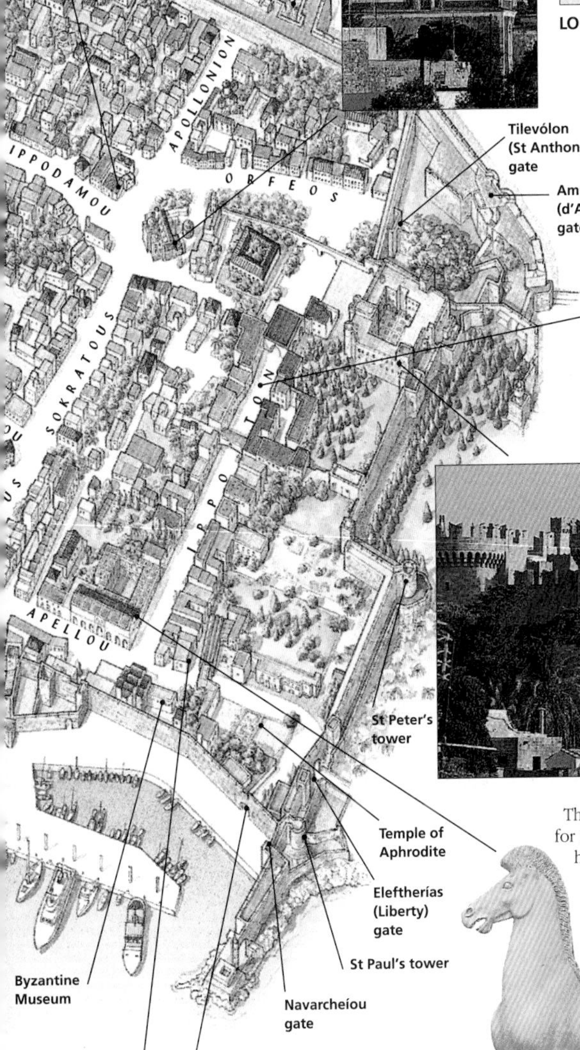

★ Street of the Knights
Lining this street are the Inns of the various Tongues, or nationalities, of the Knights. The austere gateway to the Inn of France is shown here.

★ Palace of the Grand Masters
This was the final line of defence for the Knights. The palace is now home to two permanent exhibitions about ancient and medieval Rhodes.

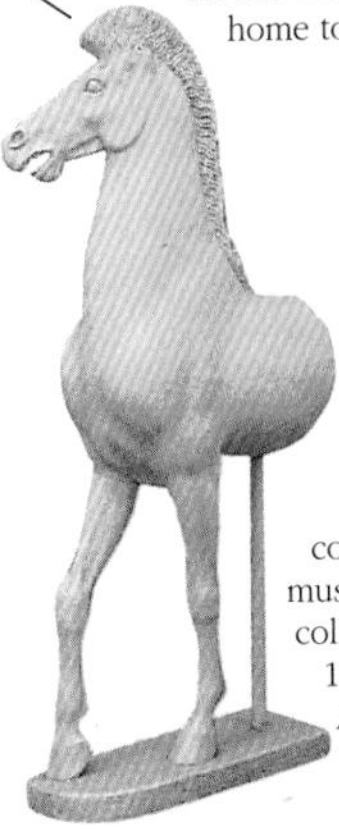

Archaeological Museum
Housed in the flamboyant Gothic Knights' hospital, completed in 1481, the museum displays a large collection, including the 1st-century BC marble Aphrodite of Rhodes, and this Hellenistic statue of a horse.

STAR SIGHTS

★ Street of the Knights

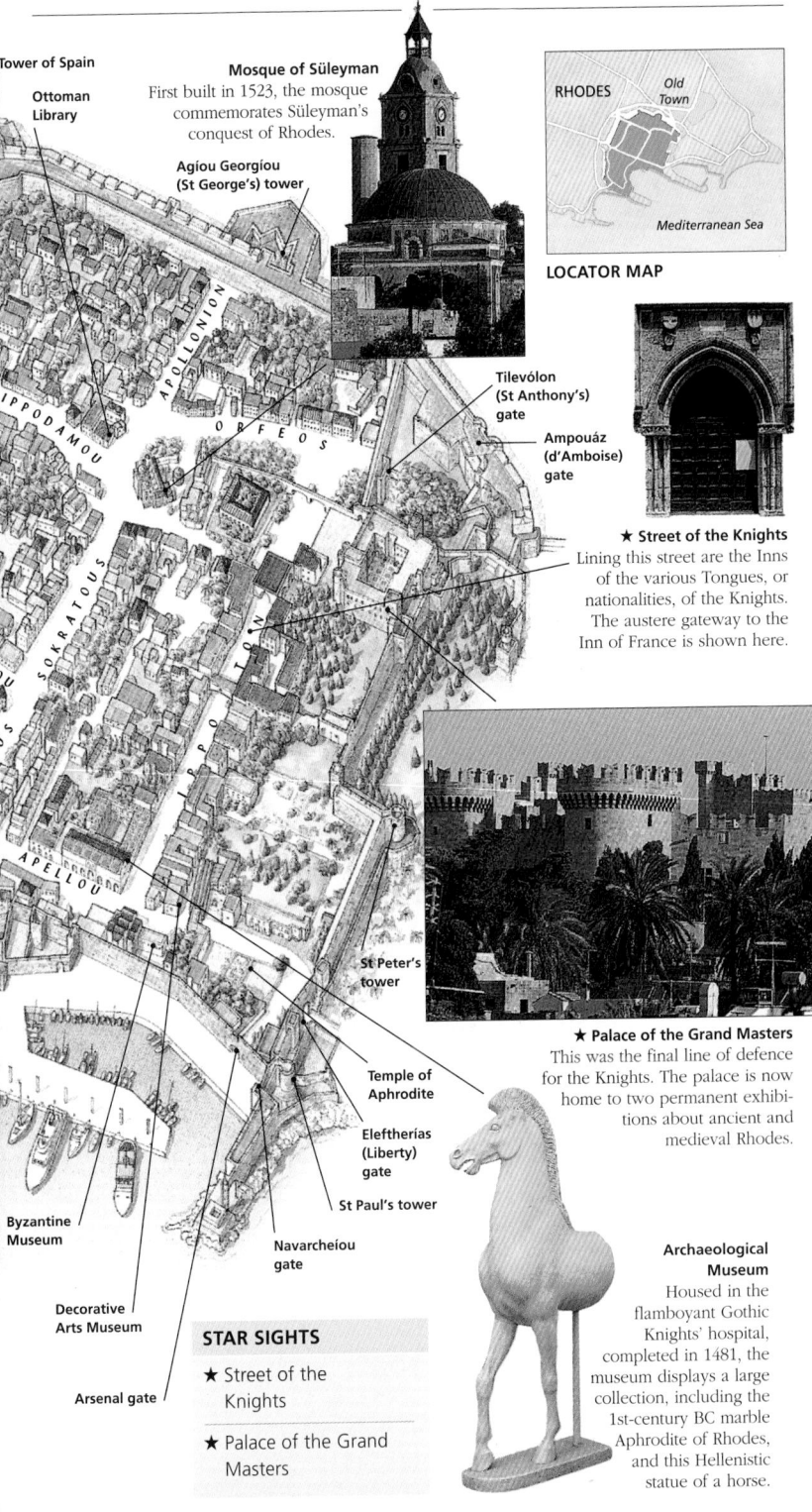

★ Palace of the Grand Masters

Crete: Irákleio

A settlement since the Neolithic era (about 7,000 years ago), Irákleio (Heraklion) served as the port for Knosós in Roman times. Under Venetian rule in the 13th century, it became known as Candia, the capital of the Aegean territories. In 1669, after withstanding a 21-year siege, the Venetians withdrew and the city fell to the Turks, who retained control for nearly 300 years until the Greek War of Independence united Crete with Greece. Today the sprawl of traffic-jammed streets and apartment buildings may detract from Irákleio's appeal. Yet, despite these first impressions, Crete's capital harbours a wealth of Venetian architecture, including the city walls and fortress. Its archaeological museum houses the world's greatest collection of Minoan art and the city provides easy access to the Palace of Knosós *(see pp324–5)*.

Venetian Fortress ①
Named *Rocca al Mare* by the Venetians and *Koulés* by the Turks, this large fortress at the northern end of Irákleio's old harbour was built between 1523 and 1540.

Historical Museum ②
Tracing the history of Crete, the Historical Museum contains sculptures, religious icons, friezes – including the 16th-century *The Prophets* – and archives from World War II.

Museum of Religious Art ⑥
Once a monastic foundation, the 16th-century Venetian church of Agía Aikateríni sof Sinai now houses the Museum of Religious Art. Among the Byzantine icons, frescoes and manuscripts are 16th-century icons painted by Michaíl Damaskinós, who taught El Greco.

EL GRECO

Domenikos Theotokopoulos (alias El Greco) was born in Crete in 1541 and by the time he had reached his early 20s he was a master painter. His style was rooted in the Cretan school of painting, an influence that permeates his extremely individualistic use of dramatic colour and elongated human forms. In Italy, El Greco became a disciple of the great Venetian painter, Titian, before moving to Spain. He died in 1614, and although his works can be seen in major collections around the world, only one of his paintings exists in Crete, at Irákleio's Historical Museum.

El Greco's *Landscape of Mount Sinai Trodden by the Gods* (c. 1570), Historical Museum

Agios Títos ③
Dedicated to Crete's patron saint, the church of Agios Títos was built by the Venetians in the 1500s. During the Turkish occupation, it was converted into a mosque, but has since been turned back into a church.

Irákleio Archaeological Museum ④
Finely carved stone vessels, exquisite jewellery and a magnificent bull's head rhyton (drinking vessel) are among the items in the vast collection of Minoan artifacts at Irákleio's Archaeological Museum.

Agios Minás ⑦
Built during the 19th century, the cathedral of Agios Minás towers over Plateía Agías Aikaterínis.

Morozini Fountain ⑤
Standing on Platéia Eleftheríou Venizélou at the heart of Irákleio, this ornate fountain was commissioned in 1628 by Francesco Morozini, then governor of the island.

KEY SIGHTS

① Venetian Fortress
② Historical Museum ★
③ Agios Títos
④ Irákleio Archaeological Museum ★
⑤ Morozini Fountain
⑥ Museum of Religious Art
⑦ Agios Minás

FACT FILE

TOURIST INFORMATION
Xanthoudidou 1.
Tel *(2810) 246298.*
Sep–Jun: daily to 3pm; Jul–Aug: daily to 8pm.

FESTIVALS
Summer Festival (Jul–Sep).

MARKETS
Fruit & vegetables Odos 1866, Irákleio; daily.

LOCAL PRODUCE
Cherries, oranges, olive oil, *Graviera* (cheese), *Mizythra* (creamy white cheese).

LOCAL SPECIALITIES
Crafts
Rugs, lace, religious icons, pottery, jewellery.
Dishes
Volvi (baked iris bulbs in olive oil and vinegar).
Choirinó kriticó (pork cutlets).
Saligkária (snails).
Salata kritiki (watercress salad).
Bougátsa (sweet pastry).
Sýka me tyrí (figs with cheese).
Loukoumádes (small deep-fried doughnuts).
Drinks
Gentilini (white wine).
Tsikoudia (raki, a local grain spirit).

EXCURSIONS
Tylissos 14 km (9 miles) SW of Irákleio. Remains of three large Minoan villas on the edge of the present-day village.
Archánes 16 km (10 miles) S of Irákleio. The town has ruins of a Minoan palace and an archaeological museum.
Vathýpetro 20 km (13 miles) S of Irákleio. Site of Minoan a villa, open mornings only.

Crete: Palace of Knossós

Built around 1900 BC, the first palace of Knossós was destroyed by an earthquake in about 1700 BC and was soon completely rebuilt. The restored ruins visible today are almost entirely from this second palace. The focal point of the site is its vast north–south aligned Central Court, off which lie many of the palace's most important areas. The original frescoes are in the Irákleio Archaeological Museum *(see p323)*.

View across the Central Court towards the northeast

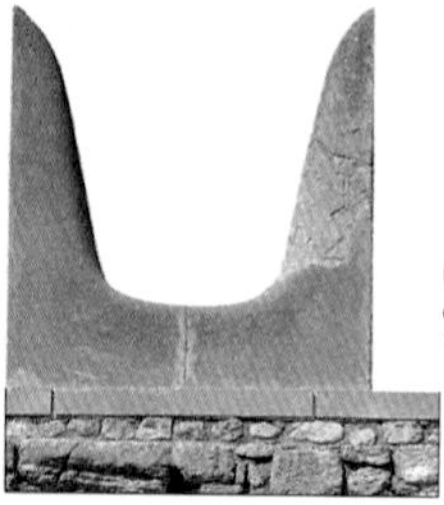

Horns of Consecration
Sitting on the south façade, these restored horns are a symbol of the sacred bull and would once have adorned the top of the palace.

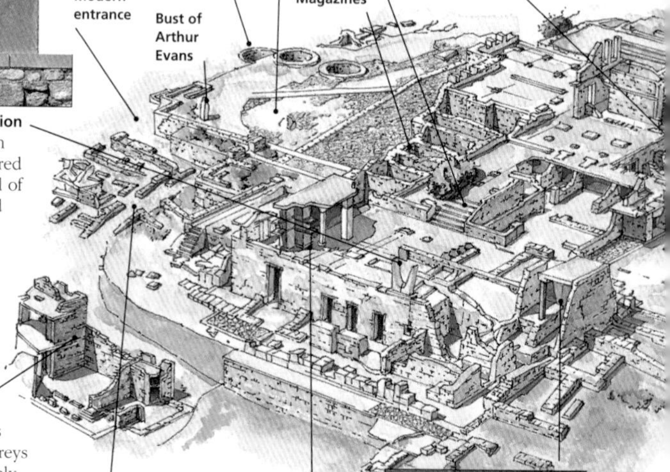

Tripartite Shrine
Formerly protected by a roof, this was one of many shrines facing on to the Central Court.

South House
Partly restored, this was once three storeys high. It was probably the residence of a palace official.

South Propylon
Entrance to the upper floor of the palace was through this pillared gateway. It is decorated with a replica of the Cup-Bearer figure, a detail from the fresco in the Corridor of the Procession.

★ Priest-King Fresco
This replica of the Priest-King fresco, also known as the Prince of the Lilies, is a detail from the Procession fresco and depicts a figure wearing a crown of lilies and feathers.

★ Throne Room

With its adjoining antechamber and lustral basin, the Throne Room is believed to have served as a shrine. The original stone throne, thought to be that of a priestess, is guarded by a restored fresco of griffins, which were sacred symbols in Minoan times.

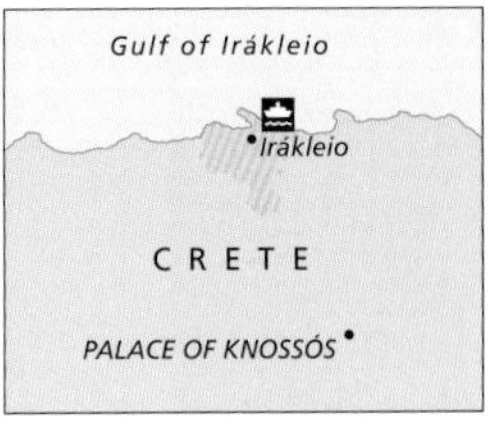

DISTANCE FROM PORT

40 km (25 miles) from city centre.

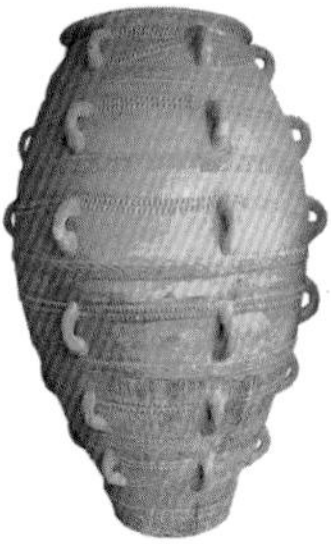

★ Giant Pithoi

Over 100 giant pithoi (storage jars) were unearthed at Knossós. The jars were used to store palace supplies.

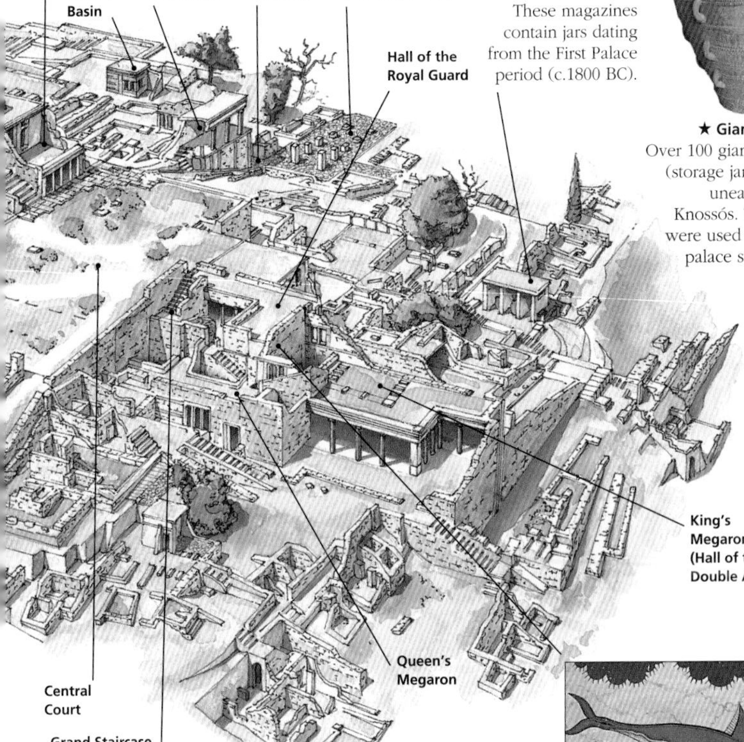

Giant Pithoi Magazines

These magazines contain jars dating from the First Palace period (c.1800 BC).

★ Royal Apartments

These rooms, built into the side of the hill upon which the palace stands, include the King's Megaron, also known as the Hall of the Double Axes. The Queen's Megaron is decorated with floral and animal motifs and has an adjoining bathroom. From the Central Court, the rooms were reached by the Grand Staircase.

STAR SIGHTS

- ★ Priest-King Fresco
- ★ Throne Room
- ★ Giant Pithoi
- ★ Royal Apartments

Olympia (Katakolo)

Detail from Pheidias' Workshop

Located at the confluence of the rivers Alfeiós and Kládeos, in a valley of pine, oak and olive trees, the Sanctuary of Olympia enjoyed over 1,000 years of esteem as a religious and athletics centre. Unlike other major archaeological sites in Greece, Olympia was never a great city, but the temples to Hera and Zeus – the latter's statue of the eponymous god was one of the seven wonders of the Ancient World – made it a place of great religious significance. In 776 BC the Olympian Games were founded here. Athletes from all over the Greek world would come every four years to compete in athletic events such as sprinting and wrestling. The games continued after the Roman invasion, but, in AD 393, they were banned by the Christian emperor Theodosius I. Soon afterwards, the sanctuary was abandoned until excavations began in the 19th century.

Olympia Archaeological Museum
Praxiteles' Classical statue of *Hermes* is just one of the ancient artifacts on display. The treasures exhibited date from the Prehistoric to the Roman eras, with the central hall dedicated to the pediment and *metope* sculptures from the Temple of Zeus.

DISTANCE FROM PORT

34 km (21 miles) from site.

KEY SIGHTS

Olympia Archaeological Museum ★

Palaestra

Temple of Zeus

FACT FILE

TOURIST INFORMATION

Praksitelous Kondili. ***Tel*** *(26240) 22262.* *Sep–Jun: Mon–Fri to 2:30pm; Jul & Aug: to 3:30pm.*

EXCURSION

Krestaena 12 km (7 miles) S of Olympia. Remains of Doric temples on outskirts of the village.

RECONSTRUCTION OF OLYMPIA (AD 100)
This shows Olympia as it was under the Romans. At that time the worship of Zeus predominated; the games were dedicated to him, and his temple was at the heart of the Olympian enclosure.

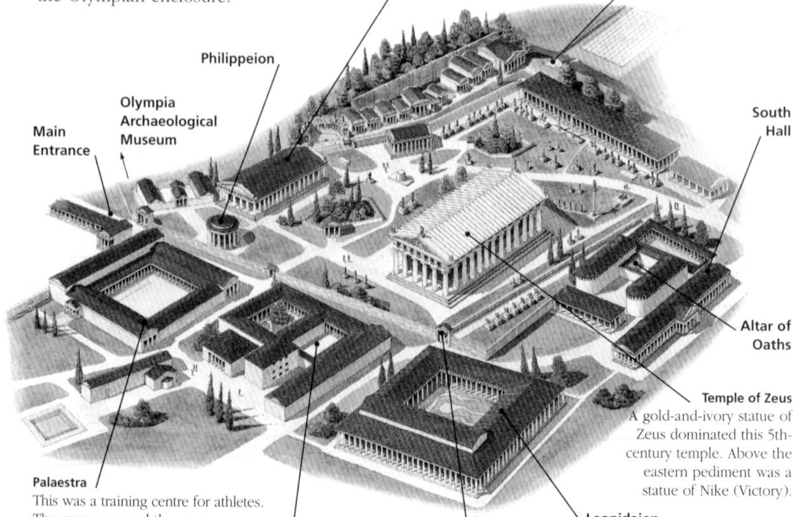
Temple of Hera
Begun in the 7th century BC, this was the third temple to the wife of Zeus built here.
Stadium Entrance
The vaulted ceiling over the entrance for athletes and jury members dates from the 3rd century BC.
Philippeion
Olympia Archaeological Museum
Main Entrance
South Hall
Altar of Oaths
Temple of Zeus
A gold-and-ivory statue of Zeus dominated this 5th-century temple. Above the eastern pediment was a statue of Nike (Victory).
Palaestra
This was a training centre for athletes. The rooms around the square were for bathing, teaching and socializing.
Pheidias' Workshop
Sanctuary entrance
Leonidaion

Corfu

Detail from Corfu Town Hall

Situated between the Greek mainland and Italy, Corfu offers the diverse attractions of secluded coves, busy resorts and traditional hill villages. Its position has given it a strategic importance, and over the centuries the island has been occupied by many invading powers; Romans, Byzantines, Venetians, French and British have all left their mark. Northern Corfu combines a rugged mountain interior with wild stretches of shoreline. In the northwest, beautiful beaches fringe a wooded headland at Palaiokastrítsa, making this one of the most popular spots on the island. Southern Corfu is less mountainous but more varied than the north; unspoiled villages dot the interior, while the lively resort of Benítses and the tranquil wildlife preserve of Korisíon Lagoon occupy opposite coasts. In Corfu town, the influences of the island's past can be clearly seen. Visitors can stroll between Italianate buildings, sip coffee in French-style colonnades or watch cricket by the Esplanade.

KEY SIGHTS

Achílleion Palace
Corfu Old Town ★
Kassiópi harbour
Korisíon Lagoon
Palaiokastrítsa coastline ★

FACT FILE

TOURIST INFORMATION

Alikes, outside new port.
Tel *(26610) 37520.*
Mon–Fri to 1:30pm.

MARKETS

Food New Fortress; daily.

LOCAL SPECIALITIES

Crafts
Olive-wood bowls.
Produce
Olive oil, kumquats.
Dishes
Pastítsio (pie with pasta and meat).
Sofríto (veal stew with wine vinegar, tomatoes and garlic).
Bourdetto (fish cooked with peppers and onions).
Bianco (whole fish served with potatoes and herbs).
Sikomaeda (fig pie).
Drinks
Mandolate (liqueur).

Maitland Rotunda
The Ionic memorial to Sir Thomas Maitland stands in the southern part of Corfu town's Esplanade. The unpopular Maitland was the first Lord High Commissioner to Corfu after the island became a British protectorate in 1814.

Kassiópi Harbour
Tavernas, shops and bars overlook the fishing boats moored in the unspoiled harbour at Kassiópi. The town has developed into one of Corfu's busiest holiday centres without losing either its charm or its character. A short walk to the west lie the ruins of a 13th-century castle.

Achílleion Palace
The stairs to the Achílleion Palace gardens lead to lush, tropical vegetation, colourful bougainvillea and numerous statues of Achilles, after whom the palace was named. The palace itself, built in the 19th century for the Empress Elizabeth of Austria, is rather less lovely, though it does contain some interesting artifacts.

Cyprus

Fought over by Persians and Greeks, Cyprus was finally captured by Ptolemy I of Egypt in 294 BC, with Páfos as the capital. This was the centre of the cult of Aphrodite, goddess of love, who was said to have been born from the sea nearby. Cyprus came under Roman rule from 58 BC to AD 395 and superb remains can be seen at Kourion and Páfos. The Byzantine era left exquisite frescoed churches, while fortifications remain from the periods of Frankish (1192 to 1453), Venetian (to 1571) and Ottoman (to 1878) rule. After independence from the British in 1960, conflict between the Greek and Turkish communities resulted in Turkish occupation of northern Cyprus in 1974. With the island still divided, southern Cyprus has made tourism its main source of income.

Tróödhos Mountains ④
Cyprus's highest point, Mount Olympus, lies in this extensive mountain range. Notable sights among the beautiful, forested scenery are nine frescoed Byzantine churches and the 11th-century Kýkko Monastery.

Akámas Peninsula ⑩
This rugged and very sparsely inhabited limestone area has some of the island's most beautiful scenery. Walking the nature trails is the ideal way to appreciate it.

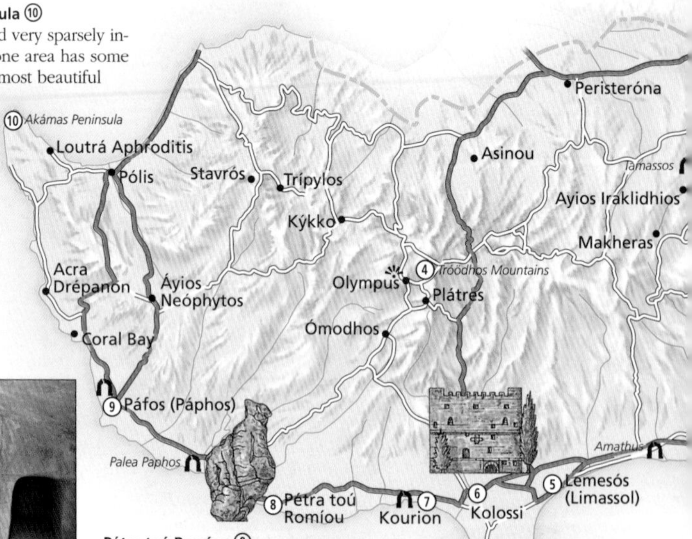

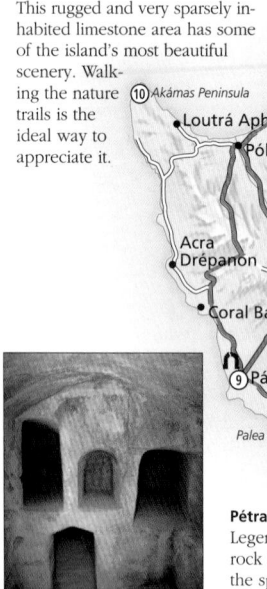

Páfos ⑨
The main attractions here are the wonderful floor mosaics of 2nd- and 3rd-century AD Roman villas and the rock-cut Tombs of the Kings, such as those above. These tombs were actually made for wealthy citizens, not kings, and date from the 3rd century BC to the 4th century AD.

Pétra toú Romíou ⑧
Legend says that this rock in the sea marks the spot where the Greek goddess Aphrodite emerged from the waves.

Kolossi Castle ⑥
The Knights of St John *(see p251)* built this castle in about 1210. The keep and courtyard date from their 15th-century renovations.

Lemesós ⑤
Southern Cyprus's chief port, this city is also the centre of its wine trade. Behind the Old Port is the castle, Lemesós's only surviving medieval building.

Kourion ⑦
This is the site of a great Greek and Roman city, among whose remains is this Roman theatre. Just 3 km (2 miles) away is the Sanctuary of Apollo Hylates, a highly revered site in Classical times.

Lefkosía ③
Famagusta Gate forms part of the Venetian city walls (1570) of Cyprus's capital, within which are the Cathedral and Icon Museum. The fine Archaeological Museum is in the New Town.

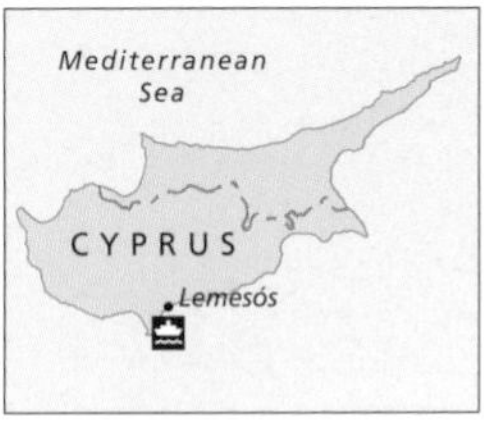

LOCATOR MAP

0 kilometres 15

0 miles 15

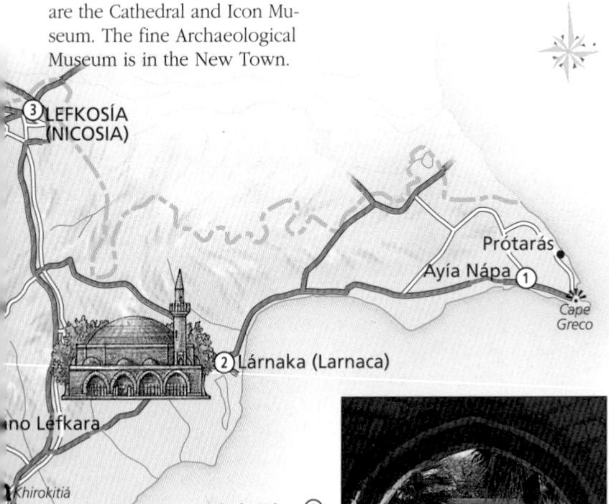

Ayía Nápa ①
The 16th-century monastery, with its attractive octagonal fountain, is an oasis of calm among Ayía Nápa's bars, nightclubs and restaurants.

Lárnaka ②
The early 10th-century Áyios Lázaros church is one of the few reminders of Lárnaka's past, along with Hala Sultan Mosque and the Turkish fort.

KEY SIGHTS

① Ayía Nápa
② Lárnaka ★
③ Lefkosía
④ Tróödhos Mountains ★
⑤ Lemesós
⑥ Kolossi Castle
⑦ Kourion ★
⑧ Pétra toú Romíou
⑨ Páfos ★
⑩ Akámas Peninsula

FACT FILE

TOURIST INFORMATION

Spyrou Araouzou 130, Lemesós. ***Tel*** *(25) 362756. ◻ Wed, Sat to 2:30pm; Mon, Tue, Thu, Fri to 6pm.*

MARKET

Fruit & vegetables Market Square, Lemesós; Mon–Sat am.

LOCAL SPECIALITIES

Crafts
Baskets, leather goods, pottery, lace, embroidery, silver filigree.

Dishes
Trahanás (wheat and yoghurt soup).
Afélia (pork in wine and coriander).
Tavás (lamb and tomato stew).
Stifádo (beef or hare with onion cooked in wine, vinegar and spices).
Halloúmi (minted ewes' cheese).
Mahlepi (rosewater syrup pudding).

Drinks
Red, white and rosé local wines.
Sherry (many local types).
Commandaria (sweet red wine).
Brandy sour (local brandy with lemon, angostura bitters and soda).

THE GREEN LINE

The demarcation line between the Greek and Turkish parts of Cyprus is known as the Green Line because, in 1974, a British officer drew the cease-fire line on a map with a green pencil. Visitors to Lefkosía (the capital of both territories) may obtain permits for day visits to the Turkish sector across the single crossing point, but not vice-versa. In the Greek sector, a stroll to view the artisans' workshops along the Green Line is popular with visitors exploring the Old Town.

Greek Mythology

The Greek myths that tell the stories of the gods, goddesses and heroes date back to the Bronze Age when they were told aloud by poets. They were first written down in the early 6th century BC and have lived on in Western literature. Myths were closely bound up with Greek religion and gave meaning to the unpredictable workings of the natural world. They tell the story of the creation and the "golden age" of gods and mortals, as well as the age of semi-mythical heroes, such as Theseus and Herakles, whose exploits were an inspiration to ordinary men. The gods and goddesses were affected by human desires and failings and were part of a divine family presided over by Zeus. He had many offspring, both legitimate and illegitimate, each with a mythical role.

Hades and Persephone were king and queen of the Underworld (land of the dead). Persephone was abducted from her mother Demeter by Hades, but was later permitted to return for six months of every year.

Poseidon, the brother of Zeus and Hades, was given control of the seas and the trident is his symbol of power. He was married to the sea-goddess Amphitrite, to whom he was not entirely faithful. This statue is from the National Archaeological Museum in Athens *(see p311)*.

Zeus was the father of the gods and ruled over them and all mortals from Mount Olympos.

Eris was the goddess of strife.

Clymene, a nymph and daughter of Helios, was mother of Prometheus, creator of mankind.

Hera, sister and wife of Zeus, was famous for her jealousy.

Athena was born from Zeus's head in full armour.

Paris was asked to award the golden apple to the most beautiful goddess.

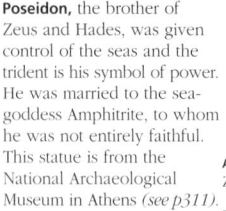

Paris's dog helped him herd cattle on Mount Ida where the prince grew up.

A DIVINE DISPUTE

This vase painting shows the gods on Mount Ida, near Troy. Hera, Athena and Aphrodite, quarrelling over who was the most beautiful, were brought by Hermes to hear the judgment of a young herdsman, the Trojan prince, Paris. In choosing Aphrodite, he was rewarded with the love of Helen, the most beautiful woman in the world. Paris abducted her from her husband Menelaos, King of Sparta, and thus the Trojan War began.

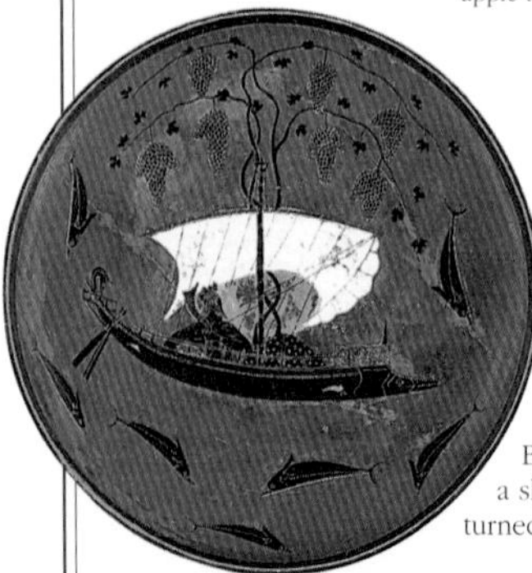

Dionysos, god of revelry and wine, was born from Zeus's thigh. In this 6th-century BC cup, beautifully painted by Exekias, he reclines in a ship whose mast has turned into a vine.

Artemis, the daughter of Zeus and twin sister of Apollo, was the virgin goddess of the hunt. Although sworn to chastity, she was also the goddess of childbirth, and is said to have helped deliver her brother, having been born slightly before him.

Happiness, here personified by two goddesses, waits with gold laurel leaves to garland the winner. Wreaths were the prizes in Greek athletic and musical contests.

Helios, the sun god, drove his four-horse chariot (the sun) daily across the sky.

Aphrodite, the goddess of love, was born from the sea. Here she has her son Eros (Cupid) with her.

Hermes was the gods' messenger.

Apollo, son of Zeus and brother of Artemis, was god of healing, plague and also music. Here he is depicted holding a lyre. He was also famous for his dazzling beauty.

THE LABOURS OF HERAKLES

Herakles (Hercules to the Romans) was the greatest of the Greek heroes, and the son of Zeus and Alkmene, a mortal woman. With superhuman strength, he achieved success, and immortality, against seemingly impossible odds in the "Twelve Labours" set by Eurystheus, King of Mycenae. For his first task he killed the Nemean lion, and wore its hide ever after.

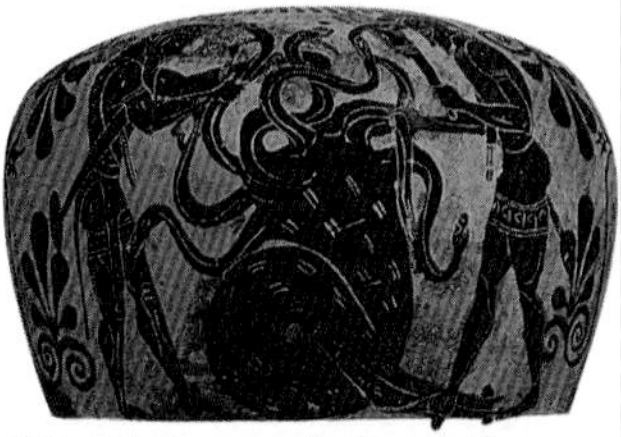

Killing the Lernaean hydra was the second labour of Herakles. The many heads of this venomous monster, raised by Hera, grew back as soon as they were chopped off. As in all his tasks, Herakles was helped by Athena.

The huge boar that ravaged Mount Erymanthus was captured next. Herakles brought it back alive to King Eurystheus who was so terrified that he hid in a storage jar.

Destroying the Stymfalían birds was the sixth labour. Herakles rid Lake Stymfalía of these brass-beaked, man-eating birds by stoning them with a sling, having first frightened them off with a pair of bronze castanets.

Aerial view of Dubrovnik, Croatia ▷

CROATIA

DUBROVNIK 334–335

Dubrovnik

Onofrio's Fountain

This architecturally unique city arose in the 12th century when the 7th-century islet settlement of Ragusa merged with the town of Dubrovnik on the mainland. The sea channel between them was filled in to become the marble-paved main street, Placa Stradun. Later, encircling ramparts were built, which remain the most complete in Europe. Dubrovnik prospered through trade until 1667, when an earthquake destroyed most of it, except for the Renaissance Pile Gate and Sponza Palace. The beautiful, red-tiled city that was rebuilt has now been largely restored after the 1991–2 shelling in the Yugoslav civil war.

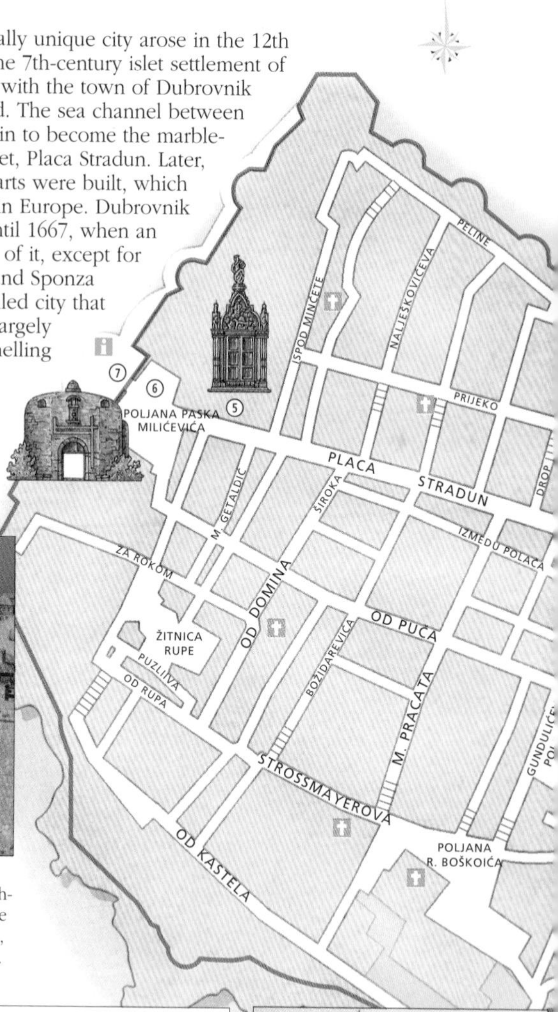

Onofrio's Fountain ⑥
A celebrated symbol of the city, this 1438 fountain was part of a supply system bringing water from a well 12 km (8 miles) away.

City Walls and Pile Gate ⑦
Access to the massive 15th- to 16th-century fortifications encircling the Old Town is next to the Pile Gate, which carries a statue of St Blaise.

KORČULA ISLAND

This island northwest of Dubrovnik is favoured by holiday-makers for its coves, villages, woods, vineyards and the still-flourishing traditional music and dance. Most famous is the Moreška Sword Dance, performed on Thursdays in July and August. The main town is Korčula in the northeast, built on a peninsula. At its tip is the medieval old town with defensive towers and a fine cathedral. Opposite, the 15th-century Gabriellis Palace houses the city museum. In Depolo Street stands the tower house, in which it is tenuously claimed that Marco Polo was born in 1254.

Korčula's Moreška Sword Dance

Cathedral of the Assumption of the Virgin ①
Completed in 1713, this Baroque church has a rich treasury. The exhibits include medieval and Renaissance gold and silver reliquaries, one holding the relics of St Blaise.

Franciscan Monastery ⑤
The portal, with a fine *Pietà* sculpted in 1498, and the 14th-century cloister are all that survived the 1667 earthquake. The rest of the monastery was rebuilt. Inside is a pharmacy that has been in business since 1317.

Dominican Monastery ④
The fortress-like exterior hides a 15th-century, Dalmation Gothic-style cloister. The monastery also has a museum with a fine collection of religious paintings.

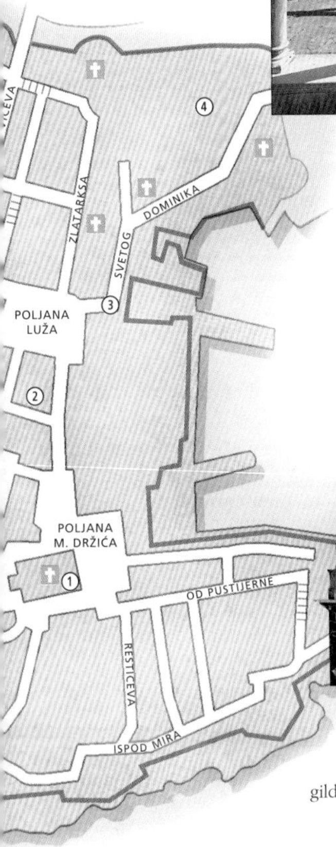

Church of St Blaise ②
Dating from 1715, this church is in ornate Baroque style. Inside, a 15th-century, gilded statue of St Blaise, patron saint of Dubrovnik, holds a model of the medieval city.

0 metres 75
0 yards 75

Sponza Palace ③
First a customs house and then a mint, this fine, 16th-century building has a Renaissance portico and second-floor windows, with Gothic windows on the first floor. The palace is now occupied by the State Archives.

KEY SIGHTS

① Cathedral of the Assumption of the Virgin
② Church of St Blaise
③ Sponza Palace
④ Dominican Monastery ★
⑤ Franciscan Monastery
⑥ Onofrio's Fountain ★
⑦ City Walls and Pile Gate ★

FACT FILE

TOURIST INFORMATION

Brsalje 1.
Tel *(020) 323 887.* ☐ *Mon–Sat to 8pm, Sun to 1pm.*

MARKETS

Food Gundulićeva Poljana; daily.

LOCAL SPECIALITIES

Crafts
Lace, embroidery.
Dishes
Brodet (rice and mixed fish stew).
Pržene lignje (fried squid in breadcrumbs). *Pršut* (Dalmatian smoked ham). *Purica s mlincima* (a turkey and pasta dish).
Pašticada (stuffed beef roasted in wine and herbs).
Čevapčići (spicy beef or pork meatballs).
Orehnjača (walnut roll dessert).
Rozata (créme caramel).
Drinks
Opolo, Merlot, Postup, Dingač, Teran, Plavac (coastal red wines).
Malvazija, Pošip, Pinot, Kujundžuša, Muškat, Grk (coastal white wines).
Prošek (dark, sweet dessert wine).
Travarica (herb-flavoured spirit).
Loza (clear, strong grape spirit).

EXCURSIONS

Elafiti Islands 8 km (5 miles) NW of Dubrovnik. Quiet archipelago. The most popular islands are Koločep, Lopud and Šipan.
Cavtat 13 km (8 miles) SE of Dubrovnik. Historic town and harbour. Monastery with good art collection.
Zaton 18 km (11 miles) NW of Dubrovnik. Town on a quiet, sandy bay, once the summer resort of Dubrovnik's aristocracy.
Korčula Island 85 km (53 miles) NW of Dubrovnik. Attractive wine-growing island with sandy beaches.

Passengers relaxing on sun deck ▷

SURVIVAL GUIDE

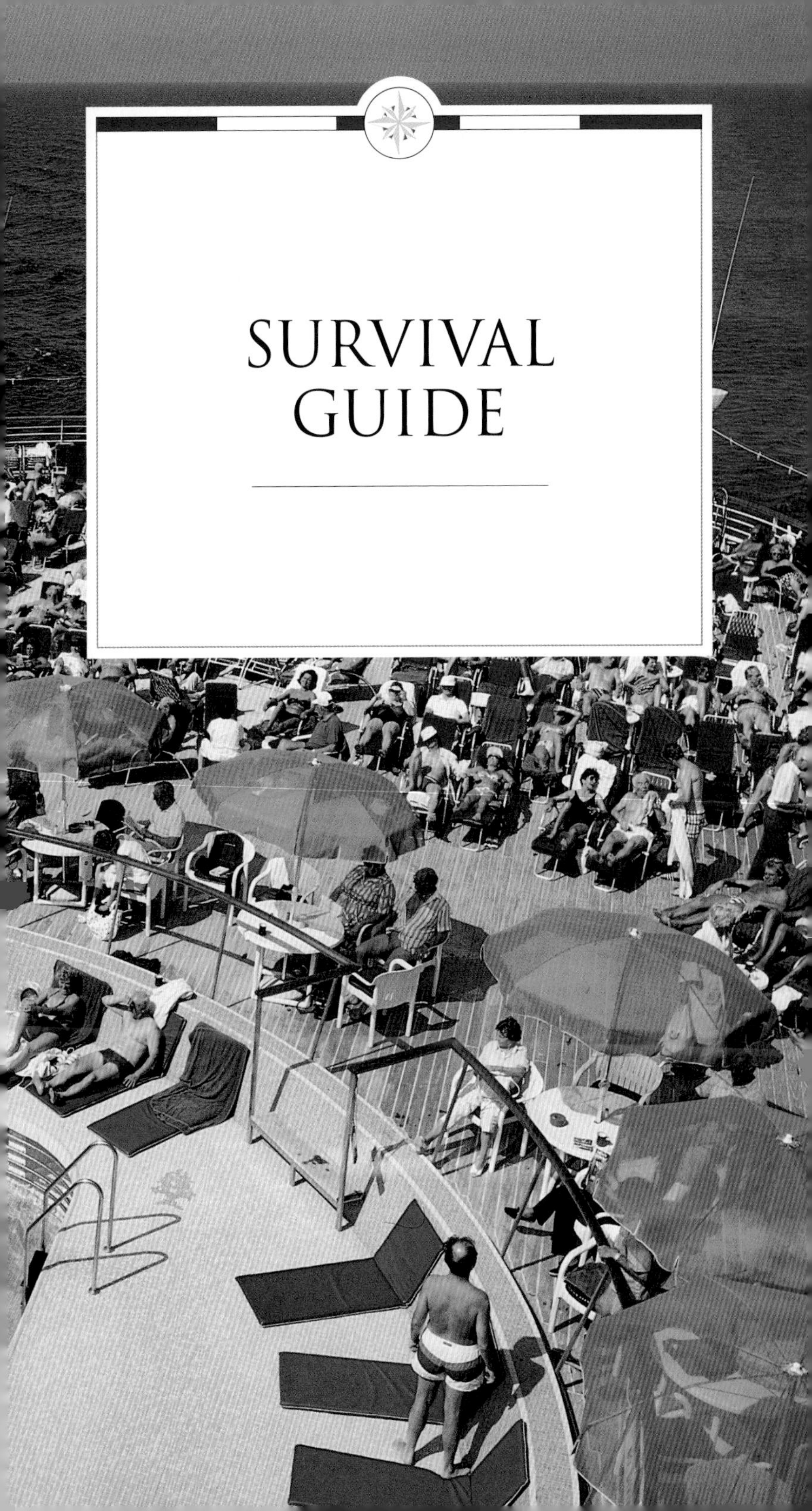

PLANNING AND BOOKING A CRUISE

It is possible to cruise all year round in Europe and the Mediterranean, with itineraries covering destinations from Scandinavia in the north to North Africa and the Middle East in the south. There is much more choice in the summer months as demand is higher, and some itineraries do not run during the winter. Passengers can catch a flight from almost anywhere in the world and join their ship in a major port, such as Barcelona, Dover, Venice or Piraeus.

As there is so much choice, it is worth doing as much research as possible – the Directory on page 339 gives some useful contact details. When it comes to booking a cruise, shop around for the best possible prices – there are hundreds of special deals being offered by cruise operators and travel agents.

RESEARCH

Requests for information can be made, by telephone or via the Internet, either directly to the cruise operators or to travel agents that specialize in cruise holiday packages. Bookings can also be made directly with the cruise lines or the agents, and both also produce a huge number of brochures and other promotional material.

The Internet is a valuable source of information about cruising, with cruise lines' and travel agents' websites usually supplying information about current programmes and giving telephone numbers for reservations. Increasingly, websites allow bookings to be made online. Some sites offer a virtual-reality tour of a ship, while some have webcams on their ships that provide live pictures direct from the bridge.

WHAT THE PRICE INCLUDES

Cruise prices may seem expensive, but, given that they always include accommodation, all meals, many non-alcoholic drinks, transportation, entertainment and, in a few cases, a limited number of shore excursions *(see pp354–7)*, it is clear that a cruise holiday offers excellent value for money. However, passengers should always pay close attention to what they have paid for. Reputable cruise companies will make it plain which items are and are not included in the price of the cruise and, by law, advertised charges should include all pre-payable taxes, such as passenger service charges.

If flights are part of the package, then airport tax and airport and port transfers should be included in the price too. Normally, passengers should expect to pay additionally for items such as holiday insurance, alcoholic drinks, port taxes, most shore excursions and personal items such as hairdressing, beauty treatments and being photographed by the ship's photographer. Some cruise lines, however, are beginning to offer "all-inclusive" deals, which usually means that all gratuities and drinks on board

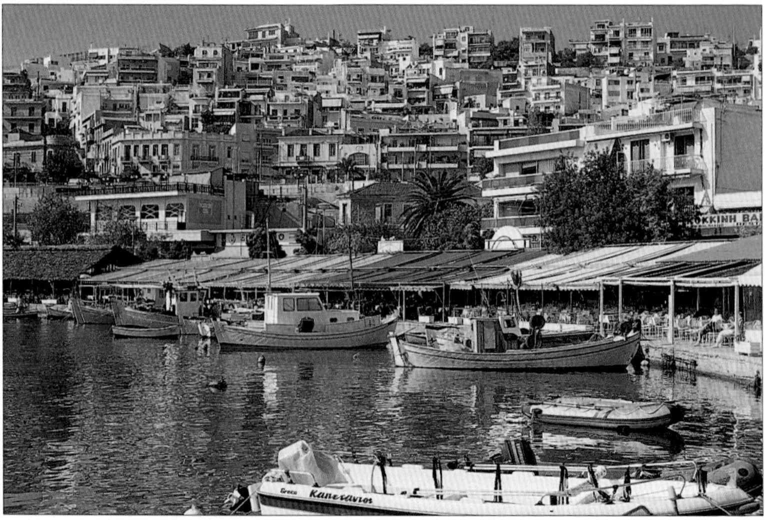

Piraeus, Greece, a typical transfer destination for those on "fly-cruise" holidays

Coaches transferring passengers to a waiting cruise ship

are included in the price, at least until the bars close. Optional shore excursions are the exception, and most must be paid for separately. A number of cruise operators supply details of shore excursions to passengers in advance of the cruise and prefer them to pre-book and pre-pay for any excursions that interest them. Others cruise operators prefer passengers to book and pay for excursions only once on board ship.

For cruises departing from a foreign port, "fly-cruise" prices should always include return air travel, airport and port transfers and airport taxes. Nevertheless, it is important that passengers take great care to check this. Some miscellaneous port charges are very often not included, and these unexpected extras can sometimes amount to a suprisingly large sum.

Gratuities *(see p346)* are another area about which passengers need to be clear – these have always been something of a bone of contention among cruise-goers, with considerable confusion as to whether tips are required or not. On some ships gratuities are included in the price, but there is evidence that this may cause standards of personal service to slip. On other ships a compulsory sum is added to passengers' accounts. Other ships leave tipping to the discretion of passengers, though guidelines are offered on how much it is appropriate to pay to whom, and when.

SPECIAL DEALS

One of the golden rules of buying cruises is to shop around. The cruising market is highly competitive and discounts, early-booking reductions and other incentives are commonplace. Many cruise lines offer some form of early-booking discount, while others have been known to offer late discounts if there are still empty berths as the sailing date approaches. In addition, offers of free or half-price cabin upgrades are very popular methods of encouraging early bookings. Cruise-specialist travel agents often have their own incentives, made possible by increased commission and special bulk contract rates with preferred suppliers. These can vary from generous "two for the price of one" deals to free cabin upgrades, free holiday insurance or free taxis to a local airport. For those on "fly-cruises" who like to travel in style it is worth enquiring about supplements for flying in business class or first class. Many cruise companies have special arrangements with their partner airlines, which enable them to offer some exceptional deals for upgraded air travel.

CHILDREN

Some cruise lines are in the business of encouraging families with children *(see p17)* to take cruise holidays, and some ships even have facilities for young children, such as kids' clubs, as well as high chairs and special menus in the restaurants. More exclusive and traditional companies tend to discourage passengers under the age of 18. No cruise ship is really suitable for babies and toddlers.

DIRECTORY

USEFUL CONTACT NUMBERS

American Society of Travel Agents (ASTA)
Tel 703 739 2782.
www.astanet.com

Association of British Travel Agents (ABTA)
Tel 020 7637 2444.
www.abta.com

Association of Canadian Travel Agents
Tel 613 237 3657.
www.acta.net

Cruise Lines International Association (CLIA)
www.cruising.org

Guild of Professional Cruise Agents
www.thelca.com

Passenger Shipping Association Retail Agent Scheme (PSARA)
Tel 020 7436 2449.
www.psa-psara.org

OTHER USEFUL WEBSITE ADDRESSES

www.cruise.com

www.cruisecommunity.com

www.seacruisevacation.com

www.cybercruises.com

www.i-cruise.com

www.seaview.co.uk

(For more details on how to contact cruise lines, see the Directory of Cruise Lines on pages 360–65.)

Choosing a Cabin

Although passengers will probably not spend that much time in their cabin, choosing the right accommodation is the single most important decision they will make. Cabins come in all shapes and sizes; a good rule of thumb is to opt for the best category that the budget will allow. If the budget permits, an outside cabin, one with a window or porthole, is well worth the extra cost. The window will prove worthwhile if seasickness is a worry, and it is always good to be able to look out when the ship is near land. In general, study the deck plan carefully to check the location of cabins in relation to the ship's facilities.

Enjoying the luxury of a room with its own private balcony

CABIN GRADINGS

If cruising for the first time, passengers should be wary of terms such as superior or deluxe, as they are only ever relative. Some ships will simply have a better standard of cabins across the full range of cabin grades than others, so the best way to guarantee value for money, and that the cabin is up to standard, is to compare like with like when looking at brochures.

As a general rule, larger ships offer a wider variety of accommodation. The more you pay, the larger the cabin and the better its position. Economy accommodation is often a small cabin in the depths of the ship, with two (sometimes four) berths and a bathroom. There is usually a choice of outside or inside cabin, window or no window. Unless your budget is really tight, it is best to avoid the lowest grades of cabin.

Better cabins are situated on the higher decks and most offer more space. A standard cabin of this type will often have large windows allowing good views, and sometimes a small balcony; cabins of this type are sometimes known as "staterooms". The highest category of accommodation are suites, which have the most space and furniture, a separate lounge area and often a balcony with chairs and a table. Suite accommodation on some cruise lines may also include butler service.

Butler service, available with some of the most luxurious suites

CABIN PLANS

Most cruise line brochures will have diagrams showing the types of cabins found on each of their ships. These are very useful as they show exactly what furniture and how much space there is in each cabin type, and will also allow passengers to see exact differences between similar cabin types on different ships.

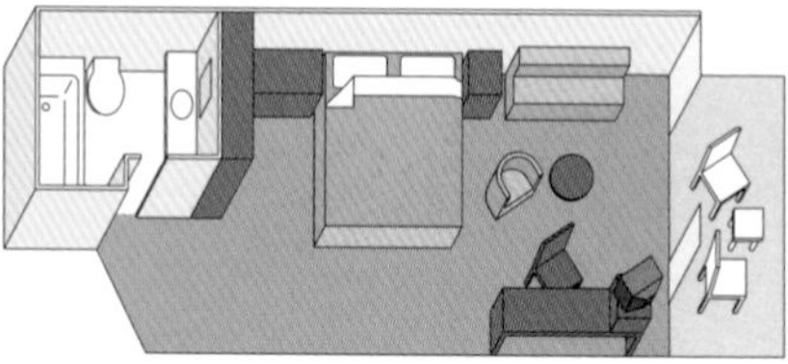

Standard cabin, or stateroom, with king-size bed and seating area

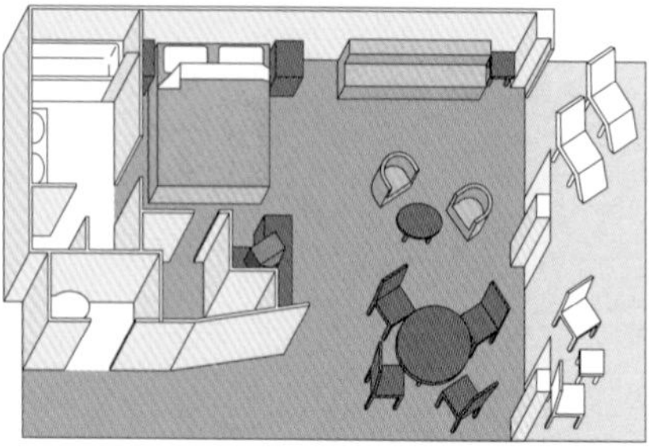

Balcony suite with separate bedroom and seating area

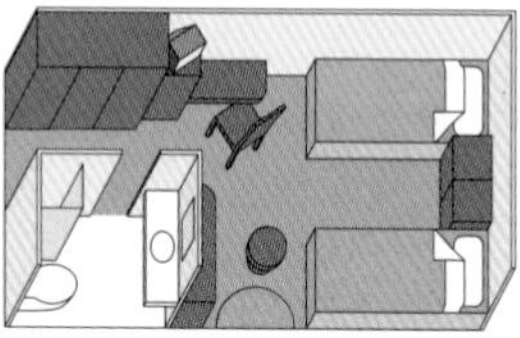

Economy cabin with twin beds

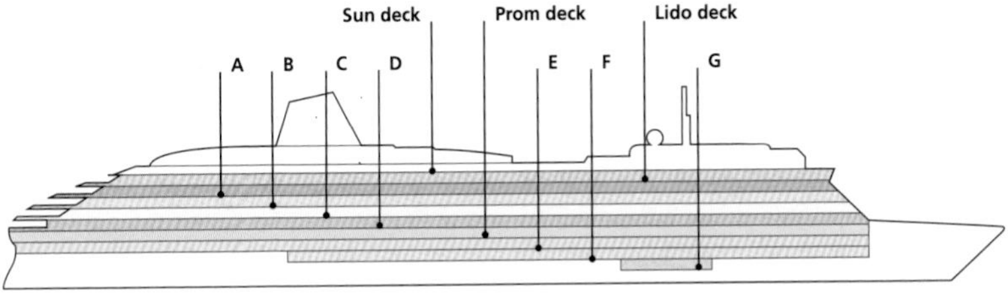

Deck hierarchy: the most expensive cabins are on A deck; some decks, such as the lido deck, have no cabins

LOCATION

Cabins nearer the centre of a ship tend to be quieter and more stable, although this is less important on larger ships. On smaller ships, noise and heat may be more noticeable on lower-deck inside cabins near the engines and funnel casing. It is important to bear in mind that some cabins can be some distance and several decks from many facilities, for example the dining room. Passengers who are less than agile will not want to walk long corridors and several flights of stairs every meal time, and if stairs are a problem, it is better to choose a cabin near lifts. Likewise, for those wanting to retire early, it would be wise not to be too near the nightclub. Cabins near the ship's bow may be exposed to unwanted early-morning noise, such as the dropping of the anchor chain. If booking an outside upper-deck cabin, check the deck plan carefully in case a lifeboat obstructs the view. Some cruise operators mention this in their brochures, but often only in the small print, simply as "restricted views."

Watching television in an outside twin-bedded economy cabin

FACILITIES

The cheapest cabins will include two single beds or an upper and lower berth. Where there are upper berths, a short ladder is provided for access and the bedframe usually tucks away out of sight during the day. Facilities include a small private bathroom with shower, toilet and wash basin (towels and soap are always provided), a chair and table, a combined vanity and desk unit with a mirror, wardrobe and drawer space, storage room for suitcases under the bed and, very importantly, a lifejacket for each person. Instructions on how to use lifejackets and on other emergency measures will be posted in each cabin *(see p343)*. There will be some form of air-conditioning, one or two electrical outlets – either 110V or 220V, possibly both – and a radio or public address system loudspeaker. There may also be a telephone, television and/or video equipment.

Higher grades of accommodation are likely to have more space, larger beds and more furniture, as well as a minibar or refrigerator, a personal safe, multichannel radio and television, even a vase of flowers.

A crew member will clean and tidy the cabin and make the beds each morning.

TIPS FOR CHOOSING A CABIN

- Study the ship's layout and deck plans very carefully.
- Select the best cabin you can afford.
- The higher price for an outside cabin is always worth it.
- The higher the deck, the better the view.
- Newer ships often have cabins specifically designed for passengers with disabilities.
- On larger ships, bear in mind that you may need to walk some distance, and up or down several levels, each time you want to reach your cabin.
- Prices for a third or fourth person sharing a three- or four-berth cabin represent exceptional value.
- If you find that the ship is not fully booked, enquire when boarding what the cost is for upgrading on the spot to a better cabin or suite.

Cabins of every variety have their own private bathroom

PRACTICAL ADVICE

For many people the perfect cruise is a complete break from all the mundane worries that beset everyday life. They book a cruise so that they can relax in elegant surroundings, be pampered in every way and visit exotic destinations that remind them that the world is still an exciting place.

To make the most of a cruise holiday, however, there are inevitably a few practicalities that need to be observed. For example, it is vital that all the right documentation is carried by passengers, and that valid credit cards or other acceptable forms of payment are readily at hand – there are bound to be some extra charges. Safety is of prime importance on board any vessel and cruise ships are no exception. There may also be a few rules that govern passengers' general behaviour, though most of these are really just common sense.

Passport and other travel documents

DOCUMENTATION

Those intending to cruise should check well in advance that all their documentation (tickets, passports, visas, travel insurance, health requirements, credit cards and so on) is in order, and that their passport is not about to expire. It is also important to obtain any visas that may be needed for some of the countries on the cruise itinerary in order to participate in any shore excursions *(see pp354–7)* offered by the cruise company. Travellers should note that visa requirements do vary according to the nationality of the passport holder: US nationals, for example, will find they need different visas from those of member states of the European Union (EU).

Photocopies should be made of all documentation and the copies should then be packed separately from the originals; they will be invaluable in the event of any problems later. It may also be worth taking a driving licence, for example to facilitate hiring a car for independent shore excursions.

Many cruise operators will offer their passengers holiday insurance. However, there is no obligation to use cover offered by the company selling the cruise; it is always worth investigating other policies offering the best deal in terms of price and cover.

PASSPORTS AND BOARDING PASSES

When passengers check in for their cruise, normal procedure is for the Purser to retain their passport and give them, in exchange, a boarding pass and cabin key. Boarding passes may have passengers' photographs displayed on them for added security. Each time passengers leave the ship they will be asked to take their boarding passes. Normally, these passes will be collected as passengers return to the ship. Often, a boarding pass is all the documentation needed to go ashore, while passengers' passports can remain safely stowed away in the Purser's office. Great care should be taken of the boarding pass while on land as it could prove difficult to reboard the ship without it.

Sometimes a visa may also be required; the cruise operator may be able to organize a group visa for some countries *(see p356)*.

Cash and credit cards – not to be left at home

MONEY

The main unit of currency on board ship, used for all transactions, will depend on the ship's nationality. Generally, cruise ships are run on a cashless basis, with an account for each cabin set up at the start of the cruise *(see p346)*. Credit cards, cash or traveller's cheques are all accepted forms of payment, when settling the account. There is usually a bureau de change for local currencies for shore excursions.

Purser's office: passports are logged in and held here for safekeeping

Communications room, a vital ship's resource when at sea

PURSER'S OFFICE

Usually located in a prominent position amidships, the office used by the Purser and his or her staff is the passengers' principal point of reference for all information, accounts, bookings and problem-solving. On some ships it may be called "Reception", "Guest Relations" or "Information Desk". Opening hours are usually advertised at the desk itself and in the ship's daily newspaper or programme of events (see p350), while on larger ships staff may be available around the clock.

A FEW RULES

Shipboard life is generally very relaxed – after all, people have paid to have an enjoyable holiday. Nevertheless there are a few rules that all passengers should be aware of, for the benefit of themselves and other travellers: bare feet and swimming attire should be restricted to cabins and the swimming pool and spa areas; those who smoke should only do so in designated areas; when taking photographs, passengers should be aware of others' personal privacy; finally, for reasons of copyright, passengers are not permitted to make video or tape recordings of shows and cabarets on board the ship.

SAFETY ON BOARD

Passengers should pay strict attention to the safety instructions that will be posted all over the ship. They should also familiarize themselves with the location of muster stations (assembly points in the case of an emergency) and make a point of attending the mandatory lifejacket drills, which will be held as soon as possible after embarkation.

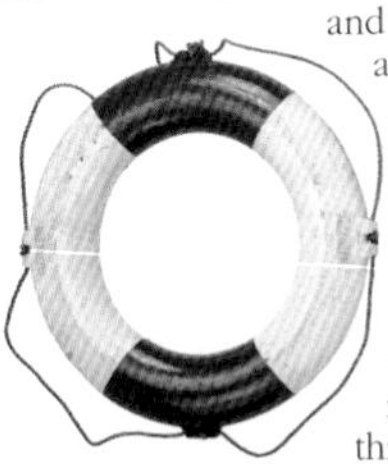

Ship's lifebelt

In addition, passengers should never throw anything over the side of the ship, and certainly not a cigarette end, which can "blow back" and cause a fire. All unwanted refuse items should always be disposed of in the proper place. When negotiating stairs, decks and gangways that are wet from rain, spray or hosing down, great care should always be taken. It is remarkably easy to slip and fall on a ship, especially if the sea is rough and the boat is small enough to enable passengers to feel it pitching.

COMMUNICATION

In these days of global telecommunications, passengers on board a cruise ship are unlikely to feel cut off from the rest of the world – unless, of course, they choose to. Though, for many, the purpose of a cruise is to take a relaxing break, there are always those who will feel the need to keep in contact with land, say for work. Cruise ships have an array of sophisticated navigation and satellite communication systems to keep in constant contact with the outside world *(see p352)*. It is these systems that also allow passengers to make calls and send e-mails worldwide. Similarly, friends and family can call while the ship is at sea; if this is important, then it is a good idea to check the ship's callsign and telephone and fax numbers in advance. Passengers should make sure they are aware of how the ship's position will make a difference to its local time. Some of the larger ships have credit card pay-phones in public areas and also ICT facilities. Mobile phones can sometimes be used, though coverage is unreliable.

SAFETY GUIDE

- When you first arrive, find out where your cabin is in relation to other parts of the ship, including muster stations.
- Instructions on how to reach your appointed muster station will be posted on the back of the cabin door. Make a point of familiarizing yourself with the details of this escape route.
- Check that there is the correct number of lifejackets in your cabin.
- Familiarize yourself with all procedures that should take place in the event of an emergency. Attend the compulsory lifejacket and safety drill that will be held as soon as possible after all passengers have embarked.
- Take all safety procedures, instructions from staff and safety drills very seriously. The lives of you, your family and other travellers may depend on your doing so.

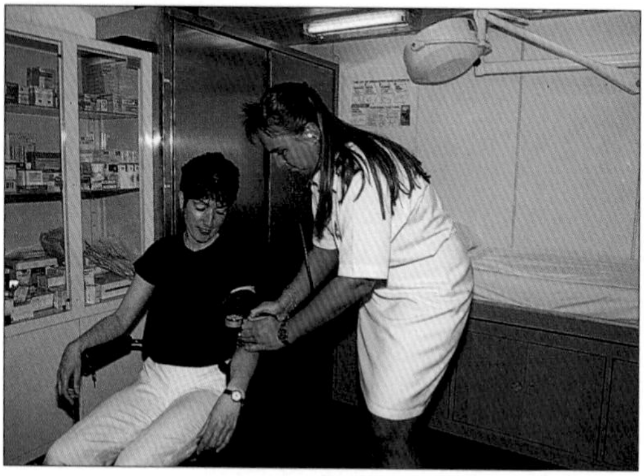
Passenger seeking medical advice from the ship's nurse

CHECKING YOUR CABIN

The first thing passengers should do when arriving at their cabin or suite is to make sure that everything is in order. Check the lights, air-conditioning, TV and water supply. If the accommodation is not what was requested, for example berths instead of beds, the matter should be raised straight away – before the ship sails – at the Purser's office. If the ship is not full, an alternative cabin may be available. If the accommodation is as booked, but more space or a better location is required, it is possible to enquire about the cost of an upgrade. Depending on availability, a move to a superior cabin or suite can cost surprisingly little extra.

MEDICAL MATTERS

Most cruise ships have a qualified doctor or nurse on board – their services will probably incur a charge, but holiday insurance will normally cover this. Ships carrying more than 100 passengers are also likely to have a small-scale hospital below decks, although standards vary since maritime regulations are not very specific on such matters. Passengers should be reassured, however, that in an emergency cruise ships in Europe are unlikely to be more than a few hours away from shore-based medical facilities.

If passengers require medication they should ensure they bring enough for the entire trip. Though most ships have a doctor and pharmacy, they may not have certain medications. Two medical essentials that most passengers will require are high protection factor sun cream (at least SPF15, as the combination of sea, wind and sun can be deceptively strong) and motion sickness pills – even the most seasoned cruise-goers take a few days to find their sea legs. People with diabetes can arrange to have insulin refrigerated if the cabin lacks a minibar or ice box.

Luggage – kept to a minimum

MOTION SICKNESS

If passengers feel they may be susceptible to motion sickness, they should talk to their doctor or pharmacist before leaving home. There are a number of remedies available, including a bracelet known as a Sea-Band, which covers pressure-points on the wrists and can be very effective. Motion sickness is rare nowadays as many ships are fitted with stabilizers; on very large ships there may be no sensation of movement at all. Nevertheless, if there is a problem, a good cure is simply to go on deck, get some air and focus on the furthest point on the horizon.

LAUNDRY

Laundry services are often available on ships, at extra cost, via the cabin steward. Larger ships may also have a self-service or full-service launderette, perhaps with dry cleaning facility. Information on these services can usually be found in the cabins.

SMOKING

As everywhere nowadays, smoking is discouraged on board ship. Most ships have non-smoking dining rooms, and smoking may only be permitted in specific areas elsewhere. Cigars and pipes are often banned, except on ships with a designated "cigar bar".

BAGGAGE

Limited space means baggage must be kept to a minimum. It should be tagged with the name of the passenger, ship and port of embarkation.

Passengers' clothes being pressed in the ship's laundry

WHAT TO PACK

Whether cruising for adventure, relaxation or even romance, there are certain essentials that passengers will need to have with them. There will be a wealth of activities to enjoy, from swimming to tennis, to evening pursuits such as cabaret, special parties and events *(see pp348–9)*. Having the right clothes *(see p346)* is important, but there are also many smaller items, without which passengers may find themselves limited in their choice of activities. For example, shore excursions *(see pp354–7)* often demand sensible walking boots and sometimes a warm jacket.

ESSENTIALS

- ☐ Passports and visas
- ☐ Currency, credit cards, traveller's cheques
- ☐ Travel insurance documents
- ☐ Cruise documents
- ☐ Medication
- ☐ Sunglasses
- ☐ Evening wear
- ☐ Deck and walking shoes
- ☐ Waterproof jacket
- ☐ Light cotton clothing
- ☐ Sun hat, baseball cap
- ☐ Toiletries
- ☐ Sun cream
- ☐ Small rucksack
- ☐ Camera and film
- ☐ Sportswear
- ☐ Light jumper, fleece
- ☐ Umbrella
- ☐ Insect repellent
- ☐ Travel alarm clock
- ☐ Flip-flops
- ☐ Swimwear

ESSENTIAL TOILETRIES AND MEDICATION

- A good supply of high factor sun cream should be taken with you and worn at all times; even when cloudy the sun can burn. More cruises have been ruined by sunstroke than by motion sickness.
- It is a good idea to bring insect repellent as some ports of call are likely to be in countries where mosquitoes and other insects are prevalent.
- If you require specific medication you should bring an ample supply that will last for the duration of your cruise.
- You should bear in mind that, while most ships have their own pharmacy, stocks may be limited; the pharmacy should be used for last-minute emergencies, not for purchasing your regular medication.
- For shore excursions, if you are going to be wearing new walking shoes, take a supply of plasters.

LIFE ON BOARD

There is something romantic and exciting about being aboard a ship as she sets sail; looking down at the quayside as the gap slowly widens and one's home for the foreseeable future takes to sea. There is always a frisson of anticipation that the future will bring exotic new locations, fabulous sightseeing opportunities, superb food and impeccable on-board service. The first evening feels like the opening night of an extravagant play, but as the days and weeks pass the ship becomes a passenger's second home.

Light, casual clothes, the norm for afternoons spent on deck

DRESS CODE

The more expensive the cruise, the more formal it it is likely to be. A good idea of the appropriate shipboard attire can be had from the brochure at the time of booking. Once on board, the ship's daily programme or newspaper usually gives advice on what to wear for the various scheduled events.

DAY WEAR

Comfort on deck is very important. Rubber-soled shoes are recommended, as are light cotton clothes, which tend to be cooler than most synthetic fabrics. It often gets chilly in the evenings, and the ship's air-conditioning keeps the atmosphere very cool, so remember to take at least one warm jumper. A number of sporting activities will also be available on board, such as aerobics, basketball and circuit training (there may even be a running track), so bring trainers and gym wear as well as the mandatory swimming outfit.

EVENING WEAR

A traditional air of glamour still surrounds evenings spent at sea. Usually, smart casual wear is acceptable, but there are at least two formal nights a week when gentlemen wear dinner jackets or lounge suits and ladies wear cocktail or evening dresses. Otherwise light summer dresses and jackets are worn by ladies, and blazers, ties and chinos by gentlemen.

GRATUITIES

Tipping continues to be a sore subject among many cruisegoers. On some ships gratuities are covered by the ticket, so tipping is unnecessary, but reports suggest that this often results in a drop in the level of service (the word 'tips' actually stands for 'to insure personal service'). To clarify this issue, many companies insist that gratuities are not included in the bill and so must be offered by passengers, particularly in the closing stages of a cruise. Many liners state quite openly the level of gratuity appropriate for the cabin steward, waiter, head waiter, wine waiter and other members of the cruise staff. Many ships have abandoned the tradition, and a service charge of up to 15% is added to all on-board beverage and beauty treatment bills instead.

SIGN FOR EVERYTHING

Cruise ships generally operate on a cashless basis; every cabin is given its own account and passengers sign for all expenditure accordingly. Credit cards or charge cards should be presented to the Purser at the beginning of the cruise, and deposits can be made using cash or traveller's cheques. Once an account is set up an identity card is given to the passenger, and this should be presented whenever anything is bought on ship, as well as before all shore excursions. Many ships carry ATM cash machines, so money can be withdrawn when needed. The currency used depends on the nationality of the cruise line.

Black ties and ballgowns, usually worn on special occasions

Ship's buffet lunch, often served on deck

DRINKS ON BOARD

Cruise ships carry a wide-range of wines, beers and spirits which often reflect the style of the ship's home port. Although these are likely to be duty-free, prices on board are rarely any less than they are on land. Drinks can be ordered at the ship's bars or from room service, and the cost will be added to the buyer's account. Soft drinks are generally available throughout the day, free of charge.

Cocktails, made to order

Consuming one's own duty-free goods in the cabin is discouraged, unless they have been purchased from the ship's own sales outlet.

MEAL ARRANGEMENTS

On some ships there are two sittings of each meal in the restaurant or dining room, and passengers are told which sitting and table they have been allocated. Tables are usually set for four or six people, very rarely for two. The cruise line will do its best to accommodate individual needs, but travellers should make enquiries about these at the time of booking, otherwise a private word with the Maître d' or Restaurant Manager will normally solve any problems. Breakfast is served in the dining room, but many ships do provide a cabin service. A buffet lunch is often served on deck as an alternative to the dining room. Informal morning coffee and afternoon tea are served daily, and on many ships a buffet is also served at around midnight each day – a lifeline for the nocturnal and anyone who misses the earlier meal.

The quality of food depends on the price of the cruise, but menus usually tally with those of onshore restaurants. On less expensive cruises the finest wines and meats can hardly be expected, but the standard is generally high. Gourmet cuisine is the much-talked-about preserve of the luxury liners, the galleys of which are regularly supplied with fresh produce. Special 'chef's choice' meals regularly appear on the menu, usually after local ingredients are taken on board, and are treats not to be missed. For that lazy evening away from the buzz of the dining room, some ships offer a pizza delivery service, which operates direct to the cabin door.

Eating in the dining room, often an intimate, lively affair

WINE WITH MEALS

Diners can order wine from what is usually an excellent range of vintages, and the wine waiter is always at hand to aid the undecided. It is often a good idea to order wine in advance, say at lunchtime for the evening's meal, so that it can be ready in plenty of time, chilled or at room temperature as appropriate. The busy galley staff appreciate such foresight.

SPECIAL DIETS

Passengers with special dietary requirements should check their options with the cruise line at the time of booking. Vegetarians are easily catered for, but low-salt, low-fat, dairy-free and gluten-free meals may only be available on larger ships. Kosher meals may also be available on a limited and unsupervised basis, but confirm this before booking. Baby food is not provided by any cruise line, and so must be supplied by the parent.

Entertainment and Events

As with all facilities on board ship, the goal of the entertainments schedule is to provide a service as good, or better, as any on land, and many ships' programmes far exceed passengers' expectations. Variety acts and traditional theatre remain popular, but dazzling performances by magicians and dancers using state-of-the-art technology are increasingly becoming the norm.

Passengers mingle with the crew during the Captain's cocktail party

WELCOME COCKTAIL PARTY

On the first or second evening of the cruise, the Captain hosts a cocktail party to introduce himself and his officers and welcome passengers aboard. This is an ideal chance to meet the Purser, the Cruise Director and the many other personnel whose duties involve looking after the passengers. A second welcoming evening may follow the next day; this is a more formal occasion, during which the chef provides gourmet food for the first of the voyage's black-tie dinners. On these evenings friendships are often made that last throughout the voyage and beyond.

SPECIAL RECEPTIONS

Cruise lines try very hard to foster passenger loyalty, and many arrange special welcoming parties for those on their first cruise. This provides an excellent opportunity for passengers to get to know the cruise staff and to resolve any queries about the trip. Cocktail receptions are also arranged for passengers who have been aboard ship at least once before. As their well-deserved reputations grow, many ships acquire such a loyal following that it is not unusual to meet passengers who are on their tenth or more cruise on the same ship.

BIRTHDAYS AND ANNIVERSARIES

Passengers who have something special to celebrate during a cruise, be it a birthday, a wedding anniversary, a honeymoon or second honeymoon, are encouraged to notify the Cruise Director or the Restaurant Manager. Wherever possible, arrangements can be made to help people celebrate in style, and the earlier the staff are informed the better. Special birthday cakes for children can usually be made and certain areas of the ship can be reserved for parties. To help the staff prepare for major celebrations, alert the booking agent in advance.

THE CAPTAIN'S TABLE

When bridge duties permit, the ship's Captain dines at a large table near the centre of the dining room. The table may be set for up to ten or twelve people, and these are usually friends of the Captain, company officials and other special guests, including the ship's entertainers. Occasionally, however, passengers are invited by the Maître d' to join the Captain; this is a genuine honour that should be accepted graciously. Senior officers also host tables, with slightly less formality; this is another great opportunity to learn more about the workings of the ship and the day-to-day running of the cruise.

ENTERTAINMENT

The level and quality of entertainment on board is usually in direct proportion to the size and class of the ship.

On smaller ships passengers tend to make their own entertainment, getting to know their fellow travellers,

Special celebration meals are enjoyed regularly in the dining room

With professional acts and the latest technology, on-board entertainment often rivals that of major cities on land

discussing the days ahead and swapping stories of past adventures and experiences.

Medium-sized ships usually have some organized entertainment each night, such as a stage show with cabaret and musical numbers; passengers may even be invited to join in a "talent contest". Whatever happens, the Entertainment Manager does his or her best to ensure everyone has a good time.

On newer and larger ships, however, the entertainment is of an altogether different nature; lavish stage productions are held in multi-level, state-of-the-art auditoriums, offering passengers the kind of entertainment they would expect in London, Las Vegas or New York. Professional dancers and choreographers work alongside well-known entertainers, singers, magicians and celebrated cabaret artists, many of whom will have performed on the international stage. Stand-up comedy is also a regular feature, and, as a rule, the routines are suitable for all the family – passengers are duly warned if there is any deviation from this.

Most entertainment schedules are tailored for week-long cruises, so passengers on longer trips should try to ration what they see during the first week of the trip to avoid repetition later in the cruise. Nevertheless, particularly good routines are always worth seeing again.

A guest speaker delivers a lecture

SPECIAL EVENTS

Many cruises also hold themed nights, for example a "Moroccan evening", for which waiters and staff dress up in costume and at which the food and accompanying music is all appropriate. Although passengers are encouraged to join in, no-one should feel obliged to dress up. Other one-off events include wine-tasting evenings, cookery demonstrations and visits by famous guest speakers, such as internationally respected journalists, biologists and historians. Some ships focus on a specific theme throughout each cruise *(see pp16–17)* and this will often determine the kind of shore excursions on offer. A gastronomical cruise, for instance, will specialize in sampling local food, while a natural history trip will study the geology, flora and fauna of an area. As with all extras, however, passengers need not feel obliged to follow any particular itinerary. The option of going ashore independently is often open *(see p356)*, and themes can be sampled when desired.

FAREWELL GALA DINNER

After bags are packed and accounts are settled, passengers can put on their finest clothes one last time for the Farewell Gala Dinner. A special menu is guaranteed by the chef, and speeches are often made by the Cruise Director, the Captain and other members of the crew. A "final fling" atmosphere pervades the occasion, and the guests and crew are more popular than ever, as this is the last chance many people have to quiz them on aspects of the cruise. As always, the ship's photographer *(see p350)* is at hand to take what, for most people, will be the final picture of the trip.

The dining room set for a gala dinner aboard the *Voyager of the Seas*

Ships' Facilities

Cruise ships are often likened to floating hotels, but many are much closer to floating towns or villages. The sheer scale of the modern-day vessels, and the range of facilities they offer, can be genuinely daunting at first, and passengers can remain spoiled for choice even after many weeks at sea. From fitness centres to shopping malls, shipboard services cater to every need.

Ship's shopping mall, much the same as those found on land

THE DAILY NEWS

Each evening a ship's newspaper is slipped under every cabin door and posted on the noticeboards. A schedule for the forthcoming day's events is included, plus vital information concerning shore excursions *(see pp354–7)*, weather reports, dress codes for special events, and customs and immigration procedures. Some include the main news headlines and even sports results. Televisions offering CNN broadcasts are gradually becoming a standard cabin feature, otherwise global news is easily received by radio. Newspapers are regularly brought on board; buying them is an essential part of reaching any sizeable port.

SHIP'S PHOTOGRAPHER

Most ships have an official-photographer who captures special moments at every opportunity. He or she is initially encountered by passengers when they step aboard for the first time; passengers have a picture taken of themselves standing in front of the ship's lifebelt, showing the date and details of the cruise. Other photographs are taken on special occasions, such as the safety drill, the Gala Dinner, shore excursions, and so on. All photographs are displayed in a gallery, usually near the Purser's office. Passengers are under no obligation to buy any pictures, but for many a professional photograph makes a memorable souvenir. Sometimes the photographs can be expensive, so remember to check the price before buying.

SHOPPING

On-board shopping facilities-can range from a simple kiosk offering the bare essentials to a glittering shopping mall; it all depends on the vessel. Special offers and discounts are usually available towards the end of the trip, which is often the time when duty-free goods are delivered; many ships hold on to these throughout the cruise to encourage passengers to use the bars, but this rarely happens on large, luxury vessels. Duty-free items are always modestly priced, but sometimes it pays to shop on land, especially in places where the products themselves are made. Many remote ports depend on passengers' custom, so a mutual fostering of interests is traditional between ports and ships. To encourage this, shipboard outlets are closed whenever the ship is in port, including disembarkation day. Nevertheless, few travellers will need any goading to go shopping on land; gathering treasures from far-flung ports of call is an essential part of the cruising experience.

GAMES ROOM AND CASINO

Larger ships often have a games room with pinball machines and video games, which is handy for passengers

Ship's casino, a vibrant part of a cruise liner's nightlife

Outdoor ship's jacuzzi, a great way to relax while on a cruise

with children. However, adults may be more interested in the casino – a traditional feature of all but the smallest vessels. The gambling opportunities depend entirely on the class of ship, with options ranging from simple slot machines and blackjack (pontoon) to roulette, craps and baccarat. Some ships also have a separate card room and library, or a quiet area where board games and reference books are kept. Generally a shipboard casino is much the same as a land-based gambling hall, but a few extra rules apply. For a start, the casino is only open while the ship is at sea, and only passengers over 18 can play (although children are allowed to watch). Also, the gambit of offering gamblers free drinks to keep them at their tables is not practised aboard ship, though a "happy hour" of cheaper drinks is common. Finally, no photography is allowed in the casino – a tradition based on simple good manners and discretion.

HEALTH SPAS AND FITNESS CENTRES

Depending on the dimensions of the ship, fitness and recreational facilities can include some or all of the following: indoor and outdoor swimming pools, a children's pool, a gymnasium, exercise machines, organized walking and jogging sessions, a sauna and steamroom, aerobics classes, a massage parlour, whirlpool spas, aromatherapy and relaxation treatments and lectures on healthy eating. Scuba-diving and snorkelling equipment is often available for those wishing to practise or learn. The very finest ships will also include tennis courts, basketball courts and volleyball courts, a rock-climbing wall and even an ice-skating rink, but few ships incorporate these into their designs.

BEAUTY SALON AND HAIRDRESSING

Appointments for hairdressing and beauty treatment should be made as soon as possible at the beginning of the cruise. Demand for appointments is usually high before special events, like the Captain's Welcome Dinner or the Farewell Dinner, with vacancies posted in the daily paper or programme. As with all products and services aboard ship, prices are consistent with those on land.

RELIGIOUS SERVICES

On many ships interdenominational services are held by the Captain or ship's Chaplain in a small chapel, or a suitably converted space. Details are posted in the daily programme, and enquiries can be made at the Purser's office.

POSTAL SERVICES

As a convenience to passengers, postcards and stamps can be bought aboard most ships, although sometimes the price can be slightly more than face value. Mail is usually taken ashore by the company's port agent just prior to sailing. Headed writing paper is provided in all cabins, and more can be obtained from the Purser's office. Faxes can be sent from most ships, but it can be very expensive.

INTERNET FACILITIES

With the availability of the Internet becoming more and more of an everyday demand, many people will only embark on ships that have e-mail facilities – a need that is catered for by all the major liners. Some ships even have computer learning centres on board, offering courses on everything from basic word processing to e-mailing and Internet navigation. Smaller ships, however, rarely have computers on board, and communications are restricted to everyday terrestrial post, radio and telephone.

Massage parlour, a popular feature of every ship's health spa

Behind the Scenes

Except on smaller ships, visits to the bridge, engine room and galley area are not permitted for security reasons. However, passengers with a particular interest in what goes on out of the public eye should mention this to the Cruise Director or one of the officers; sometimes special arrangements can be made. Otherwise, many ships have a comprehensive "Behind the Scenes" video that can be shown in passengers' cabins.

The Captain on the bridge with his Chief Officer at the helm

BRIDGE

Manned at all times, even when the ship is in port, the bridge is the ship's vital command centre. The Captain, officers and seamen all take turns on duty, each "watch" being a period of two, four or eight hours, following naval tradition. In addition to the engines, rudder, stabilizers and bow thrusters, all the ship's systems are controlled from here, and a vast array of equipment monitors every aspect of the ship's status. The steering wheel at the helm is rarely used at sea (navigation is computer-guided), but docking cannot be done without it.

Adjacent to the bridge is the chart room containing a library of maps and navigational charts. A written log of the ship's progress, recording position, heading, speed, weather, the number of people on board and all other relevant details, is required by law to be kept up to date at all times.

BERTHING

Most ships have twin areas known as "bridge wings" projecting from either side of the bridge. Duplicate engine controls are situated here, and these are used by the Captain and his officers when the ship is arriving in port (berthing). The exposed bridge wing affords an uninterrupted view of the side of the ship, all the way from stem to stern – essential when the ship is nearing the quay. Small propellers, or "bow thrusters", are built into the front of the ship; these enable the vessel to be manoeuvred precisely into place. Few passengers resist the temptation to be out on deck during berthing procedures since many of the sights are unforgettable.

RADIO ROOM

Radio, telegraph, telephone and satellite communication equipment keeps the ship in constant touch with the outside world. The radio room is where the ship's telephone exchange, radio equipment and computers are housed. While in-cabin telephones connect passengers to every part of the ship, this state-of-the-art technology allows external e-mails and telephone calls placed by passengers and crew to be sent and received via satellite all over the world.

One of the galley's many chefs, creating a special centrepiece

ENGINE ROOM AND CONTROL ROOM

Modern cruise ships make full use of the latest technology to provide reliable, efficient and environmentally friendly power, heating and air-conditioning, with computer-assisted engines and generators and instant back-up at all times. Although the engine room and control room are both off-limits to passengers, technical details of how they operate are sometimes available in a leaflet obtained from the Purser.

The control room is in direct communication with the bridge and not only monitors the power plant, but also the sophisticated automatic fire-damper and ventilation systems. The ship's complex network of watertight doors is also operated here; all can be activated manually or automatically within seconds.

The Captain and Staff Captain on the bridge wing during berthing

Staff Chief Engineer and Second Assistant Engineer in the control room

GALLEY

Staff are hard at work in the galley and bakery 24 hours a day. In addition to the kitchen with its ranges, ovens and food preparation areas, there are mixing and slicing machines, cold cabinets and huge refrigerators, plus separate freezers for fish, meat and poultry. Another area has dishwashing machines for all the plates, pots, pans and silverware. The highest standard of hygiene and cleanliness is kept aboard ship and regular inspections are made by officers and public health officials, often without warning. An Executive Chef oversees menu planning; few menus are repeated as local specialities are regularly brought on board.

MAINTENANCE

Reporting to the Chief Engineer is a large team of experienced technicians responsible for keeping all the ship's systems and facilities safe and functional at all times. The team includes electricians, mechanics, plumbers, carpenters, sound and lighting engineers and refrigeration and computer experts. This way, any fault in a passenger's cabin or a public area can be remedied quickly.

WIND VELOCITY

Wind velocity at sea is described as a "force" measured from 0 to 12 according to the Beaufort scale; a "force 12" wind (hurricane), for example, travels at over 118 kph (73 mph). This system was devised by Admiral Sir Francis Beaufort, who became hydrographer to the British Royal Navy in 1828. It was adopted by the Admiralty in 1838 and became the international standard in 1874. The strength of the wind is the single most important factor of the weather at sea.

WHO'S WHO ON BOARD

The Captain has overall responsibility for every aspect of the ship, including the welfare of passengers, crew and cruise line staff. Reporting to the Captain are senior officers, each of whom is responsible for a particular aspect of the ship's operation. Beneath them is a hierarchy of staff that ensures a safe and comfortable voyage for all passengers. There is, on average, roughly one crew member for every three passengers, though there may be a higher ratio on luxury ships. Below is an overview of the workings of a typical cruise ship.

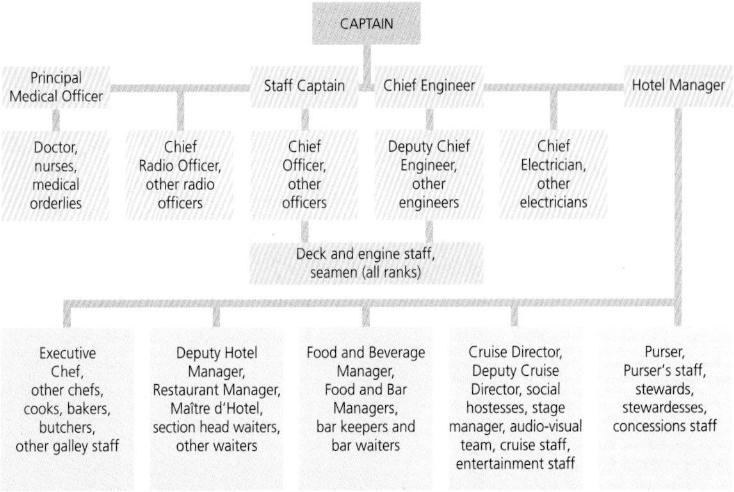

SHORE EXCURSIONS

Although modern cruise ships have so many facilities that some passengers rarely want to disembark, the opportunity to go ashore in another country is one of the highlights of the cruising experience. The term "shore excursion" is used for any outing from the ship offered by the cruise line or its agent, from an evening visit to a restaurant or nightclub to a half- or full-day sightseeing trip. It will probably have a local English-speaking guide, and include entrance fees to museums and other places where a charge is made. Appropriate meals and refreshments are also included in the price. Transport may be by road, air, train or water, or even by a combination of these. Very often cruise ship personnel accompany shore excursions in a quality-control capacity.

A cruise ship drops anchor by Akershus Castle, Oslo

ADVANTAGES OF SHORE EXCURSIONS

The main advantages of taking an organized shore excursion are that the cruise line takes responsibility for all arrangements and guarantees the return of everyone to the ship before she sails. Insurance is covered in the price, as are all extra transport and sightseeing costs, and for many passengers it is a relief not needing to worry about foreign language and currency difficulties; the guide takes care of these. An excursion is also an excellent way for passengers to get to know each other.

However, one thing to bear in mind is that when large numbers are involved it can take a long time to load a fleet of coaches, and the trip can become rather crowded.

Details of all trips ashore are usually made available well in advance, and there should be a brochure on board ship; it is worth reviewing all the options closely. The itinerary in the brochure will indicate approximately how much time will be spent in each port. Occasionally the ship will stop briefly to disembark those going ashore and then proceed to the next port of call. This way, passengers can enjoy a day's sightseeing and return to the ship in time for dinner.

Shore excursions can be expensive, and it is worth planning this expenditure in advance so you can budget accordingly. Naturally, all passengers are also welcome to go ashore by themselves or in a privately organized group *(see p356)*. This is the best arrangement for anyone wishing to spend a longer time at fewer sights, but for a comprehensive view of the area an excursion is advised.

KNOWING WHAT IS INVOLVED

Elderly or infirm passengers should check whether or not the excursion involves any climbing or extensive walking. Archaeological sites in particular can be difficult underfoot, requiring sturdy shoes and a reasonable level of fitness.

In some ports it may be possible to play tennis, enjoy a round of golf or spend a day relaxing on the beach.

The Cruise Director and excursion staff will be able to provide details of all the options. Chatting to other travellers is also an excellent way of gaining information.

ADVANCE INFORMATION

Most cruise ships provide information and maps of the next port of call, and a list of the excursions on offer will

Passengers at the Shore Excursions Desk prior to disembarking

Covent Garden, a popular London market

either be put on the notice boards or placed in passengers' cabins. Some cruise lines also offer a free talk or presentation about the excursions.

Bear in mind that a "visit" usually involves actually entering the building or site concerned, whereas "seeing" can often mean simply viewing a place from a distance, sometimes without even alighting from the coach. Passengers in any doubt about the details of a trip should ask the Cruise Director or the excursion staff.

BOOKING

Passengers who have not booked excursions in advance can do so as soon as the on-board office or help desk opens. There will probably be a high demand, so it is worth getting to the desk as soon as possible. At the time of booking it is also a good idea to make sure what the refund policy is, just in case circumstances change and the trip becomes impossible. If refunds are not given, it may be possible to sell a ticket to another passenger. On many of the newer ships excursions can be booked on in-cabin interactive screens.

PRICES

Shore excursions-are priced in the ship's currency and can usually be paid for by cash, traveller's cheque or credit card; otherwise they are charged to cabin accounts.

Before disembarking it is worth finding out about the local currency and economic climate. In some cities, such as Tunis *(see pp260–61)*, local taxi fares are very low in comparison to the European average, but in others, such as Stockholm *(see pp44–9)*, the fare can be very expensive.

In many countries bargaining is expected, while in others prices are fixed. Haggling can take a while to get used to, but most passengers acquire a talent for it during their trip.

PASSENGER BRIEFING

On many ships the Cruise Director or excursion staff hold a briefing session, which passengers are urged to attend. Information on the next port of call is provided, including a run-down of all the main sightseeing possibilities, plus advice on tipping, local currency *(see p357)* and so on. There are also regular talks on much broader cruise-related subjects, such as local culture, arts and crafts, natural history, archaeology, geology and wildlife. All passengers will be given a clear idea of what to expect before the ship draws into port, but it is always a good idea to do some research before disembarking on an excursion.

WHERE THE SHIP TIES UP

In large towns and cities cruise ships often tie up at a dock or port that may be some distance from the main area of interest, so passengers who are not on an excursion will need to hire a taxi to see the port independently. At the other extreme, when the ship arrives at a small town or island the port may be within walking distance of the town centre or tourist district; there may even be a formal "welcome centre" and tourist information office nearby. The ship may tie up at a pier or anchor slightly offshore, in which case passengers can go ashore by launch *(see p356)*. Either way, it takes a good hour for the ship to be cleared for disembarkation by the port authorities.

Arriving by coach at the Giza pyramid complex, Egypt

Heading ashore by launch from a ship anchored out of port

GOING ASHORE BY LAUNCH

Sometimes a ship will be too large to come alongside a pier, or a docking facility may not be available. In these cases the ship will drop anchor off-shore and tenders will ferry passengers to a convenient wharf or jetty. This can be a time-consuming process and there may be several queues, so it is worth finding out in advance where and when the tenders will be boarded. Details of ship-to-shore transfers are given in the ship's daily programme and are regularly announced over the public address system.

Tenders, or "launches", can be closed or open to the weather and they vary considerably in size; lifejackets may be supplied on smaller boats, otherwise these are stored on the main ship. Expedition ships often have zodiacs, which are strong rubber raft-like boats with an outboard motor. Great care should be taken when boarding these, especially if the sea is rough.

INDEPENDENT TRAVEL

Passengers who go ashore independently, whether alone or in a group, are likely to have a very different experience to those involved with the arranged excursions. Rather than seeing the whole town superficially, there is greater opportunity to get to know a couple of sights rather more intimately – an experience that many passengers prefer. Nevertheless, in the absence of a tour guide a few basic points are worth remembering. For a start, it is best to obtain a map or a street plan before disembarking and to plan carefully which of the sights are of most interest to you; time may be very limited, so making a list of priorities is essential. Also, be aware that inclement weather may cause late arrival into port and changes to the featured ports of call; in particularly bad weather the ship can still anchor off-shore, but launching tenders may occasionally prove impossible.

If a shore excursion is fully booked, it is usually possible to arrange a similar tour with a local supplier; harbour tours by boat will be prominently advertised. As for local transport, this can be anything from a modern taxi cab to an open horse and cart. Sampling local forms of transport is all part of a trip ashore, and local drivers are also a useful source of information; arranged excursions tend to avoid these, preferring to use coaches.

The main disadvantage of an independent trip is that travellers are not covered by the ship's insurance.

REEMBARKING ON TIME

Passengers who "go it alone" should also make sure they know exactly when the ship departs. Anyone who misses it will be held responsible for any extra costs incurred to reembark – these can be considerable if a taxi or plane is needed to catch the ship at its next port of call. Sailing times are rigorously adhered to, and passengers should be back at the dock no less than half an hour before the ship's departure. Anyone who misses the boat should contact the cruise line representative at the port. The time of the last shore-to-ship transfer will be clearly announced before the ship arrives at its destination.

CUSTOMS AND VISAS

For passengers on organized shore excursions, customs and immigration procedures are usually only a formality. Group visas are often issued, so individuals can leave their passports safely in the Purser's Office. Under these conditions a boarding pass *(see p342)* is generally sufficient identification. The same rules generally apply to people going ashore independently, but there are some exceptions, such as in Russia, where the individual must have a visa in advance. In other countries, such as Turkey, a visa is also required but can be obtained only on arrival. The cruise line will

A traditional horse-drawn carriage, Seville

normally arrange for these on the passenger's behalf, adding the cost to the on-board cabin account. These details should be clarified by the travel agent at the time of booking a trip as visas often take several months to process.

IDENTIFICATION AND SECURITY

Some cruise lines provide passengers with a badge or sticker to wear on excursions, usually bearing a group identification symbol. The only drawback to these is that they make the passenger conspicuous to shopkeepers and local villains; for this reason it is best to keep it out of sight.

SAFETY ON SHORE

Whether going ashore independently or in an organized group, it is always best to carry the absolute minimum, both in terms of money and personal effects. Jewellery can be left in the ship's safe deposit, and cameras and other belongings should be carried in a plain, inconspicuous bag. To the local eye, a cruise ship daytripper stands out quite noticeably in a crowd, and is therefore an easy target for thieves, many of whom operate on motorbikes. In this regard it is always important to be aware of one's surroundings. In some ports of call beggars and children can also be a problem, and for those who do not want to give them money distributing a few ballpoint pens or sweets will normally satisfy. Otherwise, if anything untoward happens the situation should be treated just as it would be at home by reporting any losses or problems to excursion staff and the local police as soon as possible.

One final point to be aware of when going ashore is the cleanliness of the water. In many countries it is best only to drink bottled spring water, or water that has been purified. If in doubt, passengers are advised to take a bottle of water ashore with them and avoid taking ice with drinks.

LOCAL CURRENCY

Passengers can change cash and traveller's cheques at the Purser's Office or onboard Bureau de Change, but many liners only deal in major currencies. The alternative is to try the banks, ATMs and exchange counters on land, which may also have better exchange rates. Most of these are situated close to the docks, and all demand a service charge. In some countries major credit cards, US dollars and other foreign currencies may be accepted.

THE EURO

The Euro (€) is the common currency of the European Union. It went into circulation on 1 January 2002. EU members using the Euro as sole official currency are known as the Eurozone. Euro notes are identical throughout the Eurozone, each one including designs of fictional architectural structures. The coins have one side identical (the value side), and one side with an image unique to each country.

100 Euros

1 cent

5 cents

20 cents

1 Euro

Cruise ships on the water in a Norwegian fjord ▷

DIRECTORY OF CRUISE LINES

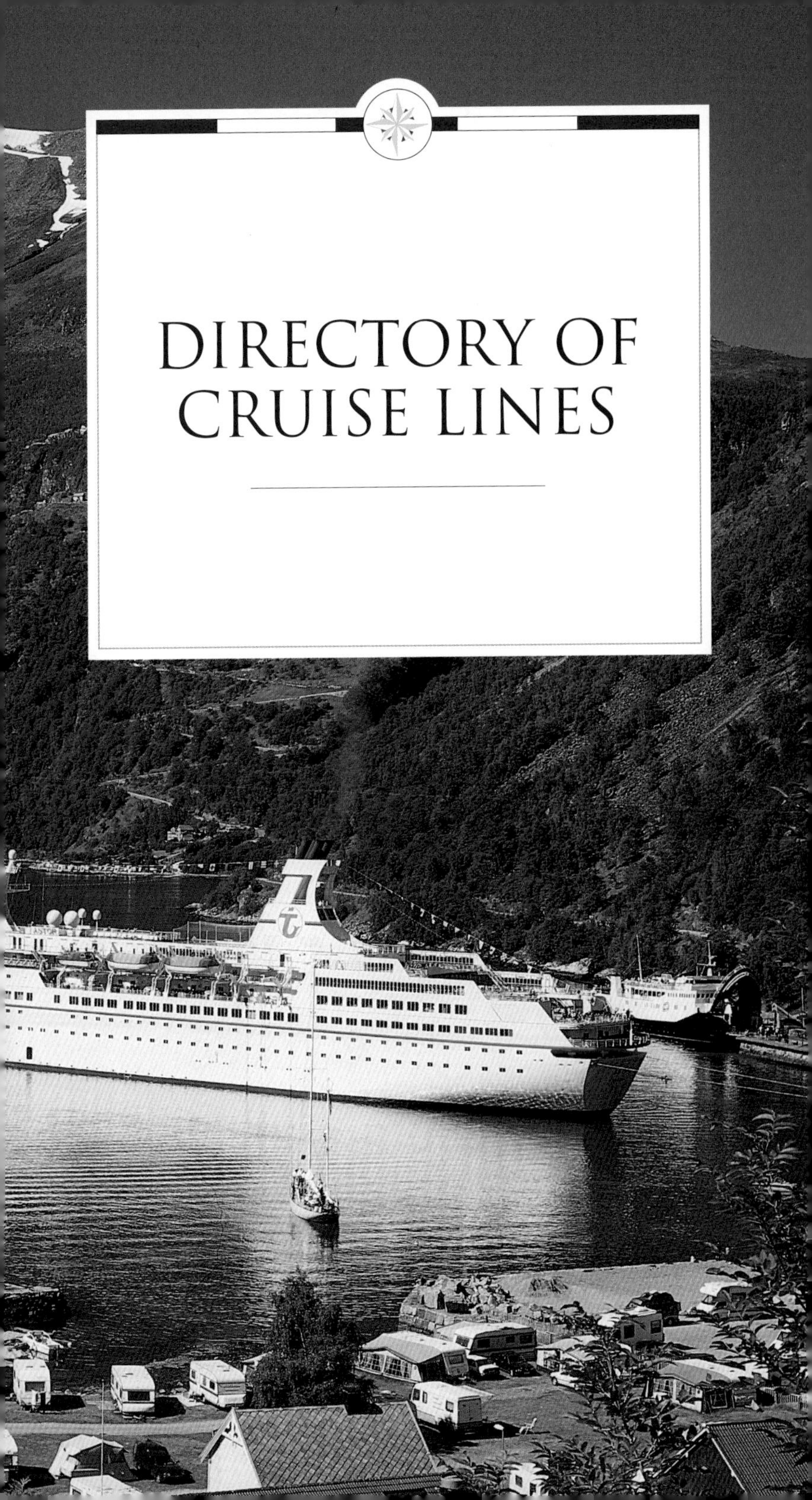

DIRECTORY OF CRUISE LINES

The directory below, though not comprehensive, represents a wide range of cruise line companies catering to a broad variety of tastes. The contact details given are for the main offices of the companies concerned. Details of local offices or sales agents can be obtained by telephoning or e-mailing the companies, or by accessing the Internet to visit their websites.

DIRECTORY

OPERATORS IN THE US

Celebrity Cruises
1050 Caribbean Way,
Miami,
FL 33132.
Tel *0800 647 2251.*
(freephone in US only).
Fax *305 373 4384.*
@ via website.
www.celebritycruises.com

Clipper Cruise Line
11969 Westline Industrial Drive,
St Louis,
MO 63146–3220.
Tel *314 655 6700.*
Fax *314 655 6670.*
@ clipper@clippercruise.com
www.clippercruise.com

Club Med Cruises
7001 North Scottsdale,
Suite 1010,
Scottsdale,
AZ 5253.
Tel *888 932 2582.*
800 258 2633
(freephone in US only).
@ via website.
www.clubmed.com

Crystal Cruises
2049 Century Park East,
Suite 1400,
Los Angeles,
CA 90067.
Tel *866 446 6625.*
Fax *310 785 0011.*
@ cruisequestions@crystalcruises.com
www.crystalcruises.com

Cunard Cruise Lines
6100 Blue Lagoon Drive, Suite 400,
Miami,
FL 33126.
Tel *305 463 3000.*
800 728 6273
(freephone in US only).
@ via website.
www.cunard.com

First European Cruises
95 Madison Avenue, Suite 1203,
New York,
NY 10016.
Tel *212 779 7168.*
888 983 8767
(freephone in US only).
Fax *212 779 0948.*
@ reser@first-european.com
www.first-european.com

Holland America Line
300 Elliot Avenue West,
Seattle,
WA 98119.
Tel *206 281 3535.*
800 426 0327
(freephone in US only).
Fax *206 281 7110.*
@ via website.
www.hollandamerica.com

Lindblad Expeditions Inc.
96 Morton St, 9th Floor,
New York, NY 10014.
Tel *212 765 7740.*
800 397 3348
(freephone in US only).
@ explore@expeditions.com
www.expeditions.com

MSC Italian Cruises
420 Fifth Avenue,
NY 10018.
Tel *201 440 4360.*
Fax *201 440 5085.*
@ cruiseinfo@cruit.mscgva.ch
www.msccruisesusa.com

Norwegian Coastal Voyage Inc.
405 Park Avenue,
New York,
NY 10022.
Tel *212 319 1300.*
800 323 7436
(freephone in US only).
Fax *212 319 1390.*
@ info@coastalvoyage.com
www.coastalvoyage.com

Norwegian Cruise Line
7665 Corporate Center
Drive, Miami,
FL 33126.
Tel *305 436 4000.*
800 327 7030
(freephone in US only).
Fax *800 329 6251.*
@ via website.
www.ncl.com

Peter Deilmann Cruises
1800 Diagonal Road, Suite 170,
Alexandria,
VA 22314.
Tel *703 549 1741.*
800 348 8287
(freephone in US only).
@ pdcmail@deilmann-cruises.com
www.deilmann-cruises.com

Princess Cruises
24305 Town Centre Drive,
Santa Clarita,
CA 91355.
Tel *661 753 0000.*
Fax *661 284 4766.*
@ via website.
www.princess.com

Radisson Seven Seas Cruise Lines
600 Corporate Drive, Suite 410,
Fort Lauderdale,
Florida 33334.
Tel *800 285 1835*
(freephone in US only).
Fax *402 501 5599.*
@ via website.
www.rssc.com

River Odysseys West
PO Box 579,
Coeur d'Alene,
ID 83816.
Tel *208 765 0841.*
800 451 6034
(freephone in US only).
Fax *208 667 6506.*
@ info@rowinc.com
www.rowinc.com

Royal Caribbean International
1050 Caribbean Way,
Miami,
FL 33132.
Tel *305 539 6000.*
800 529 6918
(freephone in US only).
@ via website.
www.rccl.com

Royal Olympia Cruises
805 3rd Avenue,
New York,
NY 10022.
Tel *800 872 6400*
(freephone in US only).
Fax *888 662 6237.*
@ via website.
www.royalolympiacruises.com

Seabourn Cruise Line
6100 Blue Lagoon Drive, Suite 400,
Miami, FL 33126.
Tel *800 929 9391*
(freephone in US only).
Tel *305 463 3010.*
@ via website.
www.seabourn.com

Sea Cloud Cruises
32–40 North Dean Street,
Englewood,
NJ 07631.
Tel *201 227 9404.*
888 732 2568
(freephone in US only).
Tel *201 227 9424.*
@ seacloud@att.net
www.seacloud.com

Silversea Cruises
110 East Broward Boulevard,
Suite 2300,
Fort Lauderdale,
FL 33301.
Tel *800 722 9955*
(freephone in US only).
Fax *954 522 4499.*
www.silversea.com

Star Clipper Cruises
4101 Salzedo Avenue,
Coral Gables,
FL 33146.
Tel *305 442 0550.*
Fax *305 442 1611.*
@ info@starclippers.com
www.starclippers.com

Swan Hellenic Cruise Line
631 Commack Road,
Suite 1A,
Commack,
NY 11725.
Tel *877 800 7926.*
Fax *631 858 1279.*
@ swanhellenic@kainyc.com
www.swanhellenic.com

Travel Dynamics International
132 East 70th Street,
New York,
NY 10021.
Tel *212 517 7555.*
800 257 5767
(freephone in US only).
www.traveldynamics
international.com

Windstar Cruises
300 Elliot Avenue West,
Seattle,
WA 98119.
Tel *800 258 7245*
(freephone in US only).
Fax *206 281 0627.*
@ info@windstarcruises.com
www.windstarcruises.com

Zeus Tours
120 Sylvian Avenue,
Englewood Cliffs,
New Jersey 07632.
Tel *201 228 5280.*
800 272 7600
(freephone in US only).
Fax *201 228 5281.*
@ tourlite@tourlite.com
www.zeustours.com

OPERATORS IN THE UK

Airtours Holidays Ltd
Holiday House,
Sandbrook Park, Sandbrook Way,
Rochdale, Lancashire OL11 1SA.
Tel *01706 742 000.*
Fax *01706 742 650.*
www.airtours.co.uk

Azamara Cruises
1050 Caribbean Way,
Miami, FL 33132.
Tel *0800 254 5067.*
www.azamaracruiselines.com

Celebrity Cruises
Royal Caribbean House,
Addlestone Road,
Weybridge,
Surrey KT15 2UE.
Tel *0800 018 2525.*
Fax *01932 820 286.*
@ infouk@rccl.com
www.celebrity.com

Club Med
Gemini House,
10–18 Putney Hill,
London, SW15 6AA.
Tel *08453 670 670.*
Fax *0208 780 8601.*
www.clubmed.co.uk

Costa Cruises
5 Gainsford Street,
London SE1 2NE.
Tel *020 7940 4499.*
Fax *020 7940 5378.*
@ client.service@uk.costa.it
www.costacruises.co.uk

Crystal Cruises
Quadrant House,
80–82 Regent Street,
London W1B 5JB.
Tel *020 7287 9040.*
Fax *020 7434 1410.*
@ cruise@cruiseportfolio.co.uk
www.crystalcruises.com

Cunard Cruise Lines
Mountbatten House,
Grosvenor Square,
Southampton SO15 2BF.
Tel *0845 071 0300.*
Fax *0238 022 5843.*
@ via website.
www.cunard.com

DFDS Seaways
Scandinavia House,
Refinery Road, Parkeston Quay,
Harwich,
Essex CO12 4QG.
Tel *0870 533 3000.*
Fax *0125 524 4382.*
@ travelsales@dfds.co.uk
www.dfdsseaways.co.uk

Fred Olsen Cruise Lines

Fred Olsen House, White House Road, Ipswich, Suffolk IP1 5LL.

Tel *01473 292 200.*

Fax *01473 292 201.*

@ cruises@fredolsen.co.uk

www.fredolsen.co.uk

Holland America Cruise Line

Carnival House, 5 Gainsford Street, London SE1 2NE.

Tel *020 7940 4477.*

Fax *020 7940 4461.*

@ via website.

www.hollandamerica.com

Louis Cruise Lines

Chesterfield House,
385 Euston Road,
London NW1 3AU.

Tel *0800 0183 883.*

Fax *020 7383 2992.*

@ cruise@louis-uk.co.uk

www.louiscruises.com

Norwegian Cruise Line

1 Derry Street,
Kensington,
London W8 5NN.

Tel *0845 658 8010 (freephone in UK only).*

Fax *020 7938 4515.*

@ via website.

www.uk.ncl.com

Orient Lines

1 Derry Street,
Kensington,
London W8 5NN.

Tel *0800 333 7300.*

Fax *020 7938 4515.*

@ info@orientlines.co.uk

www.orientlines.com

Page & Moy Limited

136–140 London Road,
Leicester LE2 1EN.

Tel *0870 010 6230.*

Fax *0870 010 6449.*

@ holiday@page-moy.co.uk

www.pageandmoy.com

P&O Cruises

Richmond House,
Terminus Terrace,
Southampton SO14 3PN.

Tel *0845 355 5333.*

Fax *0238 065 030.*

@ via website.

www.pocruises.com

Princess Cruises

Richmond House,
Terminus Terrace,
Southampton SO14 3PN.

Tel *0845 355 5800.*

Fax *0238 052 3720.*

@ via website.

www.princess.com

RSSC

Suite 3/4 Canute Chambers,
Canute Road,
Southampton SO14 3AB.

Tel *0238 068 2280.*

Fax *0238 068 2299.*

@ res@rssc.co.uk.

www.rssc.co.uk

Royal Caribbean International

Royal Caribbean House,
Addlestone Road,
Weybridge,
Surrey KT15 2UE.

Tel *01932 834 200 (freephone in UK only).*

Tel *0193 282 0286.*

@ via website.

www.royalcarib.com

Saga Holidays Limited

The Saga Building,
Endbrook Park,
Folkestone,
Kent CT20 3SE.

Tel *0130 377 1111.*
0800 096 0079 (freephone in UK only).

Fax *0130 377 6106.*

@ reservations@saga.co.uk

www.saga.co.uk

Seabourn Cruise Line

Mountbatten House,
Grosvenor Square,
Southampton SO15 2BF.

Tel *0845 070 0500 (freephone in UK only).*

Fax *0238 022 5843.*

@ via website.

www.seabourn.com

Silversea Cruises

77–79 Great Eastern Street,
London EC2A 3HU.

Tel *0870 333 7030.*

Fax *0870 333 7040.*

@ info@silversea.com

www.silversea.com

Strand Voyages

1 Adam Street,
London WC2N 6AB.

Tel *020 7921 4340.*

Fax *020 7766 8225.*

@ voyages@strandtravel.co.uk

www.strandtravel.co.uk

Swan Hellenic

Richmond House,
Terminus Terrace,
Southampton SO14 3PN.

Tel *0845 355 5111.*

Fax *0238 052 3732.*

@ reservations@swanhellenic.com

www.swanhellenic.com

Thomson Cruises
Thomson Holidays,
Greater London House,
Hampstead Road,
London NW1 7SD.
Tel *0871 231 4691.*
Fax *020 7391 0362.*
@ via website.
www.thomson-cruises.co.uk

Voyages of Discovery
Lynnem House,
1 Victoria Way,
Burgess Hill,
West Sussex RH15 9NF.
Tel *0144 446 2150.*
Fax *0144 446 2160.*
@ admin@voyagesofdiscovery.com
www.voyagesofdiscovery.com

Windstar Cruises
Carnival House, 5 Gainsford Street,
London SE1 2NE.
Tel *020 7940 4488.*
Fax *020 7940 4461.*
@ windstarcruises@carnival.com
www.windstarcruises.com

OTHER OPERATORS

Delphin Seereisen
Neu Salzer Street 22e,
63069 Offenbach, Germany.
Tel *(00 49) 69 9840 3811.*
Fax *(00 49) 69 9840 3840.*
@ delphin@delphinseereisen.de
www.delphin-kreuzfahrt.de

De Zeilvaart
Stationsplein 3,
1601 EN Enkhuizen,
Netherlands.
Tel *(00 31) 228 312 424.*
Fax *(00 31) 228 313 737.*
@ info@zeilvaart.com
www.zeilvaart.com

Golden Star Cruises
85 Akti Miaouli,
Piraeus 18538,
Greece.
Tel *(00 30) 210 429 0650.*
Fax *(00 30) 210 429 0660.*
@ gscruz@goldenstarcruises.com
www.goldenstarcruises.com

Grand Navi Veloci
Via Fieschi 17A,
16121 Genova,
Italy.
Tel *(00 39) 010 55091.*
Fax *(00 39) 010 550 9333.*
@ infopax@grimaldi.it
www.gnv.it

Grimaldi Freighter Cruises
Via Marchese Campodisola 13,
80133 Naples,
Italy.
Tel *(00 39) 081 49 6111.*
Fax *(00 39) 081 551 7401.*
@ via website.
www.grimaldi.napoli.it

Hapag-Lloyd
Ballindamm 25,
D-20095 Hamburg,
Germany.
Tel *(00 49) 40 3001 4600.*
Fax *(00 49) 40 3001 4713.*
@ via website
www.hapag-lloyd.com

Louis Cruises
150A Franklin Roosevelt &
Omonias Avenue,
3045 Lemesós,
Cyprus.
Tel *(00 357) 2557 0000.*
Fax *(00 357) 2557 3320.*
@ sales@louiscruises.com
www.louiscruises.com

Minoan Lines
25th August Street 17,
71202 Irákleio,
Crete.
Tel *(00 30) 2810 399 800.*
Fax *(00 30) 2810 330 308.*
@ info@minoan.gr
www.minoan.gr

Royal Olympia Cruises
Akti Miaouli 87,
18538 Piraeus,
Greece.
Tel *(00 30) 210 459 7000.*
Fax *(00 30) 210 429 0862.*
@ via website.
www.royalolympiacruises.com

Sea Cloud Cruises
Ballindamm 17,
D-20095 Hamburg,
Germany.
Tel *(00 49) 40 309 5920.*
Fax *(00 49) 40 3095 9222.*
@ info@seacloud.com
www.seacloud.com

Silja Line AB
Positionen 8,
S-11574 Stockholm,
Sweden.
Tel *(00 46) 8 66 63330.*
Fax *(00 49) 8 66 63548.*
@ via website.
www.silja.com

Star Clipper Cruises
Ermanno Place,
27 Boulevard Albert 1er,
98000 Monaco.
Tel *(00 377) 9797 8400.*
Fax *(00 377) 9797 8401.*
@ info@starclippers-ltd.mc
www.starclippers.com

Viking Line
Mannerheimintie 14
Fin-00100 Helsinki,
Finland.
Tel *(00 358) 91 2351.*
Fax *(00 358) 64 0705.*
@ vires@vikingline.fi
www.vikingline.fi

General Index

Page numbers in **bold** type refer to main entries.

C

D

H

Acknowledgments

Dorling Kindersley would like to thank the following people whose contributions and assistance have made the preparation of this book possible.

Contributors
Fabrizio Ardito, Rosie Ayliffe, David Baird, Rose Baring, Susie Boulton, Christopher Catling, Juliet Clough, Marc Dubin, Olivia Ercoli, Bryn Frank, Cristina Gambaro, Nina Hathway, Andrew Humphreys, Lindsay Hunt, Michael Leapman, Daniela Lepore, Emilia Marchi, Robin Pascoe, Tim Perry, Catherine Phillips, Christopher and Melanie Rice, Kaj Sandell, Martin Symington, Alan Tillier, Nigel Tisdall, Massimo Acanfora Torrefranca, Stewart J. Wild, Roger Williams, Kristina Woolnough.

Illustrations
Arcana Studios, Giorgia Boli, Richard Bonson, Stephen Conlin, Gary Cross, Chris Orr & Associates, Brian Delf, Donati Giudici Associati srl, Richard Draper, Editions Errance: Jean-Claude Golvin, Chris Forsey, Urban Frank, Nick Gibbard, Jared Gilby, Javier Gómez Morata – Acanto Arquitectura y Urbanismo S.L., Isidoro González-Adalid Cabezas, Paul Guest, Stephen Gyapay, Trevor Hill, Roger Hutchins, John Lawrence, Claire Littlejohn, Andrew MacDonald, Maltings Partnership, Jill Mumford, Mel Pickering, Robbie Polley, Simon Roulstone, Paola Spampinato, Derrick Stone, Pat Thorne, Nadia Viganò, Paul Weston, Ann Winterbotham, John Woodcock, Martin Woodward.

Photography
Richard Bonson, Demetrio Carrasco, Joe Cornish, Andy Crawford, Geoff Dann, Alistair Duncan, Mike Dunning, John Garrett, Philip Gatward, Eddie Gerald, Steve Gorton, Paul Harris, John Heseltine, Gabriel Hildebrand, Rupert Horrox, Ed Ironside, James Jackson, Alan Keohane, Adrian Lascom, Neil Lukas, Joe Cornish, Kevin Mallet, Maltings Partnership, Eric Meacher, Sue Oldfield, Ian O'Leary, Stephen Oliver, Rob Reichenfeld, Alex Saunderson, Kim Sayer, Tony Souter, Jon Spaull, Chris Stevens, Matthew Ward, Stephen Whitehorn, Linda Whitwam, Alan William, Peter Wilson, Martin Woodward, Stephen Wooster, Franceska Yorke.

Managing Editor
Anna Streiffert.

Publishing Manager
Kate Poole.

Senior Publishing Manager
Louise Bostock Lang.

Publishing Director
Gillian Allan.

Design and Editorial Assistance
Elizabeth Atherton, Sam Atkinson, Mark Bailey, Marc Bennetts, Sharon Bowker, Paula Canal, Nicola Erdpresser, Mariana Evmolpidou, Marcus Hardy, Paul Hines, Batur Kizltug, Integrated Publishing Solutions, Ben Langford, Loren Levy, Hayley Maher, Nicola Malone, Alison McGill, Sam Merrell, Jessica Nichols, Natasa Novakoic, Jane Oliver, Mary Ormandy, Johnny Pau, Lyn Parry, Mani Ramaswamy, Ellen Root, Barbara Sobeck, Andrew Szudek, Conrad Van Dyk, Mary Villabona.

Proofreaders
Michelle Clark, Stewart J. Wild.

Indexer
Hilary Bird.

Production
Marie Ingledew, Joanna Bull.

Special thanks to Captain Ian Sabet and the crew of *mv Minerva*, especially Michael Loban and Michael Marmaris, and the staff at Swan Hellenic for their help and assistance; also to Armel Dalhag, Pepito Dionisio, Nilo Francisco, Arnei Leyson, Sergiy Popov, Raju Balasubramanian, Michael Marmaris, Adam Pazdzioch, Sonja Ruppenstein, Ian Sabet and Sylvie Steinhauer for agreeing to be photographed. Thanks, also, to the passengers aboard *mv Minerva* who kindly shared their experiences and holiday tips with Dorling Kindersley's researchers during cruises in the Baltic and Mediterranean.

Picture Credits
t=top; tl=top left; tc=top centre; tr=top right; cla=centre left above; ca=centre above; cra=centre right above; cl=centre left; c=centre; cr=centre right; clb=centre left below; cb=centre below; crb=centre right below; bl=bottom left; b=bottom; bc=bottom centre; br=bottom right.

Every effort has been made to trace the copyright holders and we apologize in advance for any unintentional omissions. If any have occurred, we would be pleased to insert the appropriate acknowledgments in any subsequent edition of this publication.

The publisher would like to thank the following individuals, companies and picture libraries for permission to reproduce their photographs:

ACADEMIA ITALIANA: 243c; A.G.E. FOTOSTOCK: 190br; AGENCE FRANCE PRESS (AFP): Jean-Michel Cadiot-STF 262c; AISA BARCELONA: 190cl, 201t; AKG LONDON: 102t, 274c, 291t, 313bc; Antiquario Palatino 331bl; Erich Lessing 240t; Staatliche Antikensammlungen und Glyptotek, Munich 330bl; ANCIENT ART & ARCHITECTURE COLLECTION: 279c/b; MUSÉE DE L'ANNONCIADE, SAINT-TROPEZ: P. S. Azenia © ADAGP, Paris and DACS, London 2001 *Open Window*, 1926, Charles Camoin 157cr; ARCHAEOLOGICAL MUSEUM, NAPLES: 243b; ART DIRECTORS & TRIP: Martin Barlow 334br; Tibor Bognar 184b, 288bl; Michael Feeney 202b; John Gilbert 335c; Michael Good 288br; Juliet Highet 259c; Helene Rogers 260t, 282c; ART MUSEUM OF NORTHERN NORWAY: *From North Cape,* Peder Balke (1804—1887) 28br; ARTOTHEK: *Sea of Ice* (1823–4), Caspar David Friedrich 92t; *Morning*, 1808, Phillip Otto Runge 93bl; *Nana*, 1877 Edouard Manet 93br; ART PHOTO NEVA: Valentin Baranovsky 64bl, 65tl; A.S.A.P.: 276t; TAHSIN AYODOGMUS: 301ca, 304bl;
GONZALO M. AZUMENDI: 178b, 179t.

JAUME BALANYA; 205br; BERGEN ART MUSEUM: *From Bradbenken, Bergen,* 1924 (c) Nils Kranzt (1886–1954) 31b; BRIDGEMAN ART LIBRARY, LONDON/NEW YORK: © DACS 2001 *Long Live the Pacifist Army of the Workers*, 1920, Moor 63b; © Munch Museum/ Munch-Ellingsen Group, BONO, Oslo, DACS, London 2001, *Young Woman on the Shore*, 1896, Edvard Munch 36b; © Succession H. Matisse/DACS 2001 *La Danse*, 1910, Henri Matisse 67c; British Library, London 278bl; Giraudon 268t; Guildhall Library, Corporation of London 116cl; Musée d'Orsay/Peter Willi *L'Arlésienne*, 1888, Vincent Van Gogh 155bl; National Archaeological Museum, Athens/Bernard Cox 330cl; National Gallery of Scotland, Edinburgh 119t; National Museum of Ancient Art, Lisbon *The Temptations of St Antony*, c.1500, Hieronymus Bosch 172b; Royal Holloway and Bedford New College, *The Princes Edward and Richard in the Tower*, Sir John Everett Millais 113bl; Hermitage, St Petersburg 66t/b, 67t/b; BRITISH MUSEUM, LONDON: 315b, 331tr, 331br, Liz MacAulay 310b; BRITSTOCK-IFA Bernd Ducke 107t.

CAMERA PRESS: Roxana Artacho 65bl; CAPITOLINE MUSEUM, ROME: 230tl, 238b; A. M. CASSANDRE: 14b; JEAN-LOUP CHARMET: 243t; CAISSE NATIONALE DES MONUMENTS HISTORIQUES ET DES SITES: 149b; BRUCE COLEMAN LTD.: Hans Reinhard 207bl; Colin Varndell 207tl; COLLECTIONS: Robert Hallmann 106ca/cb; John Miller 106t; DEE CONWAY: 191ca/cb; CORBIS: Bruce Adams/Eye Ubiquitous 78–9; Paul Almasy 284c, 285t; Yann Arthus-Bertrand 256c; Craig Aurness 270tr; Dave Bartruff 257b, 297t; Jonathan Blair 329br, 332–333; Gary Braasch 213cl; Christie's Images 10t; Elio Ciol 26, 291c; Dean Conger 68–69; Margaret Courtney-Clarke 270cl, 271cla; Abbie Enock/Travel Ink 299c; Ric Ergenbright 160c; Macduff Everton 50tr; David Forman/Eye Ubiquitous 295br; Franz-Marc Frei 140bl; Robert Gill/Papilio 252–253; Shai Ginott 272–273; Robert Holmes 271clb; Aaron Horowitz 275t; Dave G. Houser 328br; Hanan Isachar 277t; Wolfgang Kaehler 27cl/bl; Lake County Museum 12–13c; Otto Lang 334c; David Lees 12cl/t, 271r; Charles & Josette Lenars 288tl/289tl; Richard List 328bl; Massimo Listri 250b; Mariner's Museum 11b, 14t; Kevin R. Morris 271tl; Michael Nicholson 284tl, 296cr, 323b; Richard T. Nowitz 276b/c, 294bl; Gianni Dagli Orti 288tr; Christine Osborne 270cr/br; Reuters/Lisbon City Museum 169bl; Enzo & Paolo Ragazzini 213cr; Fulvio Roiter 270bl; Hans Georg Roth 260cl;

Scheufler Collection 13tr; Roman Soumar 271ca; Ted Spiegel 41cla; Hubert Stadler 51t; Paul Thompson/ Eye Ubiquitous 248–249; Underwood & Underwood 12b; Francesco Ventury/Kea Publishing Services 254t, 271br; Nik Wheeler 271cr, 296t, 331tl; Roger Wood 21b, 262b, 271bl, 284t/b; Adam Woolfitt 294br; Costa Cruises: 22–23; Eric Crichton Photos: 206tr.

Danish National Museum: 41bc; DK Images: Courtesy of the National Maritime Museum, London/James Stevenson and Tina Chambers 9c; Dubrovnik Tourist Board: 334tl/bl, 335b/t. Equipo 28: 191tl; Mary Evans Picture Library: Explorer 190tl. FLPA – Images of Nature: E. & D. Hosking 207tc; Werner Forman Archive: 267c.

Getty Images: Peter Scholey 111t; Giraudon: Musée d'Art Catalan, Barcelona 313br; Glasgow Museums: Art Gallery & Museums: Museum of Transport 126b.

Hamburger Kunsthalle: Elke Walford 92c/b; Elke Walford © Munch Museum/ Munch-Ellingsen Group, BONO, Oslo, DACS, London 2001, *Girls on the Bridge*, c.1900, Edvard Munch 93c; Elke Walford, courtesy Dr. Wolfgang and Ingeborg Henze *Self Portrait with Model*, 1910, Ernst Ludwig Kirchner 93t; Archiv der Hansestadt Lübeck: 88b; Robert Harding Picture Library: 64br, 356t; Christina Gascoigne 235b, 279tr; Jeff Greenberg 354b, 351t; Gavin Hellier 354t; Dr. D. K. Holdsworth 5t; Michael Jenner 303br; John Miller 328t; G. R. Richardson 336–337; Paul van Riel 349t, 350b; Michael Short 329c/bl; Eitan Simanor 291b; Adam Woolfitt 152t; Helios Productions: Harvey Lloyd 1, 2–3; Hilti Foundation/Discovery Channel/Frank Goddio: Jerome Delafosse 267b; Crown Copyright: Reproduced by Permission of Historic Scotland: 120tr/cl; Historical Museum of Crete: 322b; Michael Holford: British Museum 330t; Hotel Sofitel Alendria Cecil: 267tl; David Martyn Hughes: 104–105; Hulton Getty: 136bl, 251b; Hunterian Art Gallery, University of Glasgow: *Sketch for Annabel Lee*, c.1868, James Abbott McNeill Whistler 124tr; Hutchison Library: Jackum Brown 254b. Images Colour Library: A.G.E. Fotostock 185b, 190br, 199cl; Imagebank, Italy: Marcella Pedone 240ca, 247t; Impact Photos: Alan Keohane 255b, 282tr; Index Fototeca: 195ca; Hanan Isachar: 277b, 278c, 296br. Jarrold Colour Publications: 136br; Michael Jenner Photography: 289tr, 290, 297b; Ann Jousiffe: 262t, 282tl; Peter Jousiffe: 282b.

Guerol Kara: 306ca; Katz Pictures: Mansell Collection 330–331c; Izzet Keribar: 306cb; Kina Nature Library: Henk Wijnja 94–95; Urs Kluyver: 91t; Kostas Kontos: 318bl, 322c; Kungliga Myntkabinettet, Stockholm: 47br. Livrustkammaren, Stockholm: Goeran Schmidt 47tl.

Magnum: Ara Gueler 303t; Mané Katz Museum, Haifa, Israel: © ADAGP, Paris and DACS, London 2001, *Three Rabbis*, c.1955, Mané Katz 277c; Marka: E. Lasagni 210c; Musée D'Orsay: *Le Déjeuner sur l'Herbe*, 1863 Edouard Manet 143t; John Miller: 182b; Ministry of Tourism, Lebanon: 283b; Monetary Research Institute: 357; Museo Correr, Venice: 216cl.

National Archaeological Museum, Naples: 243br; Reproduction Courtesy of The National Gallery of Ireland, Dublin: © J. B. Yeats Estate 134b; National Museum of Ireland, Dublin: 132br; National Museum of Denmark: 83c; © Trustees of the National Museums of Scotland: 118tr; National Trust for Scotland: 122b; Glyn Satterley 124cl; Nature Photographers: Brinsley Burbridge 207cbc; Paul Sterry 207tr; Nelli Dimoglou Folk Dance Theatre: 320t; Nicholas P. Goulandris Foundation/Museum of Cycladic and Ancient Greek Art: 311t; Nordiska Museet, Stockholm: Peter Segemark 49c; Norwegian Coastal Voyager (Hurtigruten): 17t; Richard T. Nowitz: 294t, 295c/bl, 296bl.

Office de Tourisme de Bordeaux: T. Sanson 151b; Fred Olsen Travel-Star Clippers: 16b, 348b; Oronoz Archivo Fotográfico: 188b; Museo Julia 331cr (d); Christine Osborne: 254ca, 256t; Overseas: 244tr/b, 245bl. P&O Art Collection: 8–9, 10b, 11t, 13b/cr; P&O Cruises: 16t, 17b; Panos Pictures: Morris Carpenter 283c, Jean-Leo Dugast 255t, 286–287; H. Morris 254bl; Jon Spaull 283t; Paul Quayle 258c; Pasabache Glassworks: 306t; Pictures Colour Library: 211c;

PRESSENS BILD, STOCKHOLM: 50cl/bl/br, 51b; Jeppe Wikstroem 42–43; PRINCESS CRUISES: 18b; PRISMA, BARCELONA: 178c, 179b, 180t, 181bl/br, 183bl; *El Paseante*, 1997 © J. T. Gómez Nazabal, 1997, 178t.

ZEV RADOVAN, JERUSALEM: 275b, 278br/t, 279tl; RETROGRAPH ARCHIVE: 4b, 256b; RÉUNION DES MUSÉES NATIONAUX: Arnaudet; J. Scho *Venus de Milo* 145br, *The Lacemaker* 1665, Jan Vermeer 145tl; C. Jean *Cour Marly*, 1745, Guillaume Coustou 145tr; Gérard Blot/C. Jean *Tomb of Philippe Pot* Antoine le Moiturier 146b; Gérard Blot *The Fortune Teller* c.1594, Caravaggio 146t; R. G. Ojeda *Dying Slave* Michelangelo 144bl, *Mona Lisa*, 1504, Leonardo da Vinci 144br; REX FEATURES: Stewart Cook 160b; Lehtikuva Oy/Pertti Jenytin 52–53; RIJKSMUSEUM FOUNDATION, AMSTERDAM: 102cl/b, 103c/b/t; ELLEN ROONEY: 58–59; GIULIANO ROTONDI: 246cb; ROYAL CARIBBEAN INTERNATIONAL: 4t, 15b,19t, 347b, 348b, 349b, 350t, 351b; ROYAL COLLECTION © 2001 HER MAJESTY QUEEN ELIZABETH II: 112bl/br, 113tl; ROYAL COLLECTIONS, STOCKHOLM: Alexis Daflos 44bl; FOUNDATION ROYAL PALACE AMSTERDAM: 96t.

MARÍA ÁNGELES SÁNCHEZ: 184t; SCALA GROUP S.P.A.: 215tl, 220tr, 222cb/b, 223b, 225t, 231b, 233t, 234b, 235t, 237tl/cr; SCIENCE PHOTO LIBRARY: B&C Alexander 27br; ROLF SØRENSEN: 34c/b/t, 35tl/tr/cr/bl; STATENS HISTORISKA MUSEUM, STOCKHOLM: 41cr, 44t; Peter Anderson 48b, Adrian Lascom 41t; STATENS VEGVESEN: 35br; GETTY IMAGES STONE: Glen Allison 74–75, 76bl; ST. PAUL'S CATHEDRAL: Sampson Lloyd 109crb; GOVERNING BODY OF SUOMENLINNA: 54b; SWAN HELLENIC: 18t, 340tr/ cl, 341b/t, 343c, 346b/t, 347c/t, 348t, 349c.

TAP SERVICE ARCHAEOLOGICAL RECEIPTS FUND, HELLENIC REPUBLIC MINISTRY OF CULTURE: 4th Epharat of Byzantine Antiquities 318br; A Epharat of Antiquities 312bl/br, 313c/t, 314b; Acropolis Museum 314t, 315tr/cl; Irákleio Archaeological Museum 323c, 324br; KA Epharat of Antiquities 319c/t; KG Epharat of Antiquities 324cl/bl/t, 325c/b/t; Z Epharat of Antiquities 326c; © TATE, LONDON 2001: 111b; TIVOLI FOTOARKIVET: 84t; TOPHAM PICTUREPOINT: Associated Press 15t; TOURIST OFFICE, SARDINIA: 210t; TOURIST OFFICE, SICILY: 246tl; TRAVEL INK: Ken Gibson 107b;

VAN GOGH MUSEUM, AMSTERDAM (VINCENT VAN GOGH FOUNDATION): 101b; VASA MUSEUM, STOCKHOLM: Hans Hammarskjöld 45b; RICCARDO VILLAROSA: 210b, 211b/t; VISIONS OF ANDALUCIA: 190–191c.

INGO WANDMACHER: 90tr/cr/b; WHITE STAR S.R.L.: Giulio Veggi 208–209; JEPPE WIKSTROEM: 44cl/br, 45t, 49b; PETERWILSON: 312cl.

JACKET
Front - PHOTOLIBRARY: Tsuneo Nakamura.
Back - AWL IMAGES: Julian Love clb; DORLING KINDERSLEY: Tony Souker bl, cla; Linda Whitwam tl.
Spine - PHOTOLIBRARY: Tsuneo Nakamura

Glossary of Nautical Terms

Abeam To one side of the ship, at right angles.

Aft Towards the rear of the ship.

Amidships Towards or at the middle of the ship.

Astern Behind the ship.

Beam Ship's width at its widest point.

Bearing Compass direction, expressed in degrees, from the ship to another point.

Beaufort Scale A method of measuring wind velocity, created by Commodore Francis Beaufort in 1805. The speed of the wind is related to 12 "forces" *(see p353)*.

Below The area below the main deck.

Berth Quay, dock or pier where the ship ties up, or the act of so doing. Also a term used aboard ship for a sleeping point or bed.

Bilges The very lowest parts of the ship.

Boat stations The places taken by passengers during lifeboat drill.

Bow The forward, pointed part of the ship.

Bow thrusters Small propellers at the front of the ship, used for guiding the ship into port.

Bridge The forward and upper part of the ship, which acts as a control centre.

Bulkhead Interior partition or wall aboard ship.

Bunkering Taking fuel aboard ship.

Buoy A floating marker anchored to the seabed.

Cabin Passenger's room, otherwise known as a "stateroom".

Captain Overall commander of the ship.

Cast off To release the lines that tie the ship to the quayside.

Chart A map of the coastline, sea and ocean used in navigation.

Chief Engineer Officer responsible for mechanical well-being of the ship.

Come about To turn the ship around.

Companionway Interior staircase aboard ship.

Course Ship's passage in a given direction, expressed in degrees.

Cruise Director Individual in charge of entertainment and on-board activities.

Davit A support and pulley mechanism for lowering and raising a lifeboat.

Degree (°) A unit of latitude or longitude used to define points on the Earth's surface. Also, one 360th of the circumference of a compass.

Disembark To get off a ship.

Dock Berth, pier, or quay where the ship ties up, or the act of so doing.

Draught (also Draft) Depth of water a ship requires in order to float.

Embark To join a ship for a voyage.

Fantail The rear, overhanging part of the ship.

Fathom Measurement of water depth equal to 1.82 m (6 ft).

Flagstaff A pole at the stern from which a flag of the ship's country of registry is flown.

Fore Front of the ship.

Funnel Exterior chimney to vent exhaust gases from the ship's engine room.

Galley Ship's kitchen.

Gangway The passageway or stairway that links the ship to the quayside.

Heading Direction in which the ship is travelling.

Helm The ship's steering apparatus.

Hold The area where the ship's cargo is kept.

Hotel Manager Officer in charge of passenger service.

Hull The main body of the ship, excluding the masts and superstructure.

Jack Ship's flag.

Knot Measurement of a ship's speed, originally gauged by throwing knotted rope overboard and counting the number of knots that passed a given point in a given time. One knot equals one nautical mile per hour (or 2 km / 1.15 land miles per hour).

Latitude The distance north or south of the equator, measured in degrees (°) and fractions of degrees (there are 60 "minutes" in a degree and 60 "seconds" in a minute).

Launch A small boat that transfers passengers from ship to shore when the vessel is unable to berth.

Leeward The side of the ship that is sheltered from the wind.

Lifeboat A small boat that transfers passengers to a rescue ship during emergencies.

Lifejacket An inflatable jacket that allows the wearer to float in water.

Longitude The distance east or west of the Greenwich Meridian (0°) measured in degrees and fractions of degrees.

Muster station Assembly point used in an emergency.

Nautical mile A distance of 1,853 m (6,080 ft), equal to one 60th of a degree ("minute") of the circumference of the Earth.

Passenger/ crew ratio The number of passengers divided by the number of crew gives the ratio. The lower this figure, the better the on-board service will be.

Pilot Person qualified to assist the Captain navigating into and out of harbour.

Pitching The rising and falling of the ship's bow, which may occur when the ship is moving forwards.

Plimsoll mark Mark found on the side of all ships indicating the depth to which the hull may be loaded in summer, in winter and in fresh water.

Port The left-hand side of the ship, when facing forwards.

Purser Officer in charge of finance.

Rudder Fin-like steering device at the ship's rear.

Screw Ship's propeller.

Stabilizer A retractable device that protrudes from the hull below the waterline to provide stability when the ship is moving.

Staff Captain The second in command to the Captain.

Starboard The right-hand side of the ship, when facing forwards.

Stateroom Passenger's room, otherwise known as a "cabin".

Stern The rear, flat part of a ship, opposite the bow.

Tender A small boat that transfers passengers from ship to shore when the ship is unable to berth.

Tonnage (grt) *See p19.*

Wake The area of disturbed water behind a moving ship.

Windward The side of the ship that is not sheltered from the wind.

Yawing Side to side deviation from a ship's intended course, usually caused by rough weather.

Zodiac Strong rubber raft-like boat with an out-board motor, for up to 12 passengers, used in ship-to-shore transfers.

Central Mediterranean